Sex, Gender, and Sexuality

Sex, Gender, and Sexuality
The New Basics

An Anthology

SECOND EDITION

Abby L. Ferber
University of Colorado at Colorado Springs

Kimberly Holcomb
University of Colorado at Colorado Springs

Tre Wentling
Syracuse University

New York   Oxford

OXFORD UNIVERSITY PRESS

Oxford University Press is a department of the University of Oxford.
It furthers the University's objective of excellence in research, scholarship, and
education by publishing worldwide.

Oxford New York
Auckland Cape Town Dar es Salaam Hong Kong Karachi
Kuala Lumpur Madrid Melbourne Mexico City Nairobi
New Delhi Shanghai Taipei Toronto

With offices in
Argentina Austria Brazil Chile Czech Republic France Greece
Guatemala Hungary Italy Japan Poland Portugal Singapore
South Korea Switzerland Thailand Turkey Ukraine Vietnam

For titles covered by Section 112 of the US Higher Education Opportunity Act,
please visit www.oup.com/us/he for the latest information about pricing and
alternate formats.

Published by Oxford University Press
198 Madison Avenue, New York, New York 10016
http://www.oup.com

Library of Congress Cataloging-in-Publication Data

Sex, gender, and sexuality : the new basics : an anthology /
[compiled by] Abby L. Ferber, Kimberly Holcomb, Tre Wentling.
—2nd ed.
   p. cm.
   ISBN 978-0-19-993450-8
   1. Sex.   2. Sex role.   3. Gender identity.   I. Ferber, Abby L.,
1966– II. Holcomb, Kimberly.   III. Wentling, Tre.
   HQ21.S47165 2013
   305.3—dc23   2012017143

Printing number: 9 8 7 6 5 4 3 2 1

Printed in the United States of America
on acid-free paper

For Kimberly and Tre, once my fabulous students, now my fabulous colleagues! You continue to inspire me.—*Abby Ferber*

For my sweet Avery. May this world be far more equitable before you are old enough to know otherwise. I love you to the moon and back, littlest dinosaur.—*Kimberly Holcomb*

This edition is dedicated to the Believers and those with Hope. And, to Ms. Lucinda M. Riggins for her infinite contributions, labors of love, and unconditional encouragement to Go BIG.—*Tre Wentling*

Contents

* An asterisk indicates new to the second edition

Acknowledgments

We were ecstatic when we received the invitation from our wonderful editor at Oxford University Press, Sherith Pankratz, to work on a second edition of this text. This meant that the original collection of authors, theories, and first-person narratives were circulating and that there is an eagerness to continue to engage with them. We immediately set a goal to improve the readability of the text by reorganizing it and eliminating, shortening, and adding articles, as well as integrating additional selections that would expand our focus on the social structures and institutions that shape sex, gender, and sexuality. Our commitment for this second edition was to still offer a progressive, queer collection of articles that reflect the social significance of sex, gender, and sexuality in all of our lives, every day.

We wish to thank Sherith Pankratz and Cari Heicklen at Oxford, whose support and enthusiasm for this project has sustained us. Rosemary Kelbel has provided unending clerical support, and Abby's Fall 2011 Gender and Sexuality class at the University of Colorado at Colorado Springs provided us with valuable and honest input on new essays as we made difficult decisions of what to include in this second edition. As well, we would like to acknowledge Minnie Bruce Pratt, Jackie Orr, and Margaret Himley at Syracuse University for introducing us to new and incredible theorists. We also wish to thank our families, who have continued to provide love and encouragement throughout this process.

The tremendously helpful and detailed feedback of generous reviewers was incredibly beneficial. We sincerely thank:

Brooke Ayars, Piedmont College
Siobhan Brooks, Temple University
Marie Cartier, California State University—Northridge
Stephanie Crist, Syracuse University
Amy Moff Hudec, University of Redlands
Carmen R. Lugo-Lugo, Washington State University

Greg Mullins, The Evergreen State College
Michael J. Murphy, University of Illinois at Springfield
Ann Mussey, Portland State University
Mona C. Scott, Mesa Community College

Finally, we thank the many faculty and students who read and engage this text, and we acknowledge the many sex, gender, and sexuality scholars, activists, and authors whose work constantly challenges us to re-think what we think we know.

ABOUT THE COVER ARTIST

BIOGRAPHY

Typified by arresting powers of visual imagery and spatial sophistication, Michael Gadlin's artistry is rimmed in spontaneity. His 18-year repertoire expresses a singular uninterrupted brush stroke of Mediterranean, European, and Western influences. Pushing the boundaries of contemporary art form, Michael's work epitomizes avant-garde. Michael's work reflects an improvisational inventiveness that has garnered a loyal following among the art elite. His artistic conviction that "Direct expressionism is the most meaningful reflection of life" has prompted the evolution of an extremely cogent and intriguing portfolio of 21st century art. Michael Gadlin has been exhibiting work throughout the United States for over 15 years. As a very young artist, Gadlin studied drawing and painting at the Art Students League. Directly out of high school, Gadlin attended Pratt Institute of Art And Design in New York where he began to work on his art constantly which took his art to another level. In 1999, Gadlin won "Best Of Show" at Denver's nationally renowned Cherry Creek Arts Festival, the youngest artist to do so. The Vance Kirkland Museum acquired a Gadlin work as part of its permanent collection. Gadlin's well-received public art commission, which was completed in 2004, hangs permanently in Denver's District 2 Police Station. The Fort Collins Museum of Contemporary Art selected Gadlin to be included in the Museum's 2008 "Rocky Mountain Biennial". Gadlin is currently exhibiting at his own Denver-based gallery and studio space called ArtHaus, which he co-owns with another artist.

ABOUT THE WORK…

Techniques used in Gadlin's work primarily include very loose and gestural under-painting that often involves the use of charcoal, ink and latex house paint. Gadlin then paints layers of texture, color through glazes over element of lines and shape that he creates from his head. This becomes the visual context of the work that gives a unique depth and a playground to edit forms and contextual meaning. Gadlin often incorporates collage pieces from various sources to give his surfaces dimension and variety, which for him is an integral part of the relationship between the abstractions and representational imagery that is carried through his work. The process is important for Gadlin, because it entails discoveries involving variegation by use of recycled pieces of paper, wood, and other assortments. Very thin layers of glazes, stains, and coats of color over one another achieve depth, vibrancy, and luminosity. The many techniques used to create his "interpretations of elements" are not limited to the mix of paper surfaces, torn and cut into complex shapes, collaged together for visual effect. Gadlin loves the process of discovering and "peeling the layers in art" that express, for him, what he has learned that is new and useful to his contemporary vision.

New to the Second Edition

- Moved and updated the list of key terms to the front of the text. While perhaps unconventional, we believe this helps signal its existence more easily and also encourages its use.
- Revised discussion questions for some of the reprinted articles and new discussion questions included with the articles we added.
- Part Three is one continuous, more coherent section.
- Removed twenty-two articles and added fourteen new ones.
- Part One includes two new articles. One addresses the "nature" of same-sex practices and desires transnationally and globally, and the second analyzes the social institution of heterosexuality.
- Part Two includes four new articles that invite readers to consider how constructions of body size, disability, individual and community membership(s), as well as the complicities of sexual terminology, intersect with personal experiences of sex, gender, and sexuality.
- Part Three has six new articles that present matters related to disability rights, abortion, sport, historical immigration practices, contemporary heterosexual marriage promotions, queer tourism, transnational feminism, and the global sex trade.
- Part Four incorporates two new articles: the first offers a brief autobiographical account of an androgynous person that actively practices organized religion, and the second offers a review of legal measures of "progress" in an historical and contemporary context, as well as insight into the ways in which academics can influence public policy.

Although there are nine fewer articles in this second edition, we are confident that the forty-two carefully selected articles offer important sociological insights for our contemporary landscape regarding sex, gender, and sexuality. We hope that you find it as enjoyable and transformative as we did throughout the process of building it.

Introduction

Before you read any further, take a moment to think about the key concepts examined by this text: sex, gender, and sexuality. How would you define each of these terms? Take out a piece of paper and jot down some definitions for each before we continue.

If you are anything like our students, this exercise may have been more difficult than you first imagined. Though we are bombarded with images regarding sex, gender, and sexuality every day, and tend to use these terms all the time, many of us operate with different understandings of just what, exactly, they refer to. We assume these concepts are a matter of common sense, so much so that we rarely stop to think about what they really mean. Yet as these readings will clearly demonstrate, the meanings of these terms are constantly shifting and are far from clear-cut.

Each semester we ask our students to complete this very exercise, and each semester we receive a wide array of definitions. For sex, students often reference biology, the body, genitals, hormones, chromosomes, and so on. Gender often evokes a similar roster, with a few more references to "culture" and/or "socialization." Definitions of sexuality refer to desire, sexual acts with persons of the "same" or "opposite" sex, masculinity/femininity, and/or identity markers like "gay," "lesbian," "bisexual," "heterosexual" and so on.

We can draw a number of conclusions from this exercise. First, while we use these terms all the time, we are clearly not in unison when it comes to what they actually mean. There is much confusion and overlap in our understanding of these concepts, such that we often use them interchangeably. So don't be discouraged if these terms confuse you. Keep in mind that there has been little agreement upon their meanings even among researchers and scholars who study these subjects, and the definitions change as swiftly as new discoveries are made and new theories advanced. Indeed, we hope that the chapters in this volume will behoove you to question the terms even further. The answer may not lie in finding clear-cut definitions, but in thinking about why we construct these classifications in the first place, how they operate, what social purposes they serve, and why they have become so important to us. In fact, instead of providing simple answers, our goal is to complicate readers' understandings of these terms even further.

To that end, another important fact to remember as you move through the readings is that theories involving sex, gender, and sexuality vary not only from individual to individual, but transhistorically and cross-culturally as well, making uniformity a tricky, if not impossible, business. Today many of our contemporary discussions involve words like *opposite sex* and often imply astronomical differences between males and females. Books like John Gray's *Men Are from Mars, Women Are from Venus* are best-sellers, and popular magazines are always eager to publish headlines promising to reveal "real" sex differences. However, this was certainly not always the case. The ancient Greek philosopher Aristotle theorized that men and women were essentially the same and that females actually *were* males who failed to fully form in the womb because of a lack of properly heated sperm at the time of conception. In fact, many theories of biological sameness flourished in antiquity and battled for ancient scientific proof. One such theory argued that the vagina was a sort of inside-out penis, while another suggested that the uterus was a penis that had not yet dropped outside the body. As such, women were viewed as inferior because they failed to develop fully, and the male body was posited as the full manifestation of humanness.

Sexuality in ancient Greece was also conceptualized in vastly dissimilar terms than we see today. Sexual relationships between men and women, men and men, and women and women were all common, and one's sexual or affectional desire was not a marker for social classification, stigma, or identity; however, there were strict norms governing who played what role in sexual acts. Still, ancient knowledge and attitudes toward sex and sexuality were quite different from our contemporary adherence to the heterosexual–homosexual binary, wherein the former is prized and naturalized and the latter is often demonized. This dichotomy is so pervasive today in popular culture and discourse regarding sex and sexuality that it is seen as timeless and innate, biological fate. Yet, in fact, the words *homosexual* and *heterosexual* were coined scarcely more than a hundred years ago, and they were first used discursively to posit a procreative sex imperative. That is, heterosexuality was "natural" because of its procreative potential and homosexuality—its requisite opposite—was "unnatural" for its lack of the same. The wildly popular Sigmund Freud further reinforced this idea when he claimed that exclusive heterosexuality was the ultimate sign of sexual maturation, and homosexuality a sign of neurosis or stunted development.

Fast-forward to contemporary times, and you can see quite easily how and why sexual and gender identities have become such a central form of hierarchization in our society. Indeed, the array of theories and conceptualizations involving sex and sexuality (and their social implications) from antiquity to the present make clear the ways in which our understandings of these concepts are socially constructed and change over time. Thus, it is important to study the history of theories involving sex and sexuality, because doing so allows us to expose the illusion that these categories are ageless and unchanging and rooted in biology, rather than in relations of power. Ignoring this history keeps us from looking critically at the social effects of our sex, gender, and sexual categorizations and prevents us from conceiving of a different, more equitable way of conceptualizing and ordering things. That is, it contributes to the naturalization of these definitions and ignores the vastness of human variation.

Outdated theories like essentialism and biological determinism are swiftly being replaced by more useful social constructionist models for understanding sex, gender, and sexuality. Whereas essentialists posit a basic model that assumes one's gender will automatically resonate "correctly" with one's anatomical sex and that heterosexuality will naturally result, social constructionists take a more useful approach. Rather than assuming that innate biology is the sole determinant for sex, gender, and sexuality, social constructionists recognize a complicated interplay of biology and socialization and offer a more inclusive model for understanding these concepts and the incredible variation amongst human beings. According to these theories, our ideas of gender, sexuality, and even anatomical sex are not static and immutable, but instead are socially constructed. We learn, internalize, and practice gender prescriptions to the point that they SEEM natural or inborn, but in fact they are not. Many of the chapters in this volume advance a range of social constructionist perspectives, broadly defined, and examine some of the historical and contemporary debates in conceptualizing sex, gender, and sexuality.

These discussions are not merely academic. Notions of sex, gender, and sexuality remain at the fore of political, religious, and social debate in America as well. Just open a newspaper or flip on the television, and it will become clear that we are presently in the throes of a major shift. Gay, lesbian, bisexual, transgender, transsexual, and intersexed individuals are more and more the focus of television talk shows, documentaries, and sitcoms. The issue of gay marriage continues to figure prominently in the political arena, with six states having legalized marriage between same-sex partners at the date of this publication. Mainstream media is becoming increasingly difficult to distinguish from pornography, and our exposure to all of this proliferates exponentially with increasing use of the Internet. But perhaps of more import are the ever-increasing rates of violence against those who don't conform to normative notions of gender and sexuality. The National Coalition of Anti-Violence Programs reported a 13 percent increase in reported hate crimes against GLBTIQ folks in 2010, and physical, verbal, and especially "cyber" bullying of sexual and gender variant youth is undeniably on the rise. Moreover, GLBTIQ youth are far more likely to commit suicide than their heterosexual peers, often because of bullying. It is important for us to study these concepts because new knowledge can lead to new theories and provides a foundation for building a more equitable world for all of us.

Our goal is to introduce readers to the wide range of exciting contemporary research on sex, gender, and sexuality, with particular emphasis on their intersections. Examining these new works provides a new way of thinking about sex, gender, and sexuality and considers the ways in which they are inextricably linked and mutually constitutive. Historically, our conceptualizations and theories of these categories have been intertwined, as many of the chapters in Part One reveal. Conceptualizing and studying these terms together allows us to ask ourselves important questions regarding how our sexuality is affected by our gender, or how our sex correlates (or does not) with our "performance" of gender. Would we need categories of gender today if we did not feel compelled to define ourselves as heterosexual or homosexual? Beyond this, an intersectional approach allows us to consider other social factors, such as race/ethnicity, class, age, and ability, as they relate to and shape people's experiences of sex, gender, and sexuality. In our daily lives, our experiences and opportunities are shaped by the combination of all these systems of inequality. We are never simply our gender or simply our race. It is time that our theories better grasp the complexity of our individual daily experiences. As with the definitions themselves, there is no universal with regard to these concepts. They are as multifarious as the people who experience them.

Today is an exciting moment to be studying sex, gender, and sexuality. The theoretical developments of the last thirty years have provided a rich literature to guide our understanding of the myriad ways in which the categories and identities of sex, gender, and sexuality are interdependent. The chapters included in Section One each represent contemporary contributions to rethinking our conceptualizations of sex, gender, and sexuality and the tangled relationships among them.

It is our hope that you will find the following readings engaging, challenging, and exciting and that they will help you to glean a greater understanding of contemporary debates and issues surrounding sex, gender, and sexuality, as well as to provide you with the tools and insights to reexamine your own life experience and identity. As you read, consider the ways in which the chapters relate to and complement one another and, most important, how the concepts of sex, gender, and sexuality are interrelated. Some of these readings may be challenging or make you feel uncomfortable, but as we always tell our students, that is a sure sign that you are learning and pushing the boundaries of what you already knew and took for granted.

We encourage you to take a few minutes to review the list of key terms that follows this introduction, and to turn to it frequently as you encounter new or confusing language.

Key Terms

The following definitions provide merely a starting point for readers to interrogate as language is, and especially identity categories are, embedded in state and political histories, medical and scientific discourse, and social movements. Identity terms are often advanced as tools of liberation and for community building, but they always exclude and constrict. Many of these terms and definitions will and should change over time as social actors construct new identities, demand recognition, improve theories, and provide new knowledge(s).

Ableism System of oppression that privileges (temporarily) able-bodied people over disabled people through everyday practices, attitudes, assumptions, behaviors, and institutional rules; encompasses prejudice, stereotyping, and discrimination.

Ageism System of oppression that privileges some people over others based on age through everyday practices, attitudes, assumptions, behaviors, and institutional rules; encompasses prejudice, stereotyping, and discrimination.

Androgen Insensitivity Syndrome (AIS) A medical condition in which bodies do not respond to androgen, which is described as a "male" hormone. For more information regarding AIS, visit *Intersex Society of North America* (www.isna.org).

Androgynous (1) A self-ascribed state of embodiment among individuals rejecting the binary structure of woman and man; similar to genderqueer and neutrois. (2) Also used as an adjective to describe others.

Androphilia A controversial and hotly debated term that describes sexual desire and attraction to masculinity or men without relation to the object's sex category. It is controversial because of its history in sexologist literature and diagnoses, as well as its relation to "autogynephilia."

Anti-Semitism System of oppression that privileges non-Jewish persons through everyday practices, attitudes, assumptions, behaviors, and institutional rules; it encompasses prejudice, stereotyping, and discrimination.

Asexual A self-ascribed state of being among individuals not interested in sexual expression or practice.

BDSM An abbreviation for Bondage–Discipline (or Domination)–Sadomasochism, which broadly encompasses consensual role play and performance acts of domination and submission related to sexual desire, fantasy, and gratification.

Bisexual A self-ascribed state of embodiment among people who desire emotional, physical, and/or sexual relations with persons of both sexes and genders.

Bullying Any type of repeated verbal harassment, physical assault, intimidation, or coercion that targets a person based on perceived and/or real social statuses.

Chromosomes DNA that socially is defined to categorically represent females as XX, males as XY, and intersex as a myriad of possibilities.

Cisgender Latin prefix *cis* means "same"; refers to people who embody the gender associated with their birth-assigned sex.

Classism System of oppression that privileges some people over others based on socioeconomic status through everyday practices, attitudes, assumptions, behaviors, and institutional rules; it encompasses prejudice, stereotyping, and discrimination.

Coming Out (1) A continual and selective narrative speech act among individuals who choose to publicly affirm their state of embodiment, which may also reject assumed heterosexual and/or gender identities. (2) Also used by individuals who choose to publicly reject assumptions about their person (i.e. race membership, religious membership, etc.). (3) Allies may also come out to publicly announce their commitments.

Congenital Adrenal Hyperplasia (CAH) A medical condition in which the adrenal glands release cortisol into the bloodstream, which results in higher levels of hormones and can lead to a "masculinization" of developing XX fetus' genitalia. For more information regarding the most common form of intersex conditions, visit *Intersex Society of North America* (www.isna.org).

Cross-Dresser (CD) A self-ascribed state of embodiment among individuals who wear clothing and accessories associated with a different gender, and may be inspired for both sexual and nonsexual reasons. Although antiquated and stigmatized, cross-dresser is sometimes synonymous with "transvestite."

Deep Stealth Mostly associated with transgender or transsexual individuals who have chosen to keep their sexed and gendered history private from everyone, including an intimate partner.

Diagnostic and Statistical Manual of Mental Disorders (DSM) A text developed and maintained by the American Psychiatric Association that establishes the classification standards of mental disorders and psychiatric illnesses.

Discrimination The unequal allocation of valued goods and resources based on one's social position and group membership, which includes limiting the access of some groups to full benefits, privileges, and rights.

Disorders of Sex Development (DSD) An emergent medical term that describes congenital conditions in which chromosomal, gonadal, or anatomic sex development is "atypical" from that of "standard" female and male. Some medical clinicians prefer DSD rather than "intersex" because of their shared DSD definition.

Domestic Violence (Intimate Partner Violence) Various forms of violence within partner and familial relationships, ranging from emotional (intimidation, isolation, threats) to physical, financial, and sexual abuse.

Drag Artists People who perform entertaining acts by wearing clothing and accessories associated with the different sex and gender of the performer.

Drag King A self-ascribed state of embodiment among female-bodied people who dress and perform as men, at times in a subversive way to expose some expressions of masculinity.

Drag Queen A self-ascribed state of embodiment among males who dress and perform as women.

Dyke (1) A self-ascribed identity term among female-bodied people who desire emotional, physical, and/or sexual relations with women. (2) May also be used as an epithet.

Electrolysis (Electro) A process that uses an electric current to remove facial and other body hair, eliminating the need to shave.

Endocrinologist (Endo) A medical doctor specializing in the endocrine system (i.e., hormones).

Essentialism A theoretical perspective that naturalizes differences between social groups (such as gender differences, racial differences, etc.), often positing their origins in biology (i.e., genes, chromosomes, DNA, etc.).

Estrogen Hormone most often associated with females; however, estrogen is present in all bodies.

Ethnicity A socially constructed category based on characteristics such as national origin or heritage, geography, language, customs, or cultural practices (i.e., Italian, Puerto Rican, Cuban, Kurdish, Serbian, etc.).

Ethnocentrism The practice of judging another culture using the standards of one's own culture.

Female to Male (FtM/F2M) (1) A self-ascribed state of embodiment among individuals labeled female at birth who identify as men and/or present in a masculine expression. (2) Also used as an adjective to describe a transition process.

Feminism A wide range of theoretical and political perspectives that value women and their experiences. Feminism is committed to activism, social change, and equality.

Gay (1) A self-ascribed state of embodiment among men who desire emotional, physical, and/or sexual relations with men. (2) Also used to refer to all gay men and lesbians. (3) Commonly used to describe something as stupid or dumb.

Gender Socially constructed categories that divide bodies into a binary system of women and men. Recently, new gender identities such as transgender, androgynous, and genderqueer categories have been embraced and advanced.

Gender-Bender A person who chooses to cross or violate the gender roles and/ or expressions that are associated with their socially assigned sex category.

Gender Dysphoria The controversial DSM (see definition) term used to describe some individuals seeking transition-related medical technologies.

Gender Identity Disorder (GID) A controversial DSM diagnosis that practitioners use to describe individuals who express and identify with a gender embodiment not associated with their birth-assigned sex.

Gender Ideology A set of ever-changing culturally and historically specific meanings that shape the social expectations for bodies, behaviors, emotions, and family and work roles, based on gender classifications.

Gender Image/Display The presentation of oneself through social interaction using culturally appropriate gender symbols and markers.

Genderqueer A self-ascribed state of embodiment among individuals who reject the binary gender structure of woman and man; similar to androgynous and neutrois.

Gender Reassignment Surgery (GRS) Various types of surgical procedures that some transgender individuals undergo to medically and physically align their bodies with their gender identity.

Hate Crime Crimes that are motivated by bias and hate against an individual based on perceived or actual social status membership (i.e., race, ethnicity, gender, sexuality, ability, religion, etc.).

Hegemonic Dominant beliefs or ideals that are taken for granted and thus "naturalized" in a culture at any given time.

Hermaphrodite An antiquated and stigmatizing scientific term that was used to describe individuals with varying and/or multiple sex characteristics (i.e., chromosomes, genitalia, reproductive organs, hormones, etc.) that challenge sex determinations of "female" or "male." An emergent medical literature describes sex development processes that are different from "standard" female or male as Disorders of Sex Development (DSD).

Heteronormativity A system that institutionalizes heterosexuality as the standard for legitimate and expected social and sexual relations (Ingraham).

Heterosexism System of oppression that privileges heterosexual people through everyday practices, attitudes, behaviors, and institutional rules through the promotion of heterosexuality as natural and normal.

Heterosexual (1) A self-ascribed state of embodiment among individuals who desire emotional, physical, and/or sexual relations with people of their opposite sex and gender. (2) Also used as an adjective to describe others.

Homophobia The fear, hatred, or diapproval of and discrimination against lesbian, gay, and bisexual people.

Homosexual (1) A self-ascribed state of embodiment among individuals who desire emotional, physical, and/or sexual relations with people of the same sex and/or gender. Some consider this an antiquated term linked to a medicalized history of stigma and shame.

Hormone Replacement Therapy (HRT) A medical process sometimes prescribed for or requested by women in menopause and transgender persons.

Ideology A belief system that shapes interpretations, makes sense of the world, and guides actions and behaviors. Ideologies often provide justification for inequality and oppression.

Intersex (Intersexual) A broad term that describes individuals medically labeled outside of "typical" or "standard" sex categories (i.e., female or male). There are many causes and varieties of intersex expression. For more information, visit *Intersex Society of North America* (www.isna.org).

Klinefelter Syndrome A medical condition in which male bodies inherit an extra X chromosome. For more information regarding Klinefelter Syndrome, visit *Intersex Society of North America* (www.isna.org).

Lesbian A self-ascribed state of embodiment among women who desire emotional, physical, and/or sexual relations with women.

Male to Female (MtF/M2F) (1) A self-ascribed state of embodiment among individuals labeled male at birth who identify as women and/or in a feminine expression. (2) Also used as an adjective to describe a transition process.

Matriarchy A system of inequality that privileges women and girls over men and boys.

Misogyny The hatred of women.

Neutrois A new term of self-description embraced by individuals who reject the binary structure of woman and man; similar to androgynous and genderqueer.

Non-op A popular colloquialism used in transgender communities to describe a transgender person's current embodiment and/or decision to not undergo surgical transition.

Oppression The systematic denial of access to cultural and institutional resources based on perceived or actual social status membership (i.e., race, ethnicity, gender, sexuality, ability, religion, etc.).

Outted Describes a nonconsensual public speech act or written announcement concerning an individual's identity or status that s/he wants to keep private (i.e., sexual identity, gender history, rape survivor, living with AIDS, etc.).

Pansexual A self-ascribed state of embodiment among individuals who recognize multiple sexes and genders and desire emotional, physical, and/or sexual relations with individuals, regardless of sex membership or gender embodiment.

Passing Describes a process whereby individuals are perceived in ways that affords keeping private an identity or status (i.e., sexual identity, gender history, rape survivor, living with AIDS, etc.).

Patriarchy A dynamic system of power and inequality that privileges men and boys over women and girls in social interactions and institutions.

Post-op A popular colloquialism used in transgender communities to describe a transgender person's current embodiment after surgical procedures to medically or physically transition.

Pre-op A popular colloquialism used in transgender communities to describe a transgender person's current embodiment prior to undergoing elective surgical procedures to transition (assumes decision has already been made).

Privilege The systematic access to valued cultural and institutional resources that are denied to others based on social status membership (i.e., race, ethnicity, gender, sexuality, ability, religion, etc.).

Queer Historically, and still, a controversial term that (1) is a self-ascribed state of embodiment among individuals who reject and live outside of heteronormative structures; (2) a broad umbrella term used in place of the "LGBT" acronym.

Race Socially constructed categories that group people together based on physical features, such as phenotypic expression, skin tone, and hair textures, as well as on social, cultural, and economic characteristics.

Racism System of oppression that privileges people over others based on constructed racial classifications. Racism privileges those with greater social power and oppresses others through everyday practices, attitudes, assumptions, behaviors, and institutional rules and structures.

Rape Any forced sexual act.

Secondary sex characteristics Biological attributes that most often, but not always, emerge during puberty and have social meaning related to gender and sexuality.

Sex Socially constructed categories based on culturally accepted biological attributes. In Western culture, females and males are categorized on the basis of chromosomes, genitalia, reproductive organs, and hormones.

Sexism System of oppression that privileges men over women through everyday practices, attitudes, assumptions, behaviors, and institutional rules and structures.

Sex Reassignment Surgery (SRS) Various types of surgical procedures that some transgender individuals undergo to medically and physically align their bodies with their identity.

Sexual Harassment Unwelcome sexual advances or attention, including environments that foster unsafe conditions and/or discomfort based on sexual threat or innuendo.

Sexuality A broad term that encompasses a range of concepts, ideologies, identities, behaviors, and expressions related to sexual personhood and desire.

Sexual Identity (1) Sexual desire, attraction, and practice based on sexual object choice; similar to sexual orientation. (2) Category that encompasses identity terms including lesbian, gay, bisexual, pansexual, queer, or asexual.

Social Institution An organized system that has a set of rules and relationships that govern social interactions and activities in which people participate to meet basic needs.

Sexual Orientation A self-ascribed state of embodiment that describes sexual desires and practices; also implies an essential, unchanging orientation.

Significant Other (SO) A popular colloquialism used by queer and allied communities to refer to an intimate partner.

Social Constructionism A theoretical approach that emphasizes the role of social interaction and culture in meaning-making practices including those that shape social statuses (i.e., race, ethnicity, gender, sexuality, ability, religion, etc.) and produce inequality.

Social Stratification A system by which individuals are divided into social positions that are ranked hierarchically and tied to institutional inequality.

Stealth A popular colloquialism used in transgender communities to describe individuals who have chosen to keep private various identities or statuses.

Testosterone Hormone most often associated with masculinity; however, testosterone is present in all bodies.

Transgender (TG) (1) An umbrella term that includes individuals who change, cross, and/or go beyond or through the culturally defined binary gender categories (woman/man). (2) A self-ascribed state of embodiment.

Transition A process of social and/or medical gender transition.

Transman A self-ascribed state of embodiment among female-bodied people who identify as men and/or masculine.

Transphobia/Transphobic A system of oppression that privileges nontransgender or cisgender people through everyday practices, attitudes, assumptions, behaviors, and institutional rules; encompasses prejudice, stereotyping, and discrimination.

Transsexual (TS) Rooted in the medical and sexological development of "trans" knowledge that regards people who desire to live differently than their assigned sex at birth. Historically, this term has implied medical (i.e., surgical and hormonal) transition.

Tranny/Trannie (1) A self-ascribed state of embodiment among some transgender people. (2) Extremely contextual and depends on the user's intentions and tone; may be offensive and considered an epithet.

Transvestite An antiquated medicalized term that describes individuals who cross-dress for sexual and/or nonsexual reasons.

Transwoman A self-ascribed embodiment among male-bodied people who identify as women and/or feminine.

Turner Syndrome A medical condition in which bodies do not have a second X chromosome. For more information regarding Turner Syndrome, visit *Intersex Society of North American* (www.isna.org).

REFERENCES

Intersex Society of North American (ISNA). Available online at www.isna.org

Johnson, Allan G. 2006. *Privilege, Power and Difference*, 2nd ed. Boston: McGraw-Hill.

Lober, Judith and Lisa Jean Moore. 2006. *Gendered Bodies: Feminist Perspectives*. Roxbury.

Transsexual Road Map Glossary. 2006. Available online at http://www.tsroadmap.com/index.html

Yoder, Janice D. 2007. *Women & Gender: Making a Difference*, 3rd ed. Cornwall-on-Hudson, NY: Sloan Educational Publishing.

Sex, Gender, and Sexuality

PART ONE

Rethinking Foundations: Theorizing Sex, Gender, and Sexuality

INTRODUCTION

Many of our commonsense assumptions about race, gender, and sexuality are embedded in what we call an *essentialist* approach. *Essentialism* assumes that social identities such as gender, sex, race, ability, and so on, are inherent and unchanging. They are frequently seen as intrinsic to bodies themselves and biologically determined. Cultural essentialisms, on the other hand, posit differences and traits as inherently rooted in a specific culture and impervious to change. These differences are believed to be innate and unchanging and are seen as more significant than environmental factors in explaining differences among people. Essentialism, however, is not supported by the research. For example, while our commonsense assumptions may tell us that race is rooted in biology, almost all biologists today reject such notions.

Instead, most contemporary theories of social differences fall under the broad umbrella of *social constructionism*. Social constructionist approaches have been embraced in a wide array of disciplines, including philosophy, sociology, literature, psychology, and anthropology. Social constructionist approaches emphasize the role of human interaction and culture in shaping classifications of difference and producing inequality.

Unfortunately, essentialist approaches are still sedimented in our culture. After all, identities like race and sex seem purely biological and visible, don't they? We can clearly see that there are differences among us in terms of skin color, and isn't the first thing the doctor pronounces upon the birth of a baby either "It's a boy!" or "It's a girl!"? Movies, television, and music continue to reinforce essentialist assumptions, reaffirming their status as "common sense," and making it difficult for people to grasp the social constructionist approach at first.

While there is a wide range of social constructionist approaches, along with ongoing debates among scholars that might be grouped together as social constructionists, they provide a shared critique of essentialism, arguing that:

1. There is no strictly biological basis for these categories of identity
2. Each of these categories varies tremendously across cultures
3. Each of these categories similarly varies historically

We often tend to reduce problems to a nature versus nurture perspective, however, the world is not that clear cut. The social constructionist perspective is often assumed to be a purely "nurture" account, as opposed to an essentialist "nature" perspective. However, few constructionist perspectives ignore biology and nature completely. Instead, nature and culture are seen as interconnected and inseparable. After all, we have no access to the biological realm except through the realm of culture and society. Additionally, scholars of human development have provided significant evidence that human bodies and minds develop in constant interaction with their social contexts.

Because the basic classifications and definitions of sex, gender, and sexuality are constructed by our culture, they change frequently and can be difficult to pin down. Historically, and still today, people have not agreed upon which terms to use and what the terms mean. For example, how does sex differ from gender?

In the early stages of second wave feminism, sex was seen in essentialist terms and gender assumed to loosely follow. Gender was embraced to refer to behaviors, roles, and personality traits, conceptualized as the product of social-ization processes, which were juxtaposed with the notion of a biologically sexed body. Linda Nicholson suggests that from this perspective, sexed bodies are analogous to a coat rack, upon which different cultures throw different arti-cles of clothing (the various "pieces" of gender). While gender is defined as a cross-cultural variable according to this view, the biological coat rack is taken as an unchanging, universal, and given foundation. In the past, this perspec-tive was applauded for introducing the concept of gender identity, moving us beyond a simple biologically deterministic view of sex that had long been used to rationalize women's oppression. In other words, this perspective moved one step away from essentialism by positing a socially constructed notion of gender that was assumed to follow from one's essential sex, but was more flexible and open to change.

This perspective was soon challenged. Even though gender was defined as a social construct, it ended up reifying both gender and sexuality in essentialist terms, because gender was assumed to follow from, and correspond to, one's given sex. For example, a biological male was assumed to adopt the social gender roles constructed for men and was assumed to desire women. Thus, sexuality and gender were still seen as following directly from biological sex categories.

Over the past few decades, scholars and activists have argued that not only gender, but sex itself, is socially constructed. Bodies themselves are embedded in webs of culture and open to social interpretation. This perspective does not ignore the body; instead, the body itself becomes a social variable, which can no longer ground claims about gender. For example, in his study *Making Sex: Body and Gender from the Greeks to Freud*, Thomas Laqueur has demonstrated that Western conceptions of human sexual anatomy and sexual difference have changed drastically throughout history. There is no direct access to the body, then, outside of cultural contexts.

Other critiques have reconceptualized gender as performative, and they have argued that it is through the performance of gender that sex itself is made real (Butler, 1990; West and Zimmerman, 1987). These theorists reverse the typical trajectory and argue that gender precedes sex.

Yet other critiques have brought race, class, and other forms of inequality into the picture. Essentialist notions of sex, gender, and sexuality have all assumed that there is some common essence among those in each category that in reality reflects only the experiences of the most privileged. Women of color have charged that this basis for commonality assumes a white, heterosexual, upper-middle-class ideal. This perspective, in fact, ignores within-group differences. Social movements based on gender or race throughout U.S. history have often been divisive in demanding that their constituents prioritize only one aspect of their identity. The suffrage movement was divided by race, as women of color were sacrificed by some segments in order to appeal to whites in the South and advance suffrage for white women. Women of color were asked to leave issues of race aside and focus only on the "woman question." The civil rights and second-wave women's movements repeated this pattern, again expecting women of color to focus only on race or gender, and largely excluding LGBTI issues and concerns. Intersectional theories have challenged this impossible expectation, highlighting the ways in which race, gender, sexuality, and other categories of identity are inextricably connected. Legal scholar Kimberle Crenshaw is credited with coining the term "intersectionality," and her analyses demonstrate the need for an intersectional perspective to address major social problems. She argues: "Intersectionality is a concept that enables us to recognize the fact that perceived group membership can make people vulnerable to various forms of bias, yet because we are simultaneously members of many groups, our complex identities can shape the specific way we each experience that bias. For example, men and women can often experience racism differently, just as women of different races can experience sexism differently, and so on" (Crenshaw, 3).

The theoretical developments of the last thirty years have provided a rich literature to guide our understanding of the myriad ways in which the categories and identities of sex, gender, and sexuality are interdependent. The chapters included in Part One each represent contemporary contributions to rethinking our conceptualizations of sex, gender, and sexuality, along with the tangled relationships among them.

Biologist Ann Fausto-Sterling has been a strong voice in debates over classifications of sex, gender, and sexuality. She argues that whether and how a culture creates categories of sex or sexuality are social decisions. As a scientist, she examines the physical, material world, but she argues that our understanding of this is always within the context of a specific culture shaped by our language, values, politics, and needs. Sharon Preves also examines the ways in which we decide how to classify bodies into sex categories, revealing the tremendous biological and anatomical variation that actually exists. Her work on intersex identity examines the process by which our culture transforms this variation into two and only two sexes. Leila Rupp shifts our attention away from U.S. hegemonic structures to examine those of other cultures at various historical junctures. In highlighting the tremendous cross-cultural variation in how sexuality is constructed and understood, she questions the limits of any one language or theory for exploring other times and places.

The selection by James Messerschmidt examines the *accomplishment* of gender, using cases of individuals whose gendered behavior in some settings does not reflect their sex appearance (perceived sex). He brings "sex" and the material realm more centrally into the picture and argues that we must understand human activity in the context of our embodied experience of gender. He raises the troubling issue of the extent to which masculinity depends upon aggression and violence for its performance. Messerschmidt's work also provides an excellent example of research on masculinity, a burgeoning area of inquiry.

Like Messerschmidt, Laura Carpenter examines individuals' own sense of reality—their own interpretations of sexual activity and their sense of gender and sexual identity. Carpenter demonstrates that, at the most basic level, individuals define sexual activity differently; asking a simple question such as "Are you a virgin?" can be difficult for people to answer, and their answers may change over time. Examining why this is the case reveals the complex ways in which our sense of gender and sexual identity shape our understanding of sexual practices.

While each chapter thus far has examined some aspect of the interconnections among sex, gender, and sexuality, chapters by Patricia Hill Collins and Abby Ferber bring race into the picture. Collins argues that racism, heterosexism, and gender are inseparable and cannot be understood alone. She advances an intersectional approach and demonstrates the very real dangers inherent in our attempts to theorize and conceptualize these as separate systems of oppression. Ferber integrates Collins' intersectional approach with deconstructionist theory and examines the centrality of border maintenance to the construction of identity.

Finally, author Chrys Ingraham examines the important supposition that heterosexuality is an institution. Her work exemplifies the ways in which various feminist scholars have made a critique of heterosexuality central to their analyses of gender hierarchy and inequality. Further, her work encourages us to examine the ways in which gender and heterosexuality are normalized in the minutiae of our daily existence. Her chapter explores weddings as one site where heteronormativity is naturalized.

Each of these perspectives contributes to advancing our theoretical knowledge about sex, gender, and sexuality and about the multifarious, complex ways they are interconnected and mutually constitutive. As you read through the following chapters, think about how they relate to each other. Where do you see these authors building upon the work of the others? Do you see that any contain inherent critiques or contradictions of other chapters? Which of these perspectives do you find most compelling? Which help you to reflect upon and better understand your own life experience?

REFERENCES

Butler, Judith. 1990. *Gender Trouble: Feminism and the Subversion of Identity*. New York: Routledge.

Collins, Patricia Hill. 2000. *Black Feminist Thought: Knowledge, Consciousness, and the Politics of Empowerment* (revised 10th anniversary 2nd edition). New York: Routledge.

Crenshaw, Kimberle. Intersectionality: A Primer. African-American Policy Forum. http://aapf.org

Kimmel, Michael S. 1994. "Masculinity as Homophobia: Fear, Shame, and Silence in the Construction of Gender Identity." In *Theorizing Masculinities*, ed. Harry Brod and Michael Kaufman. Thousand Oaks, CA: Sage.

Laqueur, Thomas. 1990. *Making Sex: Body and Gender from the Greeks to Freud*. Cambridge, MA: Harvard University Press.

Lorde, Audre. 1984. *Sister Outsider*. Trumansburg, PA: Crossing Press.

Nicholson, Linda. 1994. "Interpreting Gender." *Signs: Journal of Women in Culture and Society* 20 (Autumn): 79–105.

Scott, Joan W. 1988. *Gender and the Politics of History*. New York: Columbia University Press.

West, Candace, and Don H. Zimmerman. 1987. "Doing Gender." *Gender and Society* 1(2): 125–151.

1 • *Anne Fausto-Sterling*

DUELING DUALISMS

DISCUSSION QUESTIONS

1. Why does Fausto-Sterling argue that imposing categories of sex and gender are socially, not scientifically, driven?
2. How do contemporary categories of sexual identity complicate our understanding of historical findings of same-sex sexual behavior?
3. Why does the sex/gender dualism limit feminist analysis, according to Fausto-Sterling?
4. What limitations are there in using developmental systems theory?

MALE OR FEMALE?

In the rush and excitement of leaving for the 1988 Olympics, Maria Patiño, Spain's top woman hurdler, forgot the requisite doctor's certificate stating, for the benefit of Olympic officials, what seemed patently obvious to anyone who looked at her: she was female. But the International Olympic Committee (IOC) had anticipated the possibility that some competitors would forget their certificates of femininity. Patiño had only to report to the "femininity control head office," scrape some cells off the side of her cheek, and all would be in order—or so she thought.

A few hours after the cheek scraping she got a call. Something was wrong. She went for a second examination, but the doctors were mum. Then, as she rode to the Olympic stadium to start her first race, track officials broke the news: she had failed the sex test. She may have looked like a woman, had a woman's strength, and never had reason to suspect that she wasn't a woman, but the examinations revealed that Patiño's cells sported a Y chromosome, and that her labia hid testes within. Furthermore, she had neither ovaries nor a uterus. According to the IOC's definition, Patiño was not a woman. She was barred from competing on Spain's Olympic team.

Spanish athletic officials told Patiño to fake an injury and withdraw without publicizing the embarrassing facts. When she refused, the European press heard about it and the secret was out. Within months after returning to Spain, Patiño's life fell apart. Spanish officials stripped her of past titles and barred her from further competition. Her boyfriend deserted her. She was evicted from the national athletic residence, her scholarship was revoked, and suddenly she had to struggle to make a living. The national press had a field day at her expense. As she later said, "I was erased from the map, as if I had never existed. I gave twelve years to sports."

Down but not out, Patiño spent thousands of dollars consulting doctors about her situation. They explained that she had been born with a condition called *androgen insensitivity.* This meant that, although she had a Y chromosome and her testes made plenty of testosterone, her cells couldn't detect this masculinizing hormone. As a result, her body had never developed male characteristics. But at puberty her testes produced estrogen (as do the testes of all men), which, because of her body's inability to respond to its testosterone, caused her breasts to grow, her waist to narrow, and her hips to widen. Despite a Y chromosome and testes, she had grown up as a female and developed a female form.

Patiño resolved to fight the IOC ruling. "I knew I was a woman," she insisted to one reporter, "in the eyes of medicine, God and most of all, in my own eyes." She enlisted the help of Alison Carlson, a former Stanford University tennis player and biologist opposed to sex testing, and together they began to build a case. Patiño underwent examinations in which doctors "checked out her pelvic structures and shoulders to decide if she was feminine enough to compete." After two and a half years the International Amateur Athletic Federation (IAAF) reinstated her, and by 1992 Patiño had rejoined the Spanish Olympic squad, going down in history as the first woman ever to challenge sex testing for female athletes. Despite the IAAF's flexibility, however, the IOC has remained adamant: even if looking for a Y chromosome wasn't the most scientific approach to sex testing, testing *must* be done.

The members of the International Olympic Committee remain convinced that a more scientifically advanced method of testing will be able to reveal the true sex of each athlete. But why is the IOC so worried about sex testing? In part, IOC rules reflect cold war political anxieties: during the 1968 Olympics, for instance, the IOC instituted "scientific" sex testing in response to rumors that some Eastern European competitors were trying to win glory for the Communist cause by cheating—having men masquerade as women to gain unfair advantage. The only known case of a man infiltrating women's competition occurred back in 1936 when Hermann Ratjen, a member of the Nazi Youth, entered the women's high-jump competition as "Dora." His maleness didn't translate into much of an advantage: he made it to the finals, but came in fourth, behind three women.

Although the IOC didn't require modern chromosome screening in the interest of international politics until 1968, it had long policed the sex of Olympic competitors in an effort to mollify those who feared that women's participation in sports threatened to turn them into manly creatures. In 1912, Pierre de Coubertin, founder of the modern Olympics (from which women were originally banned), argued that "women's sports are all against the law of nature." If women were *by nature* not athletic competitors, then what was one to make of the sportswomen who pushed their way onto the Olympic scene? Olympic officials rushed to certify the femininity of the women they let through the door, because the very act of competing seemed to imply that they could not be true women. In the context of gender politics, employing sex police made a great deal of sense.

SEX OR GENDER?

Until 1968 female Olympic competitors were often asked to parade naked in front of a board of examiners. Breasts and a vagina were all one needed to certify one's femininity. But many women complained that this procedure was degrading. Partly because such complaints mounted, the IOC decided to make use of the modern "scientific" chromosome test. The problem, though, is that this test, and the more sophisticated polymerase chain reaction to detect small regions of DNA associated with testes development that the IOC uses today, cannot do the work the IOC wants it to do. A body's sex is simply too complex. There is no either/or. Rather, there are shades of difference.... One of the major claims I make in this book is that labeling someone a man or a woman is a social decision. We may use scientific knowledge to help us make the decision, but only our beliefs about gender—not science—can define our sex. Furthermore, our beliefs about gender affect what kinds of knowledge scientists produce about sex in the first place.

Over the last few decades, the relation between *social expression* of masculinity and femininity and their *physical underpinnings* has been hotly debated in scientific and social arenas. In 1972 the sexologists John Money and Anke Ehrhardt popularized the idea that sex and gender are separate categories.

Sex, they argued, refers to physical attributes and is anatomically and physiologically determined. *Gender* they saw as a psychological transformation of the self—the internal conviction that one is either male or female (gender identity) and the behavioral expressions of that conviction.

Meanwhile, the second-wave feminists of the 1970s also argued that sex is distinct from gender—that social institutions, themselves designed to perpetuate gender inequality, produce most of the differences between men and women. Feminists argued that although men's and women's bodies serve different reproductive functions, few other sex differences come with the territory, unchangeable by life's vicissitudes. If girls couldn't learn math as easily as boys, the problem wasn't built into their brains. The difficulty resulted from gender norms—different expectations and opportunities for boys and girls. Having a penis rather than a vagina is a sex difference. Boys performing better than girls on math exams is a gender difference. Presumably, the latter could be changed even if the former could not.

Money, Ehrhardt, and feminists set the terms so that *sex* represented the body's anatomy and physiological workings and *gender* represented social forces that molded behavior. Feminists did not question the realm of physical sex; it was the psychological and cultural meanings of these differences—gender—that was at issue. But feminist definitions of sex and gender left open the possibility that male/female differences in cognitive function and behavior could *result* from sex differences, and thus, in some circles, the matter of sex versus gender became a debate about how "hardwired" intelligence and a variety of behaviors are in the brain, while in others there seemed no choice but to ignore many of the findings of contemporary neurobiology.

In ceding the territory of physical sex, feminists left themselves open to renewed attack on the grounds of biological difference. Indeed, feminism has encountered massive resistance from the domains of biology, medicine, and significant components of social science. Despite many positive social changes, the 1970s optimism that women would achieve full economic and social equality once gender inequity was addressed in the social sphere has faded in the face of a seemingly recalcitrant inequality. All of which has prompted feminist scholars, on the one hand, to question the notion of sex itself, while on the other to deepen their inquiry into what we might mean by words such as *gender, culture,* and *experience.* The anthropologist Henrietta A. Moore, for example, argues against reducing accounts of gender, culture, and experience to their "linguistic and cognitive elements." In this book . . . I argue, as does Moore, that "what is at issue is the embodied nature of identities and experience. Experience . . . is not individual and fixed, but irredeemably social and processual."

Our bodies are too complex to provide clear-cut answers about sexual difference. The more we look for a simple physical basis for "sex," the more it becomes clear that "sex" is not a pure physical category. What bodily signals and functions we define as male or female come already entangled in our ideas about gender. Consider the problem facing the International Olympic Committee. Committee members want to decide definitively who is male and who is female. But how? If Pierre de Coubertin were still around, the answer would be simple: anybody who desired to compete could not, by definition, be a female. But those days are past. Could the IOC use muscle strength as some measure of sex? In some cases. But the strengths of men and women, especially highly trained athletes, overlap. (Remember that three women beat Hermann Ratjen's high jump.) And although Maria Patiño fit a common-sense definition of femininity in terms of looks and strength, she also had testes and a Y chromosome. But why should these be the deciding factors?

The IOC may use chromosome or DNA tests or inspection of the breasts and genitals to ascertain the sex of a competitor, but doctors faced with uncertainty about a child's sex use different criteria. They focus primarily on reproductive abilities (in the case of a potential girl) or penis size (in the case of a prospective boy). If a child is born with two X chromosomes, oviducts, ovaries, and a uterus on the inside, but a penis and scrotum on the outside, for instance, is the child a boy or a girl? Most doctors declare the child a girl, despite the penis, because of her potential to give birth, and intervene using surgery and hormones to carry out the decision. Choosing which criteria to use in determining sex, and choosing to make the determination at all, are social decisions for which scientists can offer no absolute guidelines.

REAL OR CONSTRUCTED?

I enter the debates about sex and gender as a biologist and a social activist. Daily, my life weaves in and out of a web of conflict over the politics of sexuality and the making and using of knowledge about the biology of human behavior. The central tenet of this book is that truths about human sexuality created by scholars in general and by biologists in particular are one component of political, social, and moral struggles about our cultures and economies. At the same time, components of our political, social, and moral struggles become, quite literally, embodied, incorporated into our very physiological being. My intent is to show how these mutually dependent claims work, in part by addressing such issues as how—through their daily lives, experiments, and medical practices—scientists create truths about sexuality; how our bodies incorporate and confirm these truths; and how these truths, sculpted by the social milieu in which biologists practice their trade, in turn refashion our cultural environment.

My take on the problem is idiosyncratic, and for good reason. Intellectually, I inhabit three seemingly incompatible worlds. In my home department I interact with molecular biologists, scientists who examine living beings from the perspective of the molecules from which they are built. They describe a microscopic world in which cause and effect remain mostly inside a single cell. Molecular biologists rarely think about interacting organs within an individual body, and even less often about how a body bounded by skin interacts with the world on the other side of the skin. Their vision of what makes an organism tick is decidedly bottom up, small to large, inside to outside.

I also interact with a virtual community—a group of scholars drawn together by a common interest in sexuality—and connected by something called a listserve. On a listserve, one can pose questions, think out loud, comment on relevant news items, argue about theories of human sexuality, and report the latest research findings. The comments are read by a group of people hooked together via electronic mail. My listserve (which I call "Loveweb") consists of a diverse group of scholars—psychologists, animal behaviorists, hormone biologists, sociologists, anthropologists, and philosophers. Although many points of view coexist in this group, the vocal majority favor body-based, biological explanations of human sexual behavior. Loveweb members have technical names for preferences they believe to be immutable. In addition to homosexual, heterosexual, and bisexual, for example, they speak of *hebephilia* (attracted primarily to pubescent girls), *ephebephilia* (aroused by young males in their late teens or early twenties), *pedophilia* (aroused by children), *gynephilia* (aroused by adult women), and *androphilia* (attracted to adult men). Many Loveweb members believe that we acquire our sexual essence before birth and that it unfolds as we grow and develop.

Unlike molecular biologists and Loveweb members, feminist theorists view the body not as essence, but as a bare scaffolding on which discourse and performance build a completely acculturated being. Feminist theorists write persuasively and often imaginatively about the processes by which culture molds and effectively creates the body. Furthermore, they have an eye on politics (writ large), which neither molecular biologists nor Loveweb participants have. Most feminist scholars concern themselves with real-world power relationships. They have often come to their theoretical work because they want to understand (and change) social, political, and economic inequality. Unlike the inhabitants of my other two worlds, feminist theorists reject what Donna Haraway, a leading feminist theoretician, calls "the God-trick"—producing knowledge from above, from a place that denies the individual scholar's location in a real and troubled world. Instead, they understand that all scholarship adds threads to a web that positions racialized bodies, sexes, genders, and preferences in relationship to one another. New or differently spun threads change our relationships, change how we are in the world.

Traveling among these varied intellectual worlds produces more than a little discomfort. When I lurk on Loveweb, I put up with gratuitous feminist-bashing aimed at some mythic feminist who derides biology and seems to have a patently stupid view of how the world works. When I attend feminist conferences, people howl in disbelief at the ideas debated on Loveweb. And the molecular biologists don't think much of either of the other worlds. The questions asked by feminists and Loveweb participants seem too complicated; studying sex in bacteria or yeast is the only way to go.

To my molecular biology, Loveweb, and feminist colleagues, then, I say the following: as a biologist, I believe in the material world. As a scientist, I believe in building specific knowledge by conducting experiments. But as a feminist Witness (in the Quaker sense of the word) and in recent years as a historian, I also believe that what we call "facts" about the living world are not universal truths. Rather, as Haraway writes, they "are rooted in specific histories, practices, languages and peoples." Ever since the field of biology emerged in the United States and Europe at the start of the nineteenth century, it has been bound up in debates over sexual, racial, and national politics. And as our social viewpoints have shifted, so has the science of the body.

Many historians mark the seventeenth and eighteenth centuries as periods of great change in our concepts of sex and sexuality. During this period a notion of legal equality replaced the feudal exercise of arbitrary and violent power given by divine right. As the historian Michel Foucault saw it, society still required some form of discipline. A growing capitalism needed new methods to control the "insertion of bodies into the machinery of production and the adjustment of the phenomena of population to economic processes." Foucault divided this power over living bodies (*bio-power*) into two forms. The first centered on the individual body. The role of many science professionals (including the so-called

human sciences—psychology, sociology, and economics) became to optimize and standardize the body's function. In Europe and North America, Foucault's standardized body has, traditionally, been male and Caucasian. And although this book focuses on gender, I regularly discuss the ways in which the ideas of both race and gender emerge from underlying assumptions about the body's physical nature. Understanding how race and gender work—together and independently—helps us learn more about how the social becomes embodied.

Foucault's second form of bio-power—"*a biopolitics of the population*"—emerged during the early nineteenth century as pioneer social scientists began to develop the survey and statistical methods needed to supervise and manage "births and mortality, the level of health, life expectancy and longevity." For Foucault, "discipline" had a double meaning. On the one hand, it implied a form of control or punishment; on the other, it referred to an academic body of knowledge—the discipline of history or biology. The disciplinary knowledge developed in the fields of embryology, endocrinology, surgery, psychology, and biochemistry have encouraged physicians to attempt to control the very gender of the body—including "its capacities, gestures, movements, location and behaviors."

By helping the normal take precedence over the natural, physicians have also contributed to populational biopolitics. We have become, Foucault writes, "a society of normalization." One important mid-twentieth-century sexologist went so far as to name the male and female models in his anatomy text Norma and Normman (*sic*). Today we see the notion of pathology applied in many settings—from the sick, diseased, or different body, to the single-parent family in the urban ghetto. But imposing a gender norm is socially, not scientifically, driven. The lack of research into the normal distributions of genital anatomy, as well as many surgeons' lack of interest in using such data when they do exist..., clearly illustrate this claim. From the viewpoint of medical practitioners, progress in the handling of intersexuality involves maintaining the normal. Accordingly, there *ought* to be only two boxes: male and female. The knowledge developed by the medical disciplines empowers doctors to maintain a mythology of the normal by changing the intersexual body to fit, as nearly as possible, into one or the other cubbyhole.

One person's medical progress, however, can be another's discipline and control. Intersexuals such as Maria Patiño have unruly—even heretical—bodies. They do not fall naturally into a binary classification; only a surgical shoehorn can put them there. But why should we care if a "woman" (defined as having breasts, a vagina, uterus, ovaries, and menstruation) has a "clitoris" large enough to penetrate the vagina of another woman? Why should we care if there are individuals whose "natural biological equipment" enables them to have sex "naturally" with both men and women? Why must we amputate or surgically hide that "offending shaft" found on an especially large clitoris? The answer: to maintain gender divisions, we must control those bodies that are so unruly as to blur the borders. Since intersexuals quite literally embody both sexes, they weaken claims about sexual difference.

This book reflects a shifting politics of science and of the body. I am deeply committed to the ideas of the modern movements of gay and women's liberation, which argue that the way we traditionally conceptualize gender and sexual identity narrows life's possibilities while perpetuating gender inequality. In order to shift the politics of the body, one must change the politics of science itself. Feminists (and others) who study how scientists create empirical knowledge have begun to reconceptualize the very nature of the scientific process. As with other social arenas, such scholars understand practical, empirical knowledge to be imbued with the social and political issues of its time. I stand at the intersection of these several traditions. On the one hand, scientific and popular debates about intersexuals and homosexuals—bodies that defy the norms of our two-sex system—are deeply intertwined. On the other, beneath the debates about what these bodies mean and how to treat them lie struggles over the meaning of objectivity and the timeless nature of scientific knowledge.

Perhaps nowhere are these struggles more visible than in the biological accounts of what we would today call sexual orientation or sexual preference.

Consider, for instance, a television newsmagazine segment about married women who "discovered," often in their forties, that they were lesbian. The show framed the discussion around the idea that a woman who has sex with men must be heterosexual, while a woman who falls in love with another woman must be lesbian. On this show there seemed to be only these two possibilities. Even though the women interviewed had had active and satisfying sex lives with their husbands and produced and raised families, they knew that they must "be" lesbian the minute they found themselves attracted to a woman. Furthermore, they felt it likely that they must always have been lesbian without knowing it.

The show portrayed sexual identity as a fundamental reality: a woman is either inherently heterosexual or inherently lesbian. And the act of coming out as a lesbian can negate an entire lifetime of heterosexual activity! Put this way, the show's depiction of sexuality sounds absurdly oversimplified. And yet, it reflects some of our most deeply held beliefs—so deeply held, in fact, that a great deal of scientific research (on animals as well as humans) is designed around this dichotomous formulation....

Many scholars mark the start of modern scientific studies of human homosexuality with the work of Alfred C. Kinsey and colleagues, first published in 1948. Their surveys of sexual behavior in men and women provided modern sex researchers with a set of categories useful for measuring and analyzing sexual behaviors. For both men and women, they used a rating scale of 0 to 6, with 0 being 100 percent heterosexual, 6 being 100 percent homosexual. (An eighth category—"X"—was for individuals who experienced no erotic attractions or activities.) Although they designed a scale with discrete categories, Kinsey and co-workers stressed that "the reality includes individuals of every intermediate type, lying in a continuum between the two extremes and between each and every category on the scale."

The Kinsey studies offered new categories defined in terms of sexual arousal—especially orgasm—rather than allowing terms such as *affection, marriage,* or *relationship* to contribute to definitions of human sexuality. Sexuality remained an individual characteristic, not something produced within relationships in particular social settings. Exemplifying my claim that with the very act of measuring, scientists can change the social reality they set out to quantify, I note that today Kinsey's categories have taken on a life of their own. Not only do sophisticated gays and lesbians occasionally refer to themselves by a Kinsey number (such as in a personal ad that might begin "tall, muscular Kinsey 6 seeks..."), but many scientific studies use the Kinsey scale to define their study population.

Although many social scientists understand the inadequacy of using the single word *homosexual* to describe same-sex desire, identity, and practice, the linear Kinsey scale still reigns supreme in scholarly work. In studies that search for genetic links to homosexuality, for example, the middle of the Kinsey scale disappears; researchers seek to compare the extreme ends of the spectrum in hopes of maximizing the chance that they will find something of interest. Multidimensional models of homosexuality exist. Fritz Klein, for example, created a grid with seven variables (sexual attraction, sexual behavior, sexual fantasies, emotional preference, social preference, self-identification, hetero/homo lifestyle) superimposed on a time scale (past, present, future). Nevertheless, one research team, reporting on 144 studies of sexual orientation published in the *Journal of Homosexuality* from 1974 to 1993, found that only 10 percent of these studies used a multidimensional scale to assess homosexuality. About 13 percent used a single scale, usually some version of the Kinsey numbers, while the rest used self-identification (33 percent), sexual preference (4 percent), behavior (9 percent), or, most shockingly for an academic publication, never clearly described their methods (31 percent).

Just as these examples from contemporary sociology show that the categories used to define, measure, and analyze human sexual behavior change with time, so too has a recent explosion of scholarship on the social history of human sexuality shown that the social organization and expression of human sexuality are neither timeless nor universal. Historians are just beginning to pry loose information from the historical record, and any new overviews written are sure to differ. . . .

As historians gather information, they also argue about the nature of history itself. The historian David Halperin writes: "The real issue confronting any cultural historian of antiquity, and any critic of contemporary culture, is...how to recover the terms in which the experiences of individuals belonging to past societies were actually constituted." The feminist historian Joan Scott makes a similar argument, suggesting that historians must not assume that the term *experience* contains a self-evident meaning. Instead, they must try to understand the workings of the complex and changing processes "by which identities are ascribed, resisted, or embraced and 'to note' which processes themselves are unremarked and indeed achieve their effect because they are not noticed."

For example, in her book *The Woman Beneath the Skin,* the historian of science Barbara Duden describes coming upon an eight-volume medical text. Written in the eighteenth century by a practicing physician, the books describe over 1,800 cases involving diseases of women. Duden found herself unable to use twentieth-century medical terms to reconstruct what illnesses these women had. Instead she noticed "bits and pieces of medical theories that would have been circulating, combined with elements from popular culture; self-evident bodily perceptions appear alongside things that struck [her] as utterly improbable." Duden describes her intellectual anguish as she became more and more determined to understand these eighteenth-century German female bodies on their own terms:

> To gain access to the inner, invisible bodily existence of these ailing women, I had to venture across the boundary that separates...the inner body beneath the skin, from the world around it...the body and its environment have been consigned to opposing realms: on the one side are the body, nature, and biology, stable and unchanging phenomena; on the other side are the social environment and history, realms of constant change. With the drawing of this boundary the body was expelled from history.

In contrast to Duden's anguish, many historians of sexuality have leaped enthusiastically into their new field, debating with one another as they dug into their freshly discovered resources. They delighted in shocking the reader with sentences such as: "The year 1992 marked the 100th anniversary of heterosexuality in America" and "From 1700–1900 the citizens of London made a transition from three sexes to four genders." What do historians mean by such statements? Their essential point is that for as far back as one can gather historical evidence (from primitive artwork to the written word), humans have engaged in a variety of sexual practices, but that this sexual activity is bound to historical contexts. That is, sexual practices and societal understandings of them vary not only across cultures but over time as well.

The social scientist Mary McIntosh's 1968 article, "The Homosexual Role," provided the touchstone that pushed scholars to consider sexuality as a historical phenomenon. Most Westerners, she pointed out, assumed that people's sexuality could be classified two or three ways: homosexual, heterosexual, and bisexual. McIntosh argued that this perspective wasn't very informative. A static view of homosexuality as a timeless, physical trait, for instance, didn't tell us much about why different cultures defined homosexuality differently, or why homosexuality seemed more acceptable in certain times and places than in others. An important corollary to McIntosh's insistence on a history of homosexuality is that heterosexuality, and indeed all forms of human sexuality, have a history.

Many scholars embraced McIntosh's challenge to give human sexual expression a past. But disagreement about the implications of this past abounds. The authors of books such as *Gay American History* and *Surpassing the Love of Men* eagerly searched the past for role models that could offer psychological affirmation to members of the nascent gay liberation movement. Just as with the initial impulses of the women's movement to find heroines worthy of emulation, early "gay" histories looked to the past in order to make a case for social change in the present. Homosexuality, they argued, has always been with us; we should finally bring it into the cultural mainstream.

The initial euphoria induced by these scholars' discovery of a gay past was soon complicated by heated debates about the meanings and functions of history. Were our contemporary categories of sexuality inappropriate for analyzing different times and places? If gay people, in the present-day sense, had always existed, did that mean that the condition is inherited in some portion of the population? Could the fact that historians found evidence of homosexuality in whatever era they studied be seen as evidence that homosexuality is a biologically determined trait? Or could history only show us how cultures organize sexual expression differently in particular times and places? Some found the latter possibility liberating. They maintained that behaviors that might seem to be constant actually had totally different meanings in different times and places. Could the apparent fact that in ancient Greece, love between older and younger men was an expected component of the development of free male citizens mean that biology had nothing to do with human sexual expression? If history helped prove that sexuality was a social construction, it could also show how we had arrived at our present arrangements and, most important, offer insights into how to achieve the social and political change for which the gay liberation movement was battling.

Many historians believe that our modern concepts of sex and desire first made their appearance in the nineteenth century. Some point symbolically to the year 1869, when a German legal reformer seeking to change antisodomy laws first publicly used the word *homosexuality.* Merely coining a new term did not magically create twentieth-century categories of sexuality, but the moment does seem to mark the beginning of their gradual emergence. It was during those years that physicians began to publish case reports of homosexuality—the first in 1869 in a German publication specializing in psychiatric and nervous illness. As the scientific literature grew, specialists emerged to collect and systematize the narratives. The now-classic works of Krafft-Ebing and Havelock Ellis completed the transfer of homosexual behaviors from publicly accessible activities to ones managed at least in part by medicine.

The emerging definitions of homo- and heterosexuality were built on a two-sex model of masculinity and femininity. The Victorians, for example, contrasted the sexually aggressive male with the sexually indifferent female. But this created a mystery. If only men felt active desire, how could two women develop a mutual sexual interest? The answer: one of the women had to be an *invert,* someone with markedly masculine attributes. This same logic applied to male homosexuals, who were seen as more effeminate than heterosexual men. [T]hese concepts linger in late-twentieth-century studies of homosexual behaviors in rodents. A lesbian rat is she who mounts; a gay male rat is he who responds to being mounted.

In ancient Greece, males who engaged in same-sex acts changed, as they aged, from feminine to masculine roles. In contrast, by the early part of the twentieth century, someone engaging in homosexual acts *was,* like the married lesbians on the TV news show, a homosexual, a person constitutionally disposed to homosexuality. Historians attribute the emergence of this new homosexual body to widespread social, demographic, and economic changes occurring in the nineteenth century. In America, many men and eventually some women who had in previous generations remained on the family farm found urban spaces in which to gather. Away from the family's eyes, they were freer to pursue their sexual interests. Men seeking same-sex interactions gathered in bars or in particular outdoor spots; as their presence became more obvious, so too did attempts to control their behavior. In response to police and moral reformers, self-consciousness about their sexual behaviors emerged—a budding sense of identity.

This forming identity contributed to its own medical rendering. Men (and later women) who identified themselves as homosexual now sought medical help and understanding. And as medical reports proliferated, homosexuals used them to paint their own self-descriptions. "By helping to give large numbers of people an identity and a name, medicine also helped to shape these people's experience and change their behavior, creating not just a new disease, but a new species of person, 'the modern homosexual.'"

Homosexuality may have been born in 1869, but the modern heterosexual required another decade of gestation. In Germany in 1880 the word *heterosexual* made its public debut in a work defending homosexuality. In 1892, heterosexuality crossed the ocean to America, where, after some period of debate, a consensus developed among medical men that "heterosexual referred to a normal 'other-sex' Eros. [The doctors] proclaimed a new heterosexual separatism—an erotic apartheid that forcefully segregated the sex normals from the sex perverts."

Through the 1930s the concept of heterosexuality fought its way into the public consciousness, and by World War II, heterosexuality seemed a permanent feature of the sexual landscape. Now, the concept has come under heavy fire. Feminists daily challenge the two-sex model, while a strongly self-identified gay and lesbian community demands the right to be thoroughly normal. Transsexuals, transgendered people, and a blossoming organization of intersexuals all have formed social movements to include diverse sexual beings under the umbrella of normality.

The historians whose work I've just recounted emphasize discontinuity. They believe that looking "for general laws about sexuality and its historical evolution will be defeated by the sheer variety of past thought and behavior." But some disagree. The historian John Boswell, for instance, applies Kinsey's classification scheme to ancient Greece. How the Greeks interpreted the *molle* (feminine man) or the *tribade* (masculine woman), in Boswell's view, did not necessarily matter. The existence of these two categories, which Boswell might consider to be Kinsey 6s, shows that homosexual bodies or essences have existed across the centuries. Boswell acknowledges that humans organized and interpreted sexual behaviors differently in different historical eras. But he suggests that a similar range of bodies predisposed to particular sexual activities existed then and now. "Constructions and context shape the articulation of sexuality," he insists, "but they do not efface recognition of erotic preference as a potential category." Boswell regards sexuality as "real" rather than "socially constructed." While Halperin sees desire as a product of cultural norms, Boswell implies we are quite possibly born with particular sexual inclinations wired into our bodies. Growth, development, and the acquisition of culture show us how to express our inborn desires, he argues, but do not wholly create them.

Scholars have yet to resolve the debate about the implications of a history of sexuality. The historian Robert Nye compares historians to anthropologists. Both groups catalogue "curious habits and beliefs" and try, Nye writes, "to find in them some common pattern of resemblance." But what we conclude about people's past experiences depends to a large extent on how much we believe that our categories of analysis transcend time and place. Suppose for a minute that we had a few time-traveling clones—genetically identical humans living in ancient Greece, in seventeenth-century Europe, and in the contemporary United States. Boswell would say that if a particular clone was homosexual in ancient Greece, he would also be homosexual in the seventeenth century or today. The fact that gender structures differ in different times and places might shape the invert's defiance, but would not create it. Halperin, however, would argue that there is no guarantee that the modern clone of an ancient Greek heterosexual would also be heterosexual.... The identical body might express different forms of desire in different eras.

There is no way to decide whose interpretation is right. Despite surface similarities, we cannot know whether yesterday's *tribade* is today's butch or whether the middle-aged Greek male lover is today's pedophile.

NATURE OR NURTURE?

While historians have looked to the past for evidence of whether human sexuality is inborn or socially constructed, anthropologists have pursued the same questions in their studies of sexual behaviors, roles, and expressions found in contemporary cultures around the globe. Those examining data from a wide variety of non-Western cultures have discerned two general patterns. Some cultures, like our own, define a permanent role for those who engage in same-sex coupling—"institutionalized homosexuality," in Mary McIntosh's terminology.

In contrast are those societies in which all adolescent boys, as part of an expected growth process, engage in genital acts with older men. These associations may be brief and highly ritualized or may last for several years. Here oral-genital contact between two males does not signify a permanent condition or special category of being. What defines sexual expression in such cultures is not so much the sex of one's partner as the age and status of the person with whom one couples.

Anthropologists study vastly differing peoples and cultures with two goals in mind. First, they want to understand human variation—the diverse ways in which human beings organize society in order to eat and reproduce. Second, many anthropologists look for human universals. Like historians, anthropologists are divided about what information drawn from any one culture can tell them about another, or whether underlying differences in the expression of sexuality matter more or less than apparent commonalities. In the midst of such disagreements, anthropological data are, nevertheless, often deployed in arguments about the nature of human sexual behavior.

The anthropologist Carol Vance writes that the field of anthropology today reflects two contradictory strains of thought. The first she refers to as the "cultural influences model of sexuality," which, even as it emphasizes the importance of culture and learning in the molding of sexual behavior, nevertheless assumes "the bedrock of sexuality... to be universal and biologically determined; in the literature it appears as the 'sex drive' or 'impulse.'" The second approach, Vance says, is to interpret sexuality entirely in terms of social construction. A moderate social constructionist might argue that the same physical act can carry different social meanings in different cultures, while a more radical constructionist might argue that "sexual desire is itself constructed by culture and history from the energies and capacities of the body."

Some social constructionists are interested in uncovering cross-cultural similarities. For instance, the anthropologist Gil Herdt, a moderate constructionist, catalogs four primary cultural approaches to the organization of human sexuality. *Age-structured homosexuality,* such as that found in ancient Greece, also appears in some modern cultures in which adolescent boys go through a developmental period in which they are isolated with older males and perform fellatio on a regular basis. Such acts are understood to be part of the normal process of becoming an adult heterosexual. In *gender-reversed homosexuality,* "same-sex activity involves a reversal of normative sex-role comportment: males dress and act as females, and females dress and behave as males." Herdt used the concept of *role-specialized homosexuality* for cultures that sanction same-sex activity only for people who play a particular social role, such as a shaman. Role-specialized homosexuality contrasts sharply with our own cultural creation: *the modern gay movement.* To declare oneself "gay" in the United States is to adopt an identity and to join a social and sometimes political movement.

Many scholars embraced Herdt's work for providing new ways to think about the status of homosexuality in Europe and America. But although he has provided useful new typologies for the cross-cultural study of sexuality, others argue that Herdt carries with him assumptions that reflect his own culture. The anthropologist Deborah Elliston, for instance, believes that using the term *homosexuality* to describe practices of semen exchange in Melanesian societies "imputes a Western model of sexuality . . . that relies on Western ideas about gender, erotics and personhood, and that ultimately obscures the meanings that hold for these practices in Melanesia." Elliston complains that Herdt's concept of age-structured sexuality obscures the composition of the category "sexual," and that it is precisely this category that requires clarification to begin with.

When they turn their attention more generally to the relationships between gender and systems of social power, anthropologists face the same sorts of intellectual difficulties when studying "third" genders in other cultures. During the 1970s European and North American feminist activists hoped that anthropologists could provide empirical data to support their political arguments for gender equality. If, somewhere in the world, egalitarian societies existed, wouldn't that imply that our own social structures were not inevitable? Alternatively, what if women in every culture known to humankind had a subordinate status? Didn't such cross-cultural similarity mean, as more than one writer suggested, that women's secondary standing must be biologically ordained?

When feminist anthropologists traveled around the world in search of cultures sporting the banner of equity, they did not return with happy tidings. Most thought, as the feminist anthropologist Sherry Ortner writes, "that men were in some way or other 'the first sex.'" But critiques of these early cross-cultural analyses mounted, and in the 1990s some prominent feminist anthropologists reassessed the issue. The same problem encountered with collecting information by survey emerges in cross-cultural comparisons of social structures. Simply put, anthropologists must invent categories into which they can sort collected information. Inevitably, some of the invented categories involve the anthropologists' own unquestioned axioms of life, what some scholars call "incorrigible propositions." The idea that there are only two sexes is an incorrigible proposition, and so too is the idea that anthropologists would know sexual equality when they saw it.

Ortner thinks that argument about the universality of sexual inequality has continued for more than two decades because anthropologists assumed that each society would be internally consistent, an expectation she now believes to be unreasonable: "no society or culture is totally consistent. Every society/culture has some axes of male prestige and some of female, some of gender equality, and some (sometimes many) axes of prestige that have nothing to do with gender. The problem in the past has been that all of us . . . were trying to pigeonhole each case." Now she argues instead that "the most interesting thing about any given case is precisely the multiplicity of logics operating, of discourses being spoken, of practices of prestige and power in play." If one attends to the dynamics, the contradictions, and minor themes, Ortner believes, it becomes possible to see both the currently dominant system *and* the potential for minor themes to become major ones.

But feminists, too, have incorrigible propositions, and a central one has been that all cultures, as the Nigerian anthropologist Oyeronke Oyewumi writes, "organize their social world through a perception of human bodies" as male or female. In taking European and North American feminists to task over this proposition, Oyewumi shows how the imposition of a system of gender—in this case, through colonialism followed by scholarly imperialism—can alter our understandings of ethnic and racial difference. In her own detailed analysis of Yoruba culture, Oyewumi finds that relative age is a far more significant social organizer. Yoruba pronouns, for example, do not indicate sex, but rather who is older or younger than the speaker. What they think about how the world works shapes the knowledge that scholars produce about the world. That knowledge, in turn, affects the world at work.

If Yoruba intellectuals had constructed the original scholarship on Yoruba-land, Oyewumi thinks that "seniority would have been privileged over gender." Seeing Yoruba society through the lens of seniority rather than that of gender would have two important effects. First, if Euro-American scholars learned about Nigeria from Yoruba anthropologists, our own belief systems about the universality of gender might change. Eventually, such knowledge might alter our own gender constructs. Second, the articulation of a seniority-based vision of social organization among the Yoruba would, presumably, reinforce such social structures. Oyewumi finds, however, that African scholarship often imports European gender categories. And "by writing about any society through a gendered perspective, scholars necessarily write gender into that society. . . . Thus scholarship is implicated in the process of gender-formation."

Thus historians and anthropologists disagree about how to interpret human sexuality across cultures and history. Philosophers even dispute the validity of the words *homosexual* and *heterosexual*—the very terms of the argument. But wherever they fall along the social constructionist spectrum, most argue from the assumption that there is a fundamental split between nature and culture, between "real bodies" and their cultural interpretations. I take seriously the ideas of Foucault, Haraway, Scott, and others that our bodily experiences are brought into being by our development in particular cultures and historical periods.

But especially as a biologist, I want to make the argument more specific. As we grow and develop, we literally, not just "discursively" (that is, through language and cultural practices), construct our bodies, incorporating experience into our very flesh. To understand this claim, we must erode the distinctions between the physical and the social body.

DUALISMS DENIED

"A devil, a born devil, on whose nature nurture can never stick." So Shakespeare's Prospero denounces Caliban in *The Tempest*. Clearly, questions of nature and nurture have troubled European culture for some time. Euro-American ways of understanding how the world works depend heavily on the use of dualisms—pairs of opposing concepts, objects, or belief systems. This book focuses especially on three of these: sex/gender, nature/nurture, and real/constructed. We usually employ dualisms in some form of hierarchical argument. Prospero complains that nature controls Caliban's behavior and that his, Prospero's, "pains humanely taken" (to civilize Caliban) are to no avail. Human nurture cannot conquer the devil's nature. In the chapters that follow we will encounter relentless intellectual struggle over which element in any particular pair of dualisms should (or is believed to) dominate. But in virtually all cases, I argue that intellectual questions cannot be resolved nor social progress made by reverting to Prospero's complaint. Instead, as I consider discrete moments in the creation of biological knowledge about human sexuality, I look to cut through the Gordian knot of dualistic thought. I propose to modify Halperin's *bon mot* that "sexuality is not a somatic fact, it is a cultural effect," arguing instead that sexuality *is* a somatic fact *created by* a cultural effect.

Why worry about using dualisms to parse the world? I agree with the philosopher Val Plumwood, who argues that their use makes invisible the interdependencies of each pair. This relationship enables sets of pairs to map onto each other. Consider an extract of Plumwood's list:

Reason	Nature
Male	Female

Mind	Body
Master	Slave
Freedom	Necessity (nature)
Human	Nature (nonhuman)
Civilized	Primitive
Production	Reproduction
Self	Other

In everyday use, the sets of associations on each side of the list often run together. "Culture," Plumwood writes, accumulates these dualisms as a store of weapons "which can be mined, refined and redeployed. Old oppressions stored as dualisms facilitate and break the path for new ones." For this reason, even though my focus is on gender, I do not hesitate to point out occasions in which the constructs and ideology of race intersect with those of gender.

Ultimately, the sex/gender dualism limits feminist analysis. The term *gender,* placed in a dichotomy, necessarily excludes biology. As the feminist theorist Elizabeth Wilson writes: "Feminist critiques of the stomach or hormonal structure...have been rendered unthinkable."... Such critiques remain unthinkable because of the real/constructed divide (sometimes formulated as a division between nature and culture), in which many map the knowledge of the real onto the domain of science (equating the constructed with the cultural). Dichotomous formulations from feminists and nonfeminists alike conspire to make a sociocultural analysis of the body seem impossible.

Some feminist theorists, especially during the last decade, have tried—with varying degrees of success—to create a nondualistic account of the body. Judith Butler, for example, tries to reclaim the material body for feminist thought. Why, she wonders, has the idea of materiality come to signify that which is irreducible, that which can support construction but cannot itself be constructed? We have, Butler says (and I agree), to talk about the material body. There *are* hormones, genes, prostates, uteri, and other body parts and physiologies that we use to differentiate male from female, that become part of the ground from which varieties of sexual experience and desire emerge. Furthermore, variations in each of these aspects of physiology profoundly affect an individual's experience of gender and sexuality. But every time we try to return to the body as something that exists prior to socialization, prior to discourse about male and female, Butler writes, "we discover that matter is fully sedimented with discourses on sex and sexuality that prefigure and constrain the uses to which that term can be put."

Western notions of matter and bodily materiality, Butler argues, have been constructed through a "gendered matrix." That classical philosophers associated femininity with materiality can be seen in the origins of the word itself. "Matter" derived from *mater* and *matrix,* referring to the womb and problems of reproduction. In both Greek and Latin, according to Butler, matter was not understood to be a blank slate awaiting the application of external meaning. "The matrix is a...formative principle which inaugurates and informs a development of some organism or object...for Aristotle, 'matter is potentiality, form actuality.'...In reproduction women are said to contribute the matter, men the form." As Butler notes, the title of her book, *Bodies That Matter,* is a well-thought-out pun. To be material is to speak about the process of materialization. And if viewpoints about sex and sexuality are already embedded in our philosophical concepts of how matter forms into bodies, the matter of bodies cannot form a neutral, pre-existing ground from which to understand the origins of sexual difference.

Since matter already contains notions of gender and sexuality, it cannot be a neutral recourse on which to build "scientific" or "objective" theories of sexual development and differentiation. At the same time, we have to acknowledge and use aspects of materiality "that pertain to the body." "The domains of biology, anatomy, physiology, hormonal and chemical composition, illness, age, weight, metabolism, life and death" cannot "be denied." The critical theorist Bernice Hausman concretizes this point in her discussion of surgical technologies available for creating male-to-female versus female-to-male transsexual bodies. "The differences," she writes, "between vagina and penis are not merely ideological. Any attempt to engage and decode the semiotics of sex...must acknowledge that these physiological signifiers have functions in the real that will escape...their function in the symbolic system."

To talk about human sexuality requires a notion of the material. Yet the idea of the material comes to us already tainted, containing within it pre-existing ideas about sexual difference. Butler suggests that we look at the body as a system that simultaneously produces and is produced by social meanings, just as any biological organism always results from the combined and simultaneous actions of nature and nurture.

Unlike Butler, the feminist philosopher Elizabeth Grosz allows some biological processes a status that pre-exists their meaning. She believes that biological instincts or drives provide a kind of raw material for the development of sexuality. But raw materials are never enough. They must be provided with a set of meanings, "a network of desires" that organize the meanings and consciousness of the child's bodily functions. This claim becomes clear if one follows the stories of so-called wild children raised without human constraints or the inculcation of meaning. Such children acquire neither language nor sexual drive. While their bodies provided the raw materials, without a human social setting the clay could not be molded into recognizable psychic form. Without human sociality, human sexuality cannot develop. Grosz tries to understand how human sociality and meaning that clearly originate outside the body end up incorporated into its physiological demeanor and both unconscious and conscious behaviors.

Some concrete examples will help illustrate. A tiny gray-haired woman, well into her ninth decade, peers into the mirror at her wrinkled face. "Who *is* that woman?" she wonders. Her mind's image of her body does not synchronize with the mirror's reflection. Her daughter, now in her mid-fifties, tries to remember that unless she thinks about using her leg muscles instead of her knee joint, going up and down the stairs will be painful. (Eventually she will acquire a new kinesic habit and dispense with conscious thought about the matter.) Both women are readjusting the visual and kinesic components of their body image, formed on the basis of past information, but always a bit out of date with the current

physical body. How do such readjustments occur, and how do our earliest body images form in the first place? Here we need the concept of the psyche, a place where two-way translations between the mind and the body take place—a United Nations, as it were, of bodies and experiences.

In *Volatile Bodies,* Elizabeth Grosz considers how the body and the mind come into being together. To facilitate her project, she invokes the image of a Möbius strip as a metaphor for the psyche. The Möbius strip is a topological puzzle..., a flat ribbon twisted once and then attached end to end to form a circular twisted surface. One can trace the surface, for example, by imagining an ant walking along it. At the beginning of the circular journey, the ant is clearly on the outside. But as it traverses the twisted ribbon, without ever lifting its legs from the plane, it ends up on the inside surface. Grosz proposes that we think of the body—the brain, muscles, sex organs, hormones, and more—as composing the inside of the Möbius strip. Culture and experience would constitute the outside surface. But, as the image suggests, the inside and outside are continuous and one can move from one to the other without ever lifting one's feet off the ground.

As Grosz recounts, psychoanalysts and phenomenologists describe the body in terms of feelings. The mind translates physiology into an interior sense of self. Oral sexuality, for example, is a physical feeling that a child and later an adult translates into psychosexual meaning. This translation takes place on the inside of the Möbius surface. But as one traces the surface toward the outside, one begins to speak in terms of connections to other bodies and objects—things that are clearly not-self. Grosz writes, "Instead of describing the oral drive in terms of what it feels like...orality can be understood in terms of what it does: creating linkages. The child's lips, for example, form connections...with the breast or bottle, possibly accompanied by the hand in conjunction with an ear, each system in perpetual motion and in mutual interrelation."

Continuing with the Möbius analogy, Grosz envisions that bodies create psyches by using the libido as a marker pen to trace a path from biological processes to an interior structure of desire. It falls to a different arena of scholarship to study the "outside" of the strip, a more obviously social surface marked by "pedagogical, juridical, medical, and economic texts, laws, and practices" in order to "carve out a social subject . . . capable of labor, or production and manipulation, a subject capable of acting as a subject." Thus Grosz also rejects a nature versus nurture model of human development. While acknowledging that we do not understand the range and limits of the body's pliability, she insists that we cannot merely "subtract the environment, culture, history" and end up with "nature or biology."

BEYOND DUALISMS

Grosz postulates innate drives that become organized by physical experience into somatic feelings, which translate into what we call emotions. Taking the innate at face value, however, still leaves us with an unexplained residue of nature. Humans are biological and thus in some sense natural beings *and* social and in some sense artificial—or, if you will, constructed entities. Can we devise a way of seeing ourselves, as we develop from fertilization to old age, as simultaneously natural and unnatural? During the past decade an exciting vision has emerged that I have loosely grouped under the rubric of developmental systems theory, or DST. What do we gain by choosing DST as an analytic framework?

Developmental systems theorists deny that there are fundamentally two kinds of processes: one guided by genes, hormones, and brain cells (that is, nature), the other by the environment, experience, learning, or inchoate social forces (that is, nurture). The pioneer systems theorist, philosopher Susan Oyama promises that DST: "gives more clarity, more coherence, more consistency and a different way to interpret data; in addition it offers the means for synthesizing the concepts and methods . . . of groups that have been working at cross-purposes, or at least talking past each other for decades." Nevertheless, developmental systems theory is no magic bullet. Many will resist its insights because, as Oyama explains, "it gives less . . . guidance on fundamental

truth" and "fewer conclusions about what is inherently desirable, healthy, natural or inevitable."

How, specifically, can DST help us break away from dualistic thought processes? Consider an example described by systems theorist Peter Taylor, a goat born with no front legs. During its lifetime it managed to hop around on its hind limbs. An anatomist who studied the goat after it died found that it had an S-shaped spine (as do humans), "thickened bones, modified muscle insertions, and other correlates of moving on two legs." This (and every goat's) skeletal system developed as part of its manner of walking. Neither its genes nor its environment determined its anatomy. Only the ensemble had such power. Many developmental physiologists recognize this principle. As one biologist writes, "enstructuring occurs during the enactment of individual life histories."

A few years ago, when the neuroscientist Simon LeVay reported that the brain structures of gay and heterosexual men differed (and that this mirrored a more general sex difference between straight men and women), he became the center of a firestorm. Although an instant hero among many gay males, he was at odds with a rather mixed group. On the one hand, feminists such as myself disliked his unquestioning use of gender dichotomies, which have in the past never worked to further equality for women. On the other, members of the Christian right hated his work because they believe that homosexuality is a sin that individuals can choose to reject. LeVay's, and later geneticist Dean Hamer's, work suggested to them that homosexuality was inborn or innate. The language of the public debate soon became polarized. Each side contrasted words such as *genetic, biological, inborn, innate,* and *unchanging* with *environmental, acquired, constructed,* and *choice.*

The ease with which such debates evoke the nature/nurture divide is a consequence of the poverty of a nonsystems approach. Politically, the nature/nurture framework holds enormous dangers. Although some hope that a belief in the nature side of things will lead to greater tolerance, past history suggests that the opposite is also possible. Even the scientific architects of the nature argument recognize the dangers. In an extraordinary passage in the pages of *Science,* Dean Hamer and his collaborators indicated their concern: "It would be fundamentally unethical to use such information to try to assess or alter a person's current or future sexual orientation. Rather, scientists, educators, policy-makers and the public should work together to ensure that such research is used to benefit all members of society."

The feminist psychologist and critical theorist Elisabeth Wilson uses the hubbub over LeVay's work to make some important points about systems theory. Many feminist, queer, and critical theorists work by deliberately displacing biology, hence opening the body to social and cultural shaping. This, however, is the wrong move to make. Wilson writes: "What may be politically and critically contentious in LeVay's hypothesis is not the conjunction neurology-sexuality per se, but the particular manner in which such a conjunction is enacted." An effective political response, she continues, doesn't have to separate the study of sexuality from the neurosciences. Instead, Wilson, who wants us to develop a theory of mind and body—an account of psyche that joins libido to body—suggests that feminists incorporate into their worldview an account of how the brain works that is, broadly speaking, called connectionism.

The old-fashioned approach to understanding the brain was anatomical. Function could be located in particular parts of the brain. Ultimately function and anatomy were one. This idea underlies the corpus callosum debate,...for example, as well as the uproar over LeVay's work. Many scientists believe that a structural difference represents the brain location for measured behavioral differences. In contrast, connectionist models argue that function emerges from the complexity and strength of many neural connections acting at once. The system has some important characteristics: the responses are often nonlinear, the networks can be "trained" to respond in particular ways, the nature of the response is not easily predictable, and information is not located anywhere—rather, it is the net result of the many different connections and their differing strengths.

The tenets of some connectionist theory provide interesting starting points for understanding human sexual development. Because connectionist networks, for example, are usually nonlinear, small

changes can produce large effects. One implication for studying sexuality: we could easily be looking in the wrong places and on the wrong scale for aspects of the environment that shape human development. Furthermore, a single behavior may have many underlying causes, events that happen at different times in development. I suspect that our labels of homosexual, heterosexual, bisexual, and transgender are really not good categories at all, and are best understood only in terms of unique developmental events affecting particular individuals. Thus, I agree with those connectionists who argue that "the developmental process itself lies at the heart of knowledge acquisition. Development is a process of emergence."

In most public and most scientific discussions, sex and nature are thought to be real, while gender and culture are seen as constructed. But these are false dichotomies. I start...with the most visible, exterior markers of gender—the genitalia—to illustrate how sex is, literally, constructed. Surgeons remove parts and use plastic to create "appropriate" genitalia for people born with body parts that are not easily identifiable as male or female. Physicians believe that their expertise enables them to "hear" nature telling them the truth about what sex such patients ought to be. Alas, their truths come from the social arena and are reinforced, in part, by the medical tradition of rendering intersexual births invisible.

Our bodies, as well as the world we live in, are certainly made of materials. And we often use scientific investigation to understand the nature of those materials. But such scientific investigation involves a process of knowledge construction. I illustrate this in some detail in chapter 5, which moves us into the body's interior—the less visible anatomy of the brain. Here I focus on a single scientific controversy: Do men and women have differently shaped corpus callosums (a specific region of the brain)? In this chapter, I show how scientists construct arguments by choosing particular experimental approaches and tools. The entire shape of the debate is socially constrained, and the particular tools chosen to conduct the controversy (for example, a particular form of statistical analysis or using brains from cadavers rather than Magnetic Resonance Image brain scans) have their own historical and technical limitations.

Under appropriate circumstances, however, even the corpus callosum is visible to the naked eye. What happens, then, when we delve even more deeply—into the body's invisible chemistry? In chapters 6 and 7, I show how in the period from 1900 to 1940 scientists carved up nature in a particular fashion, creating the category of sex hormones. The hormones themselves became markers of sexual difference. Now, the finding of a sex hormone or its receptor in any part of the body (for example, on bone cells) renders that previously gender-neutral body part sexual. But if one looks, as I do, historically, one can see that steroid hormones need not have been divided into sex and nonsex categories. They could, for example, have been considered to be growth hormones affecting a wide swath of tissues, including reproductive organs.

Scientists now agree about the chemical structure of the steroid molecules they labeled as sex hormones, even though they are not visible to the naked eye. In chapter 8, I focus in part on how scientists used the newly minted concept of the sex hormone to deepen understanding of genital development in rodents, and in part on their application of knowledge about sex hormones to something even less tangible than body chemistry: sex-related behavior. But, to paraphrase the Bard, the course of true science never did run smooth. Experiments and models depicting the role of hormones in the development of sexual behaviors on rodents formed an eerie parallel with cultural debates about the roles and abilities of men and women. It seems hard to avoid the view that our very real, scientific understandings of hormones, brain development, and sexual behavior are, nevertheless, constructed in and bear the marks of specific historical and social contexts.

This book, then, examines the construction of sexuality, starting with structures visible on the body's exterior surface and ending with behaviors and motivations—that is, with activities and forces that are patently invisible—inferred only from their outcome, but presumed to be located deep within the body's interior. But behaviors are generally social activities, expressed in interaction with distinctly separate objects and beings. Thus, as we move from genitalia on the outside to the invisible psyche, we find ourselves suddenly walking along the surface of a Möbius strip back toward, and beyond, the body's exterior. In the book's final chapter, I outline research approaches that can potentially show us how we move from outside to inside and back out again, without ever lifting our feet from the strip's surface.

---

2 • *Sharon E. Preves, Ph.D.*

INTERSEX NARRATIVES
Gender, Medicine, and Identity

DISCUSSION QUESTIONS

1. Given the relatively common occurrence of intersex births, why do you think people are so much more knowledgeable and willing to talk about cystic fibrosis or Down syndrome, which occur with similar frequency?

Sharon E. Preves, "Intersex Narratives: Gender, Medicine, and Identity." Written for this volume.

2. Why do you think intersex children are treated medically? What are the consequences of medical treatment for these individuals? For society?

3. Imagine that you are intersexed. How would you have wanted your parents and/or the medical community to respond? What do you think would be the most difficult issues you would face?

4. If you became the parent of an intersex child, what, if anything, would you do? Would your response be any different after reading this chapter?

If doctors really want to do something for their intersexed patients, I would say the first thing is [to] put the intersex person in touch with other people who are intersexed. Number two is see number one. And number three is see number one. That's it. Doctors think that you're going to kill yourself if you find out the truth. People kill themselves because they feel alone and isolated and helpless; that's why they kill themselves. When doctors don't tell their patients the truth, certainly they're cutting them off then from the opportunity of incredible support.

(Excerpt from interview with Sherri)[1]

BEYOND PINK AND BLUE

I recently participated in a cultural diversity field trip with twenty-two second graders in St. Paul, Minnesota. When I arrived at their school, the kids were squirrelly with anticipation. They were a colorful and varied bunch—some were tall and thin, others short and stout. Moreover, they were from a variety of racial and ethnic backgrounds and spoke nearly half a dozen native languages. When it was time to begin our community walking tour, the teachers attempted to bring the busy group to order quickly. How did they go about doing so? They told the children to form two lines: one for girls and the other for boys. The children did so seamlessly, since they had been asked to line up in this manner countless numbers of times before. Within moments, the children were quiet and attentive. I was struck then, as I had been many times before, by how often and in the most basic ways societies are organized by a distinction between sexes. With children of every shape and color, the gender divide worked as a sure way to bring order to chaos. "Girls in one line, boys in the other." Sometimes the choice between the lines— and sexes—isn't so easy.

Which line would you join? Girls' or boys'? Think about it seriously for a minute. How do you even know whether to line up with the girls or the boys? For that matter, what sex or gender *are* you, and how did you *become* the gender you are? Moreover, how do you *know* what sex and gender you are? Who decides? These questions may seem ridiculous. You may be saying to yourself, "Of course, I know what gender I am; forget this article." But really stop to think about how you know what sex you are and how you acquired your gender. Most of us have been taught that sex is anatomical and gender is social. What's more, many of us have never had the occasion to explore our gender or sexual identities because neither has given us cause for reflection. Much like Caucasians who say they "have none" when asked to explore their racial identity, many women and men find it difficult to be reflective about how they know and "do" gender (West and Zimmerman, 1987).

This article explores what happens to people who, from the time of their birth or early adolescence, inhabit bodies that do not afford them an easy choice between the gender lines. Every day babies are born with bodies that are deemed sexually ambiguous, and with regularity they are surgically altered to reflect the sexual anatomy associated with "standard" female or male sex assignment. There are numerous ways to respond to this plurality of physical type, including no response at all. Because sex and gender operate as inflexible and central organizing principles of daily existence in this culture, such indifference is rare if not nonexistent. Instead, interference with sex and gender norms is cast as a major disturbance to social order, and people go to remarkable lengths to eradicate threats to the norm, even though they occur with great regularity.

Recent estimates indicate that approximately one or two in every two thousand infants are born with anatomy that people regard as sexually ambiguous. Frequency estimates vary widely and are, at best, inconclusive. The estimates I provide here are based on a review of the recent medical literature (Blackless et al., 2000). This review suggests that approximately one or two per two thousand children are born with bodies that are considered appropriate for genital reconstruction surgery because they do not conform to socially accepted norms of sexual anatomy. Moreover, nearly 2 percent are born with chromosome, gonad, genital, or hormone features that could be considered "intersexed"; that is, children born with ambiguous genitalia, sexual organs, or sex chromosomes. Additional estimates report the frequency of this sexual variance as approximately 1 percent to 4 percent of all births. (Edgerton, 1964; Fiedler, 1978; Money, 1989).

These estimates differ so much because definitions of sexual ambiguity vary tremendously (Dreger, 1998b; Kessler, 1998). This is largely because distinctions between female and male bodies are actually on more of a continuum than a dichotomy. The criteria for what counts as female or male, or sexually ambiguous for that matter, are human standards. That is, bodies that are considered normal or abnormal are not inherently that way. They are, rather, classified as aberrant or customary by social agreement (Hird, 2000). We have, as humans, created categories for bodies that fit the norm and those that do not, as well as a systematic method of surgically attempting to correct or erase sexual variation. That we have done so is evidence of the regularity with which sexual variation occurs.

Melanie Blackless and her colleagues (2000) suggested that the total frequency of nongenital sexual variation (cases of intersexed chromosomes or internal sexual organs) is much higher than one in two thousand. They concluded that using a more inclusive definition of sexual ambiguity would yield frequency estimates closer to one or two per one hundred births, bringing us back to the 1 percent to 2 percent range.

To put these numbers in perspective, although its occurrence has only recently begun to be openly discussed, physical sexual ambiguity occurs about as often as the well-known conditions of cystic fibrosis and Down syndrome (see Desai, 1997; Dreger, 1998b; Roberts et al., 1998). Since approximately 4 million babies are born annually in the United States, a conservative estimate is that about two thousand to four thousand babies are born per year in this country with features of their anatomy that vary from the physical characteristics that are typically associated with females and males.[2] Some are born with genitalia that are difficult to characterize as clearly female or male. Others have sex chromosomes that are neither XX nor XY, but some other combination, such as X, XXY, or chromosomes that vary throughout the cells of their bodies, changing from XX to XY from cell to cell. Still others experience unexpected physical changes at puberty, when their bodies exhibit secondary sex characteristics that are surprisingly "opposite" their sex of assignment. Some forms of sexual ambiguity are inherited genetically, while others are brought on by hormonal activity during gestation or prescription medication that women take during pregnancy. Regardless of their particular manifestation or cause, most forms of physical sexual anatomy that vary from the norm are medically classified and treated as forms of inter-sexuality, or hermaphroditism.

INTERSEX IS A SOCIAL, NOT A MEDICAL, PROBLEM

While being born with indeterminate sexual organs indeed problematizes a binary understanding of sex and gender, several studies have shown—and there seems to be a general consensus (even among doctors who perform the "normalizing" operations)—that most children with an ambiguous sexual anatomy do not require medical intervention for their physi-ological health (Diamond and Sigmundson, 1997; Dreger, 1998a; Kessler, 1998). Nevertheless, the majority of sexually ambiguous infants are medically assigned a definitive sex, often undergoing repeated genital surgeries and ongoing hormone treatments to "correct" their variation from the norm.

I argue that medical treatments to create genitally *unambiguous* children are not performed entirely or even predominantly for the sake of preventing stig-matization and trauma to the children. Rather, these elaborate, expensive, and risky procedures are per-formed to maintain social order for the institutions and adults that surround these children. Newborns are oblivious to the rigid social conventions to which their families and caregivers adhere. Threats to the duality of sex and gender undermine inflex-ibly gendered occupational, education, and family structures, as well as heterosexuality itself. After all, if one's sex is in doubt, how would one's sexual orientation be identified, given that heterosexuality, homosexuality, and even bisexuality are all based on a sexual binary? So, when adults encounter a healthy baby with a body that is not easily "sexed," they may understandably be unable to imagine a happy and successful future for that child. They may won-der how the child will fit in at school and with its peers and will negotiate dating and sexuality, as well as family and a career. But most parents do not feel a real need to address these questions until years after a child's birth. Furthermore, I contend that parents and caregivers of intersexed children do not need

to be so concerned about addressing the "personal troubles" of their children either. Rather, we should all turn our attention to the "public issues" and problems that are wrought by an unwavering, mer-ciless adherence to sex and gender binarism (Mills, 1959:8).

Take Claire's experience as an example. Claire is a middle-class white woman and mother of two teenage daughters who works as a writer and editor. She was forty-four years old when she conveyed the following story to me during a four-hour interview that took place in her home. Claire underwent a clitorectomy when she was six years old at her parents' insistence, after clinicians agreed that her clitoris was just "too large" and they had to intervene. The size of her clit-oris seemed to cause problems not for young Claire, but for the adults around her. Indeed, there was noth-ing ambiguous about Claire's sex before the surgery. She has XX chromosomes, has functioning female reproductive organs, and later in life went through a physically uneventful female puberty and pregnan-cies. Claire's experience illustrates that having a large clitoris is perceived as a physical trait that is danger-ous to existing notions of gender and sexuality, despite the sexual pleasure it could have given Claire and her future sexual partners. In fact, doctors classify a larger clitoris as a medical condition referred to as "clitoral megaly" or "clitoral hypertrophy." Conversely, small penises for anatomical boys are classified as a medical problem called "micro-penis."

Reflecting on the reasons for the clitorectomy she underwent at age six, Claire said, "I don't feel that my sex was ambiguous at all. There was never that question. But I'm sure that [clitorectomies] have been done forever because parents just [do not] like big clitorises because they look too much like a penis." Even more alarming may be the physical and emotional outcomes of genital surgery that may be experienced by the patient. About the after effects of her surgery, Claire said:

> They just took the clitoris out and then whip stitched
> the hood together, so it's sort of an odd-looking
> thing. I don't know what they were hoping to pre-
> serve, although I remember my father thinking that

if someone saw me, it would look normal because there's just a little skin poking out between my lips so it wouldn't look strange. I remember I was in the hospital for five days. And then it just got better and everything was forgotten, until I finally asked about it when I was twelve. [There was] total and complete silence. You know, it was never, never mentioned. I know you know what that does. I was just in agony trying to figure out who I was. And, you know, why…what sex I was. And feeling like a freak, which is a very common story. And then when I was twelve, I asked my father what had been done to me. And his answer was, "Don't be so self-examining." And that was it. I never asked again [until I was thirty-five].

During the course of my research, I spoke with many other adults across North America who had childhood experiences remarkably similar to Claire's. Their stories are laden with family and medical secrecy, shame, and social isolation, as well as perseverance, strength of spirit, and eventual pride in their unique bodies and perspectives.

RESEARCH METHODS

I was astonished to find that so little research had been conducted with former patients or families about the experience and outcome of medical "normalization" procedures. When I began this research more than ten years ago, some adult intersexuals began coming forward to tell their stories. From this point, they began to form intersex support and advocacy groups, spurring the beginning of a burgeoning intersex social movement. Because these events coincided with my own research on intersex, I became aware of the important opportunity to speak with intersexuals about their experiences and perspectives firsthand.

Initially, recruiting willing interviewees for my study was a challenge because sexual ambiguity is generally not visible, and members of this population typically do not self-identify to others as intersexed and therefore are generally not mobilized. During the course of my research, however, several intersex support and advocacy groups either

emerged or came to my attention. Because they are a self-selected group, members of these organizations cannot be expected to represent the diversity of experience within the intersex population. In fact, given the difficulty of identifying members of this population, it is not possible to get a truly representative sample. Rather, these organizations served as a strategic and theoretically promising sampling base, given the social context of an emerging intersex social movement and my interest in the experience and process of social marginalization.

In the end, I interviewed thirty-seven intersexed adults from March of 1997 to September of 1998. The research participants ranged in age from twenty to sixty-five, with a mean age of forty, and lived in nineteen states and Canadian provinces. At the time of the interviews, 24 percent of the participants were living as a gender different from their sex of assignment and rearing; six were transitioning or had transitioned from female to male, and three from male to female. In 51 percent of the sample, intersexuality was apparent at birth or in infancy owing to genital ambiguity; for forty-nine percent, intersexuality was not apparent until puberty. I conducted the interviews in a private, face-to-face format, primarily in the participants' homes.

MEDICALIZATION, STIGMA, SECRECY, AND SHAME

The participants' experiences with medical attempts to "normalize" their bodies were amazingly consistent, despite the widespread variation of intersex diagnoses among those I interviewed. For example, intersexuals who underwent medical sex assignment in childhood experienced consistently negative and confusing messages about their bodies and their identities. In sum, the participants reported that they received the following three messages about themselves through medical sex assignment: (1) that they were objects of medical interest and treatment, (2) that they were not to know what was wrong with them or why they were receiving medical treatment, and (3) that such procedures were in their best interest and should remain uncontested and undisclosed. This model led the participants to lack information about their own bodies; open and honest communication within their familial, clinical, and friendship networks; and association with a potential peer group of intersexuals with whom to relate.

The objective of contemporary intersex medical treatment is to decrease social stigma and optimize the formation of clear and uncomplicated gender and sexual identities. The participants stated that because they were given false or incomplete information about their bodies and medical treatments and because they were encouraged to keep silent about their differences and surgical alterations, they experienced feelings of isolation, stigma, and shame—the very feelings that such procedures attempt to alleviate. The participants spoke frequently of wanting autonomy over their bodies, of longing to talk with others who had a similar anatomy, and of wanting to participate in decision making related to medical intervention. Feelings of shame were most intense in those who had recurring medical examinations or treatments to impose clarity on ambiguous sexual anatomy. These individuals spoke of feeling "monstrous, Other, and freakish." In stark contrast, when the same people spoke of gaining accurate information about their bodies, telling others openly about their physical differences, and finding other intersexuals with whom to relate, they relayed feelings of "relief, acceptance, and pride" about their difference and their identities.

As a means of illustrating the extent to which medicine alienates and objectifies intersexuals in its effort to study and control intersex variation, I quote extensively from intersexuals' life histories in the following sections. Each of these individuals speaks directly about the procedures of medicalization, the consequences of receiving ongoing negative attention to their difference, and the process of coming to accept and cherish their intersexuality.

BEING AN OBJECT OF STUDY

If identity formation is interactive, as symbolic interactionist social psychologists suggest, then receiving repeated messages that one's own body is socially unacceptable leads to a lasting and damaging impact on one's concept of self (Becker, 1963; Cooley, 1964 [1902]; Davis, 1995; Goffman, 1963; Hewitt, 1989; Holstein and Gubrium, 2000; Jones et al. 1984; Mead, 1934; Plummer, 1975; 1995; Strauss and Corbin, 1991). Such is the case for intersexuals who undergo repeated group examinations and operations on their genitalia. Conversely, if individuals receive positive feedback about their health and adequacy from the reflection of self offered by others, they will develop a sense of self that reflects that input (Jones et al., 1984). Because children are less discerning about the world, they are more passive in the socialization process during their early years. As George Herbert Mead (1934), John Hewitt (1970), and others have argued, reflected appraisal of the self may carry considerably more weight in childhood than in other periods of the life course.

Symbolic interactionists see social realities as dependent upon a shared definition of the situation. In this sense, both deviance and stigma are social products that emerge from social encounters and negotiations (Plummer, 1975, 1995). In other words, no one is inherently "normal" or "deviant"; such characteristics do not lie objectively within a person; instead what is considered normal or abnormal is culturally variable and dependent on human reactions (Goffman, 1963; Jones et al. 1984). When characteristics central to one's core concept of self, such as sex/gender, race, age, or overall physical appearance, become stigmatized, it is difficult to deemphasize the importance of these characteristics. In these cases, damage to one's self-concept may be dramatic, leaving a mark or stigma associated with a predominant characteristic upon which the self-concept is based. Here, the stigmatized characteristic becomes so central to one's overall identity that a concept of self will be developed around it, leading to a pervasive self-stigmatization that is generalized and associated with other, seemingly unrelated, aspects of oneself. In this sense, the stigmatized characteristic may become a dominating aspect of self from which (all) other concepts of self take their meaning (Jones et al., 1984). For example, an intersexed child whose sexual anatomy is repeatedly assessed as problematic may come to view herself or himself as a misfit in other matters as well.

The contrast in self-concept between participants who did not undergo medical sex assignment and those who did is striking. Drew, who was thirty years old at the time of our interview, was one of only two people in my study who did not undergo surgical or hormonal sex assignment in childhood. Drew spoke of first encountering the notion that her body was somehow pathological when she went to see a gynecologist for a routine exam at the age of twenty:

> When I was twenty, I had my first medical experience as an intersexed person. [The gynecologist] said, "Has your clitoris always been this large? I'd like to do some tests 'cause I think maybe something's not normal." And she used the word "normal" specifically like something was not normal. It was the first negative association I'd had, and [I] started [having] this feeling that I wasn't normal.

Until this interaction, Drew had received feedback from other medical professionals, her family, and peers that she was healthy, adequate, and normal, and her obvious physical differences were without negative association until that point. The gynecologist's negative assessment of her clitoris, compounded by the authority of the doctor's medical position, led Drew to question her former concept of self in light of this new and contrary information (Fisher and Groce, 1985).

Similarly, Suegee was raised without medical attempts to diminish her/his sexual ambiguity. Despite identifying her/his own gender as intersexed, Suegee was raised as female and when we met was living as a man, legally married to a woman with a young child. Here thirty-five-year-old Suegee describes how she/he experienced positive reactions to her/his body:

> It was at some point in my youth when I was playing doctor with other kids, or playing take off your clothes and show and tell, and realizing that I was different from anybody else there. And I also remember it wasn't a big deal at all.
>
> Everybody was like, "Wow! That's cool. Hey, you look like this, I look like this. Oh, yeah cool, fine, whatever." And that wasn't really a big deal at all.

Similar to Drew, Suegee did not have negative associations with her/his genitalia until she/he went to see a gynecologist at the age of sixteen.

> When I was 16 and I went off to see a gynecologist for the first time, which I was so excited [about]; I was like, "Oh boy! I'll get a whole bunch of answers." And she could just stutter out that she could recommend a good surgeon. And that was about it. She decided to examine my genitals and she was way too interested in examining my genitals. She was like... got me up in the stirrups and she's going, "Wow. Wow, that's... that's big! That's, that's real big!" And she was totally insensitive and completely just mesmerized by what she found.

But unlike Suegee and Drew, 95 percent of the people I spoke with underwent repeated medical examinations and procedures to downplay their physiological differences. And because they received extensive and prolonged reflections of themselves as pathological, many internalized feelings of inadequacy and shame. The inability to deflect negative interpretations of self may be one of the most harmful and traumatizing aspects of being intersexed in a society that adheres to the medical "correction" of such variation. As a result, the attempt to develop a coherent and positive concept of self amid continuous attempts to "fix" or change one's sex may be a project doomed to failure. According to J8, who was a thirty-six-year-old graduate student when we spoke,[3]

> The primary challenge [of being born intersexed] is childhood; parents and doctors thinking they should fix you. That can be devastating not just from the perspective of having involuntary surgery, but it's even more devastating to people's ability to develop a sense of self. I have heard from people who are really shattered selves, they don't have a concept of who they are. The core of their being is shame in their very existence. And that's what's been done to them by people thinking that intersexuality is a shameful secret that needs to be fixed. So I think for most people the biggest challenge is not the genital mutilation, but the psychic mutilation.

According to Goffman, differences that become socially stigmatized are those that are easily seen, such as the differences found among wheelchair users, amputees, and people with obvious facial scarring. Because clothing typically covers genitalia, genital differences are not readily visible (Goffman, 1963). Thus, intersexuals' genitalia must be made visible in order to allow for stigmatization. Repeated genital exams are a part of the medical protocol for assessing intersex patients' physiological development. Often, these examinations are performed with several doctors present, for the purpose of teaching medical residents, interns, and other clinicians about sexual ambiguity firsthand. The participants spoke frequently of the shame associated with such public displays of their "private parts." As Goffman noted, lacking control over others' access to one's body leaves individuals feeling threatened and out of control, as though "the stigmatized individual is a person who can be approached by strangers at will" (Goffman, 1963:16).

Several participants relayed stories about lacking autonomy during group medical examinations. Because these group examinations were a common element of their histories, several developed their own names for the alienating genital exam to express their feelings of being put on display. Some of these labels reflect the participants' feelings of being exhibited in a contemporary medical version of the freak show, such as "the dog and pony show" and "the parade." Carol, a thirty-eight-year-old social worker, wife, and mother, whose intersexuality was not apparent until her teenage years, was also the object of study at grand rounds when she was hospitalized for her upcoming orchiectomy, which is a procedure that removes abdominal testicles to ward off the possibility that they will become cancerous. At the time, Carol did not know that she was intersexed or that she had testicles or even the reason for her impending surgery. She spoke candidly of the shame and humiliation of one of the many "parades" to which she was subjected during her hospitalization at the age of nineteen:

> A few hours after I [checked in], the parade started. I stopped counting after one hundred. But I'm guessing about one hundred and twenty-five physicians, interns, [and] residents paraded by my bed over those five days that I was admitted to the hospital. I counted

literally one hundred and then quit counting because I didn't want to know. They came in groups. They just stood around my bed in a semicircle and talked. The doctor would give a little bit of a case history. He just said things like, "One hundred twenty-four pounds...five foot eleven and three quarters"...and things like that. I got so numb to it that I was eating and a parade of about ten came in at once and I kept eating, and I just lifted my gown and kept eating. And they all touched, poked, looked, mumbled, and then left. And I don't even remember looking at them. [I] put [my gown] down [and] kept eating.

What makes Carol's experience with hospitalization at the age of nineteen even more alarming is that when she went to the hospital, she thought she was simply there for a checkup and had no idea that surgery to remove her abdominal testicles was impending. After she overheard the hospital staff discussing her surgery, she inquired as to its purpose and was given little to no information. In her words,

> [I said to the doctor] as he was leaving, "Excuse me, the nurse said I'm having surgery," and he said, "Yes it'll be first thing in the morning." And I said, "For what?" and he said, "Don't worry, everything will be fine." And I said, "Why? Fine from what? Why am I having surgery?" And he said, "Well, your condition has gonads that could have abnormal cell growth, and we must remove them before it gets out of hand." And I said, "I have cancer, don't I?" And he said, "Oh don't worry about it. Don't worry about it, you're just fine. No, no, no, don't be silly. No, you don't have cancer. Don't worry." I said, "Well, then, why do I have...." "Don't worry about it, you're just fine." And I thought, "He's lying. He is lying; I have cancer." 'Cause that was the best diagnosis I'd come up with yet.

FEARING THE UNKNOWN: "WHAT KIND OF MONSTER AM I?"

As was true of Carol's experience, one of the most common themes in intersexuals' stories centers on the lack of full disclosure by clinicians and family members regarding the true nature of their intersexed conditions. Withholding information from the individuals only compounds their feelings of confusion and shame because they are told that there is something wrong with them, but they cannot and should not know the specific details of their condition. For example, Sarah, a fifty-six-year-old retired community college professor and library cataloger, spoke of the silence and secrecy she experienced in her late twenties when trying to ascertain the details of her own anatomy from her physicians. As she put it:

> They wouldn't tell me anything. I knew that there was more to it than all this. I knew that I wasn't being told the truth, but there was no way anybody was gonna tell me the truth. It was such a mess. There was so much lying and symboling going on that it's a wonder I ever figured it out. Mostly everybody figured it out for themselves.

In another case, Flora had the following experience with a genetic counselor when she was twenty-four:

> [The geneticist] said, "I'm obliged to tell you that certain details of your condition have not been divulged to you, but I cannot tell you what they are because they would upset you too much." So she's telling us we don't know everything, but she can't tell us what it is because it's too horrible.

Indeed, lacking peer contact with other intersexuals only served to further the participants' difficulty in formulating a coherent and stable self-concept because the participants had few, if any, accurate points of social comparison (Jones et al., 1984). Of this alienation, Tiger, who was subjected to sixteen failed genital surgeries in the hope that he would eventually be able to urinate from the tip of his penis, said, "The isolation is the *most* punishing aspect of this. You *really* do grow up with the internal sense of absolute freakishness." Having dealt with her difference in complete isolation all her life before finding a support group, Sherri, a thirty-nine-year-old lawyer said,

> The cruelest punishment we inflict on prisoners is solitary confinement. And intersex people have lived lives of solitary confinement. And I think that that is such a personal holocaust. Because to be completely separated from others, to not know that there are others, to only know it intellectually, but not know it viscerally is, without a doubt, solitary confinement.

In addition to experiencing their bodies as frightening and worthy of shame, many who had genital surgeries emphasized that the very operations that were intended to assuage their feelings of difference only served to deepen their sense of alienation. In reflecting upon the clitoral recession she underwent at age seven, Faye, a thirty-year-old scholar, spouse, and mother, said:

> I looked back on it and thought, this must have been really necessary. And that sort of went with me through childhood. If they would do this to me, it must be that I'm unacceptable as I am. The point is the emotional damage you do by telling someone that "You're so fuckin' ugly that we couldn't send you home to your parents the way you were." I mean, give the parents some credit. Teach them. Help them to deal with their different child.

SEEDS OF CHANGE—SEEKING COMPREHENSIVE INFORMATION AND SIMILAR OTHERS

Regardless of how the quest for information was initiated, the participants invariably made a commitment to learning more about themselves, ultimately seeking additional information about their bodies. In doing so, they turned to medical professionals and their families for answers. Such efforts often proved to be irritating or fruitless when many medical professionals denied them access to accurate information about their diagnoses or medical histories. For this reason, the participants often found it necessary to be both cunning and assertive in their quest for information. Carol recalled one such attempt to acquire additional information from the surgeon who removed her abdominal testicles when she was nineteen years old. Here, she relays a conversation with this doctor when she was twenty-one years old, during which she chose to lie to elicit her true chromosomal makeup. Her method was successful in the end:

I said [to my doctor], "I have one more question for you. I would like to know what I have that necessitated that you removed my gonads." And he said, "Well, you're just fine, there's nothing wrong." I said, "Listen, for *years* I thought I had a debilitating condition. I thought I perhaps had a progressive disease. I really believed that I possibly could still have cancer, even though you removed the unusual cells. I need to know what I have." And he said, "You don't need to worry about it, *really.* It's not something that you need to know." I said, "I need to know." And I thought, "He's not going to tell me. He's not gonna tell me. I *know* he's not going to tell me." And so I thought, "I've gotta either walk out and find somebody else [to tell me the truth] or I gotta nail this guy to the wall." And all of a sudden it hit me, I said, "Listen, I need to know because I am going into the Olympics this summer and I need to know if I'm going to test XY or XX." And he just froze. And he just looked totally panicked. And then he just dropped all pretense and he leaned over, he shook my hand with those great big long penetrating fingers, and he said, "Congratulations. You are such an intelligent woman. Congratulations for figuring it out." I said, "What did I figure it out? Do I have [androgen insensitivity syndrome]? And am I XY?" and he said, "Yes." And I said, "Well thanks for finally telling me the truth. Do I have cancer?" and he said, "No." And I said, "So, why did you remove them? Did my gonads have cancer? Were they cancerous?" He said, "There was some abnormal cell growth, but, no they weren't cancerous per se." "Where are my gonads?" I said. And he said, "Well, I sent them to the Clark Institute for inclusion in a research project." And I said, "And *what* did they learn about my gonads?!" and he said, "Um, ah, well, ah, I, I . . ." I said, "I would like to have copies of the research, please. Would you be able to get me copies of my research? I would like to find out *what* my gonads were all about, please." And he said, "Well I suppose I could," and I said, "I would also like to know if you have any more information on [androgen insensitivity syndrome] because I would like to read about it and learn more about it." He said, "If you insist."

Having successfully moved to a place of externalizing the dissatisfaction with their bodies and themselves and refocusing it on the source of that shame, as Carol conveyed, the participants were able to progress toward a greater acceptance and understanding of themselves. This development was easily notable in the participants' rejection of pathological references to the self. As Jana explained:

> Intersexuality is not a disease. Nobody dies from Klinefelter's syndrome, for example. It's not a disease. I'm not even gonna say it's an abnormality. I simply say it's a variation. Now I like my body, and I think I would have liked my body when I didn't like my body if I had known *why* it was like it is. This is the way I am, and I can accept that now. And I think I could have accepted it then, had I known, but I didn't know.

Learning to demedicalize their identities and accept themselves as healthy human beings often left the participants with feelings of pride in their difference. As Robin said,

> I feel special. My [intersex] has made me feel special, and it finally makes me understand why I am the way I am. It has made a big difference because I feel complete. I have found a part of myself that was lost.

Through this process of self-discovery, several participants became aware of other intersexuals' existence via electronic and print media, such as the Internet, television, and newspapers. While this initial association was certainly powerful, the connection remained incomplete for some until actual face-to-face meetings took place. The opportunity to meet other intersexuals signaled the end to a lifetime of seclusion. Melody, Claire, and Martha articulated the power of finding out they were not the only intersexuals after a lifetime of being sure that they would never encounter another human being with a body like theirs. In Melody's words, "You can't imagine what it was like! What a relief to find people and not to be alone! It was just incredible. It's like being green in a world of blue, and suddenly you find another green person. It was unbelievable. It was just really unbelievable." In Claire's account, "It's been incredibly freeing because there is that sense of not only finding someone like you, but finding a whole community where you belong. There's that wonderful sense of, 'Oh my god, I'm not alone.'" In a similar conversation, Martha added:

> After having lived all my life in isolation with this, suddenly to hear another person speak the words that I have spoken in the past; share the thoughts that I've had. Well what it felt like was that I've been living on this alien planet, portraying myself, passing myself off as an earthling, and I've met someone from, one of my people, from this other planet. You know?

HERMAPHRODITES WITH ATTITUDE: EVIDENCE OF INTERSEX PRIDE

Having found others with whom to relate, many participants spoke directly to the importance of using social visibility as a strategy for destigmatization and empowerment. Here, Tiger speaks of his appearances on television talk shows in an effort to educate lay audiences about intersex and externalize his prior feelings of shame:

> Becoming a person who is comfortable standing up in public, literally on television and saying, "No matter what you think of how I look or how I speak, no matter what I've done to fit into this world, I am not male or I am not female. And probably neither are you." To be in the position [of] making those kinds of statements and having all the signs and facts to back up my position, it's very exciting. This is a dramatic level of self-acceptance that I have fought with and been tortured by all my life. And to have come to a place where I realize that mine is a position of strength, *not* of disadvantageous exclusion, which is all it had ever been before… it's a good place to come to.

Similarly, in a rather gutsy and subversive move, the founding director of the Intersex Society of North America chose to embrace the alienating and shameful word *hermaphrodite* in the title of the group's newsletter. Speaking of her decision to do so, Cheryl said:

> I was so tickled with the fact that we had made this incredibly traumatic thing into something with humor

in it. And we came up with the name *Hermaphrodites with Attitude.* I thought of myself as incredibly subversive here. Here are all these little subversive messages winding their way out into the world. And [the newsletter] got *all* over the place. So many people told me, "I just saw the words *Hermaphrodites with Attitude,* and it changed my life in that moment. I was petrified and traumatized, that word had been so painful and yet, there it was out there. Just out there and then I picked up the newsletter, and it was my story on every page."

IMPLICATIONS

The implementation of radical, invasive, and life-changing medical sex-assignment procedures for children who are born with bodies whose sexual anatomy is labeled as different from the norm was standard practice until recently. However, the intersex patient advocacy and medical reform movement that began in the 1990s has gained tremendous legitimacy and ground in a short time. What's more, the patients' rights movement has upset this formerly unquestioned approach in medical education and practice and placed it into its current state of flux, controversy, crisis, and reform (Zucker, 2002).

One of the major lessons from these narratives is that sexual variation is nothing to be ashamed of and that it would not be experienced as shameful if it were recast as normal. Because sexual anatomy occurs on a continuum, diversity and variety are to be expected. Doctors, parents, and teachers have the ability and authority to reframe sexual variation in this way by responding to it with indifference. In addition to suspending unnecessary surgery on people with a sexual anatomy that is deemed ambiguous, these key socializing agents can truly destigmatize sexual variation by paying little attention to it.

Doctors, parents, and others have the ability to normalize sexual variation. In the meantime, they can help those who are labeled as intersexed by clearing the skeletons out of the closet and focusing on how best to love and support people who are cast as different. As the people in my study demonstrate, one of the most effective means of coping with difference is through relationships with others who are similarly alienated. Doctors and parents can easily assist those they care for by connecting them with the tremendous resources offered by intersex support and advocacy organizations. Doctors and parents can also engage in their own networking with the rapidly developing groups that are aimed at family and medical support, advocacy, and information exchange.

TO THE STORIES ONE LAST TIME

I opened this article with the words of one of the women I interviewed. I return to her words again, at the close, because she so eloquently conveyed the value of normalizing intersex through peer support, humor, and advocacy. Throughout her interview, Sherri spoke of feeling both grateful for and indebted to her support group for literally "saving her life." In closing, I turn to her resolution to carry her activism to her grave:

> I'll never repay, *ever,* in this lifetime I will never repay what I've been given. After I die, it all goes to the support group. My will is set up so that it all goes to the support group. My instructions in my will are to make my funeral as cheap as possible so that more money will go to the support group. That's where I want it to go. That's all I want it to go for. With the instruction that my headstone have the [support group's] web site address on it so that at least after I'm dead, people can still, I hope, pass by my gravestone and find information.

NOTES

1. Most research participants chose their own pseudonyms to be used in the presentation and publication of this research. Notably, 27 percent of those I interviewed chose to use their real names. I do not distinguish here or elsewhere between those who chose pseudonyms and those who did not.

2. National Center for Health Statistics (2001). Note that others have projected an annual birth rate of 1,500 to 2,000 intersexed children in the United States (Beh and Diamond, 2000).

3. This participant chose "J8" as her/his pseudonym. Rather than impose my own names on participants for the sake of legibility, I honored their choices in naming themselves.

REFERENCES

Becker, Howard. 1963. *The Outsiders.* New York: Free Press.

Beh, Glenn Hazel, and Milton Diamond. 2000. "An Emerging Ethical and Medical Dilemma: Should Physicians Perform Sex Assignment Surgery on Infants with Ambiguous Genitalia?" *Michigan Journal of Gender & Law* 7(1):1–63.

Blackless, Melanie, Anthony Charuvastra, Amanda Derryck, Anne Fausto-Sterling, Karl Lauzanne, and Ellen Lee. 2000. "How Sexually Dimorphic Are We?" *American Journal of Human Biology* 12:151–166.

Cooley, Charles Horton. 1964 [1902]. *Human Nature and Social Order.* New York: Charles Scribner's Sons.

Davis, Lennard J. 1995. *Enforcing Normalcy: Disability, Deafness, and the Body.* New York: Verso.

Desai, Sindoor S. 1997. "Down Syndrome: A Review of the Literature." *Oral Surgery, Oral Medicine, Oral Pathology, Oral Radiology, and Endodontics* 84: 279–285.

Diamond, Milton, and Keith Sigmundson. 1997. "Management of Intersexuality: Guidelines for Dealing with Persons with Ambiguous Genitalia." *Archives of Pediatric Adolescent Medicine* 151:1046–1050.

Dreger, Alice Domurat. 1998a. "'Ambiguous Sex'—or Ambivalent Medicine? Ethical Issues in the Treatment of Intersexuality." *Hastings Center Report* 28(3):24–36.

———. 1998b. *Hermaphrodites and the Medical Invention of Sex.* Cambridge, Mass.: Harvard University Press.

Edgerton, Robert. 1964. "Pokot Intersexuality: An East African Example of the Resolution of Sexual Incongruity." *American Anthropologist* 66: 1288–1299.

Fiedler, Leslie. 1978. *Freaks: Myths and Images of the Secret Self.* New York: Anchor Books, Doubleday.

Fisher, Sue, and Stephen B. Groce. 1985. "Doctor-Patient Negotiation of Cultural Assumptions." *Sociology of Health & Illness* 7:342–374.

Goffman, Erving. 1963. *Stigma: Notes on the Management of Spoiled Identity.* Englewood Cliffs: Prentice-Hall.

Hewitt, John P. 1970. *Social Stratification and Deviant Behavior.* New York: Random House.

———. 1989. *Dilemmas of the American Self.* Philadelphia: Temple University Press.

Hird, Myra J. 2000. "Gender's Nature: Intersexuality, Transsexualism and the 'Sex'/'Gender' Binary." *Feminist Theory* 1:347–364.

Holstein, James A., and Jaber F. Gubrium. 2000. *The Self We Live By: Narrative Identity in a Postmodern World.* New York: Oxford University Press.

Jones, Edward E., Amerigo Farina, Albert H. Hastorf, Hazel Markus, Dale T. Miller, and Robert A. Scott. 1984. *Social Stigma: The Psychology of Marked Relationships.* New York: W. H. Freeman.

Kessler, Suzanne J. 1998. *Lessons from the Intersexed.* New Brunswick, N.J.: Rutgers University Press.

Mead, George Herbert. 1934. *Mind Self and Society.* Chicago: University of Chicago Press.

Mills, C. Wright. 1959. *The Sociological Imagination.* New York: Oxford University Press.

Money, John. 1989 "Hermaphrodites: The Sexually Unfinished." *The Geraldo Rivera Show.* National Broadcasting Company, July 27.

National Center for Health Statistics. 2001. "Births: Preliminary Data for 2000." *National Vital Statistics Reports* 49 (5). (PHS) 2001–1120. Washington, D.C.: U.S. Government Printing Office.

Plummer, Ken. 1975. *Sexual Stigma.* Boston: Routledge & Kegan Paul.

———. 1995. *Telling Sexual Stories: Power, Change and Social Worlds.* New York: Routledge.

Preves, Sharon E. 2003 *Intersex and Identity: The Contested Self.* New Brunswick, N.J.: Rutgers University Press.

Roberts, Helen E., Janet D. Cragan, Joanne Cono, Muin J. Khoury, Mark R. Weatherly, and Cynthia A. Moore. 1998. "Increased Frequency of Cystic Fibrosis Among Infants with Jejunoileal Atresia." *American Journal of Medical Genetics.* 78:446–449.

Strauss, Anselm, and Juliet Corbin. 1991. "Experiencing Body Failure and a Disrupted Self-Image." In *Creating Sociological Awareness,* ed. Anselm Strauss, 341–359. New Brunswick, N.J.: Transaction Publishers.

West, Candace, and Don H. Zimmerman. 1987. "Doing Gender." *Gender and Society* 1:125–151.

Zucker, Kenneth J. 2002. "Intersexuality and Gender Identity Differentiation." *Journal of Pediatric Adolescence and Gynecology* 15:3–13.

3 • *Leila J. Rupp*

TOWARD A GLOBAL HISTORY OF SAME-SEX SEXUALITY

DISCUSSION QUESTIONS

1. Why is it so difficult to identify a term such as "gay" or "same-sex sexuality" that can be employed in historical and anthropological research?
2. Identify some of the factors that have been most salient in other times and places in structuring sexual relationships and desires.

Leila Rupp, "Toward a Global History of Same-Sex Sexuality." *Journal of the History of Sexuality* 10(2):287–302. Copyright © 2001 by University of Texas Press. Reprinted with permission by the publisher.

3. Rupp poses the provocative question: "How can we know for sure what is a sexual act?" Does your answer to this question change after reading this chapter?
4. How does even a cursory review of the construction of sexuality in various different cultures throughout history help us to better understand our own?

The blossoming of research on a wide range of manifestations of same-sex sexuality calls for an attempt at global thinking. Although my own work is rooted in U.S. and European history, I would like to make use of the work of scholars focusing on different parts of the world to reflect on what patterns might emerge. I take up this task from the perspective of one firmly committed to a social constructionist perspective on sexuality. Thus, I recognize that making transhistorical comparisons can be a risky business. Nevertheless, I think we can learn something by thinking about same-sex sexuality from a global viewpoint.

I favor the term "same-sex sexuality" as one that gets beyond the use of terms such as "queer," "gay," "lesbian," or "homosexual." Yet I would like to proceed by looking at manifestations of what we call "same-sex sexuality" in different times and places both to explore global patterns and to consider how those patterns make the two parts of the term "same-sex sexuality" problematic. That is, sometimes such manifestations cannot really be considered "same-sex," and sometimes they should not really be labeled "sexuality." These complications suggest that even the attempt to avoid assumptions about the meanings of desires, acts, and relationships by using a term such as "same-sex sexuality" may inadvertently lump together phenomena that are quite different. This is the difficulty of thinking about a global history of same-sex sexuality.

There are various ways that sexual acts involving two genitally alike bodies may in fact not be best conceptualized as "same-sex." In some cases, what is more important than genital similarity is the fact of some kind of difference: age difference, class

difference, gender difference. As numerous scholars have pointed out, across time and space those differences have in more cases than not structured what we call same-sex acts in ways that are far more important to the people involved and to the societies in which they lived than the mere fact of the touching of similar bodies.[1] (My favorite way to explain this to my students is through the story of my colleague's five-year-old son, who was one day playing with the family dog and a girl from his school. The girl said, "I love Lily [the dog] so much I wish I could marry her. But I can't because she's a girl." My colleague's son, viewing the relevant categories in a different way, responded, "That's not the reason you can't marry Lily. You can't marry Lily because she's a dog!") Looking at the whole question of sameness and difference from an entirely different angle, Jens Rydström's work on homosexuality and bestiality in rural Sweden reminds us that these two categories of deviant acts were not conceptually distinct in the past.[2] Thus, the lines between same-sex and different-species acts were not clearly drawn.

To start, probably the most familiar example is from ancient Athenian society where age difference between older and younger men determined the ways they engaged in sex acts, and such relationships had educative functions that were as much the point as the sex. Furthermore (although this is a bit controversial), the lack of an age or other differential was considered deviant, while same-sex and different-age (or different-status) relationships were not. Adult male citizens of Athens could penetrate social inferiors, including women, boys, foreigners, and slaves.[3] The privilege of elite men to penetrate anyone other than their equals lingered on into early modern Europe. "Missing my whore, I bugger my page," wrote the Earl of Rochester in Restoration England.[4] Were such men "bisexual," or was the whole notion of sexual object choice irrelevant? Was this "same-sex sex"? Or are such relations or acts best described as "different-status sex"?

We find examples of age differences structuring sexual acts in other parts of the world as well. In seventeenth-century Japan, men expected to desire sexual relations with both women and boys.[5] Two different words described love of women and love of boys. Styles of dress and distinct haircuts differentiated youths from men, thus creating visible categories of difference based on age. When a youth became a man, ceremonially donning the proper garment and having his forelocks shaved, he would cease his role as the anally penetrated partner and take on the adult male penetrator role in a new relationship.

Yet age itself could become a socially constructed category. That is, although it was a violation of the norms, men might keep the boy role well past youth. In *The Great Mirror of Male Love*, a collection of short stories published in Japan in 1687, "Two Old Cherry Trees Still in Bloom" tells of two samurai lovers in their sixties who had first met when one was sixteen and the other nineteen. "Han'emon still thought of Mondo as a boy of sixteen. Though his hair was thinning and had turned completely white, Mondo sprinkled it with 'Blossom Dew' hair oil and bound it up in a double-folded topknot anyway.... There was no sign that he had ever shaved his temples; he still had the rounded hairline he was born with."[6] John Boswell, who vehemently denied that age difference structured male same-sex relations in ancient Athens and the Roman Empire, suggests that the term "boy" might simply mean "beautiful man" or one who was beloved.[7] Boswell took this to signify that age difference was irrelevant, but it is also possible that this means, as in Japan, that age difference was crucial but that the concept of age might be only loosely tied, or not tied at all, to the number of years a person had lived.

In some societies, transgenerational same-sex relations are thoroughly institutionalized. We know

the most about a number of cultures in New Guinea in which boys cannot grow into men without incorporating the semen of older men into their bodies, either through oral sex, anal sex, or simply smearing it on the skin.[8] Such "boy-inseminating rituals" transmit life-giving semen, which produces masculinity and a warrior personality. What is critical here is that all boys take part in the ritual, and once they become men (sometimes through marriage, sometimes through fathering a child), they take on the adult role. Different cultures prescribe different lengths of time for such same-sex relations, different rules for which men should penetrate which boys (sometimes a mother's brother, sometimes a sister's husband), and different ways to transmit the semen.

Note that almost all of the information we have about age-differentiated relationships is about men.... Perhaps...comparable is a ritual among the Baruya in Melanesia in which lactating mothers nourish young girls who are not their own daughters by offering a breast, believing that breast milk is produced from men's semen and thus essential to womanhood.[9] A young girl at the breast, however, is reminiscent of motherhood, while a boy enclosing a penis has nothing to do with traditional men's roles. A more convincing, if still very sketchy, example can be found in Big Nambas society in the New Hebrides, where higher-ranking women took younger girls as sexual partners.[10]

The point here, of course, is that our construction of these interactions as same-sex may be totally foreign to the people involved. That is even more true for transgenderal relations, which can be found in a variety of cultures throughout history and around the globe. For a number of reasons—spiritual, political, economic, social, cultural—individuals take on (or are forced to take on) the social role, dress, and other markers of the (here our language fails us) "other" sex. Sexual relations may then occur between biological males of female gender and biological males of male gender, or biological females of male gender and biological females of female gender. (Here again, our language describes just two genders where other cultures may see three or more.) Such "gender-transformed relationships" can be found in many parts of the world.

We know the most about transgenderal relations among North American native peoples. The term "berdache," a derogatory French word bestowed by the horrified European invaders, emphasized the sexual aspects of the role, but in fact the spiritual characteristics of what some scholars now call the "two-spirit person" were sometimes more important.[11] The male transgendered role could be found in over a hundred American Indian tribes, the female in about thirty.[12] Among the Mohave Indians in the western United States, both male (*alyha*) and female (*hwame*) two-spirit roles existed. A two-spirit male would take a female name, engage in female occupations, and even enact menstruation and childbirth. "Manly-hearted women" would take on male characteristics and have children with their wives through adoption. Men–women sought orgasm through anal sex, while women-men engaged in tribadism or genital rubbing, with the two-spirit on top.[13]

Third-gender roles also existed in a number of Polynesian societies. From the late eighteenth century, European explorers and missionaries commented on men dressed as women who were sexually involved with men in Tahiti. *Mahus*, as they are known, according to an English missionary, "chose this vile way of life when young; putting on the dress of a woman they follow the same employments, are under the same prohibitions with respect to food, etc., and seek the courtship of men as women do, nay are more jealous of the men who cohabit with them, and always refuse to sleep with women."[14] More recently, *mahus* tend to be effeminate and interested in women's household tasks but do not dress entirely as women. They seek oral sex with men, who may ridicule them in public but also seek them out for fellatio.

Other examples of transgenderal relations involve transformation of the body in some way. The *hijras* of India are defined by their sexual impotence with women.[15] Some are born hermaphrodites, but others simply lack desire for women and as a result undergo the surgical removal of their male genitals. They wear women's clothes and hairstyles, imitate women's walk and talk, and prefer male sexual

partners. But they also exaggerate femininity and exhibit an aggressive sexuality that is unlike that of Indian women. They also have religious and ceremonial functions, performing at marriages and the birth of male children and serving as servants of Matar, the Mother goddess, at her temples. This is not to say that this is a high-status role in Indian society, for the *hijras* are much despised.

Not all cases of transgenderal relations have spiritual or religious origins or implications. The *travestis* of Brazil are transgendered prostitutes who, beginning at a young age, take female names and wear women's clothes as a result of their desire to attract men.[16] Although they do not, like the *hijras*, remove their genitals, they do take female hormones and inject silicone in order to enlarge their buttocks, thighs, and breasts. They work as prostitutes, attracting men who define themselves as resolutely heterosexual.

In the case of women who passed as men in early modern Europe, the motivation may have been a desire for occupational or literal mobility, although this is undoubtedly something we will never know for sure.[17] Women who dressed in men's clothing in order to join the army or take a man's job had to impersonate men in all ways, including in their relations with women. When discovered, punishment could be swift and severe for the usurpation of male privilege, particularly if it involved the use of what were called "material instruments" to "counterfeit the office of a husband," as a 1566 case put it.[18] In Germany in the early eighteenth century, a woman named Catharine Margaretha Linck dressed as a man, served in the army, and, after discharge, worked as a cotton dyer. She married a woman who, following a quarrel, confessed to her mother that her husband was not what he seemed. When the outraged mother took Linck to court and produced what another trial transcript in a similar case described as "the illicit inventions she used to supplement the shortcomings of her sex," Linck was sentenced to death for her crimes.[19] Were women who risked death looking only for better job prospects, or were these gender-crossers what we would today consider transgendered?

The connection between women's cross-dressing and same-sex desire becomes tighter over time. Lisa Duggan, in her analysis of the case of Alice Mitchell, a nineteen-year-old Memphis woman who murdered the girl she loved when their plans to elope came to naught, ties together the threads of romantic friendship, gender transgression, and the emerging definitions of lesbianism.[20] Jennifer Robertson's pathbreaking work on cross-dressing women in the Japanese Takarazuka Revue, founded in 1913, does much the same thing in a very different context. Exploring a rash of lesbian double suicides in Japan in the 1930s, Robertson details the erotics of fandom inspired by the Revue.[21] Like Duggan and Robertson, Lucy Chesser, in her dissertation on cross-dressing in Australia, shows the development over time of the idea that cross-dressing had something to do with same-sex desire.[22]

The point of all these examples is, once again, that sexual relations between two genitally alike (or originally alike) bodies are in many cases better defined as different-gender than same-sex relations. This seems clear in the case of two-spirit people or the *hijras* or *travestis*, but as the spectrum of transgendered relations moves from those who alter their bodies to those who simply take on some characteristics traditionally associated with the other/another gender, the lines get blurry. What about the "mollies" of eighteenth-century London? Like men in subcultures in other large European cities, including Paris and Amsterdam, "mollies" were effeminate men who frequented taverns, parks, and public latrines; sought out male sexual partners; and shared a style of feminine dress and behavior.[23] An agent of the English Societies for the Reformation of Manners entered a London club in 1714 and found men "calling one another my dear, hugging and kissing, tickling and feeling each other, as if they were a mixture of wanton males and females; and assuming effeminate voices, female airs."[24] What about the "roaring girls" of London or the "randy women" of Amsterdam, cross-dressed but not entirely? Mary Frith, known by her pseudonym, Moll Cutpurse, the model for a number of early-seventeenth-century English accounts, struck one observer as "both man and woman."[25] Examples of gender-differentiated pairings—the *bichas* (faggots) and *bofes* (real men) of Brazil, the *jotas* (homosexuals) and *mayates* (men who have sex with *jotas*) of Mexico City, the butches and fems of 1950s American bar culture, the "mine wives" and "husbands" of South Africa—can be found in many parts of the world, and how much they are perceived within their own cultures as different-gender and how much as same-sex is a tricky question.[26]

In the narrowest sense, then, "same-sex sexuality" may best refer to modern Western notions of relations between individuals undifferentiated by gender, age, class, or any other factors—in other words, those (or some of those) who adopt a "gay" or "lesbian" identity. That is an irony of a term designed to do just the opposite.

The second part of my critique of the term "same-sex sexuality" is already implicit here. That is, how do we determine what is "sexuality" and what is something else in these different interactions? Scholars have argued that "sexuality" itself is a relatively modern concept, that, for example, acts of fellatio or anal penetration in ancient Athens were expressions of power, acts of domination and submission, not "sexuality."[27] In the case of the Sambia boys in New Guinea who ingest semen through acts of fellatio on older men, we can ask, "Is that a sexual act? Or akin to taking vitamins?" Is it significant that the boys swallow the semen directly from a penis rather than from a bowl with a spoon?[28]

How can we know for sure what is a sexual act? There are really two questions here. How do we think about acts—such as fellatio, cunnilingus, anal penetration—that seem clearly sexual yet may have other meanings? What do we make of acts—such as kissing, hugging, cuddling—that may or may not be considered "sex"? These questions in turn raise a third: Are certain acts associated with specific forms of relationships?

We have already considered the possibility that fellatio and a girl's mouth on the breast of a woman not her mother may be about a kind of spiritual nutrition rather than sexuality; and even that a whole range of acts might be the assertion of elite male privilege, a sign of power. Some scholars argue that particular acts—especially anal penetration—carry meanings that are far more about power than sex and did so even before the advent of the concept "sexuality." Richard Trexler, for example, interprets the cross-gender male role in the Americas at the time of conquest as just another form of a long-lasting practice of men dominating other men by raping them, either literally or symbolically.[29] Eva Keuls, in her study of sexual politics in ancient Athens, argues that anal intercourse was an "initiatory rite of submission to the desires of the established class," an assertion of superiority rather than a source of pleasure. Agreeing with Trexler, Keuls asserts that "anal sex is charged with aggression and domination: The submitting partner is in a helpless position, penetration can be painful, and opportunity for the gratification of the passive participant is limited."[30] If these are accurate conclusions (and I know that a chorus of voices will be raised to shout that they are not!), can we think of such interactions as "same-sex sexuality" at all, or are they, rather, "same-sex domination"?

What about societies that make room for loving relations that seem sexual to outsiders but not to the participants? In Basotho society in contemporary Lesotho, girls and women exchange long kisses, putting their tongues in each others' mouths; they fondle each other and endeavor to lengthen the labia minora; they rub their bodies together and engage in cunnilingus without defining any of this as sexual. They fall in love and form marriage-like unions. In this context sex requires a penis and marriage means sex with a man, so there is no such concept as lesbian sex or lesbian relationships.[31] Are these sexual acts? . . .

Although I am bold enough to dare to address a global history of same-sex sexuality, I am not foolish enough to pretend to have answers to all of these questions. As the Euramerican nature of most of the evidence I use to consider the nature of sexual acts makes plain, we (or, certainly, I) do not know enough about such questions in other parts of the world to say anything even suggestive. But I do think these are good questions for future research.

NOTES

1. Stephen O. Murray, "Homosexual Categorization in Cross-Cultural Perspective," in *Latin American Male Homosexualities*, ed. Stephen O. Murray (Albuquerque: University of New Mexico Press, 1995), 3–32, cites a number of schemes for the social structuring of homosexuality and adopts that of Barry Adam, "Age, Structure, and Sexuality," *Journal of Homosexuality* 11 (1986): 19–33. This includes age-structured, gender-defined, profession-defined, and egalitarian. In Murray's most recent book, *Homosexualities* (Chicago: University of Chicago Press, 2000), he includes "profession-defined" under "gender-defined." John Howard, in his comment on the paper I delivered at Oslo, added race and ethnicity to this list, citing Nayan Shah's work on Indian and Chinese men arrested in British Columbia for their sexual relations with Anglo-Canadian men, along with his own work on African American and white same-sex interactions in the U.S. South. See Nayan Shah, "The Race of Sodomy: Asian Men, White Boys, and the Policing of Sex in North America" (paper presented at the Organization of American Historians conference, St. Louis, April 2000); John Howard, *Men Like That: A Southern Queer History* (Chicago: University of Chicago Press, 1999).

2. Jens Rydström, "Beasts and Beauties: Bestiality and Male Homosexuality in Rural Sweden, 1880–1950" (paper presented at the 19th International Congress of Historical Sciences, Oslo, Norway, August 2000).

3. The classic work is K. J. Dover, *Greek Homosexuality* (New York: Vintage, 1978). More recent studies include Eva C. Keuls, *The Reign of the Phallus: Sexual Politics in Ancient Athens* (New York: Harper and Row, 1985); David Halperin, *One Hundred Years of Homosexuality and Other Essays on Greek Love* (New York: Routledge, 1990); Eva Cantarella, *Bisexuality in the Ancient World* (New Haven, CT: Yale University Press, 1992); and Wayne R. Dynes and Stephen Donaldson, eds., *Homosexuality in the Ancient World* (New York: Garland, 1992). See also Craig A. Williams, *Roman Homosexuality: Ideologies of Masculinity in Classical Antiquity* (New York: Oxford University Press, 1999). John Boswell, "Revolutions, Universals, and Sexual Categories," in *Hidden From History: Reclaiming the Gay and Lesbian Past*, ed. Martin Bauml Duberman, Martha Vicinus, and George Chauncey, Jr. (New York: New American Library, 1989), 17–36, disputes the notion that an age or status difference was essential to same-sex relations in Athenian society, and, more recently, Murray, in *Homosexualities*, has argued that undifferentiated (what

he calls "egalitarian") relationships between men existed in ancient Greece and Rome (as well as in other premodern places) and that age difference did not always determine sexual role.

4. Quoted in James M. Saslow, "Homosexuality in the Renaissance: Behavior, Identity, and Artistic Expression," in *Hidden From History*, 90–105, quotation on 92. See Alan Bray, *Homosexuality in Renaissance England* (New York: Columbia University Press, 1982); Michael Rocke, *Forbidden Friendships: Homosexuality and Male Culture in Renaissance Florence* (New York: Oxford University Press, 1996); Louise Fradenburg and Carla Freccero, eds., *Premodern Sexualities* (New York: Routledge, 1996); Carolyn Dinshaw, *Getting Medieval: Sexualities and Communities, Pre- and Postmodern* (Durham, NC: Duke University Press, 1999); James M. Saslow, *Pictures and Passions: A History of Homosexuality in the Visual Arts* (New York: Viking, 1999); Glenn Burger and Steven F. Kruger, eds., *Queering the Middle Ages* (Minneapolis: University of Minnesota Press, 2001).

5. Paul Gordon Schalow, ed., *The Great Mirror of Male Love* (Stanford, CA: Stanford University Press, 1990); Stephen O. Murray, "Male Homosexuality in Japan before the Meiji Restoration," in *Oceanic Homosexualities*, ed. Stephen O. Murray (New York: Garland, 1992), 363–70; Gary P. Leupp, *Male Colors: The Construction of Homosexuality in Tokugawa Japan* (Berkeley: University of California Press, 1995).

6. Quoted in Paul Gordon Schalow, "Male Love in Early Modern Japan: A Literary Depiction of the 'Youth,'" in *Hidden from History*, 118–28, quotation on 126.

7. John Boswell, *Christianity, Social Tolerance, and Homosexuality* (Chicago: University of Chicago Press, 1980), 28–30.

8. David F. Greenberg, *The Construction of Homosexuality* (Chicago: University of Chicago Press, 1988), 26–40; Gilbert Herdt, *Same Sex, Different Cultures* (Boulder, CO: Westview Press, 1997), 64–88; Murray, *Oceanic Homosexualities*.

9. Greenberg, *Construction of Homosexuality*, 29.

10. Herdt, *Same-Sex, Different Cultures*, 86.

11. Herdt, *Same-Sex, Different Cultures*, 90–102; Walter L. Williams, *The Spirit and the Flesh: Sexual Diversity in American Indian Culture* (Boston: Beacon Press, 1986); Sue-Ellen Jacobs, Wesley Thomas, and Sabine Lang, eds., *Two-Spirit People: Native American Gender Identity, Sexuality, and Spirituality* (Urbana: University of Illinois Press, 1997). There is disagreement about the status of transgendered individuals in the Americas. For a contrary view to those cited above, see Richard

C. Trexler, *Sex and Conquest: Gendered Violence, Political Order, and the European Conquest of the Americas* (Ithaca, NY: Cornell University Press, 1995).

12. Herdt, *Same Sex, Different Cultures*, 91.

13. Herdt, *Same Sex, Different Cultures*, 92–94.

14. Quoted in Greenberg, *Construction of Homosexuality*, 58. See also Raleigh Watts, "The Polynesian Mahu," in Murray, *Oceanic Homosexualities*, 171–84.

15. Serena Nanda, "Hijras: An Alternative Sex and Gender Role in India," in *Third Sex, Third Gender: Beyond Sexual Dimorphism in Culture and History*, ed. Gilbert Herdt (New York: Zone Books, 1996), 373–417.

16. Don Kulick, *Travesti: Sex, Gender and Culture among Brazilian Transgendered Prostitutes* (Chicago: University of Chicago Press, 1998).

17. Rudolf M. Dekker and Lotte C. van de Pol, *The Tradition of Female Transvestism in Early Modern Europe* (London: Macmillan Press, 1989).

18. Quoted in Lillian Faderman, *Surpassing the Love of Men* (New York: William Morrow, 1981), 51.

19. Faderman, *Surpassing the Love of Men*, 51–52.

20. Lisa Duggan, *Sapphic Slashers: Sex, Violence, and American Modernity* (Durham, NC: Duke University Press, 2001).

21. Jennifer Robertson, *Takarazuka: Sexual Politics and Popular Culture in Modern Japan* (Berkeley: University of California Press, 1998); Jennifer Robertson, "Dying to Tell: Sexuality and Suicide in Imperial Japan," *Signs: Journal of Women in Culture and Society* 25: 1–36 (1999).

22. Lucy Sarah Chesser, "'Parting with My Sex for a Season': Cross-Dressing, Inversion and Sexuality in Australian Cultural Life, 1850–1920," (Ph.D. diss., La Trobe University, 2001). See also Lucy Chesser, "'A Woman Who Married Three Wives': Management of Disruptive Knowledge in the 1879 Australian Case of Edward De Lacy Evans," *Journal of Women's History* 9:53–77 (winter 1998).

23. Rictor Norton, *Mother Clap's Molly House: The Gay Subculture in England 1700–1830* (London: GMP Publishers, 1992); Michael Rey, "Parisian Homosexuals Create a Lifestyle, 1700–1750: The Police Archives," *Eighteenth-Century Life* 9, new series 3: 179–91 (1985); Jeffrey Merrick, "Sodomitical Scandals and Subcultures in the 1720s," *Men and Masculinities* 1:365–84 (April 1999); Arend H. Huussen, Jr., "Sodomy in the Dutch Republic during the Eighteenth Century," *Unauthorized Sexual Behavior during the Enlightenment*, ed. Robert P. Maccubbin (Williamsburg, VA: College of William and Mary Press, 1985), 169–78.

24. Randolph Trumbach, "The Birth of the Queen: Sodomy and the Emergence of Gender Equality in Modern Culture, 1660–1750," in *Hidden from History*, 129–40, quotation on 137. See also Randolph Trumbach, *Sex and the Gender Revolution: Heterosexuality and the Third Gender in Enlightenment London* (Chicago: University of Chicago Press, 1998).

25. Quoted in Faderman, *Surpassing the Love of Men*, 57. "Randy women" is a rough translation of *lollepotten*, a term analyzed by Myriam Everard in "Ziel en zinnen: Over liefde en lust tussen vrouwen in de tweede helft van de achttiende eeuw" (Ph.D. diss., Rijksuniversiteit Leiden, 1994).

26. See James N. Green, *Beyond Carnival: Male Homosexuality in Twentieth-Century Brazil* (Chicago: University of Chicago Press, 1999); Annick Prieur, *Mema's House, Mexico City: On Transvestites, Queens, and Machos* (Chicago: University of Chicago Press, 1998); Elizabeth Lapovsky Kennedy and Madeline D. Davis, *Boots of Leather, Slippers of Gold: The History of a Lesbian Community* (New York: Routledge, 1993); Stephen O. Murray and Will Roscoe, eds., *Boy-Wives and Female Husbands: Studies of African Homosexualities* (New York: St. Martin's, 1998).

27. David M. Halperin, "Sex before Sexuality: Pederasty, Politics, and Power in Classical Athens," in *Hidden from History*, 37–53.

28. This is a point made by Carole S. Vance, "Social Construction Theory: Problems in the History of Sexuality," in *Which Homosexuality?*, ed. Dennis Altman et al. (Amsterdam: Dekker/Schorer, 1989), 13–34. Vance credits a student with the incisive question about the bowl and spoon. On a Sambia man who sought out fellatio with initiates, see Gilbert H. Herdt, "Semen Depletion and the Sense of Maleness," in Murray, *Oceanic Homosexualities*, 33–68.

29. Trexler, *Sex and Conquest*.

30. Keuls, *The Reign of the Phallus*, 276.

31. Kendall, "'When a Woman Loves a Woman' in Lesotho: Love, Sex, and the (Western) Construction of Homophobia," in Murray and Roscoe, *Boy-Wives and Female Husbands*, 223–41.

4 • *Laura M. Carpenter*

THE AMBIGUITY OF SEX AND VIRGINITY LOSS

Insights from Feminist Research Methods

DISCUSSION QUESTIONS

1. How do *you* define "sex"? Why? Has your definition changed at all over time?

2. What new insights and complexities are revealed in Carpenter's research because of the feminist methodological approach she employs?

3. What factors account for individuals' changing definitions and interpretations of virginity loss?

Laura Carpenter, "The Ambiguity of Sex and Virginity Loss: Insights from Feminist Research Methods." Written for this volume.

4. What are the implications of recognizing that the distinction between "sex" and "not sex" are not as clear-cut as we might have assumed?

Studying sexuality can pose particular difficulties because sexuality is generally seen as a private aspect of social life, and it is difficult to know when people are being truthful about their sexual beliefs and behavior. Using feminist research methods can help to illuminate often-overlooked ambiguities and complexities in young Americans' understandings and experiences of sexual life. My qualitative study of the meanings and experiences of virginity loss in the contemporary United States offers a useful example of how.

Sociologists are perennially concerned that even their most careful research efforts may not yield an accurate picture of what people's lives are like. After all, our research derives much of its value from the degree to which it reflects—tells the "truth" about—the social world.[1] In the context of survey or interview research, where social scientists hope that the questions they ask are soliciting the information they desire, this is called *response error*. Response error can occur for a variety of reasons, including respondents' memory, motivation, and knowledge, as well as (mis)communication between respondents and researchers (Sudman and Bradburn, 1982). Qualitative and quantitative research are both affected by response error; however, it has been more thoroughly discussed in the latter context....

Although most Americans think of sexuality as biologically driven, in fact it is profoundly shaped by social forces (Stein, 1989). Even questions as basic as "When did you first have sex?" can be open to interpretation, depending on the concepts and categories a person has learned socially, through interaction with her or his friends, family, educators, clergy, and the mass media. Examining response error—or what appears to be response error—in research on virginity loss helps to highlight just how social a phenomenon sexuality is....

METHODS FOR THIS STUDY

My qualitative study of virginity loss in the United States offers one example of how feminist research methods can help scholars of sexuality to overcome certain aspects of response bias and to develop insights into when and how people speak truthfully about sex. To learn how young Americans interpret and experience virginity loss, I conducted in-depth, semistructured interviews with sixty-one women and men, aged eighteen to thirty-five. I consciously adopted feminist methods in the study design by seeking a diverse sample, asking primarily open-ended questions about subjective aspects of experience, and planning to share information with the participants if they inquired.

To locate potential participants, I used purposive snowball sample techniques (Biernacki and Waldorf, 1981), selecting for diversity in terms of gender and sexual identity; racial/ethnic, socioeconomic, and religious backgrounds; and extent of sexual experience.[2] My intent in assembling such a diverse sample was to gain insights into how different social locations—standpoints—shape people's interests and experiences. I personally conducted the interviews, which lasted an average of one hundred minutes each, using a semistructured interview guide composed primarily of open-ended questions....

Of the thirty-three women in the study, twenty-two described themselves as heterosexual, seven as lesbians, and four as bisexual. Of the twenty-eight men, seventeen self-identified as heterosexual, nine as gay, and two as bisexual. Forty-eight were white, six were African American, four were Latino, and three were Asian American. One-third came from working-class backgrounds, and two-thirds came from middle-class families (measured by parental education and occupation)—55 percent were white and middle class. Twenty-one were raised as mainline Protestants, sixteen as Roman Catholics, ten as conservative Christians (mostly evangelical Protestants), eight as Jewish, and six outside of organized religion. All but two participants (one heterosexual woman and one lesbian) had engaged in either vaginal intercourse or oral sex at least once; only five considered themselves virgins at the time of the interview. Most resided within two hours of the Philadelphia metropolitan area when I spoke with them, although about half grew up elsewhere in the United States.

DEFINING VIRGINITY LOSS

Although scholarly and popular writers almost always define virginity loss as the first time a man or woman engages in vaginal–penile intercourse (Jessor and Jessor, 1975; Solin, 1996; Sprecher and Regan, 1996), beliefs about the types of sexual encounters that are necessary to achieve this sexual/social transition have varied considerably over time and across cultures (Schlegel, 1995). For example, I spoke with many people who believed that not only first vaginal sex, but first same-sex encounters, can result in virginity loss. Many women and men also excluded coerced sex (including vaginal rape) from their definitions of virginity loss (Carpenter, 2001). Given my interest in virginity loss as a social phenomenon, rather than as a mere physiological event, my analyses refer to whichever sexual encounters the participants personally identified as the point at which they lost their virginity. For all of the heterosexuals and all but one of the bisexuals, that encounter was first vaginal sex; for most of the gay men and lesbians, it was first oral or anal intercourse (for further details, see Carpenter, 2001).

FINDINGS: EXPLORING AMBIGUITY AND LISTENING TO DIVERSITY

...My study suggests that much insight into the reality of sexual lives is to be gained from accepting and exploring the complexity and ambiguity of human experience, especially as seen from the perspective of the people being studied. Most studies of sexuality, especially those that have relied on survey methods, have assumed that every sexual encounter can be categorized simply as either "sex" or "not sex." Yet, some sexual encounters are physically ambiguous in ways that may leave people uncertain as to whether they did, in fact, have sex. Other experiences are ambiguous in a psychological sense, as when a sexual encounter is unpleasant enough (or a partner undesired enough) that a person feels justified in choosing not to "count" it as "sex." Still other phenomena—coerced sexual encounters and secondary virginity—are ambiguous in a definitional sense....

PHYSICALLY AMBIGUOUS EXPERIENCES

Six of the people I interviewed told me about sexual encounters—involving partial vaginal or anal penetration—that were physically so ambiguous that determining whether they had "actually" had sex was left to their own interpretation. Ettrick Anderson (aged nineteen, gay, and African American) recounted:

> I'm not really sure if I've had anal sex....I've heard that anal sex is not supposed to be painful if you're relaxed and if you're comfortable with the person you're having sex with....I've also heard that it hurts like a bitch, especially the first time. And I didn't feel anything [laughs]. So I don't know if he was just there and sort of like, you know...just rubbing up against me, or if it was there and actually inside and I was just relaxed and it was wonderful and, like. It's probably one of the best orgasms that I've ever had....And I also heard that you were supposed to bleed afterward, you know, just a little bit, but you're supposed to notice. And, I remember, feeling like, it might have happened, but I didn't bleed....Like I knew it was there, somewhere, but I didn't know like, where it was in relation to where I was. So I don't know if I've actually had anal sex.

The other five men and women chose to interpret phenomenologically ambiguous sexual encounters in unambiguous ways. Because they stopped vaginal or anal penetration when it proved too painful or difficult, they did not interpret those encounters as "really counting" as sex. Kelly Lewis (aged twenty-four, heterosexual, and white) told me about her first attempt at vaginal intercourse:

> Well, when I first tried to have sex, I was fourteen years old. And I just remember, the person I was with, he was also a virgin. And I, like, we stopped. I'm like, "This hurts, it's horrible, this is not what it's supposed to be." And so I don't consider that being. Like, the first time I had sex was a year later, when I was fifteen.

Because she interpreted it as "almost sex/virginity loss," Kelly would have omitted this physically ambiguous experience from an inventory of her experiences with vaginal sex. However, a researcher's assessment of STI transmission or the broader process of becoming sexually active would be incomplete without it.

How the participants interpreted physically ambiguous encounters depended on how they wished to appear to themselves and others, which, in turn, depended on their general beliefs about virginity and sex. In other words, their responses were also affected by motivation-based error. All five participants who interpreted partial-penetration experiences as "not sex" were virgins at the time of the encounter, saw their virginity as highly valuable, and wanted to lose it under "perfect" circumstances. In contrast, Ettrick Anderson was neither a virgin at the time of his partial-penetration experience nor saw virginity as a desirable personal trait. (For an example from the 1920s, see Brumberg, 1997, p. 155.)

PSYCHOLOGICAL AMBIGUITY

Unpleasant sexual encounters are, at least for some people, psychologically ambiguous in a way that can result in response error. Seven participants told me that, for all intents and purposes, they treated their especially unpleasant virginity-loss experiences as though they had never really happened,

in effect defining those encounters as "not sex" (see also Thompson, 1984). For example, because the first time she engaged in coitus was extremely painful and she subsequently felt that she had been too young, Hannah Cooper (aged twenty-nine, heterosexual, and white) routinely chose to speak of her second partner if asked about her first. She said:

> I basically excluded my first experience from the account of how I lost my virginity—made it the second person—to most of my friends.... It was pretty, could have been really romantic. If it hadn't been for the pain. Except that I was bleeding like [trails off]. So, yeah, so I totally excluded that.

People who "erase" unpleasant experiences from the sexual histories they share with friends may very well opt to erase these same experiences when participating in a study. Such omissions would be more likely (and more difficult to detect) in a survey-based study, not the least because qualitative interviews offer a better chance for the researcher and participant to develop rapport, which tends to encourage fuller disclosure by the participant (Weiss, 1994).

Most participants who excluded unpleasant experiences from their sexual histories simply did not consider those experiences "real" sex; in so doing, they interpreted "sex" differently than do most researchers. A few even appeared to have all but forgotten about these experiences until they spontaneously came to mind during our interviews. For example, Fernando Garcia (aged twenty-one, gay, and Cuban American) paused suddenly in his description of the ideal virginity-loss encounter and exclaimed:

> Actually. Oh my God, I guess I'm not a virgin. Oh my God, I just totally. Yeah. I must have, it's not that I blocked it out, but I, it, like. I guess going definitionwise, then I'm not a virgin....But it was a random hook-up, like. In April of last year. I penetrated him and then he penetrated me. But it was like, in and that was it, and then it was in and that was it. And that was the end of the encounter. I guess I'm on my second virginity [laughs]. Yeah, that's weird.

I can't believe I didn't remember that. Normally I do...but I don't know why I just totally forgot; it just came to me now. But I guess I didn't look at that as being like, a sexual experience, in that sense....At the emotional connection.

Motivation to present oneself as having had only positive encounters may also be involved; however, "erasing" experiences did not appear to be systematically related to the participants' beliefs about the value of virginity.

COERCED SEX

Coerced sexual encounters are ambiguous in definitional terms and thus may contribute to communication-related error. One-third (twenty-two) of the people I interviewed said that they would consider someone who had been raped, but had not otherwise been sexually active, a virgin. For instance, Jason Cantor (aged 24, heterosexual, and white) believed that rape could not result in the loss of virginity because, "In my mind, losing your virginity is sort of willfully having sex with someone. Rape and abuse are...not something that [people have] chosen to participate in." Another thirteen respondents believed that although a person who was raped was technically (i.e., physiologically) no longer a virgin, in many ways she or he still was. As Carrie Matthews (aged twenty, heterosexual, and white) put it, "If their only sexual experience has been something like a rape, I would call them a virgin even though technically something did happen." Such ambiguity—which would determine whether or not a person would include coerced sexual experiences in her or his sexual history—would not be revealed by survey research.

Of the three participants who first experienced vaginal-penile intercourse as the result of rape or sexual abuse, one drew a clear distinction between being abused during elementary school and her loss of virginity. Juliette Jordan (aged nineteen, lesbian, and African American) explained:

If you want to go like, in medical terms, no I wasn't [a virgin after being abused]. But, I don't know. I think

virginity is so much more than just a medical term. To most people.... I think, they mean more than just like, did you have sex?

The remaining two interpreted the encounters in which they were raped by acquaintances as the point at which they lost their virginity; however, they also argued that rape should not be seen as resulting in virginity loss. (They simply did not go back and reinterpret their own experiences in this light; see Carpenter, 2005.) Susheela Singh and Jacqueline Darroch (1999) noted that estimates of sexual activity among young women in the National Survey of Family Growth decreased slightly when involuntary sexual experiences were excluded, showing that some people do report nonconsensual acts as sexual experiences. Conversely, my research demonstrates that at least some people *exclude* nonconsensual encounters when they report sexual experiences. In either case, scholars should be careful to specify to study participants which sorts of sexual experiences—voluntary or involuntary—they are interested in hearing about.

SECONDARY VIRGINITY

"Secondary" virginity is another definitionally—and possibly a psychologically—ambiguous phenomenon. In my study, three women and one man described themselves as "secondary" or "born-a-gain" virgins. That is, at some point after they lost their "true" virginity (through vaginal sex in each case), they decided to refrain from vaginal sex until either marriage or involvement in a committed relationship.[3] All four secondary virgins in my study presented themselves as "technically, not [a virgin]; but...emotionally yes" (Charlotte Brandt, aged twenty-eight, heterosexual, and white). For instance, when I asked Kate O'Connor (aged twenty-four, heterosexual, and white) if she was a virgin, she said "Yes," then laughed and said "No." She elaborated:

See, I don't know, I never really think of it that way. Like, it depends. I mean...I don't consider myself a virgin. I don't think that I can erase a physical fact....But

I know in the eyes of God, I have been forgiven and that it's not an issue....If you took someone who was a virgin and me, on our wedding day, and put us in front of the altar...there is no difference, because God promises that when you repent of a sin, he just wipes it away and forgets it....If someone asked me, "Are you a virgin?" I would say no. But I would probably also...say, "Well, I'm not having sex now." I mean, it gets a little weird when you go to the gynecologist and he says, "Are you sexually active?" I'm like, "Well, sort of, I was, but I'm not." Which they never believe anyway [laughs].

However, it stands to reason that some secondary virgins may opt not to report their primary virginity-loss experiences to a researcher, instead treating their secondary virginity loss as the "real" one. Or—in the context of a closed-ended survey—a born-again virgin might respond affirmatively to the question, "Are you a virgin?" but negatively to the question, "Have you ever had vaginal sex?" Every secondary virgin I spoke with saw virginity as valuable (not surprisingly), which suggests that what researchers call motivation-based error is also in play.

RELATIVE SALIENCE

Researchers tend to assume that first vaginal sex (which they often, if problematically, equate with virginity loss) is an experience of sufficient salience that virtually all people will be able to recall the circumstances under which it occurred. In my study, however, four respondents simply did not find first coitus to be particularly salient.[4] Consequently, they all had some difficulty recalling how old they were at the time. When I asked Jessica Tanaka (aged twenty-seven, bisexual, and Japanese American) how old she had been when she lost her virginity (which she defined in terms of first vaginal sex), she said:

You know, I'm not exactly sure. I was either fourteen or fifteen. It was right around winter [laughs]. That's funny, like. It's frightening that I can't remember when it was. It was sometime in January or February. My birthday was in January, so it was somewhere right around there.

Encounters that occur near birthdays may be especially problematic, as Jessica suggested. Two additional respondents had difficulty recalling details about sexual experiences because they deemed them significant only in retrospect. For example, after Seth Silber (aged nineteen, gay, and white) came out as gay, he decided that any kind of genital sex could constitute virginity loss. He therefore retrospectively determined that he had lost his virginity the first time he engaged in oral sex with a woman (some years before he had oral sex with a man), but had difficulty pinpointing when, exactly, that encounter took place.[5]

DISCUSSION AND CONCLUSION

Following a feminist ethos in my research methods helped to reveal how sex is socially constructed in ways shaped by gender and sexual identity. My interviews with young women and men again and again showed that sexual acts have meaning only in context and only through individuals' interpretation of them. My research also inspires a reevaluation of common assumptions about early sexual experiences. More specifically, listening to diverse women and men voice their beliefs and experiences in their own terms helped me to reveal ambiguities in the physical, psychological, and definitional dimensions of virginity loss. Recognizing and exploring these ambiguities would not have been possible using the methods of traditional survey research.

My investigation moreover illuminates the vexing issue of the rescission of sexual behavior in survey studies. By asking open-ended questions and remaining open-minded about the ambiguity of social life, I discovered that certain sexual encounters are physically ambiguous to the point where young people—especially relatively inexperienced young people—find it difficult to determine whether they have had sex. I expect that such cases are one reason why some participants in longitudinal studies report different ages at first coitus in earlier and later waves of data collection. In between the waves, some young people may gain additional sexual experience (e.g., experiencing full penetration), prompting them to reevaluate a past experience (e.g., of partial penetration as "not sex"). This interpretation is supported by research that has found that inconsistent reports of first vaginal sex are more common among younger respondents (Lauritsen and Swicegood, 1997; Upchurch et al., 2002). Psychologically ambiguous experiences, like unpleasant encounters that seem better forgotten; definitionally ambiguous states of being, like secondary virginity; and individual variations in the relative salience of first vaginal sex may also prompt inconsistent responses in longitudinal studies.

Although I have used the mainstream language of response error throughout this article, I believe that my research raises the question of whether response error is, in fact, the appropriate lens through which to understand the participants' accounts of their experiences. The concept of response error derives from a positivist perspective that all social life can be broken down into discrete categories, such that there is one correct answer to sociologists' questions. Such a perspective therefore fails to recognize the real ambiguity that is inherent in life, sexual and otherwise. The participants' stories are not "right" or "wrong"; rather, they are caught in the ambiguity of sex. In effect, my research suggests not only why what social scientists traditionally call response error occurs, but what is more important, why it may not be helpful to think of sexual activity in those terms.

To conclude, I would like to consider how what I learned from analyzing the impact of feminist methods on my study may help to inform future research and to develop feminist methods further. On a general level, my findings underline the importance of attending closely to individuals' own interpretations of their experiences, especially areas of potential ambiguity—or, at least, of acknowledging more explicitly the limitations of research that fails to do so. Any study that presumes to know exactly into which categories people's experiences are going to fall is liable to miss subtle gradations of experience, such as physically ambiguous sexual acts.

I would also encourage researchers to attempt to place specific sexual activities (e.g., first vaginal sex)

in the broader context of individuals' sexual histories (see also Ehrhardt, 1996; Irvine, 1994). In practical terms, sexuality researchers would do well to inquire about genital sexual activities other than vaginal sex and to ask which sexual experiences are most significant to the people who participate in their studies. Because sexuality is a highly complex aspect of life, gathering data using only a couple of questions (as do most surveys) forces participants to oversimplify their experiences (in ways that may be systematically biased). Ideally, large-scale studies with samples selected using probability techniques should gather more complete sexual histories from participants. The National Health and Social Life Survey and Longitudinal Study of Adolescent Health represent steps in the right direction. Insofar as sexual and social life are constantly changing, further studies of sexuality-related meanings and processes will always be welcome as well.

NOTES

1. I do not believe that there is one objective truth about any given person's experiences; rather, there are multiple truths—the same story can be told in different truthful ways (Denzin, 1989; Riessman, 1993).

2. Specifically, I made a point of speaking with self-described virgins, people who were more and less satisfied with their virginity-loss encounters, who identified themselves as born-again (or secondary) virgins and who reported losing their virginity as the result of sexual assault.

3. Several conservative sex education curricula, such as True Love Waits and Sex Respect, promote this option, as do many conservative Christian denominations. For popular accounts, see (Dobie, 1995; Ingrassia, 1994; Keller, 1999); for an academic treatment, see (Carpenter, 2005).

4. Although most participants emphasized the social and personal salience of virginity and virginity loss, two-thirds (forty-one) reported having at least one sexual experience that they perceived as equally or more significant than virginity loss or first coitus.

5. Which sexual experiences people considered most significant was, broadly speaking, patterned by sexual identity. Yet I urge others not to assume that every member of a single group will see the same experience

as most salient (Thompson, 1995). For example, the gay men I spoke with disagreed as to whether a gay man who has not engaged in same-gender anal intercourse is "really" sexually active (three of nine said no; the remaining six saw giving or receiving fellatio as resulting in virginity loss).

REFERENCES

Biernacki, Patrick, and Dan Waldorf. 1981. "Snowball Sampling: Problems and Techniques of Chain Referral Sampling." *Sociological Methods and Research* 10:141–163.

Brumberg, Joan Jacobs. 1997. *The Body Project.* New York: Random House.

Carpenter, Laura M. 2001. "The Ambiguity of 'Having Sex': The Subjective Experience of Virginity Loss in the United States." *Journal of Sex Research* 38:127–139.

———. 2005. *Virginity Lost: An Intimate Portrait of First Sexual Experiences.* New York: New York University Press.

Denzin, Norman. 1989. *Interpretive Biography.* Newbury Park, Calif.: Sage.

Dobie, Kathy. 1995. "Hellbent on Redemption." *Mother Jones* (January–February): 50–54.

Ehrhardt, Anke A. 1996. "Editorial: Our View of Adolescent Sexuality—A Focus on Risk Behavior Without the Developmental Context." *American Journal of Public Health* 86:1523–1525.

Ingrassia, Michelle. 1994. "Virgin Cool." *Newsweek* (October 17): 58–69.

Irvine, Janice M. 1994. "Cultural Differences and Adolescent Sexualities." In *Sexual Cultures and the Construction of Adolescent Identities,* ed. Janice M. Irvine, pp. 3–28. Philadelphia: Temple University Press.

Jessor, Shirley L., and Richard Jessor. 1975. "Transition from Virginity to Non-virginity Among Youth: A Social-Psychological Study Over Time." *Developmental Psychology* 11:473–484.

Keller, Wendy. 1999. *The Cult of the Born-again Virgin: How Single Women Can Reclaim Their Sexual Power.* Deerfield Beach, Fla.: Health Communications.

Lauritsen, Janet L., and C. Gray Swicegood. 1997. "The Consistency of Self-reported Initiation of Sexual Activity." *Family Planning Perspectives* 29:215–221.

Riessman, Catherine Kohler. 1993. *Narrative Analysis.* Newbury Park, CA: Sage.

Schlegel, Alice. 1995. "The Cultural Management of Adolescent Sexuality." In *Sexual Nature, Sexual Culture,* ed. Paul R. Abramson and Steven D. Pinkerton, pp. 177–194. Chicago: University of Chicago Press.

Singh, Susheela, and Jacqueline E. Darroch. 1999. "Trends in Sexual Activity Among Adolescent American Women: 1982–1995." *Family Planning Perspectives* 31:212–219.

Solin, Sabrina. 1996. *The Seventeen Guide to Sex and Your Body.* New York: Simon & Schuster.

Sprecher, Susan, and Pamela C. Regan. 1996. "College Virgins: How Men and Women Perceive Their Sexual Status." *Journal of Sex Research* 33:3–15.

Stein, Arlene. 1989. "Three Models of Sexuality." *Sociological Theory* 7:1–13.

Sudman, Seymour, and Norman M. Bradburn. 1982. *Asking Questions: A Practical Guide to Questionnaire Design.* San Francisco: Jossey-Bass.

Thompson, Sharon. 1984. "Search for Tomorrow: On Feminism and the Reconstruction of Teen Romance." In *Pleasure and Danger: Exploring Female Sexuality,* ed. Carole S. Vance, pp. 350–384. Boston: Routledge.

———. 1995. *Going All the Way: Teenage Girls' Tales of Sex, Romance, and Pregnancy.* New York: Hill & Wang.

Upchurch, Dawn M., Lee A. Lillard, Carol S. Aneshensel, and Nicole Fang Li. 2002. "Inconsistencies in Reporting the Occurrence and Timing of First Intercourse Among Adolescents." *Journal of Sex Research* 39:197–206.

Weiss, Robert S. 1994. *Learning from Strangers: The Art and Method of Qualitative Interview Studies.* New York: Free Press.

5 • *James W. Messerschmidt*

GOODBYE TO THE SEX–GENDER DISTINCTION, HELLO TO EMBODIED GENDER

On Masculinities, Bodies, and Violence

DISCUSSION QUESTIONS

1. What does the author mean when he says "sex differences do not precede gender differences; rather the former is an effect of the latter"?
2. Describe and discuss the political/power struggles that have determined, at different points in time, the way we see sex and gender and the relationship between them.
3. Messerschmidt argues that gender performance is fluid, changing in different contexts, such as the school and the home. Do you agree? Describe any differences you see in your own gendered behavior in the contexts that are most significant in your life.
4. What is "embodied gender"? How does this concept recast previous conceptualizations of the relationship between sex and gender?

In the early 1970s, feminist sociologists adopted the newly developed *sex–gender distinction* (Stoller, 1968; Oakley, 1972) to redefine women's condition in social rather than in biological terms. Because the term *sex* suggested the immutability of biological differences and inequalities between men and women, feminist sociologists embraced *gender* to emphasize the social over the biological. Feminist sociologists of the second wave shifted the analysis of women and girls from biological determinism to social determinism, arguing that there is nothing about women's biology that causes women's subordination; rather, difference and inequality between women and men are socially determined phenomena that can be socially changed.

However, the concept of gender did not wholly erase "sex" from the feminist agenda, since feminist scholars often argued that gender is *related* to, but not simply *derived* from, sex. Feminist sociologists have refuted continually and soundly any claim that gender is *derived* from sex (Miller and Costello, 2001; Kennelly, Merz, and Lorber, 2001; Risman, 2001; Lorber, 2005). Yet feminist sociologists never have confronted the important question: If sex does not play a causal role in gender, how exactly then is gender *related* to sex? (Cealey Harrison and Hood-Williams,

James W. Messerschmidt, "Goodbye to the Sex–Gender Distinction, Hello to Embodied Gender." Written for this volume.

2002:15–31) Although the distinction between "sex" and "gender" allowed feminist scholars to investigate women's and men's gendered experiences without reverting to biological determinism, for many feminist sociologists "gender" is constructed socially, but "sex" is not. Accordingly, "sex" has remained an "undertheorized backdrop" within feminist gender theory—a phenomenon seemingly best left to biological scrutiny (Davis, 1997).

REVISITING "SEX"

A reconsideration of the relationship between "sex" and "gender" is now necessary because in historical studies of attempts to define "sex," gender has proved always to be already involved. For example, Thomas Laqueur (1990) showed in his book, *Making Sex,* that for two thousand years, a "one-sex model" dominated scientific and popular thought in which male and female bodies were not conceptualized in terms of difference. From Antiquity to the beginning of the seventeenth century, male and female bodies were seen as fundamentally similar, even in terms of genitalia, with the vagina regarded as an interior penis, the vulva as foreskin, the uterus as scrotum, and the ovaries as testicles. Although women were considered inferior to men, the sexes were not seen as different in *kind* but rather in *degree*—women's parts were simply arranged differently than men's. As Laqueur (p. 8) pointed out, *"Sex,* or the body, must be understood as the epiphenomenon, while *gender,* what we would take to be a cultural category, was primary or 'real.'" Inequality was imposed on bodies from the *outside,* not from the *inside,* and any physical differences were seen as God's "markers" of a male and female distinction. To be a man or a woman was to have a specific place in society decreed by God, "not to *be* organically one or the other of two incommensurable sexes. Sex before the seventeenth-century, in other words, was still a sociological and not an ontological category" (p. 8).

The shift in thinking to a "two-sex model," consisting now of two different types of human and sexual natures, corresponded to the emergence of the public-private split: It was now "natural" for men to enter the public realm of society, and it was "natural" for women to remain in the private sphere. Explaining these distinct gendered spaces was "resolved by grounding social and cultural differentiation of the sexes in a biology of incommensurability" (p. 19). In other words, "gender" became subordinated to "sex," and biology was now primary: *the* foundation of difference and inequality between men and women.

Laqueur made clear that the change to a two-sex model was not the result of advances in science, inasmuch as the reevaluation of the body as primary occurred approximately 100 years before alleged supporting scientific discoveries appeared (p. 9). And although anatomical and physiological differences clearly exist between male and female bodies, what counts as "sex" is determined socially (p. 10):

> To be sure, difference and sameness, more or less recondite, are everywhere; but which ones count and for what ends is determined outside the bounds of empirical investigation. The fact that at one time the dominant discourse construed the male and female bodies as hierarchically, vertically, ordered versions of one sex and at another time as horizontally ordered opposites, as incommensurable, must depend on something other than even a great constellation of real or supposed discoveries.

In short, natural scientists had no interest in "seeing" two distinct sexes at the anatomical and concrete physiological level "until such differences became politically important," and "sex" therefore became "explicable only within the context of battles over gender and power" (pp. 10, 11).

Similarly, Michel Foucault (1980:vii) showed that during roughly the same period, Western cultures came to reject "the idea of a mixture of two sexes in a single body, and consequently to limiting the free choice of indeterminate individuals. Henceforth, everybody was to have one and only one sex." For example, individuals accepted previously as "hermaphrodites" were now required to submit to expert medical diagnosis to uncover their "true" sex. As Foucault (p. vii) continued:

Everybody was to have his or her primary, profound, determined and determining sexual identity; as for the elements of the other sex that might appear, they could only be accidental, superficial, or even quite simply illusory. From the medical point of view, this meant that when confronted with a hermaphrodite, the doctor was no longer concerned with recognizing the presence of the two sexes, juxtaposed or intermingled, or with knowing which of the two prevailed over the other, but rather with deciphering the true sex that was hidden beneath ambiguous appearances.

The work of both Laqueur and Foucault suggests that "sex differences" do not precede "gender differences"; rather, the former is an effect of the latter. Indeed, as Wendy Cealey Harrison (2006) insightfully observed, it is virtually impossible ever to entirely separate the body and our understanding of it from its socially determined milieu. Arguably, what is now necessary is a reconceptualization of "the taken-for-grantedness of 'sex' as a form of categorization for human beings and examining the ways in which such a categorization is built" (p. 43).

THE CURRENT STUDY

Over the past five years, my research has permitted me to begin investigating how the category of "sex" is built during social interaction and how it is situationally related to the body, gender, and violence/nonviolence. Sociologists have reported little about the life histories of violent adolescents and especially little about when, and under what type of social conditions, they may also be nonviolent. In fact, no life-history research on adolescent gendered violence exists, and no study on youth violence has explored the similarities between boys and girls or the role of the body in the practices of violence and nonviolence. However, this is the subject of the current study. The research has concentrated on life-history interviews of thirty equally divided white working-class New England violent and nonviolent teenage boys and girls. I diversified the sample by obtaining a "mix" of youth from different family configurations, such as adoptive versus biological parents and violent versus nonviolent households (the presence or absence of domestic violence). This "maximum-variation" sampling procedure provided a selection of boys and girls from a wide range of home life and other background situations. Nevertheless, the vast majority of the boys and girls grew up in the same milieu (that is, they often lived in the same neighborhood and attended the same school). The race and social class of the entire sample remained constant (white working class). Data collection involved tape-recorded interviews of at least two, three-hour meetings. The interviews were structured to grasp each respondent's personal vision of the world and his or her sense of place in it. Moreover, each interview reconstructed the respondents' life histories by relating later events to earlier choices, interactions, and practices and concentrated on three "sites"—the home, the school, and the street. By examining these distinct settings, we are able to capture how people negotiate gender relations differently in and through specific spaces. I focus the following analysis on two individual biographies in the sample.[1]

Single biographies, of course, can provide extremely rich data that reveal the heart of "sex" and "gender" construction, as well as provide a fertile source for further research and theorizing. One of the first to examine the relationship between sex and gender in a single biography was Harold Garfinkel (1967) in his analysis of the male-to-female transsexual, "Agnes." Garfinkel showed how sex and gender are embodied through interaction and that accomplishing both requires persistent monitoring of the body and bodily signs and practices. Garfinkel studied the embodied methods that Agnes used to "pass" as a "normal natural female" and how Agnes acquired a public "femaleness" by utilizing the appropriate "female" bodily skills, capacities, appearances, and practices. Garfinkel concluded that the study of such "violation cases" as that of Agnes demonstrated what we all do: The naturalness of the world, in which there are two unequal "sexes," is realized through conventional, self-regulated, often unreflective management of the body.

Since Garfinkel's famous analysis of Agnes, research attention among gender scholars has broadened to include a variety of transgenderists (Devor, 1999; Dozier, 2005; Rubin, 2003; Kessler and McKenna, 1978; Namaste, 2000; Prosser, 1998; Cromwell, 1999; Halberstam, 1998). *Transgenderists* are people who specifically construct their gender display and/or practice so as not to match their perceived sex—*transgender* is an umbrella term that includes transsexuals, cross-dressers, and other "gender deviants." As part of the research genre, a recent article by Raine Dozier (2005) is particularly relevant to the discussion here, since Dozier showed, through interviews with female-to-male "trans men," how "sex" is conceptualized during social interaction as an expression of "gender." In other words, Dozier concluded that the social construction of gender relies on both sex appearance and gender behavior. More specifically, Dozier found that for "trans men," when secondary sex characteristics (such as the presence of facial hair) do not align with gender behavior, the latter becomes more important to gender expression and interpretation, and when secondary sex characteristics are congruent with gender behavior, the latter is allowed greater fluidity in asserting gender. Thus, the social perception of "sex" is salient to the interpretation of behavior as masculine or feminine because of the cultural notion that gender is "supposed" to follow from sex.

Dozier's work is important and has contributed greatly to our understanding of the relationship between sex and gender. Although my research built on Dozier's work by similarly investigating the relationship between sex appearance and gender behavior, my sample consisted of individuals who did *not* self-identify as transgenderist. Yet, all the boys and girls I interviewed can be categorized—depending upon the social setting—as either "gender deviants" or "gender conformists." Those I label *gender deviants* are individuals who are perceived *by others* as either failing or refusing to follow established bodily displays and/or practices of their "sex" in specific settings. In other words, for gender deviants, their sex is not ambiguous. Rather, according to co-present interactants in certain situations, their bodily display and/or behavior contradict their sex

appearance, and, thus, their femininity or masculinity may be questioned. As Goffman (1963:12) put it, such an individual is negatively stigmatized by others and thus reduced "from a whole and usual person to a tainted, discredited one."

Situationally labeled "gender deviants" are useful in studying the relationship between "sex" and "gender" for several reasons. First, they add a new dimension to the relationship because they are, by definition, situated outside the *self-identified* transgender arena; that is, none of the gender deviants I interviewed identified as specifically transgenderists. Second, inasmuch as gender deviants experience negative stigmatizing interactions, they highlight the nature of both sex and gender attribution and how that nature may be related to involvement in assaultive violence. Third, by definition, gender deviants cannot take their embodied gendered self for granted. Consequently, they spotlight the various dimensions of agency and how such agency is intertwined with sex and gender. Finally, by locating gender deviants in different "sites" (such as the home, the school, and the street), we can uncover the fluidity of sex and gender conformity or nonconformity, as well as the changing nature of acceptance and rejection of one's behavior as masculine or feminine.

In what follows, I outline some of the ways in which the social construction of both sex and gender are related to specific gender relations in the three settings of home, school, and street and how bodily interaction leads to violence and nonviolence. I focus my analysis on two teenage gender deviants who were included in the larger sample, a boy (Lenny) and a girl (Kelly). These teenagers are nicely juxtaposed because they were perceived by others as either failing or refusing to follow the established bodily displays and/or practices of their sex in specific settings, and they eventually engaged in assaultive violence.

GENDER CONFORMITY AND NONVIOLENCE AT HOME

Let us turn now to the data, and summarize Lenny's and Kelly's accounts of gender conformity and nonviolence in their respective home settings. We begin with Lenny.

LENNY

Lenny is a short, obese, and somewhat shy fifteen year old. He has short dark hair and was wearing blue jeans, a sweatshirt, and tennis shoes at each interview. Although he also wore a cap emblazoned with "Give Blood, Play Hockey," he spoke in a skittish and soft-spoken manner. At the time of the interviews, Lenny was undergoing private counseling for assaultive violence against several neighborhood boys.

Lenny lives in a working-class community with his mother and father, an older brother (aged 18), and a younger sister (aged 13). Their home is a two-bedroom upstairs apartment. Lenny's earliest family memory is of the first time they went camping: "We had a great time together, right by a lake, canoeing, hiking, roasting marshmallows, and stuff."

Although both parents worked as unskilled laborers, the mother and sister were responsible for all domestic labor (the father did no domestic labor); they received only limited help from Lenny and his brother. Lenny also reported a warm and affectionate family environment: "My parents have a kinda family thing. We do things together. We go to beaches, camping, have cookouts, go to the movies. A lot of things I guess." However, Lenny mostly liked doing things with his father. Asked about his favorite activities, Lenny replied: "We go hunting each year—my father, my brother, and me. My father bought me a 30/30. And I got my hunting license. My father helped me study to get my license. I studied with him. That was fun." Asked further about hunting, Lenny said: "It's exciting to get ready 'cause we eat a big supper before and get up early and go. It's fun to be with my dad." I inquired about other activities that Lenny did with his father, and he emphasized "fishing, swimming, catch, play darts. The whole family, we play board games; that's real fun."

Lenny's mother never disciplined Lenny and the other children. The father "took control" when he came home from work: "He never actually hit me; he just would get mad and talk serious to me. We didn't make him mad that much. We'd do what my dad and mom says."

At home, then, Lenny grew up under a conventional gender division of labor. Both parents performed "appropriate" gendered labor and other home-related activities—the father embodied the culturally idealized form of masculinity (hegemonic), and the mother embodied the culturally idealized form of femininity (emphasized), in the home setting.[2] Although the father was never physically violent, he clearly exercised power in the family and used that power to control all decisional issues. For example, even when Lenny wanted to do something outside the home (e.g., go bike riding), he was not allowed to do it unless his father approved ahead of time. Lenny identified with his father—his initial model for developing an embodied conception of masculinity—and engaged in accountably male sex appearance and situational masculine practices (e.g., hunting, fishing, and playing catch). In other words, there existed a balance between Lenny's sex appearance and gender behavior in the home setting. And given Lenny's success at constructing such a balance between his male appearance and masculine practices, he never engaged in assaultive violence in the home milieu. Thus, Lenny embodied an accountably complicit—yet simultaneously subordinate (through age)—masculine presence and *place* in the in-home gender relations.

KELLY

Kelly is a short, stocky, seventeen year old who eloquently presented her life history. At each interview, she arrived without makeup, with her shoulder-length blonde hair pulled back in a ponytail, and wore the same worker boots, baggy jeans, and hooded sweatshirt. At this time, Kelly was on probation for assaulting several boys at school.

Kelly lived with her biological mother, a stepfather (she had never met her biological father), a younger sister (by three years), and an older sister (by four years). Her stepfather was a factory worker, and her mother "just stayed at home." When I asked Kelly if her mother was a homemaker, she responded: "Yeah, if that's what you call it. A drunken home-maker!" Although Kelly's mother occasionally cleaned parts of the house, did some of the laundry, and cooked a few family meals, she spent most of her daily hours "drinking alcohol and watching TV." The household labor Kelly's stepfather did included taking the trash to the town dump, building household furniture, and "keeping his cars and snowmobiles running." As such, and like Lenny, Kelly grew up among an explicit gender division of household labor. But different from Lenny, Kelly's stepfather was physically and verbally abusive of Kelly's mother. As Kelly put it:

> My stepfather would come home from work, like every night, and start to yell and beat on my mom. She was always drunk and hardly did what he wanted, like clean and have dinner ready. So he would yell at her for that, you know, and she'd try to block him but she couldn't. She was too weak. He'd hit her, punch her, kick her, throw her all over the house.

Thus, Kelly grew up confronting patriarchal relations at home in which her stepfather (local hegemonic masculinity) frequently wielded power through physical and verbal abuse of her mother (local emphasized femininity).

The family never did anything together "as a whole family," since it was divided profoundly between the mother and sisters on the one side and Kelly and her stepfather on the other side. Because her mother was either occupied with her younger sister or "too drunk" to interact with her, Kelly spent most of her time with her stepfather. Kelly had turned to her stepfather for warmth and affection and considered him to be her primary parent because they did "everything" together: "We played around with cars, played games, built furniture and stuff, and worked on his cars and snowmobile." Kelly's stepfather ignored all other members of the family—except when he was physically and verbally abusing them—yet engaged in "quality time" with Kelly.

Although he practiced a violent and physically powerful masculinity at home, Kelly became extremely attached to her stepfather. This mutual affection and devotion between Kelly and her stepfather provided an escape from her overtly oppressive environment: Kelly consciously adopted what her stepfather practiced. That is, she appropriated his type of masculinity as her own, rather than the femininity of her mother or her older sister. Consider the following response when I asked Kelly what she learned from her stepfather: "He'd teach me guy stuff, you know. He kinda made me into a tomboy, I guess you could say. He always said that he didn't have any boys of his own, so he wanted me to be the boy. And I kinda really liked it." Kelly's stepfather did not "make" her into a "tomboy"; rather, the gender relations and overall interaction at home led Kelly to embody accountably complicit masculine display and practices. In other words, *initially* at home Kelly's embodied gender consisted of an imbalance between her sex appearance and gender behavior. For example, one aspect of Kelly's masculine behavior at home that contradicted her sex appearance was practicing certain gendered privileges. Kelly explained how the special bond with her stepfather empowered her to practice such privileges:

> I could be messy, and my sisters couldn't. And they had to keep their room clean, and I didn't. They had to do dishes and help my mom with stuff. I could just throw my clothes on the floor, and they couldn't. Oh, and when we were eating dinner in front of the TV, it was only my stepfather and me. My sisters and mom had to eat at the kitchen table. And I'd like just watch him [stepfather], you know. When he'd be finished he'd just throw his plate to the side, and he'd look at me and he'd go like, "You can, go ahead." And I'd throw my plate to the side like he did.

Kelly's stepfather ordered her older sister and mother to pick up after Kelly. The two never protested because "If they did, he'd come down on them. My sister hated me for that, and I think my mom did, too." Moreover, Kelly's stepfather taught her how to ride a dirt bike, a four-wheeler, and a snowmobile. The two watched sports together, such as the New England Patriots football games on TV, and "We tossed the football around alot." Neither sister engaged in these types of practices and interaction with their stepfather.

Confronting patriarchal gender relations at home, then, Kelly understood the advantages and benefits of being "Daddy's boy," since this allowed her, for example, to "be messy," to avoid domestic labor, and to escape the repercussions of her stepfather's physical and verbal abuse. Accordingly, Kelly exercised agency and reflexively became accountably masculine—"I just decided I didn't want to act like a girl; it was more fun to act boyish" and thereby occupied a unique *place* in the in-home gender relations.[3] Thus, a principal requirement of her complicit masculinity entailed distancing herself from all that is feminine. In fact, Kelly "hated" to dress and act like a girl. For example, she disliked dresses because they made it difficult to play sports and climb trees, and they would inevitably become "all torn up by the end of the day from playing outside with boys." Eventually her mother stopped pressuring her to "act" and "dress like a girl," and she has since worn baggy jeans, work boots, sweatshirts, and occasionally a duckbill hat. Kelly thought it made life easier to dress "like a boy," and it was "more fun to act like a boy because I could do anything I wanted. My stepfather even taught me that it was ok to burp out loud. He taught me how to make a mess and that it was ok to fart out loud whenever I wanted." Kelly therefore seemingly embodied a contradiction between her female appearance and masculine practices (and bodily display) at home, a contradiction that eventually was "accepted" by all family members in this setting.

Rejecting femininity and embodying masculinity also provided Kelly power through violence. For example, when I asked Kelly whether it bothered her that her stepfather physically abused her mother, she responded that her mother "had it comin' 'cause she always hassled my stepfather, you know. She got what she deserved." Kelly defined her mother as a "hassle" to her stepfather because she "just got drunk all the time, give him shit, not do anything around the house, just lazy, you know." In contrast,

Kelly looked up to her stepfather because "He taught me all kinds of things, and he didn't take no shit from my mom. So that had a lot of influence on me, you know. My mom didn't really care about me, you know, but my stepfather did." Despite this endorsement of violence and her embodied masculine presence, Kelly never engaged in assaultive violence at home.

REFLECTION

What do these two life stories teach us about the relationship among sex, gender, and nonviolence in the home setting? Beginning with Lenny, we "see" him confronting the constraints and possibilities established through patriarchal gender relations at home and his active adoption of certain forms of social action. Lenny's embodied practices at home articulated primarily with those of his father—his favorite things to do were activities that he and "Dad" did together, such as hunting, fishing, playing catch, and playing darts. These activities represent the salient available practices in the home milieu that Lenny engaged in. Accordingly, Lenny embodied a complicit but subordinate masculinity as he benefited from gender privilege, yet was simultaneously subordinated to his father in this setting. He primarily oriented his actions for his father's approval, and given that Lenny successfully engaged in such practices—Lenny's father was "real proud" of him when he shot his first deer—his masculinity never was challenged in this milieu by his father or by others. Lenny was accountably masculine at home as he engaged in situationally normative masculine conduct that aligned with his male appearance, and such embodied masculinity helped reproduce in-home gender relations; Lenny was an accountable gender conformist in this setting. Distancing himself from the feminine practices of his mother and sister (who performed the vast majority of domestic labor), Lenny confidently and, for the most part unreflectively, embodied a masculine presence and *place* at home and developed a close relationship with his father through kindred embodied interaction that seemed smooth, uneventful, socially coordinated, and nonviolent.

Kelly was similar to Lenny in that she actively rejected femininity; she did so however for a different reason—practicing femininity was painfully confining and required unexciting domestic labor. Accordingly, in her negotiation of patriarchal gender relations at home, Kelly distanced herself from in-home emphasized feminine practices (as represented by her sisters and mother), even to the extent of discounting her mother as a mentor: For Kelly, her mother was an intoxicated and weak person living a lackluster life. There was, however, an additional advantage from Kelly's point of view: Eschewing femininity and practicing masculinity permitted Kelly to enjoy tranquil (rather than tumultuous) interaction with her stepfather. For Kelly, then, practicing femininity restricted bodily mobility and freedom; practicing masculinity offered a semblance of autonomous self-rule in the home when compared to the status of her sisters and mother. Although Kelly's interaction at home and alliance with her stepfather clearly included tension and fear, Kelly allied with her stepfather, in part, to avoid succumbing to his violence and to avoid being rendered "weak" like her mother. While enjoying greater privileges than her mother and sisters, Kelly remained subordinate to, and under the domination of, her stepfather. Kelly's negotiation in this setting was different from Lenny's partly because of the presence of patriarchal violence.

Through intimate attachment to her stepfather, then, Kelly actually became accountably "Daddy's boy" and reaped the gendered benefits that such embodied social action promised. Arguably, Kelly drew on the practices at home and, like Lenny, constructed a complicit (albeit subordinate) masculinity in this setting by benefiting from the oppression of her sisters and her mother. Kelly was accountable to—and wholly endorsed—her stepfather's in-home hegemonic masculine project. Yet her path to complicit masculinity was not the smooth social process that Lenny experienced, primarily because of the imbalance between her female appearance and her masculine behavior. Given Kelly's explicit "gender deviance," Kelly's mother, for example, consistently pressured her to "act" and "dress like a girl"—her mother focused on Kelly's "sex" to disparage her gender behavior. Nevertheless, Kelly uniformly struggled against her mother's efforts and seamlessly subverted emphasized femininity. In addition, because of the stable and substantial support of the person in power—the stepfather (who exercised his ability to overrule her mother)—Kelly's sex and gender imbalance was situationally erased: The stepfather *honored* Kelly above all other family members as "Daddy's boy," and thus his power situationally rendered invisible any sex-gender asymmetry. Kelly's stepfather held her accountable to masculine embodiment, and Kelly did not resist. In fact, Kelly literally *became* "Daddy's boy," and this gender embodiment eventually was normalized in this setting. Kelly practiced nonviolent masculinity: She had no need to engage in violence at home because her stepfather recognized and respected her complicit masculinity. Consequently, Kelly occupied a specific masculine presence and *place* in in-home gender relations as an accountable gender conformist.

FROM SCHOOL TO STREET: VARIETIES OF VIOLENCE AND GENDER CONFORMITY OR DEVIANCE

We turn now to the remaining two sites investigated in the study—the school and the street—and how assaultive violence relates to gender conformity or deviance. Let us begin once again with Lenny.

LENNY

Lenny did reasonably well in elementary and junior high school. For the most part, he liked his teachers and the schools, and he earned average grades. Nevertheless, at school Lenny received constant verbal abuse because of his physical size and shape (he is much shorter and heavier than the other boys and girls), often being referred to as a "fat pig" and a "punk." Because of this peer abuse, Lenny developed a dislike of school: "I hated to go to school." When asked if he discussed this abuse with his mother and father, Lenny replied: "My dad said that if somebody punches me, then I get the right to punch him back. If I'm being teased, I tease him right back. Call him names back. If they [sic] teasing me always, then my dad tells me that I should punch 'em back."

Lenny felt embarrassed at school because of his physical size and shape. Moreover, since he was physically smaller and much heavier than the boys who were abusing him, he felt insecure about responding as his father taught him. He stated that the people who were abusing him were the "cool tough guys" (the local hegemonic masculinity) in the school: "They was the popular tough guys, and everyone laughed when I didn't do nothin'. I couldn't. I felt really small in front of everybody." Consequently, because of his embodied emasculation at school, Lenny became a loner and attempted to avoid the "cool tough guys"; he was generally frightened of social interaction at school and, accordingly, attempted to avoid school as much as possible.

Lenny wanted to be like the "cool tough guys" and longed to go home and tell his father that he did not let anyone push him around at school. However, he was unable to practice masculinity as interaction with his father (and at school) had emphasized—and this terrified him: "I couldn't tell my dad that I was afraid, 'cause then even him would call me a wimp, a scaredy-cat." By the time Lenny was fourteen, then, he lacked masculine bodily resources and thus felt extremely inferior at school. Although the other students perceived Lenny as "male," because of his bodily size and shape as well as his "failure" to engage in situationally defined masculine practices, he was effeminized in this setting. Lenny was unable to embody a masculine presence at school, yet one school event did provide an opportunity for Lenny to attempt such embodiment:

Q: Tell me about that.

A: There was this nerd of a kid that even I made fun of. He would wear high-waters.

Q: What are high-waters?

A: Kids that wear high pants.

Q: Okay, go on.

A: This high-water is real skinny and ugly. I'm bigger than him. So I go: "You look funny in those pants," and stuff like that. I called him a "nerd," and he said the same back to me. There was all these kids around, and so I beat him up in the hallway 'cause he called me a "nerd" and nobody liked him.

Q: Why did you hit him?

A: 'Cause he called me a name that I didn't like, and I wasn't afraid of him.

Q: What did the other kids say who saw you beat him up?

A: Some kids was happy 'cause nobody likes him. But some said I should pick on kids my own size. Plus I got ISS [in-school suspension].

Q: Did you tell your dad about this fight?

A: Yeah. I ran home and told him that this kid was making fun of me, so I beat him up and got ISS for it.

Q: Did your father talk to the school officials about the fight?

A: Nope. He was just happy I beat up the kid.

Q: Is that the only fight in school?

A: Yeah, 'cause he is the kid I can beat up at school. I can beat up kids in my neighborhood.

Lenny said the assault of the "high-water" was his only school fight. He then provided detailed information about his involvement in neighborhood violence, the setting where his assaultive behavior concentrated. According to Lenny, numerous neighborhood boys would constantly challenge him to physical fights. However, he developed specific criteria for his participation in such challenges:

I fight if I can beat the kid. I got this kid next door, he calls me a "fag." I mean, there is no reason why he calls me a "fag," and my father said next time he does that "Beat him up." My father says if I don't fight him, he'll [father] fight me. So I beat the kid up, and my father was happy.

Q: Was this kid smaller than you?

A: Oh yeah; I only fight kids I can beat up. My father says that's smart; you should only "pick the battles you can win."

Q: How did it make you feel when you beat up neighborhood kids?

A: It made me feel real good inside. I knew I wasn't a wimp anymore.

Q: Did it bother you that the boys you beat up were smaller than you?

A: No, 'cause of what my dad said. And I fought kids that called me names or said stuff about Mom.

Q: Who are your friends?

A: I don't have friends at school. Only kids in my neighborhood. I play with kids that are younger than me. We have fun together.

I asked Lenny about homosocial boys' groups at his school, and he mentioned four major cliques in his school—the "jocks" (the cool tough guys), the "nerds," the "smart kids," and the "losers." Although he felt he belonged to none of these groups, he believed that some of the "jocks" most likely considered him a "nerd" and a "wimp" because they always verbally abused him—not only for his size and shape, but because he did not "fight back" and did not participate in any sport. "The jocks always tease the nerds and make fun of them for not playing sports." According to the "jocks," those (including Lenny) who did not play sports (especially football) and who did not retaliate in kind when bullied were "wimps" and "nerds." In fact, Lenny stated that "jocks" often called him a "wimp" because he did not play football and because he was not tough. "The jocks called me a wimp because they said I was afraid of gettin' tackled and afraid of fighting."

Q: Did you feel you were a "wimp" and a "nerd"?

A: Yeah, I did. I wanted to be tough like them, and I was tough to some kids.

Q: How did it make you feel when you were tough with some kids?

A: I didn't feel like I was a wimp anymore. I felt good. My dad said there's always someone bigger. And that goes for the big kids, too. There are people who can beat them up.

Q: What does it mean, then, to be a "real man"?

A: To be tough, have muscles. Just big like my father, he's about six feet something. A good fighter like the guys at school.

Q: Do you want to be a "real man"?

A: Yeah! I want to get muscles because I want to be kinda strong in case people fight me. I want to be able to get them down, not to hurt them, but to get them down so they don't hurt me. I don't want them to fight me. I want to be strong enough to get them down.

Given that Lenny was often verbally abused at school for his physical size and shape and for not being "a man," he accepted the notion that being masculine meant responding to provocation with physical violence. However, because he was physically small and obese in relation to the "cool tough guys," he was unable generally to respond in such a "manly" fashion. In other words, there existed an imbalance between Lenny's male appearance and both his bodily and behavioral effeminization at school that was revealed through interaction with the "cool tough guys." Consequently, Lenny was socially constructed as a gender deviant in this setting. Although Lenny embodied masculine presence and was accountably complicit at home, at school he was essentially emasculated.

Nevertheless, Lenny wanted to satisfy his father's criteria as well as be like the cool tough guys at school—he wanted to practice hegemonic masculinity as defined both at home and at school. Consequently, Lenny felt comfortable verbally abusing a "high-water." When the "high-water" retaliated verbally, Lenny understood through the embodied discourses at home and at school that he was permitted then to assault him publicly at school; accordingly, he exercised agency and reflexively assaulted this boy in the school hallway. Because this did not completely work out as planned—numerous students criticized him for not picking on someone his own size—he failed once again to embody a masculine presence at school and restricted his assaultive violence to his neighborhood. If the smaller and younger neighborhood boys verbally abused him, Lenny willingly fought them in the street setting and won! Thus Lenny practiced embodied masculine power over a few neighborhood boys through assaultive violence; he was a gender conformist in the street setting because his male appearance and gender behavior were now aligned, and his obesity was never questioned by the neighborhood boys because of his bodily response to verbal abuse. In turn, this gave him a sense of masculine self-esteem—he became hegemonically and accountably masculine in the street setting— because of the favorable appraisal he received from, in particular, his father.

KELLY

Through the sixth grade, Kelly enjoyed school, had a few friends, got along well with her teachers, and maintained a "C" average. She considered that she and her friends were the "jocks" at school, who never did anything wrong and had great fun together playing sports on the playground. Kelly described the structure of girls' groups at school as consisting of three major cliques—the "preppies," the "jocks," and the "badass"—and a variety of not-so-distinct girl groups. The preppies were the touchstone of localized emphasized femininity that complemented and catered to the "cool guys" (boy preppies) in this setting. The "jocks" constructed a type of "sporty femininity" that combined the confluence of female appearance with athletic bodily skills. The "jocks" were not organized into one specific group; rather, a variety of smaller groups "just played sports together." As Kelly noted, "Us

jocks hung out with all kinds of people." The "badass" (oppositional femininity) were seen as "slutty" girls who engaged in sexuality with the badass boys and would occasionally engage in physical violence against other girls—they presented a female appearance with a tough "bad-girl" persona. Kelly described a tendency toward hierarchy in this group relationship: the preppy girls being the most popular and setting the feminine trends at school—with social isolation and verbal abuse marking feminine and group boundaries.

However, in the seventh grade, Kelly became a loner because her friends had suddenly rejected her. And often she was the victim of peer abuse:

> I would get bullied, mostly by the jocks, for the clothes I would wear and because I shaved the back of my head. My clothes weren't up to fashion, and they started to call me names 'cause I looked like a boy, you know, and acted like a boy. So I'd get picked on about that. And my old friends would always be talking behind my back.

Kelly explained that she wore "boys' clothes" because "It was easier to do boy stuff, and I didn't want to look like a girl, you know." Kelly also shaved the back of her head and wore a duck-bill sports hat to enhance her effort to avoid "looking like a girl." Kelly's friends did not have a problem with her overall "boyish" embodiment, but when she shaved the back of her head, they began to reject her, the girls in particular talking behind her back: "They'd stare at me and then whisper stuff to each other. Then they'd walk by me and call me a 'dyke,' and then they'd all laugh. And once someone drew a picture of me looking like a guy with a 'big dick,' and they put it on my gym locker." Kelly also was subjected to peer abuse by boys, who often called her a "wimp," told her that she simply "was a fucking girl," and bellowed at her to "stop acting like a guy 'cause you can't do guy stuff." Thus, Kelly experienced peer interaction that initially accentuated the imbalance between her female appearance and her masculine gender display (e.g., her clothing style, social practices, and the shaved back of her head). In short, Kelly was deemed a gender deviant at school simply because her sex appearance and gender display/practices (including her bodily inscription) did not correspond.

Because Kelly was the sole female "jock" who dressed in such a manner, she attributed her head-shaving rejection as "going too far for them." However, what especially and continually concerned Kelly was the peer abuse by the boys, particularly being told she was a "wimp," allegedly unfit to do "guy stuff." As Kelly stated: "That really bothered me the most, 'cause I didn't like being hassled, but I couldn't fight like guys do. I kinda felt like a wimp when guys would like hassle me, you know, about that." Because of her physical size—Kelly was shorter than most of the boys who verbally abused her—she lacked confidence in "fighting back" as the masculine culture of the school dictated. Consequently, Kelly talked with her stepfather about the peer abuse at school, "And he said I needed to threaten the boys, you know. To go after the boys, not the girls, so everyone can see me, you know. To do it so kids could see. Like, 'You keep it up and I'll take you down.' And then when they [boys and girls] saw what I did to a couple of guys at school, they just left me alone."

Kelly's stepfather told her to threaten the boys because if they "backed down," then the girls would likewise stop abusing her. Kelly explained to her stepfather that she felt ill prepared physically to threaten the boys who verbally abused her. So he taught her specifically how to, as Kelly put it, "fight like a guy": "He taught me that being short made me faster, you know. He said the lower you are to the ground, the faster you are. He taught me how I had that advantage, you know." Kelly and her stepfather would "play fight," and he taught her to "scrooch down when he'd swing a punch at me. And then I'd just swipe his feet out from under him or tackle him. My stepfather taught me that. And then he told me to punch them in the face." Kelly exercised agency and reflexively used this method of fighting in response to peer abuse *by boys* at school. The following is a representative example:

> One day a kid [a boy] walked by me in the hall at school and called me a "wimp." He said I was just

a "fucking girl," like that. Just a "girl," you know. He'd been hasslin' me like that, sayin' stuff like that, that I couldn't fight, you know. So I was tired of him, you know what I mean? So I decided to fight him right there in the hall. I wanted kids to see what I could do, you know. I ended up breaking his jaw. And I got excused for one day, and then I got to come back the next day.

I asked Kelly if this boy was physically bigger or smaller than her:

> He was a little bigger, but I knew I could take him. I felt I could take care of myself—I was shorter but stronger than a lot of kids. I thought about what my stepfather told me and kids kept sayin', "You're not gonna take any shit, are ya?" And so I did it to him. There were lotsa kids around, so I ran up to him and just like tackled him, you know. I mean I real fast like got down on him and just grabbed his legs and pulled him down. He didn't even try to hit me. He just laid right there and let me pound on his face. He kinda seemed afraid to fight back, you know.

Kelly told her stepfather about the fight; he was "real proud" that she "didn't take any shit from this kid." I then asked Kelly if she was involved in other fights at school and she said:

> Oh, yeah. After that anyone who called me names like "wimp" or "fucking girl." They thought they were bigger and better than I was. So I proved them wrong. I'd take them down and pound on them with my fists and slam their head on the floor and tell them to shut the fuck up. And they would.

Kelly never fought girls at school, only boys: "about three dozen fights at school, and I'd always win the fights with guys. Because of that, I didn't need to fight girls. They saw what I could do, and so they just left me alone. I was someone not to mess with, you know." Kelly's old "jock" girlfriends stopped verbally abusing her as well.

Despite her assaultive violence, Kelly remained marginalized at school as Other by both the boys and the girls because of the imbalance between her female appearance and now masculine behavior.

Although Kelly continued to be a loner, she did gain some masculine confidence and respect at school. She "handled" each conflictual situation in a personal and individual way. She specifically targeted boys her "size" prior to any verbal abuse and was accorded, to a certain extent, the deference she felt she deserved. That is, through her masculine (albeit subordinate) presence at school, the boys who verbally abused her (or may do so) eventually stopped because Kelly either "took them down" or threatened to do so.

Subsequently, in the eighth grade, Kelly began to "hang out" on the street with the "badass guys," a group of boys who represented an oppositional form of masculinity to the local hegemonic masculinity of the preppy boys at school. According to Kelly, the badass boys were oppositional inasmuch as they frequently challenged the authority of the school (some even physically fought teachers); they regularly "skipped class" and "beat up people" at school. However, on the street they embodied a local hegemonic masculinity and engaged in robberies, burglaries, and group violence. Kelly joined this group because at school "I didn't have any friends. And they liked to do what I liked to do. And they accepted me 'cause I'm a good fighter. They were doing things like I'd seen all my life. They liked to party and get drunk and didn't take any shit from anyone. And that was normal to me." The "badass guys" Kelly joined formed a group in which she was "the only girl who 'hung' with the guys. I was the only one that didn't dress like a girl and didn't act like a girl. All the other girls who would hang with us {the 'badass girls'} wore really tight jeans and sexy tops." Kelly referred to these girls as "slutty badass girls" because "they had slept with like over a hundred guys." Kelly "hung out" with the guys (not the girls), yet although she considered herself heterosexual, she never engaged in sexuality with these guys because, as she put it:

> I would have sex with them if they wanted. But they don't treat me that way, you know. I'm one of them, you could say. I'd get called "ladybug" because female and male ladybugs look the same and act the same.

> I just got the nickname "ladybug" because I was a girl that acted like a boy. So we never talk about sex, and they never come on to me and I don't come on to them.

I asked Kelly if the "slutty badass girls" fought boys like she did, and she responded: "No way; they only fight girls. And so that kinda raised my status 'cause I would fight boys, just go after boys for no reason, you know. That kinda raised my status." The slutty badass girls fought girls "mostly over shit I couldn't care about, you know. They'd give each other shit about the way they looked and then fight about it." These girls never "hassled" Kelly because "They're afraid of me, you know. They know what would happen if they did. So they didn't mess with me." Moreover, these girls rarely "hung out" with Kelly and the guys but, rather, "They'd go walking around stores and the Mall. Or they'd sit down, listen to music, get high. And that was about it. They never really did anything with the guys except fuck them, you know."

Instead of going to the mall and engaging in sexuality, Kelly would play video games with the guys, wrestle with them, throw a football around with them, and occasionally would "go out driving" and "stompin" (group fighting with other street groups) with them. Eventually Kelly even came to "strut" like the boys. As she pointed out: "I'd walk like them, you know. Kinda big steps with my arms hangin' down and my shoulders swaying back and forth. They liked that, and I got called 'ladybug' for it." Kelly noted that her gait was quite different from the slutty badass girls because "They walked like girls, you know, with their butts tight, and short steps, standin' straight up, like that."

Another embodied masculine practice Kelly participated in on the street—but the "slutty badass girls" did not—were "power barfs," which she described as follows:

> Let's see. You drink beer and salt, and you'd gargle it in your mouth until it gets all foamy and then you swallow it. And then someone would hit you in the stomach and you just puke it all up. And the biggest splash and mess is the winner.

Because Kelly joined in many of the same activities practiced by the boys in the group, she "was seen as a girl, but cool like a guy. I wasn't a guy, but I was in the guy group." Although Kelly embodied a masculine presence at school and on the street, she did not "pass" as a "male." Kelly had more status in the badass group than the "slutty badass girls," yet she nevertheless was subordinate to both the preppy boys at school and the badass boys at school and on the street. As Kelly expressed her relationship with the latter boys: "The guys would always tell me what to do 'cause I'm a girl, you know. They'd say I don't know shit and stuff like that, you know. A lot of guys are sexist and didn't want me around a lot."

Q: How were they sexist?

A: You know. They'd think that 'cause they're guys, they are tougher and better. But I can beat the shit out of a lot of the guys. But they got to do things I didn't.

Q: Can you give me an example?

A: Ah, you know. Like they always got to go on robberies and burglaries, you know, and stompin', just 'cause they're guys.

Q: You didn't always participate when the boys were involved in those crimes?

A: No, 'cause sometimes they thought I'd get hurt, and then they'd have to deal with me. I'd get in the way and stuff like that, you know, when they gonna use knives, guns, and baseball bats.

At school Kelly navigated the structural relations among girls' groups and between badass girls and boys (for the most part, she and the preppy boys ignored each other). Although initially accepted as a "jock," when Kelly enthusiastically rejected feminine bodily display by shaving the back of her head, numerous girls and boys verbally abused her and labeled her a "dyke" (by girls) and a "wimp" (by boys) in an attempt to discredit the asymmetry between her female appearance and gender display. This public degradation hurt Kelly, and she initially felt physically unable to "fight back." Predictably,

Kelly discussed the situation with her stepfather. His response was to "fight back" *against boys,* and he proceeded to teach Kelly the bodily skills necessary to succeed. Kelly learned from her stepfather to manage her body in such a way as to win—and she did. Thus, when the contradiction between Kelly's sex appearance and masculine behavior was challenged by boys her size—insightfully, she carefully avoided physical confrontations with taller and stronger boys—she would not physically "back down." And often she would target boys prior to any verbal abuse. Consequently, Kelly managed to "hold her own" in front of her peers, embodying a masculine presence and becoming accountably masculine (albeit subordinate) at school. For this conduct, Kelly received her admired stepfather's and badass boys' approval for "fighting back" against the peer abuse at school.

Simultaneously, then, Kelly enjoyed a certain degree of masculine presence at school and on the street—over boys and girls—yet attained only a subordinate masculine status in school or as a member of the badass group because of her sex appearance.

REFLECTION

Lenny's and Kelly's life stories both show how motivation for assaultive violence is embedded in specific gender relations in distinct social settings and an imbalance between sex appearance and gender behavior in those settings. The three settings of home, school, and street contain different gender relations and different forms of accountability, each of which constructs specific meanings of "sex" and "gender" that *may* result in violent practices.

Regarding Lenny, at home he was easily accountably masculine because he effortlessly engaged in the available masculine practices, and his masculinity was never in question in this milieu: He maintained a complicit (yet subordinate) *nonviolent* masculine presence and self-confidence at home as his male appearance and masculine behavior aligned in this setting. However, at school Lenny faced different gender relations. Constructed as a "wimp," Lenny was disallowed participation in hegemonic masculine practices at school because of a now-situationally defined imbalance between his sex appearance and his bodily/behavioral effeminization—according to in-school co-present interactants, Lenny "failed" to exhibit both a masculine body and masculine behavior that situationally conformed to his male appearance. That is, Lenny's body (size and shape) and behavior were featured by other students, especially the "cool tough guys," as controverting his sex. As a result, Lenny was often verbally abused at school for his physical size and shape and for not demonstrating that he was "a man" through appropriate practices. Lenny's "sex" was invalidated because he did *not* exhibit the competence and willingness to sustain situational masculine displays and practices (Goffman, 1979). Lenny accepted the in-school criteria that being hegemonically masculine meant having a powerful, tall, and muscular body and required responding to provocation with physical violence. But because he was physically small and obese relative to the "cool tough guys," Lenny was unable to respond in such a "manly" fashion. He did not meet the criteria by which masculine competence was judged in school and accordingly was labeled a gender deviant. Lenny *initially* responded to this situation by becoming a loner, avoiding the "cool tough guys" as often as possible, and running home immediately after school.

Nevertheless, Lenny longed to be a "cool tough guy"—he wanted accountably to embody masculinity at school—and to be able to tell his father that he did not let others push him around. He experienced verbal pressure from his father to be a "real man" at school, and so in negotiating these situationally discursive constructs, he exercised agency and reflexively schemed and staged an attempt to "do" in-school hegemonic masculinity by verbally abusing and then assaulting a physically weaker boy in school—a "high-water." In other words, he changed his gender strategy to engage in bullying and assaultive violence *only* against this particular boy to create some type of balance between his male appearance and bodily/behavioral effeminization. In negotiating in-school gender relations, then,

Lenny now interacted with and through his body in a specific way: He prudently averted retaliating against the bullies while carefully creating a situation in which he believed masculine domination would be "successful" and would be recognized as such by others. Lenny chose the school hallway as an appropriate site for the bodily domination of an easily vulnerable boy because in this setting the violence, he hoped, would be confirmed as masculine by his peers. However, it did not work out completely as he wished: Many in the school "audience" told him to "pick on" someone his own size. Accordingly, Lenny disconcertingly failed to change his *place* within in-school gender relations, and his emasculated presence remained unchanged.

Realizing he was unable to embody masculinity at school—because the "high-water" was the only boy he could "beat up"—Lenny restricted his effort at masculine recognition to his neighborhood. Because the behavioral expressions activated by the contextual bullying at school could now be directed only outside the school situation, he had to move to another "site" to become accountably masculine. In other words, Lenny's embodied interaction at school directed him toward courses of masculine social action that were realizable physically and that could be accomplished outside the boundaries of school. Lenny had a desperate need to abandon his unmanly position and to fit into the hegemonic masculine model offered by the "cool tough guys" at school. For Lenny, then, the dominant masculine practices and thus in-school discursive criteria were not rejected. Rather, physical subordination directed him toward fixating on a specific site, his neighborhood, and on a particular form of body deployment, assaultive violence, where such practices—and thus a balance between sex appearance and gender behavior—could be realized. Moreover, Lenny had access to less powerful people in his neighborhood and therefore to the means by which his body could attain dominant physical expression. Given that Lenny was removed from any type of recognized and embodied masculine status in school—he was even criticized verbally for assaulting the "high-water"—interaction with the available younger and smaller boys in his neighborhood was especially attractive and became a powerful means of embodying hegemonic masculinity in the street setting.

In attempting to masculinize his body within the captivating discursive criteria of "cool tough guy" masculinity, then, Lenny engendered a powerful sense of self by "taking charge" on his neighborhood street and by conquering younger and smaller boys' bodies through assaultive violence. It was in the setting of the neighborhood street where Lenny's body took on a relatively new size and shape (he was physically larger and stronger than the younger boys), where it moved in a different way than at school (he was physically competent and dominant in this setting) and inevitably established a novel image for Lenny through the way he presented himself to the neighborhood boys and how he was "read" eventually by these boys. By concentrating his interactional efforts within the context of the neighborhood, Lenny was now able to transform how he interacted with and through his body: He was now hegemonically masculine *in this setting* because his male appearance and masculine behavior were aligned—he now validated his "sex" through his gender behavior. Lenny was living his body in a new way, as force and power were now embodied in Lenny—whereas at school neither existed—and he took on a new *place* in the power hierarchy among boys and, therefore, a new embodied self in the setting of the street. His conscious choice to be violent in his neighborhood was a situational resource in which Lenny could be dominant, powerful, and masculine through bodily practice—he embodied masculine presence in the street setting. Lenny reflexively created a situation entailing new gender relations among boys in which he was in masculine control and in which he could not be criticized and rejected by an emasculating audience. In short, Lenny constructed a nonthreatening gendered context in which masculinity could be performed according to the in-school dominant criteria. In the brief, illusory moment of each assaultive violent incident against smaller and younger neighborhood boys who challenged his masculinity (e.g., calling him a "fag"), Lenny felt morally justified in reacting

through assaultive violence. And in the process, the emasculated became the masculine because his male appearance and gender behavior now complemented each other. In short, Lenny's behavior on the street constructed a new meaning assigned to his sex, and it influenced the nature of his overall interaction with the neighborhood boys—he was now a gender conformist.

In Kelly's negotiation of the in-school gender relations among girls, she initially positioned herself as a "jock." Yet because of her masculine appearance—especially shaving the back of her head—she was ostracized and labeled a "dyke" by the girls. In particular, for the preppy girls, Kelly was not a "real" girl because of her bodily inscription. But Kelly was also labeled a "wimp" by the boys. That is, although the girls attempted to discredit her bodily display, Kelly's sex was featured by the boys to disparage her behavior. Kelly wanted to challenge both these attempts to "make" her accountably feminine by responding in a situationally masculine way—assaultive violence—but her body initially *restrained* her agency. For Kelly, her body did not live up to the contextual in-school masculine expectations: physically fighting back when verbally abused. Kelly was socially constructed as Other—a gender deviant—by both the boys and the girls; she was neither accountably feminine nor accountably masculine.

Determined, Kelly turned to her stepfather for help, and he did *not* emphasize changing her sex appearance but, rather, taught her how to manage her bodily behavior in an accountably masculine fashion. Kelly's body became the object of her social action as she worked on it in an attempt to transform her body into an "appropriate" masculine force for the particular school setting. Although prudently avoiding boys physically larger than her—the vast majority of whom ignored Kelly anyway—she exercised agency and reflexively created situations in which physical domination of boys would be seen by others as admirable. Her physical sense of masculinity was derived, in part, then, from her ability to change her body through social practice into a "proper" fighting machine—she constructed a more confident sense of self, a new way of interacting with and through her body in the school setting. Indeed, Kelly specifically concentrated on beating up boys (similar in physical size) who verbally abused her at school and intentionally chose spaces (e.g., the hallway) where her assaultive violence would be confirmed as masculine by her peers. She developed a "Don't-mess-with-me" persona and reputation and simultaneously satisfied her stepfather's criteria for doing appropriate masculine violence.

Differing from Lenny, Kelly actually established a sense of masculine presence at school. Even though there was an imbalance between her female appearance and masculine behavior, her gender conduct secured for her the competence to engage in violence when confronted with verbal abuse. Thus, the in-school Lenny–Kelly juxtaposition demonstrates a somewhat unique situation in which a person with a female appearance (Kelly) engages in masculine behavior while a person with a male appearance (Lenny) is emasculated. Despite her actual accomplishment of masculine practices, however, because of the continued imbalance between her sex appearance and gender behavior, Kelly remained severely marginalized as Other at school. Kelly's sex and behavior reciprocally influenced the meaning assigned to both (to the girls, her behavior contradicted her sex; to the boys, her sex belied her behavior) and, thus, she was conceptualized at school as a gender deviant, she had no friends, and she subsequently became a loner.

Turning to the badass street group for social acceptance and recognition, Kelly did not position herself as a "slutty badass girl" but, rather, attempted to become "one of the guys" (Miller, 2001). Kelly's embodied practices—such as engaging in assaultive violence against boys, participating in "power barfs," and performing the appropriate "strut"—minimized gender difference, all the while maintaining a female appearance. Moreover, Kelly occasionally would be included—alongside the boys—in "stompin'," or group assaultive violence against other groups of boys. Nevertheless, and in a similar manner at school, perception of her female sex ensured that Kelly's experience as a member of a

masculine badass-group could never be the same as the boys'. Given that hegemonic masculinity in the badass group was based, in part, on being physically tough, using the body as a weapon, and constructing a don't-mess-with-me demeanor, Kelly successfully used her body in these ways, yet had no intention to "pass" completely as male. Indeed, as at school, the badass boys perceived a female body under all the masculine display and practice. Thus, Kelly was deemed inadequate by the boys for specific activities, such as robberies, burglaries, and certain forms of stompin'. In other words, and in a similar way at school, Kelly was considered to be unfeminine but not unfemale. Kelly's sex appearance influenced the ultimate meaning assigned to her behavior by the badass boys and the nature of the overall social interaction between Kelly and these boys. Kelly's interaction on the street once again illustrates the reliance on both sex appearance and gender practices in validating sex or gender. In other words, since Kelly's sex appearance did not align with her gender behavior—and such nonalignment was accentuated by those in power—her masculine practices were not simply questioned; they were also subordinated.

FROM SEX-GENDER DISTINCTION TO EMBODIED GENDER

As I noted at the beginning of this article, the emergence of a two-sex model gave rise to a cultural emphasis on male genitalia as now different from female genitalia in *kind,* rather than in *degree,* and this new difference signified an essential bodily distinction of men from women. In other words, the "truth" of *two and only two sexes* is fashioned primarily through the application of genitalia as the ultimate criterion in making sex assignments. However, in our daily interactions, we continually make sex assignments and attributions with a complete lack of information about others' genitals (Kessler and McKenna, 1978; West and Zimmerman, 1987). Our recognition of another's *sex* is thus dependent upon the presentation of such visible bodily characteristics as hair, clothing, physical appearance, and other aspects of personal front (including behavior)—a combined bodily sex and gender presentation that becomes the substitute for the concealed genitalia. Consequently, although biological differences clearly exist between male and female bodies, during social interaction, sex is always already a social interpretation. That is, sex is achieved through the application and social acceptance of identificatory characteristics that proclaim one as "male" or as "female." The meaning of sex, then, is socially "read" through interpretations placed on the visible body; during social interaction, there exists a prior belief in *two and only two sexes,* which motivates a search for its support. As Suzanne Kessler and Wendy McKenna (1978:7) put it, "the element of social construction is primary in all aspects of being female and male." Indeed, recognition of both "sex" and "gender" is always already a social act—part of everyday interaction—that occurs simultaneously. And consequently, during most interpersonal interactions, "sex" and "gender" are indistinguishable from one another because we unreflectively recognize their congruence.

However, people who present ambiguous "bodily emblems" of "sex"—such as transsexuals in transition from one sex to another—produce hesitation in an otherwise smooth social process of sex assignment and attribution. Yet by so doing, they simultaneously bring the social construction of sex (and gender) to light. The research reported here adds further light to this social process because neither Lenny nor Kelly claimed transgender status nor did others have a problem recognizing their bodily presentation as male or female. Instead, according to co-present interactants within particular social settings, Lenny *failed* and Kelly *refused* to engage in gender behavior "appropriate" to their assigned sex. These two life stories then represent an interesting juxtaposition for understanding the relationship between sex and gender because for both, in specific spaces, their *sex appearance* was judged to be incongruent with their *gender behavior.* In other words, both Lenny and Kelly attempted to accomplish masculinity, yet Lenny "failed" to do so (at school) in terms of gender behavior (and in bodily appearance), and Kelly "failed" in terms of sex appearance

(at school and on the street). Consequently, the meaning assigned to Lenny's sex was influenced through his perceived behavior, and the meaning assigned to Kelly's behavior was influenced through her perceived sex. Both life stories thus show in different ways that during social interaction, a balance between sex appearance and gender behavior is essential for validating masculinity (and femininity). Indeed, during social interaction, we generally *read* "sex" and "gender" as an inextricable, seamless whole, which is why incongruency produces a cognitive dissonance in us for which people like Lenny and Kelly get punished.[4]

In addition, by examining the different "sites" of home, school, and street, we can capture the fluidity of the relationship between sex appearance and gender behavior and the changing nature of acceptance and rejection of behavior as masculine. Indeed, such a comparative analysis of Lenny's and Kelly's accounts has richly revealed that (1) social interaction and interpretation in specific sites shape the character, definition, and meaning of both "sex" and "gender"; (2) social interaction relies on the inseparability of sex appearance and gender behavior; and (3) given the nature of the interaction, an imbalance in sex appearance and gender behavior *may* motivate assaultive violence. Moreover, regarding the last point, to be "read" by others as masculine, Lenny and Kelly were required to ensure that their proffered selves presented a balance between sex appearance and gender behavior. The meaningfulness of accomplishing masculinity was based on the reaction of others to their gender *and* sex embodiment, and whether this embodiment was judged accountable was highly important to their sense of self. Embodied accountability is vital to any individual's situational recognition as a competent social agent. If an individual's sex appearance and gender behavior are categorized by others as inconsonant, that degradation may result in a spoiled self-concept (Goffman, 1968). It was this situationally recognized "failure" by contextually powerful individuals that motivated both Lenny and Kelly, in different ways, to engage in assaultive violence to *correct* the subordinating social situation. Given that such interaction questioned, undermined, and threatened Lenny's and Kelly's "masculinity," both reflexively assumed that only contextually "appropriate" masculine practices (in this case, assaultive violence) were *the* means of overcoming the challenge.

I began this essay by posing the question, How is gender *related* to sex? The data reported here suggest the following answer: Practicing masculinity (and femininity) relies on the coexistence of *sex* appearance and *gender* behavior. When sex appearance and gender behavior are congruent—or accepted by those in power to be harmonious—masculinity (and femininity) is validated and gender conformity occurs. However, when sex appearance does not align with gender behavior—and that nonalignment is emphasized by those in power—masculinity (and femininity) may be questioned and gender deviance results. And, in addition, assaultive violence is more likely to occur when there is an imbalance between sex appearance and gender behavior.

In short, the evidence from this study suggests that feminist sociologists should focus on "embodied gender"—the confluence and symbiosis of sex appearance and gender behavior in the social validation or invalidation of masculinity and femininity—rather than concentrate solely on gender. *Embodied gender* is an interactive process involving both a sex (body)/gender (behavior) presentation and a reading of that presentation by co-present interactants. Particular forms of embodied gender emerge in specific settings and, therefore, shift over time and across sites. For example, Lenny and Kelly were both socially constructed as "masculine boys" in the home setting, but at school, Lenny became a "feminine boy" and Kelly became a "masculine girl." Indeed, in all three sites of home, school, and street, the social perception of both body and behavior were salient to "seeing" masculinity. Consequently, one's embodied gender is interactively and situationally produced simultaneously through sex appearance and gender behavior.

But in addition, these two life stories reveal that the body is an inescapable and integral part of practicing masculinities and femininities. Lenny's and Kelly's bodies participated in social action by delineating courses of social conduct: Their bodies were *agents* of social practice and, given the context (at school for instance), would do certain things and not others. Indeed, their bodies constrained and facilitated social action and therefore mediated and influenced future social practices (Connell and Messerschmidt, 2006). Lenny's and Kelly's bodies were *lived* in terms of what they could "do" and the consequence of their bodily practice was historicity, or the transformation of social situations—their bodies were drawn into history, and history was constituted through their bodies (Connell, 1998). In short, the body is a participant in shaping and generating social practice and, consequently, it is impossible to consider human agency without taking embodied gender into account.

NOTES

1. Although this article concentrates solely on two life stories, sampling continued throughout the study until no new information or themes emerged from the interviews; that is, with thirty interviews "data saturation" was easily reached, and, thus, these two case studies are representative of sample reliability. For an interesting study on "data saturation" that argues that such reliability actually can be achieved through twelve interviews, see Guest et al. (2006).
2. "Hegemonic masculinity" and "emphasized femininity" are the culturally idealized forms of gender in a given historical and social setting (local, regional, and global), and they are defined in relation to each other as well as to "complicit," "subordinated," and "oppositional" forms of gender construction. See Connell and Messerschmidt (2006), Messerschmidt (2004), and Kimmel (chapter 5 in this volume) for a fuller discussion.
3. For an excellent discussion of when gender is "reflexive" and "unreflective," see Martin (2003, 2006).
4. Thanks to Wendy Cealey Harrison (personal communication) for this important insight.

REFERENCES

Cealey Harrison, W. 2006. "The Shadow and the Substance: The Sex/Gender Debate." In *Handbook of Gender and Women's Studies,* ed. K. Davis, M. Evans, and J. Lorber, 35–52. Thousand Oaks, Calif.: Sage.

Cealey Harrison, W., and J. Hood-Williams. 2002. *Beyond Sex and Gender.* Thousand Oaks, Calif.: Sage.

Connell, R. W. 1998. "Making Gendered People: Bodies, Identities, Sexualities." In *Revisioning Gender,* ed. M. M. Ferree, J. Lorber, and B. B. Hess, 449–471. Thousand Oaks, Calif.: Sage.

———. 2000. *The Men and the Boys.* Sydney: Allen & Unwin.

Connell, R. W., and J. W. Messerschmidt. 2006. "Hegemonic Masculinity: Rethinking the Concept." *Gender & Society* 19:829–859.

Cromwell, J. 1999. *Transmen and FTMs: Identities, Bodies, Genders, and Sexualities.* Urbana: University of Illinois Press.

Davis, K. 1997. "Embody-ing Theory: Beyond Modernist and Postmodernist Readings of the Body." In *Embodied Practices: Feminist Perspectives on the Body,* ed. K. Davis, 1–23. Thousand Oaks, Calif.: Sage.

Devor, H. 1997. *FTM: Female-to-Male Transsexuals in Society.* Bloomington: Indiana University Press.

Dozier, R. 2005. "Beards, Breasts, and Bodies: Doing Sex in a Gendered World." *Gender & Society* 19:297–316.

Foucault, M. 1980. *Herculine Barbin,* trans. R. McDougall. New York: Pantheon.

Garfinkel, H. 1967. *Studies in Ethnomethodology.* Englewood Cliffs, N.J.: Prentice Hall.

Goffman, E. 1963. *Behavior in Public Places.* New York: Free Press.

———. 1968. *Stigma.* Englewood Cliffs, N.J.: Prentice Hall.

———. 1979. *Gender Advertisements.* New York: Harper & Row.

Guest, G., A. Bunce, and L. Johnson. 2006. "How Many Interviews Are Enough? An Experiment with Data Saturation and Variability." *Field Methods* 18(1):59–82.

Halberstam, J. 1998. *Female Masculinity.* Durham, N.C.: Duke University Press.

Kennelly, I., S. N. Merz, and J. Lorber. 2001. "What Is Gender?" *American Sociological Review* 66:598–605.

Kessler, S., and W. McKenna. 1978. *Gender: An Ethnomethodological Approach.* New York: John Wiley & Sons.

Laqueur, T. 1990. *Making Sex: Body and Gender from the Greeks to Freud.* Cambridge, Mass.: Harvard University Press.

Lorber, J. 2005. *Breaking the Bowls: Degendering and Feminist Change.* New York: W. W. Norton.

Martin, P. Y. 2003. "'Said and Done' Versus 'Saying and Doing': Gender Practices, Practicing Gender at Work." *Gender & Society* 17:342–366.

——— 2006. "Practicing Gender at Work: Further Thoughts on Reflexivity." *Gender, Work and Organization* 13:254–276.

Messerschmidt, J. W. 2004. *Flesh and Blood: Adolescent Gender Diversity and Violence.* Lanham, Md.: Rowman & Littlefield.

Miller, E. M., and C. Y. Costello. 2001. "The Limits of Biological Determinism." *American Sociological Review* 66:592–598.

Miller, J. 2001. *One of the Guys: Girls, Gangs, and Gender.* New York: Oxford University Press.

Namaste, V. 2000. *Invisible Lives: The Erasure of Transsexual and Transgendered People.* Chicago: University of Chicago Press.

Oakley, A. 1972. *Sex, Gender and Society.* San Francisco: Harper & Row.

Prosser, J. 1998. *Second Skins: The Body Narratives of Transsexuality.* New York: Columbia University Press.

Risman, B. J. 2001. "Calling the Bluff of Value-Free Science." *American Sociological Review* 66:605–611.

Rubin, H. 2003. *Self-Made Men: Identity and Embodiment Among Transsexual Men.* Nashville, Tenn.: Vanderbilt University Press.

Stoller, R. J. 1968. *Sex and Gender: On the Development of Masculinity and Femininity.* New York: Science House.

West, C., and D. H. Zimmerman. 1987. "Doing Gender." *Gender and Society* 1:125–151.

6 • *Patricia Hill Collins*

PRISONS FOR OUR BODIES, CLOSETS FOR OUR MINDS
Racism, Heterosexism, and Black Sexuality

DISCUSSION QUESTIONS

1. What are some of the specific problems that have resulted from seeing racism and heterosexism as two distinct systems of oppression?
2. According to Collins, what are some of the ways that racism and heterosexism have been institutionalized? Can you identify additional means?
3. How does heterosexism impact heterosexual African Americans?
4. How have the interconnected systems of racism and heterosexism produced gender-specific consequences?

> White fear of black sexuality is a basic ingredient of white racism.
>
> —Cornel West

For African Americans, exploring how sexuality has been manipulated in defense of racism is not new. Scholars have long examined the ways in which "white fear of black sexuality" has been a basic ingredient of racism. For example, colonial regimes routinely manipulated ideas about sexuality in order to maintain unjust power relations.[1] Tracing the history of contact between English explorers and colonists and West African societies, historian Winthrop Jordan contends that English perceptions of sexual practices among African people reflected preexisting English beliefs about Blackness, religion, and animals.[2] American historians point to the significance of sexuality to chattel slavery. In the United States, for example, slaveowners relied upon an ideology of Black sexual deviance to regulate and exploit enslaved Africans.[3] Because Black feminist analyses pay more attention to women's sexuality, they too identify how the sexual exploitation of women has been a basic ingredient of racism. For example, studies of African American slave women routinely point to sexual victimization as a defining feature of American slavery.[4] Despite the important contributions of this extensive literature on race and sexuality, because much of the literature assumes that sexuality means *hetero*sexuality, it ignores how racism and heterosexism influence one another.

In the United States, the assumption that racism and heterosexism constitute two separate systems of oppression masks how each relies upon the other for meaning. Because neither system of oppression makes sense without the other, racism and heterosexism might be better viewed as sharing one history with similar yet disparate effects on all Americans differentiated by race, gender, sexuality, class, and nationality. People who are positioned at the margins of both systems and who are harmed by both typically raise questions about the intersections of racism and heterosexism much earlier and/or more forcefully than those people who are in positions of privilege. In the case of intersections of racism and heterosexism, Black lesbian, gay, bisexual, and transgendered (LGBT) people were among the first to question how racism and heterosexism are interconnected. As African American LGBT people point out, assuming that all Black people are heterosexual and that all LGBT people are White distorts the experiences of LGBT Black people. Moreover, such comparisons misread the significance of ideas about sexuality to racism and race to heterosexism.[5]

Until recently, questions of sexuality in general, and homosexuality in particular, have been treated as crosscutting, divisive issues within antiracist African American politics. The consensus issue of ensuring racial unity subordinated the allegedly crosscutting issue of analyzing sexuality, both straight and gay alike. This suppression has been challenged from two directions. Black women, both heterosexual and lesbian, have criticized the sexual politics of African American communities that leave women vulnerable to single motherhood and sexual assault. Black feminist and womanist projects have challenged Black community norms of a sexual double standard that punishes women for behaviors in which men are equally culpable. Black gays and lesbians have also criticized these same sexual politics that deny their right to be fully accepted within churches, families, and other Black community organizations. Both groups of critics argue that ignoring the heterosexism that underpins Black

patriarchy hinders the development of a progressive Black sexual politics. As Cathy Cohen and Tamara Jones contend, "Black people need a liberatory politics that includes a deep understanding of how heterosexism operates as a system of oppression, both independently and in conjunction with other such systems. We need a black liberatory politics that affirms black lesbian, gay, bisexual, and transgender sexualities. We need a black liberatory politics that understands the roles sexuality and gender play in reinforcing the oppression rooted in many black communities."[6] Developing a progressive Black sexual politics requires examining how racism and heterosexism mutually construct one another.

MAPPING RACISM AND HETEROSEXISM: THE PRISON AND THE CLOSET

> We regarded the struggle in prison as a microcosm of the struggle as a whole. We would fight inside as we had fought outside. The racism and repression were the same; I would simply have to fight on different terms.
>
> —Nelson Mandela

Like Nelson Mandela's view, when it comes to racism in the United States, life for African American women and men can be compared to being in prison.[7] Certainly the metaphor of the prison encapsulates the historical placement of African Americans in the U.S. political economy. The absence of political rights under chattel slavery and Jim Crow segregation and the use of police state powers against African Americans in urban ghettos have meant that Black people could be subjugated, often with little recourse. Moreover, prisons are rarely run solely by force. Routine practices such as strip searches, verbal abuse, restricting basic privileges, and ignoring physical and sexual assault among inmates aim to control prisoners by dehumanizing them. Visiting his brother Robbie, who was incarcerated on a life sentence in a Pennsylvania prison, author John Wideman describes this disciplinary process:

> The visitor is forced to become an inmate. Subjected to the same sorts of humiliation and depersonalization. Made to feel powerless, intimidated by the might of the state. Visitors are treated like both children and ancient, incorrigible sinners. We experience a crash course that teaches us in a dramatic, unforgettable fashion just how low a prisoner is in the institution's estimation. We also learn how rapidly we can descend to the same depth.... We suffer the keepers prying eyes, prying machines, prying hands. We let them lock us in without any guarantee the doors will open when we wish to leave. We are in fact their prisoners until they release us. That was the idea. To transform the visitor into something he despised and feared. A prisoner.[8]

As direct recipients of the anti–civil rights agenda advanced under conservative Republican administrations, contemporary African Americans living in inner cities experienced the brunt of punitive governmental policies that had a similar intent.[9] Dealing with impersonal bureaucracies often subjected them to the same sorts of "humiliation and depersonalization" that Wideman felt while visiting his brother. Just as he was "made to feel powerless, intimidated by the might of the state," residents of African American inner-city neighborhoods who deal with insensitive police officers, unresponsive social workers, and disinterested teachers report similar feelings.

African American reactions to racial resegregation in the post–civil rights era, especially those living in hyper-segregated, poor, inner-city neighborhoods, resemble those of people who are in prison. Prisoners that turn on one another are much easier to manage than ones whose hostility is aimed at their jailers. Far too often, African Americans coping with racial segregation and ghettoization simply turn on one another, reflecting heightened levels of alienation and nihilism.[10] Faced with no jobs, crumbling public school systems, the influx of drugs into their neighborhoods, and the easy availability of guns, many blame one another. Black

youth are especially vulnerable.[11] As urban prisoners, the predilection for some Black men to kill others over seemingly unimportant items such as gym shoes, jewelry, and sunglasses often seems incomprehensible to White Americans and to many middle-class Black Americans. Privileged groups routinely assume that all deserving Americans live in decent housing, attend safe schools with caring teachers, and will be rewarded for their hard work with college opportunities and good jobs. They believe that undeserving Blacks and Latinos who remain locked up in deteriorating inner cities get what they deserve and do not merit social programs that will show them a future. This closing door of opportunity associated with hyper-segregation creates a situation of shrinking opportunities and neglect. This is the exact climate that breeds a culture of violence that is a growing component of "street culture" in working-class and poor Black neighborhoods.[12]

Given this context, why should anyone be surprised that rap lyrics often tell the stories of young Black men who feel that they have nothing to lose, save their respect under a "code of the street."[13] Ice Cube's 1993 rap "It Was a Good Day," describes a "good" day for a young Black man living in Los Angeles. On a "good" day, he didn't fire his gun, he got food that he wanted to eat, the cops ignored him and didn't pull him over for an imaginary infraction, and he didn't have to kill anyone. Is this art imitating life, or vice versa? Sociologist Elijah Anderson's ethnographic studies of working-class and poor Black youth living in Philadelphia suggests that for far too many young African American males, Ice Cube's bad days are only too real.[14] Just as male prisoners who are perceived as being weak encounter relentless physical and sexual violence, weaker members of African American communities are preyed upon by the strong. Rap artist Ice T explains how masculinity and perceived weakness operate:

> You don't understand anyone who is weak. You look at gay people as prey. There isn't anybody in the ghetto teaching that some people's sexual preferences are predisposed. You're just ignorant. You got to get educated, you got to get out of that jail cell called the

ghetto to really begin to understand. All you see is a sissy. A soft dude. A punk.[15]

Women, lesbian, gay, bisexual, and transgendered people, children, people living with HIV, drug addicts, prostitutes, and others deemed to be an embarrassment to the broader African American community or a drain upon its progress or simply in the wrong place at the wrong time become targets of silencing, persecution, and or abuse. This is what prisons do—they breed intolerance.

The experiences of people in prison also shed light on the myriad forms of African American resistance to the strictures of racial oppression. No matter how restrictive the prison, some prisoners find ways to resist. Often within plain sight of their guards, people who are imprisoned devise ingenious ways to reject prison policies. Nelson Mandela recounts the numerous ways that he and his fellow prisoners outwitted, undermined, tricked, and, upon occasion, confronted their captors during the twenty-seven years that he spent as a political prisoner in South African prisons. Craving news of the political struggle outside, prisoners communicated by writing in milk on blank paper, letting it dry to invisibility and, once the note was passed on, making the words reappear with the disinfectant used to clean their cells. They smuggled messages to one another in plastic wrapped packages hidden in food drums.[16] In the case of solitary confinement where an inmate could be locked up for twenty-three hours a day in a dark cell, just surviving constituted an act of resistance. As Mandela observes, "Prison is designed to break one's spirit and destroy one's resolve. To do this, the authorities attempt to exploit every weakness, demolish every initiative, negate all signs of individuality—all with the idea of stamping out that spark that makes each of us human and each of us who we are."[17] Mandela and his fellow prisoners recognized the function of actual prisons under racial apartheid and of apartheid policies as an extension of prison.

Recognizing that their everyday lives resemble those of prison inmates often politicizes individuals. Autobiographies by African Americans who were imprisoned because of their political beliefs, for example, Angela Davis and Assata Shakur, or who became politicized during their imprisonment, for example, Malcolm X or George Jackson, point to the significance of actual incarceration as a catalyst for resistance. In the 1980s, many poor and working-class African American youth who were locked up in urban ghettos and facing the closing door of opportunity refused to turn their rage upon one another. Instead, many chose to rap about the violence and intolerance around them and, in the process, created an influential hip-hop culture that reached youth all over the world. Crafted in the South Bronx, an urban landscape that had been abandoned by virtually everyone, African American, Latino, and Afro-Caribbean youth created rap, break dancing, tagging (graffiti), fashions and other cultural creations.[18] Ice Cube's rap about his good day represents the tip of an immense hip-hop iceberg. With few other public forums to share their outrage at a society that had so thoroughly written them off, Black youth used rap and hip-hop to protest the closing door of opportunity in their lives and to claim their humanity in the face of the dehumanization of racial segregation and ghettoization. Without strategies of non-cooperation such as those exhibited by Mandela and his colleagues and without developing new forms of resistance such as hip-hop, Black people simply would not have survived.

What is freedom in the context of prison? Typically, incarcerated people cannot voluntarily "come out" of prison but must find a way to "break out." Under chattel slavery, the history of the Underground Railroad certainly reflected the aspirations of enslaved Africans to break out of the prison of slavery and to flee to the quasi freedom offered by Northern states. But just as gender, age, skin color, and class affect the contours of oppression itself, these very same categories shape strategies of resistance. As African American women's slave narratives point out, men and young people could more easily break out by running away than women, mothers, and older people. Then as now, African American women are often reluctant to leave their families, and many sacrifice their own personal freedom in order to stay behind and care for children and for others who depend on them. Under Jim Crow segregation, very light-skinned African Americans faced the difficult choice of "passing" and leaving their loved ones behind. More recently, as prime beneficiaries of the antidiscrimination and affirmative action policies of the civil rights movement, many middle-class and affluent African Americans have moved to distant White suburbs. Such actions certainly reflect a desire to escape the problems associated with poor and working-class Black neighborhoods. If one can "buy" one's freedom, as Nike ads proclaim, why not exercise personal choice and "just do it"?

In other situations, African Americans have recognized the confines of the prison and, through unruly, spontaneous uprisings or through organized political protests, have turned upon their jailers. A series of urban uprisings in cities such as New York, Detroit, Miami (1980), Los Angeles (1992), and Cincinnati (2001) typify the explosive reactions of many poor and working-class African Americans to bad schools, terrible housing, no jobs, little money, and dwindling prospects. The catalyst is usually the same—police brutality against unlucky African American citizens. More organized Black protests also reflect this process of turning upon the jailers of racism and refusing to cooperate with unjust laws and customs. Historically, social formations that kept African Americans impoverished and virtually powerless—chattel slavery, labor exploitation of the Jim Crow Southern agriculture, and the continuing growth of urban ghettos—all sparked organized African American political protest. The abolitionist movement, the formation of the NAACP (1909) and the Urban League (1910), the size of Marcus Garvey's Black Nationalist United Negro Improvement Association (1920s), the many organizations that participated in the civil rights and Black Power movements, and the increased visibility of Black youth through hip-hop culture reflect resistance to racism.

Racism may be likened to a prison, yet sexual oppression has more often been portrayed using the metaphor of the "closet."[19] This metaphor is routinely invoked to describe the oppression of lesbian, gay, bisexual, and transgendered people. Historically, because religion and science alike defined homosexuality as deviant, LGBT people were forced to conceal their sexuality.[20] For homosexuals, the closet provided some protection from homophobia that stigmatized LGBT sexual expression as deviant. Being in the closet meant that most hid their sexual orientation in the most important areas of their lives. With family, friends, or at work, many LGBT people passed as "straight" in order to avoid suspicion and exposure. Passing as straight fostered the perception that few gays and lesbians existed. The invisibility of gays and lesbians helped normalize heterosexuality, fueled homophobia, and supported heterosexism as a system of power.[21]

Because closets are highly individualized, situated within families, and distributed across the segregated spaces of racial, ethnic, and class neighborhoods, and because sexual identity is typically negotiated later than social identities of gender, race, and class, LGBT people often believe that they are alone. Being in the private, hidden, and domestic space of the closet leaves many LGBT adolescents to suffer in silence. During the era of racial segregation, heterosexism operated as smoothly as it did because hidden or closeted sexualities remained relegated to the margins of society *within* racial/ethnic groups. Staying in the closet stripped LBGT people of rights. The absence of political rights has meant that sexual minorities could be fired from their jobs, moved from their housing, have their children taken away in custody battles, dismissed from the military, and be targets of random street violence, often with little recourse. Rendering LGBT sexualities virtually invisible enabled the system of heterosexism to draw strength from the seeming naturalness of heterosexuality.[22]

Since the 1980s, gay, lesbian, bisexual, and transgendered people have challenged heterosexism by coming out of the closet. If the invisibility of sexual oppression enabled it to operate unopposed, then making heterosexism visible by being "out" attacked heterosexism at its core. Transgressing sexual borders became the hallmark of LGBT politics.

The individual decision to come out to one's family or friends enabled formerly closeted LGBT people to live openly and to unsettle the normalization of heterosexuality. Transgression also came to characterize one strand of gay group politics, moving from the gay and lesbian identity politics of the first phase of "gay liberation" to more recent queer politics.[23] Gay pride marches that embrace drag queens, cross-dressers, gay men who are flamboyantly dressed, individuals with indeterminate gender identities, and mannish lesbians push the envelope beyond accepting the LGBT people who are indistinguishable from everyone else, save for this one area of sexual orientation. Through public, visible, and often outrageous acts, "queering" normal sexuality became another hallmark of LGBT politics. The phrase, "we're queer, we're here, get used to it" embraces a clear stance of defiance. At the same time, another strand of gay politics strives to be seen as "good gay citizens" who should be entitled to the same rights as everyone else. Practices such as legitimating gay marriages and supporting adoptions by gay and lesbian couples constitute another expression of transgression. By aiming for the legitimacy granted heterosexual couples and families, gay and lesbian couples simultaneously uphold family yet profoundly challenge its meaning.[24]

Racism and heterosexism, the prison and the closet, appear to be separate systems, but LGBT African Americans point out that *both* systems affect their everyday lives. If racism and heterosexism affect Black LGBT people, then these systems affect *all* people, including heterosexual African Americans. Racism and heterosexism certainly converge on certain key points. For one, both use similar state-sanctioned institutional mechanisms to maintain racial and sexual hierarchies. For example, in the United States, racism and heterosexism both rely on segregating people as a mechanism of social control. For racism, segregation operates by using race as a visible marker of group membership that enables the state to relegate Black people to inferior schools, housing, and jobs. Racial segregation relies on enforced membership in a visible community in which racial discrimination is tolerated. For

heterosexism, segregation is enforced by pressuring LGBT individuals to remain closeted and thus segregated from one another. Before social movements for gay and lesbian liberation, sexual segregation meant that refusing to claim homosexual identities virtually eliminated any group-based political action to resist heterosexism. For another, the state has played a very important role in sanctioning both forms of oppression. In support of racism, the state sanctioned laws that regulated where Black people could live, work, and attend school. In support of heterosexism, the state maintained laws that refused to punish hate crimes against LGBT people, that failed to offer protection when LGBT people were stripped of jobs and children, and that generally sent a message that LGBT people who came out of the closet did so at their own risk.[25]

Racism and heterosexism also share a common set of practices that are designed to discipline the population into accepting the status quo. These disciplinary practices can best be seen in the enormous amount of attention paid both by the state and organized religion to the institution of marriage. If marriage were in fact a natural and normal occurrence between heterosexual couples and if it occurred naturally within racial categories, there would be no need to regulate it. People would naturally choose partners of the opposite sex and the same race. Instead, a series of laws have been passed, all designed to regulate marriage. For example, for many years, the tax system has rewarded married couples with tax breaks that have been denied to single taxpayers or unmarried couples. The message is clear—it makes good financial sense to get married. Similarly, to encourage people to marry within their assigned race, numerous states passed laws banning interracial marriage. These restrictions lasted until the landmark Supreme Court decision in 1967 that overturned state laws. The state has also passed laws designed to keep LGBT people from marrying. In 1996, the U.S. Congress passed the Federal Defense of Marriage Act that defined marriage as a "legal union between one man and one woman." In all of these cases, the state perceives that it has a compelling interest in disciplining the population to marry and to marry the correct partners.[26]

Racism and heterosexism also manufacture ideologies that defend the status quo. When ideologies that defend racism and heterosexism become taken-for-granted and appear to be natural and inevitable, they become hegemonic. Few question them and the social hierarchies they defend. Racism and heterosexism both share a common cognitive framework that uses binary thinking to produce hegemonic ideologies. Such thinking relies on oppositional categories. It views race through two oppositional categories of Whites and Blacks, gender through two categories of men and women, and sexuality through two oppositional categories of heterosexuals and homosexuals. A master binary of normal and deviant overlays and bundles together these and other lesser binaries. In this context, ideas about "normal" race (whiteness, which ironically, masquerades as racelessness), "normal" gender (using male experiences as the norm), and "normal" sexuality (heterosexuality, which operates in a similar hegemonic fashion) are tightly bundled together. In essence, to be completely "normal," one must be White, masculine, and heterosexual, the core hegemonic White masculinity. This mythical norm is hard to see because it is so taken-for-granted. Its antithesis, its Other, would be Black, female, and lesbian, a fact that Black lesbian feminist Audre Lorde pointed out some time ago.[27]

Within this oppositional logic, the core binary of normal/deviant becomes ground zero for justifying racism and heterosexism. The deviancy assigned to race and that assigned to sexuality becomes an important point of contact between the two systems. Racism and heterosexism both require a concept of sexual deviancy for meaning, yet the form that deviance takes within each system differs. For racism, the point of deviance is created by a *normalized White heterosexuality* that depends on a *deviant Black heterosexuality* to give it meaning. For heterosexism, the point of deviance is created by this very same *normalized White heterosexuality* that now depends on a *deviant White homosexuality.* Just as racial normality requires the stigmatization of the sexual practices of Black people, heterosexual normality relies upon the stigmatization of the sexual

practices of homosexuals. In both cases, installing White heterosexuality as normal, natural, and ideal requires stigmatizing alternate sexualities as abnormal, unnatural, and sinful.

The purpose of stigmatizing the sexual practices of Black people and those of LGBT people may be similar, but the content of the sexual deviance assigned to each differs. Black people carry the stigma of *promiscuity* or excessive or unrestrained heterosexual desire. This is the sexual deviancy that has both been assigned to Black people and been used to construct racism. In contrast, LGBT people carry the stigma of *rejecting* heterosexuality by engaging in unrestrained homosexual desire. Whereas the deviancy associated with promiscuity (and, by implication, with Black people as a race) is thought to lie in an *excess* of heterosexual desire, the pathology of homosexuality (the invisible, closeted sexuality that becomes impossible within heterosexual space) seemingly resides in the *absence* of it.

While analytically distinct, in practice, these two sites of constructed deviancy work together and both help create the "sexually repressive culture" in America described by Cheryl Clarke.[28] Despite their significance for American society overall, here I confine my argument to the challenges that confront Black people.[29] Both sets of ideas frame a hegemonic discourse of *Black sexuality* that has at its core ideas about an assumed promiscuity among heterosexual African American men and women and the impossibility of homosexuality among Black gays and lesbians.

AFRICAN AMERICANS AND THE RACIALIZATION OF PROMISCUITY

Ideas about Black promiscuity that produce contemporary sexualized spectacles such as Jennifer Lopez, Destiny's Child, Ja Rule, and the many young Black men on the U.S. talk show circuit have a long history. Historically, Western science, medicine, law, and popular culture reduced an African-derived aesthetic concerning the use of the body, sensuality, expressiveness, and spirituality to an ideology about

Black sexuality. The distinguishing feature of this ideology was its reliance on the idea of Black promiscuity. The possibility of distinctive and worthwhile African-influenced worldviews on anything, including sexuality, as well as the heterogeneity of African societies expressing such views, was collapsed into an imagined, pathologized Western discourse of what was thought to be essentially African.[30] To varying degrees, observers from England, France, Germany, Belgium, and other colonial powers perceived African sensuality, eroticism, spirituality, and/or sexuality as deviant, out of control, sinful, and as an essential feature of racial difference.[31]

Western religion, science, and media took over 350 years to manufacture an ideology of Black sexuality that assigned (heterosexual) promiscuity to Black people and then used it to justify racial discrimination. The racism of slavery and colonialism needed ideological justification. Toward this end, preexisting British perceptions of Blackness became reworked to frame notions of racial difference that, over time, became folded into a broader primitivist discourse on race. Long before the English explored Africa, the terms "black" and "white" had emotional meaning within England. Before colonization, white and black connoted opposites of purity and filthiness, virginity and sin, virtue and baseness, beauty and ugliness, and God and the devil.[32] Bringing this preexisting framework with them, English explorers were especially taken by Africans' color. Despite actual variations of skin color among African people, the English described them as being *black,* "an exaggerated term which in itself suggests that the Negro's complexion had powerful impact upon their perceptions."[33] From first contact, biology mattered—racial difference was embodied. European explorers and the traders, colonists, and settlers who followed were also struck by the differences between their own cultures and those of continental Africans. Erroneously interpreting African cultures as being inferior to their own, European colonial powers redefined Africa as a "primitive" space, filled with Black people and devoid of the accoutrements of more civilized cultures. In this way, the broad ethnic diversity among the people of continental Africa became reduced to more generic terms such as "primitive," "savage," and "native." Within these categories, one could be an Ashanti or a Yoruba, but each was a savage, primitive native all the same. The resulting primitivist discourse redefined African societies as inferior.[34]

Western natural and social sciences were deeply involved in constructing this primitivist discourse that reached full fruition in the nineteenth and early twentieth centuries.[35] Through laboratory experiments and field research, Western science attempted to understand these perceived racial differences while creating, through its own practices, those very same differences. For example, Sarah Bartmann's dissection illustrates this fascination with biological difference as the site of racial difference, with sexual difference of women further identified as an important topic of study.[36] Moreover, this perception of Africa worked with an important idea within nineteenth-century science, namely, the need to classify and rank objects, places, living things, and people. Everything had its place and all places were ranked.[37] With its primitiveness and alleged jungles, Africa and its peoples marked the bottom, the worst place to be, and a place ripe for colonial conquest. Yet at the same time, Africa was dangerous, different, and alluring. This new category of primitive situated Africans just below Whites and right above apes and monkeys, who marked this boundary distinguishing human from animals. Thus, within Western science, African people and apes occupied a fluid border zone between humans and animals.

With all living creatures classified in this way, Western scientists perceived African people as being more natural and less civilized, primarily because African people were deemed to be closer to animals and nature, especially the apes and monkeys whose appearance most closely resembled humans. Like African people, animals also served as objects of study for Western science because understanding the animal kingdom might reveal important insights about civilization, culture, and what distinguished the human "race" from its animal counterparts as well as the human "races" from one another. Donna Haraway's study of primatology illustrates

Western scientists' fascination with identifying how apes differed from humans: "the study of apes was more about humans. Moreover, the close proximity to apes and monkeys that Africans occupied within European derived taxonomies of life such as the Great Chain of Being worked to link Africans and animals through a series of overlapping constructs. Apes and Africans both lived in Africa, a place of wild animals and wild people. In both cases, their source of wildness emerged from their lack of culture and their acting out of instinct or bodily impulses."[38] This family resemblance between African people and animals was not benign—viewing Africans and animals alike as embodied creatures ruled by "instinct or bodily impulses" worked to humanize apes and dehumanize Black people.

In this context, studying the sexual practices of African people and animals took on special meaning. Linking African people and animals was crucial to Western views of Black promiscuity. Genital sexual intercourse or, more colloquially, the act of "fucking," characterized animal sexuality. Animals are promiscuous because they lack intellect, culture, and civilization. Animals do not have erotic lives; they merely "fuck" and reproduce. Certainly animals could be slaughtered, sold, and domesticated as pets because within capitalist political economies, animals were commodities that were owned as private property. As the history of animal breeding suggests, the sexual promiscuity of horses, cattle, chickens, pigs, dogs, and other domesticated animals could be profitable for their owners. By being classified as proximate to wild animals and, by analogy, eventually being conceptualized as being animals (chattel), the alleged deviancy of people of African descent lay in their sexual promiscuity, a "wildness" that also was believed to characterize animal sexuality. Those most proximate to animals, those most lacking civilization, also were those humans who came closest to having the sexual lives of animals. Lacking the benefits of Western civilization, people of African descent were perceived as having a biological nature that was inherently more sexual than that of Europeans. The primitivist discourse thus created the category of "beast"

and the sexuality of such beasts as "wild." The legal classification of enslaved African people as chattel (animal-like) under American slavery that produced controlling images of bucks, jezebels, and breeder women drew meaning from this broader interpretive framework.[39]

Historically, this ideology of Black sexuality that pivoted on a Black heterosexual promiscuity not only upheld racism but it did so in gender-specific ways. In the context of U.S. society, beliefs in Black male promiscuity took diverse forms during distinctive historical periods. For example, defenders of chattel slavery believed that slavery safely domesticated allegedly dangerous Black men because it regulated their promiscuity by placing it in the service of slave owners. Strategies of control were harsh and enslaved African men who were born in Africa or who had access to their African past were deemed to be the most dangerous. In contrast, the controlling image of the rapist appeared after emancipation because Southern Whites' feared that the unfettered promiscuity of Black freedmen constituted a threat to the Southern way of life. In this situation, beliefs about White womanhood helped shape the mythology of the Black rapist. Making White women responsible for keeping the purity of the White race, White men "cast themselves as protectors of civilization, reaffirming not only their role as social and familial 'heads,' but their paternal property rights as well."[40]

African American women encountered a parallel set of beliefs concerning Black female promiscuity. White Americans may have been repulsed by a Black sexuality that they redefined as uncivilized "fucking," but the actions of White men demonstrated that they simultaneously were fascinated with the Black women who they thought engaged in it. Under American slavery, all White men within a slave-owning family could treat enslaved African women within their own families as sexual property. The myth that it was impossible to rape Black women because they were already promiscuous helped mask the sexual exploitation of enslaved Black women by their owners. Using enslaved Black women for medical experimentation constituted another form of control. As individuals who are trained to watch, dissect, and cast a critical eye on biological and social phenomena, scientists became voyeurs *extraordinaire* of Black women's bodies. For example, between 1845 and 1849, Marion Sims, now remembered variously as the Father of American Gynecology, the Father of Modern Gynecology, and the Architect of the Vagina, conducted surgical experiments on slave women in his backyard hospital in Montgomery, Alabama. Aiming to cure vaginal fistulas resulting from hard or extended childbirth, Sims discovered a way to peer into Black women's vaginas. Placing Lucy, a slave woman into knee-chest position for examination, Sims inserted a pewter spoon into her vagina and recounts, "introducing the bent handle of the spoon I saw everything, as no man had ever seen before. The fistula was as plain as the nose on a man's face."[41]

The events themselves may be over, but their effects persist under the new racism. This belief in an inherent Black promiscuity reappears today. For example, depicting poor and working-class African American inner-city neighborhoods as dangerous urban jungles where SUV-driving White suburbanites come to score drugs or locate prostitutes also invokes a history of racial and sexual conquest. Here sexuality is linked with danger, and understandings of both draw upon historical imagery of Africa as a continent replete with danger and peril to the White explorers and hunters who penetrated it. Just as contemporary safari tours in Africa create an imagined Africa as the "White man's playground" and mask its economic exploitation, jungle language masks social relations of hyper-segregation that leave working-class Black communities isolated, impoverished, and dependent on a punitive welfare state and an illegal international drug trade. Under this logic, just as wild animals (and the proximate African natives) belong in nature preserves (for their own protection), unassimilated, undomesticated poor and working-class African Americans belong in racially segregated neighborhoods.

This belief in Black promiscuity also continues to take gender-specific forms. African American men live with the ideological legacy that constructs Black male heterosexuality through images of wild beasts, criminals, and rapists. A chilling case was provided in 1989 by the media coverage of an especially brutal crime that came to be known as the "Central Park Jogger" panic. In this case, a White woman investment banker jogging in Central Park was raped, severely beaten, and left for dead. At the time, the police believed that she had been gang-raped by as many as twelve Black and Latino adolescents. The horror of the crime itself is not in question, for this attack was truly appalling. But as African American cultural critic Houston A. Baker points out, what was also noteworthy about the case was the way in which it crystallized issues of race, gender, class, and sexuality in the mass media. The assault occurred during a time when young Black men and hip-hop culture were becoming increasingly visible in urban public space. Lacking spacious basement recreation rooms and well-tended soccer fields, African American and Latino youth set up their equipment on streets and in public parks, creating public hip-hop theaters. Graffiti, breakdancing, and enormous boom boxes blasting the angry lyrics of gangsta rap effectively "blackened" urban spaces. Baker describes how public space became a site of controversy: "Urban public space of the late twentieth-century [became]...spaces of audiovisual contest. It's something like this: 'My billboards and neon and handbills and high-decibel-level television advertising are purely for the public good. Your boom boxes and graffiti are evil pollutants. Erase them, shut them down!'"[42]

The attack in Central Park occurred in this political, social, and cultural context. The "park panic" that followed the incident drew upon this fear of young Black men in public space, as evidenced by their loudness, their rap music, and their disrespect for order (graffiti). In doing so, it referenced the primitivist ideology of Blacks as animalistic. Media phrases such as "roving bands" and "wolf pack" that were used to describe young urban Black and Latino males during this period were only comprehensible *because* of long-standing assumptions of Black promiscuity. Drawing upon the historical discourse on Black promiscuity, the phrase "to go buck wild" morphed into the new verb of "wilding" that appeared virtually overnight. Baker is especially insightful in his analysis of how the term "wilding" sounded very much like rapper Tone-Loc's hit song "Wild Thing," a song whose content described sexual intercourse. "Wilding" and "Wild Thing" belong to the same nexus of meaning, one that quickly circulated through mass media and became a plausible (at least as far as the media was concerned), explanation for the brutality of the crime.[43] Resurrecting images of Black men as predatory and wild, rape and "wilding" became inextricably linked with Black masculinity.

The outcome of this case shows how deeply entrenched ideologies can produce scenarios that obscure the facts. Ironically, twelve years after five young Black males were convicted of the crime, doubts arose concerning their guilt. A convicted murderer and serial rapist came forward, confessed to the rape, and claimed he had acted alone. After his story was corroborated by DNA testing, the evidence against the original "wolf pack" seemed far less convincing than in the climate created by "wilding" as the natural state of young Black men. In 2003, all of the teenagers originally convicted of the crime were exonerated, unfortunately, after some had served lengthy jail terms.[44]

African American women also live with ideas about Black women's promiscuity and lack of sexual restraint. Reminiscent of concerns with Black women's fertility under slavery and in the rural South, contemporary social welfare policies also remain preoccupied with Black women's fertility. In prior eras, Black women were encouraged to have many children. Under slavery, having many children enhanced slave owners' wealth and a good "breeder woman" was less likely to be sold.[45] In rural agriculture after emancipation, having many children ensured a sufficient supply of workers. But in the global economy of today, large families are expensive because children must be educated. Now Black women are seen as producing too many children who contribute less to society than they take. Because Black women on welfare have long been seen as undeserving, long-standing ideas about Black women's promiscuity

become recycled and redefined as a problem for the state.[46]

In her important book *Killing the Black Body: Race, Reproduction, and the Meaning of Liberty,* legal scholar Dorothy Roberts claims that the "systematic, denial of reproductive freedom has uniquely marked Black women's history in America."[47] Believing the unquestioned assumption of Black female promiscuity influences how poor and working-class Black women are treated. The inordinate attention paid to the sexual lives of adolescent Black women reflects this ongoing concern with an assumed Black female promiscuity.[48] Rather than looking at lack of sex education, poverty, sexual assault, and other factors that catalyze high rates of pregnancy among young Black women, researchers and policy makers often blame the women themselves and assume that the women are incapable of making their own decisions. Pregnancy, especially among poor and working-class young Black women, has been seen as evidence that Black women lack the capacity to control their sexual lives. As a visible sign of a lack of discipline and/or immorality, becoming pregnant and needing help exposes poor and working-class women to punitive state policies.[49] Arguing that Black women have been repeatedly denied reproductive autonomy and control over their own bodies, Roberts surveys a long list of current violations against African American women. Black women are denied reproductive choice and offered Norplant, Depo-Provera, and similar forms of birth control that encourage them to choose sterilization. Pregnant Black women with drug addictions receive criminal sentences instead of drug treatment and prenatal care. Criticizing two controversial ways in which the criminal justice system penalizes pregnancy, Roberts identifies the impossible choice that faces women in these situations. When a pregnant woman is prosecuted for exposing her baby to drugs in the womb, her crime hinges on her decision to have a baby. If she has an abortion she can avoid prosecution, but if she chooses to give birth, she risks going to prison. Similarly, when a judge imposes birth control as a condition of probation, for example, by giving a defendant the choice between Norplant or jail, incarceration becomes the penalty for her choice to remain fertile. These practices theoretically affect all women, but, in actuality, they apply primarily to poor and working-class Black women. As Roberts points out, "prosecutors and judges see poor Black women as suitable subjects for these reproductive penalties because society does not view these women as suitable mothers in the first place."[50]

AFRICAN AMERICANS AND THE WHITENING OF HOMOSEXUALITY

Depicting people of African descent as symbols of embodied, natural sexuality that "fucked" like animals and produced babies installed Black people as the essence of nature. Moreover, the concern with Black fertility linked perceptions of promiscuity to assumptions of heterosexuality. Within this logic, homosexuality was assumed to be impossible among Black people because same-sex sexual practices did not result in reproduction:

> Among the myths Europeans have created about Africa, the myth that homosexuality is absent or incidental is the oldest and most enduring. For Europeans, black Africans—of all the native peoples of the world—most epitomized "primitive man." Since primitive man is supposed to be close to nature, ruled by instinct, and culturally unsophisticated, he had to be heterosexual, his sexual energies and outlets demoted exclusively to their "natural" purpose: biological reproduction. If black Africans were the most primitive people in all humanity—if they were, indeed, human, which some debated—then they had to be the most heterosexual.[51]

If racism relied on assumptions of Black promiscuity that in turn enabled Black people to "breed like animals," then Black sexual practices that did not adhere to these assumptions challenged racism at its very core. Either Black people could not be homosexual or those Blacks who were homosexual were not "authentically" Black.[52] Black people were allegedly not threatened by homosexuality because they were protected by their "natural" heterosexuality. In contrast, Whites had no such "natural" protection and thus had to work harder at proving their heterosexuality. By a curious twist of logic, these racist assumptions about an authentic Blackness grounded in a promiscuous heterosexuality helped define Whiteness as well. In this context, homosexuality could be defined as an internal threat to the integrity of the (White) nuclear family. Beliefs in a naturalized, normal hyper-heterosexuality among Black people effectively "whitened" homosexuality. Within a logic that constructed race itself from racially pure families, homosexuality constituted a major threat to the White race.[53]

Contemporary African American politics confront some real contradictions here. A discourse that constructs Black people as the natural essence of hyper-heterosexuality and White people as the source of homosexuality hinders developing a comprehensive analysis of Black sexuality that speaks to the needs of straight and gay Black people alike. Those African Americans who internalize racist ideologies that link Black hyper-heterosexuality with racial authenticity can propose problematic solutions to adolescent pregnancy, rape, sexual violence, and the troubling growth of HIV/AIDS among African Americans. Such beliefs generate strategies designed to regulate tightly the sexual practices of Black people as the fundamental task of Black sexual politics. This position inadvertently accepts racist views of Blackness and advocates an antiracist politics that advocates copying the heterosexist norms associated with White normality. Such beliefs also foster perceptions of LGBT Black people as being less authentically Black. If authentic Black people (according to the legacy of scientific racism) are heterosexual, then LGBT Black people are less authentically Black because they engage in allegedly "White" sexual practices. This entire system of sexual regulation is turned on its head when heterosexual African Americans reject promiscuity yet advocate for a Black eroticism.

In a similar fashion, visible, vocal LGBT Black people who come out and claim an eroticism that is not predicated upon heterosexuality also profoundly challenge the same system. The historical invisibility of LGBT African Americans reflects this double containment, both within the prison of racism that segregates Black people in part due to their alleged sexual deviancy of promiscuity and within the closet of heterosexism due to the alleged sexual deviancy of homosexuality. The closets created by heterosexism were just as prominent within Black communities as outside them. For example, the Black Church, one of the mainstays of African American resistance to racial oppression, fostered a deeply religious ethos within African American life and culture.[54] The Black Church remains the linchpin of African American communal life, and its effects can be seen in Black music, fraternal organizations, neighborhood associations, and politics.[55] As religious scholar C. Eric Lincoln points out, "for African Americans, a people whose total experience has been a sustained condition of multiform stress, religion is never far from the threshold of consciousness, for whether it is embraced with fervor or rejected with disdain, it is the focal element of the black experience."[56]

At the same time, the Black Church has also failed to challenge arguments about sexual deviancy. Instead, the Black Church has incorporated dominant ideas about the dangers of promiscuity and homosexuality within its beliefs and practices.[57] Some accuse the Black Church of relying on a double standard according to which teenaged girls are condemned for out-of-wedlock pregnancies but in which the men who fathered the children escape censure. The girls are often required to confess their sins and ask for forgiveness in front of the entire congregation whereas the usually older men who impregnate them are excused.[58] Others argue that the Black Church advances a hypocritical posture about homosexuality that undercuts its antiracist posture:

> Just as white people have misused biblical texts to argue that God supported slavery, and that being Black was a curse, the Bible has been misused by African Americans to justify the oppression of homosexuals. It is ironic that while they easily dismiss the Bible's problematic references to Black people, they

accept without question what they perceive to be its condemnation of homosexuals.[59]

One reason that the Black Church has seemed so resistant to change is that it has long worried about protecting the community's image within the broader society and has resisted *any* hints of Black sexual deviance, straight and gay alike. Recognizing the toll that the many historical assaults against African American families have taken, many churches argue for traditional, patriarchal households, and they censure women who seemingly reject marriage and the male authority that creates them. For women, the babies who are born out of wedlock are irrefutable evidence for women's sexual transgression. Because women carry the visible stigma of sexual transgression—unlike men, they become pregnant and cannot hide their sexual histories—churches more often have chastised women for promiscuity. In a sense, Black churches historically preached a politics of respectability, especially regarding marriage and sexuality because they recognized how claims of Black promiscuity and immorality fueled racism. In a similar fashion, the Black Church's resistance to societal stigmatization of all African Americans as being sexually deviant limits its ability to take effective leadership within African American communities concerning all matters of sexuality, especially homosexuality. Black Churches were noticeably silent about the spread of HIV/AIDS among African Americans largely because they wished to avoid addressing the sexual mechanisms of HIV transmission (prostitution and gay sex).[60]

Within Black churches and Black politics, the main arguments given by African American intellectuals and community leaders that explain homosexuality's presence within African American communities show how closely Black political thought is tethered to an unexamined gender ideology. Backed up by interpretations of biblical teachings, many churchgoing African Americans believe that homosexuality reflects varying combinations of: (1) the loss of male role models as a consequence of the breakdown of the Black family structure, trends that in turn foster weak men, some of whom turn to homosexuality; (2) a loss of traditional religious values that encourages homosexuality among those who have turned away from the church; (3) the emasculation of Black men by White oppression; and (4) a sinister plot by White racists as a form of population genocide (neither gay Black men nor Black lesbians have children under this scenario).[61] Because these assumptions validate only one family form, this point of view works against both Black straights and gays alike. Despite testimony from children raised by Black single mothers, families headed by women alone routinely are seen as "broken homes" that somehow need fixing. This seemingly pro-family stance also works against LGBT African Americans. Gay men and lesbians have been depicted as threats to Black families, primarily due to the erroneous belief that gay, lesbian, and bisexual African Americans neither want nor have children or that they are not already part of family networks.[62] Holding fast to dominant ideology, many African American ministers believe that homosexuality is unnatural for Blacks and is actually a "white disease." As a result, out LGBT African Americans are seen as being disloyal to the race.

Historically, this combination of racial segregation and intolerance within African American communities that influenced Black Church activities explains the deeply closeted nature of LGBT Black experiences. The racial segregation of Jim Crow in the rural South and social institutions such as the Black Church that were created in this context made living as openly gay virtually impossible for LGBT African Americans. In small town and rural settings of the South, it made sense for the majority of LGBT Black people to remain deeply closeted. Where was the space for out Black lesbians in Anita Hill's close-knit segregated community of Lone Tree in which generations of women routinely gave birth to thirteen children? Would coming out as gay or bisexual Black men make any difference in resisting the threat of lynching in the late nineteenth century? In these contexts, Black homosexuality might have further derogated an already sexually stigmatized population. Faced with this situation, many African American gays, lesbians, and bisexuals saw heterosexual passing as the only logical choice.

Prior to early-twentieth-century migration to Northern cities, Black gays, lesbians, and bisexuals found it very difficult to reject heterosexuality outright. Cities provided more options, but for African Americans residential housing segregation further limited the options that did exist. Despite these limitations, gay and lesbian Black urban dwellers did manage to carve out new lives that differed from those they left behind. For example, the 1920s was a critical period for African American gays, lesbians, and bisexuals who were able to migrate to large cities like New York. Typically, the art and literary traditions of the Harlem Renaissance have been analyzed through a race-only Black cultural nationalist framework. But LGBT sexualities may have been far more important within Black urbanization than formerly believed. Because the majority of Harlem Renaissance writers were middle-class, a common assumption has been that their response to claims of Black promiscuity was to advance a politics of respectability.[63] The artists of the Harlem Renaissance appeared to be criticizing American racism, but they also challenged norms of gender and sexuality that were upheld by the politics of respectability.

Contemporary rereadings of key texts of the Harlem Renaissance suggest that many had a homoerotic or "queer" content. For example, new analyses locate a lesbian subtext within Pauline Hopkins's novel *Contending Forces,* a homoerotic tone within the short stories of Black life detailed in *Cane,* and an alternative sexuality expressed in the corpus of Langston Hughes's work.[64] British filmmaker Isaac Julien's 1989 prizewinning short film *Looking for Langston* created controversy via its association of Hughes with homoeroticism. Julien's intent was not to criticize Hughes, but rather, to "de-essentialize black identities" in ways that create space for more progressive sexual politics. At a conference on Black popular culture, Julien explains this process of recognizing different kinds of Black identities: "I think blackness is a term used—in the way that terms like 'the black community' or 'black folk' are usually bandied about—to exclude others who are part of that community...to create a more pluralistic interreaction [*sic*] in terms of difference, both sexual and racial, one has to start with deessentializing the notion of the black subject."[65] Basically, rejecting the erasure of gay Black male identities, Julien's project creates a space in which Hughes can be both Black and queer.

Middle-class African Americans may have used literary devices to confront gendered and sexual norms, but working-class and poor African Americans in cities also challenged these sexual politics, albeit via different mechanisms. During this same decade, working-class Black women blues singers also expressed gendered and sexual sensibilities that deviated from the politics of respectability.[66] One finds in the lyrics of the blues singers explicit references to gay, lesbian, and bisexual sexual expression as a natural part of lived Black experience. By proclaiming that "wild women don't get no blues," the new blues singers took on and reworked long-standing ideas about Black women's sexuality. Like most forms of popular music, Black blues lyrics talk about love. But, when compared to other American popular music of the 1920s and 1930s, Black women's blues were distinctive. One significant difference concerned the blues' "provocative and pervasive sexual—including homosexual—imagery."[67] The blues took on themes that were banished from popular music—extramarital affairs, domestic violence, and the short-lived nature of love relationships all appeared in Black women's blues. The theme of women loving women also appeared in Black women's blues, giving voice to Black lesbianism and bisexuality.

When it came to their acceptance of Black gays, lesbians, and bisexuals, urban African American neighborhoods exhibited contradictory tendencies. On the one hand, Black neighborhoods within large cities became areas of racial and sexual boundary-crossing that supported more visible lesbian and gay activities. For example, one community study of the lesbian community in Buffalo, New York, found racial and social class differences among lesbians. Because Black lesbians were confined to racially segregated neighborhoods, lesbians had more house parties and social gatherings within their neighborhoods. In contrast, White working-class lesbians were more likely to frequent bars that, ironically, were typically located near or in Black neighborhoods.[68] In her autobiography *Zami,* Audre Lorde describes the racial differences framing lesbian activities in New York City in the 1950s where interracial boundaries were crossed, often for the first time.[69] These works suggest that African American lesbians constructed sexual identities within African American communities in urban spaces. The strictures placed on all African American women who moved into White-controlled space (the threat of sexual harassment and rape) affected straight and lesbian women alike. Moreover, differences in male and female socialization may have made it easier for African American women to remain closeted within African American communities. Heterosexual and lesbian women alike value intimacy and friendship with their female relatives, their friends, and their children. In contrast, dominant views of masculinity condition men to compete with one another. Prevailing ideas about masculinity encourage Black men to reject close male friendships that come too close to homoerotic bonding.

On the other hand, the presence of Black gay, lesbian, and bisexual activities and enclaves within racially segregated neighborhoods did not mean that LGBT people experienced acceptance. Greatly influenced by Black Church teachings, African Americans may have accepted homosexual individuals, but they disapproved of homosexuality itself. Relations in the Black Church illustrate this stance of grudging acceptance. While censuring homosexuality, Black churches have also not banished LGBT people from their congregations. Within the tradition of some Church leaders, homosexuality falls under the rubric of pastoral care and is not considered a social justice issue. Ministers often preach, "love the sinner but hate the sin."[70] This posture of "don't be too out and we will accept you" has had a curious effect on churches themselves as well as on African American antiracist politics. For example, the Reverend Edwin C. Sanders, a founding pastor of the Metropolitan Interdenominational Church in Nashville, describes this contradiction of accepting LGBT Black people, just as long as they are not too visible. As Reverend Sanders points out: "the unspoken message...says it's all right for you to be here, just don't say anything, just play your little role. You can be in the choir, you can sit on the piano bench, but don't say you're gay."[71] Reverend Sanders describes how this policy limited the ability of Black churches to deal with the spreading HIV/AIDS epidemic. He notes how six Black musicians within Black churches died of AIDS, yet churches hushed up the cause of the deaths. As Reverend Sanders observes, "Nobody wanted to deal with the fact that all of these men were gay black men, and yet they'd been leading the music for them."[72]

The dual challenges to racism and heterosexism in the post–civil rights era have provided LGBT Black people with both more legal rights within American society (that hopefully will translate into improved levels of security) and the potential for greater acceptance within African American communities. As a result, a visible and vocal Black LGBT presence emerged in the 1980s and 1990s that challenged the seeming separateness of racism and heterosexism in ways that unsettled heterosexual Black people and gay White people alike. Rejecting the argument that racism and heterosexism come together solely or even more intensively for LGBT African Americans, LGBT African American people highlighted the connections and contradictions that characterize racism and heterosexism as mutually constructing systems of oppression. Working in this intersection between these two systems, LGBT African Americans raised important issues about the workings of racism and heterosexism.

One issue concerns how race complicates the closeting process and resistance to it. Just as Black people's ability to break out of prison differed based on gender, class, age, and sexuality, LGBT people's ability to come out of the closet displays similar heterogeneity. As LGBT African Americans point out, the contours of the closet and the costs attached to leaving it vary according to race, class, and gender. For many LGBT Whites, sexual orientation is all

that distinguishes them from the dominant White population. Affluent gay White men, for example, may find it easier to come out of the closet because they still maintain many of the benefits of White masculinity. In contrast, in part because of a multiplicity of identities, African American gay, lesbian, bisexual, and transgendered individuals seem less likely than their White counterparts to be openly gay or to consider themselves completely out of the closet.[73] Race complicates the coming-out process. As Kevin Boykin recalls, "coming out to my family members, I found, was much more difficult than coming out to my friends. Because my family had known me longer than my friends had, I thought they at least deserved to hear the words 'I'm gay' from my own lips....On the other hand, precisely because my family, had known and loved me as one person, I worried that they might not accept me as another. Would they think I had deceived them for years?"[74] Gender and age add further layers of complexity to the coming-out process, as the difficulties faced by African American lesbians and gay African American high school youth suggest.[75]

Another related issue concerns the endorsement of "passing" and/or assimilation as possible solutions to racial and sexual discrimination. Black LGBT people point to the contradictions of passing in which, among African Americans, racial passing is routinely castigated as denying one's true self, yet sexual passing as heterosexual is encouraged. Barbara Smith, a lesbian activist who refused to remain in the closet, expresses little tolerance for lesbians who are willing to reap the benefits of others' struggles, but who take few risks themselves:

A handful of out lesbians of color have gone into the wilderness and hacked through the seemingly impenetrable jungle of homophobia. Our closeted sisters come upon the wilderness, which is now not nearly as frightening, and walk the path we have cleared, even pausing at times to comment upon the beautiful view. In the meantime, we are on the other side of the continent, hacking through another jungle. At the very least, people who choose to be closeted can speak out against homophobia....[Those] who protect their closets never think about...how their silences contribute to the silencing of others.[76]

Even if the "wilderness" is not nearly as frightening as it once was, the seeming benefits of remaining closeted and passing as straight may be more illusory than real. Because of the ability of many LGBT individuals to pass as straight, they encounter distinctive forms of prejudice and discrimination. Here racism and heterosexism differ. Blackness is clearly identifiable, and in keeping with assumptions of color blindness of the new racism, many Whites no longer express derogatory racial beliefs in public, especially while in the company of Blacks. They may, however, express such beliefs in private or behind their backs. In contrast, U.S. society's assumption of heterosexuality along with its tolerance of homophobia imposes no such public censure on straight men and women to refrain from homophobic comments in public. As a result, closeted and openly LGBT people may be exposed to a much higher degree of interpersonal insensitivity and overt prejudice in public than the racial prejudice experienced by Blacks and other racial/ethnic groups.[77]

Black churches and African American leaders and organizations that held fast in the past to the view of "don't be too out and we will accept you" faced hostile external racial climates that led [them] to suppress differences among African Americans, ostensibly in the name of racial solidarity. This version of racial solidarity also drew upon sexist and heterosexist beliefs to shape political agendas for all Black people. For example, by organizing the historic 1963 March on Washington where Martin Luther King, Jr. gave his legendary "I Have a Dream Speech," African American civil rights leader Bayard Rustin played a major role in the civil rights movement. Yet because Rustin was an out gay man, he was seen as a potential threat to the movement itself. Any hint of sexual impropriety was feared. So Rustin stayed in the background, while Martin Luther King, Jr. maintained his position as spokesperson and figurehead for the march and the movement. But the question for today is whether

holding these views on race, gender, and sexuality makes political sense in the greatly changed context of the post–civil rights era. In a context where out-of-wedlock births, poverty, and the spread of STDs threaten Black survival, preaching abstinence to teens who define sexuality only in terms of genital sexual intercourse or encouraging LGBT people to renounce the sin of homosexuality and "just be straight" simply miss the mark. Too much is at stake for Black antiracist projects to ignore sexuality and its connections to oppressions of race, class, gender, and age any longer.

RACISM AND HETEROSEXISM REVISITED

On May 11, 2003, a stranger killed fifteen-year-old Sakia Gunn who, with four friends, was on her way home from New York's Greenwich Village. Sakia and her friends were waiting for the bus in Newark, New Jersey, when two men got out of a car, made sexual advances, and physically attacked them. The women fought back, and when Gunn told the men that she was a lesbian, one of them stabbed her in the chest.

Sakia Gunn's murder illustrates the connections among class, race, gender, sexuality, and age. Sakia lacked the protection of social class privilege. She and her friends were waiting for the bus in the first place because none had access to private automobiles that offer protection for those who are more affluent. In Gunn's case, because her family initially did not have the money for her funeral, she was scheduled to be buried in a potter's grave. Community activists took up a collection to pay for her funeral. She lacked the gendered protection provided by masculinity. Women who are perceived to be in the wrong place at the wrong time are routinely approached by men who feel entitled to harass and proposition them. Thus, Sakia and her friends share with all women the vulnerabilities that accrue to women who negotiate public space. She lacked the protection of age—had Sakia and her friends been middle-aged, they may not have been seen as sexually available. Like African American girls and women, regardless of sexual orientation, they were seen as approachable. Race was a factor, but not in a framework of interracial race relations. Sakia and her friends were African American, as were their attackers. In a context where Black men are encouraged to express a hyper-heterosexuality as the badge of Black masculinity, women like Sakia and her friends can become important players in supporting patriarchy. They challenged Black male authority, and they paid for the transgression of refusing to participate in scripts of Black promiscuity. But the immediate precipitating catalyst for the violence that took Sakia's life was her openness about her lesbianism. Here, homophobic violence was the prime factor. Her death illustrates how deeply entrenched homophobia can be among many African American men and women, in this case, beliefs that resulted in an attack on a teenaged girl.

How do we separate out and weigh the various influences of class, gender, age, race, and sexuality in this particular incident? Sadly, violence against Black girls is an everyday event. What made this one so special? Which, if any, of the dimensions of her identity got Sakia Gunn killed? There is no easy answer to this question, because *all* of them did. More important, how can any Black political agenda that does not take *all* of these systems into account, including sexuality, ever hope adequately to address the needs of Black people as a collectivity? One expects racism in the press to shape the reports of this incident. In contrast to the 1998 murder of Matthew Shepard, a young, White, gay man in Wyoming, no massive protests, nationwide vigils, and renewed calls for federal hate crimes legislation followed Sakia's death. But what about the response of elected and appointed officials? The African American mayor of Newark decried the crime, but he could not find the time to meet with community activists who wanted programmatic changes to retard crimes like Sakia's murder. The principal of her high school became part of the problem. As one activist described it, "students at Sakia's high school weren't allowed to hold a vigil. And the kids wearing the rainbow flag were being punished like they had on gang colors."[78]

Other Black leaders and national organizations spoke volumes through their silence. The same leaders and organizations that spoke out against the police beating of Rodney King by Los Angeles area police, the rape of immigrant Abner Louima by New York City police, and the murder of Timothy Thomas by Cincinnati police said nothing about Sakia Gunn's death. Apparently, she was just another unimportant little Black girl to them. But to others, her death revealed the need for a new politics that takes the intersections of racism and heterosexism as well as class exploitation, age discrimination, and sexism into account. Sakia was buried on May 16 and a crowd of approximately 2,500 people attended her funeral. The turnout was unprecedented: predominantly Black, largely high school students, and mostly lesbians. Their presence says that as long as African American lesbians like high school student Sakia Gunn are vulnerable, then every African American woman is in danger; and if all Black women are at risk, then there is no way that any Black person will ever be truly safe or free.

NOTES

1. The field of postcolonial studies contains many works that examine how ideas generally, and sexual discourse in particular, was essential to colonialism and to nationalism. In this field, the works of French philosopher Michel Foucault have been pivotal in challenging prior frameworks heavily grounded in Marxism and in Freudian psychoanalysis. Here I rely on two main ideas from the corpus of Foucault's work. The first, expressed in his classic work *Discipline and Punish,* concerns the strategies that institutions use to discipline populations and get them to submit under conditions of oppression (Foucault 1979). The second idea concerns the normalization of such power through the use of hegemonic ideologies. Volume I of Foucault's *The History of Sexuality* uses sexuality to illustrate this normalization of power (Foucault 1980). Despite the enormous impact that Foucault has had on studies of power, few works analyze his treatment of race. Ann Stoler's *Race and the Education of Desire* is exemplary in this regard (Stoler 1995). Stoler examines how Foucault's analyses of sexuality in European societies can be read also as an analysis of race. In

this chapter, I rely on many of Stoler's insights. For a comprehensive overview of works on Foucault and sexuality that do not deal with race, see Stoler 1995, 19, n. 1. For a description of the specific manipulation of sexual discourse within colonialism, see McClintock 1995; Gilman 1985; and Young 1995, 90–117.

2. Jordan 1968, 3–43.

3. Jordan 1968, 136–178.

4. See, for example, White 1985a.

5. Despite the marginality of all LGBT Black people, subpopulations did not place issues of sexuality on the public agenda at the same time or in the same way. Black lesbians raised issues of heterosexism and homophobia in the 1980s, fairly early in modern Black feminism. For classic work in this tradition, see Combahee River Collective 1982; Lorde 1982; Smith 1983; and Clarke 1983. For a representative sample of more recent works, see Clarke 1995; Gomez and Smith 1994; Moore 1997; Gomez 1999; Greene 2000; Smith 1998. In contrast, works by gay Black men achieved greater prominence later. See, for example, Hemphill 1991; Riggs 1992. *Tongues Untied,* the documentary by the late Marlon Riggs, represents an important path breaking work in Black gay men's studies in the United States (*Tongues Untied* 1989). More recently, work on Black masculinity that analyzes homosexuality has gained greater visibility. See Hutchinson 1999; Riggs 1999; Thomas 1996; Carbado 1999c; Hawkeswood 1996; Simmons 1991.

6. Cohen and Jones 1999, 88.

7. Mandela 1994, 341. Foucault suggests that the prison serves as an exemplar of modern Western society (Foucault 1979). The techniques used to discipline and punish deviant populations constitute a punishment industry. Prisons operate by controlling populations via disciplining the body. Foucault's work on sexuality also emphasizes regularization and discipline, only this time via creating discourses of sexuality that also aim to control the body (Foucault 1980). For an analysis of Foucault's treatment of race, sexuality, and gender, see Stoler 1995.

8. Wideman 1984, 52.

9. For works that detail the effects of welfare state policies on African Americans, see Quadagno 1994; Brewer 1994; Neubeck and Cazenave 2001. For general works on state policy and African American economic well-being, see Squires 1994; Massey and Denton 1993; Oliver and Shapiro 1995. For analyses of jobs and urban economies, see Wilson 1996; 1987.

10. West 1993.

11. In the 1980s, homicide became one of the leading causes of death of young Black men (Oliver 1994).

For work on the vulnerability of Black youth in inner cities, see Anderson 1978; 1990; 1999; Canada 1995; Kaplan 1997; Kitwana 2002.

12. Anderson 1999.

13. Anderson 1999.

14. Anderson 1978; 1990; 1999.

15. As quoted in Cole and Guy-Sheftall 2003, 139.

16. Mandela 1994, 367–368.

17. Mandela 1994, 341.

18. Rose 1994, 21–61; George 1998, 1–21.

19. Sociologist Steve Seidman traces the emergence and decline of the closet as a metaphor describing contemporary LGBT politics (Seidman 2002). Seidman dates the closet as reaching its heyday in the 1950s and early 1960s during the early years of the cold war. In his research, he was surprised to find that many contemporary gay Americans live outside the social framework of the closet. Seidman suggests that the two main ways that gay life has been understood since 1969, namely, the coming-out narrative or the migration to gay ghettoes, may no longer be accurate: "as the lives of at least some gays look more like those of straights, as gays no longer feel compelled to migrate to urban enclaves to feel secure and respected, gay identity is often approached in ways similar to heterosexual identity—as a thread" (Seidman 2002, 11). Unfortunately, Seidman's methodology did not allow him to explore the ways in which Black LGBT people have similar and different experiences.

20. Both science and religion advanced different justifications for stigmatizing homosexuals. Until recently, Western medicine and science viewed sexuality as being biologically hardwired into the human species and obeying natural laws. Heterosexual sexual practices and reproduction were perceived as the "natural" state of sexuality, and all other forms of sexual expression were classified as deviant. Religion offered similar justifications. Promiscuity and homosexuality emerged as important categories of "unnatural" sexual activity that normalized monogamous heterosexuality within the context of marriage and for purposes of reproduction.

21. This is Foucault's argument about biopower, the normalization of practices that enable society to discipline individual bodies, in this case, sexual bodies, and groups, in this case, straights and gays, as population groups that become comprehensible only in the context of discourses of sexuality. This view prevailed until shifts within the study of sexuality in the 1980s and 1990s.

22. Seidman 1996, 6.
23. The term *queer* often serves as an umbrella term for lesbian, gay, bisexual, transgendered, and anyone else whose sexuality transgresses the status quo. Not everyone claims the term as an identity or statement of social location. Some argue that the term erases social and economic differences among lesbians and gay men, and others consider it to be derogatory. Still others use the term to acknowledge the limitless possibilities of an individual's sexuality. They see terms such as *gay, lesbian,* and *bisexual* as misleading in that they suggest stable sexual identities. Beyond these ideological differences, I do not use the term *queer* here because LGBT African American people do not prefer this term. When participants in the *National Black Pride Survey 2000* were asked which label from a very extensive list came closest to describing their sexual orientation, 42 percent self-identified as gay, 24 percent chose lesbian, 11 percent chose bisexual, and 1 percent marked transgendered. In contrast to high levels of agreement on gay and lesbian, "queer" was one of the least popular options (1 percent). As the survey reports, "Black GLBT people do not readily, or even remotely, identify as 'queer'" (Battle et al. 2002, 19).
24. LGBT politics and the "queering" of sexuality has been one important dimension of the post–civil rights era and Seidman contends that the postcloseted world of the post–civil rights era has shown greater acceptance of LGBT people. Yet, suggests Seidman, acceptance may come with a price. Today, LGBT people are under intense pressure to fit the mold of the "good gay citizen" to be monogamous and to look and act normal. This image may be safe, but it continues to justify discrimination against those who do not achieve this ideal (Seidman 2002).
25. Here I use the framework of "domains of power" to examine the convergence of racism and heterosexism. Briefly, race, sexuality, gender, class, and other systems of oppression are all organized through four main domains of power. The structural domain of power (institutional policies), the disciplinary [domain] of power (the rules and regulations that regulate social interaction), the hegemonic domain of power (the belief systems that defend existing power arrangements), and the interpersonal domain of power (patterns of everyday social interaction) are organized differently for different systems of oppression. Here I use this model as a heuristic device to build an argument about the interconnections of racism and heterosexism. For a discussion of the framework and its applicability in Black feminist politics, see chapter 12 of *Black Feminist Thought* (Collins 2000a, 273–290).
26. For a discussion of the *Loving* decision and its effects on interracial marriage, see Root 2001. For the full definition of the Defense of Marriage Act, see U.S. Census Bureau 2000.
27. Racism and heterosexism share this basic cognitive frame, and it is one shared by other systems of power.
28. Clarke 1983.
29. Both sets of ideas also serve as markers for constructing both heterosexuality and homosexuality within the wider society. Prior to the social movements of the civil rights era that called increased attention to both racism and heterosexism, racial protest was contained within the prisons of racially segregated neighborhoods and LGBT protest within the invisibility of individual closets.
30. Mudimbe 1988; Appiah 1992.
31. Young 1995, 90–117; McClintock 1995.
32. Jordan 1968, 7.
33. Jordan 1968, 5. Jordan suggests that the reactions of the English differed from those of the Spanish and the Portuguese who for centuries had been in close contact with North Africa and who had been invaded by peoples both darker and more civilized than themselves. The impact of color on the English may have been more powerful because England's principal contact with Africans came in West Africa and the Congo, areas with very dark-skinned Africans. Thus, "one of the fairest-skinned nations suddenly came face to face with one of the darkest peoples on earth" (Jordan 1968, 6).
34. Torgovnick 1990, 18–20.
35. Historically, scientific racism has made important contributions to creating and sustaining myths of Black promiscuity as well as constructing a normalized heterosexuality juxtaposed to the alleged deviancy of White homosexuality. The scientific racism of medicine, biology, psychology, anthropology, and other social sciences constructed both Black promiscuity as well as homosexuality and then spent inordinate time assisting state and religious institutions that aimed to regulate these practices. For general discussions of race and science, see Gould 1981; Harding 1993; Zuberi 2001.
36. Fausto-Sterling 1995.
37. Foucault 1979.
38. Haraway 1989, 262. In this context, studying animals that were clearly not human but close to it might reveal what granted Europeans their humanity and Africans their putative bestiality. Here the interest

in animal behavior as a form of human behavior uninterrupted by culture appears. Within primatology, monkeys and apes have a privileged relation to nature and culture, in that "simians occupy the border zones" (Haraway 1989, 1). "In Africa, the primate literature was produced by white colonists and western foreign scientists under no pressure until well after independence to develop scientific, collegial relations with black Africans. African primates, including the people imagined as wildlife, modeled the 'origin of man' for European-derived culture.... Africa became a place of darkness, one lacking the enlightenment of the West. India has been used to model not the 'origin of man,' but the 'origin of civilization.' Both are forms of 'othering' for western symbolic operations, but their differences matter" (Haraway 1989, 262).

39. Collins 2000a, 69–96.
40. Wiegman 1993, 239.
41. Quoted in Kapsalis 1997, 37. Understandings of Black women's promiscuity also build upon a deep historical theme within Western societies that links deviant sexuality with disease. The hypervisible, pathologized portion of Black women's sexuality centered on the icon of the whore, the woman who demands money for sexual favors. This image is pathologized in that prostitutes were associated with ideas about disease and pollution that bore stark resemblance to ideas about the threat of racial pollution so central to conceptions of whiteness grounded in purity (Giddings 1992, 419).
42. Baker 1993, 43.
43. Baker 1993, 33–60.
44. Dwyer 2002. This case also resembles the well-known case of the Scottsboro boys in which a group of Black men were convicted of allegedly raping White women. They too were eventually exonerated.
45. White 1985a.
46. Gould 1981; Zucchino 1997; Amott 1990; Brewer 1994; Neubeck and Cazenave 2001.
47. Roberts 1997, 4.
48. In a context in which the United States has the highest teen pregnancy rate in the Western world, the even higher rates of teen pregnancy among African American adolescents is a cause for alarm. Many factors influence high rates of pregnancy among young Black women. For example, adult men, some of whom may have coerced girls to have sex with them, father most of the babies born to teen mothers. Studies show that as many as one in four girls are victims of sexual abuse (Roberts 1997, 117).
49. See Gould 1981; Lubiano 1992; Zucchino 1997; Neubeck and Cazenave 2001.
50. Roberts 1997, 152.
51. As quoted in Cole and Guy-Sheftall 2003, 165.
52. For a discussion of the type of racial reasoning that generates ideas of racial authenticity, see Cornel West's "The Pitfalls of Racial Reasoning" (West 1993, 21–32).
53. These same pressures fostered views of homosexuals as invisible, closeted, and assumed to be White. Normalized White heterosexuality became possible and hegemonic only within the logic of both racism and heterosexism.
54. The general use of the term "the Black Church" refers to Black Christian churches in the United States. This includes any Black Christian who worships and is a member of a Black congregation. The formal use of the term refers to independent, historic, and Black-controlled denominations that were founded after the Free African Society in 1787. For a listing, see Monroe 1998, 297, n. 1. For a general history of the Black Church, see Lincoln 1999. For analyses of Black women's participation in the Black Church, see Douglas 1999; Gilkes 2001; Higginbotham 1993.
55. See, Patillo-McCoy 1999, especially Patillo-McCoy 1998.
56. Lincoln 1999, xxiv.
57. Douglas 1999.
58. Cole and Guy-Sheftall 2003, 116.
59. Cole and Guy-Sheftall 2003, 120.
60. Cohen 1999, 276–288.
61. Simmons 1991.
62. For a discussion of the family networks of Black gay men in Harlem, see Hawkeswood 1996. Also, see Battle et al. 2002, 13–17.
63. Higginbotham 1993, 185–229.
64. Somerville 2000.
65. Julien 1992, 274.
66. Davis 1998.
67. Davis 1998, 3.
68. Kennedy and Davis 1994.
69. Lorde 1982.
70. Monroe 1998, 281.
71. Comstock 1999, 156.
72. Comstock 1999, 156.
73. Boykin 1996, 90.
74. Boykin 1996, 19.
75. Moore 1997; McCready 2001.
76. Smith 1990, 66.
77. Boykin 1996, 81.
78. "Skeleton in Newark's Closet: Laquetta Nelson Is Forcing Homophobia Out into the Open" 2003.

REFERENCES

Anderson, Elijah. 1978. *A Place on the Corner.* Chicago: University of Chicago Press.

———. 1990. *Streetwise: Race, Class, and Change in an Urban Community.* Chicago: University of Chicago Press.

———. 1999. *Code of the Street: Decency, Violence and the Moral Life of the Inner City.* New York: W. W. Norton.

Appiah, Kwame Anthony. 1992. *In My Father's House: Africa in the Philosophy of Culture.* New York: Oxford University Press.

Baker, Houston A. 1993. *Black Studies, Rap, and the Academy.* Chicago: University of Chicago Press.

Battle, Juan, Cathy J. Cohen, Dorian Warren, Gerard Fergerson, and Suzette Audam. 2002. *Say It Loud, I'm Black and I'm Proud: Black Pride Survey 2000.* New York: The Policy Institute of the National Gay and Lesbian Task Force.

Boykin, Keith. 1996. *One More River to Cross: Black and Gay in America.* New York: Anchor Books.

Brewer, Rose. 1994. "Race, Class, Gender and U.S. State Welfare Policy: The Nexus of Inequality for African American Families." *Color, Class and Country: Experiences of Gender.* Ed. Gay Young and Bette J. Dickerson, 115–127. London: Zed.

Canada, Geoffrey. 1995. *Fist, Stick, Knife, Gun: A Personal History of Violence in America.* Boston: Beacon Press.

Carbado, Devon W. 1999c. "Introduction: Where and When Black Men Enter." *Black Men on Race, Gender, and Sexuality.* Ed Devon W. Carbado, 1–17. New York: New York University Press.

Clarke, Cheryl. 1983. "The Failure to Transform: Homophobia in the Black Community." *Home Girls: A Black Feminist Anthology.* Ed. Barbara Smith, 197–208. New York: Kitchen Table Press.

———. 1995. "Lesbianism: An Act of Resistance." *Words of Fire: An Anthology of African-American Feminist Thought.* Ed. Beverly Guy-Sheftall, 241–251. New York: The New Press.

Cohen, Cathy J. 1999. *The Boundaries of Blackness: AIDS and the Breakdown of Black Politics.* Chicago: University of Chicago Press.

Cole, Johnnetta Betsch, and Beverly Guy-Sheftall. 2003. *Gender Talk: The Struggle for Women's Equality in African American Communities.* New York: Ballantine.

Collins, Patricia Hill. 2000. *Black Feminist Thought: Knowledge, Consciousness, and the Politics of Empowerment.* New York: Routledge.

Combahee River Collective. 1982. "A Black Feminist Statement." *But Some of Us Are Brave.* Ed. Gloria T. Hull, Patricia Bell Scott, and Barbara Smith, 13–22. Old Westbury, N.Y.: Feminist Press.

Comstock, Gary David. 1999. "'Whosoever' Is Welcome Here: An Interview with Reverend Edwin C. Sanders II." *Dangerous Liaisons: Blacks, Gays, and the Struggle for Equality.* Ed. Eric Brandt, 142–157. New York: The New Press.

Davis, Angela Y. 1998. *Blues Legacies and Black Feminism: Gertrude "Ma" Rainey, Bessie Smith and Billie Holiday.* New York: Vintage.

Douglas, Kelly Brown. 1999. *Sexuality and the Black Church: A Womanist Perspective.* Maryknoll, N.Y.: Orbis.

Dwyer, Jim. 2002. "Reinvestigation of Park Jogger Case Leaves Some Officials with Doubts" *New York Times,* A15. September 28.

Fausto-Sterling, Anne. 1995. "Gender, Race, and Nation: The Comparative Anatomy of 'Hottentot' Women in Europe, 1815–1817." *Deviant Bodies: Critical Perspectives on Difference in Science and Popular Culture.* Ed. Jennifer Terry and Jacqueline Urla, 19–48. Bloomington: Indiana University Press.

Foucault, Michel. 1979. *Discipline and Punish: The Birth of the Prison.* New York: Schocken.

———. 1980. *The History of Sexuality. Vol. I: An Introduction.* New York: Vintage Books.

George, Nelson. 1998. *Hip Hop America.* New York: Penguin.

Giddings, Paula. 1992. "The Last Taboo." *Race-ing Justice, En-Gendering Power.* Ed. Toni Morrison, 441–465. New York: Pantheon.

Gilkes, Cheryl Townsend. 2001. *If It Wasn't for the Women: Black Women's Experience and Womanist Culture in Church and Community.* Maryknoll, N.Y.: Orbis.

Gilman, Sander L. 1985. *Difference and Pathology: Stereotypes of Sexuality, Race, and Madness.* Ithaca, N.Y.: Cornell University Press.

Gomez, Jewell, and Barbara Smith. 1994. "Taking the Home Out of Homophobia: Black Lesbian Health." *The Black Women's Health Book: Speaking for Ourselves.* Ed. Evelyn C. White, 198–213. Seattle: Seal Press.

Gould, Stephen Jay. 1981. *The Mismeasure of Man.* New York: Norton.

Greene, Beverly. 2000. "African American Lesbian and Bisexual Women." *Journal of Social Issues* 56, no. 2: 239–249.

Haraway, Donna. 1989. *Primate Visions: Gender, Race, and Nature in the World of Modern Science.* New York: Routledge, Chapman & Hall.

Harding, Sandra, ed. 1993. *The "Racial" Economy of Science: Toward a Democratic Future.* Bloomington: Indiana University Press.

Hawkeswood, William G. 1996. *One of the Children: Gay Black Men in Harlem.* Berkeley: University of California Press.

Hemphill, Essex, ed. 1991. *Brother to Brother: New Writings by Black Gay Men.* Boston: Alyson Publications.

Higginbotham, Evelyn Brooks. 1993. *Righteous Discontent: The Women's Movement in the Black Baptist Church 1880–1920.* Cambridge, Mass.: Harvard University Press.

Hutchinson, Darren Lenard. 1999. "'Claiming' and 'Speaking' Who We Are: Black Gays and Lesbians, Racial Politics, and the Million Man March." *Black Men on Race, Gender, and Sexuality.* Ed. Devon W. Carbado, 28–45. New York: New York University Press.

Jordan, Winthrop D. 1968. *White Over Black: American Attitudes toward the Negro, 1550–1812.* New York: W. W. Norton.

Julien, Isaac. 1992. "Black Is, Black Ain't: Notes on De-essentializing Black Identities." *Black Popular Culture.* Ed. Gina Dent, 255–275. Seattle: Bay Press.

Kaplan, Elaine Bell. 1997. *Not Our Kind of Girl: Unraveling the Myths of Black Teenage Motherhood.* Berkeley: University of California Press.

Kapsalis, Terri. 1997. *Public Privates: Performing Gynecology from Both Ends of the Speculum.* Durham, N.C.: Duke University Press.

Kennedy, Randall. 2002. *Nigger: The Strange Career of a Troublesome Word.* New York: Pantheon.

Kitwana, Bakari. 2002. *The Hip Hop Generation: Young Blacks and the Crisis in African-American Culture.* New York: Basic Books.

Lincoln, C. Eric. 1999. *Race, Religion, and the Continuing American Dilemma.* New York: Hill & Wang.

Lorde, Audre. 1982. *Zami, A New Spelling of My Name.* Freedom, Calif.: Crossing Press.

———. 1984. *Sister Outsider: Essays and Speeches.* Freedom, Calif.: Crossing Press.

Mandela, Nelson. 1994. *Long Walk to Freedom: The Autobiography of Nelson Mandela.* Boston: Little, Brown.

Massey, Douglas S., and Nancy A. Denton. 1993. *American Apartheid: Segregation and the Making of the Underclass.* Cambridge, Mass.: Harvard University Press.

McClintock, Anne. 1995. *Imperial Leather: Race, Gender, and Sexuality in the Colonial Contest.* New York: Routledge.

McCready, Lance. 2001. "When Fitting In Isn't an Option, or, Why Black Queer Males at a California High School Stay Away from Project 10." *Troubling Intersections of Race and Sexuality: Queer Students of Color and Anti-oppressive Education.* Ed. Kevin K. Kumashiro, 37–54. New York: Rowman & Littlefield.

Monroe, Irene. 1998. "Louis Farrakhan's Ministry of Misogyny and Homophobia." *The Farrakhan Factor: African-American Writers on Leadership, Nationhood, and the Minister Louis Farrakhan.* Ed Amy Alexander, 275–298. New York: Grove Press.

Moore, Lisa C., ed. 1997. *Does Your Mama Know? An Anthology of Black Lesbian Coming Out Stories.* Austin, Texas: Redbone Press.

Mudimbe, V. Y. 1988. *The Invention of Africa: Gnosis, Philosophy, and the Order of Knowledge.* Bloomington: Indiana University Press.

Neubeck, Kenneth J., and Noel A. Cazenave. 2001. *Welfare Racism: Playing the Race Card against America's Poor.* New York: Routledge.

Oliver, Melvin L., and Thomas M. Shapiro. 1995. *Black Wealth/White Wealth: A New Perspective on Racial Inequality.* New York: Routledge.

Oliver, William. 1994. *The Violent Social World of Black Men.* New York: Lexington Books.

Patillo-McCoy, Mary. 1998, "Church Culture as a Strategy of Action in the Black Community." *American Sociological Review* 63 (December): 767–784.

———. 1999. *Black Picket Fences: Privilege and Peril among the Black Middle Class.* Chicago: University of Chicago Press.

Platt, Larry. 2002. *New Jack Jocks: Rebels, Race, and the American Athlete.* Philadelphia: Temple University Press.

Quadagno, Jill. 1994. *The Color of Welfare: How Racism Undermined the War on Poverty.* New York: Oxford University Press.

Riggs, Marlon T. 1992. "Unleash the Queen." *Black Popular Culture.* Ed. Gina Dent, 99–105. Seattle: Bay Press.

———. 1999. "Black Macho Revisited: Reflections of a SNAP! Queen." *Black Men on Race, Gender, and Sexuality.* Ed. Devon W. Carbado, 306–311. New York: New York University Press.

Roberts, Dorothy E. 1997. *Killing the Black Body: Race, Reproduction, and the Meaning of Liberty.* New York: Pantheon Books.

Root, Maria P. P. 2001. *Love's Revolution: Interracial Marriage.* Philadelphia: Temple University Press.

Rose, Tricia. 1994. *Black Noise: Rap Music and Black Culture in Contemporary America.* Hanover, N.H.: Wesleyan University Press.

Seidman, Steven. 1996. "Introduction." *Queer Theory/ Sociology.* Ed. Steven Seidman, 1–29. Malden, Mass.: Blackwell.

———. 2002. *Beyond the Closet: The Transformation of Gay and Lesbian Life.* New York: Routledge.

Simmons, Ron. 1991. "Some Thoughts on the Challenge Facing Gay Intellectuals." *Brother to Brother: New Writings by Black Gay Men.* Ed. Essex Hemphill, 211–228. Boston: Alyson Publications.

Smith, Barbara, ed. 1983. *Home Girls: A Black Feminist Anthology.* New York: Kitchen Table Press.

———. 1990. "The NEA Is the Least of It." 65–67.

———. 1998. *The Truth That Never Hurts: Writings on Race, Gender, and Freedom.* New Brunswick, N.J.: Rutgers University Press.

Somerville, Siobhan B. 2000. *Queering the Color Line: Race and the Invention of Homosexuality in American Culture.* Durham, N.C.: Duke University Press.

Squires, Gregory D. 1994. *Capital and Communities in Black and White: The Intersections of Race, Class, and Uneven Development.* Albany: State University of New York Press.

Stoler, Ann Laura. 1995. *Race and the Education of Desire: Foucault's History of Sexuality and the Colonial Order of Things.* Durham, N.C.: Duke University Press.

Thomas, Kendall. 1996. "'Ain't Nothin' Like the Real Thing': Black Masculinity, Gay Sexuality, and the Jargon of Authenticity." *Representing Black Men.* Ed. Marcellus Blount and George P. Cunningham, 55–69. New York: Routledge.

Torgovnick, Marianna. 1990. *Gone Primitive: Savage Intellects, Modern Lives.* Chicago: University of Chicago Press.

U.S. Census Bureau. 2000. "Technical Note on Same-Sex Unmarried Partner Data from the 1990 and 2000 Censuses." Web page [accessed March 16, 2003]. Available at http://www.census.gov/population/www/cen2000/samesex.html.

West, Cornel. 1993. *Race Matters.* Boston: Beacon Press.

White, Deborah Gray. 1985a. *Ar'n't I a Woman? Female Slaves in the Plantation South.* New York: W.W. Norton.

Wideman, John Edgar. 1984. *Brothers and Keepers.* New York: Penguin.

Wiegman, Robyn. 1993. "The Anatomy of Lynching." *American Sexual Politics.* Ed. John C. Fout, and Maura Tantillo, 223–245.

Wilson, William Julius. 1987. *The Truly Disadvantaged: The Inner City, the Underclass, and Public Policy.* Chicago: University of Chicago Press.

———. 1996. *When Work Disappears: The World of the New Urban Poor.* New York: Knopf.

Young, Robert J. C. 1995. *Colonial Desire: Hybridity in Theory, Culture and Race.* New York: Routledge.

Zuberi, Tukufu. 2001. *Thicker than Blood: How Racial Statistics Lie.* Minneapolis: University of Minnesota Press.

Zucchino, David. 1997. *The Myth of the Welfare Queen.* New York: Scribner.

7 • *Abby L. Ferber*

KEEPING SEX IN BOUNDS
Sexuality and the (De) Construction of Race and Gender

DISCUSSION QUESTIONS

1. What makes deconstructionist theory different from social constructionist theories?

Abby L. Ferber, "Keeping Sex in Bounds: Sexuality and the (De) Construction of Race and Gender." Written for this volume.

2. Why do people often feel uncomfortable when they encounter someone whose sex or race is not clear?
3. Why is the construction of race and gender identity central to our understanding of human identity?
4. Historically, how has the maintenance of race, gender, and sexual boundaries been essential to the reproduction of racial inequality? Do you see these connections today?

When I began studying the contemporary white supremacist movement many years ago, I was shocked to find interracial sexuality and attacks against white masculinity referred to and discussed over and over again. I was not prepared for this. Almost all the literature I had read about the movement had focused simply on the racism and anti-Semitism of the movement, with few, if any, references to issues of gender or sexuality. Yet as I have come to realize, our analyses of the movement have been limited by our theoretical tools. Traditionally, scholars and journalists studying the movement have focused on it as an issue of race relations. After all, the Klan, neo-Nazis, and skinheads organize specifically to promote white pride, white nationalism, and white interests and often denigrate and attack Jews and people of color. While on the surface this is clearly a movement about race, I believe that an intersectional approach, bringing in issues of gender and sexuality as well, is essential to fully understanding this movement and to understanding racism more generally. Examining this movement provides us with a case study, one specific example, of the ways in which gender and sexuality are a part of *everything*, to some degree. They are so central to our identities, culture, social systems, and institutions that they always need to be a part of the analysis.

Examining white supremacist discourse provides a case study for us of the ways in which gender and sexuality are central to who we are and all aspects of our identity, even our racial identity. In this chapter, I argue that race and gender identities are constructed and inequality is maintained through the regulation of sexual practices. I offer a deconstructionist approach that is at the same time intersectional—exploring the intersections of race, sex, gender, and sexuality.

Sociologist Patricia Hill Collins contended that it is only by adopting an intersectional approach, which examines the ways in which race, gender, and other systems of inequality interact and intersect as part of a matrix of privilege and oppression, that we can fully comprehend and work to develop successful strategies for combating oppression (Collins, 2000). Recent years have seen parallel developments in the study of gender, race, and sexuality. All three systems of classification and identity have been revealed as social constructs. For example, while our commonsense assumptions may tell us that race is rooted in biology, biologists, anthropologists, and sociologists widely reject such notions. Like gender and sexuality, racial classifications are socially constructed. Racial categories lack any scientific foundation; there is greater genetic variety within racial groups than among them, and racial classifications vary both cross-culturally and historically. Michael Omi and Howard Winant (1986:60) argued convincingly that race is a "preeminently sociohistorical concept. Racial categories and the meaning of race," they explained, "are given concrete expression by the specific social relations and historical context in which they are embedded." Following this lead, a body of research that explores the construction of racialized identities in various historical contexts is accumulating.

A social constructionist approach emphasizes the critical need for researchers to "read the processes of differentiation, not look for differences" (Crosby, 1992:140). As Omi and Winant suggested, the meaning of race and racialized meanings are politically contested, and it is this contested terrain that needs to be explored. Processes of racialization are always political, taking place within relations of power and privilege. If these classifications are not rooted in nature, what gave rise to them? Why did these differences, rather than other differences, come to matter? Why at this point in time? In this place? Who benefits, and who does not? Concepts of race did not exist prior to the rise of racism. Instead, it is inequality and oppression that have produced the idea of essential racial differences. The same can be said of gender and sexuality: *inequality produces difference.*

While inequality preceded difference, these constructions of race, gender, and sexuality have become central to our understanding of what it means to be human, further reinforcing these systems of oppression and privilege in a cyclical fashion. I find particularly important the theoretical work of Judith Butler (1990, 1991, 1993) to understanding this process. Butler (1991) contended that the production of subjects actually occurs through the construction of gendered identities and that those practices that regulate the construction of coherent gender identities constitute our very understandings of identity itself. "It would be wrong," she warned, "to think that the discussion of 'identity' ought to proceed prior to a discussion of gender identity for the simple reason that 'persons' only become intelligible through becoming gendered in conformity with recognizable standards of gender intelligibility" (Butler 1991:17). It is the regulation of compulsory heterosexuality, she argued, that produces the illusion of coherent gender identities. The production of gender occurs through the performance of heterosexuality; motivating this performance is the threat of punishment, symbolized by "at least two inarticulate figures of abject homosexuality, the feminized fag and the phallicized dyke" (Butler 1993:102). Those who do not partake in the heterosexual performance are seen as not properly gendered. Perhaps the clearest example I found of this in white supremacist discourse is the many references to gays and lesbians as "the third sex." Because gays and lesbians do not define themselves as heterosexual, they are excluded from the categories of male and female.

What it means to be human is constrained and defined by norms of cultural intelligibility. In other words, our cultural norms make certain forms of living and being comprehensible to others, while at the same time making other forms unimaginable. Those who do not conform to these cultural norms are frequently excluded, attacked, and denied rights. Yet these abject identities are central to the definition of normal subjectivity. It is against this realm of the abject that the normal is defined, maintained, and privileged. Butler demonstrated one example of an abjected identity in heterosexuality's delegitimation of homosexuality. More recent work on intersexed and transgender identities has explored this process as well.

Building upon Butler's insight that gendered subjects are produced through the institution of heterosexuality, I argue that this is also a *racialized* process. Throughout U.S. history, the regulation of sexuality has been governed not only by a compulsory heterosexuality, but by a compulsory intraracial sexuality, serving to maintain the illusion of racial purity and secure racial boundaries (Butler, 1993).

While Butler demonstrates the production of culturally intelligible gender identities, suggesting that unintelligible, abject identities (those that are seen as not fully human) are simultaneously produced, I see a similar process at work in the production of coherent racial identities. Just as many transgender individuals face stares and whispers as people try to guess if they are male or female, a growing body of work by multiracial writers has detailed their daily encounters with people inquiring "What are you?"

Omi and Winant (1986) pointed out that "one of the first things we notice about people when we meet them…is their race. We utilize race to provide clues about *who* a person is. This fact is made painfully obvious when we encounter someone whom we cannot conveniently racially categorize—someone who is, for example, racially "mixed" or of an ethnic/racial group with which we are not familiar. Such an encounter becomes a source of discomfort and momentarily a crisis of racial meaning. Without a racial identity, one is in danger of having no identity at all."

Thus, racialized identities also govern our notions of what it means to be human. As this passage suggests, the production of recognizable racial identities, like the production of recognizable gender identities, requires the simultaneous production of "unviable (un)subjects" (Butler 1991:20), here, transgender, multiracial people, and others whose gender or racial identity is not readily identifiable.

Within white supremacist discourse, the regulation of heterosexual and intraracial sexuality produces culturally intelligible, racialized, and gendered identities, while at the same time relegating homosexuals, intersexuals, transgendered people, and mixed-race people to the realm of the unintelligible. Butler (1993) argued that this type of exclusion is a key point of deconstruction that is often overlooked by constructionist approaches. While constructionist analyses often argue that everything is discursively constructed, the construction of the human is always in relation to its constitutive outside, a realm of beings *not* constructed as fully human.

The deconstruction of binary oppositions, such as white/black, and male/female, directs our attention to borders and boundaries. In any given binary opposition, it is the border between the two terms that constructs them as apparently coherent and stable identities. For example, the historical construction of the opposition white/black involves defining the limits of whiteness and blackness and defining precisely who qualifies as white and who qualifies as black. To produce whiteness as a stable, natural, given identity, the boundaries of whiteness must be specified and secured. To classify the population racially, scientists, politicians, and the courts found it necessary specifically to delineate who was white and who was black. They did so over the years with laws labeling the fraction of black blood necessary to deem an individual black. This act of boundary maintenance was necessary to construct racial categories. This theory helps us to understand the threat posed by interracial sexuality. Whenever pressure

to produce secure racial classifications increased, the public outcry over interracial sexuality also increased. Interracial sexuality and the births of "mulattoes" represented boundary crossings that were widely perceived as threatening to otherwise stable racial boundaries.

Historian F. James Davis (1991) traced this history in his book *Who Is Black? One Nation's Definition.* Davis argued that when race mixing between whites and blacks in the United States became widespread for the first time in the seventeenth century, punishments, such as whipping, fines, and public humiliation, were instituted. In 1662, Virginia passed the first laws discouraging miscegenation, defining mulattoes born to slave mothers as slaves. This represented a significant departure from the tradition of English law, which, until that point, determined lineage through the father. As historian Paula Giddings (1984:37) explained, "The circle of denigration was virtually complete with this law, which managed to combine racism, sexism, greed, and piety.... Such legislation laid women open to the most vicious exploitation. For a master could save the cost of buying new slaves by impregnating his own slave, or for that matter having anyone impregnate her."

While these laws encouraged interracial relationships between white male slaveowners and their black female slaves, policy makers sought to discourage interracial liaisons between white women and black men. White women engaging in miscegenation faced forced servitude or banishment from the colony (F. J. Davis, 1991:33). A mulatto child who was born to a white woman, however, was a threat to the entire system of slavery and white supremacy. Because it was assumed that the child of a white woman would remain with his or her mother, racial segregation would be breached. Gender is central to understanding this distinction. The birth of a mulatto child to a white woman directly usurped white male power and control over both white women and black men. Mulatto children born to black women, on the other hand, were signs of white male power (A. Davis, 1983; F. J. Davis, 1991).

With the end of the Civil War and the passage of the Thirteenth Amendment, white anxieties rose, and the white population increasingly demanded sharper racial definitions and boundaries. Fears of miscegenation rose among whites, especially in the South, where it was believed that because of the postwar shortage of white men, interracial sexual relations between free black men and white women would grow rampant. This fear became an obsession with the burgeoning Ku Klux Klan (F. J. Davis 1991:43). Jim Crow laws were passed with increasing frequency to segregate blacks from whites, limit black political involvement, and prevent blacks from competing economically with whites for jobs. Thomas Dixon's novel, *The Leopard's Spots: A Romance of the White Man's Burden—1865–1900,* published in 1902, proclaimed: "The beginning of Negro equality as a vital fact is the beginning of the end of this nation's life....You cannot seek the Negro vote without asking him to your home sooner or later....And if you seat him at your table, he has the right to ask your daughter's hand in marriage" (Dixon, 1902, quoted in Mencke, 1979:210).

This fear exemplifies the frequent charge that any freedom for blacks would necessarily and inevitably lead directly to interracial sexual relations between black men and white women. Lynching was often an effort to rescue the reputation of white women who chose to associate with black men, as well as a form of terror aimed at the political and economic advances of blacks (J. F. Davis, 1991:52–53; Ware, 1992:181).

Angela Davis argued that the myth of the black male rapist originated at this time as a tool of racist terrorism. "The institution of lynching, in turn, complemented by the continued rape of Black women, became an essential ingredient of the post-war strategy of racist terror. In this way the brutal exploitation of Black labor was guaranteed, and after the betrayal of Reconstruction, the political domination of the Black people as a whole was assured" (A. Davis, 1983:185).

Representing some of the earliest examples of intersectional theorizing, the pioneering works of Ida B. Wells, Mary Church Terrell, Frances Harper, Anna Julia Cooper, and other black women at the time drew connections between lynching and rape and the weapons of racism and sexism. As Hazel Carby (1986:308) explained, "Wells knew that emancipation meant that white men lost their vested interests in the body of the Negro and that lynching and the rape of black women were attempts to regain control. The terrorizing of black communities was a political weapon that manipulated ideologies of sexuality."

As these analyses highlight, constructions of womanhood and manhood were delimited by race. Forms of sexual terror, in the mechanisms of lynching and rape, bolstered both racial and gender hierarchies that maintained white male dominance. Fears of blacks' political and economic equality with whites continued to be rearticulated as fears of interracial sexuality and black male sexuality. Emancipation, voting rights, and blacks' competition with whites for jobs all led to white violence aimed at blacks in the name of protecting white womanhood and warding off the threat of interracial sexuality. When the 1954 *Brown v. Board of Education* decision was handed down by the United States Supreme Court and the Jim Crow system was threatened, cries against miscegenation grew once more. Mississippi Circuit Court Judge Thomas Brady voiced these fears, threatening that the Supreme Court ruling in *Brown* would result in "the tragedy of miscegenation."

The intersections of race, gender, and sexuality are revealed in the entrenched paradox that while interracial sexuality has been condemned and was illegal in many states until 1967, it is only the relations between white women and black men that have been considered a threat to the white community. Today, contemporary white supremacist discourse rearticulates these fears.

Throughout white supremacist discourse, interracial sexuality is presented as the enemy of everything white supremacists desire. For white supremacists, the construction of racial purity requires a policing of the racial and gender boundaries; interracial sexuality is the greatest threat to this border maintenance. For a movement that is concerned with forging a white identity, interracial sexuality is constructed as a threat to the boundaries of whiteness, to the very possibility of a pure white identity.

White supremacist discourse frequently ridicules feminists, antiracists, and others who fight for human equality. While equality is obviously a threat to white male privilege and power, white supremacists also articulate it as a threat to the existence of the white race itself. "What's wrong with interracial sex? Well, interracial sex is immoral and unscientific. Also, interracial sex has destroyed many civilizations. What dark races have ever contributed anything to civilization comparable to the light bulb, the airplane or the automobile? A famous U.S. Senator once stated that all our armies, cities and machines could be destroyed—and we could rebuild. But he went on to say that the White Christian Race could never be restored if it were destroyed through racial mongrelization" (*The Thunderbolt,* April 1975, 10).

White supremacist discourse is obsessed with interracial sexuality. Web sites, chat rooms, and publications devote huge amounts of space to the issue. Interracial sexuality, it is argued, will erase differences and make everyone the same: brown. The construction of gender identities remains central to the discourse decrying interracial sexuality. Not only is it seen as threatening the existence of a "pure" white race, but it is constructed as a threat to white manhood as well. As one white supremacist author argued:

> Northern European males have traditionally tended throughout history to be dominant by nature, but... they are becoming submissive and passive. This phenomenon is especially obvious in the declining strength of their opposition to the interracial sexual transgressions of non-Northern European males with Northern European females. [Northern European men] repress the natural inborn tendencies of exclusivity which played an important role in preserving the biological integrity of their race during its evolution. Many carry their altruism to the point of even seeming to approve of, and to encourage, the sexual trespasses of non-Northern European males upon Northern European females whom their more vigorous and race-conscious ancestors would have

> defended from such defilements with their very lives. (*Instauration,* June 1980:8)

This author lamented the destruction of what he saw as the natural roles of men and women, attacking contemporary white men, no longer "real men," willing to prove their masculinity by protecting white women. The breakdown of these natural roles threatens to increase interracial sexuality and lead to the subsequent breakdown of the natural racial order. White men are blamed for allowing *their* women to fall into the arms of black men. This decline in white masculinity is targeted as a primary reason for the increase in interracial sexuality. Ultimately, changing gender relations are held responsible for the destruction of white racial identity.

Similarly, an article entitled "Sexuality in a Sick Society: The Changing Relationship between Men and Women is Leading to Ominous Racial Consequences for the West," contended that feminism and the sexual revolution have led to the

> demasculinization of the Western male, [and] together with the reaction of the Western female to this, [it] is a cause for grave concern.... [Men] are constrained from expressing their maleness in any of the ways which were natural in the past. One of the most important of those ways was protecting a mate....All the brave, new talk about marriage today being a partnership of equals does not change the basic, biological natures of men and women. Those natures have fitted them for *complimentary* roles, not for the *same* role...[but now the man is no longer] the master in his house. One way in which Western women have responded to the perceived demasculinization of their men has been to turn toward non-White males, who are perceived as more masculine.... [A woman will] run through a long succession of Black lovers in her fruitless, instinctual search for a man who would not only love her but also master her. (*National Vanguard* January, 1983:17)

In these examples, we see clearly the ways in which race, gender, and sexuality are inextricably interconnected. They are constructed in and through each other, and through sexual practices. It is through normative gender, heterosexual, and intraracial sexual relations that properly gendered and racialized subjects are produced. Thus, a threat to the "natural" gender order is also a threat to the "natural" racial order, and vice versa. This *National Vanguard* article succinctly summarized the situation, highlighting the interlocking nature of race and gender identity: "It is a grim reminder to us of the inextricable interdependence of the sexual and racial issues: Unless a healthy relationship between the sexes is reestablished in the West, the White race certainly will not survive" *(National Vanguard* January, 1983:21–22). In white supremacist discourse, any threat to the hierarchical binary oppositions of man/woman and white/nonwhite is represented as a threat to humanity itself. (Elsewhere, I discussed the construction of nonwhites as "mud people," people not fully human. It is only the white race that is defined as fully human; see Ferber, 1998.)

Boundaries are pivotal to the construction of any identity category. As Iris Marion Young (1990:303) explained: "Any move to define an identity, a closed totality, always depends on excluding some elements, separating the pure from the impure.... The logic of identity seeks to keep those borders firmly drawn." The construction of racial identities, then, requires a policing of the borders, maintenance of the boundaries between "one's own kind" and others. Regulations prohibiting interracial sexual relationships actually serve to produce and consolidate both racial and gender identities. It is through the construction of boundaries themselves that identities come into existence. As Butler (1990:134) pointed out, "'Inner' and 'outer' make sense only with reference to a mediating boundary that strives for stability.... Hence, 'inner' and 'outer' constitute a binary distinction that stabilizes and consolidates the coherent subject."

Throughout U.S. history, sexual relationships, or "ethnosexual frontiers," according to Nagel (2003), are the boundaries through which racialized, gendered bodies are produced and maintained and inequality is reproduced. They are the point at which male and female, white and nonwhite differences are constructed, policed, and threatened with disruption. As we have seen, throughout white supremacist

discourse, threats to inequality and white male privilege are responded to with a reinforcement of the sex, gender, racial, and sexual boundaries and essentialist categories. It is inequality that produced these differences to rationalize itself; thus, when inequality is threatened, those who feel their privilege is at risk seek to sediment these classifications further as normal and natural. By expelling these categories of race, sex, gender, and sexuality to the realm of the natural and universal, they are placed beyond question and doubt, and privilege protected. What this also suggests, then, is that any attempts to dismantle these systems of inequality require the interrogation of these categories of identity as well.

REFERENCES

Butler, Judith. 1990. *Gender Trouble: Feminism and the Subversion of Identity.* New York: Routledge.

Butler, Judith. 1991. "Imitation and Gender Insubordination." In *Inside/Out: Lesbian Theories, Gay Theories,* ed. Diana Fuss. London: Routledge.

Butler, Judith. 1993. *Bodies That Matter: On the Discursive Limits of Sex.* New York: Routledge.

Carby, Hazel. 1986. "On the Threshold of Woman's Era: Lynching, Empire, and Sexuality in Black Feminist Theory." In *"Race," Writing and Difference,* ed. Henry Louis Gates, Jr. Chicago: University of Chicago Press.

Collins, Patricia Hill. 2000. *Black Feminist Thought: Knowledge, Consciousness, and the Politics of Empowerment* (rev. 10th anniversary 2nd ed.). New York: Routledge.

Crosby, Christina. 1992. "Dealing with Differences." In *Feminists Theorize the Political,* ed. Judith Butler and Joan Scott. New York: Routledge.

Davis, Angela. 1983. *Women, Race and Class.* New York: Vintage Books.

Davis, F. James. 1991. *Who Is Black? One Nation's Definition.* University Park: Pennsylvania State University Press.

Ferber, Abby L. 1998. *White Man Falling: Race, Gender and White Supremacy.* Lanham, Md.: Rowman & Littlefield.

Giddings, Paula. 1984. *When and Where I Enter: The Impact of Black Women on Race and Sex in America.* New York: William Morrow.

Instauration, June 1980.

Mencke, John G. 1979. *Mulattoes and Race Mixture: American Attitudes and Images, 1865–1918.* Ann Arbor, Mich.: University Microfilms Research Press.

Nagel, Joanne. 2003. *Race, Ethnicity, and Sexuality: Intimate Intersections, Forbidden Frontiers.* New York: Oxford University Press.

National Vanguard, January 1983.

Omi, Michael, and Howard Winant. 1986. *Racial Formation in the United States: From the 1960s to the 1980s.* New York: Routledge.

The Thunderbolt, April 1975.

Ware, Vron. 1992. *Beyond the Pale: White Women, Racism and History.* London: Verso.

Young, Iris Marion. 1990. "The Ideal of Community and the Politics of Difference." In *Feminism/Postmodernism*, ed. Linda J. Nicholson. New York: Routledge.

Young, Robert J. C. 1995. *Colonial Desire: Hybridity in Theory, Culture and Race.* New York: Routledge.

8 • *Chrys Ingraham*

HETEROSEXUALITY

It's Just Not Natural!

DISCUSSION QUESTIONS

1. How do *you* define heterosexuality? Why does Ingraham argue that it is a *social institution*? What are the implications of seeing heterosexuality as an institution?
2. Why did second-wave feminists link heterosexuality to women's oppression?
3. How does the heterosexual imaginary normalize heterosexuality?
4. Ingraham examines weddings as one site where the heterosexual imaginary is pervasive and obscures the various relations of power at work. What are some other locations we might examine?

Since I began teaching courses on gender and sexuality in the early 1980s, I've struggled with debates that claim that heterosexuality is both 'natural and normal'. As a sociologist, I frequently find such positions lacking in that they fail to attend to the social conditions upon which most things depend. In other words, the question is not whether (hetero) sexuality is natural. *All* aspects of our social world–natural or otherwise–are given meaning. The real issue is, how we give meaning to heterosexuality and what interests are served by these meanings? . . .

Historically, we have witnessed the scientific establishment determine which phenomena can be considered normal and natural only to turn around years later and say they were wrong or that their judgement was premature. Consider the instance of women's entry into higher education. At a time when white middle-class women entering higher education was frowned upon, nineteenth-century scientists discovered that women's reproductive organs would be harmed if they were exposed to a college education. And, in an historical moment when the notion of former slaves being equal to whites was not a popular notion, it was scientists who claimed that people of African descent had smaller brains than those of European lineage. In each case, scientists succumbed to the political interests of their time in formulating and interpreting research on such topics. As social conditions shifted, so too did scientific discovery. In each instance, scientists eventually overturned their previous findings in the face of overwhelming evidence to the contrary....

Typically studied as a form of sexuality, heterosexuality is, in reality, a highly regulated, ritualized, and organized set of practices, e.g. weddings or proms. Sociologically, then, heterosexuality as an established order made up of rule-bound and standardized behavior patterns qualifies as an institution. Moreover, heterosexuality as an arrangement involving large numbers of people whose behavior is guided by norms and rules is also a *social* institution.

Heterosexuality is much more than a biological given or whether or not someone is attracted to someone of another sex. Rules on everything from who pays for the date or the wedding rehearsal dinner to who leads while dancing, drives the car, cooks dinner or initiates sex, all serve to regulate heterosexual practice. What circulates as a given in western societies is, in fact, a highly structured arrangement. As is the case with most institutions, people who participate in these practices must be *socialized* to do so. In other words, women were not born with a wedding gown gene or neo-natal craving for a diamond engagement ring! They were taught to want these things. Women didn't enter the world with a desire to practice something called dating or a desire to play with a 'My Size Bride Barbie', they were rewarded for desiring these things. Likewise,

men did not exit the womb knowing they would one day buy a date a corsage or spend two months' income to buy an engagement ring. These are all products that have been sold to consumers interested in taking part in a culturally established ritual that works to organize and institutionalize heterosexuality and reward those who participate.

HETERONORMATIVITY

In the 1970s as second wave feminists attempted to theorize and understand the source of women's oppression, the notion of heterosexuality as normative emerged. In one of the earliest examples of this effort, The Purple September Staff, a Dutch group, published an article entitled 'The normative status of heterosexuality' (1975). They maintain that heterosexuality is really a normalized power arrangement that limits options and privileges men over women and reinforces and naturalizes male dominance....

> Heterosexuality—as an ideology and as an institution—upholds all those aspects of female oppression...For example, heterosexuality is basic to our oppression in the workplace. When we look at how women are defined and exploited as secondary, marginal workers, we recognize that this definition assumes that all women are tied to men...It is obvious that heterosexuality upholds the home, housework, the family as both a personal and economic unit. (Bunch, 1975: 34)

In this excerpt from Charlotte Bunch, the link between heterosexuality and systems of oppression is elaborated.

While many of these arguments were made by heterosexually-identified feminists, some of the more famous works were produced by lesbian feminists, making a link to the interests of both feminism and lesbian and gay rights. Adrienne Rich's essay 'compulsory heterosexuality and lesbian existence' (1980), a frequently reprinted classic, confronts the institution of heterosexuality head on, asserting that heterosexuality is neither natural nor inevitable but is instead a compulsory, contrived, constructed and taken-for-granted institution which serves the interests of male dominance.

> Historians need to ask at every point how heterosexuality as institution has been organized and maintained through the female wage scale, the enforcement of middle-class women's leisure, the glamorization of so-called sexual liberation, the withholding of education from women, the imagery of high art and popular culture, the mystification of the personal sphere, and much else. We need an economics which comprehends the institution of heterosexuality, with its doubled workload for women and its sexual divisions of labor, as the most idealized of economic relations. (ibid.: 27)

Understanding heterosexuality as compulsory and as a standardized institution with processes and effects is what makes Rich's contribution to these debates pivotal.

Monique Wittig's 'The category of sex' (1976), takes the argument to a different level, declaring heterosexuality a political regime. The category of sex, she argues, is the political category that founds society as heterosexual:

> As such it does not concern being but relationships...The category of sex is the one that rules as natural the relation that is at the base of (heterosexual) society and through which half of the population, women, are heterosexualized...and submitted to a heterosexual economy...The category of sex is the product of a heterosexual society in which men appropriate for themselves the reproduction and production of women and also their physical persons by means of a contract called the marriage contract. (Wittig, 1992: 7)

This regime depends upon the belief that women are sexual beings, unable to escape or live outside of male rule.

These positions signal a paradigm shift in how heterosexuality is understood, challenging the very centrality of institutionalized heterosexuality and beginning the work of offering a systematic analysis of heterosexuality. When queer theory emerged in the 1990s, these critical analyses of heterosexuality were revisited and reinvigorated (e.g. Butler, 1990; de Lauretis, 1987; Fuss, 1991; Hennessy, 1995; Ingraham, 1994; Jackson, 1996; Sedgwick, 1990; Seidman, 1991, 1992, 1995; Warner, 1993; Wittig, 1992). In his anthology *Fear of a Queer Planet*, Michael Warner rearticulated these debates through his creation of the concept of 'heteronormativity'. According to Warner:

> So much privilege lies in heterosexual culture's exclusive ability to interpret itself as society. Het culture thinks of itself as the elemental form of human association, as the very model of intergender relations, as the indivisible basis of all community, and as the means of reproduction without which society wouldn't exist...Western political thought has taken the heterosexual couple to represent the principle of social union itself. (1993: xxi)

In this same passage Warner relates his notion of heteronormativity to Wittig's idea of the social contract. For Wittig the social contract is heterosexuality. 'To live in society is to live in heterosexuality...Heterosexuality is always there within all mental categories' (1992: 40). Like whiteness in a white supremacist society, heterosexuality is not only socially produced as dominant but is also taken-for-granted and universalizing.

Steven Seidman in his introduction to the groundbreaking work *Queer Theory/Sociology* (1996) assesses the role of queer theorists in developing a new critical view of normative heterosexuality. Given the history of sociology as a 'de-naturalizing force', he argues that it is time for queer sociologists to de-naturalize heterosexuality as a 'social and political organizing principle'. Seidman asserts that the contribution of queer sociology is to analyse normative heterosexuality for the ways it conceals from view particular social processes and inequalities.

Drawing on these early arguments heteronormativity can be defined as the view that institutionalized heterosexuality constitutes the standard for legitimate and expected social and sexual relations. Heteronormativity insures that the organization of heterosexuality in everything from gender to weddings to marital status is held up as both a model and as 'normal'. Consider, for instance, the ways many surveys or intake questionnaires ask respondents to check off their marital status as either married, divorced, separated, widowed, single, or, in some cases, never married. Not only are these categories presented as significant indices of social identity, they are offered as the only options, implying that the organization of identity in relation to marriage is universal and not in need of explanation. Questions concerning marital status appear on most surveys *regardless of relevance*. The heteronormative assumption of this practice is rarely, if ever, called into question and when it is, the response is generally dismissive. (Try putting down 'not applicable' the next time you fill out one of these forms in a doctor's office!)

Or try to imagine entering a committed relationship without benefit of legalized marriage. We find it difficult to think that we can share commitment with someone without a state-sponsored license. People will frequently comment that someone is afraid to 'make a commitment' if they choose not to get married even when they have been in a relationship with someone for years! Our ability to imagine possibilities or to understand what counts as commitment is itself impaired by heteronormative assumptions. We even find ourselves challenged to consider how to marry without an elaborate white wedding. Gays and lesbians have participated in long-term committed relationships for years yet find themselves desiring state sanctioning of their union in order to feel legitimate. Heteronormativity works in all of these instances to naturalize the institution of heterosexuality while rendering real people's relationships and commitments irrelevant and illegitimate....

To expand the analytical reach of the concept of heteronormativity, it is important to examine how heterosexuality is constructed as normative. A concept that is useful for examining the naturalization of heterosexual relations is 'the heterosexual imaginary'.[1] The 'imaginary' is that illusory relationship we can have to our real conditions of existence. It is that moment when we romanticize things or refuse to see something that makes us uncomfortable.

Applied to the study of heterosexuality it is that way of thinking that conceals the operation of heterosexuality in structuring gender (across race, class; and sexuality) and closes off any critical analysis of heterosexuality as an organizing institution. It is a belief system that relies on romantic and sacred notions in order to create and maintain the illusion of well-being. At the same time this romantic view prevents us from seeing how institutionalized heterosexuality actually works to organize gender while preserving racial, class, and sexual hierarchies as well. The effect of this illusory depiction of reality is that heterosexuality is taken for granted and unquestioned while gender is understood as something people are socialized into or learn. By leaving heterosexuality unexamined as an institution we do not explore how it is learned, what it keeps in place, and the interests it serves in the way it is practiced. Through the use of the heterosexual imaginary, we hold up the institution of heterosexuality as timeless, devoid of historical variation, and as 'just the way it is' while creating social practices that reinforce the illusion that as long as this is 'the way it is' all will be right in the world. Romancing heterosexuality–creating an illusory heterosexuality–is central to the heterosexual imaginary.

Frequently, discussions about the legalization of gay marriage depend on this illusion. Gays and lesbians are seeking equal access to economic resources such as benefits and see marriage as the site for gaining equity with heterosexuals. The central problem with this position is that it constructs the debates in terms of coupling. All those who do not couple for whatever reason are left out of the discussion. Consider some of the other consequences of participating in the heterosexual imaginary, of perpetuating the notion that heterosexuality is naturally a site for tranquility and safety. This standpoint keeps us from seeing and dealing with issues of marital rape, domestic violence, pay inequities, racism, gay bashing, and sexual harassment. Instead, institutionalized heterosexuality organizes those behaviors we ascribe to men and women–gender–while keeping in place or producing a history of contradictory and unequal social relations. The production of a division of labor that results in unpaid domestic work, inequalities of pay and opportunity, or the privileging of married couples in the dissemination of insurance benefits are examples of this. The heterosexual imaginary naturalizes the regulation of sexuality through the institution of marriage and state domestic relations laws. These laws, among others, set the terms for taxation, health care, and housing benefits on the basis of marital status. Laws and public- and private-sector policies use marriage as the primary requirement for social and economic benefits and access rather than distributing resources on some other basis such as citizenship or ability to breathe, for example. The distribution of economic resources on the basis of marital status remains an exclusionary arrangement even if the law permits gays and lesbians to participate. The heterosexual imaginary works here as well by allowing the illusion of well-being to reside in the privilege heterosexual couples enjoy while keeping others from equal access—quite a contradiction in a democratic social order.

WEDDINGS

...To study weddings using this theory of heterosexuality is to investigate the ways various practices, arrangements, relations, and rituals work to standardize and conceal the operation of this institution. It means to ask how practices such as weddings become naturalized and prevent us from seeing what is at stake, what is kept in place, and what consequences are produced. To employ this approach is to seek out those instances when the illusion of tranquility is created and at what cost. Weddings, like many other rituals of heterosexual celebration such as anniversaries, showers, and Valentine's Day become synonymous with heterosexuality and provide illusions of reality which conceal the operation of heterosexuality both historically and materially. When used in professional settings, for example, weddings work as a form of ideological control to signal membership in relations of ruling as well as to signify that the couple is normal, moral, productive,

family-centered, upstanding citizens and, most importantly, appropriately gendered....

To study weddings means to interrupt the ways the heterosexual imaginary naturalizes heterosexuality and prevents us from seeing how its organization depends on the production of the belief or ideology that heterosexuality is normative and the same for everyone—that the fairy tale romance is universal. It is this assumption that allows for the development and growth of a $32 billion per year wedding industry. This multi-billion dollar industry includes the sale of a diverse range of products, many of which are produced outside of the USA—wedding gowns, diamonds, honeymoon travel and apparel, and household equipment. Also included in the market are invitations, flowers, receptions, photos, gifts, home furnishings, wedding cakes, catering, alcohol, paper products, calligraphy, jewelry, party supplies, hair styling, make-up, manicures, music, books, and wedding accessories, e.g., ring pillows, silver, chauffeurs and limousines. In the name of normative heterosexuality and its ideology of romance the presence and size of the sometimes corrupt wedding industry escape us.

While newlyweds make up only 2.6 per cent of all American households, they account for 75 per cent of all the fine china, 29 per cent of the tableware, and 21 per cent of the jewelry and watches sold in the USA every year. Even insurers have entered the primary wedding market by offering coverage 'if wedding bells don't ring' to cover the cost of any monies already spent on the wedding preparation. Fireman's Fund Insurance Company offers 'Weddingsurance' for wedding catastrophes such as flood or fire but not for 'change of heart' (Haggerty, 1993). In fact, attach the words wedding or bridal to nearly any item and its price goes up. With June as the leading wedding month followed by August and July, summer becomes a wedding marketer's dream. According to industry estimates, the average wedding in the USA costs $19,104. Considered in relation to what Americans earn, the cost of the average wedding represents 51 per cent of the mean earning of a white family of four and 89 per cent of the median earnings for black families. The fact that

63.7 per cent of Americans earn less than $25,000 per year (US Bureau of the Census, 1997) means the average cost of a wedding approximates a year's earnings for many Americans. . . .

Probably the most significant wedding purchase is the wedding gown. Industry analysts have noted that most brides would do without many things to plan a wedding and stay within budget, but they would not scrimp when it comes to the purchase of the wedding gown. With the US national average expenditure at $823 for the gown and $199 for the veil, the bride's apparel becomes the centerpiece of the white wedding. Most of us have heard the various phrases associated with the bride and her gown, the symbolic significance attached to how she looks and how beautiful her gown is. The marketing of everything from weddings to gowns to children's toys to popular wedding films to Disney is laced with messages about fairy tales and princesses, the fantasy rewards that work to naturalize weddings and heterosexuality. Even couture fashion shows of world-class designers traditionally feature wedding gowns as their grand finale.

One particularly troubling practice widely engaged in by gown sellers is the removal of designer labels and prices from dresses. In many surveys, from *Modern Bride* to Dawn Currie's interview study (1993), brides indicate that they rely upon bridal magazines to give them ideas about what type of gown to choose. They take the ad for the gown they like best to area stores and attempt to try on and purchase that particular dress. What they encounter is a system of deception widely practiced by many bridal shops. First, sellers remove the labels. Brides ask for a Vera Wang or an Alfred Angelo or a Jessica McClintock and are told to get the number off the gown and the clerk will check their book and see which designer it is. The bride has no way of knowing if she actually has the brand she seeks. As I toured various shops and saw how widespread this practice was, I asked store owners why they removed the labels from the dresses. Without exception they told me that it was to maintain the integrity of their business and to prevent women from comparison shopping. The truth is, this practice is *illegal* and

provides shop owners with a great deal of flexibility in preserving their customer base and profit margin. In addition to this federal consumer protection law there are many states which provide similar protections. All in all, bridal gown stores have little to fear: This law is not enforced. And, perhaps more importantly, the romance with the white wedding gown distracts the soon-to-be brides from becoming suspicious of store practices.

If you look at the portion of tags gown-sellers leave in the dresses you will see that most are sewn outside the USA in countries such as Guatemala, Mexico, Taiwan, and China. Nearly 80 per cent of all wedding gowns are produced outside the USA in subcontracted factories where labor standards are nowhere near US standards and no independent unions or regulators keep watch.

The recruitment by US companies to contract offshore labor benefits manufacturers on many levels: cheap labor, low overhead, fewer regulations, and higher profits. And with the proliferation of free trade agreements such as the North Atlantic Free Trade Agreement (NAFTA) and the General Agreement on Tariffs and Trade (GATT), labor and environmental abuses abound. In a survey conducted by UNITE in April 1997 of three factories in Guatemala, it was discovered that one American manufacturer's gowns were being made by 13 year olds in factories with widespread violations of their country's child labor laws, wage and hour laws, and under life-threatening safety conditions. At two of the firms, 14 and 15 year olds worked as long as 10 hours a day earning $20.80 a week.

Another area of the wedding industry dominated by messages about romance is the marketing of diamonds. As part of the fantasy of the ever-romantic marriage proposal, the diamond ring takes center stage. In fact, for 70 per cent of all US brides and 75 per cent of first-time brides, the first purchase for the impending wedding is the diamond engagement ring. The central marketing strategy of the world's largest diamond mining organization, DeBeers, is to convince consumers that 'diamonds are forever'. Once you accept this slogan, you also believe that you are making a life-long investment, not just purchasing a bauble for your bride! In fact, DeBeers spends about $57 million each year in this advertising campaign and has 'committed to spending a large part of [their] budget–some $200 million this year–on the promotion of diamond jewelry around the world' (Oppenheimer, 1998: 8). DeBeers and its advertisers have developed a new 'shadow' campaign to sell to consumers the advice that the 'appropriate' diamond engagement ring should cost at least 'two months' salary' for the groom (*Jewelers*, 1996). This advertising strategy signals to newlyweds, grooms in particular, that anything less is not acceptable. In effect, the diamond industry has made use of heteronormativity and the heterosexual imaginary and has convinced us that purchasing a diamond engagement ring is no longer a want but is 'natural', and therefore, a must. Not surprisingly, according to wedding industry estimates, this message is reaching its target. The average annual expenditure for engagement rings is $3000 (*Modern Bride*, 1996). If that constitutes the equivalent of two months', salary, the groom is expected to earn an annual salary of approximately $26,000 per year, the income bracket many of these ads target. What gets naturalized here is not just heterosexuality and romance but also weddings and commodity consumption....

The contemporary white wedding under transnational capitalism is, in effect, a mass-marketed, homogeneous, assembly-line production with little resemblance to the utopian vision many participants hold. The engine driving the wedding market has mostly to do with the romancing of heterosexuality in the interests of capitalism. The social relations at stake–love, community, commitment, and family–become alienated from the production of the wedding spectacle while practices reinforcing heteronormativity prevail.

The heterosexual imaginary circulating throughout the wedding industry masks the ways it secures racial, class, and sexual hierarchies. For instance, in nearly all of the examples offered above, the wedding industry depends upon the availability of cheap labor from developing nations with majority populations made up of people of color. The wealth garnered by white transnational corporations both relies on racial hierarchies, exploiting people and resources of communities of color (Africa, China, Haiti, Mexico, South Asia), and perpetuates them in the marketing of the wedding industry....

CONCLUSION

Heterosexuality is just not natural! It is socially organized and controlled. To understand how we give meaning to one of our major institutions is to participate as a critical consumer and citizen actively engaged in the production of culture and the social order. Heteronormativity–those practices that construct heterosexuality as the standard for legitimate and expected social and sexual relations–has enormous consequences for all members of a democratic social order, particularly in relation to the distribution of human and economic resources that affect the daily lives of millions of people. When the expectation is that all are equal under the law and that all citizens in a democracy can participate fully in the ruling of that society, rendering one form of socio-sexual relations as dominant by constructing it as 'natural' is both contradictory and violent. In other words, the heterosexuality we learn to think of as 'natural' is anything but.

NOTE

1. See 'The heterosexual imaginary: feminist sociology and theories of gender', *Sociological Theory*, 12: 203–19. 2 July 1994 for further elaboration of this concept.

REFERENCES

Adams, Mary Louise (1997) *The Trouble with Normal: Postwar Youth and the Making of Heterosexuality*. Toronto: University of Toronto Press.

Best, Amy (2000) *Prom Night: Youth, Schools, and Popular Culture*. New York: Routledge.

Bunch, Charlotte (1975) 'Not for lesbians only', *Quest: A Feminist Quarterly*, (Fall).

Butler, Judith (1990) *Gender Trouble*. New York: Routledge.

Currie, D. (1993) 'Here comes the bride': The making of a 'modern traditional' wedding in western culture', *Journal of Comparative Family Studies*, 24 (3): 403–21.

de Lauretis, Teresa (1987) 'Queer theory: lesbian and gay sexualities'. *Differences*, 3: iii–xviii.

Field, Nicola (1995) *Over the Rainbow: Money, Class and Homophobia*. London: Pluto Press.

Fuss, Diana (1991) *Inside/Out*. New York Routledge.

Graff, E.J. (1999) *What is Marriage for?: The Strange Social History of our Most Intimate Institution*. Boston: Beacon Press.

Harman, Moses (1901) *Institutional Marriage*. Chicago: Lucifer.

Helms, Jesse (1996) 'The defense of marriage act'. *Senate Congressional Quarterly* September 9.C. 1996 Senate proceedings. *Congressional Record*, September 9.

Hennessy, Rosemary (1995) 'Incorporating queer theory on the left', Antonio Callari, Stephen Cullenberg, and Carole Beweiner (eds) *Marxism in the Postmodern Age*. New York: Guilford.

Heywood, Ezra (1876) *Cupid's Yokes*. Princeton, NJ: Co-operative Publishing Company.

Ingraham, Chrys (1994) 'The heterosexual imaginary: feminist sociology and theories of gender', *Sociological Theory*, 12, 2 (July): 203–19.

Ingraham, Chrys (1999) *White Weddings: Romancing Heterosexuality in Popular Culture*. New York: Routledge.

Jackson, Stevi (1996) 'Heterosexuality and feminist theory', in Diane Richardson (ed.), *Theorising Heterosexuality*. Buckingham: Open University Press.

Jackson, Stevi (1999) *Heterosexuality in Question*. London: Sage Publications.

Jewelers Circular-Keystone (1996) 'Diamond sales hit record', New York: Chilton.

Katz, Jonathan Ned (1995) *The Invention of Heterosexuality*. New York: Plume.

Maynard, Mary and Purvis, June (eds) (1995) *(Hetero)sexual Politics*. London: Taylor & Francis.

Modern Bride (1996) 'The bridal market retail spending study: $35 billion market for the 90's', New York: Primedia.

Oppenheimer, Nicholas (1998) 'Chairman's statement', *Annual Report*. De Beers.

Rich, Adrienne (1980) 'Compulsory heterosexuality and lesbian existence', *Signs*, 5 (Summer): 631–60.

Richardson, Diane (ed.) (1996) *Theorising Heterosexuality*. Buckingham: Open University Press.

Sears, Hal D. (1977) *The Sex Radicals: Free Love in High Victorian America*. Lawrence: Regents Press of Kansas.

Sedgwick, Eve (1990) *Epistemology of the Closet*. Berkeley, CA: University of California Press.

Seidman, Steven (1991) *Romantic Longings*. New York: Routledge.

Seidman, Steven (1992) *Embattled Eros*. New York: Routledge.

Seidman, Steven (1993) 'Identity and politics in a postmodern gay culture: some conceptual and historical notes', in M. Warner (ed.), *Fear of a Queer Planet*. Minneapolis: University of Minnesota Press.

Seidman, Steven (1996) *Queer Theory/Sociology*. Cambridge, MA: Blackwell.

US Bureau of the Census (1997) *Statistical Abstracts of the U.S.* Washington DC: Government Printing Office.

Wilkinson, Sue and Kitzinger, Celia (eds) (1993) *Heterosexuality: A Feminism and Psychology Reader*. London: Sage Publications.

Wittig, Monique (1992) *The Straight Mind and Other Essays*. Boston: Beacon Press.

PART TWO

Examining Our Lives, Expanding the Boundaries

INTRODUCTION

As Part One demonstrated, discussions of sex, gender, and sexuality are often limited to essentialist, heteronormative constructions—that is, standard assumptions of a natural binary between female and male that manifests in legitimate sexual relations. Additionally, discussions typically reify white, able-bodied, and middle-class ideologies by leaving these social statuses unmarked. This section of the volume intervenes in these discourses to expand and share the real and diverse embodied stories of people that live both within and beyond these constructed expectations. The carefully selected articles offer intimate insights of empowerment, recognition, resistance, trauma, desire, action, community solidarity, and hope. The mostly first-person narratives in this section demonstrate a kind of resistance to the "scientized," stigmatized, and highly theorized analyses that academic literatures offer. Instead, this section will traverse cutting-edge *personal* work that explores complexly gendered and sexual lives at the intersections of culture, race, ethnicity, socioeconomic status, age, nation, and geography. In recent years there has been an explosion of this type of writing, which has created space for people to share their voice and experiences. The Internet has also been an important site for individual expression, sharing, and community building. For example, consider the number of people who write blogs, tweet, or produce personal videos that are uploaded to YouTube. These mediums can allow us to recognize how we are different and yet interconnected. In this section readers may find themselves reflecting on their own personal stories of resistance, trauma, empowerment, struggle, and pride.

Ryan A. Flores, a powerful young poet, begins this section with a beautiful interrogation of the perceived and real cultural, social, political, and institutional categorizations of his embodied reality. While Flores asks, "Who *am* I?", we ask *how* and *why* he becomes a trope for these constructions that he must negotiate every day. Andrew Matzner introduces us to Kaua'i Iki, a *mahu* person living within a context of Western assimilation and Christianity on Oahu, the most densely populated island of Hawai'i. Iki raises the complexity of contemporary cultural clashes that are deeply rooted in spirituality and colonialism, and the following chapters by Naber and Navarro similarly explore the complex emotional terrain negotiated by those straddling cultural borders. Nadine Naber shares a second-generation Arab American woman's narrative in a post-9/11 San Francisco, California, while Marissa Navarro's examination of racism, sexism, classism, and homophobia as a Mexican-American woman presents the transformative *body as battleground* metaphor that resonates throughout this volume. Kate Harding explores the battleground for women who transgress body-size norms—chubby, fat, and obese. Her story viscerally exposes the traumas created by structural violence against women who are labeled fat.

Activist poet Eli Clare gently but painfully makes clear the entanglements of multiple systems of oppression. His maneuvering in/between and beyond rural/urban, heteronormative/queer, home/exile, bourgeoisie/proletariat, freak/normal, and so many more artificial binaries give us the chance to simply ask why: Why do we continue to demand that people neatly fit? Legendary trans activist Riki Anne Wilchins' frustrating experience reveals

the absurdity of the institutional demands that we neatly fit. Both Sonya Bolus and C. Jacob Hale present their intimate awareness, resistance, and empowerment in light of these demands. Finally, Tabatabai exposes the borders and boundaries of lesbian spaces and communities of solidarity, while Yon-Leau and Muñoz-Laboy offer inspiring Latino youth narratives of negotiation and opposition.

We hope that the following articles move us beyond the previously narrow confines of traditional research on sex, gender, sexuality, identities, and practices and raise new questions about how we can theorize these concepts. Together, they raise provocative and important questions including: How do we think about identity and sexual practices today? Do we even have the language for conceptualizing the complexity of these realities? As these life accounts highlight, lived experience is often more complex, varied, and fluid than our theoretical frameworks reflect. Which experiences are central and which end up excluded from our theoretical frameworks has tremendous consequences for which we need to be more responsible. What other factors are equally important to shaping sex, gender, and sexuality that we have not yet fully explored? As readers continue to read the text, we encourage a reflection on the theoretical discussions raised in Part One to connect, develop, or refine them in light of this section. Which theories do you think best help you to grasp and comprehend these experiences? What are the implications of these personal stories for developing more just social structures and social movements?

Ryan A. Flores, Guess Who?

[an exercise in lateral thinking]

to my mother I am *son*
to my father I am *hijo*
to racist hillbillies of the Midwest
I am *wetback, spic,* and *beaner*
to cholos at Armijo I am *gringo*
to officials at the State Department
I need proof of *citizenship*
to la gente de México I am *güero*

Ryan A. Flores, "Guess Who?". Reprinted with the permission of the poet.

in the Southwest I am *coyote*
at the university I am *Latino*,
Mexican-American, and *Chicano*
to the Census Bureau I am *Hispanic*
or *"more than one heritage"*
to mis abuelos I am *mezclado*
to those who hear me speak Spanish
I must be *Argentino* or *Español*
because of light skin and green eyes
because of maternal Bohemian ancestry
I muse as being *Chex-Mex*
I could be the *United States* of existence
I could be *America*
I could be your neighbor
your boss, your teacher, your student
I could mow your lawn,
cook your food
I could be you

So, who *am* I?

9 • *Andrew Matzner*

'O AU NO KEIA

Voices from Hawai'i's Mahu and Transgender Communities

Discussion Questions

1. How did Western colonization impact mahu culture, ritualism, and practice?
2. How does space and place (i.e., rural vs. city) influence mahu expressions according to the author?
3. Is being mahu the same as being gay or lesbian or transgender? Why or why not?

Kaua'i Iki from Andrew Matzner's *'O Au no Keia: Voices from Hawai'i's Mahu and Transgender Communities*. Reprinted with the permission of the author.

I was brought up in Kaua'i in a household where it was OK to be *mahu,* unlike a lot of people I know who were ostracized and kicked out of the house; I was loved within my own household. My mom and dad raised me as a *mahu.* I still did all of the tasks a boy would do, but I also did the tasks the girls would do. I was taught everything. Of course, just because my immediate family accepted me didn't mean that my other relatives were as accepting. My cousins used to make fun of me and call me "Diana." My given name is Dana, which was already *fish.* For some reason my mom had given me a name which could go either way, so it was lovely....

We lived in the countryside, in the center of a small plantation town. We ran the theater, which was right in front of our house. On my mother's side, her father was pure Filipino and her mother was pure Hawaiian. My mother's side has ten children; they were primarily farmers and fishermen. My grandfather worked on the sugar cane plantation and while he was doing that, my grandmother and the kids worked on the taro farm. We had a large taro farm which all of the *mo'opuna* took care of, and during my mom's time they also cared for that. But my mom actually went on and attained a college degree at Kaua'i Community College. She was a registered nurse. I believe that she's the only one in her family that attained a college degree. I was proud of my mother. She went to work and went to school, did all of her homework and actually raised all of us. But we were also raised by our grandparents, which is Hawaiian style. So while mom and dad were working, we were taken care of by our grandparents.

My father is Filipino-Spanish-Chinese. My father's side were laborers, too—sugar cane workers. My father was one of twelve brothers and sisters. When they were young, their mother would take them to help the father work in the fields. During my grandparents' days, they got paid a dollar a day....

My parents were very non-judgmental. They always accepted people as they were. We always had *mahus* at our house. My parents were like foster parents to many other children. When we were growing up, all the unwanted children ended up at our house. My parents took them in, even though we didn't have any legal rights or foster-home papers. They'd say, "Your mother no like you? Then get all your crap together—you're living here with us." We already had eight kids, but my parents took these other kids in, too. We never asked for money. My parents just gave the kids the love that they needed. I'm sure their parents loved them, but any kid that needed a place to go had a place to go....

Our house was located right in the middle of town. Right in front of us was the movie theater. It was very quaint, and old-fashioned style. The theater was destroyed in 1982, after hurricane Eva. The town we lived in had a strong community association. During the holidays they always had programs for the kids, treats at Christmas, Easter Egg hunts, Halloween treats, all that kind of stuff, but the proceeds from the theater went to fund all of those things. We actually ran the films and picked up and dropped off the films, rewound the films, cleaned the theater, and even ran the concession stand sometimes. We did all that. It was community. A lot of the community people would come out and help. When we had the theater cleaning, for instance, they would open up the whole theater during the daytime, and people would come with their water hoses and brooms and mops, and sweep up the whole thing. I think about two hundred people could fit in the theater.

Next to the theater was Kunamoto Stores, something like Arakawa's used to be, a plantation store where you could buy everything—clothes, shoes, fresh meat, bread, everything that you needed to survive. You could charge it on your account. Everybody had a *bango* number. Ours was 2567, and you could go there and charge whatever. Occasionally I would go to the store and charge what I wanted to eat. [laughs] It was real nice....

Our town was all dirt roads. The only paved road was the one fronting the theater and store. Also the main road in front of the town, along the beach. Those were the only paved roads at that time, so everything else was all dirt roads....

About 1970 they cut the tree down and paved the road where my house was, but not the other dirt roads. Today, it's completely torn down and taken away—all the old houses, the mango trees. . . . The town was known for mango. There was a general store, the Filipino social hall, and a post office down the road. The whole life of the town was in the center. Our house was centrally located. None of these places exist today—they were all bulldozed around 1980. That whole way of life was erased.

* * *

From a young age, I was my grandmother's *puna hele*—her favorite. She used to call me "Glamour Boy." When relatives came in from off-island, she would introduce me and say, "This is my Glamour Boy." But I don't think I got special treatment because I was *mahu*. I was special, but everybody was special, too. However, I did feel a closer affinity to my grandmother simply because she never gave me lickins. I was raised before all this child abuse stuff—I got lickins! Everybody got lickins in those days. You act up, you act silly, you bad-mouth somebody—you're gonna get lickins. And like I said, oftentimes I was just caught in the cross-fire—guilt by association.

My family knew I was *mahu*. They didn't see anything wrong with it. They didn't make a big issue of it. It was just natural. I had a very natural upbringing. I was loved no matter what. But I was *mahu*. I was *mahu* as *mahu* could be. And the thing is, my grandmother and my mom's brother were the only ones who never spanked me. They recognized how I was and loved me for that. My grandmother would always talk to me each morning, to all of us, whoever was around. She would tell us different things. From her we learned the facts of life, about having sex, who you're having sex with, when you're having sex, when not to have sex. My grandmother taught us about that kind of stuff. Because when we were young, we had sex. I had sex with girls and boys. Because everybody wanted to have sex. And I was just there. [laughs] When you're young you don't really think about it in an intimate way. You just go for the experience.

But as far as being *mahu* and being treated or raised in a special way, I really wasn't. My grandmother

would sit me down and tell me stories about this and stories about that, or take me to different places around the island. I thought that everything she told me and the places she showed me, I thought that everybody else knew these things, this family folklore. But it wasn't until her death that I realized that no one else had been told or shown these things. So then I began to think, "Why did she tell *me* these stories? I don't want to be responsible!" Because with the stories comes responsibility.

For example, she gave me the responsibility of caring for the graves of our ancestors. We have many in the mountains which are difficult to find. If you don't know they are there, you won't know. And we have ancestors buried in caves along areas that are populated now, but where the caves are still protected. If people ever want to develop certain areas, I'll have to say, "You cannot, because my ancestors are buried there!" So one of the things I was charged with was to care for our dead, our ancestors' bones. It's an important responsibility. And for some reason or other my grandmother, who had been their caretaker, had entrusted that to me.

Throughout my years, starting from childhood, I was also raised by my mom's brother. He was the oldest male child in my mother's family. He was a marine. There were times that my uncle would show up, pick me up and not come back for a few days. My mom would be hysterical—"Where the hell were you?!" And he would say, "I took him up into the mountains." Or, "I took him down to the beach." My mom would be all worried—"He doesn't know anything about the mountains." And my uncle would say, "Well, that's why I'm taking him." Throughout my childhood it was always like that. Even moreso during my high school years. When I had come back to Kaua'i for high school after going to school here on O'ahu, I was a dropout for a while. During that time, when I wasn't in school, my uncle said, "Hey—if you're not going to be in school, come to my house." So I would hitchhike to the other end of the island, all the way to Hanalei. . . .

My uncle took care of me and raised me in the mountains. I lived with him in the mountains of the Na Pali Coast, from Hanalei Valley all the way in. He taught me how to run, fish, jump and hunt. Survival skills are what he gave me. He would always brief me before an activity. "We're going to go here and there. These are the things we're going to see. These are things we're going to do. This is what I want you to do. This is what I don't want you to do." Whatever my uncle said, I followed to the T. If he told me to climb that mountain, I would climb the mountain like a goat. If he told me dive into the sea, I would dive into the sea. Whatever he told me to do. Whether it was climb that tree, build a house. Anything I had to do, I did for my uncle, to make him happy. Not just to make him happy. It was also survival.

We would often go and stay in the mountain without any supplies. We were lucky if we had a small zip-lock bag of rice or salt. Or maybe a bag of *poi*. The deal was always that if we don't catch anything then we won't eat anything. We'll just have salt and *poi* to eat. But it never worked out like that; we always had something to eat. The way my uncle worked was, we would go down to the beach and he would throw his net no more than three times, and whatever fish we caught—and we always caught, *always*—I'd clean. On the way home he'd give all the fish away, except for what we needed for the day. I mean, the people we met were so lucky because they got free fish! The first time I saw him do that I said, "Uncle, you're giving away all our fish!" He replied, "Don't worry." Because when we got home we still had our fish for dinner. The next day we went back to the sea and the same thing happened.

By the time I was in my high school years and I had dropped out of school, that was when he was able to show me and tell me more, give me more. Because I was getting to be a young adult already, going through all those changes. Everybody was looking at me, *"Oh, mahu."* But it didn't bother my uncle one bit.

In fact, the whole time my uncle knew I was *mahu*. People had the nerve to ask him in front of me, "How come you're taking him with you—he's *mahu*." My uncle would turn to them and say, "He's the only one in the family who can handle all of the things that have to be done." That's why my uncle

took me with him. I was the only one in the family who was taken with him to those places. No one else. Not any of my brothers, who today are excellent fishermen and hunters. Not any of my other cousins. No one.

My uncle was also one of the family's caretakers of our ancestors. That's why I was taken to learn about that and learn to fend for myself in the wild. He felt that no matter how I was, it was important that I knew how to survive. It was the same thing with my grandmother—how to survive, how to protect myself from any kind of evil that might be following me. Because we believe in the Hawaiian ways, which are very mysterious in a lot of ways. We do certain things to counteract those events we believe are the cause of some kind of illness or whatever. We were raised with all the *kahuna* beliefs, steeped in them. . . .

* * *

My family never made a big issue about me being *mahu*. I just was. There were no ifs, ands or buts about it. I lived like any regular child. The people who surrounded me never gave a damn I was a *mahu*. . . .

All the *mahus* who came to my house were loved and accepted by all of us. The queens would love to come and visit with my family because my family didn't care. You know how it is when you go into a room and people start whispering, "Oh, there's a *mahu* over there." They're pointing or making snide remarks under their breath. We never had that. That only happened when we went beyond the Waimea Bridge, for instance. Or when I came to Honolulu. My whole life I knew how I was and it didn't seem like a problem. It was only when I came out here to Honolulu that it became a big problem. I felt people here made a big problem out of nothing. I remember thinking, "This is nothing—why are you guys acting so stupid? This is nothing."

I was raised as a Christian and I went to Catholic school as a child. I remember reading in Leviticus about all the things you're not allowed to do and thinking, "I'm doing that, so I must be evil." But as I grew older my understanding changed. Because what did Jesus come for? He came to give us one more commandment: to love one another as you love yourself. So as a child, when I read that I said to myself, "That's why Jesus came. So that everybody can know the extra commandment, know how to pray to the Lord and know that we have to love each other the way we love ourselves. The first time he never told us that. He said to honor your mother and father, don't steal, don't covet this, don't covet that. But he forgot to tell us to love one another. That's why Jesus Christ had to come back—to remind us."

People use the word of God for their own good and to blaspheme everybody else. But I believe the word of God is a positive thing that you cannot use or manipulate. Today I don't consider myself a Christian, but I have ideals and beliefs which are the same as Christianity because they stem from a long time ago. Those are the ancient beliefs I have. I just freak out sometimes when I see religious leaders who blaspheme anybody who's gay or this or that. They keep quoting the Old Testament and don't mention that when God's son was on earth, he said to love everybody.

By the time I was around ten years old I knew that I would never fit the norm—I knew that I didn't like sleeping with girls and that I would never get married. I had slept with girls and didn't like it. Actually, by the time I was five years old I completely knew. I was attracted to boys from the time I was small. My neighbors were beautiful boys and were attracted to me for some reason, not the girls. [laughs] What could I do? We were attracted to each other. How I felt inside, though...I felt like everybody else. Its just that I had feelings for the same sex. When you're in love or you feel *aloha* for somebody, you just feel that. Maybe people looked at me like I was different, but I didn't feel different inside, and I was never made to feel different. Although I was different I felt like anybody else. I never had to hide anything....

I think the first time my being *mahu* really became an issue was when I was in intermediate school. I had come to Honolulu for boarding and went to Kamehameha Schools [which are funded specifically for the education of Hawaiian children]. On one occasion when my mother was visiting, some counselors pulled my mother to the side and said, "Oh, we think your son has tendencies...He might be gay or *mahu*." My mother turned to them and said, "So what of it?" They were shocked at her answer. They thought she was going to be concerned. In fact, they had wanted to send me for psychiatric treatment in the seventh grade because they felt it was a problem...that I was going to be a problem. In my mother's mind there was no problem. Later she told me what the counselors had said. But she didn't care. For her my being *mahu* was totally natural....

* * *

Around 1973, '74 the Glades [a well-known nightclub in Honolulu] was still going, and I used to go down there. I was about twelve, thirteen, fourteen then. I would head downtown because everybody was heading there. After living in Honolulu as a boarder, I started to get a little bit braver. I used to run away from school. On the weekends I'd check myself out of the dorms, saying I was going to a relative's, but I wouldn't go. Instead I'd just go around, cruise, meet friends. Oftentimes I would sneak in and out of the dormitory without them knowing.

Later on, after the Glades had shut down, I ended up working for the owner of the Glades. I worked for her and lived with the costume designer of the Glades. After I graduated I worked for her. The Glades was the hottest club in Hawai'i at one time. The best shows were found at the Glades. Today, female impersonation here in O'ahu, at Fusions [nightclub]—everything stems from the Glades. Any drag show in Hawai'i stems from the Glades. You have to compare it with the Glades days. Those days were fabulous, fun days, because downtown was fabulous, so alive and full of color. Unlike today—when you go downtown at night its just full of drug addicts. During that time it was full of color because of all the queens on the street. Hairdos, clothing... As a child, I was very intrigued by what they did. Being already acclimated to show business and performing, I enjoyed glamorous things—after all,

"Glamour Boy" was my nickname from my grand-mother. So I enjoyed what Honolulu had to offer. I loved the country, too, but I did enjoy Honolulu, seeing all these people on the streets. Of course, other activities were going on which I wasn't oblivious to, like prostitution....

It was a rough time, because in Honolulu if people found out you were *mahu,* they would really let you have it. When I came here it was the first time I had ever heard the words "fag" and "faggot" being used to refer to me. I was like, "What?! You're calling me a fag—what the hell is that?" I had never known about that word until I came to Honolulu, and then I found out that fag meant *mahu.* I had never been called that before. But I did-n't give a damn. I was raised with the kind of attitude that if somebody is going to come to hurt you, then you know how to take care of yourself. Teasing words—those are nothing. When they come at you and are ready to hurt you, then you know how to protect yourself. So that was my safeguard—I always knew how to protect myself. If anybody was going to come and try to hurt me, I was going to stop them from doing that before they got there. Because I was raised by a marine; I learned how to hunt, fish, kill, jump—so you're not going to do anything to me! I wasn't afraid of people. I was nonconfrontational at the same time. But just because I was nonconfrontational doesn't mean I was afraid. I just didn't waste my time.

There was another culture shock I experienced when I came to Honolulu. On Kaua'i I had been accustomed to greeting each and every person I saw. It's because we were raised with the trail mentality. If you meet someone on the trail, you always say hello. So when I came to Honolulu I was walking down the sidewalk and saying hello to everybody I saw. And people were looking at me like I was crazy. So I had culture shock when I first came to Honolulu. But being called faggot ... It hurt sometimes. It does. But the thing is, I had been so conditioned to not let words like that bother me, that it really didn't. But I have to admit that sometimes I wanted to just slap people or punch someone in the mouth for being so small-minded....

Today I'm a college graduate. A four year graduate from the University of Hawai'i in Hawaiian Studies. Art and music were my concentration. I originally started off in college going for an early education degree, and I'm two credits short of graduating from that. But I changed my major to a Bachelor of Fine Arts. I decided I would do the dance and theater thing. Then I thought, "I don't need a degree in dancing. Let me change again." So I changed to Hawaiian Studies, which was an easy road for me because I had been brought up with all of that stuff. So after twelve years of being in the university system I got my BA in 1992. I was very happy; somebody like me actually made it through a four year college....

Hula and dance took me all over the world. Had it not been for another queen I knew, a family member whose name was Tiane Clifford, it wouldn't have happened. I was in a *hula* competition in Las Vegas that year, I think it was 1987, and I hadn't seen her for a long, long time. When I went out for that *hula* competition, she was there also, and she invited me to her room. When I came in I saw it was full of beautiful clothing and beautiful jewelry, and all her implements and prizes and trophies ... there was all this stuff surrounding her. She was lying in her bed and she said to me, *"Ti,* you see that thing over there hanging? Beautiful, isn't it? You want it? You should do *hula.* All of these things—they're all from *hula.* I go here, there, here, there, and all around the world teaching this and teaching that—*all through hula."*

So she encouraged me. She said, "If you want to travel the world, if you want to have these beautiful things, do the *hula."* That's when it clicked in my mind because I actually had somebody now who was giving me a focus and a direction to go in. That summer, a month later, she came home to Kaua'i, and brought me my first *ipuheke*—my first gourd drum. I composed my first chant on the day she gave it to me. And from that day on, I have only moved forward in the *hula.* I attribute all of my successes to her—she's like my spiritual guide, my *aumakua,* in the *hula.* I feel she is always with me.

She guided me back to my grand-aunt, for instance, who was a *kumu hula,* and I went to live with her. Both Tiane and my grand-aunt were the ones who insured that I would be doing *hula* for the rest of my life. Because they gave me the direction. They said, "You're going this way. Don't turn back for anything. Look ahead and just move forward." . . .

* * *

When I think about *mahus* and think back to my time as a child growing up in Hawaiian culture and learning the *hula,* we were always told that Laka, the goddess of the *hula,* was the god of the *hula.* The god or goddess of the *hula* was in male and female form. We were always told that. They never told us that Laka was *mahu.* They said that Laka had a male and female form in one. We never questioned. All our lives we were taught that Laka was male and female. Then when I got older I realized that must have meant that *Laka was mahu.* That was my introduction to Laka and how something in Hawaiian culture was *mahu,* and that was Laka. A god, goddess of the *hula* is like this.

I also heard stories of chiefs who slept with *aikane.* We were taught about our culture and they said that each of the chiefs had *aikane.* What is *aikane*? "*Ai kane*" means "to eat men" or "to have sexual relations." And each chief had an *aikane*—a man that they ate! I kept wondering what was going on. Later I found out that every chief always had a male lover. We were told that this was because women were believed to be *haumia,* or unclean. A man or a chief who slept with a woman of lower rank than him would lose *mana.* But if he slept with another man he wouldn't be affected. That's why, according to my *kupunas,* the chiefs had these male lovers. They were there to be with the chiefs as a friend and companion. In their time it was an accepted practice and actually bisexuality seemed the norm for most people in old Hawai'i. That's the way I look at it.

The place of *mahu* . . . You can read about *mahu* in certain books. But actually it's kind of unclear about *mahu* in the old days. But in certain stories and books you can read about them. . . . Like in this Hula Perspective book, this one anthropologist who went to the area where I live on Kaua'i wrote

of seeing a "hermaphrodite"—that's the word she used—teaching the *hula.* That particular hermaphrodite was named Ho'okano and came from where we lived. And according to what the old people tell me, that's what the *mahus* did. They were the keepers of the culture, they did the *hula,* and Laka herself was male/female, which is *mahu.*

In fact, we were told that all people are androgynous. All humans are born androgynous and as they grow up, a person's male or female side becomes stronger. But for *mahu,* both sides are strong. That's why when I think about *mahus,* I think of strong people. I think of soft people. I think of sweet, beautiful people. Stern people. But they're not weaklings. All the *mahus* from my family are strong—they can do everything. They can do everything that a male can do and everything that a female can do.

Oftentimes the line between male and female in ancient Hawai'i was very clear cut. But when you had certain ceremonies that required a male and a female . . . It was like in Elizabethan England in the old days, when males played the parts of the females in the dramas. That's what *mahus* did. They played the female roles in the dramas of ancient times and danced as females in the temples where only males could go. That's what my *kupunas* always told me: the *mahu* danced the parts of Pele and Haumeia and all of these goddesses to induce the goddesses' help and to appease the goddesses. Because the women could not go in certain temples. So *mahus* could play the role of the woman in these places because they were still male. Other people might not agree, but this is what my *kupunas* told me. My source of this information is my *kupunas,* who actually lived through and experienced those things.

If you go into Mo'oku'auhau genealogies, you'll come across people who are *mahu.* But being *mahu* didn't mean that they couldn't have sex with the opposite sex. Because they did. From what I've studied, it seemed that bisexualism was the norm. Hawaiians loved whomever loved them. They didn't have animosity towards any particular sex. If they felt *aloha* for somebody then they loved them. It carries on even today. You'd be surprised—even the most butchiest-looking guys still love queens. I don't know why, but its a part of the culture which still carries over today. Our role was to satisfy and please the chiefs. And that's how I feel. Even today I feel that's our role.

As far as *mahus* in the culture, I don't associate with being gay. I associate with being *mahu*. For me, the difference between being gay and *mahu* is that there is a place for me in my culture, in my society. There was a role which we once played and still play. So I believe in my culture; I'm an accepted and integral part of my culture. That's why I don't feel anything. Because I know I'm an integral part of my culture. It's necessary for me to be here. Whereas if you're gay, you're not part of society. You're not with the norm. You're an outcast, a "faggot." So I don't like to be labeled "gay." I'd rather be called *mahu* straight to my face. Being called gay is degrading to me. Because I've been called *mahu* my whole life. I don't feel part of the group which is labeled "gay" because culturally that group is not accepted. It's not loved—they are outcasts.

I think some of the *mahus* today still carry on their traditional roles, like in *hula*. A lot of *mahus* today are prominent in *hula*. A lot of them are prominent athletes as well. You'd be surprised. A lot of people don't think *mahus* are strong, but they were strong in the old days and they're still strong today. Some *mahus* that I know are the strongest in their family! They still maintain the strength and ability to do anything. They're working in all kinds of fields today. For instance, they're healers; I know a lot of *mahus* who are doing *lomilomi* massage.

When you talk about today, because we live in Western society, all the norms of that society have been imposed on us. A lot of the old thinking and old ways have gotten shoved under the rug. Because of the new thinking, *mahu* began to alienate themselves and were alienated by the rest of society. Thats why you get the gay and the straight today. We never had that in the olden days. We never had gay and straight. Everybody was bisexual, or more open. That's the difference today—because of assimilation into Western culture and Christianity, less *mahus* are willing to or want to show their true colors. They're finding it confusing and difficult to act out their role in society today. So they become drag queens, or go into prostitution—they go into all of those things that are stereotyped for *mahus*. And those are only stereotypes because *mahus* have much more to offer society as a whole. To bring beauty and sunshine and warmth and color and *culture* to the world. It all stems from that Western concept and the Christianity concept. That's the sad part to me, because when you talk about *mahus* and Hawaiian society, they were an integral part of the society. But in today's society they are considered a *detriment*.

Even in *hula* . . . I've held the title of Queen of Hula for a year, which is a contest for *mahus* in *hula*. It's overwhelming for people to accept that a *mahu* can be skillful in dancing. And for women to accept it . . . If a *mahu* walks into a crowd and she looks better than all the ladies there, they hate it. They are upset that a *mahu* can look better than them. Or you go to an area with all these guys, and one *mahu* can lift more than all those guys, a *mahu* can shoot a pig, clean it, cook it and all of that, and they cannot. So although I'm kind of assimilated into Western culture, I will remain a remnant of my culture forever. That's my role. I am *mahu*. I will do all the things that are culturally appropriate for me. And I don't feel any pain.

I choose to live as a woman today. I'm not sure if in ancient times all *mahus* did that. I'm sure they didn't. Because diversity is what made the culture thrive. I give the fullest to my culture when I can be myself by acting out the roles I am supposed to. For example, naming children. Doing all of the different things which traditionally were—and still are—for *mahu* to do. People come to me and ask me to name their children. That's what I'm here for, that's my role. I don't have any other purpose other than to act out my role. And if it's my role to be *mahu*, then it's my role. I accept it graciously. It's not an easy role to play. It's even more difficult because of Westernization and Christianity. It's harder to be in that role and feel comfortable. But I do it. A lot of people don't feel comfortable. They have a lot of fear. They're afraid of things like gay-bashing.

Nowadays it takes a lot of courage for *mahu* to be transgender. Walking down the street, knowing you've got something hanging between your legs. But you look like this. I keep telling people: "I can't change the way that I look. This is only my physical shell; I cannot change that. I have to live with the body that I have." I'm one of those who hasn't had any surgicals done—no implants, no hormones, no nothing.

I have a husband, the man I live with. I don't consider my husband gay. Society might, but I don't. I have three children. They are his natural children. I have raised them for ten years. I'm acting out and living in the role of a woman. I'm not their mother, but I'm their guide. I have guided them all these years. It's been a very difficult role for me to live in today. Not just for me, but for my children because they are subject to the whole gamut of emotions which I go through or I might have felt before because... you know how people are in society—we might be out together and people will give looks or snide remarks and the kids will pick it up. Or even now as they're getting older, they know what gay is, they've learned about that kind of stuff, and that it's *bad*. It's made out to be *evil*. It's made out to be such a horrible thing that for my kids—growing up and knowing that I'm like this, and that their father is sleeping with me—it's difficult. But I always have to remind them, "Who's buying your food? Who's loving you? Who's taking care of you? It's us. Those other people on the outside aren't doing anything for you. I'm doing my best for you." I try to assure them because a lot of times they feel bad.

The way I was brought up, when kids had things like events and games, we'd all go and give moral support. Whereas in this situation, I want to give moral support, but sometimes my giving moral support will actually inhibit or hurt my children's performance by making them feel ashamed. So I have to give in and say, "OK, I won't go to that, then." Which is sad. To me it's sad, sad, sad. It breaks my heart not to be able to give one of my children moral support because it might make him feel funny around his friends. It's not an easy situation. I don't

know of many queens or *mahus* around today who are in the kind of situation I am in... Most of the *mahus* I know are young and single and doing their own thing. But I have a stable family life, I have children to worry about. It's very different for me. I have people I have to worry about twenty-four hours a day. When you're a transgendered person it's something, I tell you!...

Actually, I have been more fortunate than a lot of people, beyond my wildest dreams, to have left Hawai'i and traveled. I've gone all over Asia, all over the South Pacific, and all over the United States, including Alaska, as a performer. I've also worked in museums as a conservator of items, of objects. I have training in that kind of specialized work. I'm not working in that field now, but I feel one day it will come into play, because that's another role of *mahus:* to maintain and nurture the culture and art of our people, of the Polynesian people. To *maintain* and to continue the cultural side of our people because if *mahus* don't do that... I guess we've got a lot of other people doing that as well, but the role of *mahus* is, to me, to maintain the art and culture connection in Hawai'i, so people from elsewhere can learn and be nurtured by that and be able to grow from our experience here in our homeland. Because when you look at Hawai'i as a whole and Hawai'i as a place, we Hawaiians don't own Hawai'i. We are just a part of this land that you see which is so beautiful. We are the ones that make the land come to life. We give it life... the flowers blossom and grow because of us. If we don't continue to practice our culture, as fragmented as it might be, then we will not have a culture to look back on.

I believe the reason we have this wonderful culture today is because of *mahus*. *Mahus* have been the ones in the forefront, standing up when nobody else was standing up, leading and fighting. I'm an activist [for Hawaiian sovereignty], too, so I've been on countless marches and demonstrations, both big and small. I've been at demonstrations where there were only five of us. But I'm yelling like five hundred. I'm not afraid. I don't care what anybody says. If I feel there's injustice, then there's injustice. I can play the games they want me to. I can do it the American way—I can go down to the legislature, I can do all of that crap, I can lobby, I can do all that stuff. But I choose to live in my culture. I choose to do culturally related activities.

I worked as a *hula* dancer in the tourist industry for years and years and years. I worked as a performer, a singer, dancer—I did it all. I was a fire-knife dancer, you name it. All the experiences I've had . . . I've stood on the Great Wall of China. I've been everywhere. So I always ask the queens today, "Why don't you come to *hula*? Because *hula* will fill your mind, fill your soul, your spirit. And if travel is in your blood, that's what it's going to do—it's going to take you around the world, like it's taken me. It's going to

take you to places that you never imagined existed. To the places in your dreams." That's how I try to encourage my students. Be in *hula*, and you're going to travel. You're going to learn. The gay community, the *mahu* community in Hawai'i is so small. And I am known for being in *hula*, I'm known for cultural things. I'm known not just in the *mahu* community, but also in the community at large, in the *hula* community. They know I'm *mahu*; I *want* them to know I'm *mahu*. I am *mahu*, and I am proud. What are you going to do? I cannot help how I look. I'm only enhancing what the Lord has given me. What the gods have given me, I just work with.

As I listened to my mother,[1] I recalled several experiences growing up within a bicultural Arab American

---

10 • *Nadine Naber*

ARAB AMERICAN FEMININITIES
Beyond Arab Virgin/American(ized) Whore

DISCUSSION QUESTIONS

1. How does Lulu's family's understanding of American culture and identity, Christianity, and Western feminism inform their conceptualization of her sexual identity?

2. How do the normative demands of middle-class American whiteness impact Lulu and her family?

3. What is Lulu's central marker of betrayal? Who maintains the cultural markers of her insider–outsider status?

4. What is the heterosexual imperative? How does this imperative reinforce the control over women's sexual and marriage practices in Arab and Western societies?

It was a typical weeknight at my parents' home. My father was asleep since he wakes up at 4:00 a.m. to open his convenience store in downtown San Francisco. I joined my mother on the couch and we searched for something interesting to watch on TV. My mother held the remote control, flipping through the stations. Station after station a similar picture of an Anglo American male and female holding one another in romantic or sexual ways appeared on the screen. As she flipped the station, my mother remarked, "Sleep, Slept...Sleep, Slept...THAT is America!" She continued, "Al sex al hum, zay shurb al mai [Sex for them is as easy as drinking water]."

—Nadine Naber, journal entry, December 2, 1999

familial and communal context. *Al Amenkan* (Americans) were often referred to in derogatory sexualized terms. It was the trash culture—degenerate, morally bankrupt, and not worth investing in. *Al Arab* (Arabs), on the other hand, were referred to positively and associated with Arab family values and hospitality. Similarly, throughout the period of my ethnographic research among middle-class Arab American family and community networks in San Francisco, California,[2] between January 1999 and August 2001, the theme of female sexuality circumscribed the ways my research participants imagined and contested culture, identity, and belonging. The theme of female sexuality tended to be utilized as part of some Arab immigrant families' selective assimilation strategy in which the preservation of Arab cultural identity and assimilation to American norms of "whiteness" were simultaneously desired. Within this strategy, the ideal of reproducing cultural identity was gendered and sexualized and disproportionately placed on daughters. A daughter's rejection of an idealized notion of Arab womanhood could signify cultural loss and thereby negate her potential as capital within this family strategy. In policing Arab American femininities, this family strategy deployed a cultural nationalist logic that represented the categories "Arab" and "American" in oppositional terms, such as "good Arab girls" vs. "bad American(ized) girls," or "Arab virgin" vs. "American(ized) whore." I coin the term Arab

cultural re-authenticity to contextualize this process within Arab histories of transnational migration, assimilation, and racialization. Arab cultural re-authenticity, I suggest, is a localized, spoken, and unspoken figure of an imagined "true" Arab culture that emerges as a reaction or an alternative to the universalizing tendencies of hegemonic U.S. nationalism, the pressures of assimilation, and the gendered racialization of Arab women and men. I use the term hegemonic (white) U.S. nationalism to refer to the official discourses of the U.S. state and corporate media and the notion of a universalized abstract American citizen that "at the same time systematically produces sexualized, gendered, and racialized bodies and particularistic claims for recognition and justice by minoritized groups."[3]...

It situates discussions on religious identity within the context of intersecting coordinates of power (race, class, nation, and so forth) and historical circumstances. Moreover, I do not present narratives as sites from which to universalize the experiences of all Arab American women, but to provide an opportunity to think beyond misperceptions and stereotypes. I locate myself in the context of multiple, contradictory loyalties, such as Arab daughter, sister, and cousin, anthropologist, researcher, community activist, and feminist. This location rendered me at once "insider" and "outsider," collaboratively and individually deconstructing, contesting, and often

---

Nadine Naber, "Arab American Femininities: Beyond Arab Virgin/American(ized) Whore."
Reprinted with the permission of the author.

reinforcing the cultural logics that circumscribed my research participants' identities.

This article focuses on the tense and often conflictual location of Arab American femininities at the intersections of two contradictory discourses: Arab cultural re-authenticity and hegemonic U.S. nationalism. I explore the ways that the theme of sexuality permeated many Arab immigrant families' engagements with the pressures of assimilation vis-à-vis a series of racial and cultural discourses on Arabness and Americanness. I argue that although my research participants (and their parents) perceived their cultural location within a binary of Arabness and Americanness, when lived and performed, this binary constantly broke down, particularly along the lines of race, class, gender, sexuality, religion, and nation. Yet binary terms for expressing the themes of family, gender, and sexuality persisted throughout my field sites as a discursive mechanism for explaining more complex processes that implicate my research participants and their parents within a desire for a stereotypical "Americanization" that is predicated on "Arabness" as the crucial Other. A binary cultural logic of "us" and "them" that was gendered and sexualized was then a discursive reaction to the complex dichotomies of hegemonic U.S. nationalism that at once pressure racialized immigrants to assimilate into a whitened middle-class U.S. national identity while positioning them outside the boundaries of "Americanness." Both generations were mutually invested in expressing the two racial-ethnic-national categories (Arab and American) in dichotomous terms because it provided a discursive mechanism for engaging with the processes of immigration and assimilation in which Arabness and Americanness absolutely depend on each other to exist—as opposites and in unison....

This article, then, is not an analysis of *all* second-generation Arab Americans, but of how locational conditions (especially when it comes to racialized, gendered, class, and religious identities) mediate and break down an imagined "Arab" identity in the context of the San Francisco Bay area of California. It is an exploration of how binary oppositions within Arab American discourses on gender and sexuality take on particular form among my research participants, a group of educated, middle-class, young women active in progressive Arab, Arab feminist, and/or queer Arab political movements whose parents are ethnic entrepreneurs and immigrated, or were displaced, to the San Francisco Bay area—a traditionally liberal, racially/ethnically diverse location.... I argue that the phenomena of intersectionality cannot be generalized as taking one singular form for all Arab Americans; that one must be cautious about using the terms "Arab American" or "Arab American women" in a U.S. national sense; and that feminist theory and practice vis-à-vis Arab American communities should take the specific ways that the coordinates of race, class, gender, sexuality, religion, and nation intersect in different contexts seriously. For example, perhaps part of the motivation behind the policing of an Arab daughter's behavior among middle-class business entrepreneurs invested in economic mobility and the selective reproduction of patriarchal cultural ideals is that San Francisco is home to some of the most vibrant progressive Arab, queer Arab, Arab feminist, and Arab student movements alongside some of the most vibrant civil rights, racial justice, feminist, and queer movements in the nation. In the San Francisco Bay area, multiracial coalition building, transgressive sexual politics, and critiques of classism, capitalism, U.S.-led imperialism, and war heavily inspire young people, such as my research participants, who are either active in or loyal to progressive politics.

Among my research participants, the performativity of an idealized "true" Arab culture emerged in the context of "regulatory ideals" that they associated with "being Arab" and distinguished from the regulatory ideals of "being American," such as: knowing what is *abe* (shameful); knowing how to give *mujamalat* (flattery); knowing what you're supposed to do when someone greets you; drinking *shai* (tea) or coffee; talking about politics "sooo" much; getting up for an older person; respecting your elders; looking after your parents and taking care of them; judging people according to what family they are from; marrying through connections; gossiping and having a good reputation.[4]

Articulations of "selfhood" among my research participants were key sites where the oppositional logic of self/Other, us/them, Arab/American was reproduced among my research participants. Selfhood was often articulated in terms of a choice between "being an individual, being my own person, being an American," or "being connected, having family, and being 'Arab.'" Yet what ultimately distinguished "us" from "them," or *Al Arab* from *Al Amerikan,* among my research participants was a reiterated set of norms that were sexualized, gender specific, and performed in utterances such as *"banatna ma bitlaau fil lail"* (our girls don't stay out at night). Positioning the feminized subjectivities within my field sites in between the binary oppositions of good Arab daughter vs. bad American(ized) daughter, or Arab virgin vs. American(ized) whore, the discourse of Arab cultural re-authenticity reproduced a masculinist cultural nationalist assumption that if a daughter chooses to betray the regulatory demands of an idealized Arab womanhood, an imagined Arab community loses itself to the *Amerikan.* Jumana, recalling her parents' reinforcement of this distinction while she was growing up, explains,

> My parents thought that being American was spending the night at a friend's house, wearing shorts, the guy-girl thing, wearing make-up, reading teen magazines, having pictures of guys in my room. My parents used to tell me, "If you go to an American's house, they're smoking, drinking...they offer you this and that. But if you go to an Arab house, you don't see as much of that. *Bi hafzu 'ala al banat* [They watch over their daughters].

My research participants generally agreed that virginity, followed by heterosexual (ethno-religious) endogamous marriage were the key demands of an idealized Arab womanhood that together, constituted the yardstick that policed female subjectivities in cultural nationalist terms. Here, discourses around Arab American femininities allow for a cultural, versus territorial, nationalist male Arab American perspective within the United States that emerges in opposition to hegemonic (white) U.S. nationalism and in the context of immigrant

nostalgia. Here, an imagined notion of "Arab people" or an "Arab community" is inspired, in part, by a collective memory of immigrant displacement and romantic memories of "home" and "homeland culture." Among middle-class familial and communal networks in San Francisco, Arab American cultural nationalism was expressed in terms of an imagined Arab community or people that constituted "woman" as virgin or mother vis-à-vis an extended family context. Among Arab American cultural authorities in San Francisco, the ideal of marrying within one's kin group within the discourse of Arab cultural re-authenticity was refashioned in terms of marrying within the kin groups' religious group (Muslim or Christian); village of origin (Ramallah, Al Salt), economic class, national (Jordanian, Lebanese, Palestinian, or Syrian), or racialized/ethnic (Arab) group. These categories were hierarchical, as "religious affiliation" tended to supersede "national origin" and "national origin" superseded "racial/ethnicity identity" as the boundary to be protected through a daughter's marriage. Although the regulatory demands of Arab womanhood were often framed as an alternative to assimilation and Americanization, the cultural discourses that controlled a daughter's marriageability simultaneously enabled a family strategy of assimilation to an appropriate American norm of whiteness that privileges heterosexual marriage—within particular boundaries of race and class—as capital.

The following...narrative emphasizes intersections of religion and sexuality....

THE HETEROSEXUAL IMPERATIVE

Waiting for a friend at Café Macondo, in San Francisco's Mission district, graffiti reading QUEER ARABS EXIST caught my attention. Later, in conversations among Arab women activists, I learned that the graffiti artist was a Syrian American woman named Lulu. Lulu was also the coproducer of a special issue of *Bint Al Nas* on the theme of "sexuality." *Bint Al Nas* is a cyber magazine and network for queer Arab women and as part of this issue, Lulu designed the web art,

"Virgin/Whore," where a collage representing herself as "virgin" (represented by drums, pita bread, camels, Allah, a Syrian flag, and a photograph of her family members wearing blindfolds) transforms into a second collage representing her as "whore" (represented by images of dildos next to her girlfriend's name written in Arabic, handcuffs, a blurred image of the picture that represents her parents, and a photo of Madonna). A few months later, Lulu and I made plans to meet at Café Flor, a queer hang out in the Castro district of San Francisco. I recognized Lulu from the tattoo of her girlfriend's name Amina in Arabic script on her arm and the Palestinian flag sewn onto her book bag. We talked about the collage and she explained, "What I am doing with the two images is showing how they are dichotomous, or at least they have felt that way, and how really, it has been an either/or situation. Also, I think it's how my mother would see my sexuality: dirty, sinful, dark. The reason for the roll over of images is to show that the two states can't coexist."

—Naber, journal entry, December 28, 2000

EXCERPTS FROM LULU'S ORAL HISTORY: *I grew up with this all the time: "Sex is an act of love in marriage. If you're not a virgin when you get married, you're in trouble." I fought that all the time. I would ask my mom about Syria. I would say, "If good Arab women are not having sex and Arab men can have sex, then who were the Arab men having sex with?" She would answer, "The Christian women." So the Christian women were the whores. That is very prevalent in my family, the Muslim virgin and the Christian whore. The whore is either American or Christian.*

My family is unique because we talked about sex. My sister was really vocal about having boyfriends and they were always black, which was even more of a problem. My parents are into the idea that Arabs are white. I think it's more of a Syrian–Lebanese thing. But I didn't have the same problems with my parents about boyfriends as my sister because I knew I was queer since I was thirteen or fourteen. It was when I came out when things erupted for me. It got to the point where they were asking, "Don't you want to have a boyfriend?"

My mom won't come visit me at my house because she doesn't want to see that I live with a woman. The bottom line is premarital sex. Lesbian sex doesn't happen because Arab girls don't have premarital sex. When I came out, it was like, "That's fine that you're gay—but don't act on it. We don't want you having sex." Everyday I heard, "Get married with a guy and…" suppress it basically. I said, "I can't do that." And I still get that… "We (Arabs) don't do that"… or "You're the only gay Arab in the world."

It became this thing that everyone was going to fix me. My uncles would come and take me out to lunch. They would say, "Let's talk. This doesn't happen in our culture. You've been brainwashed by Americans. You've taken too many feminist classes, you joined NOW, you hate men, you have a backlash against men…." It was like…"This is what this American society has done to our daughter."

When that was the reaction I received, I totally disassociated myself from Arabs. I felt I couldn't be gay and Arab. I felt that either I have to go home and be straight or be totally out and pass as white. But later, I got a lot of support from queer Arab networks.

One of the first people I met was Samah. She was doing some research and asked if she could interview me. I did it and we both cried. Then I went to a queer Arab women's gathering. I was the youngest one and everyone knew that I came out a week after I turned eighteen and was kicked out by my parents four months later. I was the baby. They all supported me. Over the years, they've become my family.

Now my mom tells me. "Just go have sex with a man—maybe you'll change," and I say, "Maybe you should try it with a woman." She keeps finding ways to say I'm too Americanized…and when I tell her, "You don't know how many queer Arabs I know." She says, "They're American, they're American born, they're not Arab…" or "They must be Christian" or "Their fathers must not be around because no father would accept his daughter being gay."

They blamed Western feminism and said I should go to a therapist. Then they changed their mind and said not to go because they don't want it on my hospital records that I am gay—because "You know," they would say, "After you change—someone might see on your hospital records that you were gay." Their idea was that they didn't want anyone finding out "after I change" and "once I get married," that I had this dark past. Then at the very end they did try to send me to a hospital. That was when the shit hit the fan, our big final fight. I was so strong in defending myself—and they thought that too was very American. So it became this thing of like—and they make it very clear—"You chose your sexuality over us. Sex is more important than your family." Which goes back to the tight-knit family Arab thing. It's all about group dynamics.

When Lulu's mother replaces the "American whore" with the "Christian Arab" she reveals the gaps and fissures within the idea of a unified Arab American nationalist identity and the ways that Arab cultural re-authenticity shifts depending on sociohistorical circumstances. Lulu's mother's association of the category "Syrian Christian" with the classification "Westernized Other" signifies the ways that the categories "Islam" and "Arabness" have often been conflated throughout Arab history and in several cases, juxtaposed against the notion of a Christian West. According to her mother, the Syrian–Muslim self is to be protected from the corrupted, Westernized, Syrian–Christian Other.

Intersections between national origin and racial identification in Lulu's narrative further complicate Arab cultural identity in the United States. Lulu, in remembering why her parents did not accept her sister's black boyfriends, explains that identifying as white is "a Syrian–Lebanese thing." The Syrian–Lebanese distinction is common within hegemonic Arab American discourses in San Francisco. Many of my research participants agree that Syrian and Lebanese Arab Americans have had more access to the privileges of middle-class whiteness compared to other Arab Americans.[5] Steering Lulu's sister away from the racial Other, Lulu's mother, like Rime's father, secures a white middle-class positionality. Yet when it comes to Lulu's sexuality, the association of Syrians with whiteness is quickly disrupted as a

sexualized, cultural, nationalist logic disassociates them as "Arabs" from the loose, sexually immoral American "feminist" Other in the name of controlling Lulu's sexuality. In Lulu's narrative, then, the *Al Arab/Al Amerikan* boundary is permeable and shifting. As Lulu explains, her parents uphold the normative demands of middle-class American whiteness to tame her sister's sexuality while they distinguish themselves from *Al Amerikan* when it comes to taming Lulu's behaviors.

Fissures in Arab cultural re-authenticity also emerge when Lulu's mother suggests that Lulu "try sex with a man." In the case of Lulu's queer identity, a heterosexual imperative becomes a more significant symbol of the Arab virgin/American whore boundary than the "virginity" ideal. Gloria Anzaldúa writes, "For the lesbian of color, the ultimate rebellion she can make against her native culture is through her sexual behavior. She goes against two moral prohibitions: sexuality and homosexuality."[6] Lulu's queerness, the central marker of her betrayal, underwrites her marginalization as traitor-outsider-American by cultural authorities such as her mother, her father, and her uncle. The extent to which she is seen as "unacceptable, faulty, damaged," culminate in her family's attempt to send her to a hospital to fix her so that she might return "straight" home. Here, the stance of their conservativism is made possible by their inculcation and reproduction of white American middle-class norms, such as "therapy," within the discourse of Arab cultural re-authenticity. Lulu's parents thus reinforce a particular kind of assimilation constituted by the ways that Arabness and Americanness operate both as opposites and in unison in the policing of Arab American femininities throughout my field sites.

In overriding the virginity ideal with the heterosexual imperative, Lulu's mother reinforces the control over women's sexual and marriage practices that underlie the heterosexual conjugal ideal in Arab and Western societies. Yet beyond reinforcing a heterosexual imperative, Lulu's mother is also reinforcing family ideals critically inherited from Arab homelands that are not only conjugal, but include extended kin that are inscribed beyond household or nuclear terms.

In attempting to reinstate Lulu's heterosexuality, Lulu's mother seeks to protect Lulu's father's honor as well as the family honor of her nuclear and her extended family. Moreover, the intervention of Lulu's uncle can be interpreted in terms of the refashioning of a patrilineal ideal in the diaspora, in which males and elders remain responsible for female lineage members (even after marriage) and men are responsible for providing for their families, which includes their current wives and underage children and may include aged parents, unmarried sisters, younger brothers, and the orphaned children of their brothers.[7]

As a form of political critique directed against patriarchy and patrilineality, Lulu's chosen family is a sign of her resistance. In the act of choosing her family, Lulu challenges Arab and Anglo-European ideologies that read blood and heterosexual marriage ties as the key foundation of kinship, demonstrating that all families are contextually defined. In undermining the association of kinship with biology, Lulu overtly performs the social, ideological, political, and historical constructedness of kinship. Yet when she meets Samah and joins queer Arab e-mail lists, Lulu finds an alternative to the Arab/American split in the coming together of what she understood to be her "queer" and her "Arab" identities. Lulu's insistence that QUEER ARABS EXIST is an act in resisting racism, homophobia, and patriarchy on multiple fronts: it undermines the Arab virgin/American (ized) whore that seeks to control women's sexuality by marking women who transgress the heterosexual imperative of Arab cultural authenticity as "American" and it disrupts the dualistic logic of hegemonic U.S. nationalist discourses that homogenize and subordinate Arab women as either veiled victims of misogynist terrorist Arab men or exotic erotic objects accessible to white/Western male heroes. Yet cultural identity, for Lulu, is more than "separate pieces merely coming together"—it is a site of tension, pain, and alienation that is constantly in motion.

Lulu's narrative signifies the critical inheritance of the polarization between Muslim and Christian Arabs from the homeland(s) to Arab San Francisco. It exemplifies the ways that this polarization took on local form among many bourgeois Arab American Muslims with whom I interacted. Throughout my field sites, hegemonic Arab Muslim discourses often privileged Arab Muslim women as the essence of cultural re-authenticity—as opposed to Arab Christian women who were often represented as promiscuous and therefore, "Americanized." Yet although cultural authorities often deployed religion as a framework for policing feminized subjectivities throughout my field sites, religious background alone did not determine the extent to which my research participants upheld, reconfigured, or transgressed the feminized imperatives of Arab cultural re-authenticity. My research participants who transgressed "good girl" behaviors through dating before marriage, interracial, and/or same-sex relationships were religiously diverse. In addition, religious affiliation alone did not determine the extent to which parents, aunts, or uncles circumscribed their daughters' behaviors and identities.

While Lulu explained that her mother deployed her Muslim identity to reinforce the normative demands of virginity, her parents' self-identification as "white" complexified their understanding of a "normative femininity." In addition, Lulu stated that her mother deployed a pan-ethnic "Arab" identity when she asked her to suppress her lesbian identity. Thus, while the discourse of the "Muslim virgin" and the "Christian whore" policed Lulu's femininity, the "virgin/whore" dichotomy was also constituted by a series of intersecting and contradictory discourses such as white versus non-white, Arab versus American. The ways that these discourses operated to police femininities depended on the different ways that coordinates of race, class, gender, sexuality, religion, and nation intersected in each of my research participants' lives. . . .

CONCLUSION

Walking down the street between one of San Francisco's largest populations of homeless women and men and the new dot-com yuppies, I did my usual skim of graffiti on Café Macondo's walls. The

"FOR" in LESBIANS FOR BUSH had been crossed out and replaced with the word "EAT." As I turned to the wall behind me to find out whether QUEER ARABS still EXIST[ed], my eyes followed an arrow, drawn in thick black marker that pointed to the words QUEER ARABS and was connected to the words, ONE OF MANY PROBLEMS.

Looking closer, I noticed another message superimposed over QUEER ARABS EXIST in faint blue ink. A line was drawn between the words QUEER and ARABS and the letter "S" was added to the beginning of the word "EXIST." I re-read it several times before I finally understood that superimposed upon QUEER ARABS EXIST, the new message, in coupling the words ARABS and SEXIST, implied that ARABS are SEXIST. I thought about my research and the resemblance between the images on the wall and my research participants' everyday experiences. While Lulu's graffiti confronted the lumping of Arabs into the homogeneous categories "veiled victim" or "polygamous terrorist," the defacement of QUEER ARABS EXIST reinforced the binary construction of "the Arab" as Other. Similarly, while Rime, Lulu, and Nicole burst the boundaries of hegemonic Arab American and U.S. nationalisms on multiple fronts, they also rearticulate hegemonic nationalisms in binary terms as a coding for a more complex process in which the categories "Arab" and "American" are mutually constitutive and exist both as opposites and in unison, in the context of immigration, assimilation, and racialization.

As I took another glance at ARABS ARE SEXIST, superimposed over QUEER ARABS EXIST, I noticed another message, a much smaller message written in black letters in Spanish and English that framed the top right side of QUEER ARABS EXIST. It read ES ALGO BUENO. IT'S A GOOD THING.

—Naber, journal entry, June 2001

NOTES

I am grateful to Suad Joseph, Kent Ono, Ella Maria Ray, Martina Reiker, Minoo Moallem, Andrea Smith, Rabab Abdulhadi, and Evelyn Alsultany for providing me with invaluable feedback and support while I was developing this article. I would like to especially thank the editorial board members of *Feminist Studies* and the anonymous readers for their constructive suggestions and the immense time and effort they committed to seeing this article in publication. I am indebted to each and every person who participated in this project and I am grateful to Eman Desouky, Lilan Boctor, my mother, Firyal Naber, and my father, Suleiman Naber for their persistent support and encouragement throughout the period of my field research.

1. This is not a literal translation, but conveys the message of my mother's words. Throughout the rest of this article, I have edited my research participants' quotes into a readable form, maintaining the originality of the quote as much as possible. This process included cutting repetitive words and statements, rearranging the order of the narratives, and simplifying elaborate explanations. I have also altered names and places in order to protect my research participants' privacy.

2. These networks included local chapters of the American Arab Anti-Discrimination Committee, the Arab Women's Solidarity Association, the Muslim Students' Association, Students for Justice in Palestine, and the Arab Cultural Center.

3. Minoo Moallem and Ian Boal, "Multicultural Nationalism and the Poetics of Inauguration," in *Between Woman and Nation. Nationalisms. Transnational Feminism, and the State.* ed. Caren Kaplan, Norma Alarcon, and Minoo Moallem (Durham, N.C.: Duke University Press, 1999), 243–64.

4. Here, I use terms that were reiterated among my research participants to illustrate the ways that my research participants regularly associated "Americanness" with freedom and individualism and "Arabness" with family and connectivity.

5. Throughout my field sites, Palestinian and Jordanian Arab Americans tended to view Syrian and Lebanese Arab Americans as more "assimilated" than themselves. Several factors have produced this "difference." Historically, Syrian and Lebanese emigrated to the San Francisco Bay area in the early 1900s, before Palestinians and Jordanians, who first immigrated in the late 1950s.

6. Gloria Anzaldúa, *Borderlands: La Frontera* (San Francisco: Aunt Lute Books, 1987), 17.

7. Here, I build on Suad Joseph's definition of patrilineality in Arab families in "Gendering Citizenship in the Middle East," in *Gender and Citizenship in the Middle East,* ed. Suad Joseph (New York: Syracuse University Press, 2000), 3–32.

11 • *Marisa Navarro*

BECOMING *LA MUJER*

DISCUSSION QUESTIONS

1. In what ways is Navarro's article related to Naber's—especially considering the construction of race, female sexuality as whore or virgin, and the relationship to socioeconomic status?
2. Why and how do the hegemonic constructions of female sexuality vary according to membership in a particular racial category?
3. Navarro conceptualizes her body as a "battleground." What does this metaphor serve and how does it relate to contemporary feminist politics—and even contemporary politics of war?

I used to dream that Superwoman would fly into my life, her legs unshaven and her hair cropped short. She would swoop me up and take me somewhere that made me feel safe and beautiful—a place far from the hell I knew as public high school. In this distant place, I would feel sensual for the first time ever, without feeling dirty. No one would assume I was destined to be a teenage mom, or that my brown skin marked me as a criminal. I wouldn't be "too dark" or "too fat," and my intelligence would never be compromised.

Those were ambitious goals for a Mexican-American girl growing up near East Los Angeles. Every year, the drill team girl had a kid, then the prom queen. Pregnancy was so common it was almost a game to guess who the next teenage mother would be. Still, East L.A. is the only place I've lived where the scent of Aqua Net and overprocessed hair mingles with the sounds of English, Spanish, Chinese, Korean and Armenian. There was comfort in being surrounded by hundreds of other brown people. I missed that when

I went away to college and found my skin color and dark hair made me stand out in class.

I was one of the fortunate at my high school, shielded from some of Los Angeles's harshness by college prep classes. My parents stressed education all my life, so I focused on earning good grades, hoping they would be my ticket to a better life. But there was a price to pay. Since many of my female classmates wouldn't make it to graduation (pregnancy or lack of interest leading them to drop out), girls' actions became dichotomized into right and wrong. There were "good girls" (those who went to college) and "bad girls" (teenage mothers on welfare).

Early on, my parents reinforced that message, and there could be no margin of error. "It's out of love we tell you this, *mijita*," they'd say. "Be quiet. Study hard. Don't have sex. Go to college, and then get married. A good daughter doesn't dress like a slut. A good daughter doesn't pierce or tattoo herself. A good daughter doesn't rock the boat." If I

---

messed up, my whole future would be over. I must be a good *hijita*.

My parents also grew up in East L.A. I never told them what I faced at school, but I'm sure they knew. That made the parental leash even tighter. As an immigrant (my dad) and a first-generation American (my mom), they stressed hard work and success at any cost. It's a drive I don't think any person who is fourth-generation American or beyond can fully understand. Perhaps it's the stigma of the accent fresh in the memory, the blunter racism and the hard labor not even a distant memory. Either way, it fuels parents' determination that their children will not be like them.

In my family, being a good *hijita* meant more than simply being an obedient daughter. It also meant being desexualized. Being of mind but not of body. Wrapped in that word were my parents hopes for me—and for themselves. I was to transcend the racism they'd experienced and to surpass society's low expectations.

My father was the success story in the family, and he was proud of it. He came from a small town in Mexico, graduated from college in the United States and made lots of money. Somehow, my sister and I had to do even better than he had. On top of being supernaturally smart, we had to fulfill his macho idea of sensuality, a classic Madonna/whore tightrope that demanded we be attractive yet pure. We were expected to be skinny, have long hair and wear clothes that showed our womanliness. Yet, we had to carry this off in a way that let men know we were unavailable for sex.

Sex was the biggest threat to my parents' carefully laid plans. Having sex meant I'd impede my chances to succeed, to achieve an American dream greater than the one offered to my parents. It meant I'd inevitably get pregnant and become a statistic, trapped in a community that was slowly falling apart. My body (and what I did with it) could make or break our family's future. The concept of the body as a battleground had much more meaning than even the most radical feminist could conceive. I needed only to keep my legs tightly locked, and everything would be all right.

Eventually, the word *hijita* left a sour taste in my mouth. It meant I was my parents' daughter. I didn't belong to me.

When I hit puberty, my father took on a form of desexualization with me and my sister. Boys were not humans, but the makers of sperm, waiting to plant their seed in us. For some reason my father saw me as extra fertile ground that he was determined be kept fallow. The only way to accomplish this was to forbid boys into the house and into my social life. If a boy called, I was questioned about his intentions. My father would bend down, squint and stare into my eyes to make sure I wasn't lying.

To further the desexualization process, he inspected me before I went out. If I wore lipstick or a tight shirt that showed my breasts, I was criticized and called a slut. I tried being the dutiful, plain daughter, but still I lost. When I cut off my hair and started wearing baggy pants to avoid his scrutiny, my father called me a boy. Where was this invisible line that would win his acceptance? What did it take to be a good *hijita*?

Since I couldn't figure that out, I looked to my older sister. My father always had a special fondness for her. I think it was because she was just so smart—smarter than all the white kids. In high school, she defied him by experimenting with sexuality, sensuality and love. She proved she could be smart and sensual and have neither quality compromised. As an intelligent woman, she was unhappy learning about science and literature while knowing nothing about her body. She innocently assumed our father would be okay with this, since it didn't affect her grades.

Instead, he became enraged. Didn't she know that sex led to pregnancy and pregnancy led to welfare, which led to family dishonor? Although my sister didn't agree with his linear thinking, she was powerless to convince him otherwise. He would not have it. My sister became a bad *hijita* and was kicked out of the house. This terrified me; maybe *la familia* wasn't really about unconditional love after all. And if my sister and my father shared a special relationship that I would never have, what would happen to me if I did the same thing? I was too scared to find out.

I played out my teenage years like a script. More than anything, I felt I dressed in drag throughout high school, wearing clothes that would get boys to look at me, but only with vague interest. Avoiding male attention consumed my thoughts so much that men were all I thought about.

In the end, they won. I was constantly concerned that my outfits were too sensual. I had a hard time looking at my face in the mirror, much less the rest of my body. Everything was wrong with me. Caught in a paradox, I was always dissatisfied. I hated that men were attracted to me, but I also hated that I didn't have big breasts or a thinner waistline. No guy wanted a fat, small-chested girl.

I lost all sense of ownership and control over my physical self. My memories of that script are vivid, too easy to relive:

Act I: First Year—(Sur)Real World 101

My math teacher walks around the room and then stops and leans his back against mine so that my head and breasts are flattened against the desk. Two boys sitting next to me laugh. I put my head down and silently swear that I'll stick quadratic equations up his ass. Eventually, I stop paying attention in class and drop from an A to barely a B. I chalk it up to the fact that I always hated math.

Act II: Sophomore Year—Boys Will Be Boys

A boy likes me and decides to show it by grabbing me every day. He does it when my back is facing him and I'm trying to be taken seriously. In the beginning, I yell that he's a fuckin' dick/asshole/no good motherfucker. He smiles and grabs me again. Eventually, I stop reacting, hoping he'll go away if I don't pay attention to his games. He assumes that means I like it and grabs me even more. Sometimes I think I should fuck him to get it over with, because that's all he really wants. Maybe afterward he'll leave me alone. But I don't. Not because I love myself enough not to fuck an asshole, but because the thought of someone seeing me naked is terrifying.

Act III: Junior Year—Honk If You're Horny

Trying to walk down the street with my head up has become the most political act of my teenage life. I dread major roads and busy intersections because men yell at me or stick out their tongues like deranged lizards. I hate how all they see is long hair and breasts, and how with each honk they take a piece of my self-esteem with them. These are the kind of men that stick silhouettes of women with big tits and tiny waists on their cars. These are the kind of men who smell estrogen and think fuck. I start to hate everything that makes me look like a woman—the breasts, the hips, the long hair—because I'm getting lots of attention, but no self-esteem.

Act IV: Senior Year—Stand by Your Man

By now I hate myself for turning men on, for being a "slut." All I want is for someone to love me for my mind. I'm tired of having my body picked apart by my father, being a virgin but made to feel like a whore. I figure since I'm already dirty, having sex won't make it any worse.

In bed, the boy I'm dating pulls my hair and pretends to slap me to make his dick harder. He calls me a slut and a ho'. I lie flat as a board, confused, scared and sexually unfulfilled. I let him fuck me without a condom, without birth control pills, nothing. My body is too dirty to be worth protecting against AIDS or pregnancy. Everything the men on the street and my father told me seems true.

One day the boy laughs and says that the first time he saw me, he thought I looked ugly because my skin was dark. He doesn't want to take me to the beach or lie down in the park because I could get tan again. Another time, he tells me to shut up because I sound "too Mexican." What race does he think I am? I ask. He smiles, caresses my face and tells me he doesn't like to think of me as Mexican. He means it as a compliment. At eighteen, I think if this is love, then maybe I was meant to be alone in the world after all.

Act V: Pomp and Circumstance

The most beautiful song I've ever heard. I collect my diploma like a trophy of war and run far away.

I left Los Angeles for Smith College in Northampton, Massachusetts, knowing the distance of a thousand miles had to release the parental leash. I wanted the power to create my identity, a power that I didn't have before. I purposely chose a women's college because I knew I needed time away from men.

School saved my mind and body. In college, I wasn't anyone's *hijita*, and I wouldn't be anyone's slut. I was able to come out of the closet, first to myself and a year later to everyone else. Women told me I was smart and beautiful; neither quality was ever questioned. When I took up smoking and drinking, I wasn't a bad *hijita.* Good and bad vanished, and I was *la mujer.* That phrase sounded beautiful and empowering to me.

At school I met many different types of women who were smart and proud of their bodies. I had a friend who fought boys. One time she was flyering a concert about a group's homophobic lyrics, and a man shouted "dyke" at her. She grabbed a pool stick, chased him down and threatened to show him "what a real dyke can do." The guy was so dumbfounded that a woman wasn't going to put her head down and take his shit that he hid underneath a pool table and waited for others to calm her down. I met many women who felt comfortable wearing dresses and grabbing their crotches in public. Others recited Marx to their lovers as they prepared to make passionate love.

I thought racing to be a part of the queer community would save me. I enlisted in the dyke world complete with uniform—short hair, overalls, cap on backwards and body piercings. As an extra buffer, I gained twenty-five pounds to make sure men wouldn't be interested in me, and to make sure I didn't have the body of a "slut." I walked down the street with pride, knowing that men no longer honked at me. I was undesirable. There was power in that for me. I thought I was screwing the patriarchy, subverting the status quo of femininity.

I didn't realize, however, that I was still blaming myself. At twenty, I had only run away from my problems and never dealt with them. I still felt as if my body was dirty and shameful. I still believed that the unwanted sexual attention I got in high school had been my fault—as though I'd "asked for it" by trying to fit a narrow prescription of femininity.

Soon, I found myself trying to follow the status quo of a different community, complete with confining norms and stereotypes. Now, instead of wanting to be a good *hijita,* I found myself trying to be a good queer girl and a good feminist. The role was just as confining. The feminist and gay communities still had a white/classist/racist framework—one which did nothing to address the multiple-identity dilemmas that came along with being a queer Latina feminist.

When I looked in the mirror, I felt just as much in drag as I had in high school. Finally, after twenty-one years of confusion, I realized I could be happy only when I defined my own idea of beauty and sensuality. My identity had too many layers for me to wrap it into a convenient package. The most political statement I could make was to look the way I wanted and not be ashamed of it. Today, my closet reflects my philosophy with a feather boa, tuxedo shirt, overalls and platforms all peacefully cohabiting. Such nonsensical words as *butch, femme* and *drag* have disappeared from my vocabulary and my fashion style.

And naked, I'm just as sensual. I can look at myself and not feel ashamed anymore. Sure, I have stretch marks all over my ass, scars all over my body, and my breasts are lopsided. But that's what being a real *mujer* is all about. Real *mujeres* live life intensely—and their bodies show it. They feast on food, drink with revelry and play hard. I look forward to watching my body develop more, to becoming more curvaceous. I'm ready for anything that happens, whether it's cellulite or muscle definition.

Now that I wear whatever I like, I feel sensual. I can go to a club and let the beat lead my hips. That's what I like best about dancing. My mind doesn't think. The rhythms dictate how my hips will sway, how my whole body moves. I don't care if men or women are looking. My sensuality is for me.

I need to discover how my body can move. I need to know me before anyone else can. I thought if I reached this epiphany and expressed my sexuality with freedom, that men would see me as a target. I was wrong. It wasn't my body that made men yell and grab me. It was them.

And, in some ways, I have little power to change that. I can't single-handedly overturn messages telling men that women are sex objects. I can't uproot myths casting women of color as wild and sexually available. I also understand my parents' mistakes. Instead of shielding me from boys and sex, they should have prepared me for what I would come to expect. Instead of "protecting" me by teaching me body hatred, they should have taught me to cherish myself. Had I been proud of my body, I may not have let street harassers bring me down so low. I wouldn't have risked my life sleeping with assholes. I would have known how to defend myself.

I accept this now and fight to unlearn twenty-one years of conditioning. So far, I'm doing pretty well. Without realizing it, I've developed a new body language. When I walked with my head down, men picked up on my powerlessness. I believe that my confident new stride actually scares some of those assholes away. Once in a while, I get catcalls, but now those men are sure to get flipped off, barked at or blown a kiss. I realize why my friend is willing to fight boys, and ultimately, I would fight a man. I spent so many years feeling ashamed of my body that rolling in the dirt might make me feel cleaner.

In the end, no Superfeminist ever flew in from the sky to save me. It took me years to realize that nobody else could rescue me. I didn't have to be a superhero. I just had to allow myself to become *la mujer*.

---

12 • *Kate Harding*

HOW DO YOU FUCK A FAT WOMAN?

DISCUSSION QUESTIONS

1. What forms of violence manifest against women who are socially constructed as "fat" in Harding's account?
2. What roles do "cognitive dissonance" and "body image" play in shaping notions of sexual identity, desirability, attraction, and love?
3. How do constant messages of diet fads, gym memberships, and body-mass-index measures, among other things, frame notions of "chubby," "fat" and "obese" as an individual problem as opposed to a structural system that constructs beauty and body ideals?

You should consider yourself lucky that some man finds a hideous troll like yourself rape-able.

That's an actual comment left on the blog of a friend of mine, in response to a post she wrote about being raped and nearly killed. Every feminist blogger with more than four readers has dealt with comments along these lines. There are certain people who feel it's their sacred duty to inform us, again and again, that *rape is a compliment*. (Or, more precisely, "Rape is a compliment, you stupid whore.") Rape is not a violent crime meant to control and dehumanize the victim, see; it's evidence that you were just so ding-dang attractive to some perfectly average guy, he couldn't stop himself from fucking you, against your will, right then and there! He thought you were pretty! Why are you so upset?

All in a day's work for a feminist blogger, sadly— and when you're a *fat* feminist blogger, it comes with a special bonus message: No one *but* a rapist would ever, ever want you. In this iteration of the "rape is a compliment" construct, our hypothetical rapist is no longer a perfectly average guy—because perfectly average guys aren't driven to sexual incontinence by fat chicks. I mean, *duh*. No, the guy who would rape a fat chick is not only paying her a compliment, but doing her an enormous *favor*. He's a fucking philanthropist, out there busting his ass to save fat girls everywhere from vaginal atrophy.

You fat whores would be lucky to even get raped by someone. I hope you whiny cunts find your way on top of a pinball machine in the near future.

Whoever raped you could have just waited at the exit of a bar. at 3 am and gotten it consensually without the beached whale–like "struggle" you probably gave.

If any man would want to rape your gigantic ass, I'd be shocked.

It's tempting to dismiss the lowlife assholes who leave comments like that on feminist blogs as . . . well, lowlife assholes. As in, people beneath not only our contempt but also our notice. Problem is, these comments show up frequently enough that they're clearly not just the isolated thoughts of a few vicious, delusional wackjobs. They're part of a larger cultural narrative about female attractiveness in general, and fat women's sexuality in particular.

It starts here: Women's first—if not only—job is to be attractive to men. Never mind straight women who have other priorities or queer women who don't *want* men. If you were born with a vagina, your primary obligation from the onset of adolescence and well into adulthood will be to make yourself pretty for heterosexual men's pleasure. Not even just the ones you'd actually want to have a conversation with, let alone sex with—*all* of them.

So if you were born with a vagina *and* genes that predispose you to fatness, then you've got a real problem. You've already failed—fat is repulsive! Sure, there are men out there who particularly dig fat women, and plenty of other men who would be hot for the *right* fat woman if she came along. But those men, the culture helpfully explains, are outliers. Freaks. Even if you chanced upon one—which you could go a whole lifetime without doing, so exquisitely rare are they!—who would want to be with a man who's so broken, he finds fat women attractive? Besides which, as we've discussed, your job as a woman is to be attractive not only to the men who will love you and treat you well, but to *all* heterosexual men. And if you're fat? Well, as the kids on the Internet say, epic fail.

I'm against rape. Unless it's obese women. How else are they going to get sweet, sweet cock?

People really say this shit.

Whether they really *believe* it is almost immaterial. The purpose of comments like these isn't to argue sincerely that rapists are doing a favor to fat chicks; it's to wound the fat woman or women at whom they're directed, as deeply as possible. And it works, to the extent that it does (which depends on the person and the day), because too many of us fully believe the underlying premise on which that twisted leap of logic is based: *No one wants to fuck a fatty.*

When I was in college—long before I discovered, let alone joined, the fat acceptance movement— I had a months-long non-relationship with this dude whose girlfriend was studying abroad for the year. We started out as Just Friends, then moved on to Friends Who Give Each Other Backrubs, and then to Friends Who Give Each Other Half-Naked Backrubs, Like, Three Times Daily. As you do in college.

One afternoon, I was lying on my stomach on a dorm bed, shirt and bra on the floor next to me, while this dude straddled my ass. He was giving me a backrub that, as usual, involved his sliding his fingers under my waistband and kneading handfuls of side-boob as if he just didn't *notice* it wasn't back fat. Sarah McLachlan's *Fumbling Towards Ecstasy* was on the stereo (appropriately enough), a cheap vanilla votive candle was burning, and I was trying to regulate my breathing so he wouldn't notice me pretty much panting. Because, after all, we were *just friends*. He had a girlfriend, even if she was on the other side of the world. This backrub thing was just . . . I don't know, a hobby?

And then, out of nowhere, he says, "Hey, I kind of feel like making out."

Now, I wanted to make out with this dude more than anything in the world just then—I'd wanted it more than anything in the world for *months*. And he'd totally just opened the door! Finally!

So here's what I said: "*What?*"

I'm slick like that.

And here's what he said: "Oh—oh, nothing. I didn't say anything. Forget it."

And with that, I immediately convinced myself he *hadn't* just expressed interest in making out with me, for the very same reason I'd asked him to repeat himself instead of throwing him on his back and kissing him in the first place: *I didn't believe it was possible.*

Let's review. This guy was coming to my room every day, more than once, to doff substantial amounts of clothing and touch me a whole lot. On top of that, we were both nineteen. *And I didn't believe he was attracted to me.*

It sounds absurd to me now, but back then, it somehow made all the sense in the world. I was a fat girl! Nobody wants to have sex with a fat girl!

Compounding the absurdity of it all, I was just barely *chubby* back then, but of course body image doesn't necessarily have jack shit to do with reality. My closest female friends were positively waifish, both naturally thin and not yet settled into their adult bodies. The guys I was attracted to—including this one—dated only skinny girls,

at least on the record. And the guy in question had, in fact, mentioned on more than one occasion that it would be cool if I worked out more, while straddling my ass and groping side-boob. He'd made it perfectly clear that he did *not* find me especially attractive—certainly nowhere near as attractive as his girlfriend—while rubbing his hands all over my bare skin.

I didn't know what "cognitive dissonance" meant back then. I knew only this: I was fat. And that meant he *couldn't* want me. Sex was a nonissue because I was a nonsexual being—never mind what I felt, thought, or did on my own time. The important thing wasn't my *actual* sexuality, or even how this particular dude perceived me; the important thing was how *all* heterosexual men perceived me. Remember?

And the culture never failed to remind me how I was perceived, via women's magazines offering a new way to lose weight and "look good naked" every goddamned month; cheery radio jingles for fitness centers about destroying your "flubbery, rubbery gut"; Courteney Cox Arquette dancing in a fat suit on *Friends*, between ads for weight-loss programs; low-cal, low-fat menus with cutesy names like the Guiltless Grill in restaurants; sidelong glances in the dining hall; size 4 friends who were dieting; and—just in case all that was too subtle—the No Fat Chicks bumper stickers, the "How do you fuck a fat woman?" jokes, the fatcalls on the street. Women with bodies like mine were unwantable, unlovable, and *definitely* unfuckable. I was utterly, unwaveringly convinced of this.

So I really believed that dude and I were just, you know, backrub buddies. It was strictly platonic—even if I have never in thirty-three years had another platonic relationship in which a friend and I would greet each other by ripping our shirts off and getting into bed.

I have a dozen more stories like that. Add in my friends' stories, and I've got a book. *The Ones That Got Away: Fat Women on Their Own Goddamned Romantic Cluelessness*, something like that. In our thirties, with most of us partnered off, we can laugh about it—but in our teens and twenties, the pain of rejection was fierce, and we truly had no idea that probably half the time, that rejection wasn't even coming from outside us. We rejected *ourselves* as potential dates or partners or fuck buddies before anyone else got the chance.

Worse yet, some of us assumed our manifest unfuckability meant that virtually any male attention was a thing to be treasured. While I don't know any women who have bought into the "rape is a compliment" theory, I certainly know some who believed abusive boyfriends when they said, "You can't leave, because no one but me would want your fat ass." I know several who have had multiple semi-anonymous one-night stands, not because that's what floats their boats but because they were so happy to find men—any men, just about—who expressed sexual interest in their bodies. There's a reason why so many TV shows, movies, and rude jokes represent fat women as pathetically grateful to get laid; some (though nowhere near all) of us *are* grateful, because after years of being told you're too physically repulsive to earn positive male attention, yeah, it's actually kind of nice to be noticed. And from there, it's a frighteningly short leap to "You'd be lucky to be raped." Even if you never officially make that leap—and I really, really hope there aren't women out there who would—you're still essentially believing that you have no agency in your own sexual experiences. Your desires aren't important, because they can never be fulfilled anyway—you aren't pretty enough to call the shots. The best you can hope for is that some man's desire for sex will lead him to you, somewhere, some night.

Of all the maddening side effects of our narrow cultural beauty standard, I think the worst might be the way it warps our understanding of attraction. The reality is, attraction is unpredictable and subjective—even people who are widely believed to meet the standard do not actually, magically become Objectively Attractive. I fall right in line with millions of heterosexual women when it comes to daydreaming about George Clooney, but Brad Pitt does absolutely nothing for me. I think Kate Winslet is breathtaking, but my boyfriend thinks she's *meh*. Ain't no such thing as a person who's categorically

hot in the opinion of every single person who sees them.

But that's exactly what we're trained to believe: "Hot" is an objective assessment, based on a collection of easily identifiable characteristics. Thin is hot. White is hot. Able-bodied and quasi-athletic is hot. Blond is hot. Clear skin is hot. Big boobs (so long as there's no corresponding big ass) are hot. Little waists are hot. Miniskirts and high heels and smoky eyes are hot. There's a proven formula, and if you follow it, you will be hot.

Of course, very few people can follow that formula to the letter, and some of us—fat women, nonwhite women—physically disabled women, flat-chested, apple-shaped, acne-prone women—basically have no fucking prayer. That doesn't stop purveyors of the beauty standard from encouraging us to keep trying, though—with enough hard work and money spent, we can all at least move closer to the ideal. Sure, women of color can't be expected to surmount that whole white-skin requirement (sorry, gals—better luck next millennium!), but they can torture their hair with chemicals and get surgery on those pesky non-European features if they're really committed. There's something for everyone in this game!

And for fat women, the solution is actually quite simple, they tell us: You can diet. You can work out as much and eat as little as it takes until you look like your naturally thin friend who loves fast food and despises the gym. Never mind that studies have shown over 90 percent of dieters gain all the weight back within five years.[1] Never mind that twin studies show weight and body shape are nearly as inheritable as height.[2] And definitely never mind that your one friend can maintain this shape without ever consuming a leafy green vegetable or darkening the door of a gym, and another friend can maintain it while eating satisfying meals and working out for half an hour, three times a week, but for you to maintain it requires restricting your calories to below the World Health Organization's threshold for starvation and spending way more time exercising than you do hanging out with friends and family. The unfairness of that is irrelevant. You just have to *want* it badly enough.

And you must want it that badly, because fat is Not Hot. To anyone, ever.

How else are you going to get sweet, sweet cock?

It's really tempting to simply declare that fat women oppress ourselves, demean ourselves, cut off our own romantic opportunities—and the obvious solution is to knock it the fuck off. It's tempting to say that because, you know, it's kind of true. But it's ultimately a counterproductive and nasty bit of victim blaming. When you're a fat woman in this culture, *everyone*—from journalists you'll never meet to your own mother, sister, and best friend—works together to constantly reinforce the message that you are not good enough to be fucked, let alone loved. *You'd be so pretty if you just lost weight. You'd feel so much better about yourself if you just lost weight. You'd have boys beating down your door if you just lost weight.*

You'd be lucky to be raped, you fat cunt.

That's just the way it is, baby. Fat chicks are gross. Accept it.

Refusing to accept it is hard fucking work. And being tasked with doing that is, frankly, every bit as unfair as being tasked with keeping "excess" weight off a naturally fat body. We shouldn't have to devote so much mental energy to the exhausting work of *not hating ourselves*. Believing that we can be desirable, that we deserve to be loved, that that guy over there really *is* flirting should not be a goddamned daily struggle. It should not feel like rolling a boulder up a hill.

But it does. So the question is, which boulder are you going to choose to roll? The "must lose weight" boulder or the "fuck you, I will boldly, defiantly accept the body I've got and *live in it*" boulder? It's backbreaking and frequently demoralizing work either way. But only one way can lead to real sexual power, to real ownership of your body, to real strength and confidence.

Imagine for a minute a world in which fat women don't automatically disqualify themselves from the dating game. A world in which fat women don't believe there's anything intrinsically unattractive about their bodies. A world in which fat women hear that men want only thin women and laugh our asses off, because that is not remotely our experience—our experience is one of loving and fucking and navigating a big damn world in our big damn bodies with grace and optimism and power.

Now try to imagine some halfwit dickhead telling you a rapist would be doing you a favor, in that world. Imagine a man poking you in the stomach and telling you you need to work out more, moments after he comes inside you. Imagine a man going on daytime TV to announce to the world that he's thinking of getting a divorce because his wife is thirty pounds heavier than she was the day they were married. Imagine a man telling you that you can't leave him, because no one else will ever want your disgusting fat ass.

None of it makes a lick of sense in that world, does it?

It doesn't in this one, either.

Imagine if more of us could believe that.

13 • *Eli Clare*

NAMING AND LOSING HOME

DISCUSSION QUESTIONS

1. Identify the many systems of oppression Clare lives in/between.
2. What relationships between anonymity and safety, isolation and violence, and home and community are examined in this chapter?
3. Why is the loss of "home" and the experience of "exile" about class? How does the "upward scramble" relate to this loss and exile?
4. Why and how is "queer identity" and "queer culture" an urban—not rural—specificity and possibility?

NAMING

Handicapped

A disabled person sits on the street, begging for her next meal. This is how we survived in Europe and the United States as cities grew big and the economy moved from a land base to an industrial base. We were beggars, caps in hand. This is how some of us still survive. Seattle, 1989: a white man sits on the sidewalk, leaning against an iron fence. He smells of whiskey and urine, his body wrapped in torn cloth. His legs are toothpick-thin, knees bent inward. Beside him leans a set of crutches. A Styrofoam cup, half full of coins, sits on the sidewalk in front of him. Puget Sound stretches out behind him, water sparkling in the sun. Tourists bustle by. He strains his head up, trying to catch their eyes. Cap in hand. *Handicapped.*[1]

Disabled

The car stalled in the left lane of traffic is disabled. Or alternatively, the broad stairs curving into a public building disable the man in a wheelchair. That word used as a noun (the *disabled* or people with *disabilities*), an adjective (*disabled* people), a verb (the accident *disabled* her): in all its forms it means "unable," but where does our inability lie? Are our bodies like stalled cars? Or does disability live in the social and physical environment, in the stairs that have no accompanying ramp? I think about language. I often call nondisabled people able-bodied, or, when I'm feeling confrontational, *temporarily* able-bodied. But if I call myself disabled in order to describe how the ableist world treats me as a person with cerebral palsy, then shouldn't I call nondisabled people *enabled*? That word locates the condition of being nondisabled, not in the nondisabled body, but in the world's reaction to that body. This is not a semantic game.

Cripple

The woman who walks with a limp, the kid who uses braces, the man with gnarly hands hear the word *cripple* every day in a hostile nondisabled

Eli Clare, "Naming" and "Losing Home" from *Exile and Pride*. Reprinted with permission of the author.

world. At the same time, we in the disability rights movement create crip culture, tell crip jokes, identify a sensibility we call crip humor. Nancy Mairs writes:

> I am a cripple. I choose this word to name me.... People—crippled or not—wince at the word *cripple*, as they do not at *handicapped* or *disabled*. Perhaps I want them to wince. I want them to see me as a tough customer, one to whom the fates/gods/viruses have not been kind, but who can face the brutal truth of her existence squarely. As a cripple, I swagger.[2]

Gimp

Slang meaning "to limp." *Gimp* comes from the word *gammy*, which hobos in the 18th century used among themselves to describe dangerous or unwelcoming places. Hobo to hobo, passing on the road: "Don't go there. It's gammy." Insider language, hobo solidarity. And now a few centuries later, one disabled person greets another, "Hey, gimp. How ya doin?" Insider language, gimp solidarity.

Retard

I learned early that words can bruise a body. I have been called *retard* too many times, that word sliding off the tongues of doctors, classmates, neighbors, teachers, well-meaning strangers on the street. In the years before my speech became understandable, I was universally assumed to be "mentally retarded." When I started school, the teachers wanted me in the "special education" program. My parents insisted I be given yet another set of diagnostic tests, including an IQ test, and I—being a white kid who lived in a house full of books, ideas, and grammar-school English, being a disabled kid who had finally learned how to talk—scored well. They let me join the "regular" first grade. I worked overtime to prove those test results right. Still I was *retard, monkey, defect* on the playground, in the streets, those words hurled at my body, accompanied by rocks and rubber erasers. Even at home, I

heard their echoes. My father told me more than once to stop walking like a *monkey*. My mother often talked about my birth *defect*. Words bruise a body more easily than rocks and rubber erasers.

Differently Abled, Physically Challenged

Nondisabled people, wanting to cushion us from the cruelty of language, invented these euphemisms. In explaining her choice of the word *cripple*, Nancy Mairs writes:

> *Differently abled*...partakes of the same semantic hopefulness that transformed countries from *undeveloped* to *underdeveloped*, then to *less developed*, and finally *developing* nations. People have continued to starve in those countries during the shift. Some realities do not obey the dictates of language.[3]

Differently abled is simply easier to say, easier to think about than *disabled* or *handicapped* or *crippled*.

Freak

I hold fast to my dictionary, but the definitions slip and slide, tell half stories. I have to stop here. *Freak* forces me to think about naming.

Handicapped, Disabled, Cripple, Gimp, Retard, Differently Abled

I understand my relationship to each of these words. I scoff at *handicapped*, a word I grew up believing my parents had invented specifically to describe me, my parents who were deeply ashamed of my cerebral palsy and desperately wanted to find a cure. I use the word *disabled* as an adjective to name what this ableist world does to us crips and gimps. *Cripple* makes me flinch; it too often accompanied the sticks and stones on my grade school playground, but I love crip humor, the audacity of turning *cripple* into a word of pride. *Gimp* sings a friendly song, full of irony and understanding. *Retard* on the other hand draws blood every time, a sharp, sharp knife. In the world as it should be, maybe disabled people would be *differently abled*: a world where Braille and audiorecorded editions of books and magazines were a matter of course, and hearing people signed ASL; a world where schools were fully integrated, health care, free and unrationed; a world where universal access meant exactly that; a world where disabled people were not locked up at home or in nursing homes, relegated to sheltered employment and paid sweatshop wages. But, in the world as it is, *differently abled, physically challenged* tell a wishful lie.

Handicapped, Disabled, Cripple, Gimp, Retard, Differently Abled, Freak

I need to stop here. *Freak* I don't understand. It unsettles me. I don't quite like it, can't imagine using it as some politicized disabled people do. Yet I want *freak* to be as easy as the words *queer* and *cripple*.

Queer, like *cripple*, is an ironic and serious word I use to describe myself and others in my communities. *Queer* speaks volumes about who I am, my life as a dyke, my relationship to the dominant culture. Because of when I came out—more than a decade after the Stonewall Rebellion—and where—into a highly politicized urban dyke community—*queer* has always been easy for me. I adore its defiant external edge, its comfortable internal truth. *Queer* belongs to me. So does *cripple* for many of the same reasons. *Queer* and *cripple* are cousins: words to shock, words to infuse with pride and self-love, words to resist internalized hatred, words to help forge a politics. They have been gladly chosen—*queer* by many gay/lesbian/bi/trans people, *cripple*, or *crip*, by many disabled people.

Freak is another story. Unlike *queer* and *crip*, it has not been widely embraced in my communities.[4] For me *freak* has a hurtful, scary edge; it takes *queer* and *cripple* one step too far; it doesn't feel good or liberating.

This profusion of words and their various relationships to marginalized people and politicized communities fascinates me. Which words get embraced, which don't, and why? *Queer* but not *pervert*. *Cripple*, and sometimes *freak*, but not *retard*. Like most of the ugly and demeaning words used to

batter and bait marginalized peoples—racist, sexist, classist, ableist, homophobic slurs—*pervert* and *retard* nearly burst with hurt and bitterness, anger and reminders of self-hatred.[5] I doubt the l/g/b/t community and the disability community respectively will ever claim those words as our own. In contrast *crip, queer*, and *freak* have come to sit on a cusp. For some of us, they carry too much grief. For others, they can be chosen with glee and pride. *Queer* and *crip* are mine but not *freak*, and I want to know why. What is it about that word? What bitterness, what pain, does it hold that *cripple*, with its connotations of pitiful, broken bodies, and *queer*, with its sweeping definitions of normality and abnormality, do not? . . .

LOSING HOME

I must find the words to speak of losing home. Then I never want to utter them again. They throb like an abscessed tooth, simply hurt too much. *Homesick* is a platitude. I need to grab at seemingly unrelated words. *Queer. Exile. Class.* I reach for my red and gold *American Heritage Dictionary* but restrain myself. I know the definitions. I need to enter the maze created by dyke identity, class location, and rural roots.

Let me start with *queer*, the easiest point of entry. In its largest sense, queer has always been where I belong. A girl child not convinced of her girlness. A backwoods hick in the city. A dyke in a straight world. A gimp in an ableist world. The eldest child of a poor father and a working-class mother, both teachers who tried to pull themselves up by their own bootstraps, using luck and white-skin privilege.

In its narrower sense, queer has been home since I became conscious of being a dyke. At age 17, I left the backwoods of Oregon with a high school diploma and a scholarship to college, grateful not to have a baby or a husband. A year later, after months of soul-searching, I finally realized that I was a dyke and had been for years. Since then, I have lived among dykes and created chosen families and homes, not rooted in geography, but in shared passion, imagination, and values. Our collective dyke household in Oakland with its vegetable garden in the front yard and chicken coop in the back. The women's circle on the Great Peace March from Los Angeles to Washington, D.C. The Women's Encampment for a Future of Peace and Justice in upstate New York. Queer potlucks in Ann Arbor, where I now live. Whether I've been walking across the country for peace or just hanging out listening to lesbian gossip, learning to cook tofu, or using red-handled bolt cutters to cut fence at the Army Depot, being a dyke in dyke community is as close as I've ever felt to belonging. And still I feel queer.

Exile

If *queer* is the easiest, then *exile* is the hardest. I lie when I write that home is being a dyke in dyke community. Rather, home is particular wild and ragged beaches, specific kinds of trees and berry brambles, the exact meander of the river I grew up near, the familiar sounds and sights of a dying logging and fishing town. Exile is the hardest because I have irrevocably lost that place as actual home....

...Let me take you to my maternal grandfather's funeral. At the service I sat with family, my sister to the right, my great aunt Esther to the left, my aunt Margaret in front of us, her lover of many years to her right. Barb is an African-American dyke, unmistakable whether or not she's in heels and a skirt. I am quite sure my aunt has never introduced Barb to Uncle John or Aunt Esther, Uncle Henry or Aunt Lillian as her partner, lover, or girlfriend. Yet Barb is unquestionably family, sitting with my grandfather's immediate relatives near the coffin, openly comforting my aunt. My grandfather was a mechanic in Detroit; his surviving brothers and sisters are Lutheran corn farmers from southern Illinois. Most of them never graduated from high school, still speak German at home, and have voted Republican all their lives. From the perspective of many middle- and upper-class urban folks, they are simple rednecks, clods, hillbillies. Working-class writer and activist Elliott maps out three definitions of the word *redneck*. Its denotation: "A member of

the white rural laboring class...."[6] Its connotation: "A person who advocates a provincial, conservative, often bigoted sociopolitical attitude characteristic of a redneck...."[7] And lastly its usage by progressives, including many queers: "1. Any person who is racist, violent, uneducated and stupid (as if they are the same thing), woman-hating, gay-bashing, Christian fundamentalist, etc. 2. Used as a synonym for every type of oppressive belief except classism."[8] Many urban queer folks would take one look at my great aunts and uncles and cast them as over-the-top rednecks and homophobes.

Yet in this extended working-class family, unspoken lesbianism balanced against tacit acceptance means that Barb is family, that Aunt Margaret and she are treated as a couple, and that the overt racism Barb would otherwise experience from these people is muffled. Not ideal, but better than frigid denial, better than polite manners and backhanded snubs, better than middle-class "don't ask, don't tell," which would carefully place Barb into the category marked "friend" and have her sit many pews away from immediate family at her lover's father's funeral.

At the same time, it is a balance easily broken. In Port Orford I would never walk down Main Street holding hands with a woman lover. That simple act would be too much. It is also a balance most readily achieved among family or folks who have known each other for decades. If I moved back and lived down the road from a dyke—closeted or not—who hadn't grown up in Port Orford, whose biological family didn't live in town, who was an "outsider," I would worry about her safety.

It isn't that outside the bounds of this fragile balance these rural white people are any more homophobic than the average urban person. Rather the difference lies in urban anonymity. In Ann Arbor if a group of frat boys yells, "Hey, lezzie!" at me or the man sitting next to me on the bus whispers "queer" and spits at me, I'll defend myself in whatever ways necessary, knowing chances are good that I'll never see these men again, or if I do, they won't remember me. On the other hand, in Port Orford if someone harassed me—the balance somehow broken, some invisible line overstepped, drunken bravado overcoming tacit acceptance—I would know him, maybe work with his wife at the cannery, see his kids playing up the river at Butler Bar, encounter him often enough in the grocery store and post office. He would likewise know where I lived, with whom I lived, what car I drove, and where I worked. This lack of anonymity is a simple fact of rural life, one that I often miss in the city, but in the face of bigotry and violence, anonymity provides a certain level of protection.

If I moved back to Port Orford, the daily realities of isolation would compete with my concerns about safety. Living across the street from the chainsaw shop, I would have to drive an hour to spend an evening at a dyke potluck, three hours to hang out at a women's bookstore or see the latest queer movie, seven hours to go to a *g/l/b/t* pride march. I don't believe I could live easily and happily that isolated from queer community, nor could I live comfortably while always monitoring the balance, measuring the invisible lines that define safety. My loss of home is about being queer.

Let me return now to *exile*. It is a big word, a hard word. It implies not only loss, but a sense of allegiance and connection—however ambivalent—to the place left behind, an attitude of mourning rather than of good riddance. It also carries with it the sense of being pushed out, compelled to leave. Yes, my loss of home is about being queer, but is it *exile?* To answer that, I need to say another thing about anonymity, isolation, and safety, a messier thing.

Throughout my childhood and young adulthood, my father, along with a number of other adults, severely sexually and physically abused me, tying me up, using fire and knives and brute force on my body. My father, who taught for 30 years at the local high school. My father, whom everyone in town knew and respected, even if they thought he was quirky, odd, prone to forgetfulness and unpredictable anger. He no longer lives there, although some of the other adults who abused me still do. In the years since leaving Port Orford, I have been able to shake my perpetrators' power away from me, spending long periods of time uncovering the memories and working through persistent body-deep terror, grief, and confusion. I've done this work in community, supported by many friends, a few good professionals,

and a political framework that places the violence I experienced into a larger context. For much of that time, I could not have returned to Port Orford and been physically safe. I lived a kind of exile, knowing I needed the anonymity of a small city halfway across the country to protect me, a city where no one knew my father, where not a single person had participated either tangentially or centrally in my abuse. Today my safety depends less on anonymity and more on an internal set of resources. Even so, I don't know how I would deal, if I moved back, with seeing a small handful of my perpetrators on a regular basis, being known as Bob's kid everywhere I went. Simply put, my desire for community, for physical safety, for emotional well-being and psychological comfort compelled me to leave. Being a queer is one piece of this loss, this exile; abuse is another.

And class is a third. If *queer* is the easiest and *exile* the hardest, then *class* is the most confusing. The economics in Port Orford are simple: jobs are scarce. The life of a Pacific Northwest fishing and logging town depends on the existence of salmon and trees. When the summer salmon runs dwindle and all the old growth trees are cut, jobs vanish into thin air. It is rumored that fishermen now pay their boat mortgages by running drugs—ferrying marijuana, crack, and cocaine from the freighters many miles out at sea back to the cannery where they are then picked up and driven inland. Loggers pay their bills by brush cutting—gathering various kinds of ferns to sell by the pound to florists—and collecting welfare. What remains is the meager four-month-a-year tourist season and a handful of minimum-wage jobs—pumping gas, cashiering, flipping burgers. The lucky few work for the public school district or own land on which they run milk cows and sheep. In short, if I moved back, I probably wouldn't find work. Not only are jobs scarce, but my CP makes job-hunting even harder. Some jobs, like cashiering or flipping burgers, I simply can't do; I don't have enough manual dexterity. Other jobs, like clerical work that requires a lot of typing, I can do but more slowly than many people. Still other jobs I can do well, but potential employers are reluctant to hire me, confusing disability with inability. And if, miraculously, I did find work, the paycheck probably wouldn't stretch around food, gas, and rent.

To leap from economic realities to class issues in Port Orford holds no challenge. The people who live in dying rural towns and work minimum- or sub-minimum-wage jobs—not temporarily but day after day for their whole working lives—are working-class and poor people. There are some middle-class people who live in Port Orford: the back-to-the-land artists who grow marijuana for money (or did until the federal crackdown more than a decade ago), the young teachers whose first jobs out of college bring them to Pacific High School, the retirees who have settled near Port Orford, lured to Oregon by cheap land. But these people don't stay long. The artists bum out. The young teachers find better jobs in other, more prosperous towns. The retirees grow older and find they need more services than are available in Curry County. The people who stay are poor and working-class. I left because I didn't want to marry and couldn't cashier at Sentry's Market. I left because I hoped to have money above and beyond the dollars spent on rent and food to buy books and music. I left because I didn't want to be poor and feared I would be if I stayed. I will never move back for the same reasons. My loss of home, my exile, is about class.

Leaving is a complicated thing. I left with a high school diploma and a scholarship to college, grateful to be leaving, but this is only half the truth. The other half is that everyone around me—my parents, teachers, classmates and friends, the women who cashiered at Sentry's Market, the men who drove logging trucks—assumed I would leave, go to college, and become "successful." No one expected me to marry a week after graduation and move up the road from my parents, to die in a drunk-driving car accident or a high-speed game of chase down Highway 101, to have a baby and drop out of school at 15. A high school diploma and a college scholarship were givens in my life.

This is all about class location, which is where class gets confusing. In Port Orford, my family and I were relatively well off: we always had enough to eat; my father was securely employed at the high school; my mother bragged that she had the only Ph.D. in

town. We eventually built a big house of our own. Books filled my childhood. We borrowed them by the arm-load from the public library; we bought them by mail-order from book clubs; we cherished trips to the one bookstore in Coos Bay, a town of 10,000 an hour's drive away. We always had health care. I grew up among people for whom none of these things were givens. On the other hand, we wore hand-me-downs and home-made clothes, for years rented tiny two-bedroom houses, owned one beat-up car, and balanced dental bills against new school shoes. I didn't know that in a middle-class town or neighborhood these things would have marked my family and me as something other than well-off.

Who left and who stayed measured in part the class differences at Pacific High School. My best friend from sixth to twelfth grade was poor. She and I spent high school together in college-prep classes, poring over pre-calculus problems and biology experiments. We both wanted to go to college, to leave rural Oregon, and yet in our senior year as I filled out college applications, Judy made plans to marry her boyfriend of four years. I know now that her decision arose out of financial desperation—her father had just died, and her family was falling deeper into poverty—but at the time, I thought Judy was copping out. I walked away, glad to be leaving Port Orford behind me. Or so I thought.

Only later did I understand what I lost by leaving. Loss of a daily sustaining connection to a landscape that I still carry with me as home. Loss of a rural, white, working-class culture that values neighbors rather than anonymity, that is both tremendously bigoted—particularly racist—and accepting of local eccentricity, that believes in self-sufficiency and depends on family—big extended families not necessarily created in the mold of the Christian right. Loss of a certain pace of life, a certain easy trust. I didn't know when I left at 17 that I would miss the old cars rusting in every third front yard. Miss the friendly chatting in the grocery store, the bank, the post office. Miss being able to hitchhike home, safe because I knew everyone driving by....

My siblings and I inherited this halfway successful scramble. Our grandparents and great uncles and aunts were farmers, gravediggers, janitors, mechanics; our parents, teachers; and we were to be professors, lawyers, or doctors. As I try to sort the complexity out, I have to ask, does this upward scramble really work: this endless leaving of home, of deeply embodied culture and community, in search of a mirage called the "American Dream"? Instead of professor, lawyer, or doctor, my brother is a high school teacher, my sister, a low-level administrator, and I, a bookkeeper. Did my parents become middle class in their scramble? Did my siblings and I?

The answers are not that important except for the betrayal that can creep up behind us, make home under our skins. If we leave, never come back, somehow finding ourselves in the middle class, will we forget—or worse, start mocking—the men who can't read, the women who can make a bag of potatoes and five pounds of Velveeta last nearly forever? Will we train the accents out of our voices so far that we'll wake up one day and not recognize ourselves? And what about the people we leave behind? The last time I saw Judy, her two sons playing hide-and-go-seek nearby, we could find nothing to say to each other, that woman who had been my best—and sometimes only—friend for so many years. How do we deal with the loss? For decades my mother missed living in a big, industrial, working-class city; my father would drive every day to the ocean just to see a long, flat horizon like the one he left behind in North Dakota. My brother has returned to rural Oregon, my sister dreams of leaving Seattle for some small town in the North Cascades, and I entertain fantasies of a rural queer community. Is the upward scramble worth the loss? This question leads me back to being queer, to another, similar question: is queer identity worth the loss?

Queer identity, at least as I know it, is largely urban. The happening places, events, dialogues, the strong communities, the journals, magazines, bookstores, queer organizing, and queer activism are all city-based. Of course rural lesbian, gay, bi, and trans communities exist, but the people and institutions defining queer identity and culture are urban.

For me, coming into my queer identity and untangling my class location have both been rooted in urban life. In moving to an urban, private, liberal arts college, I found what I needed to come out as a dyke: the anonymity of a city, the support of lesbian-feminist activists, and access to queer culture. In that same move, I also found myself living among middle-class people for the first time. Because in Port Orford my family had always defined itself as middle-class—and in truth we were well-educated people who lived somewhere between the working-class loggers and the middle-class retirees—I believed the class differences I felt in my bones amounted to my being a country bumpkin. I assumed my lack of familiarity with trust funds, new cars, designer clothes, trips to Paris, and credit cards was the same as my lack of familiarity with city buses, skyscrapers, one-way streets, stop lights, and house keys.

Even now after a decade of urban living, the two are hard to separate. I am remembering the first time I went to OutWrite, a national queer writer's conference. From the moment I walked into the posh Boston hotel where the conference was being held, I gawked, staring unbelievingly at the chandeliers, shiny gold railings, ornate doors, in the same way I used to gawk at twenty-story buildings. Saturday night before the big dance party, to which I couldn't afford to go, I had dinner with an acquaintance and a group of her friends, all white, lesbian writers from New York City. We ate at the hotel restaurant, where I spent too much money on not enough food, served by brown-skinned men who were courteous in spite of our ever-changing party and ever-changing food orders. Jo and her friends were all going to the party after dinner and were dressed accordingly, in black plastic miniskirts and diamond earrings, three-piece suits and gold cufflinks, hair carefully molded and shaved in all the right places. In my blue jeans and faded chamois shirt, I felt conspicuous and embarrassed.

At some point the conversation turned to gossip about queer writers not at the conference. Cathy, an editor for a well-known lesbian press, started in on one of "her" writers, a novelist from rural Oregon. Having heard me talk earlier about growing up there, Cathy turned to me and asked, "When Laura asks me to send stuff to her P.O. box because during the winter rains the mail carrier might not be able to navigate the dirt road to her mailbox, is she serious?" I wanted to laugh, to have some clever retort to slide off my tongue. Instead, I politely explained about dirt roads and months of rain. What this New York femme didn't know about rural living didn't offend me; rather it was the complete urban bias of the evening that did. Was I uncomfortable, feeling conspicuous and embarrassed, because of class or because of urban/rural differences? I can't separate the two....

Just how urban is the most visible of queer identities, how middle class, how consumer-oriented? I am remembering Stonewall 25, media shorthand for New York City's celebration of the 25th anniversary of the Stonewall Rebellion. If one were to believe the mainstream media and much of the queer media, it was a defining event of queer identity in the '90s. I didn't go. I can't tolerate New York City: its noise, crowds, grime, heat, concrete, and traffic. I inherited my father's rural fear of cities as big and tall as New York. I've gone to queer pride marches for the last 15 years, but Stonewall 25 was different, a commercial extravaganza of huge proportions. From the reports I heard, the tickets for many of the events cost outrageous amounts of money. Who could afford the benefit dance at $150, the concert at $50, the t-shirt at $25? I know that at the 1993 March on Washington trinkets and souvenirs flourished. Not only could one buy 14 different kinds of t-shirts but also coffee mugs, plastic flags, freedom rings, and posters. I can only assume this proliferation was even more astonishing at Stonewall 25. And sliding-scale prices? They're evidently a thing of the past. Stonewall 25 strikes me not so much as a celebration of a powerful and life-changing uprising of queer people, led by transgendered people of color, by drag queens and butch dykes, fed up with the cops, but as a middle- and upper-class urban party that opened its doors only to those who could afford it.

Why does the money that creates Stonewall 25 and events like it rarely find its way to working-class and poor queers? Why does the money stay urban? What about AIDS prevention programs, l/g/b/t youth services, hate-crime monitoring, queer theater

in the mountains of rural Oregon, the cornfields of rural Nebraska, the lowlands of rural South Carolina? Have we collectively turned our backs on the small towns in Oregon that one by one are passing local anti-gay ordinances? Are we in effect abandoning them to the Oregon Citizens Alliance, the Christian right coalition which spearheaded the outrageously homophobic Proposition 9 in 1992 and which, after losing that vote, has directed its attention toward local initiatives? Will we remember and support Brenda and Wanda Hansen of Camp Sister Spirit, white, rural, working-class lesbians who are building and maintaining lesbian and feminist space in rural Mississippi, when the homophobic violence they face—dead dogs in their mailbox, gunfire at night—no longer makes the headlines?...

My leaving gave me a dyke community but didn't change my class location. Before I left, I was a rural, mixed-class, queer child in a straight, rural, working-class town. Afterwards, I was an urban-transplanted, mixed-class, dyke activist in an urban, mostly middle-class, queer community. Occasionally I simply feel as if I've traded one displacement for another and lost home to boot. Most of the time, however, I know that living openly in relative safety as a queer among queers; living thousands of miles away from the people who raped and tortured me as a child; living in a place where finding work is possible; living with easy access to books and music, movies, and concerts, when I can afford them—this is lifeblood for me. But I hate the cost, hate the kind of exile I feel....

...My displacement, my exile, is twined with problems highlighted in the intersection of queer identity, working-class and poor identity, and rural identity, problems that demand not a personal retreat, but long-lasting, systemic changes. The exclusivity of queer community shaped by urban, middle-class assumptions. Economic injustice in the backwoods. The abandonment of rural working-class culture. The pairing of rural people with conservative, oppressive values. The forced choice between rural roots and urban queer life. These problems are the connective tissue that brings the words *queer, class,* and *exile* together. Rather than a relocation back to the Oregon mountains, I want a redistribution of economic resources so that wherever we live—in the backwoods, the suburbs, or the city—there is enough to eat, warm, dry houses for everyone, true universal access to health care and education. I want queer activists to struggle against homophobic violence in rural areas with the same kind of tenacity and creativity we bring to the struggle in urban areas. I want rural queers, working-class queers, poor queers to be leaders in our communities, to shape the ways we will celebrate the 50th anniversary of Stonewall. I want each of us to be able to bring our queerness home.

NOTES

1. The word *handicap* means to compensate each participant in a contest differently in order to equalize the chances of winning and derives from a lottery game called "hand in cap," in which players held forfeits in a cap. In spite of this derivation, the word play "cap in hand" resonates ironically with the ways in which disabled people have survived as beggars.
2. Mairs, Nancy, *Plaintext* (Tucson: University of Arizona Press, 1986), p. 9.
3. Mairs, p. 10.
4. *Freak* actually is used by a number of marginalized peoples: hippies, drug users, and l/g/b/t people, as well as disabled people.
5. *Pervert* is sometimes used by queer people in leather and s/m communities who feel marginalized within the larger queer culture. The point here isn't that *pervert* and *retard* are never spoken with affection or pride but that they haven't been embraced and used to construct both individual and communal identities.
6. Elliott, "Whenever I Tell You the Language We Use is a Class Issue, You Nod Your Head in Agreement—And Then You Open Your Mouth," in *Out of the Class Closet: Lesbians Speak*, Penelope, Julia, ed. (Freedom, California: The Crossing Press, 1994), p. 277.
7. Elliott, p. 278.
8. Elliott, p. 280.

CLICK, HELLO?

DISCUSSION QUESTION

1. Although you may not have had this exact experience, have you experienced similar types of frustrating bureaucratic processes?

CLICK. Hello?

Yes. Hello, I'm a transexual woman and I—

CLICK.

Hello? Hello?

Yes. Hello, I'm interested in changing the sex on my driver's—

CLICK.

Hello? Hello?

Yes. Hi. I'm just your normal female woman and I notice they've made a mistake on my driver's license, ha-ha, and put me down, ha-ha, wait till you get this, as a man. Can you tell me how I can get this changed? What?...I'll have to bring my birth certificate down with my correct sex on it so you can verify it? Okay.

CLICK.

Hello? County Records Office? I'm a transexual and I—

CLICK.

Hello? Hello?

Yes? County Records Office? I'm trying to get my driver's license corrected. You see, it lists me as a man and they told me that to get it changed I have to get a copy of my birth certificate and—

CLICK.

Hello? Hello?

County Records? Yes. I'm just your average woman here in the county, and yesterday, just looking through some old papers, I noticed a couple errors on my birth certificate and I was just kind of wondering, you know, woman-to-woman here, how I could get them corrected...uh-huh...submit a doctor's statement contemporaneous with my birth from the attending physician or else a notarized statement from my current personal physician and a second notarized statement from a physician here in the county of origin. Thank you.

CLICK.

Yes. Doctor's office? I'd like to speak with—

Please hold, Sir.

CLACK....

...

...

...

...

...

CLICK.

Hello, doctor's office? Yes, I just called. Please don't put me on—

Can you hold please, Sir?

CLACK ...

...

...

CLICK.

Yes. I've been put on hold twice. Can I please talk to Dr. Sprocket?

I'm connecting you now, Sir.

Doctor Sprocket? This is Riki Anne Wilchins. Right. I know you've only seen me a couple of times but now that I've started hormones and everything I'm having trouble finding work as a woman and I need to change—

CLONCK.

Hello? Hello?

Yes. Doctor? Yes, well we were cut off. As I was saying, I'm trying to change my driver's license so I can get a job but they want my birth certificate and that's still male so I have to get that changed and to do that I'll need a statement from you that—no, I can't take time off from work to come in to see you. . . . Well, first I can't because I have no job to take time from and second because I can't afford another $150 visit—no, I'm not trying to be difficult. . . . Yes, I know surgeons are very busy and they save lives and all but . . . look, if you could please just see your way clear to—

CLICK.

Hello? Hello?

Doctor? Doctor Sprocket? Yes. I'm sorry I got angry, Doctor. Look, is there any way you could sign a statement that I'm female so I can get my paperwork done and get a job? . . . I know you can't be certain yet but how many men want to take estrogen and grow bosoms? . . . Oh, really? I had no idea. . . . Yes, I know I still sleep with women and that's not very normal for a transexual. . . . No, I haven't looked very feminine when I've come for my appointments. Have you ever tried walking around the city in a push-up bra, pantyhose, three-inch heels, and—Oh, really? I had no idea. Then you know what I— No, I wasn't aware you wear women's panties under your smock when you operate, but I can certainly sympathize with— What? You want me to see what? . . . Who? . . . Is there any way we could avoid this? . . . Okay. Okay, yes. I'm sure you're looking out for my interests. Good-bye.

CLICK.

Hello? Hello? Dr. Farvis? Dr. Francis Farvis? Yes. This is Riki Anne Wilchins. Yes. That's right . . . from Dr. Sprocket. Yes, Thursday is fine . . . afternoon is fine. How much? You said how much?? Is that absolutely necessary? . . . Okay, okay. Yes, I want to get my paperwork done. . . . Yes, I'll be there at four o'clock sharp. . . . No, believe me, Doctor, it won't be any trouble getting off work. . . . No, I haven't been in therapy before. . . . Yes, I'll try to come properly dressed. Speaking of which, did you know that Dr. Sprocket—No, never mind, just thinking out loud. . . . Yes, I know thinking out loud could be a sign of— Well, of course I sound a little agitated and defensive, Doctor. Now let me ask you a question: Do you have any idea at all how frustrating it can be going through all this stuff and getting a sex-change operation and—Oh really? I had no idea. Yes . . . yes . . . okay, I'll see you Thursday. Good-bye, Doctor.

CLICK.

Hello? City Court? Yes, I'm a transexual woman and I need to get my name changed and—

CLICK.

Hello? Hello?

LOVING OUTSIDE SIMPLE LINES

DISCUSSION QUESTIONS

1. In general, how might a person's development, growth, and/or experience of major life changes affect their intimate partner(s)?
2. More specifically, how might a person's decision to gender transition, both socially and medically, affect their intimate partner(s)?
3. Imagine yourself in a relationship with someone who decided to gender transition. How might you respond to their decisions? What particular challenges would be most difficult for you?

Leaning over you in bed, I run my hand across your shirted torso, caressing breast and muscle, smoothing abdomen and flank. My touch on your female body does not emasculate you. You are not a woman to me. You are butch. My fingers tell you I understand.

My stone butch; I am prepared for you to pull away every time I reach for you. I don't understand the strange sense that guides my approach to you, but it is innate, instinctive, natural.

You gaze at me with trust and wonder that you can let me touch you so freely. I tell you I could make love to you for hours. I, young and novice femme, could make love to you, skilled and knowing butch, for hours. And you, tough from years of living as you do, lie quiet beneath my touch.

Sometimes I have to trick you. We pretend you are fucking me, so you don't have to think about what I am doing to you. I make my body available to you as a distraction.

Sometimes I use words: "Let me suck your dick." Whether I go down on a dildo or a cunt, I am sucking your dick. I see it. I feel it. I know it. We both believe in this absolutely, and there is a shift from role play into another kind of reality.

Always, I give you my body, completely. I luxuriate in how well you know my needs, how well you match me and capture every strength and grace I hold within. I give over to you, and you take me to total release, drive me to sexual madness, then bring me back to safety in your embrace.

Without knowing that anyone like you existed, I searched for you. And now that I've found you, I feel such relief to know that you are real. Now I want to know the wealth of your mind, body, and soul, the hell of being you in this world, and the joy that also comes from living outside simple lines.

You ask me to marry you. "Yes" is my answer. And I say yes to life. I say yes with my eyes wide open. You will be my husband, for you are butch, and I can call you no other way. You will be my husband because you are worthy of that title, far more than any man I have known. You'll not own me, but I'll be your wife. I am already your femme and your girl, and I feel my own strength and power as never before. I marry you, and it is more than words or license or tax break, more than a church wedding or a white dress/tuxedo affair, more than a political statement, commitment ceremony, holy union. Marriage with you is life. You extend your hand to me. I step into your world and unite you to mine.

Comes the day you tell me you want your breasts removed. Top surgery. Chest reconstruction. I am oddly not surprised. I think I always knew we would do this together someday. And somewhere in me, though you have not said it aloud, I know this is the first step of a profound transition.

I love you. So I go with you to the computer, and we look up different transgender Web sites (places I have already been because I knew that someday you would want this information). We read about procedures and options. We have an animated and revelatory conversation. But inside me, a deep, overwhelming panic begins to build.

I want to scream, "I love you…as you are!" My desire for you is not confused. I'm a femme who loves butches, who knows butches. I understand your body. Why can't that be enough?

Ever since I met you, I have struggled to reconcile your breasts with your masculine face, your cunt with your masculine presentation, your body with your masculine soul. I have wanted to "figure you out," using an intellect fettered by narrow expectations, so implicit in my culture that even I have rarely, if ever, questioned them.

You, simply by existing, question all gender assumptions. Gradually I have learned not to try to understand you with my intellect but instead to trust my heart, so clear in its acceptance and love for you.

Yet now, I fear, I want you to agree with me: "Perhaps if you had been recognized, accepted and validated as you are, maybe now you would not want to alter your body." Please, my eyes beg. I want there to be an easier way. I want that you should not need to do this. I want even the possibility that there might have been a chance for you not to need to do this.

You patiently shake your head. "The world is only part of this," you tell me. "The rest of it is inside me."

And my heart knows better. I know you better. You were transgendered before socialization tried to force you to choose "one or the other."

"Are you a boy or a girl?" has been ringing in your ears from earliest memory.

"What do you think?" you flip to them now, tired of explaining. Confusion turns in their eyes. What they say is: freak. What they do is: turn away. Stare. Laugh. Spit. Kill. Beat the spirit from your heart.

You fight them. Survival. Best defense is Get Them First. Show your menace; you are not to be toyed with. "Dangerous" is the message in your eyes, clothes, walk. The razor edge walks with you. You anticipate attack or threat at every turn, exchange, and glance. You talk through. Survival. And "tough" encases your heart.

End of the day and your voice is cold. Your eyes, too old for your years. Tears backed up, held in at what cost? I draw you into the circle of my arms and feel your tension ease. You breathe, and I know you are quietly bringing yourself to me. You can hardly believe you can let it all down, that you can let the tears fall. You can. I know your strength; you have nothing to prove to me. Every part of you that they hate and fear gives me delight. In loving you, I am assured of my own normality.

It is this I fear losing.

The next morning I am driving to work. As I hand my $2 to the toll collector at the bridge, I try to calm myself. "Whatever happens, she will still be my Mary," I whisper again and again, like a mantra. But then I realize you will not be Mary anymore; you will have a new name. And as if that were not enough, you will not even be "she."

We are in uncharted territory.

One night, several weeks later, I awaken to see you sleeping next to me. Your breasts—dusky in the half-light—are spilling onto the bed. Your breasts, which I never touch without knowing a part of you shrinks from my hand. Beautiful, womanly breasts.

Suddenly I can't lie beside you another moment. Tears from nowhere stream hot down my cheeks. In the bathroom I leave the light off, sit on the edge of the bathtub, double over in the moonlight. I rock against my confusion.

Anger. How dare you throw my universe into disarray! Just when I think I finally know myself! When I think I know you!

Fear. This is too much to ask of me! I can't bear this weight. It is impossible. I feel insane!

Betrayal. Who are you? Are you a butch only because there was no other choice! Am I really a lesbian? What does this mean? How can I be a femme if you are a man?

I want to scream at you. Hate you. Instead I stifle my crying in a towel until at last the tears come silent, flow gently. In the morning you find me curled on the couch in the living room. You hold me. Your eyes are so sad. You tell me how sorry you are.

For what? For being true to yourself? I don't want you to apologize for this. I don't know what I want!

I let you hold me, and it does feel better. But I berate myself for being so angry. For hurting you. I wish I could just get to the other side without going through the pain.

Every day I feel different: I drift in and out of anger and pride, excitement and fear. I grapple with monumental theories and insignificant—but suddenly important—consequences of your transition.

My greatest fear is of how this might affect my own sense of self. "Just don't ask me to be straight," I tell you. "It took me too much pain and time and struggle to come out queer, lesbian, and femme-proud. I can't go back." But you never step on or dictate my identity, and for this I am grateful beyond words.

Instead you inspire me to look with courage at my self-definitions. I see how they are true to me. I also see how they sometimes limit me. Though they have often given me security and a means to self-awareness, I notice parts of myself I have suppressed: the attraction I once felt for men, the desire I feel now for other femmes, the need to examine my own "othergenderedness."

Some days I feel very alone in the world, like the biggest "freak among the freaks," and I turn old internalized hatred upon myself. Other days I feel like part of an ancient, unspoken tradition, as one who is particularly "wired" to partner a transperson. I feel almost sacred.

Months pass quickly. Every time you bleed, you feel a little more insane, and I feel less able to be your safe harbor. We go to meetings, get to know other transmen and their lovers and wives. We search the Internet for surgeons. We figure out which credit cards can hold the weight of this surgery. Time eases pain, it is true. I love your breasts, but now I release this part of you so beautiful and mysterious to me.

I am changing. Part of me begins to address this surgery with a note of erotic anticipation. I notice that much of my desire is linked to the disparity between your gender expression and your body. When you bind your breasts, pack a dick, when you wear a suit and tie, T-shirt and boxers, when you shift before my eyes from woman into man, I am aroused, excited beyond belief.

I relish the way you construct your gender despite the dictates this world links to your body, which further manifests your particular gender.

Christmas week we travel from San Francisco to Maryland for your surgery. We make love in the cheap motel room near the surgeon's office. I want to touch you, but you tell me you just can't. I could cry.

Later I ask if I can kiss your breasts goodbye. You grant me this, though I know what an effort it is. But I have to ask for this; I'll never have another chance. I kiss your nipples as tenderly as if they were made of snow. I let my tears fall onto your soft skin. I know I will always remember how your nipples quietly harden, even under such a gentle touch.

The next day we go to the clinic. You leave me in the hallway as you make your way to the operating room, looking back to mouth, "I love you." Your eyes are wide in fright, but you are smiling.

Then you are gone. I spend four hours waiting.

There is a strip mall next door. In the coffee shop, I write in my journal. In the drugstore, I buy you a card and makeshift bandages. I try to be objective about whether sanitary pads or diapers will be more comfortable and absorbent against your wounds.

The lady at the checkout counter asks me how I'm spending my holidays. I tell her, "Quietly."

After three hours, I come back to the waiting room. It is a cosmetic surgery office, so a little like a hotel lobby, underheated and expensively decorated, with candy in little dishes, emerald-green plush chairs, and upscale fashion magazines artfully displayed against the wall.

A young woman comes in, frantic to get a pimple "zapped" before she sees her family over the holidays. An older woman comes in with her daughter for a follow-up visit to a face-lift. She is wearing a scarf and dark glasses. The nurse examines her bruises right out in the waiting room.

And you are in the operating room having your body and your gender legally altered. I feel like laughing, but I know it makes me sound like a lunatic.

After a lifetime of waiting, I am finally called to the recovery room. You are woozy and weak but smile at me when I take your hand. I remember why I am willing to nurse you through this and anything.

Over the course of the next several months we embark upon a journey filled with dramatic peaks and valleys. You start testosterone treatments and your very thinking is changed, along with your body. Most profound is the change in your sexuality. You are more driven, yet more open and vulnerable. You want me like men have wanted me. Sometimes I am so frightened; it is only your love that makes sex possible.

And yet, if anything, you are more sensual to me now. On you, "more masculine" seems like "more butch." I never thought it possible that you could be more butch.

You strut more. Sometimes I find you looking at yourself in the mirror, curious and even delighted. I never saw you take such an interest in your body before. You let me touch you more.

There is a giddy feeling to our lives. Clothes shopping, making love, just being together in this journey is funny, surreal, and filled with a strange, joyful expectation.

And there are stray moments when I stop in my tracks, suddenly realizing my own transition, how I have also changed. How I am changing even now.

On one such day I make a word for myself: *transensual*. And in naming myself, I feel substantial—connected. I am reminded of when I discovered the word *lesbian* and later *femme*. These words name me and help create me at once. My self has reached for these identifiers, found them and filled them out. Now I make them unique to me. Transensual femme lesbian.

I often bless this path you have taken, for your own sake and for mine; it has propelled me into my own journey, and I have found a part of me which needed to emerge. I see people, the world, differently. I am different.

I am trans-formed.

When you came out over 30 years ago, a young butch in the Chicago bars before the lesbian-feminist movement swept you up in its passion, did you ever long for this second chance?

When you burned your last bra and wore your last dress, did you ever think your path would lead you to this future?

When you swore to yourself as a child that you would somehow find a way to put your elbow in your ear if it would change you into a boy, did you ever think your wish would come true?

You are a boy now. And you are a transgendered butch with a 50-year history. Your politics and passion, your anger and hurt, your emotional capacity and human consciousness—these can never be erased. When I move against you, when I hold you to my breast, when I take you in my mouth, I take in your whole self. You feel my soul and I respond to you, as a femme, as a lesbian, as a transensual woman…as myself.

Tonight I wake up to see you lying next to me, your chest softly rising and falling with each breath. I hardly notice the scars, you are so beautiful. Sleep well, my butch, my boy, my man. I will be here when you wake.

WHOSE BODY IS THIS ANYWAY?

DISCUSSION QUESTIONS

1. What social systems or institutions regulate Hale's personal experience of embodiment and identity?
2. How might identity politics play a role in finding support for transition-related decisions among trans people?
3. Why do you think there is such an emphasis placed on genitalia in our society as essential markers of "real" maleness or femaleness?

There was the doctor who told me that if I wanted testosterone, I should be looking for a surgeon to cut on my genitals.

There was the passport agency official who told me that if I want an M on my passport, I should have already had a surgeon cut on my genitals.

There was the human relations employee who told me that if I wanted a faculty ID card with a current picture and a name matching the one on my driver's license, I should have already had a surgeon cut on my genitals.

There are FTMs who tell me that if I want to go to their meetings, if I am a real/true/genuine transexual, if I am one of them, I should be looking for a surgeon to cut on my genitals.

There are FTMs who tell me that if I want to be one of them, I should be delighted and congratulatory when one of them finds a surgeon to cut on his genitals.

There are FTMs who tell me that if I want to be one of them, I should be filled with pity or disdain when another FTM finds a surgeon to cut on his genitals.

There are FTMs who tell me that I should want to look at the results when one of them has had a surgeon cut on his genitals.

There was the psychiatrist who told me that if I want to have sex, I should get a surgeon to cut on my genitals first.

There was the nontransexual butch leatherman who told me that if I want to suck his cock, I should have plans to find a surgeon to cut on my genitals.

There was the MTF who shoved her tits in my face and told me that I should give her a call after I had gotten a surgeon to cut on my genitals because I'm just so cute.

There is Donald Laub, who says that if I am to have sex that isn't lesbian sex, I should have him cut on my genitals—but only if I quit my job first.

There are the leathermen of Hellfire who say that if I want to be one of them, I must have had a surgeon cut on my genitals because Inferno is for people without vaginas.

There is David Gilbert, who says that if he cuts on my genitals, he will remove my vagina no matter what I want because otherwise he would be making a chick with a dick, and no one wants that.

There was the nontransexual gay man who told a group of FTMs how glad he is that not all of us have surgeons cut on our genitals because he likes fucking our hot sexy wetness.

There was the nontransexual bi-guy who told a group of FTMs how glad he is that not all of us have surgeons cut on our genitals because we are the best of both worlds—male psyches in female bodies.

There are MTFs who tell me that if I am really transexual, I should define myself according to whether or not I have, or intend to have, a surgeon cut on my genitals. "Pre-op or post-op or non-op?"

Which op?

There was the social service agency director who shook my hand—the first FTM hand he had knowingly shaken—after a political meeting and asked if I'd had a surgeon cut on my genitals.

There are people in the audiences at the academic trans theory talks I give who don't ask about the content of my work but do ask about whether or not I've had a surgeon cut on my genitals.

There are shrinks who tell me that if I want testosterone, I should get myself diagnosed with a mental disorder and seek a surgeon to cut on my genitals when the shrinks tell me I am ready to have a surgeon cut on my genitals.

There are all those nontransexuals who tell me that if I get some surgeon to cut on my genitals, I will be mutilating myself or sinning or making myself into a monster or a freak.

There is Sheila Jeffreys who says that Janice Raymond didn't go far enough and that surgeons should be prohibited from cutting on transexuals' genitals because it is mutilation.

There are all those transexuals who tell me that if I want to have a surgeon cut on my genitals, I must believe myself to be mentally disordered or disabled or suffering from a birth defect.

There are some nontransgendered academic theorists who tell me that if I am a transexual rather than a cross-dresser or a transvestite or a butch lesbian, this must mean I want a surgeon to cut on my genitals. And they tell me that if I get a surgeon to cut on my genitals, this will show my internalized misogyny or my internalized homophobia or my lack of agency or my complicity with the medical regime, consumer capitalism, or the bipolar gender system.

There are all those transexuals who tell me that if I get a surgeon to cut on my genitals, I will no longer be a transexual but a complete man who blends into society, pays his taxes, and lives a normal life.

I'm tired of listening to other people talking about whether or not I should have a surgeon cut on my genitals. And I'm also tired of people talking about whether or not my trans sisters should have some surgeon cut on their genitals. Whose genitals are these anyway?

PROTECTING THE LESBIAN BORDER: THE TENSION BETWEEN INDIVIDUAL AND COMMUNAL AUTHENTICITY

DISCUSSION QUESTIONS

1. How do the concepts of "border" and "boundary" inform sexual identifications/labels among the women participants, as well as their community membership?
2. In what ways do the women participants resist being perceived as "not straight," and why is this important?
3. How does public space become an important site of identification and authentic membership for the women participants?

The stories of lesbians who begin relationships with men inform us not only about the complex ways in which sexuality is lived but also about how individuals account for potential changes in their identities, how they navigate issues of belonging and the embodiment of desire, and how they connect identity and community. Their negotiations with notions of authenticity and belonging can inform how such matters are engaged in a variety of other scenarios. I begin here with the story of Jennifer, a woman who, after many years of living as a lesbian, became involved with a man.

Jennifer, a 39-years-old white professional, came out as a lesbian in her early 20s. She was politically active and involved in AIDS prevention work. She recalls that her parents were at first taken aback but then settled into acceptance of her identity, going as far as becoming active in Parents, Families, and Friends of Lesbians and Gays (PFLAG), a support organization for friends and family members of gay and lesbian individuals. In her late 20s, while on a trip away from home, Jennifer met Tom. It was a friend who pointed out that Jennifer might be attracted to Tom. "I was embarrassed," she says "that I hadn't noticed." Of the moment she noticed her attraction to Tom, Jennifer says she was "kind of horrified because that meant that everything was going to be different." At first, she tried to hide her involvement.

> I kept it a secret for a good while...[but once] it became clear that this is not going to go away, and he was not going to somehow miraculously become a woman, and that I had to really stop being closeted, I started telling people.

Jennifer eventually married Tom, something about which she still expresses mixed emotions. She explains feeling "absolutely horrible about it....I often lie to people and say that we did not." She does not refer to Tom as her husband, preferring instead the term "partner." They have two children together. Today, Jennifer refrains from using the word lesbian to define herself.

> The label of lesbian was tremendously important. I identified as a radical lesbian, feminist and as a dyke and all of those terms were absolutely empowering and my complete identity. They were powerful, powerful important words in my life and there's nothing that remotely compares to that now. And lesbian also still counts as that core of my identity, so it feels kinda dishonest also to identify as anything else. Those terms still feel like important terms for me, but I don't use those terms because I think it's politically very damaging for the lesbian community.

She continues.

> I absolutely feel like I have lost my, I can't think of how to say it, I think I lost my right to claim my identity and the terms that feel right for me for defining my identity.

For Jennifer, the change to a partner of a different gender brings about a change in identity, not an identity that she considers her "core," but the identity with which she publicly affiliates.

COMMUNITIES

Many authors have discussed the fact that sexual identities are socially constructed (Esterberg, 1997; Gagnon and Simon, 1973; Garber, 1995; Green, 2002; Kitzinger and Wilkinson, 1995; McIntosh, 1968; Plummer, 1995; Rust, 2000, 1993; Stein, 1993; Weeks, 1985). Identities have shifting meanings that are dependent on the social context in which they exist. But despite their shifting meanings, identities continue to inform notions of belonging and community. Identities serve as anchors to the self and as entry points into particular communities.

The definition of a lesbian community and what it means to belong to such a community is contested (Esterberg, 1997). But what remains true is that the lesbian community is a powerful concept in the lives of American lesbians (Esterberg, 1997; Inness, 1997; Rothblum, 2008). Kitzinger and Wilkinson (1995) show that for many women, being a part of the lesbian community is a significant part of living as a lesbian. Many stage models of gay and lesbian identity development put community integration as the final and most positive indicator of a healthy identity (Floyd and Stein, 2002). As Shugar notes, lesbian communities are important sites of security, safety and political activism. Community is central to identity and in turn, identity is central to the "production, maintenance, and continuation of lesbian communities" (Shugar, 1999: 13). Heterosexual women, on the other hand, tend to not accord as much importance to a community based on sexual identity (Rothblum, 2008).

Although community has been a central tenet of the lesbian identity, the idea of membership in such communities is itself contested. Much of the debate about who belongs in the lesbian community and who does not has centered on bisexual women. Some have questioned whether bisexual women, because of their presumed attraction to and involvement with men, can be considered members of a lesbian community. Involvement with men has emerged as a central criterion for exclusion from lesbian communities (Jeffreys, 1999, 1994; MacKinnon, 1982; Walters, 1996).

Some lesbians do end up having sexual relationships with men on a short-term, or long-term basis. Other lesbians do not. The difference between lesbians and heterosexual women may be "one of degree rather than kind" (Diamond, 2005: 119), but previous research shows that the border between the two groups is heavily policed not only by group members but also scholars who study sexual communities.

The desire on the part of academics to organize lesbians into groups based on their involvement with men is an example of the way the boundary between "real" lesbian and others is maintained. Diamond (2005) classifies women who do not engage in relationships with men as "stable lesbians" and the women who do as "fluid lesbians." . . .

This boundary keeping is visible even in the very limited media representations of lesbians who are involved with men. An example includes the character of Tina on the Showtime mini-series *The L-Word*. Of course, it is not surprising that there would be a need to police the boundaries of a community that is stigmatized (Plummer, 1982). Nevertheless, this border, or boundary, although socially constructed, is very much real. There may be little difference between the experiences of lesbians who do and do not get involved with men. But this "border" is socially important. Labels matter to people. They create communities (Esterberg, 1997; Green, 2002; Phelan, 1994).

This study examines how women who experience a change to a partner of a different gender, use categories of gender, sexual identity, and sexual orientation to make sense of this shift both to themselves and to others. In examining these categories, the study contributes to the area of research concerned with the way sexual identity categories, although socially constructed and at times fluid, are shaped and become powerful forces in shaping people's lives and their communities (Green, 2002; Esterberg, 1997; Phelan, 1994). More specifically, I examine the women's narratives of change in partners. Since narrative analysis gives prominence to human agency, it is well suited for studies of identity (Riessman, 1993). . . .

For lesbian women who have begun relationships with men, few scripts are readily available. There is no readily available way of being a lesbian who is now partnered with a man, partially because the women are no longer part of a "community of discourse" (Swidler, 2001) that gives them resources and allows them the opportunity to articulate identities. There are no stories readily available of lesbians dating men. The exception to this is a handful of Hollywood representations like the character of Tina on the Showtime miniseries *The L-Word*, the

1997 film *Chasing Amy*, and a brief mention in the 1994 film *Go Fish*.

When I tell people what my research is about, most venture the guess that women who were once partnered with women and are now with men think of themselves as bisexual. But this is not how the women thought of themselves; in fact, most emphatically rejected the label of bisexual. In other words, although the label of bisexual is one that many would associate with these women, and although bisexuality provides a ready-made alternative identity, the women in this study do not feel at home under the banner of bisexuality. It becomes clear that the women consider the common perceptions of bisexuality to be a hindrance to their ability to fully embrace the label. Among the stereotypes associated with bisexuality, one that is most difficult to surmount is that of non-monogamy. Bisexuals are assumed to be non-monogamous (Garber, 1995; Rust, 2000). The women themselves bring up this matter time and again. Non-monogamy implies a desire to or a propensity to be involved with more than one partner at one time. The combination of bisexuality and non-monogamy implies switching to partners of different genders, or going "back and forth" between the two genders. The trouble for the women in this study is that they wish to guard against this notion of "back and forth." They want to embody something more stable. In order not to be mistaken for someone who would go "back and forth," the women painstakingly express their commitment to their male partners. A legitimate claim to their identities, the women believe, is grounded in stability. They see themselves as authentic when they can also present their identity as stable. The label of bisexual does not offer them authenticity in this way because it lacks that element of stability. The women make attempts to uncouple stability and authenticity but nevertheless fall back on notions of stability to make their claim to authenticity. They claim to be the "same person" as they were when involved with women, and they claim to be attracted to the "same qualities" in men and in women. The label of bisexual is thus rejected. The notion of a stable self is maintained.

Interestingly, the identity of "straight" or heterosexual is one that is also actively rejected by the majority of women in the study, but for different reasons. Being straight implies a lot of things that the women do not wish to take part in, such as being traditionally feminine and sexually submissive. Being perceived as "not straight" is both a goal and an ongoing task. Despite their efforts, the women are often read as straight, or as they themselves indicate, they are not read as "anything at all." The women acknowledge that when they are assumed to be straight, in fact, it is because their sexuality goes under the radar, so to speak. And so, during any given interaction, the women have a choice to make. They can let assumptions stand, and not challenge the fact that they are perceived as straight. They do this on occasion. Or, they have to work not to appear straight. The desire not to appear straight requires a particular set of negotiations. It requires the women to make choices about disclosure and requires them to challenge, sometimes verbally, unspoken assumptions. This proves to be difficult or nearly impossible at times.

...This research shows that there are limitations to what identity can be embraced. Self-identified lesbian women who begin relationships with men are not free to embrace any label that they feel reflects their identities, as Jennifer's story shows. Instead, in the process of settling on an identity after their involvement with men, these women not only negotiate what feels authentic to them, but also consider their obligations towards their previous lesbian communities, communities to which they no longer belong. The fluidity in the identities is balanced by their commitment to real communities.

When individuals move out of a community, as opposed to into one, the notion of authenticity is made more complex. In the case of a woman who once identified as lesbian and now is partnered with a man, there may be many different authenticities, in relation to families or in-laws, other lesbians, or ex-partners (Vannini, 2007). This does not imply that the notion of an authentic self is any less important than it was before. What is different in the case of the women in this study is that they have

many sources of authentification (Gubrium and Holstein, 2009). The women show a concern for what might be considered localized authenticity or multiple authenticities.

INVESTMENT IN IDENTITY

According to Stein (1997), lesbians who get involved with men are dissatisfied with their lesbian identity and, by extension, with the lesbian community. In fact, according to Stein, the lesbians who do partner with men are different from those who do not. These women, ex-lesbians as Stein calls them, are motivated by a sense of pursuit for their real identity. They get involved with men and cease to be lesbians and thus settle into an identity that feels more authentic to them. No doubt this is true for some people, but recent research shows that women who relinquish lesbian and bisexual identities do not differ significantly from women who do not in terms of their sexual milestones of first same-sex attraction, conduct, questioning, and most importantly identification (Diamond, 2003; Peplau and Garnet, 2000; Rothblum, 2000; Rust, 2000).

For lesbians who become involved with men, notions of community and belonging are deeply tied into the process of self-identification. Esterberg (1997) finds that for lesbians who become involved with men, involvement in the lesbian community, which she translates into a political commitment to lesbian rights, can affect what identity is settled into after involvement with men. She examines the stories of two women who left relationships with women to begin relationships with men. One woman, Cheryl, chose to label herself bisexual after partnering with a man and the other, Sally, chose to maintain her lesbian label. Esterberg explains this difference in terms of involvement in a lesbian community. Involvement in the lesbian community made the lesbian identity more salient for Sally and so she felt more connected to the label of lesbian and sought to preserve it despite her marriage to a man. Cheryl, on the other hand, having been less politically involved, chose to re-label herself. According to Esterberg, the process of re-labeling was not straining for Cheryl because bisexuality was not a source of political identity and community belonging for her....

Commitment and salience are partially consequences of relationships in which the individual is invested. If an identity is implicated in many commitments, if many relationships are based on it, the identity is more likely to be salient. A salient identity is less likely to change. Thus, relationships have a role in maintaining identities. This would lead one to believe, as Esterberg has shown, that the women in this study would try any means necessary to keep their lesbian labels, especially if they, like Jennifer, are deeply involved in a lesbian community. However, this is not what I found.

DATA COLLECTION AND METHOD

I collected data through semi-structured interviews with 32 women who had at some point in their lives self-identified as lesbian, bisexual or queer but who were subsequently involved with men. This article concerns itself with the 14 women out of the initial 32 who specifically identified as lesbian prior to their involvement with men, as opposed to bisexual or queer. The women ranged in age from 20 to 43. At the time of the interview, four women had begun relationships with women once again. Of the 14 self-identified lesbian women, 9 women identified as white and/or Caucasian, 2 identified as African American, one identified as Iranian, one identified as Chinese and another identified as "other." The women all lived or had ties to the same mid-size Midwestern city in the USA. The group consisted of a mix of students and professionals. All women either had or were working toward a university degree (BA, MA, Ph.D.), except for one woman who ended her formal education after high school.

As Esterberg (1997) notes, the meaning of sexual identities depends on the social and historical context in which they are produced. Being a lesbian, bisexual or queer woman in the USA is different than being lesbian, bisexual or queer elsewhere in the world. And even in the context of the USA, being in the part of the country known as the Midwest may give identities a different character than being in larger coastal cities such as New York and San Francisco, which are known for their large and visible LGBTQ populations. This fact certainly contributes to the limitations of this study. But a preliminary study such as this can and should lead to further research that examines the impact that regionality can have on these particular identity processes. A second limitation of the study is the overrepresentation of professionals and students, although this group represents racial and ethnic diversity, which is generally lacking in LGBTQ research. People occupy intersections of identities and since sociocultural factors, such as race, ethnicity, and class, affect sexual identities; they have to be accounted for in research (Garnets, 2002)....

As Gagnon (2004: 127) states "Conducting research on this movement from same to other-gender erotic preference is very difficult in that the persons involved may be treated as socially dead by the gay and lesbian communities." The methods for participant recruitment were sensitive to this issue and I made attempts to seek out as many diverse women as possible. The women with whom I spoke are those who do not mind "being found" and thus this makes them particular kinds of individuals. This is, of course, a symptom of doing research in a homophobic society. I have attempted to recruit participants through gay and lesbian organizations as well as social-networking websites that do not necessarily cater to LGBTQ persons. This was done in hopes of capturing anyone who, since the move to a male partner, has abandoned their lesbian, bisexual or queer label. Through my own personal contacts, I was able to include the accounts of two women who had previously identified as lesbian but who now identify as heterosexual and seek to keep their previous identity "private."...

SYMBOLIC AND PHYSICAL PROTECTIONISM

Of the 14 women who previously self-identified as lesbian, none sought to retain the label of lesbian after their involvement with men. The women in this study showed a great deal of protectionism towards the lesbian label. By distancing themselves from lesbian spaces, both physical and symbolic, they sought to preserve the authenticity of those spaces. In some cases the distancing was not one of their choosing, but in most cases it was.

This protectionism toward "lesbianism" manifested itself in two different ways. First, women exhibited a great sense of preservation towards the label of lesbian. They sought to keep the label untainted by removing themselves from under its umbrella, as in the case of Jennifer, although they still felt that the label captures something about their true identity. Second, they physically sought to preserve lesbian public spaces either by not occupying them anymore or at the very least, not occupying them with their male partners. In the following sections, I outline the ways in which this sense of protectionism manifests itself in the process of (1) self-labeling or symbolic protectionism, and (2) navigating public spaces or physical protectionism. I then show how investment in identity coupled with notions of fluidity create a boundaried fluidity in which the women find spaces to define who they are.

SELF-LABELING

The process of choosing an identity label is by no means uncomplicated. None of the women with whom I spoke had an essentialist notion of what it means to be lesbian. They acknowledged variability in the lesbian experience. Despite this fact, the women, through their own experiences, sought to make room for an authentic lesbian experience that they no longer took part in. What exactly counted as an authentic lesbian experience, of course, varied from woman to woman, and sometimes varied within the same interview. Although the women were quick to explain that they knew of many lesbians who in the past had been or were currently in a relationship with a man, none of the women with whom I spoke currently identified as lesbian. I asked the women to explain this choice. If there is

so much variety in the lesbian experience, why not continue to use the label?

Karen, a 29-year-old white professional, who had previously identified as lesbian-queer, explains why she no longer identified as lesbian.

> 'Cause I'm a word-fiend, I like definitions to actually mean something and what I hate about labels for myself is also what I love about words, that they mean something and so, if I say tree you might picture a palm tree and somebody else may picture an oak tree and that's fine, just like when I say lesbian you might picture lipstick and curly hair and I might picture flannel or whatever and that's fine but, like we would all agree that a tree is a plant and it has roots, they go down in the ground, it takes up water, chlorophyll, whatever some kind of leaves or pine needles, brown and green, and so there's a general framework that everybody understands and I think it makes the word tree very powerful because it's universal, it's understood. There's variations on it but we know what it means, and what I would love about more flexible labels and just having a jillion labels for people's sexuality is also what I would hate if it happened to the rest of my words, like I want them to be kinda boxed in just a little bit so that there's a universal understanding.

Despite the fact that she mentions that many different types of "trees" exist, Karen considers her choice to be with a man as a difference of kind and not of degree, a universally understood difference. Although she refrains from completely framing her argument in essentialist terms, by arguing that sexuality is innate, Karen nevertheless creates space for a discussion of a "real" lesbian experience. Just where that threshold of difference resides is unclear, or perhaps differs from woman to woman. The implication of Karen's reasoning for no longer considering herself a lesbian is that including her experience in the definition would make the definition itself meaningless. It would, in short, take power away from the word lesbian and this is clearly something that Karen does not wish to take part in. The fact that she offers no universally accepted definition of lesbian seems not to be of concern. Heather, a 41-year-old white student, makes a point similar to Karen.

> I called myself lesbian for a while when I was, when I started dating my [male] partner. But I feel like that's not, I feel like I'm taking away somehow, from women who are exclusively with women, if I use the word lesbian.

As Heather's statement hints, the process of choosing a label is not an individually isolated process. Her assumption that she is "taking away somehow" outlines her feelings that her choice to keep the label does injury to women who do not have relationships with men. It seems that her very existence as a lesbian with a male partner is a threat to the legitimacy of a community that she cares greatly about. As a way to reconcile that, Heather, like Jennifer and Karen, gives up a label that she otherwise would want to use in order to preserve the authenticity of the community in which she used to belong.

Why would these women's choice to keep the label have any implication for anyone other than themselves? This is precisely because of the central role that the community plays in defining a lesbian identity. While involved with women, many of these women, like many other LGBTQ women have been bombarded by messages that their attraction and involvement with other women is a phase, or is otherwise not to be taken seriously. As Diamond (2009:52) notes, there is an "assumption among scientists and laypeople alike that authentic sexual orientation develops early and is consistent through one's life." What is authentic is what is stable. "So the familiar battlegrounds are drawn: fixed ¼ biological ¼ deserving of acceptance and protection, whereas variable ¼ chosen ¼ fair game for stigma and discrimination" (Diamond, 2009: 246).

Amy, a white 36-year-old student, recalls:

> I sometimes felt a sort of eye rolling, like it was some sort of phase for me or something, or a novelty of some kind.

Meg, a 30-year-old white student, recalls her discomfort with the assumption.

> I think they feel, and not just like my parents, my extended family my grandma, grandpa, like we're talking and I'll be like "we're not in a monogamous

relationship and I may still sleep with women" just because I want them to realize that this wasn't a phase and whatever.

The idea that their attraction to women can be read by others as having been a phase is a constant backdrop to the women's personal narratives. So they find themselves in a difficult place. On one hand, they need to make it clear that their attraction to women and the identities that they embraced previously were authentic, and not an experimental phase. They seek to make their previous choices authentic by confirming that they still find themselves attracted to other women. But they can only take this point so far. They refrain from continuing to identify as lesbian, in order to not fall into the stereotype that as Jennifer states: "All lesbians need is to meet the right man." Emily, a 32-year-old white student, explains the situation as follows:

> Part of my fear is that I think that, you know, to the ears of someone who doesn't understand what it means to be gay, I think that unfortunately that my experience makes the case that it's a choice and I know that, I think that, I know that's not true for so many people that I love. It's not, you know, so I do feel guilt about that. . . . I think my guilt is that it sounds like I make the case for choice, which I think is a very unhelpful, not even, it's a harmful experience to talk about to the biased ear, to the ear that wants to already reject and hate.

The women's experience, as they explain, can too easily serve as an example of "choice." The lesbian community as they understand it, is built around notions of essentialism, or being born a lesbian. The women fear that their experience will harm . . . the lesbian community. The women's choice of identity after involvement with men is not about settling on a label that feels right to them alone. Their choice is also motivated by the consequences of their choice for the lesbian community.

Jennifer remembers some direct feedback from friends.

> A couple of people specifically said I can't believe that you would do this, you know, this is exactly the

stereotype that people have about gay people and specifically about lesbians and now you've proven them right and why not just not date this guy because it's really really bad.

Now involved with men, these women's fear is that they will further serve as an example of the perceived impermanence and the inauthentic nature of a lesbian identity. These women have to come to terms with exactly the idea that lesbians really just haven't found the right man. On the matter of becoming an example of choice, Jennifer explains:

> I think it's too damaging. It fits into the stereotypes and I think does a lot of damage to the lesbian, gay, bisexual and transgendered queer movement too, there's so much of the civil rights activism that rests on, and I think inappropriately so, but that rests on we're born gay, we can't help it and my story flies in the face of that and I think would be used as an example by people in the ex-gay movement and in the, you know, people that want to change people's sexual orientation, who say that it's a choice, you can just choose something else, that I would be more fodder for that crap and I don't want to be that. So, in many ways, I think it's oppressive heterosexual society, you know, I talk about how I lost friends like that's, and I did, but I think I lost friends because of heterosexist oppression not because my friends were bad people although I'm pissed it wasn't, they weren't wrong about what image that creates.

When navigating the events following their partnership with men, these women are constantly working against the backdrop of their lesbian experiences having been a choice, and thus inauthentic. Their sense of personal authenticity is in conflict with a community's authenticity. On one hand, they work to explain that their involvement with women was not a phase. On the other hand, they work to not make the case for choice. This is an extremely difficult balance to maintain. In addition to maintaining this balance, the women distance themselves from the community, despite sometimes feeling profound loss. Karen, a 29-year-old white professional, puts it simply:

> I think the biggest hesitance is about like going back into the closet or whatever, you know, you've set up

your community and then how does this affect the rest of your community.

Explaining her sense of loss, Tina, a 38-year-old white professional, states:

> You know, I love watching *The L-Word* and sometimes I feel like this isn't really your show anymore. You're not a lesbian anymore. I used to get *Curve Magazine* and I, you know, like you're not really a lesbian anymore so I do, I feel like I kinda lost, part, being part of the club or whatever. And I feel like I lost that sense of solidarity.

Tina expresses her sense of loss but is inadvertently implying that there is an authentic lesbian whom she no longer embodies. By placing *Curve Magazine* and *The L-Word* together and placing herself out, Tina is drawing a circle around what she considers to be "real" lesbian. She herself serves as an example of what is not real; and through that process of exclusion, she inadvertently solidifies the notion of a real lesbian.

PUBLIC SPACES

Not only do some women relinquish the label of lesbian, but their desire to maintain an authentic lesbian community extends to avoiding lesbian public spaces, or at least, avoiding such places when in the company of their male partners. Riley, a 24-year-old white student, explains this in terms of respect for a space that is made for a particular purpose. She says:

> I wouldn't enjoy them if I was with a man but also that I would feel, like honestly, being disrespectful, and I know that, you know, in theory that's ridiculous, but you know, I'm slightly sort of keeping it that way by respecting those kind of boundaries but there's something I kinda like about things being separate. I think it's important to have spaces that are not necessarily explicitly exclusive but that especially for, for the lack of a better word, minority groups, incredibly important, you know, and also I love feeling like there's almost this like social service quality to my social behavior…there is something that's like, this isn't accessible for everyone.

Riley feels that bringing a man into a space that is considered lesbian would be disrespectful. She does what she considers "social service" by helping to maintain the integrity of the lesbian space.

Celia, a 33-year-old white student, echoes these sentiments:

> I'm always concerned too, I want to remain respectful, like I won't be really affectionate with my husband in a gay bar. I do try to, you know, be respectful. And I don't go overboard, like I don't make sure that everybody knows he's my husband but at the same time, I don't deny that he's my husband. But, I'm conscious of that balance.

Celia wants to be respectful of the queer space she occupies. Somehow being affectionate with her husband is a sign of disrespect. One could assume that, according to Celia, it is not the affection that is disrespectful but the heteronormativity it signals. The relationship is a symbol of the structurally privileged social position of heterosexuality.

I ask Meg, a 30-year-old white student, about her experience of being in a gay bar with her husband. In this context, gay bar is used as a descriptor for a space that caters to lesbian women. She explains:

> I think certainly, I felt uncomfortable dancing with him and being straight in a gay bar. But still if I were not with him I probably wouldn't have an issue with dancing with him in a gay bar, if he wasn't my partner.

The issue that Meg highlights is interesting. It is not the presence of a man in a gay bar that is of concern. Meg explains that she would dance with men at gay bars. The issue is bringing her heterosexual relationship into a gay bar, the same sentiment echoed by Celia. All three women show great reverence for a space that they consider serving a particular purpose, that of letting those who occupy it interact outside of the heterosexual gaze. The women perform the same level of policing of public spaces as they do of symbolic spaces. They physically refrain from coming into lesbian public spaces, thus protecting those spaces. They symbolically

avoid such identity spaces, by refraining from identifying as lesbian.

As some authors have noted, the legitimacy accorded to heterosexuality is not just a by-product of individual interactions (Jackson, 2006). Heteronormativity and heterosexuality are not synonymous (Berlant and Warner, 2000; Ward and Schneider, 2009; Schlichter, 2004). The term heteronormativity captures the "taken-for-granted and simultaneously compulsory character of institutionalized heterosexuality" (Nielson et al., 2000: 284). Despite this difference, the women in this study see their individual relationships and interactions as symbols of the legitimacy of heterosexuality and its privileged position with regards to other forms of sexuality....

CONCLUSION

Some sociologists argue that in a postmodern era there is more fluidity in all identities. Gergen (2000) for example argues that today, individuals experience self-multiplication, or the capacity to be present in many places at once. This diversification makes identity commitment nearly impossible. Individuals are no longer bound to particular locales, as they were in modern times, that is they are in the presence of a variety of "going concerns" or identity resources (Holstein and Gubrium, 2000). Gergen argues that this lack of commitment allows for fluidity in many identities and that the traditional goal of a stable self (self as object) has been replaced with a fluid self (self as process). The self, as Gergen argues, is in jeopardy (2000: 6). Although he does not specifically theorize about sexuality, one could assume that the same mechanism would be at play in navigating postmodern sexual identities. One could assume that individuals are no longer bound by any social structures and that they are free to define themselves, however temporarily in whatever way they wish. But the idea that we live in a time where anything goes in terms of identity is not supported by these accounts. Plummer (2003) notes that not everyone's life is marked by the lack of commitment that Gergen sees as possible. He argues that many individuals are still bound by very traditional understandings of sexuality with strict guidelines about appropriate behavior. In the case of the majority of the women in this study, that is not entirely true either. The women in this study occupy the uncharted territory between these two identity extremes; they are neither liberated by fluidity nor confined by tradition. They do not necessarily hold an essentialist notion of lesbianism but they do have a commitment to the lesbian community. These women themselves draw and redraw boundaries around their communities. Plummer is correct in stating that it is perhaps premature to assume that in the current social arrangement, sexual identities are fluid beyond any concrete boundaries. But it is not that these women have somehow accepted an essentialist notion of sexuality. They are aware that no real definition of lesbian exists. But they also know, based on first hand experience that a real lesbian community does exist. Although they can no longer actively participate in the social aspects of that community, they still have a hand in shaping it. They see this "shaping" as part of their responsibility. The last thing that these women desire is to have their experiences used as a platform to erode the sense of authenticity of the community that they cherish.

REFERENCES

Baudrillard J (1995) The Gulf War Did Not Take Place. Bloomington: Indiana University Press.

Berlant L and Warner M (2000) Sex in public. In: Berlant L (ed.) Intimacy. Chicago, IL: University of Chicago Press, 311–360.

Burke PJ (1991) Identity processes and social stress. American Sociological Review 56(3): 836–849.

Burke PJ (2006) Identity change. Social Psychology Quarterly 69(1): 81–96.

Callero PL (1985) Role-identity salience. Social Psychology Quarterly 48(3): 203–214.

Denzin NK (1991) Images of Postmodern Society: Social Theory and Contemporary Cinema. Newbury Park, CA: SAGE.

Diamond LM (2003) Was it a phase? Young women's relinquishment of lesbian/bisexual identities over a 5-year period. Journal of Personality and Social Psychology 84(2): 352–364.

Diamond LM (2005) A new view of lesbian subtypes: Stable versus fluid identity trajectories over an 8-year period. Psychology of Women Quarterly 29(2): 119–128.

Diamond LM (2009) Sexual Fluidity: Understanding Women's Love And Desire. Cambridge, MA: Harvard University Press.

Esterberg KG (1997) Lesbian and Bisexual Identities: Constructing Communities, Constructing Selves. Philadelphia, PA: Temple University Press.

Floyd F and Stein TS (2002) Sexual orientation identity formation among gay, lesbian, and bisexual youths: Multiple patterns of milestone experiences. Journal of Research on Adolescence 12(2): 167–191.

Gagnon JH (2004) An Interpretation of Desire. Chicago, IL and London: University of Chicago Press.

Gagnon JH and Simon W (1973) Sexual Conduct: The Social Sources of Human Sexuality. Chicago, IL: Aldine.

Garber M (1995) Vice Versa: Bisexuality and The Eroticism of Everyday Life. Simon & Schuster: New York.

Garnets LD (2002) Sexual orientations in perspective. Cultural Diversity and Ethnic Minority Psychology 8(2): 115–129.

Gergen KJ (2000) The Saturated Self: Dilemmas of Identity in Contemporary Life. New York: Basic Books.

Green AI (2002) Gay but not queer: Toward a post-queer study of sexuality. Theory and Society 31(4): 521–545.

Gubrium JF and Holstein JA (2009) Analyzing Narrative Reality. London: SAGE Publications.

Holstein JA and Gubrium JF (2000) The Self We Live By: Narrative Identity in a Postmodern World. New York, NY: Oxford University Press.

Inness SA (1997) The Lesbian Menace: Ideology, Identity, and the Representation of Lesbian Life. Amherst: University of Massachusetts Press.

Jackson S (2006) Gender, sexuality and heterosexuality: The complexity (and limits) of heteronormativity. Feminist Theory 7(1): 102–121.

Jeffreys S (1994) The queer disappearance of lesbians. Women's Studies International Forum 17(5): 459–472.

Jeffreys S (1999) Bisexual politics: A superior form of feminism? Women's Studies International Forum 22(3): 273–285.

Kitzinger C and Wilkinson S (1995) Transitions from heterosexuality to lesbianism: The discursive production of lesbian identities. Developmental Psychology 31(1): 95–104.

MacKinnon C (1982) Feminism, Marxism, method and the state: An agenda for theory. Signs 7(3): 515–544.

McIntosh M (1968) The homosexual role. Social Problems 17(2): 262–270.

Nielson JM, Walden G and Kunkel CA (2000) Gendered heteronormativity empirical illustrations in everyday life. Sociological Quarterly 41(2): 283–296.

Peplau LA and Garnets LD (2000) A new paradigm for understanding women's sexuality and sexual orientation. Journal of Social Issues 56(2): 329–350.

Phelan S (1994) Getting Specific: Postmodern Lesbian Politics. Minneapolis: University of Minnesota Press.

Plummer K (1982) Symbolic interactionism and sexual conduct: An emergent perspective. In: Brake M (ed.) Human Sexual Relations: Towards a Redefinition of Sexual Politics. New York: Pantheon, 223–241.

Plummer K (1995) Telling Sexual Stories: Power, Change and Social Worlds. London and New York: Routledge.

Plummer K (2003) Queers, bodies and postmodern sexualities: A note on revisiting the 'sexual' in symbolic interactionism. Qualitative Sociology 26(4): 515–530.

Ponse B (1978) Identities in the Lesbian World: The Social Construction of Self. Westport CT: Greenwood Press.

Riessman CK (1993) Narrative Analysis. London: SAGE.

Rothblum E (2000) Sexual orientation and sex in women's lives: Conceptual and methodological issues. Journal of Social Issues 56(2): 193–204.

Rothblum E (2008) Finding a large and thriving lesbian and bisexual community: The costs and benefits of caring. Gay and Lesbian Issues and Psychology Review 4(2): 69–79.

Rust P (1993) Coming out in the age of social constructionism. Gender and Society 7(1): 50–77.

Rust P (2000) Bisexuality: A contemporary paradox for women. Journal of Social Issues 56(2): 205–221.

Schlichter A (2004) Queer at last? Straight intellectuals and the desire for transgression. GLQ 10(4): 543–564.

Shugar DR (1999) To(o) queer or not? Journal of Lesbian Studies 3(3): 11–20.

Stein A (ed.) (1993) Sisters, Sexperts, Queers: Beyond the Lesbian Nation. New York: Penguin.

Stein A (1997) Sex and Sensibility: Stories of a Lesbian Generation. Berkeley, Los Angeles, London: University of California Press.

Stryker S and Burke PJ (2000) The past, present and future of an identity theory. Social Psychology Quarterly 63(4): 284–297.

Stryker S and Serpe RT (1994) Salience and psychological centrality: equivalent, overlapping, or complementary concepts? Social Psychology Quarterly 57(1): 16–35.

Swidler A (2001) Talk of Love: How Culture Matters. Chicago, IL and London: University of Chicago Press.

Vannini PA (2007) The changing meanings of authenticity: An interpretive biography of professors' work experiences. Studies in Symbolic Interaction 29: 63–90.

Walters SD (1996) From here to queer: Radical feminism, postmodernism, and the lesbian menace (or why can't a woman be more like a fag?) Signs 21(4): 830–869.

Ward J and Schneider B (2009) The research of heteronormativity: An introduction. Gender and Society 23(4): 433–439.

Weeks J (1985) Sexuality and its Discontents: Meanings, Myths and Modern Sexualities. New York: Routledge.

"I DON'T LIKE TO SAY THAT I'M ANYTHING"

Sexuality Politics and Cultural Critique among
Sexual-Minority Latino Youth

DISCUSSION QUESTIONS

1. What does using a social constructionist approach offer our understanding of sexual practice, desire, and identity, and how does it challenge a singular coming-out process?
2. How do ethnicities, cultural practices, and sexualities interact according to the participants' narratives? How do participants resist discrimination and normalization?
3. What are the limitations to this research? What questions might you pose as a social researcher interested in constructions and experiences of sexuality among youth?

The scientific study of bisexuality among Latinos is scant and mostly focused on behavior rather than in the subjective experience of sexuality. This absence is particularly important as it limits the understanding of personal, social and political dimensions shaping sexuality, including sexual behavior. Research exploring sexual meanings and identities from the perspective of the subjects themselves—that is, an *experience-near approach* (Geertz 1974)—is needed for a critical analysis of the relevance and limitations of conceptual approaches and scientific labeling in sexuality research on Latino bisexualities.

Research in the 1970s and 1990s on masculinity and sexuality in Latin America (e.g., Cáceres 1996; Carrier 1995; De Moya and Garcia 1996; Liguori et al. 1996; Parker 1991; Ramirez 1999; Schifter

2000) stumbled on bisexuality when researchers found that self-identified heterosexual or straight married men (or those who had girlfriends) engaged regularly in anal intercourse with other men but their sexual orientation or identity was not threatened as long as they remained the penetrative or active partner during the sexual encounter. Although a particular contribution of these studies is their comprehensive approach to cultural and sociopolitical contexts shaping gender and sexuality, they have served unintentionally to support a behavioral-based definition or type of bisexuality: *Latin bisexuality* (e.g., Fox 1995; Ross 1991).

Latin bisexuality refers to male individuals who take only the insertive role in anal or oral sex with another male, and consider themselves heterosexuals

Carmen Yon-Leau and Miguel Muñoz-Laboy, "'I Don't Like to Say that I'm Anything': Sexuality Politics and Cultural Critique among Sexual-Minority Latino Youth." *Sexuality Research and Social Policy* 7:105–117. Copyright © February 23, 2010, by Springer Science+Business Media, LLC. Reprinted with permission by the publisher.

(Fox 1995). This concept used to study bisexuality among Latinos might be a useful starting point to address a relationship between culture and sexual diversity, suggesting that ethnic minorities, such as Latinos, may not resist lesbian or gay identities exclusively. However, as established, the concept of Latin bisexuality is problematic because it assumes a generalized and static experience of bisexuality within the Latino population who participate in the mentioned studies. Moreover, as Latin bisexuality is defined basically from Latino men's behavior, sexual attraction, and self-identification of men and women are overlooked (Muñoz-Laboy 2004).

Other important reference about Latino bisexuality is HIV-related research (e.g., Agronick et al. 2004; Chu et al. 1992; Diaz 1998; Diaz et al. 1993; Marks et al. 1998). Prior to the emergence of the AIDS epidemics, this topic was rarely investigated in the USA (Muñoz-Laboy 2004). Several of these studies have contributed to demonstrate that Anglo-Western categories of sexual orientation and identity—homosexual–heterosexual–bisexual or gay–lesbian–straight—are culturally specific and could not be imposed on Latinos in the USA without creating misnomers (e.g., Alonso and Koreck 1989; Carballo-Dieguez and Dolezal 1994; Carballo-Dieguez et al. 2000; 1997 Diaz). However, because most of the literature about Latino bisexuality is under the framework of HIV-related research, it tends to medicalize Latino bisexuality. Sexuality became sexual behavior, and individuals were defined by their behavior or by risk groups.[1] This approach was particularly salient for Latino bisexuals and, more recently, for Latina bisexuals (Muñoz-Laboy and Yon-Leau 2010).

This article will analyze the sexual identities of sexual minority[2] Latino youth focusing on their views and critical responses regarding social categories of sexual identity. Following a social constructionist approach,[3] we will explore sexual identity not as an essence to be discovered in a coming-out process, but as a complex, dynamic, and interactional process by which subjects construct their sexual identities in dialogue with existent cultural possibilities, and in the context of their everyday

social relations (Blumstein and Schwartz 1990; Rust 1993). Furthermore, taking into account that individuals or groups are not mere bearers of the norms and values of their cultures, we will explore sexual identities as "sites of varying degrees of conflict and contestation for groups and individuals" (Watney 1993 p. 13). Particularly, we will focus on sexual identity labeling as a site of cultural and political agency (Gamson 1989). In this article, we understand by agency the capacity of the individuals to act or intervene in a certain established social order (Giddens 1979). Informed by practice theory,[4] we address agency as both socially structured and shaped by particular historical contexts and cultural logics of the subjects (Bourdieu 1998; Karp 1986; Ortner 1996). We refer by cultural agency to the capacity to participate in the creation and reproduction of the symbolic world, including meanings, symbols and labels. Political agency is understood as the capacity to use, challenge, or refuse to collaborate with, current forms of power.

METHOD

STUDY POPULATION

The target group for this study included both youth who self-identified with a bisexual identity and those who were sexually active[5] with both male and female partners but who did not have a bisexual identity. To qualify for this study the youth had to be of Latino ancestry. We defined Latinos/as as individuals whose birthplace, or that of one of their parents or grandparents, was in any territory of Latin America or the Spanish Caribbean. Individuals were eligible to participate in this study whether they spoke English, Spanish, or Portuguese (however, there were no Portuguese speakers in the sample). Although the term *Latino* is in some ways a useful ethnic identity label, it is also a simplifying construct, missing much of the complexity and variation among members of this group, with conceptual and empirical shortcomings that have been discussed in other publications (Asencio 2002). Thus, making broad generalizations about the cultural background of Latino youth in a group as diverse as Latinos should be avoided.

With these conceptual definitions in mind, the authors conducted a qualitative study with participants drawn from four predominantly Latino neighborhoods in the city of New York. These neighborhoods were selected based on our prior research on Latino bisexuality in the city (Muñoz-Laboy 2008; Muñoz-Laboy and Dodge 2005). Within the spaces of these neighborhoods, flyers were distributed outside high schools and in collaboration with youth organizations, and person-to-person outreach was conducted with key youth leaders in these communities. This recruitment strategy yielded a mostly second-generation Latino sample from a working-class background with high levels of education.

SAMPLE CHARACTERISTICS

Of a total of 58 Latino youth screened, 25 met the aforementioned study criteria and consented to be part of the study[;] 16 of these youth, 11 boys and five girls, participated in the sexual history interviews analyzed in this article. Of the 16 participants, four self-identified as both from a Spanish Caribbean nation (Cuba, Dominican Republic, or Puerto Rico) and from African American or West Indian (Jamaica, Barbados, or Trinidad, and Tobago) descent. The rest of the youth self-reported their ethnic affiliation as mostly Spanish Caribbean with the exception of one Peruvian and two who reported dual Latino ethnic affiliations: Honduran and Puerto Rican, Dominican and Puerto Rican. All but three of the youth were born in the USA (i.e., second-generation Latinos). In terms of education, 13 youth were in high school or had just completed high school, two were in their 1st year of college, and one had dropped out of high school. The sample ranged from 15 to 19 years of age. The mode (i.e., the number that occurred most often) was 17 years of age. In terms of experience of sexual intercourse, two of the five young women reported not having experienced intercourse at the time of the interview, contrary to the young men, all of whom reported having had intercourse....

...The two central analytical questions were How do Latino youth use, question, or negotiate labels of sexual identity to define themselves? and How is sexual identity self-definition connected to the social experiences and forms of agency of the Latino youth in the study?

A thematic analysis in this study refers to how the analytical code of sexual identity links with broader themes within the research participants' narrative accounts, including those related to their family, friends, neighborhood, school, work, and their social experiences of discrimination and acceptance or integration. The central focus was to identify common themes in answering our research questions....

FINDINGS

All of the youth interviewed expressed that they had felt sexual attraction to both women and men, and most of them had been involved in romantic or sexual relations with both of them. These commonalities regarding sexual attraction, relationships, or behavior are not the same regarding these young people's self-definition in terms of their sexual identity. Eight out of the 16 interviewed defined themselves as bisexuals or bi, one defined himself as a gay, one as a "confused lesbian"; three considered themselves "non-straight," expressing their dislike for being labeled, and three did not define themselves in sexual terms (e.g., "labels are a waste of time"; "I shun definitions").

When youth used the words *bisexual* or *bi* during the interview, they primarily were referring to their sexual attraction for both men and women ("I am bisexual because I do like both men and women"), citing their current and past history of sexual and romantic relationships, and their future or potential affective or sexual relationships. Youth highlighted that the particular meanings and ways of being bi vary in different sexual cultures, communities, and groups in which they were involved. These differences referred to diverse aspects or a combination of them, including the kinds of ties established with their sexual partners (e.g., affective or sexual, stable or temporary), having a single partner or two simultaneously, and the relevance or not of their sexual partners' gender.

Patricia, a Cuban girl self-defined as bi, suggested that being bisexual did not imply for her having at the same time two sexual partners, a boy and a girl. Moreover, she was critical about this practice and way of understanding bisexuality by most of her friends. She said:

> Everybody wants to be bi. Everybody wants to be with a girl and a guy. I don't think that's right if you are supposed to be with one person, but a lot of my friends are bi. Everybody has their own interpretation of what bi is. [Q: What is your interpretation?] It's one, if I find a guy that I like and have interest in, I'll go with that. If I don't find a guy, and I find a girl that I have interest, then, I go with that . . . you know.

Diego, a second-generation Dominican boy, ultimately self-identified as bisexual and expressed his interest of establishing a nonmonogamous relationship with a woman and a man in a polyamorous relationship. Polyamory is different from hooking up or dating because polyamory implies emotional ties and a partner relationship with two people. He referred to polyamory in this way:

> I usually date one after the other; I'm not a huge believer in dating two people at a time. Although, I think it's interesting, and I am willing to give it a try if I can find two other partners, preferably male and female, who are willing to try the polyamory thing. I did look up on it. If they're willing to try, I am for it, because it takes communication and maturity in order to do it—I'm so up for it but I've never tried it.

Tom, who defined himself as African American and bi, said that for him and other members of the *down-low* culture and community,[6] being bi is related to hooking up with boys and girls and maintaining a low profile of his sexual attraction to both sexes. Tom highlighted that these relationships do not involve commonly stable or affective ties because the major focus is on sexual pleasure regardless of the gender of sexual partners:

> Let's have sex and forget about it the next day. Sex, to me, is sex. In this generation nowadays, it's not about "Oh, you care about someone and want to be with someone." It's about getting off. It's about if you're a chick you want to climax, you want to get your cootie licked, or you're a dude you just want to bust a nut. Sex is not about, for most people, love, it's about getting off, feeling good for the time being or moment.

CONSTRUCTION OF SEXUAL IDENTITY IN AN ADVERSE SOCIAL ENVIRONMENT

Most of the interviewees approached their sexuality as an ongoing and interactional process characterized by questioning, self-reflection, and transformations. With the exception of one boy, who believed that his sexual orientation (bisexual) was given from the time that he born, the other youth suggested that both their sexual orientation and self-identification were not stable realities to discover. One girl's self-descriptive term expressed constant questioning: Jessie, a girl with Cuban and Jamaican background, defined herself as a "confused lesbian" because she had been experiencing transformations related to the subjects of her desire, who were attractive for her independently of their sex. She reflected:

> I'm a confused lesbian, I guess. I don't know, hahaha. . . . But I lean more towards girls so, but I do like guys. . . . When I was younger, I thought: "OK, I like guys." As I got older, I was like: "OK, no, no, no, I like girls." Now, that I'm all in the mix, I realize that I still like guys. Like, I don't know, anything beautiful I'm attracted to. It could be guys or girls— so long as it's beauty.

Youth processes of sexual-orientation exploration and sexual-identity construction are depicted as particularly difficult because of the adverse familiar and social environment to homosexuality and bisexuality in which they live. José, a Puerto Rican boy self-identified as bi, accounted for the complex process of exploration and acceptance of his sexual attraction for both boys and girls in a context in which the so-called normal was associated with same-sex relationships and heterosexual marriage. He recalled:

> It was big decision.... I'm supposed to like girls, not guys because that's how I grew up with. I always grew up with girls going out with guys, and having kids, and getting married. I wasn't growing up with guys-guys, girls-girls getting off. I wouldn't think that was normal. I would put myself down by "You're not supposed to have that." I would talk to a girl and it would make me feel better and I would talk to a guy and it would also make me feel better. And it's just at that time. I was really down on myself. Now, I'm more accepting of myself. I like a girl—cool; I like a guy—cool. I'm accepting of myself.

Melissa, a second-generation Dominican girl who defined herself as "not straight," explained how a gendered socialization particularly protective of girls limited her thinking about her sexuality and sexual identity until she went to high school. There, she had the opportunity to meet gay friends or youth who were exploring their sexual orientation. Melissa said:

> Before I got into high school, my family didn't let me go anywhere. I was usually kept in the house. I wouldn't be able to go with my friends. My mom and dad were protective. Then, I got into high school and they opened up to more things. And my first friends when I went into high school were gay, so I was given, I got a sneak peek of what it felt like because I never had any friends before, and I was exposed to, oh my god, wow!

The quotidian social contexts in which Latino youth live not only are restrictive regarding same-sex sexual relations but also can be hurtful and violent when youth come out as gay, lesbian, or bisexual, or are suspected of being not straight. Most of the interviewees had to deal with familiar pressure or rejection, losing friends, stigmatization in the school, verbal violence, or fear of being attacked in the streets due to their sexual identity. Diego remembered that after coming out, a series of events occurred in his family and at school that brought him to a social and personal isolation:

> My mom was extremely shocked. My grandmother was perturbed, and I use that word to all extent of the negative connotation it brings to your imagination. She was mortified that I was this way, and that really hit to me because she was my heart and soul. Our relationship immediately thereafter went into extreme disrepair. After time, it became an issue of less dominance. That's the only prevalent memories I have.... My family did ostracize me for a time. In school, I was made fun of and teased—it may not have been as hard as other people. I did wake up in the middle of the night. I did wake up in the morning crying because I was different than everybody else, so there's a huge difference.

Probably, the rejection of the family is one of the most painful experiences that the interviewees had. A close relationship with the family is especially desirable in youth definitions of what it meant to be good sons or daughters. However, these youth sexual identity or orientation contravenes their families' expectations about their children. A frequent response to the questions about being good daughters and sons is illustrated by this quotation from one study participant: "In my family, it would have to be for you to be straight. Yes, be straight, bring the best grades home, and don't go out to parties; stay home, clean the house, and that's it."

Likewise, emotional and material support provided by young people's families was depicted as conditional to expectations of heterosexuality, gender conformity, and so-called acceptable social behavior. Boys' familiar socialization was shaped by expectations about a heterosexual masculinity. Francisco, a Peruvian boy self-defined as gay, illustrated how his familiar expectations about masculinity and heterosexuality intermingled:

> So I guess since I'm a guy, everyone wants me to be much into sports, they want me always—soccer is a big thing, my father wants me to play soccer, he wants me to have a lot of girlfriends.... They're always initiating some conversation like "Oh, how many girlfriends do you have right now? Oh, you are going to see a girl Oh, is that a girl calling you." Small things,

trying to lead me towards going, having something with a girl, but other than the pressure.

Negative reactions of the family when sexual-minority youth came out ranged from disappointment to asking the youth to leave the house. The idea of bisexuality was found to be confusing by the parents and difficult to understand. Being gay or lesbian, albeit heavily stigmatized, was perceived to be less problematic to understand for participants' families than being bisexual. Four of the youth in the sample left the house, two of them returned, and another two stayed in the New York City shelter system. Siblings served as a source of support for those youth who came out or were outed to their parents. Likewise, some youth had been expulsed from social events, such as parties, for being gay or bisexual. In addition to suffering the harassment of people attending these events, they had to face the menace of institutional forms of repression exercised by the police. These forms of sexual discrimination interacted with other forms of segregation experienced by youth.

Particularly, ethnic discrimination was constantly mentioned in the youth narratives, and compared with sexual discrimination. Experiencing discrimination because of their Hispanic or African American origin was a common situation referred by youth to depict segregation, persecution, verbal and physical violence, and the fear of being harassed for their sexual orientation or identity. For Martin, a Puerto Rican boy who defined himself as not straight, sexual discrimination was expressed in phobias that make sexual minority youth drop out of school and hide their sexual identity to avoid suffering violence. Although he noticed certain favorable changes in schools regarding sexual discrimination (they become, in his words, "more liberal"), the current situation was depicted as hostile for [people] who are non-straight, in similar way that it is for people excluded because [of] their religious beliefs.

Developing a self-notion of bisexuality seemed to be accompanied by a clear awareness of the consequences of sexual labels. Some youth referred to negative value connotations of bisexuality by contrast with only same-sex or heterosexual attraction, saying that being bi was associated with confusion or, in their words, "being greedy" (defined as "wanting to have everything, girls and boys"). Moreover, some teens had experienced negative attitudes of youth from the lesbian and gay communities. These attitudes were related to the fear of being abandoned and replaced with someone of a different gender.

On the other hand, being bi as synonymous with hooking up with boys and girls had a positive connotation within some groups of youth. These youth considered being bi as trendy. In Patricia's words, "Hooking up with boys and girls is the new thing. Everybody wants to be bi."

Strategies, Cultural Agency, and Critique of Social Categories

Interviewees described themselves neither as passive victims of social discrimination and violence based on their sexual identity, nor as subjects determined by heteronormative sexual taxonomies and stereotypes. Their narratives talked about both limitations and impositions, as well as strategies or forms of resistance to face discrimination and normalization. It is important to mention that most of the participants were not active in organizations for lesbian, gay, bisexual, transgender, and queer or questioning individuals, but some of them had been exposed to scholarly and political language regarding gender and sexuality at school, community centers, or services oriented to sexual-minority youth.

Keep Your Business to Yourself

Approximately half of the youth interviewed faced the negative values and stereotypes associated to bisexuality by keeping their emotional and sexual relationships with girls and boys as private information in their families, neighborhood or schools. Annika, a second-generation Puerto Rican who shunned sexual-identity labels, illustrated a common strategy of youth to avoid conflicts with their family. She explained that silencing her sexual attraction and relationships in their home was a response to a realistic assessment of the cultural background of her parents and negative experiences of other youth with similar cultural heritage who had come out. For Annika, her parents' Hispanic cultural norms and values can predict their negative responses regarding non-straight sexual identities. Being aware of it, she reflected, allowed her to deal with a potential conflict with her parents while experiencing her sexuality according to her feelings and decisions.

Being selective or wholesome regarding the display of sexuality was also a common response of the participants when faced with social discrimination and violence. Such displays entail an evaluation of the contexts or forms in which it is appropriate or not to tell one's business and express one's sexuality. Annika and Diego illustrated two different approaches among the interviewees. For Annika, it was important to consider what was respectful or disrespectful for diverse groups of people surrounding her, according to their morals and views about same-sex relationships. In her opinion:

> You have to have respect. I wouldn't go around kissing another girl knowing the way our world is pretty much, and how everyone sees gays and lesbians, and how some people are disgusted by it, and just don't like it, and religion, and all that stuff. So, I wouldn't do that. I don't care if it's a group or a gay party and you're just making out with a girl, I don't care or it's just a group of gay people and two girls are making out, who cares. But when you do it in front of people you know don't like it, then I feel that's disrespectful. You have to have some respect.

Diego criticized the display of sexuality, and judged it in terms of what was considered wholesome or not. He suggested that one of the sources of discrimination was related to individuals' presentation and expression of their sexuality. He said:

> I haven't been oppressed. The main part of it is because of the way I carry myself. . . . I think this is where a lot of the discrimination comes from, when you make sexuality a major part of your lifestyle. . . . Because I carry myself in a wholesome manner, if you ask me

about my sexuality, I'll be open with you and let you know. But if you carry yourself in a wholesome way which doesn't flaunt your sexuality, I think it will be no problem. So, I think, it's more about personal display or . . . the way you present yourself has a lot to do with discrimination and the way that people perceive you.

Other youth hid their sexual identity according to their potential or current sexual partner. For instance, Tom was particularly careful to be identified as bisexual by gay people because he knew that they disliked the way in which bi individuals from the down-low community approached their sexual relationships. He said:

> Not if there was a gay person I wouldn't tell them. If it comes up, it's not their business whether I'm gay or bisexual. To a gay person I wouldn't be bisexual. To anybody that knows I've slept around with a dude I would define myself as bisexual, but they're straight—it doesn't matter whether I'm bisexual, gay or straight. You don't just put your business out there for everyone.

Not all the youth considered "keeping your business to yourself" as a strategy for dealing with social and, especially, parental rejection. Some of them did it as a nondesired and painful choice. Moreover, most of the participants suggested tensions and contradictions related to this situation. Tom viewed his sexuality as "none of their business," but at the same time he "does not want to talk to his family because I'm afraid of what they say and what they might think." Krista said she had avoided speaking to her family about her personal or romantic life because she dislikes lying to her parents.

Selecting and Negotiating Labels

Participants, both those who use specific sexual labels—such as bisexual, gay, or confused lesbian—to define themselves and those who do not, had to deal with the stable meanings or boundaries suggested by these social categories. Existent sexual-identity classifications contrasted with the changeable and ongoing character of these adolescents' objects of desire (e.g., boys sometimes felt more sexual attraction for boys than for girls) and sexual identity (e.g., initial identification as gay, and then in the process of accepting as bisexual); the different ways in which they felt sexual attraction to boys and girls (e.g., boys liked other boys in a different way than girls), or if they felt sexual attraction regardless of gender or sex; and the kinds of relationships in which they were or wanted to be involved with boys or girls (e.g., to whom they imagine being married).

The cases of Lucas and Diego exemplify some of these youth difficulties to use sexual-identity labels to define them. These two boys suggested that although they ultimately could consider themselves bisexuals because they like boys and girls, they are really, in their words, "undefined" (not defined). They found that there was no category into which they could fit exactly because they were mostly but not exclusively attracted to boys, which would be inconsistent with gay and bisexual labels. For this reason, Diego initially identified himself as a gay. He said:

> I am undefined. One minute I like girls, one minute I like guys, one minute I like birds—just kidding. It's so sporadic. I'm preferably attracted to guys. For me, to date a girl, she has to be astounding; not really astounding in beauty, she has to have this one characteristic. That's why I usually identify as being gay at first glance. But, ultimately, I think I am bisexual. I identify myself as being bisexual because I do like girls and guys.

Youth are constantly selecting and negotiating labels and identities according to the different scenarios and interactions in which they are involved, the sexual identity of their potential or actual sexual partners, or the information they have about them. Diego's account about how presenting himself to potential partners shows the complexities of dealing with both other people's fears and expectations and changes of his sexual desires ("you never know what you want"). His narrative suggests that self-ascribed identity labels are at the same time related to both a personal interpretation of the self according to cultural definitions and an interactional process of negotiation with potential partners. In Diego's words:

> Being bisexual in dating it's definitely an issue. A lot of guys and girls are not attracted to guys who are bisexual because they say it's double the risk—you're with a girl and with a guy. That's why I try to stay on one end of the spectrum. I tell them I'm gay if I'm dating a guy. With a girl I'll say I do have strong feelings for guys and you'll just have to understand it. If they want to work with me, they can; if they don't, they guess that the doors are the other way. I think being bisexual is ... not as hard as people think it seems. I don't think it's fun, it's not a fun and party crazed thing. It's not that hard, but then again, it's not that easy. It's undefined because you never know what you want.

I Don't Want Others to Define Me

Most of the youth who rejected particular labels to define their sexual orientation or identity made critical commentaries about assumed linkages between sexual behavior, sexual attraction, and sexual identity. For instance, Annika preferred to keep herself unlabeled and questioned the association between "hooking up with boys and girls" and being bisexual. Francisco liked boys and dated girls, rejected being labeled either as bisexual or as homosexual, and expressed his political membership to the gay community and called himself gay. In reflecting about these categories, youth critiqued existent labels that could not capture their sexual experiences and views about romantic and sexual relationships, rejected being defined by others through systems of classification imposed by the larger society, or proposed a nongendered approach to sex, beauty, and love ("sex is sex"; "feelings are feelings"; "beauty is beauty"). Francisco expressed a frequent claim among interviewees regarding sexual classifications and labels imposed by society according to individuals' sexual attractions, behaviors, or relationships:

> I actually don't like the word *homosexuality*, I don't like defining myself, it's too much, its I just don't

like labels. I do like guys, though I don't think it should be just labeled but in society's views I'm a homosexual. . . . I dated many girls back in my class, so I don't want to be considered bisexual either. If I happen to meet the right person. . . . I mean, love shouldn't have boundaries.

Sexual Behavior Does Not Define a Man

For most of the boys, having same-sex sexual relations has raised initial doubts, confusion, or fears regarding losing masculinity. These concerns were related to cultural assumptions about a naturalized correspondence between biological male sex, masculine gender identity, and a dominant or active role in sexual interactions. However, during the process of exploring their sexuality and reflecting about it, these youth had overcome their doubts and reframed or challenged traditional patterns of Latino masculinity in different ways. Some of these boys did not question dual classifications of masculine and feminine characteristics, but considered that adopting or having feminine or feminine-like qualities or roles did not challenge their identity as men. Asked about his gender identity, Carlos, a second-generation Puerto Rican boy, defined himself as a bisexual man "with at times feminine qualities." In his narrative, manhood seemed to conflate male sex and masculine gender identity, whereas feminine qualities existed as showed or performed. He said:

I am definitely a man, a man with at times feminine qualities. I don't know because I like female stuff. I didn't put any on today, but I like lip gloss. I should have put some on. I'm definitely a man. That's how it is: I'm a bisexual man.

Other boys challenged traditional ideas of masculinity and the definition of masculinity itself. They critiqued certain characteristics assigned to masculinity, such as the nonexpression of emotions. Furthermore, some of these youth questioned the heteronormative character of hegemonic Latino masculinity, which tends to naturalize and normalize gender relationships and roles according to top–bottom (or dominant–submissive and

active–passive) roles in sexual relationships. In these male youth reflections, the idea that sexual behavior and sexual attraction does not necessarily define a man was a key dimension. Martin's accounts illustrate a critical view of masculinity:

When I have sex with guys, in the beginning, I was always, like, this makes me less of a man, and that's where I think the top and bottom issue is huge in terms of heteronormativity. In heteronormativity, we expect there's a submissive and dominant role, and when you bring in the top–bottom issue into play . . .—oh, I'll [be] less of a man if I take it, I'm more of a man if I give it—that's when it becomes a major issue. But I don't feel less of a man because I'm sleeping with a man, I don't feel more of a man because I'm sleeping with a girl. Sexual behavior doesn't define a man. Your ability to handle conflict and situations and the way you apply yourself to problem solving is what makes a man and what builds character.

By contrast to boys' experiences, girls did not mention fears or doubts regarding their gender identity when they discovered their sexual attraction to other girls or had sexual relations with them. These girls related sexual and gender identity in a complex and heterogeneous spectrum, which included challenging traditional patterns of gender identity, not problematizing or thinking much about the connections between these aspects (some of the girls were starting a process of exploration of their sexual attraction to both girls and boys), and assuming different gender roles with different sexual partners according to a dichotomic view of femininity and masculinity. Krista and Jessie illustrate two extremes of this spectrum. On the one hand, Krista framed gender as a social construction not determined by her sexual orientation or sexual practices. In her words:

[T]he very concept of woman is such a social term, like what is a woman versus what is a man, so . . . I feel like definitions like that kinda connect you to this larger group. . . . I'm not going for the whole gender-neutral thing, but I don't think I'm defined as a woman in any way, really, by who I want to have sex with....I'm totally a woman, whatever that means, because that's what society says I am.

On the other hand, Jessie assumed different gender roles according to the sex of her partners: a masculine role in same-sex relationships and a feminine role in different-sex relationships. For her, masculinity is related to domination and strength, femininity to subordination and softness. Jessie's accounts suggest that gender identity can be best conceived as relational. Moreover, she challenged a naturalized correspondence between sex and gender, transgressing expected feminine gender roles and identity (she likes to be called Daddy) in the context of same-sex relationships. She explained:

Because I'm with girls, I'm the guy. Like, I'm the masculine one completely. My girl can't even talk back to me....My girls have to call me Daddy. I have to be catered to, know what I'm saying? You have to treat me like your king. When I'm with guys, that's how I treat the guys, I'm soft with the guys. But I'm harder with the girls....I know I'm a girl, but when I'm with girls I feel like a guy; when I'm with guys I feel like a girl-guy, know what I'm saying? It's crazy.

DISCUSSION

...Our study illustrates the relational (as opposed to individual and natural or fixed) character of sexual- and gender-identity constructions, as well as the complex relationships between Latino youth subjective experience of sexuality and the social and cultural contexts in which they live.

This relational approach to sexual identity integrates personal, interpersonal, and collective dimensions of identity: The subjective experience of sexuality is constructed in the context of different interactions (e.g., depending on whom someone is sexually involved with, or what specific activities one does with those partners) and interpreted in relation to collective cultural possibilities to define themselves (i.e., sexual-identity labels) with which youth identify or dis-identify.

Thus, our data suggest that sexual identity might not be best studied as an individual-level variable, or as the predictable result of existent sexual taxonomies. This article can also be a contribution, from a Latino perspective, to the body of literature discussing dis-identification and politics of resistance (e.g., Dean 2008; Medina 2003; Muñoz 1999; Raby 2005), or arguing that sexual-minority youth may not desire traditional identities or simply refuse any sexual-identity label (e.g., Savin-Williams 2005, 2008). However, because our data are not comparative, we are particularly cautious to draw cultural explanations about forms of Latino identification or dis-identification with existent labels of sexual identity (e.g., straight, gay, lesbian, bisexual, queer).

Further studies with larger and more diverse samples of sexual-minority young women and men are needed to address differences and similarities among sexual-minority youth sexual identification or dis-identification, across and within different ethnic groups. Likewise, future interdisciplinary research is important for a nuanced understanding of the ways in which Latino youth deal with diverse social (e.g., belonging to gay, down-low, or catholic communities) and cultural (e.g., having Hispanic, Caribbean, or African American background) boundaries shaping their sexual identities and interactions.

NOTES

1. The inclusion of bisexual Latino men in HIV-related studies responds to the hypothesis that they can be what is called a *bridge population*, a term that refers to the fact that HIV infections among Latinas are frequently attributed to the bisexual behavior of their male partners.
2. We use the term *sexual minority* to refer to people who are not members of the heterosexual majority, including gay, lesbian, bisexual, and unlabeled individuals.
3. Social constructionism is a broad theoretical approach proposing that social reality, including social identities, is a product of social and historical practices, as well as everyday human interactions (Berger and Luckman 1966).

4. Practice theory is a sociological analytical framework addressing the complex relations among agents' strategies, their cultural logics, and the distribution of power in society (Karp 1986; also see Bourdieu and Wacquant 1992; Ortner 1996).

5. We defined the term *sexually active* as applying to a person who has had any type of sexual encounter, non-penetrative to penetrative, with both female and male partners, more than once over the past 12 months.

6. The down low (DL) refers to an identity based on ethnic affinity and sexuality observed among circles of African American and Latino men in urban settings such as New York City (Mays et al. 2004). Men who say that they are "on the DL" have sex with other men without self-identifying as gay or homosexual, and strive to maintain a low profile of their sexual activities or attraction to both sexes. Implicit in the notion of the DL is the idea of avoiding the cultural stigma attached to nonheterosexual identities and, for this reason, keeping nonheterosexual sexual matters private (Muñoz-Laboy 2008).

REFERENCES

Abarca, H. (2001). Las fuerzas que configuran el deseo [The forces shaping desire]. In J. Olavarria & R. Parrini (Eds.), *Masculinidades: Identidad, sexualidad y familia* (pp. 105–112). Santiago: FLACSO.

Agronick, G., O'Donnell, L., Stueve, A., Doval, A., Duran, R., & Vargo, S. (2004). Sexual behaviors and risks among bisexually- and gay-identified young Latino men. *AIDS and Behavior, 8*, 185–197.

Alonso, A., & Koreck, T. (1989). Silences: "Hispanics", AIDS, and sexual practices. *Differences: A Journal of Feminist Cultural Studies, 1*(1), 110–125.

Asencio, M. (2002). *Sex and sexuality among New York's Puerto Rican youth.* Boulder, CO: Lynne Rienner.

Berger, P., & Luckman, T. (1966). *The social construction of reality: A treatise in the sociology of knowledge.* Garden City, NY: Doubleday.

Blumstein, P., & Schwartz, P. (1990). Intimate relationships and the creation of sexuality. In D. McWhirter, S. Sanders, & J. Reinisch (Eds.), *Homosexuality/heterosexuality: Concepts of sexual orientation* (pp. 307–320). New York: Oxford University Press.

Bourdieu, P. (1998). *Practical reason: On the theory of action.* Palo Alto, CA: Stanford University Press.

Bourdieu, P., & Passeron, J. C. (1990). *Reproduction in education, society, and culture.* Newbury Park, CA: Sage.

Bourdieu, P., & Wacquant, L. J. (1992). *An invitation to reflexive sociology.* Chicago: University of Chicago Press.

Cáceres, C. (1996). Male bisexuality in Peru and the prevention of AIDS. In P. Aggleton (Ed.), *Bisexualities and AIDS: International perspectives* (pp. 136–147). Bristol, PA: Taylor & Francis.

Carballo-Dieguez, A., & Dolezal, C. (1994). Contrasting types of Puerto Rican men who have sex with men (MSM). *Journal of Psychology & Human Sexuality, 6*, 41–47.

Carballo-Dieguez, A., Dolezal, C., Nieves-Rosa, L., & Diaz, F. (2000). Similarities in the sexual behavior and HIV risk factors of Latino men residing in New York City. *Journal of Psychology & Human Sexuality, 12*, 49–67.

Carballo-Dieguez, A., Dolezal, C., Nieves-Rosa, L., Diaz, F., & Decena, C. (2004). Looking for a tall, dark, macho man: Sexual-role behavior variations in Latino gay and bisexual men. *Culture, Health & Sexuality, 6*, 159–171.

Carrier, J. (1995). *De los otros: Intimacy and homosexuality among Mexican men.* New York: Columbia University Press.

Cass, V. (1979). Homosexual identity formation: A theoretical model. *Journal of Homosexuality, 4*(3), 219–235.

Chu, S. Y., Peterman, T. A., Doll, L. S., Buehler, J. W., & Curran, J. W. (1992). AIDS in bisexual men in the United States: Epidemiology and transmission to women. *American Journal of Public Health, 82*, 220–224.

Coleman, E. (1982). Developmental stages of the coming-out process. *American Behavioral Scientist, 25*, 469–482.

Dean, J. (2008). "The lady doth protest too much": Theorising disidentification in contemporary gender politics [Working paper]. Retrieved September 8, 2009, from http://www.essex.ac.uk/idaworld/paper240708.pdf

De Moya, A., & Garcia, R. (1996). AIDS and the enigma of bisexuality in Dominican Republic. In P. Aggleton (Ed.), *Bisexualities and AIDS: International perspectives* (pp. 121–135). Bristol, PA: Taylor & Francis.

Diamond, L. (2008). Female bisexuality from adolescence to adulthood: Results from a 10-year longitudinal study. *Developmental Psychology, 44*, 5–14.

Diaz, R. (1998). *Latino gay men and HIV: Culture, sexuality and risk behavior.* New York: Routledge.

Diaz, T., Chu, S. Y., Frederick, M., Herman, P., Levy, A., & Mokoloff, E. (1993). Sociodemographic and HIV risk behaviors of bisexual men with AIDS:

Results from a multistate interview project. *AIDS, 7,* 1227–1232.

Dowsett, G. (1996). *Practicing desire: Homosexual sex in the era of AIDS.* Palo Alto, CA: Stanford University Press.

Dubé, E., Savin-Williams, R., & Diamond, L. (2001). Intimacy development, gender and ethnicity among sexual-minority youths. In A. D'Augelli & C. Patterson (Eds.), *Lesbian, gay and bisexual identities and youth* (pp. 129–152). Oxford: Oxford University Press.

Floyd, F., & Stein, T. (2002). Sexual orientation identity formation among gay, lesbian, and bisexual youths: Multiple patterns and milestone experiences. *Journal of Research on Adolescence, 12,* 167–191.

Fonseca, C. (2001). Philanderers, cuckolds, and wily women: A reexamination of gender relations in a Brazilian working-class neighborhood. *Men and Masculinities, 3,* 261–277.

Fox, R. (1995). Bisexual identities. In A. R. D'Augelli & C. J. Patterson (Eds.), *Lesbian, gay and bisexual identities over the lifespan* (pp. 24–47). New York: Oxford University Press.

Fuller, N. (2001). The social constitution of gender identity among Peruvian men. *Men and Masculinities, 3,* 316–331.

Gamson, J. (1989). Silence, death and the invisible enemy: AIDS activism and social movement "Newness." *Social Problems, 36,* 351–365.

Gatter, P. (1995). Anthropology, HIV and contingent identities. *Social Science and Medicine, 41,* 1523–1533.

Geertz, C. (1974). From the native point of view: On the nature of anthropological understanding. *Bulletin of the American Academy of Arts and Sciences, 28*(1), 26–45.

Giddens, A. (1979). *Central problems in social theory: Action, structure, and contradiction in social analysis.* Berkeley: University of California Press.

Karp, I. (1986). Agency and social theory: A review of Anthony Giddens. *American Ethnologist, 13,* 131–137.

Liguori, A. L., Gonzalez-Block, M., & Aggleton, P. (1996). Bisexuality and HIV/AIDS in Mexico. In P. Aggleton (Ed.), *Bisexualities and AIDS: International perspectives* (pp. 76–98). Bristol, PA: Taylor & Francis.

Marks, G., Cantero, P. J., & Simoni, J. M. (1998). Is acculturation associated with sexual risk behaviors? An investigation of HIV-positive Latino men and women. *AIDS Care, 10,* 283–295.

Mays, V., Cochran, S., & Zamudio, A. (2004). HIV prevention research: Are we meeting the needs of African American men who have sex with men? *Journal of Black Psychology, 30,* 78–105.

McDonald, G. (1982). Individual differences in the coming out process for gay men: Implications for theoretical models. *Journal of Homosexuality, 8*(1), 47–60.

Medina, J. (2003). Identity trouble: Disidentification and the problem of difference. *Philosophy & Social Criticism, 29,* 655–680.

Miceli, M. (2002). Gay, lesbian and bisexual youth. In D. Richardson & S. Seidman (Eds.), *Handbook of lesbian and gay studies* (pp. 199–214). London: Sage.

Muhr, T. (2004). *ATLASti (Version 5) {Computer software}.* Berlin: Scientific Software Development.

Muñoz, J. E. (1999). *Disidentifications: Queers of colour and the performance of politics.* Minneapolis: University of Minnesota Press.

Muñoz-Laboy, M. (2004). Beyond "MSM": Sexual desire among bisexually-active Latino men in New York City. *Sexualities, 7,* 55–80.

Muñoz-Laboy, M. (2008). Familism and sexual regulation among bisexual Latino men. *Archives of Sexual Behavior, 37,* 773–782.

Muñoz-Laboy, M., & Dodge, B. (2005). Bi-sexual practices: Patterns, meanings, and implications for HIV/STI prevention among bisexually-active Latino men and their partners. *Journal of Bisexuality, 5,* 81–100.

Muñoz-Laboy, M., & Yon-Leau, C. (2010). Boundaries and bisexuality: Reframing the discourse on Latina/o bisexualities. In Asencio, M. (Ed.), *Latina/o sexualities.* New Brunswick, NJ: Rutgers University Press.

Ortner, S. (1996). *Making gender: The politics and erotics of culture.* Boston: Beacon Press.

Parker, R. (1991). *Bodies, pleasures and passions: Sexual culture in contemporary Brazil.* Boston: Beacon Press.

Parker, R. (1999). *Beneath the equator: Cultures of desire, male homosexuality and emerging gay communities in Brazil.* New York: Routledge.

Plummer, K. (1983). *Documents of life: An introduction to the problems and literature of a humanistic method.* London: George Allen & Unwin.

Raby, R. (2005). What is resistance? *Journal of Youth Studies, 8,* 151–171.

Ramirez, R. L. (1999). *What it means to be a man: Reflections on Puerto Rican masculinity.* New Brunswick, NJ: Rutgers University Press.

Ross, M. (1991). A taxonomy of global behavior. In R. A. Tielman, M. Carballo, & A. Hendriks (Eds.), *Bisexuality and HIV/AIDS: A global perspective* (pp. 21–26). Buffalo, NY: Prometheus Books.

Rust, P. C. (1993). Coming out in the age of social constructionism: Sexual identity formation among lesbian and bisexual women. *Gender & Society, 7,* 50–77.

Savin-Williams, R. (2005). *The new gay teenager.* Cambridge, MA: Harvard University Press.

Schifter, J. (2000). *Public sex in a Latin society.* Binghamton, NY: Haworth Hispanic/Latino Press.

Troiden, R. (1989). The formation of homosexual identities. *Journal of Homosexuality, 17*(1/2), 43–73.

Watney, S. (1993). Emergent sexual identities and HIV/AIDS. In P. Aggleton, G. Gart, & P. Davies (Eds.), *AIDS: Facing the second decade* (pp. 13–28). London: Falmer Press.

Weeks, J. (1986). *Sexuality.* London: Tavistock.

Young, R., & Meyer, I. (2005). The trouble with "MSM" and "WSM": Erasure of the sexual-minority person in public health discourse. *American Journal of Public Health, 95,* 164–168.

PART THREE

Context Matters:
Power, Knowledge,
and Institutions

INTRODUCTION

In this section we examine the importance of power and context, along with the many attendant factors that shape our understandings of sex, gender, and sexuality. These chapters examine politics and power in different social settings and institutional locations. Sex, gender, and sexuality are constructed differently across time and place. Part Three asks, What factors shape the specific forms that those constructions take? It is not just random, but instead specific economic, social, and cultural interests and relations of power that produce those varied incarnations. In order to understand what form these constructs take, and why, we must ask critical questions about how they are defined, maintained, and reinforced, and to whose benefit.

Many chapters in this section begin to answer these questions by examining specific institutional contexts. Furthermore, they highlight the ways in which we "perform" gender differently in diverse contexts—the various factors that shape those performances, including organizational practices and structural forces that contribute to defining our identities, practices, and desires. Throughout all of these chapters, we see the ways in which the constructions and lived realties of sex, gender, and sexuality are intertwined and mutually constitutive.

The section begins with a contribution from Marsha Saxton, who complicates stale abortion debates by introducing a disability studies perspective.

Many disability rights activists situate selective abortion within the history of eugenics, while many in the pro-choice movement have avoided engaging with the issue altogether. She highlights the ways in which reproductive rights and women's control over their own bodies become more complicated when we engage in difficult dialogues about what kinds of life are worthy of living. Saxton argues that more inclusive dialogue is precisely what is needed. This chapter provides a perfect transition from the narratives in Part Two in its insistence that we ground our debates, analyses, and theories in the lived experiences of real people, whose lives cannot be reduced to an issue of gender divorced from ability, class, race, and other systems of oppression and privilege.

The next set of chapters continue to examine aspects of science and medicine. For instance, Martin discusses the ways in which many authors of scientific textbooks have described male and female reproductive functions in terms of stereotypical male/female gender roles. Descriptions of "valiant" sperm and "passive" eggs demonstrate the extent to which our notions of gender are ingrained, so much so that they become apparent even in the way we personify and describe biological *activity*. Likewise, Siobhan Somerville examines scientific–medical constructions focused on racial and homosexual bodies and their intersecting origins. Phyllis Burke goes one step further to reveal the disturbing consequences of rigid medical theories of gender, documenting the ways in which children who do not conform to gender roles and stereotypes are abused and manipulated by medical and psychiatric "professionals." These methods include everything from forced play with gender-specific toys to insisting that children dress in gender-specific clothing and shocking the genitals of children who refuse to conform to gender ideals in the hopes of "preventing homosexuality" later in life.

Wentling and Blackledge each take up the phenomenon of medicalization from other angles, examining the power of the medical establishment to define what is or isn't a "disorder" with regard to gender and sexuality. Wentling focuses on the effects that the inclusion of "gender dysphoria" in the *Diagnostic Statistical Manual* ultimately has on transgender persons, while Blackledge discusses the turn-of-the-century control of women's bodies through the construction of sexual "frigidity" as a psychological disorder. Each of these pieces examines an historically specific slice of the full picture, so that we get multiple glimpses of the effects of our scientific and medical constructs of sex, gender, and sexuality at different points throughout history. While the specific discourses have evolved, their consequences are similarly problematic and demonstrate the productive exercise of institutional power.

Simone Weil Davis focuses directly on the body, discussing the relatively new phenomenon of labial plastic surgery and the power of cultural and economic forces to determine what qualifies as "good-looking" female genitals. This article demonstrates, like a number of preceding pieces, the ways in which sex, gender, and sexuality are conflated, and it describes how normative expectations of sex and gender ensure heteronormativity. While continuing to examine the medical industry, media and consumer culture are also under the microscope here.

McGrath and Chananie-Hill further move us into the realm of popular culture, shifting our attention to the world of sports as a site of cultural production and staging ground for contests over gender performance. They examine the tightrope walked by women body builders forced to balance their pursuit of muscularity with limited definitions of femininity, exploring the strategies used by women to both resist and reinscribe the gender order.

Other chapters in this section discuss the power of the state to regulate our sexed, gendered, and sexualized bodies. For instance, both Luibhéid and Heath examine state control over marriage, and they study the ways in which normative definitions of the "appropriate" American family are both reproduced and enforced. In doing so, they reveal the reliance of heterosexuality as an institution upon specific gendered, racialized identities. While we hear often about the role of the state in allowing or prohibiting same-sex marriage, we often fail to realize the extent to which the state has historically regulated who can marry, which immigrants are permitted to bring their spouses and families with them to the United States, which families "appropriately" qualify for welfare, and so on. It was not until 1967, for example, that the Supreme Court struck down state laws prohibiting interracial marriage. We provide here two very different cases that exemplify the ways in which state control operates.

The chapters by Cantu and Kempadoo move us away from the confines of U.S. policy to examine global dynamics, discussing, for example, the impact of transnational migration, development policies, border policing, and international tourism on changing dynamics of gender and sexuality in specific locales. Andrea Smith's chapter asks us to further contemplate a subject addressed by Kempadoo and, in one way or another, by many of the authors in this volume: Whose lives do we value? She explores the many ways in which Native women and their bodies have been and continue to be abused and manipulated and yet continue to remain invisible even in movements for social justice. How do our definitions of sex, gender, and sexuality construct certain bodies as valuable and others as disposable? Who has the power to construct or contest these assumptions? Barbara Perry widens this discussion, placing violence within the broader context of the construction of gender and sexuality and examining various forms of violence as mechanisms of social control. Her disturbing discussion of domestic violence and hate crimes supports her conclusion that violence is readily used within various institutional and social contexts to ensure conformity to normative standards of sex, gender, and sexuality and to maintain unequal relations of power and privilege.

The voices in this section teach us to *see* the reproduction and enforcement of sex, gender, and sexual identities and inequality all around us, every day. They make visible the structural and cultural mechanisms that are constantly working to make sex, gender, and sexuality invisible and seemingly natural.

NELLIE WONG, WHEN I WAS GROWING UP

I know now that once I longed to be white.
How? you ask.
Let me tell you the ways.

when I was growing up, people told me
I was dark and I believed my own darkness
in the mirror, in my soul, my own narrow
vision

when I was growing up, my sisters
with fair skin got praised
for their beauty, and in the dark
I fell further, crushed between high walls

when I was growing up, I read magazines
and saw movies, blonde movie stars, white skin,
sensuous lips and to be elevated, to become
a woman, a desirable woman, I began to wear
imaginary pale skin

when I was growing up, I was proud
of my English, my grammar, my spelling
fitting into the group of smart children
smart Chinese children, fitting in,
belonging, getting in line

when I was growing up and went to high school,
I discovered the rich white girls, a few yellow girls,
their imported cotton dresses, their cashmere sweaters,
their curly hair and I thought that I too should have
what these lucky girls had

when I was growing up, I hungered
for American food, American styles,
coded: white and even to me, a child
born of Chinese parents, being Chinese
was feeling foreign, was limiting,
was unAmerican

when I was growing up and a white man wanted
to take me out, I thought I was special,
an exotic gardenia, anxious to fit
the stereotype of an oriental chick

Nellie Wong, "When I Was Growing Up" from *The Death of Long Steam Lady*. West End Press, 1986. Reprinted with permission by the author.

when I was growing up, I felt ashamed
of some yellow men, their small bones,
their frail bodies, their spitting
on the streets, their coughing,
their lying in sunless rooms,
shooting themselves in the arms

when I was growing up, people would ask
if I were Filipino, Polynesian, Portuguese.
They named all colors except white, the shell
of my soul, but not my dark, rough skin

when I was growing up, I felt
dirty. I thought that god
made white people clean
and no matter how much I bathed,
I could not change, I could not shed
my skin in the gray water

when I was growing up, I swore
I would run away to purple mountains,
houses by the sea with nothing over
my head, with space to breathe,

uncongested with yellow people in an area
called Chinatown, in an area I later learned
was a ghetto, one of many hearts
of Asian America

I know now that once I longed to be white.
How many more ways? you ask.
Haven't I told you enough?

19 • *Marsha Saxton*

DISABILITY RIGHTS AND SELECTIVE ABORTION

DISCUSSION QUESTIONS

1. How is our understanding of reproductive rights complicated when we bring in the voices of disability activists?
2. Why do many disabilitity rights activists and scholars call selective abortion the "new eugenics"?
3. How might reproductive technologies presented as offering more "choices" to women actually shift power into the hands of a commercialized medical institution and limit women's control over their own reproduction?
4. In what ways does the birth of a disabled child constitute a social problem, rather than a medical one?

Disability rights activists are now articulating a critical view of the widespread practice of prenatal diagnosis with the intent to abort if the pregnancy might result in a child with a disability. Underlying this critique are historical factors behind a growing activism in the United States, Germany, Great Britain, and many other countries, an activism that confronts the social stigmatization of people with disabilities.

For disabled persons, women's consciousness-raising groups in the 1960s and 1970s offered a model for connecting with others in an "invisible" oppressed social group and confirming the experience of pervasive social oppression. ("That happened to you, too?") Participants in such groups began to challenge a basic tenet of disability oppression: that disability *causes* the low socioeconomic status of disabled persons. Collective consciousness-raising has made it clear that stigma is the cause.

Effective medical and rehabilitation resources since the 1950s have also contributed to activism.

Antibiotics and improved surgical techniques have helped to alleviate previously fatal conditions. Consequently, disabled people are living longer and healthier lives, and the population of people with severely disabling conditions has increased. Motorized wheelchairs, lift-equipped wheelchair vans, mobile respirators, and computer and communication technologies have increased the mobility and access to education and employment for people previously ostracized because of their disabilities.

Effective community organizing by blind, deaf, and mobility-impaired citizen groups and disabled student groups flourished in the late 1960s and resulted in new legislation. In 1973 the Rehabilitation Act Amendments (Section 504) prohibited discrimination in federally funded programs. The Americans with Disabilities Act of 1990 (ADA) provides substantial civil rights protection and has helped bring about a profound change in the collective self-image of an estimated

45 million Americans. Today, many disabled people view themselves as part of a distinct minority and reject the pervasive stereotypes of disabled people as defective, burdensome, and unattractive.

It is ironic that just when disabled citizens have achieved so much, the new reproductive and genetic technologies are promising to eliminate births of disabled children—children with Down's syndrome, spina bifida, muscular dystrophy, sickle cell anemia, and hundreds of other conditions. The American public has apparently accepted these screening technologies based on the "common-sense" assumptions that prenatal screening and selective abortion can potentially reduce the incidence of disease and disability and thus improve the quality of life. A deeper look into the medical system's views of disability and the broader social factors contributing to disability discrimination challenges these assumptions.

REPRODUCTIVE RIGHTS IN A DISABILITY CONTEXT

There is a key difference between the goals of the reproductive rights movement and the disability rights movement regarding reproductive freedom: the reproductive rights movement emphasizes the right to have an abortion; the disability rights movement, the right *not to have to have* an abortion. Disability rights advocates believe that disabled women have the right to bear children and be mothers, and that all women have the right to resist pressure to abort when the fetus is identified as potentially having a disability.

Women with disabilities raised these issues at a conference on new reproductive technologies (NRTs) in Vancouver in 1994.[1] For many of the conference participants, we were an unsettling group: women in wheelchairs; blind women with guide dogs; deaf women who required a sign-language interpreter; women with scarring from burns or facial anomalies; women with missing limbs, crutches, or canes. I noticed there what we often experience from people who first encounter us: averted eyes or stolen glances, pinched smiles,

awkward or overeager helpfulness—in other words, discomfort accompanied by the struggle to pretend there was none.

It was clear to me that this situation was constraining communication, and I decided to do something about it. I approached several of the non-disabled women, asking them how they felt about meeting such a diverse group of disabled women. Many of the women were honest when invited to be: "I'm nervous. Am I going to say something offensive?" "I feel pretty awkward. Some of these women's bodies are so different!" One woman, herself disabled, said that she'd had a nightmare image of a disabled woman's very different body. One woman confessed: "I feel terrible for some of these unfortunate disabled women, but I know I'm not supposed to feel pity. That's awful of me, right?"

This awkwardness reveals how isolated the broader society and even progressive feminists are from people with disabilities. The dangerous void of information about disability is the *context* in which the public's attitudes about prenatal diagnosis and selective abortion are formed. In the United States this information void has yielded a number of unexamined assumptions, including the belief that the quality and enjoyment of life for disabled people is necessarily inferior, that raising a child with a disability is a wholly undesirable experience, that selective abortion will save mothers from the burdens of raising disabled children, and that ultimately we as a society have the means and the right to decide who is better off not being born.

What the women with disabilities were trying to do at the Vancouver conference, and what I wish to do in this essay, is explain how selective abortion or *eugenic abortion*, as some disability activists have called it, not only oppresses people with disabilities but also hurts all women.

EUGENICS AND THE BIRTH CONTROL MOVEMENT

The eugenic interest that stimulates reliance on prenatal screening and selective abortion today has had a central place in reproductive politics for more than half a century. In the nineteenth century, eugenicists believed that most traits, including such human "failings" as pauperism, alcoholism, and thievery, as well as such desired traits as intelligence, musical ability, and "good character," were hereditary. They sought to perfect the human race through controlled procreation, encouraging those from "healthy stock" to mate and discouraging reproduction of those eugenicists defined as socially "unfit," that is, with undesirable traits. Through a series of laws and court decisions American eugenicists mandated a program of social engineering. The most famous of these was the 1927 U.S. Supreme Court ruling in *Buck v. Bell*.[2]

Leaders in the early birth control movement in the United States, including Margaret Sanger, generally embraced a eugenic view, encouraging white Anglo-Saxon women to reproduce while discouraging reproduction among nonwhite, immigrant, and disabled people. Proponents of eugenics portrayed disabled women in particular as unfit for procreation and as incompetent mothers. In the 1920s Margaret Sanger's group, the American Birth Control League, allied itself with the director of the American Eugenics Society, Guy Irving Burch. The resulting coalition supported the forced sterilization of people with epilepsy, as well as those diagnosed as mentally retarded and mentally ill. By 1937, in the midst of the Great Depression, twenty-eight states had adopted eugenics sterilization laws aimed primarily at women for whom "procreation was deemed inadvisable." These laws sanctioned the sterilizations of over 200,000 women between the 1930s and the 1970s.[3]

While today's feminists are not responsible for the eugenic biases of their foremothers, some of these prejudices have persisted or gone unchallenged in the reproductive rights movement today.[4] Consequently, many women with disabilities feel alienated from this movement. On the other hand, some pro-choice feminists have felt so deeply alienated from the disability community that they have been willing to claim, "The right wing wants to force us to have defective babies."[5] Clearly, there is work to be done.

DISABILITY-POSITIVE IDENTITY VERSUS SELECTIVE ABORTION

It is clear that some medical professionals and public health officials are promoting prenatal diagnosis and abortion with the intention of eliminating categories of disabled people, people with Down's syndrome and my own disability, spina bifida, for example. For this reason and others, many disability activists and feminists regard selective abortion as "the new eugenics." These people resist the use of prenatal diagnosis and selective abortion.

The resistance to selective abortion in the disability activist community is ultimately related to how we define ourselves. As feminists have transformed women's sense of self, the disability community has reframed the experience of having a disability. In part, through developing a sense of community, we've come to realize that the stereotyped notions of the "tragedy" and "suffering" of "the disabled" result from the *isolation* of disabled people in society. Disabled people with no connections to others with disabilities in their communities are, indeed, afflicted with the social role assignment of a tragic, burdensome existence. It is true, most disabled people I know have told me with certainty, that the disability, the pain, the need for compensatory devices and assistance can produce considerable inconvenience. But the inconvenience becomes minimal once the disabled person makes the transition to a typical everyday life. It is discriminatory attitudes and thoughtless behaviors, and the ensuing ostracism and lack of accommodation, that make life difficult. That oppression is what's most disabling about disability.

Many disabled people have a growing but still precarious sense of pride in an identity as "people with disabilities." With decades of hard work, disability activists have fought institutionalization and challenged discrimination in employment, education, transportation, and housing. We have fought for rehabilitation and Independent Living programs, and we have proved that disabled people can participate in and contribute to society.

As a political movement, the disability rights community has conducted protests and effective civil disobedience to publicize our demand for full citizenship. Many of our tactics were inspired by the women's movement and the black civil rights movement in the 1960s. In the United States we fought for and won one of the most far-reaching pieces of civil rights legislation ever, the Americans with Disabilities Act. This piece of legislation is the envy of the international community of disability activists, most of whom live in countries where disabled people are viewed with pity and charity, and accorded low social and legal status. Disability activists have fought for mentor programs led by adults with disabilities. We see disabled children as "the youth" of the movement, the ones who offer hope that life will continue to improve for people with disabilities for generations to come.. . .

MIXED FEELINGS: DISABLED PEOPLE RESPOND TO SELECTIVE ABORTION

The disability *activist* community has begun to challenge selective abortion. But among disabled people as a whole, there is no agreement about these issues. After all, the "disability community" is as diverse as any other broad constituency, like "the working class" or "women." Aspects of this issue can be perplexing to people with disabilities because of the nature of the prejudice we experience. For example, the culture typically invalidates our bodies, denying our sexuality and our potential as parents. These cultural impulses are complexly intertwined with the issue of prenatal testing. Since the early 1990s, disability rights activists have been exploring and debating our views on selective abortion in the disability community's literature.[6] In addition, just like the general population's attitudes about *abortion*, views held by people with disabilities about *selective abortion* relate to personal experience (in this case, personal history with disability) and to class, ethnic, and religious backgrounds.

People with different kinds of disabilities may have complex feelings about prenatal screening tests. While some disabled people regard the tests as a kind of genocide, others choose to use screening tests during their own pregnancies to avoid the birth of a disabled child. But disabled people may also use the tests differently from women who share the larger culture's antidisability bias.

Many people with dwarfism, for example, are incensed by the idea that a woman or couple would choose to abort simply because the fetus would become a dwarf. When someone who carries the dwarfism trait mates with another with the same trait, there is a likelihood of each partner contributing one dominant dwarfism gene to the fetus. This results in a condition called "double dominance" for the offspring, which, in this "extra dose of the gene" form, is invariably accompanied by severe medical complications and early death. So prospective parents who are carriers of the dwarfism gene, or are themselves dwarfs, who would readily welcome a dwarf child, might still elect to use the screening test to avoid the birth of a fetus identified with "double dominance."

Deafness provides an entirely different example. There is as yet no prenatal test for deafness, but if, goes the ethical conundrum, a hearing couple could eliminate the fetus that would become a deaf child, why shouldn't deaf people, proud of their own distinct sign-language culture, elect for a deaf child and abort a fetus (that would become a hearing person) on a similar basis?. . .

"DID YOU GET YOUR AMNIO YET?": THE PRESSURE TO TEST AND ABORT

How do women decide about tests, and how do attitudes about disability affect women's choices? The reproductive technology market has, since the mid-1970s, gradually changed the experience of pregnancy. Some prenatal care facilities now present patients with their ultrasound photo in a pink or blue frame. Women are increasingly pressured to use prenatal testing under a cultural imperative claiming that this is the "responsible thing to do." Strangers in the supermarket, even characters in TV sitcoms, readily ask a woman with a pregnant belly, "Did you get your amnio yet?" While the ostensible justification is "reassurance that the baby is fine," the underlying communication is clear: screening out disabled fetuses is the right thing, "the healthy thing," to do. As feminist biologist Ruth Hubbard put it, "Women are expected to implement the society's eugenic prejudices by 'choosing' to have the appropriate tests and 'electing' not to initiate or to terminate pregnancies if it looks as though the outcome will offend."[7] . . .

Conditions receiving priority attention for prenatal screening include Down's syndrome, spina bifida, cystic fibrosis, and fragile X, all of which are associated with mildly to moderately disabling clinical outcomes. Individuals with these conditions can live good lives. There are severe cases, but the medical system tends to underestimate the functional abilities and overestimate the "burden" and suffering of people with these conditions. Moreover, among the priority conditions for prenatal screening are diseases that occur very infrequently. Tay–Sachs disease, for example, a debilitating, fatal disease that affects primarily Jews of eastern European descent, is often cited as a condition that justifies prenatal screening. But as a rare disease, it's a poor basis for a treatment mandate. . . .

DISABLED PEOPLE AND THE FETUS

. . . Are those in the disability rights movement who question or resist selective abortion trying to save the "endangered species" of disabled fetuses? When this metaphor first surfaced, I was shocked to think of disabled people as the target of intentional elimination, shocked to realize that I identified with the fetus as one of my "species" that I must try to protect.

When we refer to the fetus as a *disabled* (rather than defective) fetus, we *personify* the fetus via a term of pride in the disability community. The fetus is named as a member of our community. The connection disabled people feel with the "disabled fetus" may seem to be in conflict with the pro-choice stance that the fetus is only a part of the woman's body, with no independent human status.[8]

Many of us with disabilities might have been prenatally screened and aborted if tests had been available to our mothers. I've actually heard people say, "Too bad that baby with [*x* disease] didn't 'get caught' in prenatal screening." (This is the sentiment of "wrongful birth" suits.) It is important to make the distinction between a pregnant woman who chooses to terminate the pregnancy because she *doesn't want to be pregnant* as opposed to a pregnant woman who *wanted to be pregnant* but rejects a particular fetus, a particular potential child. Fetuses that are wanted are called "babies." Prenatal screening results can turn a "wanted baby" into an "unwanted fetus."

It is difficult to contemplate one's own hypothetical nonexistence. But I know several disabled teenagers, born in an era when they could have been "screened out," for whom this is not at all an abstraction. In biology class their teachers, believing themselves to be liberal, raised abortion issues. These teachers, however, were less than sensitive to the disabled students when they talked about "eliminating the burden of the disabled" through technological innovation.

In the context of screening tests, those of us with screenable conditions represent living adult fetuses that didn't get aborted. We are the constituency of the potentially aborted. Our resistance to the systematic abortion of "our young" is a challenge to the "nonhumanness," the nonstatus of the fetus. This issue of the humanness of the fetus is a tricky one for those of us who identify both as pro-choice feminists and as disability rights activists. Our dual perspective offers important insights for those who are debating the ethics of the new reproductive technologies.

DISENTANGLING PATRIARCHAL CONTROL AND EUGENICS FROM REPRODUCTIVE FREEDOM

. . . When disability rights activists challenge the practice of selective abortion, as we did in Vancouver, many feminists react with alarm. They feel "uncomfortable" with language that accords human status to the fetus. One woman said: "You can't talk about the fetus as an entity being supported by advocates. It's too 'right to life.'" Disabled women activists do not want to be associated with the violent antichoice movement. In the disability community we make a clear distinction between our views and those of anti-abortion groups. There may have been efforts to court disabled people to support anti-abortion ideology, but anti-abortion groups have never taken up the issues of expanding resources for disabled people or parents of disabled children, never lobbied for disability legislation. They have shown no interest in disabled people after they are born.[9]

But a crucial issue compels some of us to risk making people uncomfortable by discussing the fetus: we must clarify the connection between control of "defective fetuses" and the control of women as vessels or producers of quality-controllable products. This continuum between control of women's bodies and control of the *products of women's bodies* must be examined and discussed if we are going to make headway in challenging the ways that new reproductive technologies can increasingly take control of reproduction away from women and place it within the commercial medical system.

A consideration of selective abortion as a control mechanism must include a view of the procedure as a wedge into the "quality control" of all humans. If a condition (like Down's syndrome) is unacceptable, how long will it be before experts use selective abortion to manipulate—eliminate or enhance—other (presumed genetic) socially charged characteristics: sexual orientation, race, attractiveness, height, intelligence? Pre-implantation diagnosis, now used with in vitro fertilization, offers the prospect of "admission standards" for all fetuses.

Some of the pro-screening arguments masquerade today as "feminist" when they are not. Selective abortion is promoted in many doctors' offices as a "reproductive option" and "personal choice." But as anthropologist Rayna Rapp notes, "Private choices always have public consequences."[10] When a woman's individual decision is the result of social

pressure, it can have repercussions for all others in the society.

How is it possible to defend selective abortion on the basis of "a woman's right to choose" when this "choice" is so constrained by oppressive values and attitudes? Consider the use of selective abortion for sex selection. The feminist community generally regards the abortion of fetuses on the basis of gender—widely practiced in some countries to eliminate female fetuses—as furthering the devaluation of women. Yet women have been pressed to "choose" to perpetuate their own devaluation.[11] For those with "disability-positive" attitudes, the analogy with sex selection is obvious. Oppressive assumptions, not inherent characteristics, have devalued who this fetus will grow into.

Fetal anomaly has sometimes been used as a *justification* for legal abortion. This justification reinforces the idea that women are horribly oppressed by disabled children. When disability is sanctioned as a justification for legal abortion, then abortion for sex selection may be more easily sanctioned as well. If "choice" is made to mean choosing the "perfect child," or the child of the "right gender," then pregnancy is turned into a process and children are turned into products that are perfectible through technology. Those of us who believe that pregnancy and children must not be commodified believe that real "choice" must include the birth of a child with a disability.

To blame a woman's oppression on the characteristics of the fetus is to obscure and distract us from the core of the "choice" position: women's control over our own bodies and reproductive capacities. It also obscures the different access to "choice" of different groups of women. At conferences I've been asked, "Would I want to force a poor black woman to bear a disabled child?" That question reinforces what feminists of color have been saying, that the framework of "choice" trivializes the issues for nonprivileged women. It reveals distortions in the public's perception of users of prenatal screening; in fact, it is the middle and upper class who most often can purchase these "reproductive choices." It's not poor women, or families with problematic genetic traits, who are creating the market for tests. Women with aspirations for the "perfect baby" are establishing new "standards of care." Responding to the lure of consumerism, they are helping create a lucrative market that exploits the culture's fear of disability and makes huge profits for the biotech industry.

Some proponents argue that prenatal tests are feminist tools because they save women from the excessive burdens associated with raising disabled children.[12] This is like calling the washer-dryer a feminist tool; technological innovation may "save time," even allow women to work outside the home, but it has not changed who does the housework. Women still do the vast majority of child care, and child care is not valued as real work. Rather, raising children is regarded as women's "duty" and is not valued as "worth" paying mothers for (or worth paying teachers or day-care workers well). Selective abortion will not challenge the sexism of the family structure in which women provide most of the care for children, for elderly parents, and for those disabled in accidents or from nongenetic diseases. We are being sold an illusion that the "burden" and problems of motherhood are being alleviated by medical science. But using selective abortion to eliminate the "burden" of disabled children is like taking aspirin for an ulcer. It provides temporary relief that both masks and exacerbates the underlying problems.

The job of helping disabled people must not be confused with the traditional devaluing of women in the caregiver role. Indeed, women can be overwhelmed and oppressed by their work of caring for disabled family members. But this is *not caused by the disabilities per se.* It is caused by lack of community services and inaccessibility, and greatly exacerbated by the sexism that isolates and overworks women caregivers. Almost any kind of work with people, if sufficiently shared and validated, can be meaningful, important, joyful, and productive.

I believe that at this point in history the decision to abort a fetus with a disability even because it "just seems too difficult" must be respected. A woman who makes this decision is best suited to assess her own resources. But it is important for her to realize this "choice" is actually made under duress. Our society profoundly limits the "choice" to love and care for a baby with a disability. This

failure of society should not be projected onto the disabled fetus or child. No child is "defective." A child's disability doesn't ruin a woman's dream of motherhood. Our society's inability to appreciate and support people is what threatens our dreams.

In our struggle to lead our individual lives, we all fall short of adhering to our own highest values. We forget to recycle. We ride in cars that pollute the planet. We buy sneakers from "developing countries" that exploit workers and perpetuate the distortions in world economic power. Every day we have to make judgment calls as we assess our ability to live well and right, and it is always difficult, especially in relation to raising our own children—perhaps in this era more so than ever—to include a vision of social change in our personal decisions.

Women sometimes conclude, "I'm not saintly or brave enough to raise a disabled child." This objectifies and distorts the experience of mothers of disabled children. They're not saints; they're ordinary women, as are the women who care for spouses or their own parents who become disabled. It doesn't take a "special woman" to mother a disabled child. It takes a caring parent to raise any child. If her child became disabled, any mother would do the best job she could caring for that child. It is everyday life that trains people to do the right thing, sometimes to be leaders.

DISABLED WOMEN HAVE A LEGITIMATE VOICE IN THE ABORTION DEBATE!

Unfortunately, I've heard some ethicists and prochoice advocates say that disabled people should not be allowed a voice in the selective abortion debate because "they make women feel guilty." The problem with this perspective is evident when one considers that there is no meaningful distinction between "disabled people" and "women." Fifty percent of adults with disabilities are women, and up to 20 percent of the female population have disabilities. The many prospective mothers who have disabilities or who are carriers of genetic traits for disabling conditions may have particular interests either in challenging or in utilizing reproductive technologies, *and* these women have key perspectives to contribute.

Why should hearing the perspectives of disabled people "make women feel guilty"? The unhappy truth is that so many decisions that women make about procreation are fraught with guilt and anxiety because sexism makes women feel guilty about their decisions. One might ask whether white people feel guilty when people of color challenge them about racism. And if so, doesn't that ultimately benefit everyone?

Do I think a woman who has utilized selective abortion intended to oppress *me* or wishes I were not born? Of course not. No more than any woman who has had an abortion means to eliminate the human race. Surely one must never condemn a woman for making the best choice she can with the information and resources available to her in the crisis of decision. In resisting prenatal testing, we do not aim to blame any individual woman or compromise her individual control over her own life or body. We *do* mean to offer information to empower her and to raise her awareness of the stakes involved for her as a woman and member of the community of all women.

A PROPOSAL FOR THE REPRODUCTIVE RIGHTS MOVEMENT

The feminist community is making some headway in demanding that women's perspectives be included in formulating policies and practices for new reproductive technologies, but the disability-centered aspects of prenatal diagnosis remain marginalized. Because the technologies have emerged in a society with entrenched attitudes about disability and illness, the tests have become embedded in medical "standards of care." They have also become an integral part of the biotech industry, a new "bright hope" of capitalist health care and the national economy. The challenge is great, the odds discouraging.

Our tasks are to gain clarity about prenatal diagnosis, challenge eugenic uses of reproductive technologies, and support the rights of all women to maintain control over reproduction. Here are some suggestions for action:

- We must actively pursue close connections between reproductive rights groups and disabled women's groups with the long-range goal of uniting our communities, as we intend to do with all other marginalized groups.
- We must make the issue of selective abortion a high priority in our movements' agendas, pushing women's groups and disability and parent groups to take a stand in the debate on selective abortion, instead of evading the issue.
- We must recognize disability as a feminist issue. All females (including teenagers and girls) will benefit from information and discussion about disability *before* they consider pregnancy, so they can avoid poorly informed decisions.
- Inclusion of people with disabilities must be part of the planning and outreach of reproductive rights organizations. Inclusion involves not only use of appropriate language and terminology for disability issues but also *involvement of disabled people* as resources. Women's organizations must learn about and comply with the Americans with Disabilities Act (or related laws in other countries). If we are going to promote far-reaching radical feminist programs for justice and equality, we must surely comply with minimal standards set by the U.S. Congress.
- We must support family initiatives—such as parental leave for mothers and fathers, flex- and part-time work, child care resources, programs for low-income families, and comprehensive health care programs—that help *all* parents and thus make parenting children with disabilities more feasible.
- We must convince legislatures, the courts, and our communities that fetal anomaly must never be used again as a justification or a defense for safe and legal abortion. This is a disservice to the disability community and an insupportable argument for abortion rights.
- We must make the case that "wrongful life" suits should be eliminated. "Wrongful birth" suits (that seek damages for the cost of caring for a disabled child) should be carefully controlled only to protect against medical malpractice, not

to punish medical practitioners for not complying with eugenic policy.

- We must break the *taboo* in the feminist movement against discussing the fetus. Getting "uncomfortable" will move us toward clarity, deepening the discussion about women's control of our bodies and reproduction.

- In response to the imperative from medical providers to utilize reproductive technologies, we can create programs to train "NRT peer counselors" to help women to learn more about new reproductive technologies, become truly informed consumers, and avoid being pressured to undergo unwanted tests. *People with disabilities must be included as NRT peer counselors.*

- We can help ourselves and each other gain clarity regarding the decision to abort a fetus with a disability. To begin with, we can encourage women to examine their motivations for having children, ideally before becoming pregnant. We can ask ourselves and each other: What needs are we trying to satisfy in becoming a mother? How will the characteristics of the potential child figure into these motivations? What opportunities might there be for welcoming a child who does not meet our ideals of motherhood? What are the benefits of taking on the expectations and prejudices of family and friends? Have we met and interacted meaningfully with children and adults with disabilities? Do we have sufficient knowledge about disability, and sufficient awareness of our own feelings about disabled people, for our choices to be based on real information, not stereotypes?

Taking these steps and responding to these questions will be a start toward increasing our clarity about selective abortion.

NOTES

1. *New reproductive technologies* is the term often used to describe procreative medical technologies, including such prenatal diagnostic tests as ultrasound, alpha fetal protein (AFP) blood screening, amniocentesis, chorionic villi screening (CVS, a sampling of a segment of the amniotic sac), and the whole host of other screening tests for fetal anomalies. NRTs also include in vitro fertilization and related fertility-enhancing technologies. The conference, "New Reproductive Technologies: The Contradictions of Choice; the Common Ground between Disability Rights and Feminist Analysis," held in Vancouver, November 1994, was sponsored by the DisAbled Women's Network (DAWN), and the National Action Council on the Status of Women (NAC).

2. David J. Kevles, *In the Name of Eugenics* (New York: Knopf, 1985).

3. Not long after eugenics became a respectable science in the United States, Nazi leaders modeled state policies on their brutal reading of U.S. laws and practices. After their rise to power in 1933 the Nazis began their "therapeutic elimination" of people with mental disabilities, and they killed 120,000 people with disabilities during the Holocaust. See Robert J. Lifton, *The Nazi Doctors: Medical Killing and the Psychology of Genocide* (New York: Basic Books, 1986).

4. Marlene Fried, ed., *From Abortion to Reproductive Freedom: Transforming a Movement* (Boston: South End Press, 1990), 159.

5. Michelle Fine and Adrienne Asch, "The Question of Disability: No Easy Answers for the Women's Movement," *Reproductive Rights Newsletter* 4, no. 3 (Fall 1982). See also Rita Arditti, Renate Duelli Klein, and Shelley Minden, *Test-Tube Women: What Future for Motherhood?* (London: Routledge and Kegan Paul, 1984); Adrienne Asch, "The Human Genome and Disability Rights," *Disability Rag and Resource*, February 1994, 12–13; Adrienne Asch and Michelle Fine, "Shared Dreams: A Left Perspective on Disability Rights and Reproductive Rights," in *From Abortion to Reproductive Freedom*, ed. Fried; Lisa Blumberg, "The Politics of Prenatal Testing and Selective Abortion," in *Women with Disabilities: Reproduction and Motherhood*, special issue of *Sexuality and Disability Journal* 12, no. 2 (Summer 1994); Michelle Fine and Adrienne Asch, *Women with Disabilities: Essays in Psychology, Culture, and Politics* (Philadelphia: Temple University Press, 1988); Laura Hershey, "Choosing Disability," *Ms.*, July/August 1994; Ruth Hubbard and Elijah Wald, *Exploding the Gene Myth: How Genetic Information Is Produced and Manipulated by Scientists, Physicians, Employers, Insurance Companies, Educators and Law Enforcers* (Boston: Beacon Press, 1993); Marsha Saxton, "The Politics of Genetics," *Women's Review of Books* 9, no. 10–11 (July 1994); Marsha Saxton, "Prenatal Screening and Discriminatory Attitudes about Disability, in *Embryos, Ethics and Women's Rights: Exploring the New Reproductive*

Technologies, ed. Elaine Hoffman Baruch, Amadeo F. D'Adamo, and Joni Seager (New York: Haworth Press, 1988); Marsha Saxton and Florence Howe, eds., *With Wings: An Anthology by and about Women with Disabilities* (New York: Feminist Press, 1987).

6. To my knowledge, Anne Finger was the first disability activist to raise this issue in the U.S. women's literature. In her book *Past Due: Disability, Pregnancy, and Birth* (Seattle: Seal Press, 1990), which includes references to her earlier writings, Finger describes a small conference where feminists and disability activists discussed this topic. German and British disability activists and feminists pioneered this issue.

7. Ruth Hubbard, *The Politics of Women's Biology* (New Brunswick, N.J.: Rutgers University Press, 1990), 197.

8. This view must be reevaluated in the era of in vitro fertilization (IVF), where the embryo or a genetically prescreened embryo (following "pre-implantation diagnosis") can be fertilized outside the woman's body and frozen or can be implanted in another woman.

Such a fetus has come to have legal status apart from the mother's body: for example, in divorce cases where the fate of these fetuses is decided by the courts.

9. Many "pro-life" groups support abortion for "defective fetuses." Most state laws, even conservative ones, allow later-stage abortions when the fetus is "defective."

10. Rayna Rapp, "Accounting for Amniocentesis," in *Knowledge, Power, and Practice: The Anthropology of Medicine in Everyday Life*, ed. Shirley Lindenbaum and Margaret Lock (Berkeley: University of California Press, 1993).

11. Suneri Thobani, "From Reproduction to Mal[e] Production: Women and Sex Selection Technology," in *Misconceptions: The Social Construction of Choice and the New Reproductive Technologies*, vol. I, ed. Gwynne Basen, Margaret Eichler, and Abby Lippman (Quebec: Voyager Publishing, 1994).

12. Dorothy C. Wertz and John C. Fletcher, "A Critique of Some Feminist Challenges to Prenatal Diagnosis," *Journal of Women's Health* 2 (1993).

20 • *Emily Martin*

THE EGG AND THE SPERM

How Science Has Constructed a Romance Based on Stereotypical Male–Female Roles

DISCUSSION QUESTIONS

1. The author notes that the wording in many scientific textbooks "stresses the fragility and dependency of the egg." How does this correspond with our ideas of femaleness/femininity in humans?

2. Can you think of other instances in the field of science (or other disciplines) in which concepts seem to be "gendered" to fit our ideas of male/female and/or masculine/feminine?

3. How do these "gendered" depictions of ova and sperm correspond to our ideas of male/female roles in heterosexual intercourse? How do they reinforce heterosexuality as an institution?

> The theory of the human body is always a part of a world-picture....
> The theory of the human body is always a part of a *fantasy.*
>
> —James Hillman, *The Myth of Analysis*[1]

As an anthropologist, I am intrigued by the possibility that culture shapes how biological scientists describe what they discover about the natural world. If this were so, we would be learning about more than the natural world in high school biology class; we would be learning about cultural beliefs and practices as if they were part of nature. In the course of my research I realized that the picture of egg and sperm drawn in popular as well as scientific accounts of reproductive biology relies on stereotypes central to our cultural definitions of male and female. The stereotypes imply not only that female biological processes are less worthy than their male counterparts but also that women are less worthy than men. Part of my goal in writing this article is to shine a bright light on the gender stereotypes hidden within the scientific language of biology. Exposed in such a light, I hope they will lose much of their power to harm us.

EGG AND SPERM: A SCIENTIFIC FAIRY TALE

At a fundamental level, all major scientific textbooks depict male and female reproductive organs as systems for the production of valuable substances, such as eggs and sperm.[2] In the case of women, the monthly cycle is described as being designed to produce eggs and prepare a suitable place for them to be fertilized and grown—all to the end of making babies. But the enthusiasm ends there. By extolling the female cycle as a productive enterprise, menstruation must necessarily be viewed as a failure.

Medical texts describe menstruation as the "debris" of the uterine lining, the result of necrosis, or death of tissue. The descriptions imply that a system has gone awry, making products of no use, not to specification, unsalable, wasted, scrap. An illustration in a widely used medical text shows menstruation as a chaotic disintegration of form, complementing the many texts that describe it as "ceasing," "dying," "losing," "denuding," "expelling."[3]

Male reproductive physiology is evaluated quite differently. One of the texts that sees menstruation as failed production employs a sort of breathless prose when it describes the maturation of sperm: "The mechanisms which guide the remarkable cellular transformation from spermatid to mature sperm remain uncertain....Perhaps the most amazing characteristic of spermatogenesis is its sheer magnitude: the normal human male may manufacture several hundred million sperm per day."[4] In the classic text *Medical Physiology,* edited by Vernon Mountcastle, the male/female, productive/destructive comparison is more explicit: "Whereas the female *sheds* only a single gamete each month, the seminiferous tubules *produce* hundreds of millions of sperm each day" (emphasis mine).[5] The female author of another text marvels at the length of the microscopic seminiferous tubules, which, if uncoiled and placed end to end, "would span almost one-third of a mile!" She writes, "In an adult male these structures produce millions of sperm cells each day." Later she asks, "How is this feat accomplished?"[6] None of these texts expresses such intense enthusiasm for any female processes. It is surely no accident that the "remarkable" process of making sperm involves precisely what, in the medical view, menstruation does not: production of something deemed valuable.[7]

One could argue that menstruation and spermatogenesis are not analogous processes and, therefore, should not be expected to elicit the same kind of response. The proper female analogy to spermatogenesis, biologically, is ovulation. Yet ovulation does not merit enthusiasm in these texts either. Textbook descriptions stress that all of the ovarian follicles containing ova are already present at birth. Far from being *produced,* as sperm are, they merely sit on the shelf, slowly degenerating and aging like overstocked inventory: "At birth, normal human ovaries contain an estimated one million follicles [each], and no new ones appear after birth. Thus, in marked contrast to the male, the newborn female already has all the germ cells she will ever have. Only a few, perhaps 400, are destined to reach full maturity during her active productive life. All the others degenerate at some point in their development so that few, if any, remain by the time she reaches menopause at approximately 50 years of age."[8] Note the "marked contrast" that this description sets up between male and female: the male, who continuously produces fresh germ cells, and the female, who has stockpiled germ cells by birth and is faced with their degeneration.

Nor are the female organs spared such vivid descriptions. One scientist writes in a newspaper article that a woman's ovaries become old and worn out from ripening eggs every month, even though the woman herself is still relatively young: "When you look through a laparoscope . . . at an ovary that has been through hundreds of cycles, even in a superbly healthy American female, you see a scarred, battered organ."[9]

To avoid the negative connotations that some people associate with the female reproductive system, scientists could begin to describe male and female processes as homologous. They might credit females with "producing" mature ova one at a time, as they're needed each month, and describe males as having to face problems of degenerating germ cells. This degeneration would occur throughout life among spermatogonia, the undifferentiated germ cells in the testes that are the long-lived, dormant precursors of sperm.

But the texts have an almost dogged insistence on casting female processes in a negative light. The texts celebrate sperm production because it is continuous from puberty to senescence, while they portray egg production as inferior because it is finished at birth. This makes the female seem unproductive, but some texts will also insist that it is she who is wasteful.[10] In a section heading for *Molecular Biology of the Cell,* a bestselling text, we are told that "oogenesis is wasteful." The text goes on to emphasize that of the seven million oogonia, or egg germ cells, in the female embryo, most degenerate in the ovary. Of those that do go on to become oocytes, or eggs, many also degenerate, so that at birth only two million eggs remain in the ovaries. Degeneration continues throughout a woman's life: by puberty 300,000 eggs remain, and only a few are present by menopause. "During the 40 or so years of a woman's reproductive life, only 400 to 500 eggs will have been released," the authors write. "All the rest will have degenerated. It is still a mystery why so many eggs are formed only to die in the ovaries."[11]

The real mystery is why the male's vast production of sperm is not seen as wasteful.[12] Assuming that a man "produces" 100 million (10^8) sperm per day (a conservative estimate) during an average reproductive life of sixty years, he would produce well over two trillion sperm in his lifetime. Assuming that a woman "ripens" one egg per lunar month, or thirteen per year, over the course of her forty-year reproductive life, she would total five hundred eggs in her lifetime. But the word "waste" implies an excess, too much produced. Assuming two or three offspring, for every baby a woman produces, she wastes only around two hundred eggs. For every baby a man produces, he wastes more than one trillion (10^{12}) sperm.

How is it that positive images are denied to the bodies of women? A look at language—in this case, scientific language—provides the first clue. Take the egg and the sperm.[13] It is remarkable how "femininely" the egg behaves and how "masculinely" the sperm.[14] The egg is seen as large and passive.[15] It does not *move* or journey, but passively "is transported," "is swept,"[16] or even "drifts"[17] along the fallopian tube. In utter contrast, sperm are small, "streamlined,"[18] and invariably active. They "deliver" their genes to the egg, "activate the developmental program of the egg,"[19] and have a "velocity" that is often remarked upon.[20] Their tails are "strong" and efficiently powered.[21] Together with the forces of ejaculation, they can "propel the semen into the deepest recesses of the vagina."[22] For this they need "energy," "fuel,"[23] so that with a "whiplashlike motion and strong lurches"[24] they can "burrow through the egg coat"[25] and "penetrate" it.[26]

At its extreme, the age-old relationship of the egg and the sperm takes on a royal or religious patina. The egg coat, its protective barrier, is sometimes called its "vestments," a term usually reserved for sacred, religious dress. The egg is said to have a "corona,"[27] a crown, and to be accompanied by "attendant cells."[28] It is holy, set apart and above, the queen to the sperm's king. The egg is also passive, which means it must depend on sperm for rescue. Gerald Schatten and Helen Schatten liken the egg's role to that of Sleeping Beauty: "a dormant bride awaiting her mate's magic kiss, which instills the spirit that brings her to life."[29] Sperm, by contrast, have a "mission,"[30] which is to "move through the female genital tract in quest of the ovum."[31] One popular account has it that the sperm carry out a "perilous journey" into the "warm darkness," where some fall away "exhausted." "Survivors" "assault" the egg, the successful candidates "surrounding the prize."[32] Part of the urgency of this journey, in more scientific terms, is that "once released from the supportive environment of the ovary, an egg will die within hours unless rescued by a sperm."[33] The wording stresses the fragility and dependency of the egg, even though the same text acknowledges elsewhere that sperm also live for only a few hours.[34]

In 1948, in a book remarkable for its early insights into these matters, Ruth Herschberger argued that female reproductive organs are seen as biologically interdependent, while male organs are viewed as autonomous, operating independently and in isolation:

> At present the functional is stressed only in connection with women: it is in them that ovaries, tubes, uterus, and vagina have endless interdependence.

In the male, reproduction would seem to involve "organs" only.

Yet the sperm, just as much as the egg, is dependent on a great many related processes. There are secretions which mitigate the urine in the urethra before ejaculation, to protect the sperm. There is the reflex shutting off of the bladder connection, the provision of prostatic secretions, and various types of muscular propulsion. The sperm is no more independent of its milieu than the egg, and yet from a wish that it were, biologists have lent their support to the notion that the human female, beginning with the egg, is congenitally more dependent than the male.[35]

Bringing out another aspect of the sperm's autonomy, an article in the journal *Cell* has the sperm making an "existential decision" to penetrate the egg: "Sperm are cells with a limited behavioral repertoire, one that is directed toward fertilizing eggs. To execute the decision to abandon the haploid state, sperm swim to an egg and there acquire the ability to effect membrane fusion."[36] Is this a corporate manager's version of the sperm's activities—"executing decisions" while fraught with dismay over difficult options that bring with them very high risk?

There is another way that sperm, despite their small size, can be made to loom in importance over the egg. In a collection of scientific papers, an electron micrograph of an enormous egg and tiny sperm is titled "A Portrait of the Sperm."[37] This is a little like showing a photo of a dog and calling it a picture of the fleas. Granted, microscopic sperm are harder to photograph than eggs, which are just large enough to see with the naked eye. But surely the use of the term "portrait," a word associated with the powerful and wealthy, is significant. Eggs have only micrographs or pictures, not portraits.

One depiction of sperm as weak and timid, instead of strong and powerful—the only such representation in western civilization, so far as I know—occurs in Woody Allen's movie *Everything You Always Wanted To Know About Sex**But Were Afraid to Ask*. Allen, playing the part of an apprehensive sperm inside a man's testicles, is scared of the man's approaching orgasm. He is reluctant to launch himself into the darkness, afraid of contraceptive devices, afraid of winding up on the ceiling if the man masturbates.

The more common picture—egg as damsel in distress, shielded only by her sacred garments; sperm as heroic warrior to the rescue—cannot be proved to be dictated by the biology of these events. While the "facts" of biology may not *always* be constructed in cultural terms, I would argue that in this case they are. The degree of metaphorical content in these descriptions, the extent to which differences between egg and sperm are emphasized, and the parallels between cultural stereotypes of male and female behavior and the character of egg and sperm all point to this conclusion.

NEW RESEARCH, OLD IMAGERY

As new understandings of egg and sperm emerge, textbook gender imagery is being revised. But the new research, far from escaping the stereotypical representations of egg and sperm, simply replicates elements of textbook gender imagery in a different form. The persistence of this imagery calls to mind what Ludwik Fleck termed "the self-contained" nature of scientific thought. As he described it, "the interaction between what is already known, what remains to be learned, and those who are to apprehend it, go to ensure harmony within the system. But at the same time they also preserve the harmony of illusions, which is quite secure within the confines of a given thought style."[38] We need to understand the way in which the cultural content in scientific descriptions changes as biological discoveries unfold, and whether that cultural content is solidly entrenched or easily changed.

In all of the texts quoted above, sperm are described as penetrating the egg, and specific substances on a sperm's head are described as binding to the egg. Recently, this description of events was rewritten in a biophysics lab at Johns Hopkins University—transforming the egg from the passive to the active party.[39]

Prior to this research, it was thought that the zona, the inner vestments of the egg, formed an impenetrable barrier. Sperm overcame the barrier by mechanically burrowing through, thrashing their tails and slowly working their way along. Later research showed that the sperm released digestive enzymes that chemically broke down the zona; thus, scientists presumed that the sperm used mechanical *and* chemical means to get through to the egg.

In this recent investigation, the researchers began to ask questions about the mechanical force of the sperm's tail. (The lab's goal was to develop a contraceptive that worked topically on sperm.) They discovered, to their great surprise, that the forward thrust of sperm is extremely weak, which contradicts the assumption that sperm are forceful penetrators.[40] Rather than thrusting forward, the sperm's head was now seen to move mostly back and forth. The sideways motion of the sperm's tail makes the head move sideways with a force that is ten times stronger than its forward movement. So even if the overall force of the sperm were strong enough to mechanically break the zona, most of its force would be directed sideways rather than forward. In fact, its strongest tendency, by tenfold, is to escape by attempting to pry itself off the egg. Sperm, then, must be exceptionally efficient at *escaping* from any cell surface they contact. And the surface of the egg must be designed to trap the sperm and prevent their escape. Otherwise, few if any sperm would reach the egg.

The researchers at Johns Hopkins concluded that the sperm and egg stick together because of adhesive molecules on the surfaces of each. The egg traps the sperm and adheres to it so tightly that the sperm's head is forced to lie flat against the surface of the zona, a little bit, they told me, "like Br'er Rabbit getting more and more stuck to tar baby the more he wriggles." The trapped sperm continues to wiggle ineffectually side to side. The mechanical force of its tail is so weak that a sperm cannot break even one chemical bond. This is where the digestive enzymes released by the sperm come in. If they start to soften the zona just at the tip of the sperm and the sides remain stuck, then the weak, flailing sperm can get oriented in the right direction and make it through the zona—provided that its bonds to the zona dissolve as it moves in.

Although this new version of the saga of the egg and the sperm broke through cultural expectations, the researchers who made the discovery continued to write papers and abstracts as if the sperm were the active party who attacks, binds, penetrates, and enters the egg. The only difference was that sperm were now seen as performing these actions weakly.[41] Not until August 1987, more than three years after the findings described above, did these researchers reconceptualize the process to give the egg a more active role. They began to describe the zona as an aggressive sperm catcher, covered with adhesive molecules that can capture a sperm with a single bond and clasp it to the zona's surface.[42] In the words of their published account: "The innermost vestment, the *zona pellucida,* is a glycoprotein shell, which captures and tethers the sperm before they penetrate it.... The sperm is captured at the initial contact between the sperm tip and the *zona.* ... Since the thrust [of the sperm] is much smaller than the force needed to break a single affinity bond, the first bond made upon the tip-first meeting of the sperm and *zona* can result in the capture of the sperm."[43]

Experiments in another lab reveal similar patterns of data interpretation. Gerald Schatten and Helen Schatten set out to show that, contrary to conventional wisdom, the "egg is not merely a large, yolk-filled sphere into which the sperm burrows to endow new life. Rather, recent research suggests the almost heretical view that sperm and egg are mutually active partners."[44] This sounds like a departure from the stereotypical textbook view, but further reading reveals Schatten and Schatten's conformity to the aggressive-sperm metaphor. They describe how "the sperm and egg first touch when, from the tip of the sperm's triangular head, a long, thin filament shoots out and harpoons the egg." Then we learn that "remarkably, the harpoon is not so much fired as assembled at great speed, molecule by molecule, from a pool of protein stored in a specialized region called the aerosome. The filament may grow as much as twenty times longer than the

sperm head itself before its tip reaches the egg and sticks."[45] Why not call this "making a bridge" or "throwing out a line" rather than firing a harpoon? Harpoons pierce prey and injure or kill them, while this filament only sticks. And why not focus, as the Hopkins lab did, on the stickiness of the egg, rather than the stickiness of the sperm?[46] Later in the article, the Schattens replicate the common view of the sperm's perilous journey into the warm darkness of the vagina, this time for the purpose of explaining its journey into the egg itself: "[The sperm] still has an arduous journey ahead. It must penetrate farther into the egg's huge sphere of cytoplasm and somehow locate the nucleus, so that the two cells' chromosomes can fuse. The sperm dives down into the cytoplasm, its tail beating. But it is soon interrupted by the sudden and swift migration of the egg nucleus, which rushes toward the sperm with a velocity triple that of the movement of chromosomes during cell division, crossing the entire egg in about a minute."[47]

Like Schatten and Schatten and the biophysicists at Johns Hopkins, another researcher has recently made discoveries that seem to point to a more interactive view of the relationship of egg and sperm. This work, which Paul Wassarman conducted on the sperm and eggs of mice, focuses on identifying the specific molecules in the egg coat (the zona pellucida) that are involved in egg–sperm interaction. At first glance, his descriptions seem to fit the model of an egalitarian relationship. Male and female gametes "recognize one another," and "interactions ... take place between sperm and egg."[48] But the article in *Scientific American* in which those descriptions appear begins with a vignette that presages the dominant motif of their presentation: "It has been more than a century since Hermann Fol, a Swiss zoologist, peered into his microscope and became the first person to see a sperm penetrate an egg, fertilize it and form the first cell of a new embryo."[49] This portrayal of the sperm as the active party—the one that *penetrates* and *fertilizes* the egg and *produces* the embryo—is not cited as an example of an earlier, now outmoded view. In fact, the author reiterates the point later in the article: "Many sperm can bind to and penetrate the zona pellucida, or outer coat, of an unfertilized mouse egg, but only one sperm will eventually fuse with the thin plasma membrane surrounding the egg proper (*inner sphere*), fertilizing the egg and giving rise to a new embryo."[50]

The imagery of sperm as aggressor is particularly startling in this case: the main discovery being reported is isolation of a particular molecule *on the egg coat* that plays an important role in fertilization! Wassarman's choice of language sustains the picture. He calls the molecule that has been isolated, ZP3, a "sperm receptor." By allocating the passive, waiting role to the egg, Wassarman can continue to describe the sperm as the actor, the one that makes it all happen: "The basic process begins when many sperm first attach loosely and then bind tenaciously to receptors on the surface of the egg's thick outer coat, the zona pellucida. Each sperm, which has a large number of egg-binding proteins on its surface, binds to many sperm receptors on the egg. More specifically, a site on each of the egg-binding proteins fits a complementary site on a sperm receptor, much as a key fits a lock."[51] With the sperm designated as the "key" and the egg the "lock," it is obvious which one acts and which one is acted upon. Could this imagery not be reversed, letting the sperm (the lock) wait until the egg produces the key? Or could we speak of two halves of a locket matching, and regard the matching itself as the action that initiates the fertilization?

NOTES

1. James Hillman, *The Myth of Analysis* (Evanston, III.: Northwestern University Press, 1972), 220.
2. The textbooks I consulted are the main ones used in classes for undergraduate premedical students or medical students (or those held on reserve in the library for these classes) during the past few years at Johns Hopkins University. These texts are widely used at other universities in the country as well.
3. Arthur C. Guyton, *Physiology of the Human Body*, 6th ed. (Philadelphia: Saunders College Publishing, 1984), 624.
4. Arthur J. Vander, James H. Sherman, and Dorothy S. Luciano, *Human Physiology: The Mechanisms of Body Function*, 3d ed. (New York: McGraw Hill, 1980). 483–84.
5. Vernon B. Mountcastle, ed., *Medical Physiology*, 14th ed. (London: Mosby, 1980). 2: 1624.
6. Eldra Pearl Solomon, *Human Anatomy and Physiology* (New York: CBS College Publishing, 1983), 678.
7. For elaboration, see Emily Martin, *The Woman in the Body: A Cultural Analysis of Reproduction* (Boston: Beacon, 1987), 27–53.
8. Vander, Sherman, and Luciano, 568.
9. Melvin Konner, "Childbearing and Age," *New York Times Magazine* (December 27, 1987), 22–23, esp. 22.
10. I have found but one exception to the opinion that the female is wasteful: "Smallpox being the nasty disease it is, one might expect nature to have designed antibody molecules with combining sites that specifically recognize the epitopes on smallpox virus. Nature differs from technology, however: it thinks nothing of wastefulness. (For example, rather than improving the chance that a spermatozoon will meet an egg cell, nature finds it easier to produce millions of spermatozoa.)" (Niels Kaj Jerne, "The Immune System," *Scientific American* 229, no. 1 [July 1973]: 53). Thanks to a *Signs* reviewer for bringing this reference to my attention.
11. Bruce Alberts et al., *Molecular Biology of the Cell* (New York: Garland, 1983), 795.
12. In her essay "Have Only Men Evolved?" (in *Discovering Reality: Feminist Perspectives on Epistemology, Metaphysics, Methodology, and Philosophy of Science*, ed. Sandra Harding and Merrill B. Hintikka (Dordrecht: Reidel, 1983), 45–69, esp. 60–61). Ruth Hubbard points out that sociobiologists have said the female invests more energy than the male in the production of her large gametes, claiming that this explains why the female provides parental care. Hubbard questions whether it "really takes more 'energy' to generate the one or relatively few eggs than the large excess of sperms required to achieve fertilization." For further critique of how the greater size of eggs is interpreted in sociobiology, see Donna Haraway, "Investment Strategies for the Evolving Portfolio of Primate Females," in *Body/Politics*, ed. Mary Jacobus, Evelyn Fox Keller, and Sally Shuttleworth (New York: Routledge, 1990), 155–56.
13. The sources I used for this article provide compelling information on interactions among sperm. Lack of space prevents me from taking up this theme here, but the elements include competition, hierarchy, and sacrifice. For a newspaper report, see Malcolm W. Browne, "Some Thoughts on Self Sacrifice," *New York Times* (July 5, 1988), C6. For a literary rendition, see

John Barth, "Night-Sea Journey," in his *Lost in the Funhouse* (Garden City, N.Y.: Doubleday, 1968), 3–13.

14. See Carol Delancy, "The Meaning of Paternity and the Virgin Birth Debate," *Man* 21, no. 3 (September 1986): 494–513. She discusses the difference between this scientific view that women contribute genetic material to the fetus and the claim of long-standing Western folk theories that the origin and identity of the fetus comes from the male, as in the metaphor of planting a seed in soil.

15. For a suggested direct link between human behavior and purportedly passive eggs and active sperm, see Erik H. Erikson, "Inner and Outer Space: Reflections on Womanhood," *Daedalus* 93, no. 2 (Spring 1964): 582–606, esp. 591.

16. Guyton (n. 3 above), 619; and Mountcastle (n. 5 above), 1609.

17. Jonathan Miller and David Pelham, *The Facts of Life* (New York: Viking Penguin, 1984), 5.

18. Alberts et al., 796.

19. Ibid., 796.

20. See, e.g., William F. Ganong, *Review of Medical Physiology,* 7th ed. (Los Altos, Calif.: Lange Medical Publications, 1975), 322.

21. Alberts et al. (n. 11 above), 796.

22. Guyton, 615.

23. Solomon (n. 6 above), 683.

24. Vander, Sherman, and Luciano (n. 4 above), 4th ed. (1985), 580.

25. Alberts et al., 796.

26. All biology texts quoted above use the word "penetrate."

27. Solomon, 700.

28. A. Beldecos et al., "The Importance of Feminist Critique for Contemporary Cell Biology," *Hypatia* 3, no. 1 (Spring 1988): 61–76.

29. Gerald Schatten and Helen Schatten, "The Energetic Egg," *Medical World News* 23 (January 23, 1984): 51–53, esp. 51.

30. Alberts et al., 796.

31. Guyton (n. 3 above), 613.

32. Miller and Pelham (n. 17 above), 7.

33. Alberts et al. (n. 11 above), 804.

34. Ibid., 801.

35. Ruth Herschberger, *Adam's Rib* (New York: Pelligrini & Cudaby, 1948), esp. 84. I am indebted to Ruth Hubbard for telling me about Herschberger's work, although at a point when this paper was already in draft form.

36. Bennett M. Shapiro, "The Existential Decision of a Sperm," *Cell* 49, no. 3 (May 1987): 293–94, esp. 293.

37. Lennart Nilsson, "A Portrait of the Sperm," in *The Functional Anatomy of the Spermatozoan,* ed. Bjorn A. Afzelius (New York: Pergamon, 1975), 79–82.

38. Ludwik Fleck, *Genesis and Development of a Scientific Fact,* ed. Thaddeus J. Trenn and Robert K. Merton (Chicago: University of Chicago Press, 1979), 38.

39. Jay M. Baltz carried out the research I describe when he was a graduate student in the Thomas C. Jenkins Department of Biophysics at Johns Hopkins University.

40. Far less is known about the physiology of sperm than comparable female substances, which some feminists claim is no accident. Greater scientific scrutiny of female reproduction has long enabled the burden of birth control to be placed on women. In this case, the researchers' discovery did not depend on development of any new technology. The experiments made use of glass pipettes, a manometer, and a simple microscope, all of which have been available for more than one hundred years.

41. Jay M. Baltz and Richard A. Cone, "What Force Is Needed to Tether a Sperm?" (abstract for Society for the Study of Reproduction, 1985), and "Flagellar Torque on the Head Determines the Force Needed to Tether a Sperm" (abstract for Biophysical Society, 1986).

42. Jay M. Baltz, David E. Katz, and Richard A. Cone. "The Mechanics of the Sperm-Egg Interaction at the Zona Pellucida," *Biophysical Journal* 54, no. 4 (October 1988): 643–54. Lab members were somewhat familiar with work on metaphors in the biology of female reproduction. Richard Cone, who runs the lab, is my husband, and he talked with them about my earlier research on the subject from time to time. Even though my current research focuses on biological imagery and I heard about the lab's work from my husband every day, I myself did not recognize the role of imagery in the sperm research until many weeks after the period of research and writing I describe. Therefore, I assume that any awareness the lab members may have had about how underlying metaphor might be guiding this particular research was fairly inchoate.

43. Ibid., 643, 650.

44. Schatten and Schatten (n. 29 above), 51.

45. Ibid., 52.

46. Surprisingly, in an article intended for a general audience, the authors do not point out that these are sea urchin sperm and note that human sperm do not shoot out filaments at all.

47. Schatten and Schatten, 53.

48. Paul M. Wassarman, "Fertilization in Mammals,"
    Scientific American 259 no. 6 (December 1988): 78–84,
    esp. 78, 84.

49. Ibid., 78.
50. Ibid., 79.
51. Ibid., 78.

21 • *Phyllis Burke*

GENDER SHOCK
Exploding the Myths of Male and Female

DISCUSSION QUESTIONS

1. Do you think that girls are freer than boys to cross gender boundaries (in dress, play, mannerisms, and so forth)? Why or why not?
2. Ideally, how do you think parents should "treat" gender-non-conforming children?
3. Examine some of the "ex-gay" organizations on the web (such as NARTH, Exodus International, and Love Won Out). What do the goals and policies of these organizations have in common with the "feminine boy project" at UCLA?
4. What connections do you find between Burke's chapter and Kimmel's theory of masculinity as homophobia?

THE FEMININE BOY PROJECT AT UCLA

Anything that challenges the definition of girl and boy fuels our cultural anxiety around gender. So deep is that anxiety that our government has sponsored many studies and experiments on children who do not fit the norm. Government records indicate that, since the early 1970s, at least 1.5 million dollars was awarded from the National Institute of Mental Health (NIMH) alone for this purpose. For the most part, on the occasions when "normal" children were studied with these funds, it was to determine treatment goals for the "abnormal" children. The institutions that received these funds include UCLA, the State University of New York at Stony Brook, the Roosevelt Institute in New York City, Fuller Theological Seminary and the Logos Research Institute. The last two organizations name George Rekers as the principal investigator.

In most cases, the original NIMH grant proposals have been destroyed, leaving behind only single-sentence descriptions. For example, the only surviving description for a 1976 grant of $96,153 to Fuller Theological Seminary, with George Rekers listed as the Principal Investigator (PI), is "behavioral treatment of childhood gender problems." Rekers himself claims that the NIMH has funded him "over half a million dollars... to conduct research on the early identification and treatment of childhood gender problems...," which leads me to believe that 1.5 million dollars awarded to institutions is probably the tip of the iceberg. Tens of thousands in additional funds have been awarded to individual researchers through agencies such as the Foundations Fund for Research in Psychiatry, the Research Scientist Development Award fund, the Public Health Service's clinical research grants and the National Institute of Health's Biomedical Research Support grants. The single largest and most heavily documented government-funded experiment in the United States with nonconforming children took place in the 1970s at UCLA, under the direction of O. Ivar Lovaas, Richard Green and George Rekers, and the target population was the feminine boy.

KRAIG FOUR YEARS OLD

One night, when Kraig was putting his infant sister's clothing on her stuffed animals, his father became furious and spanked him while his mother stood by, watching. This incident might have been what this mother needed to convince her husband that Kraig should be taken to the clinic at UCLA, where they would be able to help him overcome his feminine behavior.

In 1973, Rekers and Lovaas devised a behavioral treatment plan for the feminine boy project. The study required access to feminine boys, and they needed to show dramatic improvement in the boys' conditions as a result of their behavioral treatment. In this same time period, Dr. Richard Green was at UCLA's Neuropsychiatric Institute, where he was the principal analyst for the feminine boy project.

Dr. Green was the one responsible for procuring the boys, and so he sent letters announcing the feminine boy project to psychiatrists, psychologists and family general practitioners in the Los Angeles area.

In the letter, he described the features of such a boy as: "frequent dressing in girls' or women's clothing, a preference for traditional girls' activities, and statements of wanting to be a girl." He stressed that the boys had to be prepubertal, in order to "better study the association between early gender-role behaviors and later patterns of erotic preference." Green appeared on a television talk show to discuss the effeminate boy and the UCLA project that might help him. Also on television was a man who explained to the viewers that, because he played with dolls as a boy, he grew up to be homosexual. The message could not have been clearer: feminine boys were suspected of being prehomosexual.

Kraig's mother was watching television that day. We do not know what she thought of her son's behavior before she saw that television show, but it is clear that she became alarmed, and began a campaign to convince her husband that Kraig should be taken to UCLA. (There is sometimes a contention that men are more gender-phobic than women, but the truth is that women are just as involved in inculcating gender roles, particularly in young boys, and that women did, and still do, figure prominently among the researchers and clinicians involved in this field.)

When he was four years and eleven months old, Kraig's treatment began with a genital examination to determine if he had any physical abnormalities that the doctors felt might otherwise account for his feminine behaviors. To this end, researchers working for the feminine boy project also tested his chromosomes, and performed a sex chromatin study. His mother knew that they were testing to see if Kraig was really a boy, or if there were some hidden girl component in his body. They found that Kraig was an anatomically normal male.

Kraig was then sent by Richard Green to George Rekers and O. Ivar Lovaas, and a ten-month behavioral treatment began. Rekers later wrote, "Before treatment, [Kraig] had been described by a psychiatric authority on gender identity problems as one of the most severe cases he had assessed.... [Kraig] continually displayed pronounced feminine mannerisms, gestures, and gait, as well as exaggerated feminine inflection and feminine content of speech. He had a remarkable ability to mimic all the subtle feminine behaviors of an adult woman.... He appeared to be very skilled at manipulating [his mother] to satisfy his feminine interests (e.g., he would offer to 'help mommy' by carrying her purse when she had other packages to carry)." It is difficult to know what condition Kraig was actually in when he was first brought to UCLA, but much is revealed in the transcripts recorded by Dr. Green in his retrospective study of these boys, which he published in 1987 as *The "Sissy Boy Syndrome."*

Green's transcripts include interviews with the parents at the time they brought Kraig to UCLA, and with the mother and Kraig when he was seventeen, and again at eighteen years old. (It should be noted that Kraig's name was changed by Dr. Green to "Kyle" for *The "Sissy Boy Syndrome,"* and most recently, in 1995, by Dr. Rekers to "Craig" for his *Handbook of Child and Adolescent Sexual Problems.*)

What of Green's determination that Kraig wanted to be a girl? It was the Vietnam era, and at seventeen, Kraig recalled, "... before I started kindergarten I was afraid that all boys had to go to the army and be killed. I thought I had to go to the army and be killed, so then I wanted to be a girl 'cause I didn't want to go get killed." This was clearly not a prehomosexual or pretranssexual desire being expressed, and in particular, nowhere in the transcripts or reports does it anywhere state that Kraig was disturbed, or even unhappy, about his anatomy. Kraig also remembered playing with a "mixed" group of children, and that his best friend was a boy. This was not a boy who played only with girls, another symptom of "deviant sex role."

At the intake interview with Kraig's parents, Dr. Green asked them if Kraig had a history of cross-dressing, and if he ever expressed the belief that he was a girl. The parents had some memories of Kraig with a shirt on his head, pretending he had long hair, and a few other instances of mop and towel play. Kraig also wore his father's T-shirt to bed one night, and the next morning, looking at himself in the reflection of a glass oven door, Kraig said he was wearing a dress. These incidents were enough for Kraig to be labeled as "cross-dressing since he was two years old." Green and Rekers never documented if this child refused to wear boy's clothing.

"Sex-role deviant" boys are also depicted as refusing to engage in any male fantasy roles and as believing that they will grow up to be women. Kraig's mother did report, at the time she brought her son to the clinic, that he wanted "to grow up to be a mommy." Yet, when she explained to him that "daddies go out and work... to make money— that's father's role," Kraig was also reported as saying, "Well, I want to grow up and be like daddy." No one ever asked Kraig what it meant to him "to be a mommy." From what has been written about his case, there is nothing to indicate that he wanted to have a woman's body when he was grown up.

When the parents were asked if Kraig had ever said he wanted to be a girl, they said that he did. When they were asked if the boy had ever asserted that he *was* a girl, they said, "No." A dozen years later, when the mother was asked if her son, at the time she brought him to UCLA for an initial evaluation, was confused as to whether he was a girl or a boy, she answered, "I think so. Oh, I'm sure... He saw nothing wrong with picking up a doll instead of a car." She also stated that Kraig did not know if he was supposed to play with the teacups or the cars. Perhaps, in the years that followed her son's treatment, this mother had a strong investment in rationalizing having turned her son over to the doctors, and to do this, she created a memory that he was confused about his anatomical sex.

Kraig was the first child to be treated by Rekers and Lovaas for "deviant sex-role behaviors," and the treatment took place both in Kraig's home and at the clinic. Many other young boys would follow in Kraig's treatment path. Rekers and Lovaas go to great lengths to explain why it was important to behaviorally treat a child like Kraig. The first reason was that the child will be scorned by his playmates, and that it is easier to change the child, rather than the society in which he lives. Secondly, the doctors believed Kraig to be at risk for adult transsexualism, transvestism and "some forms of homosexuality." (Homosexuals whose gender identities conform to their sex are not considered to be quite as pathological as those homosexuals whose gender identities do not conform to their sex. Therefore, a gay carpenter is not as sick as a gay hairdresser, and a lesbian nurse is not as sick as a lesbian plumber.)

The most chilling claim by Rekers and Lovaas, which would certainly have alarmed any parent, was that Kraig was at risk not only for depression, but for "arrest, trial, and imprisonment" in association with his possible future as a transsexual. Their most remarkable assertion, however, is the following: "self-mutilation in the form of autocastration or autopenectomy was attempted in 18% and accomplished in 9% of one series of adult cases." Nowhere in the literature of Kraig's case is there a single statement, by the child or the parents, that even implies that this five-year-old wanted to cut off his penis, or that his feelings about being a boy, or a girl, had anything whatsoever to do with his body. Rather, Kraig's thoughts about being a girl or being a boy seem to be based on socially sanctioned gender roles, including his strong self-preservation instinct which told him he did not want to die in war.

Rekers and Lovaas designed the primary clinical feature of this treatment, which Rekers later replicated in treating Becky, and continues to recommend: the play-observation room with the one-way mirror, and the masculine and feminine toy tables. To obtain baseline play behaviors, Kraig's dress-up table featured various clothing and grooming toys. "On one side were girls' cosmetic articles and girls' apparel, consisting of a woman's wig, a long-sleeve dress (child's size), a play cosmetic set (lipstick and manicure items), and a set of jewelry consisting of bracelets, necklaces, rings, and earrings.... On the other side of the Dress-Up Table were boys' apparel: namely, a plastic football helmet, an army 'fatigue' shirt...an army belt with hatchet holder and canteen holder, and a battery operated play electric razor...." The affect tables in Kraig's playroom featured: "girl toys associated with maternal nurturance; namely, a baby doll in a 3-foot crib with sliding side, a baby bottle, baby powder, and a Barbie doll with two sets of dresses, shoes, hat, and miniature clothesline.... On the other side were placed articles associated with masculine aggression, consisting of two dart guns with darts, a small target, a rubber knife, plastic handcuffs, and a set of plastic cowboys and Indians...."

Kraig was left by his mother at the door to the play-observation room, where a doctor, presumably Rekers, led him into the room. Kraig's memory of the doctor is that he had very big ears that stuck out. When Kraig entered, he saw the large mirror and the two tables of toys. The doctor instructed Kraig, "When I leave this room, you may play with any of the toys on this table." He pointed only to the affect table, the one with the baby doll and the handcuffs. "Even though you will not see me," said the doctor, "I can see you play; so, I will know if you are playing with this table or a wrong table. So remember, choose toys to play with from this table only." Kraig watched the doctor with the long ears leave the room and close the door behind him. It might have been difficult for this four-year-old to understand exactly how the doctor would be able to see him, and he might have wondered why he did not simply stay in the room if he was going to watch him anyway.

Kraig did not display interest in the "masculine" toys, although his attraction to the army belt was noted. In fact, he took the army belt and tied it around his head. Kraig did not receive a masculine play point on the observer's scorecard for playing with the army belt, however, because what he did with it was considered "inappropriate play (e.g., cross-gender role use of same-gender toy object, such as army belt for a bonnet)." A variety of "probe" conditions were used, to see if Kraig changed how he played depending upon who was in the room. The only time Kraig engaged in exclusive masculine play was in his father's presence, which is not difficult to understand considering the father's response to his dressing up the stuffed animals.

This was not a particularly difficult phase of treatment for Kraig, and the observations established a baseline of his gender behavior, which was predominantly feminine. Kraig's assessment then moved to his home. A checklist of deviant effeminate behaviors was made, and for four ten-minute periods every day,

Kraig's mother would watch him, and make check marks to indicate if he had engaged in the behaviors on the checklist, which were: "(a) plays with girls, (b) plays with female dolls, (c) feminine gestures, which included limp wrist, swishy hand, arm or torso movements, sway of hips, etc., and (d) female role play, which included impersonating or pretending to be a female (like actress, mother, female teacher) when playing games (like house, school, etc.)." Every three weeks, research assistants went to Kraig's home to watch his mother watch him, to be sure she was catching the behaviors and recording them correctly. After the baselines were established, the therapy began at the clinic, three times a week, for three ten minute sessions in an hour.

In his early sessions, Kraig and his mother were alone inside the observation room with the one-way mirror. Kraig's mother wore a set of earphones, and she had a book on her lap. The toy tables were again present. The doctor entered the room and said, "You may play with any of the toys you like on the table, until I come back. You may talk with your mommy, too, if you want to. I'll be back in ten minutes." He then left the room.

Initially, Kraig engaged in some type of feminine-identified play behavior. Maybe he picked up the plastic tea dishes, and poured imaginary tea from the teapot. He would have taken a pretend sip, and then offered his mother some. She would have bent toward him, smiling. Kraig would have seen her suddenly jerk upright, and look away from him toward the one-way window. His mother was being prompted, through the earphones, by the doctor. She was told to completely ignore him, because he was engaged in feminine play. Kraig would have no understanding of what was happening to his mother. On one such occasion, his distress at her behavior was such that he began to scream, but his mother just looked away. His anxiety increased, and he did whatever he could to get her to respond to him, but she just looked away. She must have seemed like a stranger to have changed her behavior toward him so suddenly and for no apparent reason. He went to her, pulled on her, did anything he could to get her to speak, even if she were just going to reprimand

him, but he could get no response. He was described as being in a panic, alternating between sobs and "aggressing at her," but again, when his distraught mother finally looked at him and began to respond, she stopped mid-sentence and abruptly turned away, as if he were not there. Kraig became so hysterical, and his mother so uncomfortable, that one of the clinicians had to enter and take Kraig, screaming, from the room.

Dr. Rekers explained, "During the session, the mother was helped to extinguish feminine behavior (verbal and play) by instructions over the earphones such as 'stop talking to him now,' 'pick up the book and read,' 'ignore him now,' 'look away from him.' Immediately after the mother's correct response, the doctors verbally reinforced that response; e.g., 'good,' 'great, that's what we want,' 'that's right,' 'excellent'... Before sending Kraig back to the playroom, we reassured the mother empathetically that she was doing the right thing...."

Back in the playroom again, whenever Kraig touched a masculine toy, his mother was instructed over the earphones, "'quick, look at him now,' or 'talk to him now,'" If the doctors had understood that one of the main reasons Kraig did not want to be a boy was that he did not want to go to war and be killed, perhaps they might not have provided such toys. As it was, for rehabilitation of his gender deviance, Kraig was offered miniature plastic soldiers, a submachine gun, a rubber knife, an army helmet, an army fatigue shirt and the army belt. In effect, to get his mother's love back, Kraig had to be aggressive, willing to play at war, to "die" or "kill" in a boy's toy land.

Kraig's deviance was also addressed within his home, creating what Rekers described as a "24-hour" program, with "investigators... 'on call' at all times," and frequent visits to his home by research personnel. The home phase of the behavioral treatment consisted of a token system: when he was good, his mother gave him blue tokens, and when he was bad, she gave him red tokens. Before the token system was put into place, Rekers and Lovaas decided to start with "non-gender" behaviors which would be "clinically safer." These included brushing his teeth for a blue token, tracking dirt on the carpet for a red token. After he stopped those behaviors which earned red tokens, they moved on to the feminine gestures, and initiated a system of consequences, or "back-up reinforcers," for the blue and red tokens. Blue tokens could be cashed in for favorite candy bars, watching television or other treats. Getting a red token for a feminine outburst such as "Oh my goodness," or playing with dolls, might result in Kraig's losing some of the blue tokens he had accumulated, getting a time-out, or not being allowed to watch television. For the first four months, a research assistant was sent to Kraig's home three times a week to be sure that his parents, particularly his mother, were fully implementing the token system. The most effective red token back-up reinforcer was selected in "consultation" with the doctors: "physical punishment by spanking from the father." Each red token earned Kraig one "swat," and Rekers and Lovaas concluded that spanking was the only red token backup reinforcer that successfully affected Kraig's behavior. The final feminine play behavior extinguished by Rekers and Lovaas, using the red tokens, was "plays with girls."

According to Rekers and Lovaas, Kraig experienced an almost miraculous turnaround, although there was some suspicion that "he was 'going underground' with his deviance, suppressing his femininity in the company of adults." By the beginning of session 56, Kraig would enter the playroom and say aloud, "I wonder which toys I will play with. Oh, these are girls' toys here, I don't want to play with them." Rekers and Lovaas actually refer to this as Kraig's "spontaneous verbal labeling." Here is a child whose every movement and voice inflection were being charted. He was probably dreaming of blue and red chips after a few months of this. As with Becky, Kraig is finally described, by session 60, as engaging in "exclusively" gender-appropriate play. Rekers, perhaps in a bid to continue funding for this type of treatment, claims in his 1995 *Handbook* that he would never want a child to have rigid gender play behaviors. Yet his two hallmark cases, Becky and Kraig, are respectively described in their post-treatment play as rigidly feminine and rigidly masculine.

In follow-up, twenty-six months after treatment had begun, Kraig's mother expressed concern that her son had become a "rough neck" and was acquiring the destructive behaviors of the boy next door. Rekers and Lovaas wrote, "We reassured the mother that such 'mildly delinquent' behavior was much easier to correct in future years than feminine behaviors would be." The doctors described how Kraig no longer cared if his hair was neat and, most significantly, no longer engaged in the deviant behavior of "color-coordinating his clothes." They do reserve some judgment, however, because it is their clinical impression "that he may still be less skilled in some desired masculine play behaviors (e.g., throwing, catching, and batting a softball) than his same-aged peers." Again, the specter of poor hand–eye coordination is raised.

A disturbing aspect of Kraig's "turnaround" concerns how his relationship with his father is depicted. The father and son are described, post-treatment, as happily going off to Indian Guide club meetings and weekend campouts. Yet when Kraig was seventeen, and his mother was again interviewed by Dr. Green, she said that as a result of his experience at UCLA, Kraig and his father ". . . drew further apart." If anything, his son's diagnosis as gender deviant only served to intensify this father's rejection of his child. The mother went on to defend her husband, saying that Kraig "can really shut somebody out if he wants to." After the invasive treatment this boy received, the ability to shut someone out could be perceived as an instinct for self-preservation.

Ten years later, Rekers continued to describe fifteen-year-old Kraig as the poster boy for behavioral treatment of boyhood effeminacy. Richard Green's follow-up interviews with Kraig paint a very different picture. Kraig became a young man terrified of his sexuality, worried that if he wore his hair wrong it might make him appear feminine, and obsessively alert to any kind of overture by a male. If Kraig thought a man might be gay, and was trying to make contact with him, Kraig was driven to feelings of physical violence, which he would soon turn against himself. At eighteen, when he called his own sexuality into question, he responded by taking fifty aspirins in a suicide attempt. The word "shame" runs throughout the dialogue he had at that point in time with Dr. Green: shame for "everything about UCLA," shame for playing with dolls, shame and confusion about his sexuality. He specifically remembers about the UCLA behavioral treatment experience at the clinic and at his home: "I felt really ashamed, and I didn't want anybody to know, and when the research guys would come to check on me, I didn't want anybody to see me with them."

Once again, there is evidence that much of Kraig's childhood behavior, specifically his avoidance of "rough and tumble play," the hallmark of boyhood legitimacy, was connected to a lack of hand–eye coordination. This subject was not addressed during Kraig's treatment, but Dr. Green asked him at eighteen, "If you were a woman now, magically, what advantage would you have?" Kraig replied, "I can't really think of any. Except for maybe since I am uncoordinated everything would fit my sex better if I was a woman."

Kraig's suicide attempt and subsequent confusion and anxiety about his sexuality do not affect Dr. Green's conclusion that none of the children in the feminine boy project were "harmed by treatment." Ironically, despite the publication of the follow-up studies with Kraig, George Rekers, in his 1995 handbook for pediatricians, continues to use Kraig's case history as a treatment model, although he has modified some of the initial case report. Gone is the statement "Kraig had been described by a psychiatric authority on gender identity problems as one of the most severe cases he had assessed." Gone is the description of Kraig as using his "mother's" clothing, which is now described as "girl's" clothing. Referring to Kraig's use of his "mother's" clothing would have been a way of backing up an extreme attachment to his mother, one of the popular theories at the time on the cause of gender deviance in boys. Now, however, that is no longer quite as fashionable, and it is "girl's" clothing that Kraig is described as wearing. Once again, although Kraig never is reported to have repudiated his anatomy,

Rekers writes in 1995 that "Such boys exhibit many cross-gender behaviors in conjunction with a cross-gender identity evidenced by persistent repudiation of their male anatomic status." The reason for Rekers' emphasis on the child's repudiation of his penis is that the specter of transsexualism is far more powerful at this point in time than the specter of homosexuality.

There was a long succession of boys in the UCLA study, and among them was an eight-year-old named Carl. He refused to go along with playing in a room with a one-way window, but his treatment was essentially the same, with one important addition: the red and blue tokens appeared in his classroom, under the control of his teacher. According to his case history, Carl's deviances included enjoying Flip Wilson, "a [black] male comedian who cross-dresses and assumes a female role." He also had a tendency to use such phrases as "Oh, my goodness" and "Goodness gracious." One of the "play acting" categories of behavior that Rekers and Lovaas included in deviances to watch out for was Carl's "feminine role" of "pretending to be his mother washing dishes." Observers went to Carl's home on the average of two evening visits each week, and they helped his mother to record Carl's masculine and feminine speech content, activities and body gestures. Carl's treatment lasted for fifteen months.

One of Carl's treatment components included athletic training, to cure his "deficits in throwing a football." At follow-up twelve months after the treatment program had ended, the parents' "only remaining concern was that Carl would occasionally make self-critical remarks about his athletic abilities." Hand–eye coordination problems were marching again under the psychiatric flag of gender identity disorder of childhood in boys.

Carl was another of Dr. Rekers' and Dr. Lovaas' miracle cures. We do not have the extensive cross-references about Carl that we have about Kraig. We do know that they found him at risk for transvestism, transsexualism and probably autopenectomy. They also wrote, "After our behavioral treatment, the two independent psychologists could find no evidence of feminine behavior or identification in

Carl's test responses or interview behavior." Perhaps Carl's feminine behavior had gone underground, as the doctors suggested with Kraig, yet of all the things in this report, the most disturbing are Carl's own "volunteered" words, that he "used to be a queer, but not anymore."

One of the strangest phases of treatment for these boys involved their group therapy. Picture a large group of feminine boys on a playground with male coaches reinforcing any sign, however minuscule, however "inept," of masculine behavior, shouting constantly with deliberate emphasis on masculine nouns: "That's a good *boy*." "Come on, *guys*." "You're getting taller; you're going to be a big *man* when you grow up." When feminine gestures are exhibited by a boy, the therapist/coach says, "Hey, don't run like that." We are told that "the boys know what the admonition refers to." Any type of female role taking, which typically surfaced during rest periods from sports or enforced "rough housing," was met with immediate negative reinforcement: "You don't *look* much like a stewardess. You look more like a *pilot*. I think you'd make a better pilot." According to Dr. Green, who supervised this arena of therapy, there was a particularly distinct advantage to this type of treatment. At first, the boys would allow each other to take on female roles, but soon, they turned on each other, and in Dr. Green's view, this was an important aspect of their rehabilitation. "For example, one boy with an effeminate lisp took severe exception to another boy's speech, citing a lisping quality. When the therapist wondered whether the criticizing boy had ever *also* had difficulty in his manner of speaking, this was adamantly denied."

These boys also turned on themselves, exhibiting what Green describes as "Identifying with the aggressor. A potentially feminine toy, such as a stuffed animal, may be, with great display, rejected as a 'sissy' object, a feminine boy thus identifying with the masculine boys who usually tease him." Oppressed individuals often turn on each other in frustration and shame, and they often try to take power by identifying with their oppressors. It is disheartening that the National Institute of Mental Health underwrote this treatment.

In the course of my research on UCLA's feminine boy project, the name of O. Ivar Lovaas was prominent. Dr. Lovaas still works at UCLA, where he is the head of the Clinic for Behavioral Treatment of Children. His specialty at present is autism, and he now dissociates himself from what now is known as Gender Identity Disorder of childhood. Dr. Lovaas agreed to be interviewed on the condition that he tape-record our conversation. During the conversation, Dr. Lovaas was defensive and frequently explosive. Like others in the field, such as Dr. Myrick in Florida, who treated Jerry, Dr. Lovaas wishes to distance himself from this work in regard to questions of sexuality.

Dr. Lovaas began by claiming that the feminine boy project took place in the early 1960s, and that his role in the project was minor. I refreshed his memory by pointing out that the National Institute of Mental Health grant checks to UCLA for all of the research on the children in 1973, 1974 and 1975 were written with the understanding that he was the principal investigator. He often interrupted, raising his voice as if being attacked, in a bid to prevent this simple fact from being acknowledged: over and above the funds that Richard Green brought with him from SUNY–Stony Brook, $218,945 went to UCLA from the NIMH with Dr. Lovaas as Principal Investigator (PI) in this project. For the early 1970s, this was an extraordinary amount of money for such a research grant, and because he was the PI, Dr. Lovaas was also the kingpin, the one whose reputation secured the grant, and the one who determined how the money would be allocated.

He now describes his role as tangential, explaining that he was simply on a committee that evaluated the research of a young assistant professor, George Rekers, who was working on gender deviation. Dr. Lovaas says that gender deviation was of absolutely no interest to him, which might be news to the National Institute of Mental Health.

When asked who specifically examined the children's genitals before they were admitted into the program, he became enraged, denying that anyone had ever looked at the children's bodies in any way. When told that it was reported by the NIMH, and in Dr. Rekers' own studies, that the children's genitals were examined by *someone,* along with other physical tests to rule out anatomical deviances in feminine boys, he denied knowledge of that.

He then explained that at the time this research was performed, UCLA was heavily involved in psycho-sexual reassignment. He believes that transsexualism results from living a life of rejection and accusation by peers, which drives these men to undergo hormonal treatments and genital changes, that they might live as women. Dr. Lovaas contends that these men were so seriously emotionally disturbed by the time they were thirty years old that they contemplated suicide, and wanted to have their bodies changed. Dr. Lovaas said that some of those who underwent the reas-signment were pleased, and others were not. In the 1970s, he believed that if he could prevent the chil-dren from experiencing peer rejection, such as being called a sissy, they would not grow up to be disturbed to the point of wanting to change their bodies. This statement would indicate that gender deviation actu-ally was of interest to him.

When asked why Kraig's treatment included spankings by his father, he stated that the father or mother decided to do that, not him. When asked why he, as the UCLA psychologist in charge of a government-funded study, did not insist that hit-ting the boy was not a sound psychological tool for growth and self-esteem, he stated that he just gave parents advice on what to do.

During the interview with Dr. Lovaas, my suspi-cions were confirmed that the boys in the study were not necessarily in as dire a condition as the reports might lead one to think. "Many of the boys did not exhibit any cross-dressing or any behaviors like that in the presence of the father. Only in the presence of the mother," said Dr. Lovaas. "When the issue came up, the father said, 'I never saw that.' That was a com-mon observation of ours." Yet the children were por-trayed in the case studies as compulsively performing these behaviors, with little or no choice. One could speculate that this would enhance the position of the researchers by highlighting profound gender devi-ance. The more deviant the child is to begin with, the more impressive their post-treatment, gender-appropriate behavior would be to funding sources.

Lovaas described the boys as playing with cos-metics, wigs and other female grooming items, which were made available to them on dress-up tables. "They were like superwomen," he said. The concept of these boys performing like "super-women" is very revealing. Kraig is described as "swishing" around the clinic, "fully dressed as a woman with a long dress, wig, nail polish, high screechy voice, slatternly, seductive eyes..." (Another UCLA gender behaviorist, Lawrence Newman, used the phrase "slovenly seductive eyes" when describing Kraig's case.) This behavior sug-gested to the doctors that Kraig was suffering from "irreversible neurological and biochemical deter-minants." If a five-year-old girl were performing as Kraig did, she would not be diagnosed as gender deviant, although she might be viewed as prac-ticing to be a "superwoman." Perhaps these boys were treated because they frightened the adults around them when they reflected an exaggerated and stylized female gender role performance in such a devastatingly accurate manner. Ironically, many doctors still believe that this type of behav-ior is caused in some girls and women by "irrevers-ible neurological and biochemical determinants," when it is actually the product of a series of choices and coercions, conscious and otherwise.

In terms of the boys who engaged in this behav-ior, Dr. Lovaas stated that they would not be able to develop friendships until they were seventeen, eighteen or nineteen years old, at which time "they could meet people like themselves." Dr. Lovaas said it was very, very easy to change behaviors, but that it was simply "just not interesting" after the first three or four children were seen. Despite this observation, he allowed treatment to proceed with sixty-six boys between the ages of four and twelve, at taxpayers' expense.

After six to twelve months of treating the boys, Lovaas said, "they'd dress like boys, talk like boys, gesture like boys. To me, this was easy to do, and as far as I was concerned, that ful-filled the intent of the study." When asked about treatment goals regarding the boys' adult sexu-alities, he responded hotly, "The issue of sexual orientation is of no interest to me." It seems disingenuous of Dr. Lovaas to claim a "disinterest" in sexual orientation, when his own reports on Kraig and Carl reveal a very clear agenda. For example, in June of 1974, Dr. Lovaas coauthored the article on Carl, in which Carl stated that he "'used to be a queer, but not anymore.'" The doctors follow up his statement with: "The treatment has clearly changed Carl's overt gender-related behaviors, suggesting that his sex-role development may have become normalized." In the spring of 1977, Lovaas was coauthor of a study of a child with gender behavior disturbance which speculated: "He may also be high risk for a homosexual adjustment."

I again broached with Dr. Lovaas the fact that Kraig had been touted as a poster boy for gender treatment, only to become suicidal. By self-report, Kraig said that he knew he was being brought to UCLA to prevent him from growing up to be a homosexual because, among other things, he played with dolls and wanted his hair to be neat. Dr. Lovaas said, "I am not responsible for that. I don't know what happened to these kids in follow-up. My responsibility was to help George Rekers set up a scientific study." I asked Dr. Lovaas if he had read Richard Green's book, from which this follow-up information on Kraig comes, and he answered, "I think I did. It didn't provide any information to me which I thought was all that helpful."

---

22 • Tre Wentling

AM I OBSESSED?
Gender Identity Disorder, Stress, and Obsession

DISCUSSION QUESTIONS

1. What are the consequences of pathologizing transgender people? For society more generally? What theoretical assumptions about sex, gender, and sexuality are embedded in this perspective?
2. How may other socially constructed categories, such as race or class, shape the experience and opportunities of transgender people?
3. What social institutions and structures are missing from the article that a transgender person must navigate? How can nontransgender people support gender-variant individuals within these social institutions?

I do my best not to speed when I am driving, and not for the sake of following the laws of the road. I try to schedule medical appointments with my life partner

or, at least, with a supportive friend. I wait until the last possible moment to use a public restroom. I am always alert, constantly suspecting everyone as a

Tre Wentling, "Am I Obsessed? Gender Identity Disorder, Stress, and Obsession." Written for this volume.

potential perpetrator. I wear clothes that never even hint at my body's actual shape and size.

On the surface, it may seem that these are just idiosyncratic tendencies. However, upon further inspection, my actions are precise, deliberate, and carried out with such tenacity that they may even be considered *obsessive*. Yes, obsessive. I find I experience recurrent thoughts, images, and impulses that center on my gender and gender expression. Most of the time, obsession is considered a psychological disorder; however, my obsession has social foundations, and, I will argue, it is quite reasonable given the social context. Society is literally making me obsessed.

BRIEF HISTORY

Medical discourse on transgender identity began appearing in journals at the end of the nineteenth and early twentieth centuries. Historically, conceptions and explanations of gender variance focused on transsexuals. Today, the term *transgender* operates as an overarching umbrella to include multiple gender-variant identities, not just transsexuals; individuals who have moved further away from the so-called standard male and standard female identities.

Magnus Hirschfeld, a medical doctor from Germany, is credited with identifying "transsexualism." He advocated on behalf of transsexual people considering them "like homosexuals, to be one of innumerable types of 'sexual intermediaries' who existed on a spectrum from a hypothetical 'pure male' to 'pure female'" (Stryker and Whittle, 2006:28). Hirschfeld argued that transsexualism was too complex to reduce the understanding to some form of fetishism or psychopathology (Stryker and Whittle, 2006). Contrary to Hirschfeld, Richard von Krafft-Ebing, an influential professor of psychiatry in Vienna, can be partially credited with pathologizing nonprocreative sexual behavior because he thought that persons engaging in such behavior were "profoundly disturbed, and considered their desire for self-affirming transformation to be psychotic" (Stryker and Whittle 2006:21). There was

considerable emphasis on complete medical surgical changes during the early twentieth century in the initial development of transsexual "treatment." A real tension between medicine and psychology arose that affected the progress made in the United States.

If we fast-forward into the middle of the twentieth century, U.S. medical doctors were separately trying to identify an internal source of gender expression and conformity. A few private medical doctors, like Harry Benjamin,[1] advocated surgically altering the body. However, many doctors simply refused surgery as an option, basing their decisions on "moral and/or religious grounds," along with their "fear of a malpractice suit and reluctance to explain their actions to a local medical society" (Califia, 1997:65).

The increasing rejection of surgery as a legitimate option provided room for psychologists and psychoanalysts during the middle of the twentieth century to emerge as "experts." Developments among many psychologists and psychoanalysts understood gender and sexuality as separate from the body; thus, many saw gender "contradictions" as a psychological condition. In fact, Robert Stoller, an American psychoanalytic psychologist, in collaboration with his colleague Ralph Greenson (Meyerowitz, 2002), developed the three-part model of human psychosexual structures: "biological sex, social gender role, and subjective or psychological gender identity" (Stryker and Whittle, 2006:53). This theory of a psychological gender identity is still used today to understand a person's sense of herself or himself as a woman or man. Another influential contributor to the field of psychosexual understandings of gender variance is Richard Green, also an American psychiatrist. Green suggested that, "Ultimately a comprehensive understanding, evaluation, and management of transsexualism will take into account the extensively rooted sources of this psychosexual phenomenon" because he realized the existence of cross-gender identified persons and the varied embodiments of gender expression among different cultures and across times (Califia, 1997:62).

Many psychologists who were concerned with cross-gender identification focused on prevention among young people (Meyerowitz, 2002). Several gender-identity clinics were established throughout the 1960s and 1970s that ultimately produced the needed medical terminology, meticulously describing gender nonconformity and prescribing "cures." Countless children were institutionalized in these psychiatric evaluation centers because their parents or guardians thought their gender behavior and expression contradicted their anatomically assigned sex category. Psychological rehabilitation seemed to be the mission of some of the most famous private and government-funded gender identity clinics housed at UCLA,[2] SUNY Stony Brook, the Roosevelt Institute in New York City, Fuller Theological Seminary, and the Logos Research Institute (Burke, 1996; Califia, 1997). Thus, "as funding for the study and treatment of gender nonconforming children increased, a need to create a specific psychiatric diagnosis for the condition" emerged (Burke, 1996:60).

While gay and lesbian activists successfully fought for the removal of homosexuality from the *Diagnostic and Statistical Manual of Mental Disorders* in 1973 (Piontek, 2006), both gender identity disorder (GID) in children and discrete psychiatric syndromes in adult transsexual and transvestite individuals were introduced seven years later in the third edition. As Eve Kosofsky Sedgwick (1991:21) explained, "The *de*pathologization of an atypical sexual object-choice can be yoked to the *new* pathologization of an atypical gender identification" [italics in original]. Despite inconclusive scientific evidence, many scientists continue this line of research with scholarly hopes of identifying hormones and genes that determine or, at least, influence an individual's gender expression and sexual desire.

GENDER IDENTITY (DIS)ORDER: A SOCIAL STIGMA

The construction of gender variance as a pathology and a "disorder" is extremely problematic. I am not psychologically disturbed, nor do I consider myself to have an illness, and many other transgender persons feel the same (see Finney Boylan, 2003; Green, 2004; Kailey, 2005). One outcome of the GID diagnosis is the development of social stigma. Erving Goffman (1963) described stigma as discrediting attributes that are considered failings, shortcomings, or handicaps. These psychological classifications enforce dichotomous social constructs of gender and define any deviation as a problem of individual character (Goffman, 1963). So, while some members of the transgender community embrace the "transgender" label, others resist it and see it as a form of "othering."[3] Rejecting the label is tricky, however. Accessing partial or complete insurance benefits to cover transgender-related procedures, which few insurance policies include, requires the GID diagnosis.

> The Harry Benjamin International Gender Dysphoria Association's Standards of Care for the Treatment of Gender Identity Disorders require that the transgender-specific medical interventions of hormone therapy and sex reassignment surgery be recommended by a mental health provider after a thorough psychological evaluation and, in most cases, a period of psychotherapy (Bockting et al., 2004:279).

Since the GID diagnosis is needed for hormones and/or surgery, many choose to embrace it strategically. Judith Butler (2006:280) questioned, however, "whether submitting to the diagnosis does not involve, more or less consciously, a certain subjection to the diagnosis such that one does end up internalizing some aspect of the diagnosis, conceiving of oneself as mentally ill or 'failing' in normality, or both, even as one seeks to take a purely instrumental attitude toward these terms."

I have been forced to ask myself, do I have GID? Have I internalized these medical and psychosexual constructions? Did I have this *mental disorder* as a child, or do I still have it as an adult? Did I ever try urinating in a standing position? Did I think I might grow a penis? Did I ever believe I was born the wrong sex? Am I distressed because I am uncomfortable with my physical body? These questions highlight my obsession with gender expression and, even more important, the social origins of this obsession. It is the pathological construction of sex and gender variation that pushes anyone who does not conform to become obsessed.

MY OBSESSIONS

VIOLENCE

The first and most important issue is others' perceptions of me. One transgender murder per month[4] in the United States would make *you* obsessive about your gender appearance and acceptance, too. Transgender persons have an elevated risk of becoming victims of various types of transphobic[5] crimes. In the past few years, the media have shone a spotlight on the dangers of being transidentified. Films like *Boys Don't Cry* and *A Girl Like Me: The Gwen Araujo Story* have presented the true stories of transgender teenagers who were murdered. These violent crimes have a chilling effect on the transgender community nationwide.

"Gender based violence and discrimination results in an environment in which covert if not overt permission is given to society to 'punish' people for gender transgression" (Lombardi et al., 2001:91). As Califia (1997:82) wrote, "It is our fear and hatred of people who are differently-gendered that need to be cured, not their synthesis of the qualities we think of as maleness and femaleness, masculinity and femininity." If this fear and hatred continue, so will my obsession with how I appear to others.

Murder is just one form of violence that is perpetrated against transgender people. In fact, Lombardi et al. (2001) surveyed 402 transgender persons in 1997 and found that over half the participants had experienced verbal harassment at some point during their lifetime and 25 percent had experienced a violent incident. The same study indicated that being stalked was the second most common experience, and being assaulted without a weapon was the third most common event. Participants younger than age 18 were underrepresented (0.5 percent) in this study, leaving transgender youths' experiences of violence unrecorded.

Most transgender youths face significant prejudice and discrimination at school from their teachers, staff, and administrators, as well as from other students (Grossman and D'Augelli, 2006; Guiterrez, 2004). From abusive language to teachers' prejudice to unapproachable school counselors, school environments are unsafe for most lesbian, gay, bisexual, and transgender (LGBT) students (Price and Telljohann, 1991; Telljohann et al., 1995). "Nearly 70 percent of lesbian, gay, bisexual and transgendered youth report experiencing some form of harassment or violence in school, and they are three times more likely to attempt suicide than other youth, according to the National Mental Health Association" (Boykin, 2004).

Internalized homophobia and transphobia must also be examined. A San Francisco-based study of 515 transgender persons, conducted by Clements-Nolle, Marx, and Katz (2006), revealed that attempted suicide was higher for transgender persons younger than age twenty-five (47 percent) than transgender persons older than age twenty-five (30 percent). I am thankful to have passed the twenty-five year mark but am concerned that transgender youths have minimal space (literally and figuratively) to share experiences and gender "obsessions" with others in a safe environment.[6]

DRAMATIZING MY LIFE: THE MEDIA

The media provide viewers with exposure to gender specialists, gender therapists, psychotherapists, and psychologists, presenting authority figures who use medical and pathologizing language to establish a psychological framework. These trained professionals ultimately gain the audience's trust using highly specialized language that reinforces the medical paradigm and the "need" for gender transitions.

Television is a popular medium that spectacularizes gender variance through investigative lenses of "unbelievable" transformations, capitalizing on before-and-after photographs. For instance, clips of transgender women applying makeup or practicing their voice lessons on *Oprah* (October 12, 2004) and dramatized presentations of their wives devastated over the loss of their once-heterosexual relationship and questions about the wives' own heterosexuality on *Grey's Anatomy* (November 9, 2006) have made these stories about real-life experiences voyeuristically engaging. Nancy Nangeroni, a transgender community activist, writer, and musician, began her own radio program after feeling poorly represented on numerous public television and radio shows (MacKenzie and Nangeroni, 2004). Aware of the media's goal to sensationalize transgender persons, I often feel obsessed with trying to offer an alternative analysis to these representations when I am aware of their showings.

I personally feel the effects of "TV knowledge" when people around me seek to understand my transgender identity with questions akin to, "So you're stuck inside a female body, but you really feel like a man?" because some transgender representatives who are portrayed in the media use these types of statements. Although they may not mean to, they simplify and maintain the gender binary of man and woman. This is not meant to discount those who feel trapped but, rather, to raise awareness of the complex realities of biological sex and gender expression and diversity within the transgender community. When I am asked this question, I explain that I am not "stuck" anywhere and that I do not think framing gender this way is useful. However, my own experience and expertise are often challenged as these people attempt to take on the "expert" role, and I become the pathologized one. This only reinforces my obsession with depathologizing gender variation.

The professional "transexperts" who are seen on television call upon the GID diagnosis and therefore supply their viewers with a psychological framework to comprehend transgender people. I have yet to witness one of these experts share the scientific evidence of the immense biological variation found within humans—that is, chromosomally, hormonally, and genitally. Nor do these experts invoke history to explain the ever-changing expression of gender in the United States that relies on hegemonic notions of white, Christian, middle-class, male, able-bodied heterosexuality. Perhaps the most interesting aspect of the authoritative psychological voice is the intentional exclusion of when or how GID became a diagnosable mental illness. This omission helps naturalize what is actually a constructed diagnosis. The limited perspective provided by the media leaves me in the position of having to refute this "knowledge" and provide alternative perspectives. Taking responsibility for challenging other people's understanding of sex, gender, and sexuality becomes extremely stressful.

MY BODY

My resistance to the sex and gender binaries, as well as GID, could potentially be misunderstood, since I have made "transitional" decisions. For instance, my determination to have "top surgery," otherwise known as a double mastectomy, and to receive testosterone injections (t-shots) may seem to reinforce dichotomous gender categories. However, masculinizing my chest is just one part of who I am, not my entire being. This surgery will free me from my obsession with how my chest appears and is perceived by others, but it will not erase my living and being addressed as a girl and woman for twenty-two years. The decision to take testosterone stems from my desire to have a deeper voice, not because I feel like a man in a woman's body. This wish does not negate my navigation through and appreciation of androgynous space and embodiment. I am not intentionally supporting the binary sex and gender systems but, rather, acting to limit my obsessions within these strictly controlled structures. My choices are constrained by the social context I must live in. These decisions led to new obsessions and stress, however. I became concerned about my family and how they would respond once they noticed the effects of t-shots, for example.

FAMILY: TAKING CONTROL

I have spent many hours thinking about my family's response and reaction to me as I safely become the person I am. How will my mother handle others seeing me as a man? Will she take responsibility for my identity, believing she has somehow failed me as a white, single, working mother of two? Will she succumb to the societal stereotypes that deviant and disturbed children come out of so-called broken families? Will my decisions push her over the edge? How is my homophobic brother going to respond? Will he use GID as a justification for keeping me away from his two-year-old daughter, my niece? Will I be allowed to watch her alone? Will he teach her to call me uncle? What is my distant father going to say? Will he blame my mother? Will he be willing to replace the old pictures of me with long hair, so my half-sisters can recognize me? What about my mother's parents, my only grandparents? Will Oma be just as emotionally devastated as she was when I came out to her as a lesbian? Will Opa stop talking to me because of his strongly committed Baptist beliefs? What about our longtime family friends? Will Oma and Opa still speak proudly about me to them? Will I still exist? Or will I disappear from their conversations altogether? Should I move to another city, so I do not have to confront my obsession and deal with the stress of explaining who I am?

It took many years to become confident with the idea that my life is my own, I can take control of it, and I am not responsible for anyone else. I told my mother I was starting testosterone almost a full year before I actually began. It was one of the hardest confessions I have ever had to make. I took a two-step approach: First, since I no longer lived at home, I wrote her a letter and left it on her bed to find when she arrived home. The final line read, *Please call me when you are finished reading this so I know you still love me.* The second step was meeting face to face to talk about my decision. My heart broke as I watched tears stream down her face that night. I devastated every dream she ever had for me. I was on the brink of changing the gender composition of her first-born child. And although I was to blame, I do not regret having that conversation with her. I knew I would never be able to mend her broken heart, but my decisions were important in order to live my life. I left my mother that night with swollen red eyes and tissues in hand.

The letter and conversation with my mother was the only premeditated session I had. Rather than obsessing and stressing over each conversation I would face, I decided it would be easier to inform my family and friends along the way as needed. Opportunities arose just a few short weeks after I started testosterone; some people noticed the subtle voice change immediately. On the one hand, I was thrilled to feel and hear an alteration in my voice, but in the midst of my excitement, I wondered what my brother and others thought when they heard my new tone—many never said a word. My plan to avoid stress was not entirely successful, however, as I spent hours stressing about what people thought, since their silence was indeed a response. Over time, my resolution to take the path of least resistance and not tell family members and friends about my decisions until needed began to disintegrate as I lost my courage to explain to my family *why* my voice was changing. Each time I spoke with my Oma on the phone, she would ask, *Are you sick? You sound sick. Are you sick?* My responses were like a broken record, constantly reassuring her that I was in good health. But I never had the nerve to tell her why my voice sounded the way it did. I had become so stressed about how my family was going to react that I literally stopped calling and became ultimately disconnected from the people I loved.

Isolation from my family took its toll, and for a time, my life at home did not fare any better, since the transition affected the intimacy I shared with my lover, my partner, my best friend. I was afraid that she, too, might resist my decisions and have difficulty with the changes it would bring to our relationship. Would her self-proclaimed identity as a lesbian deny our relationship if I no longer identified as such, or if strangers did not see us as a lesbian couple? How would she respond to my ever-changing body: the growth in body hair, the change in my sex drive, my skin shifting to a rougher texture, the modification in my pheromones, and the surgical procedure removing the breasts she had already redefined as masculine pecs? My fears that she only partially accepted me emerged when we disagreed or spoke about future plans. I always assumed she was angry with me because of my choices. Her commitment, dedication, and, most importantly, love won out. She fought me long and hard, refusing to let me push her away. Instead, she transitioned with me. Through countless hours of encouragement and confirmation that her love is unconditional, she proved herself and, not surprisingly, became a part of the movement for transgender rights.

HEALTH CARE (MIS) TREATMENT

Most transgender persons have at least one horror story of institutional discrimination. I have one story of my own that has forcefully shaped each subsequent encounter I have had with the medical community. At age twenty-three, before I began testosterone, I was without health insurance. This should come as no surprise, considering that more than 43 million people younger than age sixty-five were uninsured in 2000 (Jillson, 2002). Unable to get rid of a powerful cold, I decided to visit the university student health center. I entered the office in what I considered "comfortable clothes" (e.g., a sweatshirt, sweatpants, T-shirt, and baseball cap), and, as with any first-time visit, I completed all the required paperwork. After my basic vitals were measured (blood pressure, fever, weight, height, and so forth), I patiently waited in a treatment room.

A male doctor and a female physician's assistant entered the room confidently and began to review my file while simultaneously asking me about my ailments and the reasons for my visit. Maybe the doctor's multitasking is what got him befuddled. He initially used male pronouns when speaking about me to his assistant but became confused when he looked at my intake form, which I had marked with the letter *F*. He did a sort of double-double-take: he looked at the chart, then back at me, then back at the chart, and right back at me. In a matter of seconds, something quite inappropriate transpired. To alleviate his confusion, he lifted the neckline of my shirt to look for the presence or absence of breasts to gauge my sex without permission or warning. Not having any prior experience with this sort of abuse and invasion, I waited for the diagnosis and subsequent prescription and then left the clinic as fast as I could. This incident, which was out of my control,

has produced more obsessive thoughts: am I going to be mistreated if, and when, I go to the doctor in the future? Will they humiliate me again? Will it be in the waiting room next time, in front of others? Will they tell me I am a "sick" person, yet refuse to treat my actual illness, as they did to transgender- and lesbian-identified Leslie Feinberg (1999) who had a temperature of 104 degrees but was refused treatment? Whenever I have to visit a medical or dental office, not to mention any other professional setting, I now experience high levels of stress.

Despite this stress, I am well aware that as a white middle-class person, my privilege mitigates this stress. As a consumer of health insurance, I have the privilege of seeking out transpositive health care providers. Besides having a comfortable and high-quality physician's visit, I am also ensured access to safe[7] prescription hormones and syringes. I do not have to rely on street hormones and shared needles like many young, poor, uninsured, urban, and transgender persons of color (Grossman and D'Augelli, 2006; Lombardi et al., 2001). One result of "black-market" hormones is the increased risk of HIV transmission from shared needles (Grossman and D'Augelli, 2006; Lombardi et al., 2001; Pettiway, 1996). I am free from this risk and stress, since I inject testosterone with clean needles in the comfort of my home. I have routine blood tests to measure the proper function of my liver and to monitor my cholesterol levels in case of increased hypertension. When it comes to health care, the most stress I have is finding a transpositive doctor.

EMPLOYMENT (MIS) FORTUNES

In 2005, I met an African American transwoman in Philadelphia, and we discussed some of our common stressors regarding employment. She had just obtained part-time employment working for a local community-based program designed by and for gender-variant persons. This program provides comprehensive HIV prevention and health education to many different clients.

At the time she was hired, her responsibilities included handing out information about safe-sex and safe-injection techniques to transgender persons working on the street. In what would be deemed an otherwise virtuous effort to discourage risky behaviors, she was extremely anxious about the work. Her stress resulted because of her shift: 10:00 p.m. to 2:00 a.m. Not only did she face the threat of physical assault, she was also at risk of harassment by the police. She explained, "I mean, I don't want to be arrested while I'm at work. I'll be scared to be doing my job. They'll [the police] think I'm selling or something and take me in." At that moment, I was reminded of just how pervasive gendered and racialized obsessions and stressors are in the transgender community.

She was, in fact, worried about being arrested or, at a minimum, being harassed by police officers who would be operating under the assumption that she was a sex worker. A simultaneous layer of complexity is the fact that whomever she talks to may become suspicious targets for the police as well. Her stress about the blatant presumption by the police force that transgender people who are out at night *must* be sex workers is a reality, especially in poverty-stricken urban areas. Our shared obsessions about physical safety—what to wear, how and with whom to communicate, what time our shifts are, and our geographic locations—are similar stressors. My relative privilege, however, provides a buffer, since I work at a university, and her responsibilities place her in a more vulnerable position.

Workplace obsession and stress seem to have two components. The first is being accepted and supported on the job. The second is the type of job a gender-variant person occupies. Discrimination claims are a little tricky, since there are currently no federal protections in place for gender-variant persons.[8] I am unaware of research that offers statistical data[9] on which professions value (e.g., invite and support) gender diversity and devalue (e.g., deny, demote, or fire) gender-variant persons; however, it is likely that there are systematic patterns adversely affecting transgender people by age, race, income, and ability. These struggles that directly affect living arrangements, the resources to pay for medical treatment, and the means to clothe and feed oneself (and others), are not shown on *Oprah* or *Grey's Anatomy*.

In fact, most of the stressors I face are not portrayed on the talk shows, docudramas made for television, or evening soap operas. Where is the portrayal of the real lives of transgender people in the United States? Who wants to know about the everyday violence perpetrated against transgender people? About the countless cases of employment discrimination? Or the transgender persons who are turned away from emergency rooms? The transgender parents who lose the rights to their biological children? Who shares these obsessions and stressors with us?

CONCLUSION

It is safe to say that both my mother and Oma obsess about my safety, too. They are fully aware of gender-based violence and do not want me added to the yearly statistics. My aunt always calls when she has watched a transgender-specific television show, mostly to share what she has learned and to ask for my perspective. My ever-increasingly tolerant brother has never invoked the constructed GID to deny a relationship with my niece, but instead playfully acknowledges my masculine appearance and my quasi-uncle status. A recent family vacation corroborated my mother's understanding of my (and other transgender people's) discomfort and the complications of sex-segregated facilities. We had to ask multiple park personnel if and where a family bathroom was located, walked fifteen minutes (one way) out of our intended direction, and made my overzealous cousins wait so I could visit the restroom *once* on our fifteen-hour-long outing.

I have found that sharing my obsessions and stressors with my family has since brought us together. I am no longer the only one worrying about my physical safety, experience with medical doctors, abuse by the authorities, and need for protection from my employers. The same family members I spent so much time worrying about have become a tremendous source of support. Just yesterday, my mother told me that one of her friend's grandchildren is expressing the desire to be a girl and said, "It's OK because the parents are very supportive." My obsessions and stress all have social, not psychological, foundations. They are a product of a social order that defines anyone who does not conform to our two-gender system as deviant and pathological. Because they are the result of social and cultural factors, they require social, not psychological, change. I have found it heartening in my own life to see this change begin in my own family.

AUTHOR'S NOTE

As we publish a second edition, I wanted to share an update on my obsessions. I have recognized that my privilege (as a white, educated, able-bodied transman) substantially diminishes my life chances of being a victim of violence; my social statuses systematically offer financial and employment opportunities as well as access to places and spaces that others assume I belong in, or at least am not suspect when in them. The obsessions about my mother were all valid, and in three years I can proudly and admirably say that she has become an advocate. We have participated in our local PFLAG chapter to share our transition, together. She also, by herself, attended PFLAG specifically to support a mother as her child began the social and medical journey. And, I am just as proud of my brother as he has been the most cognizant and supportive of using *he, him,* and calling me his *brother*. We have never taught my niece about desired pronouns or my social role, as she has called me Uncle since the time she could speak the words. Recently she asked my aunt, *why is Uncle Tre wearing a girl's bathing suit?* referencing a picture as they surfed the album. My father, step mom, and two sisters have become much less distant and are transitioning too. The trans-advocate partner and I have taken different paths, and I know that her dedication and love are perfectly placed within the social justice projects that she has always fought for. In all of the relationships that I have committed to over the years, *I* still *exist*. They are still *proud of me*. And, they still *love me*.

APPENDIX: DIAGNOSTIC CRITERIA FOR GENDER IDENTITY DISORDER

A. *A strong persistent cross-gender identification* (not merely a desire for any perceived cultural advantages of being the other sex). In children, the disturbance is manifested by four (or more) of the following:

1. Repeatedly stated desire to be, or insistence that he or she is, the other sex.
2. In boys, preference for cross-dressing or simulating female attire; in girls, insistence on wearing only stereotypical masculine clothing.
3. Strong and persistent preferences for cross-sex roles in make believe play or persistent fantasies of being the other sex.
4. Intense desire to participate in the stereotypical games and pastimes of the other sex.
5. Strong preference for playmates of the other sex.

In adolescents and adults, the disturbance is manifested by symptoms such as a stated desire to be the other sex, frequent passing as the other sex, desire to live or be treated as the other sex, or the conviction that he or she has the typical feelings and reactions of the other sex.

B. *Persistent discomfort with his or her sex or sense of inappropriateness in the gender role of that sex.* In children, the disturbance is manifested by any of the following: In boys, assertion that his penis or testes are disgusting or will disappear or assertion that it would be better not to have a penis, or aversion toward rough-and-tumble play and rejection of male stereotypical toys, games, and activities. In girls, rejection of urinating in a sitting position, assertion that she has or will grow a penis, or assertion that she does not want to grow breasts or menstruate, or marked aversion toward normative feminine clothing.

In adolescents and adults, the disturbance is manifested by symptoms such as preoccupation with getting rid of primary and secondary sex characteristics (e.g., request for hormones, surgery, or other procedures to physically alter sexual characteristics to simulate the other sex) or belief that he or she was born the wrong sex.

C. *The disturbance is not concurrent with physical intersex condition.*

D. *The disturbance causes clinically significant distress or impairment in social, occupational, or other important areas of functioning.*

Code based on current age:

302.6 Gender Identity Disorder in Children
302.85 Gender Identity Disorder in Adolescents or Adults

Specify if (for sexually mature individuals):

Sexually Attracted to Males
Sexually Attracted to Females
Sexually Attracted to Both
Sexually Attracted to Neither

NOTES

1. Benjamin, a native German who immigrated to the United States before World War I, popularized the term *transsexual* through his advocacy on behalf of transgender persons. He did not support psychotherapy as a "cure." His relationship with Christine Jorgenson and his publication of *The Transsexual Phenomenon* in 1966 carved out a space for him to establish much of the medical practices that transgender persons go through today.
2. Stoller helped establish this clinic (Stryker and Whittle, 2006).
3. For example, Guiterrez (2004:72) shared the voice of a young self-identified woman, who said, "I don't consider myself transgendered, you know. I feel like me. We're women . . . it's a label that shouldn't be used."
4. *Remembering Our Dead,* a product of Gender Education & Advocacy, states that more than one antitransgender murder has been reported in the U.S. media every month since 1989, and many fatal assaults go unreported as gender-based violence, making this statistic low.
5. *Transphobic* is simply an adaptation of *homophobic* and expresses a phobia and hatred toward gender-nonconforming persons.
6. For more information on gender-based violence against youth, visit Gender Public Advocacy Coalition at www.gpac.org.
7. "Safe" is in quotes because no research that I am aware of has provided conclusive evidence of the safety of injecting androgens.
8. For more on transgender policies and issues in the workplace, visit Transgender Law and Policy Institute (www.transgenderlaw.org), National Center for Transgender Equality (www.nctequality.org), Sylvia Rivera Law Project (www.srlp.org), and Human Rights Campaign (www.hrc.org).
9. See Schilt (2006) for a qualitative project on transmen's experiences in the workplace and thus the visibility of gendered workplace disparities and disadvantages.

REFERENCES

Balagot, J. 2002. "In Memory of Gwen Araujo." Retrieved December 9, 2006, from http://www.transyouth.net/stories/gwen_araujo.html

Bockting, W., B. Robinson, A. Benner, and K. Scheltema. 2004. "Patient Satisfaction with Transgender Health Services." *Journal of Sex & Marital Therapy,* 30:277–294.

Boykin, K. 2004. "Sakia Gunn Remembered." Retrieved December 9, 2006, from http://www.keithboykin.com/arch/2004/05/11/sakia_gunn_reme

Burke, P. 1996. *Gender Shock: Exploding the Myths of Male and Female.* New York: Anchor Press.

Butler, J. 2006. "Undiagnosing Gender." In *Transgender Rights,* ed. P. Currah, R. M. Juang, and S. P. Minter, pp. 274–298. Minneapolis: University of Minnesota Press.

Califia, P. 1997. *Sex Changes: The Politics of Transgenderism.* San Francisco: Cleis Press.

Clements-Nolle, K., R. Marx, and M. Katz. 2006. "Attempted Suicide Among Transgender Persons: The Influence of Gender-based Discrimination and Victimization." *Journal of Homosexuality,* 51:53–69.

Feinberg, L. 1999. *TransLiberation: Beyond Pink or Blue.* Boston: Beacon Press.

Finney Boylan, J. 2003. *She's Not There: A Life in Two Genders.* New York: Broadway Books.

Fleener, P. E. n.d. "Diagnostic Criteria for Gender Identity Disorder." *Gender Identity Disorder Today.* Retrieved March 22, 2007, from http://www.mental-health-today.com/gender/dsm.htm#gid9

Goffman, E. 1963. *Stigma: Notes on the Management of Spoiled Identity.* New York: Simon & Schuster.

Green, J. 2004. *Becoming a Visible Man.* Nashville, Tenn.: Vanderbilt Press.

Grossman, A. H., &. A. R. D'Augelli. 2006. "Transgender Youth: Invisible and Vulnerable." *Journal of Homosexuality,* 51:111–128.

Guiterrez, N. 2004. "Resisting Fragmentation, Living Whole: Four Female Transgender Students of Color Speak About School." *Journal of Gay and Lesbian Social Services,* 16:69–79.

Hussey, W. 2006. "Slivers of the Journey: The Use of Photovoice and Storytelling to Examine Female to

Male Transsexuals' Experience of Health Care Access." *Journal of Homosexuality,* 51:129–158.

Jillson, I. A. 2002. "Opening Closed Doors: Improving Access to Quality Health Services for LGBT Populations." *Clinical Research and Regulatory Affairs,* 19(2–3):153–190.

Kailey, M. 2005. *Just Add Hormones: An Insider's Guide to the Transsexual Experience.* Boston: Beacon Press.

Kenagy, G. P. 2005. "Transgender Health: Findings from Two Needs Assessment Studies in Philadelphia." *Health and Social Work,* 30:19–26.

Kosofsky Sedgwick, E. 1991. "How to Bring Your Kids Up Gay." *Social Text,* 29:18–27.

Lombardi, E., R. A. Wilchins., D. Priesing., and D. Malouf. 2001. "Gender Violence: Transgender Experiences with Violence and Discrimination." *Journal of Homosexuality,* 42:89–101.

Lucal, B. 1999. "What It Means to Be Gendered Me: Life on the Boundaries of a Dichotomous Gender System." *Gender and Society,* 13:781–797.

MacKenzie, G., and N. Nangeroni. 2004. "Gender Talk—Labor of Love." In *Pinned Down by Pronouns,* ed. M. Davies and T. Amato, pp. 109–112. Jamaica Plain, Mass.: Conviction Books.

Meyerowitz, J. 2002. *How Sex Changed: A History of Transsexuality in the United States.* Cambridge, Mass: Harvard University Press.

Pettiway, L. E. 1996. *Honey, Honey, Miss Thang: Being Black, Gay, and on the Streets.* Philadelphia: Temple University Press.

Piontek, T. 2006. *Queering Gay and Lesbian Studies.* Urbana: University of Illinois Press.

Price, J. H., and S. K. Telljohann. 1991. "School Counselors' Perceptions of Adolescent Homosexuals." *Journal of School Health,* 61:433–439.

Schilt, K. 2006. "Just One of the Guys?: How Transmen Make Gender Visible at Work." *Gender and Society* 20:465–490.

Stryker, S., and S. Whittle. 2006. *The Transgender Studies Reader.* New York: Routledge.

Telljohann, S. K., J. H. Price, M. Poureslami, and A. Easton. 1995. "Teaching About Sexual Orientation by Secondary Health Teachers." *Journal of School Health,* 65:18–23.

Wise, T. 2001. "Why Whites Think Blacks Have No Problems." Retrieved April 5, 2005, from http://www.alternet.org/story/11192.

23 • *Siobhan Somerville*

SCIENTIFIC RACISM AND THE INVENTION OF THE HOMOSEXUAL BODY

DISCUSSION QUESTIONS

1. What was the role of comparative anatomy in the creation of classifications of racial and sexual differences?
2. Why does Somerville argue that in the beginning, sexology was related to and dependent on eugenics and antimiscegenation campaigns?

Siobhan Somerville, "Scientific Racism and the Invention of the Homosexual Body" from *The Journal of the History of Sexuality* Vol. 5, No. 2 (1994): 243–266. Copyright © 1994 by The University of Texas Press. Reprinted with the permission of The University of Texas Press.

3. How is medicine used to naturalize and legitimate dominant cultural myths?
4. Does this historical perspective offer any insight into understanding today's knowledge and debates around homosexuality and transgender identity?

One of the most important insights developed in the fields of lesbian and gay history and the history of sexuality is the notion that homosexuality and, by extension, heterosexuality are relatively recent inventions in Western culture, rather than transhistorical or "natural" categories. As Michel Foucault and other historians of sexuality have argued, sexual acts between two people of the same sex had been punishable through legal and religious sanctions well before the late nineteenth century, but they did not necessarily define individuals as homosexual per se.[1] Only in the late nineteenth century did a new understanding of sexuality emerge in which sexual acts and desires became constitutive of identity. Homosexuality as the condition, and therefore identity, of particular bodies is thus a production of that historical moment.

Medical literature, broadly defined to include the writings of physicians, sexologists, and psychiatrists, has been integral to this historical argument. Although medical discourse was by no means the only—nor necessarily the most powerful—site of the emergence of new sexual identities, it does nevertheless offer rich sources for at least partially understanding the complex development of these categories in the late nineteenth and early twentieth centuries. Medical and sexological literature not only became one of the few sites of explicit engagement with questions of sexuality during this period but also held substantial definitional power within a culture that sanctioned science to discover and tell the truth about bodies.

As historians and theorists of sexuality have refined a notion of the late nineteenth-century "invention" of the homosexual, their discussions have drawn primarily upon theories and histories of gender. George Chauncey, in particular, has provided an invaluable discussion of the ways in which paradigms of sexuality shifted according to changing ideologies of gender during this period.[2] He notes a gradual change in medical models of sexual deviance, from a notion of sexual inversion, understood as a reversal of one's sex role, to a model of homosexuality, defined as deviant sexual object choice. These categories and their transformations, argues Chauncey, reflected concurrent shifts in the cultural organization of sex/gender roles and participated in prescribing acceptable behavior, especially within a context of white middle-class gender ideologies.

While gender insubordination offers a powerful explanatory model for the "invention" of homosexuality, ideologies of gender also, of course, shaped and were shaped by dominant constructions of race. Indeed, although it has received little acknowledgment, it is striking that the "invention" of the homosexual occurred at roughly the same time that racial questions were being reformulated, particularly in the United States. This was the moment, for instance, of *Plessy v. Ferguson,* the 1896 U.S. Supreme Court ruling that insisted that "black" and "white" races were "separate but equal." Both a product of and a stimulus to a nationwide and brutal era of racial segregation, this ruling had profound and lasting effects in legitimating an apartheid structure that remained legally sanctioned for more than half of the twentieth century. The *Plessy* case distilled in legal form many fears about race and racial difference that were prevalent at the time. A deluge of "Jim Crow" and anti-miscegenation laws, combined with unprecedented levels of racial violence, most visibly manifested in widespread lynching, reflected an aggressive attempt to classify and separate bodies as either "black" or "white."

Is it merely a historical coincidence that the classification of bodies as either "homosexual" or "heterosexual" emerged at the same time that the United States was aggressively policing the imaginary boundary between "black" and "white" bodies?

Although some historians of sexuality have included brief acknowledgments of nineteenth-century discourses of racial difference, the particular relationship and potentially mutual effects of discourses of homosexuality and race remain unexplored.[3] This silence around race may be due in part to the relative lack of explicit attention to race in medical and sexological literature of the period. These writers did not self-consciously interrogate race, nor were those whose gender insubordination and/or sexual transgression brought them under the medical gaze generally identified by race in these accounts.[4] Yet the lack of explicit attention to race in these texts does not mean that it was irrelevant to sexologists' endeavors. Given the upheavals surrounding racial definition during this period, it is reasonable to assume that these texts were as embedded within contemporary racial ideologies as they were within contemporary ideologies of gender.

Take, for instance, the words of Havelock Ellis, whose massive *Studies in the Psychology of Sex* was one of the most important texts of the late nineteenth-century medical and scientific discourse on sexuality. "I regard sex as the central problem of life," began the general preface to the first volume. Justifying such unprecedented boldness regarding the study of sex, Ellis said the following:

> And now that the problem of religion has practically been settled, and that the problem of labour has at least been placed on a practical foundation, the question of sex—*with the racial questions that rest on it*—stands before the coming generations as the chief problem for solution.[5]

Despite Ellis's oddly breezy dismissal of the problems of labor and religion, which were far from settled at the time, this passage points suggestively to a link between sexual and racial anxieties. Yet what exactly did Ellis mean by "racial questions"? More significantly, what was his sense of the relationship between racial questions and the "question of sex"? Although Ellis himself left these issues unresolved, his elliptical declaration nevertheless suggested that a discourse of race—however elusively—somehow hovered around or within the study of sexuality.

In this article, I offer speculations on how late nineteenth- and early twentieth-century discourses of race and sexuality might be, not merely juxtaposed, but brought together in ways that illuminate both. I suggest that the concurrent bifurcations of categories of race and sexuality were not only historically coincident but in fact structurally interdependent and perhaps mutually productive. My goal, however, is not to garner and display unequivocal evidence of the direct influence of racial categories on those who were developing scientific models of homosexuality. Nor am I interested in identifying whether or not individual writers and thinkers are racist. Rather, my focus here is on racial ideologies, the systems of representation and cultural assumptions about race through which individuals understood their relationships within the world.[6] My emphasis is on understanding the relationships between the medical/scientific discourse around sexuality and the dominant scientific discourse around race during this period, that is, scientific racism.

My approach combines literary and historical methods of reading, particularly that which has been so crucial to lesbian, gay, and bisexual studies: the technique of reading to hear "the inexplicable presence of the thing not named,"[7] of being attuned to the queer presences and implications in texts that do not otherwise name them. Without this collective and multidisciplinary project to see, hear, and confirm queer inflections where others would deny their existence, it is arguable that the field of lesbian, gay, and bisexual studies itself, and particularly our knowledge and understanding of the histories, writing, and cultures of lesbians, gay men, and bisexuals, would be impoverished, if not impossible. In a similar way, I propose to use the techniques of queer reading, but to modulate my analysis from a focus on sexuality and gender to one alert to racial resonances as well.

My attention, then, is focused on the racial pressure points in exemplary texts from the late nineteenth-century discourse on sexuality, including those written by Ellis and other writers of the period who made explicit references to homosexuality. I suggest that the structures and methodologies that drove dominant ideologies of race also fueled the pursuit of scientific knowledge about the homosexual body: both sympathetic and hostile accounts of homosexuality were steeped in assumptions that had driven previous scientific studies of race.[8] My aim is not to replace a focus on gender and sexuality with one on race but rather to understand how discourses of race and gender buttressed one another, often competing, often overlapping, to shape emerging models of homosexuality.

I suggest three broadly defined ways in which discourses of sexuality seem to have been particularly engaged—sometimes overtly, but largely implicitly—with the discourse of scientific racism. All of these models pathologized to some degree both the non-white body and the non-heterosexual body. Although I discuss these models in separate sections here, they often coexisted, despite their contradictions. These models are speculative and are intended as a first step toward understanding the myriad and historically specific ways in which racial and sexual discourses shaped each other at the moment in which homosexuality entered scientific discourse.

VISIBLE DIFFERENCES: SEXOLOGY AND COMPARATIVE ANATOMY

Ellis's *Sexual Inversion,* the first volume of *Studies in the Psychology of Sex* to be published, became a definitive text in late nineteenth-century investigations of homosexuality.[9] Despite the series' titular focus on the psychology of sex, *Sexual Inversion* was a hybrid text, poised in methodology between the earlier field of comparative anatomy, with its procedures of bodily measurement, and the nascent techniques of psychology, with its focus on mental development.[10] In *Sexual Inversion,* Ellis hoped to provide scientific authority for the position that homosexuality should be considered not a crime but rather a congenital (and thus involuntary) physiological abnormality. Writing *Sexual Inversion* in the wake of England's 1885 Labouchère Amendment, which prohibited "any act of gross indecency" between

men, Ellis intended in large part to defend homosexuality from "law and public opinion," which, in his view, combined "to place a heavy penal burden and a severe social stigma on the manifestations of an instinct which to those persons who possess it frequently appears natural and normal."[11] In doing so, Ellis attempted to drape himself in the cultural authority of a naturalist, eager to exert his powers of observation in an attempt to classify and codify understandings of homosexuality.[12]

Like other sexologists, Ellis assumed that the "invert" might be visually distinguishable from the "normal" body through anatomical markers, just as the differences between the sexes had traditionally been mapped upon the body. Yet the study of sexual difference was not the only methodological precedent for the study of the homosexual body. In its assumptions about somatic differences, *Sexual Inversion,* I suggest, also drew upon and participated in a history of the scientific investigation of race.

Race, in fact, became an explicit, though ambiguous, structural element in Ellis's *Sexual Inversion.* In chapter 5, titled "The Nature of Sexual Inversion," Ellis attempted to collate the evidence from case studies, dividing his general conclusions into various analytic categories. Significantly, "Race" was the first category he listed, under which he wrote, "All my cases, 80 in number, are British and American, 20 living in the United States and the rest being British. Ancestry, from the point of view of race, was not made a matter of special investigation" (264). He then listed the ancestries of the individuals whose case studies he included, which he identified as "English…Scotch…Irish…German…French…Portuguese…[and] more or less Jewish" (264). He concluded that "except in the apparently frequent presence of the German element, there is nothing remarkable in this ancestry" (264). Ellis used the term "race" in this passage interchangeably with national origin, with the possible exception of Jewish ancestry. These national identities were perceived to be at least partially biological and certainly hereditary in Ellis's account, though subordinate to the categories "British" and "American." Although he dismissed "ancestry, from the point of view of race" as a significant category, its place as the first topic within the chapter suggested its importance to the structure of Ellis's analysis.[13]

Ellis's ambiguous use of the term "race" was not unusual for scientific discourse in this period, during which it might refer to groupings based variously on geography, religion, class, or color.[14] The use of the term to mean a division of people based on physical (rather than genealogical or national) differences had originated in the late eighteenth century, when Johann Friedrich Blumenbach first classified human beings into five distinct groups in *On the Natural Variety of Mankind.* This work in turn became a model for the nineteenth-century fascination with anthropometry, the measurement of the human body.[15] Behind these anatomical measurements lay the assumption that the body was a legible text, with various keys or languages available for reading its symbolic codes. In the logic of biological determinism, the surface and interior of the individual body, rather than its social characteristics, such as language, behavior, or clothing, became the primary sites of its meaning. "Every peculiarity of the body has probably some corresponding significance in the mind, and the cause of the former are the remoter causes of the latter," wrote Edward Drinker Cope, a well-known American paleontologist, summarizing the assumptions that fueled the science of comparative anatomy.[16] Although scientists debated which particular anatomical features carried racial meanings—skin, facial angle, pelvis, skull, brain mass, genitalia—the theory that anatomy predicted intelligence and behavior nevertheless remained remarkably constant. As Nancy Stepan and Sander Gilman have noted, "The concepts within racial science were so congruent with social and political life (with power relations, that is) as to be virtually uncontested from inside the mainstream of science."[17]

Supported by the cultural authority of an ostensibly objective scientific method, these readings of the body became a powerful instrument for those seeking to justify the economic and political disenfranchisement of various racial groups within systems of slavery and colonialism. As Barbara Fields has noted, however, "Try as they would, the scientific racists of the past failed to discover any objective criterion upon which to classify people; to their chagrin, every criterion they tried varied more within so-called races than between them."[18] Although the methods of science were considered to be outside the political and economic realm, in fact, as we know, these anatomical investigations, however professedly innocent their intentions, were driven by racial ideologies already firmly in place.[19]

Ideologies of race, of course, shaped and reflected both popular and scientific understandings of gender. As Gilman has argued, "Any attempt to establish that the races were inherently different rested to no little extent on the sexual difference of the black."[20] Although popular racist mythology in the U.S. in the nineteenth century focused on the supposed difference between the size of African-American and white men's genitalia, the male body was not necessarily the primary site of medical inquiry into racial difference.[21] Instead, as a number of medical journals from this period demonstrate, comparative anatomists repeatedly located racial difference through the sexual characteristics of the female body.[22]

In exploring the influence of scientific studies of race on the emerging discourse of sexuality, it is useful to look closely at a study from the genre of comparative anatomy. In 1867, W. H. Flower and James Murie published their "Account of the Dissection of a Bushwoman," which carefully catalogued the "more perishable soft structures of the body" of a young Bushwoman.[23] They placed their study in a line of inquiry concerning the African woman's body that had begun at least a half-century earlier with French naturalist Georges Cuvier's description of the woman popularly known as the "Hottentot Venus," or Saartje Baartman, who was displayed to European audiences fascinated by her "steatopygia" (protruding buttocks).[24] Significantly, starting with Cuvier, this tradition of comparative anatomy located the boundaries of race through the sexual and reproductive anatomy of the African female body, ignoring altogether the problematic absence of male bodies from their studies.

Flower and Murie's account lingered on two specific sites of difference: the "protuberance of the buttocks, so peculiar to the Bushman race" and "the remarkable development of the labia minora," which were "sufficiently well marked to distinguish these parts from those of any ordinary varieties of the human species" (208). The racial difference of the African body, implied Flower and Murie, was located in its literal excess, a specifically sexual excess that placed her body outside the boundaries of the "normal" female. To support their conclusion, Flower and Murie included corroborating "evidence" in the final part of their account. They quoted a secondhand report, "received from a scientific friend residing at the Cape of Good Hope," describing the anatomy of "two pure bred Hottentots, mother and daughter" (208). This account also focused on the women's genitalia, which they referred to as "appendages" (208). Although their account ostensibly foregrounded boundaries of race, their portrayal of the sexual characteristics of the Bushwoman betrayed Flower and Murie's anxieties about gender boundaries. The characteristics singled out as "peculiar" to this race, the (double) "appendages," fluttered between genders, at one moment masculine, at the next moment exaggeratedly feminine. Flower and Murie constructed the site of *racial* difference by marking the sexual and reproductive anatomy of the African woman as "peculiar." In their characterization, sexual ambiguity delineated the boundaries of race.

The techniques and logic of late nineteenth-century sexologists, who also routinely included physical examinations in their accounts, reproduced the methodologies employed by comparative anatomists like Flower and Murie. Many of the case histories in Krafft-Ebing's *Psychopathia Sexualis,* for instance, included a paragraph detailing any anatomical peculiarities of the body in question.[25] Although Krafft-Ebing could not draw any conclusions about somatic indicators of "abnormal" sexuality, physical examinations remained a staple of the genre. In Ellis's *Sexual Inversion,* case studies often focused more intensely on the bodies of female "inverts" than those of their male counterparts.[26] Although the specific sites of anatomical inspection (hymen, clitoris, labia, vagina) differed, the underlying theory remained constant: women's genitalia and reproductive anatomy held a valuable and presumably visual key to ranking bodies according to norms of sexuality.

Sexologists reproduced not only the methodologies of the comparative anatomy of races but also its iconography. One of the most consistent medical characterizations of the anatomy of both African-American women and lesbians was the myth of an unusually large clitoris.[27] As late as 1921, medical journals contained articles declaring that "a physical examination of [female homosexuals] will in practically every instance disclose an abnormally prominent clitoris." Significantly, this author added, "This is particularly so in colored women."[28] In an earlier account of racial differences between white and African-American women, one gynecologist had also focused on the size and visibility of the clitoris; in his examinations, he had perceived a distinction between the "free" clitoris of "negresses" and the "imprisonment" of the clitoris of the "Aryan American woman."[29] In constructing these oppositions, such characterizations literalized the sexual and racial ideologies of the nineteenth-century "Cult of True Womanhood," which explicitly privileged white women's sexual "purity," while implicitly suggesting African-American women's sexual accessibility.[30]

It is evident from the case histories in *Sexual Inversion* that Ellis gave much more attention to the presumed anatomical peculiarities of the women than to those of the men. "As regards the sexual organs it seems possible," Ellis wrote, "so far as my observations go, to speak more definitely of inverted women than of inverted men" (256). Ellis justified his greater scrutiny of women's bodies in part by invoking the ambiguity surrounding women's sexuality in general: "we are accustomed to a much greater familiarity and intimacy between women than between men, and we are less apt to suspect the existence of any abnormal passion" (204). To Ellis, the seemingly imperceptible differences between "normal" and "abnormal" intimacies between women called for closer scrutiny of the subtleties of their anatomy. He included the following detailed account as potential evidence for distinguishing the fine line between the lesbian and the "normal" woman:

> *Sexual Organs.*—(a) Internal: Uterus and ovaries appear normal. (b) External: Small clitoris, with this irregularity, that the lower folds of the labia minora, instead of uniting one with the other and forming the frenum, are extended upward along the sides of the clitoris, while the upper folds are poorly developed, furnishing the clitoris with a scant hood. The labia majora depart from normal conformation in being fuller in their posterior half than in their anterior part, so that when the subject is in the supine position they sag, as it were, presenting a slight resemblance to fleshy sacs, but in substance and structure they feel normal (136).

This extraordinary taxonomy, performed for Ellis by an unnamed "obstetric physician of high standing," echoed earlier anatomical catalogues of African women. The exacting eye (and hand) of the investigating physician highlighted every possible detail as meaningful evidence. Through the triple repetition of "normal" and the use of evaluative language like "irregularity" and "poorly developed," the physician reinforced his position of judgment. Although he did not provide criteria for what constituted "normal" anatomy, the physician assumed abnormality and simply corroborated that assumption through sight and touch. Moreover, his characterization of what he perceived as abnormal echoed the anxious account by Flower and Murie. Although the description of the clitoris is a notable exception to the tendency to exaggerate its size, the account nevertheless scrutinized another site of genital excess. The "fleshy sacs" of this woman, like the "appendages" fetishized in the earlier account, invoked the anatomy of a phantom male body inhabiting the lesbian's anatomical features.[31]

Clearly, anxieties about gender shaped both Ellis's and Flower and Murie's taxonomies of the lesbian and the African woman. Yet their preoccupation with gender cannot be understood as separate from the larger context of scientific assumptions during this period, which one historian has characterized

as "the full triumph of Darwinism in American thought."[32] Gender, in fact, was crucial to Darwinist ideas. One of the basic assumptions within the Darwinian model was the belief that, as organisms evolved through a process of natural selection, they also showed greater signs of differentiation between the (two) sexes. Following this logic, various writers used sexual characteristics as indicators of evolutionary progress toward civilization. In *Man and Woman,* for instance, Ellis himself cautiously suggested that since the "beginnings of industrialism," "more marked sexual differences in physical development seem (we cannot speak definitely) to have developed than are usually to be found in savage societies."[33] In this passage, Ellis drew from theories developed by biologists like Patrick Geddes and J. Arthur Thomson. In their important work *The Evolution of Sex,* which traced the role of sexual difference in evolution, Geddes and Thomson stated that "hermaphroditism is primitive; the unisexual state is a subsequent differentiation. The present cases of normal hermaphroditism imply either persistence or reversion."[34] In characterizing the bodies of lesbians or African-American women as less sexually differentiated than the norm (always posited as white heterosexual women's bodies), anatomists and sexologists drew upon notions of natural selection to dismiss these bodies as anomalous "throwbacks" within a scheme of cultural and anatomical progress.

THE MIXED BODY

The emergence of evolutionary theory in the late nineteenth century foregrounded a view of continuity between the "savage" and "civilized" races, in contrast to earlier scientific thinking about race, which had focused on debates about the origins of different racial groups. Proponents of monogeny argued that all races derived from a single origin. Those who argued for polygeny believed that each race descended from its own biological and geographical source, a view, not coincidentally, that supported segregationist impulses.[35] With Darwin's publication of *The Origin of Species* in 1859, the debate between polygeny and monogeny was superseded by evolutionary theory, which was appropriated as a powerful scientific model for understanding race. Its controversial innovation was its emphasis on the continuity between animals and human beings. Evolutionary theory held out the possibility that the physical, mental, and moral characteristics of human beings had evolved gradually over time from ape-like ancestors.[36] Although the idea of continuity depended logically on the blurring of boundaries within hierarchies, it did not necessarily invalidate the methods or assumptions of comparative anatomy. On the contrary, notions of visible differences and racial hierarchies were deployed to corroborate Darwinian theory.

The concept of continuity was harnessed to the growing attention to miscegenation, or "amalgamation," in social science writing in the first decades of the twentieth century. Edward Byron Reuter's *The Mulatto in the United States,* for instance, pursued an exhaustive quantitative and comparative study of the "mulatto" population and its achievements in relation to those of "pure" white or African ancestry. Reuter traced the presence of a distinct group of mixed-race people back to early American history: "Their physical appearance, though markedly different from that of the pure blooded race, was sufficiently marked to set them off as a peculiar people."[37] Reuter, of course, was willing to admit the viability of "mulattoes" only within a framework that emphasized the separation of races. Far from using the notion of the biracial body to refute the belief in discrete markers of racial difference, Reuter perpetuated the notion by focusing on the distinctiveness of this "peculiar people."

Miscegenation was, of course, not only a question of race, but also one of sex and sexuality. Ellis recognized this intersection implicitly, if not explicitly. His sense of the "racial questions" implicit in sex was surely informed by his involvement with eugenics, the movement in Europe and the United States that, to greater or lesser degrees, advocated selective reproduction and "race hygiene."[38] In the United States, eugenics was both a political and scientific

response to the growth of a population beginning to challenge the dominance of white political interests. The widespread scientific and social interest in eugenics was fueled by anxieties expressed through the popular notion of (white) "race suicide." This phrase, invoked most notably by Theodore Roosevelt, summed up nativist fears about a perceived decline in reproduction among white Americans. The new field of eugenics worked hand in hand with growing anti-miscegenation sentiment and policy, provoked not only by the attempts of African-Americans to gain political representation but also by the influx of large populations of immigrants.[39] As Mark Haller has pointed out, "Racists and [immigration] restrictionists...found in eugenics the scientific reassurances they needed that heredity shaped man's personality and that their assumptions rested on biological facts."[40] Ellis saw himself as an advocate for eugenics policies. As an active member of the British National Council for Public Morals, he wrote several essays on eugenics, including *The Problem of Race Regeneration,* a pamphlet advocating "voluntary" sterilization of the unfit as a policy in the best interest of "the race."[41] Further, in a letter to Francis Galton in 1907, Ellis wrote, "In the concluding volume of my Sex 'Studies' I shall do what I can to insinuate the eugenic attitude."[42]

The beginnings of sexology, then, were related to, and perhaps even dependent on, a pervasive climate of eugenic and anti-miscegenation sentiment and legislation. Even at the level of nomenclature, anxieties about miscegenation shaped sexologists' attempts to find an appropriate and scientific name for the newly visible object of their study. Introduced into English in 1892 through the translation of Krafft-Ebing's *Psychopathia Sexualis,* the term "homosexuality" itself stimulated a great deal of uneasiness. In 1915, Ellis reported that "most investigators have been much puzzled in coming to a conclusion as to the best, most exact, and at the same time most colorless names [for same-sex desire]."[43] Giving an account of the various names proposed, such as Karl Heinrich Ulrichs's "Uranian" and Carl von Westphal's "contrary sexual feeling," Ellis admitted that "homosexuality" was the most widely used term. Far from the ideal "colorless" term, however, "homosexuality" evoked Ellis's distaste because of its mixed origins: in a regretful aside, he noted that "it has, philologically, the awkward disadvantage of being a bastard term compounded of Greek and Latin elements" (2). In the first edition of *Sexual Inversion,* Ellis stated his alarm more directly: "'Homosexual' is a barbarously hybrid word."[44] A similar view was expressed by Edward Carpenter, an important socialist organizer in England and an outspoken advocate of homosexual and women's emancipation. Like Ellis, Carpenter winced at the connotations of illegitimacy in the word: "'[H]omosexual,' generally used in scientific works, is of course a bastard word. 'Homogenic' has been suggested, as being from two roots, both Greek, i.e., 'homos,' same, and 'genos,' sex."[45] Carpenter's suggestion, "homogenic," of course, resonated both against and within the vocabularies of eugenics and miscegenation. Performing these etymological gyrations with almost comic literalism, Ellis and Carpenter expressed pervasive cultural anxieties around questions of racial origins and purity. Concerned above all else with legitimacy, they attempted to remove and rewrite the mixed origins of "homosexuality." Ironically, despite their suggestions for alternatives, the "bastard" term took hold among sexologists, thus yoking together, at least rhetorically, two kinds of mixed bodies: the racial "hybrid" and the invert.

Although Ellis exhibited anxieties about biracial bodies, for others who sought to naturalize and recuperate homosexuality, the evolutionary emphasis on continuity offered potentially useful analogies. Xavier Mayne, for example, one of the earliest American advocates of homosexual rights, wrote, "Between [the] whitest of men and the blackest negro stretches out a vast line of intermediary races as to their colours: brown, olive, red tawny, yellow."[46] He then invoked this model of race to envision a continuous spectrum of gender and sexuality: "Nature abhors the absolute, delights in the fractional.... Intersexes express the half-steps, the between-beings."[47] In this analogy, Mayne reversed dominant cultural hierarchies that privileged purity

over mixture. Drawing upon irrefutable evidence of the "natural" existence of biracial people, Mayne posited a direct analogy to a similarly mixed body, the intersex, which he positioned as a necessary presence within the natural order.

Despite Carpenter's complaint about "bastard" terminology, he, like Mayne, also occasionally appropriated the scientific language of racial mixing in order to resist the association between homosexuality and degeneration. In *The Intermediate Sex,* he attempted to theorize homosexuality outside of the discourse of pathology or abnormality; he too suggested a continuum of genders, with "intermediate types" occupying a place between the poles of exclusively heterosexual male and exclusively heterosexual female. In an appendix to *The Intermediate Sex,* Carpenter offered a series of quotations supporting his ideas, some of which drew upon racial analogies:

> Anatomically and mentally we find all shades existing from the pure genus man to the pure genus woman. Thus there has been constituted what is well named by an illustrious exponent of the science "The Third Sex".... As we are continually meeting in cities women who are one-quarter, or one-eighth, or so on, *male*...so there are in the Inner Self similar half-breeds, all adapting themselves to circumstances with perfect ease.[48]

Through notions of "shades" of gender and sexual "half-breeds," Carpenter appropriated dominant scientific models of race to construct and embody what he called the intermediate sex. These racial paradigms, along with models of gender, offered Carpenter a coherent vocabulary for understanding and expressing a new vision of sexual bodies.

SEXUAL "PERVERSION" AND RACIALIZED DESIRE

By the early twentieth century, medical models of sexuality had begun to shift in emphasis, moving away from a focus on the body and toward psychological theories of desire. It seems significant that this shift took place within a period that also saw a transformation of scientific notions about race. As historians have suggested, in the early twentieth century, scientific claims for exclusively biological models of racial difference were beginning to be undermined, although, of course, these models have persisted in popular understandings of race.[49]

In what ways were these shifts away from biologized notions of sexuality and race related in scientific literature? One area in which they overlapped and perhaps shaped one another was through models of interracial and homosexual desire. Specifically, two tabooed sexualities—miscegenation and homosexuality—became linked in sexological and psychological discourse through the model of "abnormal" sexual object choice.

The convergence of theories of "perverse" racial and sexual desire shaped the assumptions of psychologists like Margaret Otis, whose "A Perversion Not Commonly Noted" appeared in a medical journal in 1913. In all-girl institutions, including reform schools and boarding schools, Otis had observed widespread "love-making between the white and colored girls."[50] Both fascinated and alarmed, Otis remarked that this perversion was "well known in reform schools and institutions for delinquent girls," but that "this particular form of the homosexual relation has perhaps not been brought to the attention of scientists" (113). Performing her ostensible duty to science, Otis carefully described these rituals of interracial romance and the girls' "peculiar moral code." In particular, she noted that the girls incorporated racial difference into courtship rituals self-consciously patterned on traditional gender roles: "One white girl…admitted that the colored girl she loved seemed the man, and thought it was so in the case of the others" (114). In Otis's account, the actions of the girls clearly threatened the keepers of the institutions, who responded to the perceived danger with efforts to racially segregate their charges (who were, of course, already segregated by gender). Otis, however, did not specify the motivation for segregation: Did the girls' intimacy trouble the authorities because it was homosexual or because it was interracial? Otis avoided exploring

this question and offered a succinct theory instead: "The difference in color, in this case, takes the place of difference in sex" (113).

Otis's explicit discussion of racial difference and homosexuality was extremely unusual in the burgeoning social science literature on sexuality in the early twentieth century.[51] Significantly, Otis characterized this phenomenon as a type of "the homosexual relation" and not as a particular form of interracial sexuality. Despite Otis's focus on desire rather than physiology, her characterization of the schoolgirls' "system" of romance drew upon stereotypes established by the earlier anatomical models. She used a simple analogy between race and gender in order to understand their desire: black was to white as masculine was to feminine.

Recent historical work on the lesbian subject at the turn of the century in the United States offers a useful context for considering the implications of Otis's account. In a compelling analysis of the highly publicized 1892 murder of Freda Ward by her lover, Alice Mitchell, Lisa Duggan has argued that what initially pushed the women's relationship beyond what their peers accepted as normal was Mitchell's decision to pass as a man.[52] Passing, according to Duggan, was "a strategy so rare among bourgeois white women that their plan was perceived as so radically inappropriate as to be insane."[53] Duggan characterizes passing as a kind of red flag that visually marked Mitchell and Ward's relationship. Suddenly, with the prospect of Mitchell's visible transformation from "woman" to "man," the sexual nature of their relationship also came into view—abnormal and dangerous to the eyes of their surveyors.

Following Duggan's line of analysis, I suggest that racial difference performed a similar function in Otis's account. In turn-of-the-century American culture, where Jim Crow segregation erected a structure of taboos against any kind of public (non-work-related) interracial relationship, racial difference visually marked the alliances between the schoolgirls as already suspicious. In a culture in which Ellis could remark that he was accustomed to women being on intimate terms, race became a visible marker for the sexual nature of that liaison.

In effect, the institution of racial segregation and its cultural fiction of "black" and "white" produced the girls' interracial romances as "perverse."[54]

It is possible that the discourse of sexual pathology, in turn, began to inform scientific understandings of race. By 1903, a southern physician drew upon the language of sexology to legitimate a particularly racist fear: "A perversion from which most races are exempt, prompts the negro's inclinations towards the white woman, whereas other races incline toward the females of their own."[55] Using the medical language of perversion to naturalize and legitimate the dominant cultural myth of the black rapist, this account characterized interracial desire as a type of congenital abnormal sexual object choice. In the writer's terms, the desire of African-American men for white women (though not the desire of white men for African-American women) could be understood and pathologized by drawing upon emergent models of sexual orientation.[56]

DIVERGENCES IN RACIAL AND SEXUAL SCIENCE

The "invention" of homosexuality and heterosexuality was inextricable from the extraordinary pressures attached to racial definition at this particular historical moment in the late nineteenth century. Although sexologists' search for physical signs of sexual orientation mirrored the methods of comparative racial anatomists, the modern case study marked a significant departure from comparative anatomy by attaching a self-generated narrative to the body in question. As Jeffrey Weeks has written, Krafft-Ebing's *Psychopathia Sexualis* was a decisive moment in the "invention" of the homosexual because "it was the eruption into print of the speaking pervert, the individual marked, or marred, by his (or her) sexual impulses."[57]

The case study challenged the tendency of scientific writers to position the homosexual individual as a mute body whose surface was to be interpreted by those with professional authority. Whether to grant a voice, however limited, to the homosexual body was a heavily contested methodological question among sexologists. The increasingly central position of the case study in the literature on homosexuality elicited concern from contemporary professionals, who perceived an unbridgeable conflict between autobiography and scientific objectivity. Invested in maintaining authority in medical writing, Morton Prince, a psychologist who advocated searching for a "cure" to homosexuality, described in exasperation his basic distrust of the case history as a source of medical evidence, especially in the case of "perverts":

> Even in taking an ordinary medical history, we should hesitate to accept such testimony as final, and I think we should be even more cautious in our examination of autobiographies which attempt to give an analysis, founded on introspection, of the feelings, passions and tastes of degenerate individuals who attempt to explain their first beginnings in early childhood.[58]

For Prince, the "speaking pervert" was a challenge to the "truth" of medical examination and threatened to contradict the traditional source of medical evidence, the patient's mute physical body as interpreted by the physician. In Prince's view, the case history also blurred the boundaries between the legal and medical spheres:

> Very few of these autobiographies will stand analysis. Probably there is no class of people whose statements will less stand the test of a scorching cross-examination than the moral pervert. One cannot help feeling that if the pervert was thus examined by an independent observer, instead of being allowed to tell his own story without interruption, a different tale would be told, or great gaps would be found, which are now nicely bridged, or many asserted facts would be resolved into pure inferences.[59]

A "different tale" indeed. Prince's focus on "testimony" and "cross-examination" illustrated the overlapping interests and methods of the medical and the legal spheres. His tableau of litigation placed the homosexual individual within an already guilty body, one that defied the assumption that it was a readable text; its anatomical markers did not necessarily correspond to predictable sexual behaviors. The sure duplicity of this body demanded investigation by the prosecutor/physician, whose professional expertise somehow guaranteed his access to the truth.

Ellis, who sought legitimacy both for himself as a scientist and for the nascent field of sexology, also worried about the association between autobiographical accounts and fraud. In *Sexual Inversion,* he stated that "it may be proper, at this point, to say a few words as to the reliability of the statements furnished by homosexual persons. This has sometimes been called in[to] question" (89). Although he also associated the homosexual voice with duplicity, Ellis differed from Prince by placing this unreliability within a larger social context. He located the causes of insincerity not in the homosexual individual but in the legal system that barred homosexuality: "[W]e cannot be surprised at this [potential insincerity] so long as inversion is counted a crime. The most normal persons, under similar conditions, would be similarly insincere" (89).

With the movement toward the case study and psychoanalytic models of sexuality, sexologists relied less and less upon the methodologies of comparative anatomy and implicitly acknowledged that physical characteristics were inadequate evidence for the "truth" of the body in question. Yet the assumptions of comparative anatomy did not completely disappear. Although they seemed to contradict more psychological understandings of sexuality, notions of biological difference continued to shape cultural understandings of sexuality, particularly in popular representations of lesbians, gay men, and bisexuals.

TROUBLING SCIENCE

My efforts here have focused on the various ways in which late nineteenth- and early twentieth-century scientific discourses around race became available to sexologists and physicians as a way to articulate emerging models of homosexuality. Methodologies and iconographies of comparative anatomy attempted to locate discrete physiological markers

of difference through which to classify and separate types of human beings. Sexologists drew upon these techniques to try to position the "homosexual" body as anatomically distinguishable from the "normal" body. Likewise, medical discourses around sexuality appear to have been steeped in pervasive cultural anxieties about "mixed" bodies, particularly the "mulatto," whose literal position as a mixture of black and white bodies acquires a symbolic position in scientific accounts. Sexologists and others writing about homosexuality borrowed the model of the mixed body as a way to make sense of the "invert." Finally, racial and sexual discourses converged in psychological models that understood "unnatural" desire as a marker of perversion: in these cases, interracial and same-sex sexuality became analogous.

Although scientific and medical models of both race and sexuality held enormous definitional power at the turn of the century, they were variously and complexly incorporated, revised, resisted, or ignored both by the individuals they sought to categorize and within the larger cultural imagination. My speculations are intended to raise questions and to point toward possibilities for further historical and theoretical work. How, for instance, were analogies between race and sexual orientation deployed or not within popular cultural discourses? In religious discourses? In legal discourses? What were the material effects of their convergence or divergence? How have these analogies been used to organize bodies in other historical moments, and, most urgently, in our own?

In the last few years alone, for example, there has been a proliferation of "speaking perverts" in a range of cultural contexts, including political demonstrations, television, magazines, courts, newspapers, and classrooms. Despite the unprecedented opportunities for lesbian, gay, bisexual, and queer speech, however, recent scientific research into sexuality has reflected a determination to discover a biological key to the origins of homosexuality. Highly publicized new studies have purported to locate indicators of sexual orientation in discrete niches of the human body, ranging from a particular gene on the X chromosome to the hypothalamus, a structure of the brain.[60] In an updated and more technologically sophisticated form, comparative anatomy is being granted a peculiar cultural authority in the study of sexuality.

These studies, of course, have not gone uncontested, arriving as they have within a moment characterized not only by the development of social constructionist theories of sexuality but also, in the face of AIDS, by a profound and aching skepticism about prevailing scientific methods and institutions. At the same time, some see political efficacy in these new scientific studies, arguing that lesbians, gay men, and bisexuals might gain access to greater rights if sexual orientation could be proven an immutable biological difference. Such arguments make an analogy, whether explicit or unspoken, to the previous understanding of race as immutable difference. Reverberating through these arguments are echoes of late nineteenth- and early twentieth-century medical models of sexuality and race, whose earlier interdependence suggests a need to understand the complex relationships between constructions of race and sexuality during our own very different historical moment. How does the current effort to re-biologize sexual orientation and to invoke the vocabulary of immutable difference reflect or influence existing cultural anxieties and desires about racialized bodies? To what extent does the political deployment of these new scientific "facts" about sexuality depend upon reinserting biologized racial categories? These questions, as I have tried to show for an earlier period, require a shift in the attention and practices of queer reading and lesbian, gay, and bisexual studies. We must begin to see questions of race as inextricable from the study of sexuality. To date, these connections have only been a part of our peripheral vision; we must make them a central focus.

NOTES

1. See, for example, Michel Foucault, *The History of Sexuality,* vol. 1, *An Introduction* (New York: Vintage, 1980); George Chauncey, "From Sexual Inversion to Homosexuality: Medicine and the Changing Conceptualization of Female Deviance," *Salmagundi,* nos. 58–59 (Fall 1982–Winter 1983): 114–46; Jeffrey Weeks, *Sex, Politics, and Society: The Regulation of Sexuality since* 1800 (New York: Longmans, 1981); and David Halperin, "Is There a History of Sexuality?" in *The Lesbian and Gay Studies Reader,* ed. Henry Abelove, Michèle Aina Barale, and David M. Halperin (New York: Routledge, 1993), 416–31. On the invention of the classification "heterosexual," see Jonathan Katz, "The Invention of Heterosexuality," *Socialist Review* 20 (1990): 17–34. For a related and intriguing argument that locates the earlier emergence of hierarchies of reproductive over non-reproductive sexual activity, see Henry Abelove, "Some Speculations on the History of 'Sexual Intercourse' during the 'Long Eighteenth Century' in England." *Genders* 6 (1989): 125–30.

2. Chauncey, "From Sexual Inversion to Homosexuality."

3. In "Homosexuality: A Cultural Construct," from his *One Hundred Years of Homosexuality; and Other Essays on Greek Love* (New York: Routledge, 1990), David Halperin has briefly and provocatively suggested that

> all scientific inquiries into the aetiology of sexual orientation, after all, spring from a more or less implicit theory of sexual races, from the notion that there exist broad general divisions between types of human beings corresponding, respectively, to those who make a homosexual and those who make a heterosexual object-choice. When the sexual racism underlying such inquiries is more plainly exposed, their rationale will suffer proportionately—or so one may hope. (50)

In a recent article, Abdul R. JanMohamed offers a useful analysis and critique of Foucault's failure to examine the intersection of the discourses of sexuality and race. See his "Sexuality on/of the Racial Border: Foucault, Wright, and the Articulation of 'Racialized Sexuality,'" in *Discourses of Sexuality: From Aristotle to AIDS,* ed. Domna C. Stanton (Ann Arbor: University of Michigan Press, 1992), 94–116. I explore a different (though related) set of questions in this essay.

4. In *Disorders of Desire: Sex and Gender in Modern American Sexology* (Philadelphia: Temple University Press, 1990), Janice Irvine notes that, for example, "the invisibility of Black people in sexology as subjects or researchers has undermined our understanding of the sexuality of Black Americans and continues to be a major problem in modern sexology." She adds that Kinsey, the other major sexologist of the twentieth century, planned to include a significant proportion of African-American

case histories in his *Sexual Behavior in the Human Male* (1948) and *Sexual Behavior in the Human Female* (1953) but failed to gather a sufficient number of them and so "unwittingly colluded in the racial exclusion so pervasive in sex research" (43).

5. Havelock Ellis, *Studies in the Psychology of Sex,* vol. 1, *Sexual Inversion* (1897; London, 1900), x, emphasis added.

6. My use of the concept of ideology draws upon Barbara Fields, "Slavery, Race, and Ideology in the United States of America," *New Left Review* 181 (1990): 95–118; Louis Althusser, "Ideology and Ideological State Apparatuses (Notes towards an Investigation)," in his *Lenín and Philosophy and Other Essays,* trans. Ben Brewster (New York: Monthly Review Press, 1971), 121–73; and Teresa de Lauretis, "The Technology of Gender," in her *Technologies of Gender: Essays on Theory, Film, and Fiction* (Bloomington: Indiana University Press, 1987), 1–30.

7. I borrow this phrase from Willa Cather's essay "The Novel Démeublé," in her *Not under Forty* (New York, 1922), 50.

8. I am not implying, however, that racial anxieties caused the invention of the homosexual, or that the invention of the homosexual caused increased racial anxieties. Both of these causal arguments seem simplistic and, further, depend upon separating the discourses of race and sexuality, whose convergence, in fact, I am eager to foreground.

9. Havelock Ellis, *Studies in the Psychology of Sex,* vol. 2, *Sexual Inversion,* 3d ed. (Philadelphia, 1915). Further references to this edition will be noted parenthetically unless otherwise stated. Although *Sexual Inversion* was published originally as volume 1, Ellis changed its position to volume 2 in the second and third editions, published in the United States in 1901 and 1915, respectively. In the later editions, volume 1 became *The Evolution of Modesty.*

   Ellis originally coauthored *Sexual Inversion* with John Addington Symonds. For a discussion of their collaboration and the eventual erasure of Symonds from the text, see Wayne Koestenbaum, *Double Talk: The Erotics of Male Literary Collaboration* (New York: Routledge, 1989). 43–67.

10. In "Sex and the Emergence of Sexuality," *Critical Inquiry* 14 (Autumn 1987): 16–48, Arnold I. Davidson characterizes Ellis's method as "psychiatric" (as opposed to "anatomical") reasoning. Arguing that "sexuality itself is a product of the psychiatric style of reasoning" (23), Davidson explains that "the iconographical representation of sex proceeds by depiction of the body,

more specifically by depiction of the genitalia. The iconographical representation of sexuality is given by depiction of the personality, and it most usually takes the form of depiction of the face and its expressions" (27). The case studies in *Sexual Inversion,* and especially those of women, however, tend to contradict this broad characterization. My understanding of Ellis differs from that of Davidson, who readily places Ellis in a psychiatric model. Instead, Ellis might be characterized as a transitional figure, poised at the crossroads between the fields of comparative anatomy and psychiatry. To borrow Davidson's terms, anatomical reasoning does not disappear; it stays in place, supporting psychiatric reasoning.

11. Ellis, *Sexual Inversion* (1900), xi. Ironically, upon publication in 1897, *Sexual Inversion* was judged to be not a scientific work but "a certain lewd, wicked, bawdy, scandalous libel." Effectively banned in England, subsequent copies were published only in the United States. See Jeffrey Weeks, "Havelock Ellis and the Politics of Sex Reform," in *Socialism and the New Life: The Personal and Sexual Politics of Edward Carpenter and Havelock Ellis,* ed. Sheila Rowbotham and Jeffrey Weeks (London: Pluto Press, 1977), 154; and Phyllis Grosskurth, *Havelock Ellis: A Biography* (New York: Knopf, 1980), 191–204.

12. For further discussion of Ellis's similarity to Charles Darwin as a naturalist and their mutual interest in "natural" modesty, see Ruth Bernard Yeazell, "Nature's Courtship Plot in Darwin and Ellis," *Yale Journal of Criticism* 2 (1989): 33–53.

13. Elsewhere in *Sexual Inversion,* Ellis entertained the idea that certain races or nationalities had a "special proclivity" to homosexuality (4), but he seemed to recognize the nationalistic impulse behind this argument and chided those who wielded it: "The people of every country have always been eager to associate sexual perversions with some other country than their own" (57–58).

14. Classic discussions of the term's history include Peter I. Rose, *The Subject Is Race: Traditional Ideologies and the Teaching of Race Relations* (New York: Oxford University Press, 1968), 30–43; and Thomas F. Gossett, *Race: The History of an Idea in America* (Dallas: Southern Methodist University Press, 1963). For a history of various forms and theories of biological determinism, see Stephen Jay Gould, *The Mismeasure of Man* (New York: Norton, 1981).

15. John S. Haller, Jr., *Outcasts from Evolution: Scientific Attitudes of Racial Inferiority, 1859–1900* (Urbana: University of Illinois Press, 1971), 4.

16. Ibid., 196. On Cope, see also Gould, *The Mismeasure of Man,* 115–18.

17. Nancy Leys Stepan and Sander Gilman, "Appropriating the Idioms of Science: The Rejection of Scientific Racism," in *The Bounds of Race: Perspectives on Hegemony and Resistance,* ed. Dominick LaCapra (Ithaca, NY: Cornell University Press, 1991), 74.

18. Fields, "Slavery, Race, and Ideology in the United States of America," 97, n. 3.

19. Haller, "Outcasts from Evolution," 48.

20. Sander Gilman, *Difference and Pathology: Stereotypes of Sexuality, Race, and Madness* (Ithaca, NY: Cornell University Press, 1985), 112.

21. According to Gilman, "When one turns to autopsies of black males from [the late nineteenth century], what is striking is the absence of any discussion of the male genitalia" (ibid., 89).

    The specific absence of male physiology as a focus of nineteenth-century scientific texts, however, should not minimize the central location of the African-American male body in popular cultural notions of racial difference, especially in the spectacle of lynching, which had far-reaching effects on both African-American and white attitudes toward the African-American male body. One might also consider the position of the racialized male body in one of the most popular forms of nineteenth-century entertainment, the minstrel show. See Eric Lott, *Love and Theft: Blackface Minstrelsy and the American Working Class* (New York: Oxford University Press, 1993).

22. The *American Journal of Obstetrics (AJO)* was a frequent forum for these debates. On the position of the hymen, for example, see C. H. Fort, "Some Corroborative Facts in Regard to the Anatomical Difference between the Negro and White Races," *AJO* 10 (1877): 258–59; H. Otis Hyatt, "Note on the Normal Anatomy of the Vulvo-Vaginal Orifice," *AJO* 10 (1877): 253–58; A. G. Smythe, "The Position of the Hymen in the Negro Race," *AJO* 10 (1877): 638–39; Edward Turnipseed, "Some Facts in Regard to the Anatomical Differences between the Negro and White Races," *AJO* 10 (1877): 32–33. On the birth canal, see Joseph Taber Johnson, "On Some of the Apparent Peculiarities of Parturition in the Negro Race, with Remarks on Race Pelves in General," *AJO* 8 (1875): 88–123.

    This focus on women's bodies apparently differed from earlier studies. In her recent work on gender and natural history, Londa Schiebinger discusses how eighteenth-century comparative anatomists and anthropologists developed their theories by examining male bodies. See *Nature's Body: Gender in the Making of Modern Science* (Boston: Beacon, 1993), especially 143–83.

23. W. H. Flower and James Murie, "Account of the Dissection of a Bushwoman," *Journal of Anatomy and Physiology* 1 (1867): 208. Subsequent references will be noted parenthetically within the text.

    Flower was the conservator of the Museum of the Royal College of Surgeons of England; Murie was prosector to the Zoological Society of London. For brief discussions of this account, see Gilman, *Difference and Pathology,* 88–89; and Anita Levy, *Other Women: The Writing of Class, Race, and Gender, 1832–1898* (Princeton, NJ: Princeton University Press, 1991), 70–72. Although she does not consider questions surrounding the lesbian body, Levy offers an astute reading of this case and its connection to scientific representations of the body of the prostitute.

24. Georges Cuvier, "Extraits d'observations faites sur le cadavre d'une femme connue à Paris et à Londres sous le nom de Vénus Hottentote," *Mémoires du Musée d'histoire naturelle* 3 (1817): 259–74. After her death in 1815 at the age of twenty-five, Baartman's genitalia were preserved and re-displayed within the scientific space of the Musée de I'Homme in Paris.

    On Baartman, see Schiebinger, *Nature's Body,* 160–72; and Stephen Jay Gould, *The Flamingo's Smile: Reflections in Natural History* (New York: Norton 1985), 291–305.

25. Richard von Krafft-Ebing, *Psychopathia Sexualis,* 12th ed., trans. Franklin S. Klaf (1902; reprint, New York: Putnam, 1965).

26. This practice continued well into the twentieth century. See, for example, Jennifer Terry's discussion of the anatomical measurement of lesbians by the Committee for the Study of Sex Variants in the 1930s, in "Lesbians under the Medical Gaze: Scientists Search for Remarkable Differences," *Journal of Sex Research* 27 (August 1990): 317–39; and "Theorizing Deviant Historiography," *differences* 3 (Summer 1991): 55–74.

27. In the first edition of *Sexual Inversion,* Ellis, who did search the lesbian body for masculine characteristics, nevertheless refuted this claim about the clitoris: "there is no connection, as was once supposed, between sexual inversion and an enlarged clitoris" (98).

28. Perry M. Lichtenstein, "The 'Fairy' and the Lady Lover," *Medical Review of Reviews* 27 (1921): 372. In "Lesbians under the Medical Gaze," Terry discusses sexologists' conjectures about the size of lesbians' genitalia in a report published in 1941. Researchers were somewhat uncertain whether perceived excesses were congenital or the result of particular sex

practices. On the history of scientific claims about the sexual function of the clitoris, see Thomas Laqueur, *Making Sex: Body and Gender from the Greeks to Freud* (Cambridge: Harvard University Press, 1990), 233–37.

29. Morris, "Is Evolution Trying to Do Away with the Clitoris?" (paper presented at the meeting of the American Association of Obstetricians and Gynecologists, St. Louis, September 21, 1892), Yale University Medical Library, New Haven, CT.

30. See Hazel Carby, *Reconstructing Womanhood: The Emergence of the Afro-American Woman Novelist* (New York: Oxford University Press, 1987), 20–39; and Barbara Welter, "The Cult of True Womanhood, 1820–1860," in her *Dimity Convictions: The American Woman in the Nineteenth Century* (Columbus: Ohio University Press, 1976), 21–41.

31. Characterizing this passage as "punitively complete," Koestenbaum in *Double Talk* has suggested that Ellis also had personal motivations for focusing so intently on the lesbian body: "Ellis, by taking part in this over-description of a lesbian, studied and subjugated the preference of his own wife; marrying a lesbian, choosing to discontinue sexual relations with her, writing *Sexual Inversion* with a homosexual [Symonds], Ellis might well have felt his own heterosexuality questioned" (54, 55).

32. George Fredrickson, *The Black Image in the White Mind: The Debate on Afro-American Character and Destiny, 1817–1914* (New York: Harper and Row, 1971), 246.

33. Havelock Ellis, *Man and Woman: A Study of Human Secondary Sexual Characters* (1894; New York, 1911), 13. Of course, the "beginnings of industrialism" coincided with the late eighteenth century, the period during which, as Schiebinger has shown, anatomists began looking for more subtle marks of differentiation. See Londa Schiebinger, *The Mind Has No Sex? Women in the Origins of Modern Science* (Cambridge: Harvard University Press, 1989), 189–212.

34. Patrick Geddes and J. Arthur Thomson, *The Evolution of Sex* (London, 1889; New York, 1890), 80. Ellis no doubt read this volume closely, for he had chosen it to inaugurate a series of popular scientific books (the Contemporary Science Series) that he edited for the Walter Scott Company. For more on this series, see Grosskurth, *Havelock Ellis,* 114–17.

35. For a full account of the debates concerning monogeny and polygeny, see Gould, *The Mismeasure of Man,* 30–72. Polygeny was a predominantly American theoretical development and was widely referred to as the "American school" of anthropology.

36. See Nancy Stepan, *The Idea of Race in Science: Great Britain, 1800–1960* (Hamden, CT: Archon Books, 1982), 53.

37. Edward Byron Reuter, *The Mulatto in the United States: Including a Study of the Role of Mixed-Blood Races throughout the World* (Boston, 1918), 338. Interestingly, in a paper delivered to the Eugenics Society of Britain in 1911, Edith Ellis (who had at least one long-term lesbian relationship while she was married to Havelock Ellis) had also used the phrase "peculiar people" to describe homosexual men and women. See Grosskurth, *Havelock Ellis,* 237–38.

38. Francis Galton (a cousin of Charles Darwin) introduced and defined the term "eugenics" in his *Inquiries into Human Faculty and Its Development* (1883; reprint, New York: AMS Press, 1973) as "the cultivation of the race" and "the science of improving stock, which . . . takes cognisance {sic} of all influences that tend in however remote a degree to give to the more suitable races or strains of blood a better chance of prevailing speedily over the less suitable than they otherwise would have had" (17).

39. For a discussion of Roosevelt's place within the racial ideology of the period, see Thomas G. Dyer, *Theodore Roosevelt and the Idea of Race* (Baton Rouge: Louisiana State University Press, 1980). See also John Higham, *Strangers in the Land: Patterns of American Nativism, 1860–1925* (New Brunswick, NJ: Rutgers University Press, 1955; reprint, New York: Atheneum, 1963), 146–57.

40. Mark H. Haller, *Eugenics: Hereditarian Attitudes in American Thought* (New Brunswick, NJ: Rutgers University Press, 1963), 144.

41. Jeffrey Weeks, *Sexuality and Its Discontents: Meanings, Myths, and Modern Sexualities* (Boston: Routledge and Kegan Paul, 1985), 76; Grosskurth, *Havelock Ellis,* 410. See also Havelock Ellis, "The Sterilization of the Unfit," *Eugenics Review* (October 1909): 203–6.

42. Quoted by Grosskurth, *Havelock Ellis,* 410.

43. Ellis, *Sexual Inversion* (1915), 2.

44. Ellis, *Sexual Inversion* (1900), 1n.

45. Edward Carpenter, "The Homogenic Attachment," in his *The Intermediate Sex: A Study of Some Transitional Types of Men and Women,* 5th ed. (London, 1918), 40n.

46. Xavier Mayne [Edward Irenaeus Prime Stevenson], *The Intersexes: A History of Similisexualism as a Problem in Social Life* ([Naples?], ca. 1908); reprint, New York: Arno Press, 1975), 14.

47. Ibid., 15, 17.

48. Quoted in Carpenter, *The Intermediate Sex,* 133, 170. Carpenter gives the following citations for these

quotations: Dr. James Burnet, *Medical Times and Hospital Gazette* 34, no. 1497 (November 10, 1906); and Charles G. Leland, "The Alternate Sex" (London, 1904), 41, 57.

49. In *New People: Miscegenation and Mulattoes in the United States* (New York: Free Press, 1980), Joel Williamson suggests that a similar psychologization of race was underway: "By about 1900 it was possible in the South for one who was biologically purely white to become behaviorally black. Blackness had become not a matter of visibility, not even, ironically, of the one-drop rule. It had passed on to become a matter of inner morality and outward behavior" (108). See also Elazar Barkan, *The Retreat of Scientific Racism: Changing Concepts of Race in Britain and the United States between the World Wars* (New York: Cambridge University Press, 1992).

Legal scholars have begun to explore the analogies between sodomy laws and anti-miscegenation statutes. See, for example, Andrew Koppelman, "The Miscegenation Analogy: Sodomy Law as Sex Discrimination," *Yale Law Journal* 98 (November 1988): 145–64. See also Janet Halley, "The Politics of the Closet: Towards Equal Protection for Gay, Lesbian, and Bisexual Identity," *UCLA Law Review* 36 (1989): 915–76. I am grateful to Julia Friedlander for bringing this legal scholarship to my attention.

50. Margaret Otis, "A Perversion Not Commonly Noted," *Journal of Abnormal Psychology* 8 (June–July 1913): 113–160. Subsequent references will be noted parenthetically within the text.

51. In "From Sexual Inversion to Homosexuality," Chauncey notes that "by the early teens the number of articles of abstracts concerning homosexuality regularly available to the American medical profession had grown enormously" (115, n. 3).

52. Lisa Duggan, "The Trials of Alice Mitchell: Sensationalism, Sexology, and the Lesbian Subject in Turn-of-the-Century America," *Signs: Journal of Women in Culture and Society* 18 (Summer 1993): 791–814.

53. Ibid., 798.

54. In a useful discussion of recent feminist analyses of identity, Lisa Walker suggests that a similar trope of visibility is prevalent in white critics' attempts to theorize race and sexuality. See her "How to Recognize a Lesbian: The Cultural Politics of Looking like What You Are," *Signs* 18 (Summer 1993): 866–90.

55. W. T. English, "The Negro Problem from the Physician's Point of View," *Atlanta Journal-Record of Medicine* 5 (October 1903): 468.

56. On the other hand, anti-lynching campaigns could also invoke the language of sexology. Although the analogy invoked sadism, rather than homosexuality, in 1935 a psychologist characterized lynching as a kind of "Dixie sex perversion...[m]uch that is commonly stigmatized as cruelty is a perversion of the sex instinct." Quoted in Phyllis Klotman, "'Tearing a Hole in History': Lynching as Theme and Motif," *Black American Literature Forum* 19 (1985): The original quote appeared in the *Baltimore Afro-American,* March 16, 1935.

57. Weeks, *Sexuality and Its Discontents.* Weeks points out that beginning with Krafft-Ebing's *Psychopathia Sexualis,* the case study became the standard in sexological writing. The dynamic between medical literature and a growing self-identified gay (male) subculture is exemplified by the growth of different editions of this single work. The first edition of *Psychopathia Sexualis,* published in 1886, contained 45 case histories and 110 pages; the twelfth edition, published in 1903, contained 238 case histories and 437 pages. Many of the subsequent case histories were supplied by readers who responded to the book with letters detailing their own sexual histories. This information suggests that, to at least some extent, an emerging gay male subculture was able to appropriate the space of "professional" medicolegal writing for its own uses, thus blurring the boundaries between professional medical and popular literature.

58. Morton Prince, "Sexual Perversion or Vice? A Pathological and Therapeutic Inquiry," *Journal of Nervous and Mental Disease* 25 (April 1898): 237–56; reprinted in *Psychotherapy and Multiple Personality: Selected Essays,* ed. Nathan G. Hale (Cambridge: Harvard University Press, 1975), 91.

59. Prince, *Psychotherapy and Multiple Personality*, 92.

60. Simon LeVay, *The Sexual Brain* (Cambridge: MIT Press, 1993); and Dean Hamer, *The Science of Desire: The Search for the Gay Gene and the Biology of Behavior* (New York: Simon and Schuster, 1994).

THE FUNCTION OF THE ORGASM

DISCUSSION QUESTIONS

1. The author writes, "It seems that western women couldn't win—they were either inferior to men because they were lacking in sexual feeling, or abnormal because they enjoyed and displayed their feelings of sexual pleasure." Do you think this mentality persists today? Why or why not?
2. How does the medicalization of women's sexual pleasure correspond with gendered expectations of women?
3. The author explains that, "sperm transport is primarily a female-dominated affair." How does this contradict the medical texts discussed in Martin's chapter?

Pleasure or pain? Ecstasy or agony? Gianlorenzo Bernini depicted the moment as one of voluptuous rapture. St. Teresa swoons backwards, lost in the moment, surrendering to her sacred vision. She moans, her lips parted, her face suffused with sensation, her eyes closed. The folds of her clothing stream and flow from her body, fluid as water, caressing her contours, as above golden rays of light surge down from heaven, and the angel of her lord prepares to pierce his flame-tipped spear through her heart, again and again, "The Ecstasy of St. Teresa," Bernini's sculpture of the Spanish saint of Avila in intimate communion with her god, is both glorious and disturbing, supremely capable of inducing shudders in unsuspecting onlookers.

For many, what Bernini's seventeenth-century hands created—an image of religious, saintly ecstasy—verges on the blasphemous. However, to others it is pure splendour—an emblem of eternal orgasm. St. Teresa herself described her moments of mystical communion with Christ in terms imbued with intense passion. In her manuscript *Life,* written in 1565, she describes how "The pain was so great that I screamed aloud; but simultaneously I felt such infinite sweetness that I wished it to last eternally. It was not bodily but psychic pain, although it affected to a certain extent also the body. It was the sweetest caressing of the soul by God."

Perhaps it is not surprising that St. Teresa was lost as to how to describe her intense sensations, and onlookers remain split as to what they see. Descriptions of orgasm often defy exactitude. What, after all, is one expressing? A pinnacle of pleasure and passion, or simply seconds of sweet, streaming, exquisite suffering? Is it a blissful evanescent and ecstatic moment when a person can stand outside one's conscious life and self, or just deliciously pleasant muscular contractions centred on and around a person's genitalia? Orgasm, it seems, is paradoxical. Language tells us the word derives from the Greek *orgasmos,* itself from the term *orgon,* which means to grow ripe, swell or be lustful, words which carry sexual and genital connotations. The Sanskrit *urira* means "sap" or "strength"—conveying a sense of sexual energy. However, such words fail somewhat when addressing the complexity and emotion of the experience.

Other English orgasmic expressions—climax, come, spend oneself and the big O—also pale beside the real thing. Latin sexual language utilised metaphors of reaching a goal or arriving (*peruenies*) or accomplishing something (*patratio*) to describe orgasm. French highlights the step to an altered consciousness with *la petite morte,* and expresses the pleasures of orgasm using the verb *jouir*—literally to enjoy or delight in something. However, French perplexes somewhat with the phrase *vider ses burettes* to describe female orgasm. This phrase literally means "the emptying of her *burettes,*" *burettes* being the receptacles for wine and holy water at Mass, but also in Old French a jug or pitcher with a wide mouth. It's also possible that this expression relates to the phenomenon of female ejaculation too. Meanwhile, German adds a bit of fizz with a descriptor of orgasm as *höchste Wallung,* that is "maximum bubbling"—a deliciously effervescent portrayal of the pleasure phenomenon.

The difficulty of grasping the heart of orgasm is reflected in the language of other cultures too. Anthropological evidence highlights how, for the Mangaian people, orgasm is *nene,* a word used figuratively to refer to perfection. Synonymous with this is *nanawe,* used for either "luxuriously comfortable" or "the pleasantness of a person's talk or of music." In the Trobiand Islands, the fine line between orgasm and ejaculation is somewhat blurred. *Ipipisi momona* describes the moment of orgasm, but translates literally as "the sexual fluid squirts/the seminal fluid discharges." *Ipipisi momona* also refers to nocturnal orgasms, be they female or male, yet the act of ejaculation is described using the word *isulumomoni*—which means "the sexual fluid boils over."

Interestingly, the language of the Polynesian people of the Marquesas Islands uses different words to describe different aspects of orgasm, as well as attitudes. First of all they describe orgasm with the word *manini,* meaning literally sweet. However,

while *manini* refers mainly to the sensations of pleasure, release and well-being associated with orgasm, Marquesans also describe orgasm in terms of what happens to a person's genitals. This word for orgasm, *hakate'a,* translates literally as "make semen," i.e., ejaculate, but also possesses overtones of the aspects of *manini.* Neither of these orgasm terms are viewed as being suitable for polite usage—in such circumstances, *pao,* meaning finish, is substituted. This separation into *manini, hakate' a* and *pao* is, I feel, similar to English with orgasm, ejaculate and come. Somewhat worryingly, the influence of the sexual views of missionaries on the Marquesan people is evident in their rejigged sexual lexicon. In the southern group of the Marquesas archipelago, both *pe* (rotten) and *hau hau* (bad) are now used to depict orgasm. The phrase *ua pe nei au* translates, disconcertingly, as "I am rotten now; I have had an orgasm."

ORGASMS FOR ALL

The desire to describe, name, quantify, and, in doing so, understand orgasm is an age-old itch. Indeed, a multitude of minds—medical, moral, philosophical and just plain curious—have pondered on such questions as "What is an orgasm?"; "Why do orgasms exist?"; "Why do they feel so good?" and, crucially, for an understanding of the vagina, "What do they say about genitalia?" Ancient western medicine was no exception in this. "I must now tell why a great pleasure is coupled with the exercise of the generative parts and a raging desire precedes their use," says Greek physician Galen in *On the Usefulness of the Parts.* Galen, following the lead of Hippocrates, viewed orgasm as a signal of the release of an individual's procreative genital fluids—the seed or semen that they believed both women and men contributed to the conception of a child. That is, orgasm, in their minds, was the means by which genitalia shook forth both sexes' essential generative seed.

Within this two-seed model of conception (as it has come to be known), orgasm could be described as follows. It was associated with a great pleasure that was felt by both sexes and was intimately tied to successful sexual reproduction; both sexes typically emitted genital fluids; the pleasurable sensations felt were a result of both the qualities of the substance emitted, as well as its rapid propulsion; and the woman's womb both secreted her own fluids and then drew up and retained a mixture of her fluids and the male's. Critically, this theory viewed both female and male orgasm during sexual intercourse as essential for ensuring successful sexual reproduction. If female orgasm did not occur, a woman would not release her seed, and conception, therefore, could not take place. That is, this view saw both female and male genitalia, and female and male pleasure, having a meaningful role to play in procreation.

Not all early western philosophers of medicine agreed with Galen and Hippocrates' orgasmic views. Aristotle had distinctly different ideas about the nature of both female and male orgasm. Whereas the two-seed theory of conception tied the pleasure of orgasm and the emission of sexual fluids firmly together for both women and men, Aristotle's view of orgasm was completely dissociated from the explosive release of generative seed. Moreover, he underlined this view by refuting that orgasm was a signaller of ejaculation in either sex. For Aristotle, orgasm, or "the vehemence of pleasure in sexual intercourse," as he put it, was a result of "a strong friction wherefore if this intercourse is often repeated the pleasure is diminished in the persons concerned." Orgasm, for him, was not the sensation associated with emission of genital fluids.

In order to back up his "orgasm separate from seed" theory, Aristotle pointed to his observations that women could conceive without orgasm (although he stressed that this was the exception rather than the rule). And he also highlighted how orgasm was possible for both young boys and old men without the concomitant spurt of ejaculate. Significantly, Aristotle also commented on the changes that occurred in female genitalia during orgasm, noting that as a woman came her cervix acted as a "cupping vessel," seeming to serve to draw in semen. Aristotle suggested, rather astutely,

as we shall see, that "when this is so there is a readier way for the semen of the male to be drawn into the uterus." In his view then female orgasm may not be essential for conception, but it and the changes it wrought in the vagina could certainly improve the chances of conception occurring.

The musings of Aristotle on female and male orgasm were not, however, the ones that gained widespread acceptance in the western world. Rather, it was the Hippocratic idea that female orgasm was crucial for conception that remained in common currency up until and during the eighteenth century. For example, in 1745, French scientist Pierre de Maupertuis still felt confident enough to describe female orgasm in his work *The Earthy Venus* as "the pleasure which perpetuates mankind, that moment so rich in delight, which brings to life a new being."

FEMALE ORGASM IS ESSENTIAL FOR CONCEPTION

The theory that female orgasm is essential for conception to occur is, I believe, one of the most influential ideas in the history of the vagina and female sexual pleasure. This is because it had particularly far-reaching consequences for how western women and their genitalia were treated. For with female orgasm understood as a necessary part of the procreation equation, female sexual pleasure, and how to evoke it, could be viewed in a positive light. Religion could sanction female sexual pleasure and medics could advise on how best to bring about female orgasm because of its intimate connection to creation. The result: female sexual pleasure was deemed acceptable, moral even, by the most important authorities of the day—the church and science.

Delightfully, fertility advice from physicians emphasised the importance of ensuring that a woman's shudder of orgasm was felt during sexual intercourse. If "in the very coitional act itself, she notes a certain tremor...she is pregnant," Äetius of Amida, physician to the Byzantine emperor

Justinian, advised. Moreover, suggesting how best to stimulate a woman to this sexual bliss was also perceived as part of a medic's remit. Soranus' influential second-century medical text, *Gynaecology*, prescribes appropriate foods and massage as the prerequisite preludes to orgasm. He writes of tempting women with meals of aphrodisiacal foods "to give the inner turbulence an impetus towards coition," and of giving a massage, as it "naturally aids the distribution of food [and] also helps in the reception and retention of the seed." Such conception prescriptions were enduring, as the seventeenth-century recommendation of "sweet embraces with lascivious words mixed with lascivious kisses" shows. History also records the 1740s' story of the young Habsburg princess Maria Theresa, who found herself unable to conceive after her recent marriage. Her physician's advice was: "I think the vulva of Her Most Holy Majesty should be titillated before intercourse." This seems to have worked, as Maria Theresa went on to bear more than a dozen children.

The timing—and not just the occurrence—of female orgasm during sexual intercourse was seen as a crucial component of the two-seed theory of successful sexual reproduction. Hippocrates, like his later Greek fellow, Aristotle, noted changes in a woman's genitalia on orgasm. His interpretation was that a woman's womb contracted and closed up after its orgasmic ejaculation, barring entry to any male latecomers. And so the belief that simultaneous orgasm was necessary for conception was born. Rhythm and timing became all important. If a woman came before a man, she could not conceive because her uterus would already be drawn up and closed. If a man orgasmed before a woman, his sperm would douse and extinguish "both the heat and pleasure for woman." But if both sexes could come to orgasm together, Hippocrates envisaged, it is as if wine is sprinkled on a naked flame—the flames shoot higher, the heat of the woman's womb blazes most brilliantly, and post-mutual-orgasmic shiver, her womb seals. Success.

Over the centuries many opinions were offered as to what was the best way to ensure a woman came at the same time as a man. Certain times of the day or night were suggested to be better than others, aphrodisiacs could help, as could the right sexual technique. The medieval manuscript *Women's Secrets* advised how "After the middle of the night or before daybreak the male should begin to excite the woman to coitus. He should speak to her in a jesting manner, kiss and embrace her, and rub her lower parts with his fingers. All this should be done to arouse the woman's appetite for coitus so the male and the female seed will run together in the womb at the same time." And according to this anonymous male adviser: "When the woman begins to speak as if she were babbling the male ought to become erect and mix with her." The final piece of advice? A "sign of conception is if the man feels his penis drawn and sucked into the closure of the vulva."

The belief that changes in the structure of female genitalia at orgasm were an integral part of ensuring procreation meant that coital fertility advice was quite far-reaching. The sixteenth-century French surgeon Ambroise Paré counselled on the wisdom of not withdrawing from a woman too soon after her womb had opened from orgasm, "lest aire strike the open womb," he says, and cool the freshly sown warm seeds, thus harming conception. It seems that sex for women—if a man was aiming to procreate—may well have been more enjoyable than others have presumed. Sweet talk and kisses, good food and wine, a sensual massage, mutual orgasm and a long, close embrace afterwards. It sounds good to me.

But sadly for women, the notion that female and mutual orgasm was necessary for conception did not last. Aristotle's beliefs did not disappear entirely and rumours had been circulating the medical world for centuries that female orgasm was not a prognosticator of semination. In the twelfth century, Arabic philosopher and author of a major medical encyclopaedia Averroes reported on the case of a woman who got pregnant from semen floating in her bath water. The death knell sounded in the 1770s when Lazzaro Spallanzani successfully artificially inseminated a water spaniel. Dogs and other animals, at least, the theorists concluded, did not need to enjoy orgasm to conceive. As one doctor commented sagely and succinctly, syringes could not "communicate or meet with joy." And what about women and orgasm? Although it took a while longer for the equation of female orgasm with conception to be erased from public consciousness, by the start of the nineteenth century, medical opinion was reaching a consensus. Human female orgasm was not necessary for successful sexual reproduction. What a come-down.

Some entrepreneurial spirits discovered the truth about orgasm and contraception for themselves. Mabel Loomis Todd was one such person. This nineteenth-century American woman, who later became the lover of poet Emily Dickinson's brother, kept a deliciously explicit diary of her sex life, her menstrual cycle, her orgasms (noting them all, including masturbation) and more. May 15, 1879, "barely eight days over my illness [period]," is the day she chose to put her beliefs about orgasm to the test. "With me," she writes, "the only fruitful time could be at the climax moment of my sensation—that once passed, I believed the womb would close, & no fluid could reach the fruitful point."

And so she proceeded to test this idea out by having sex with her husband and deliberately coming before he did. As she put it: "Not at all from uncontrollable passion, but merely from the strongest conviction of the truth of my idea, I allowed myself to receive the precious fluid, at least six or eight moments after my highest point of enjoyment had passed, and when I was perfectly cool & satisfied, getting up immediately, thereafter, and having it all apparently escape." The result of Mabel's home fecundation experiment—her only child, Millicent.

ORGASMS FOR HEALTH—THE MAKINGS OF AN ORGASM INDUSTRY

Despite the severing in the eighteenth and nineteenth centuries of a link between female orgasm and conception, one strand of the original two-seed theory remained as part of medical practice. It even flourished as the nineteenth century became the twentieth, evolving into a major part of medical practice. This portion of the two-seed theory

was the idea that female orgasm was necessary to maintain a woman's health. As Hippocrates perceived it, orgasm was essential in releasing both sexes' retained seed. However, if this seed was not expelled regularly via orgasm shaking it out, ill health would result from the build-up of seed and subsequent imbalance of bodily fluids. As the medieval manuscript the *Trotula,* in *Treatments for Women,* states: "Women, when they have immoderate desire to have intercourse and they do not do so, if they do not satiate the desire they incur grave suffering." As we shall see, though, this conclusion that female orgasms were necessary in order to maintain physical and mental health had major repercussions for how women, and the diseases attributed to them, were treated by the medical profession.

From Galen's time onwards (129–200 ce), medical texts record, in great detail, how manipulation to orgasm was the standard medical treatment for these non-specific "women's diseases." This was because these ailments, which were variously called "suffocation of the womb"; *suffocatio matricis* ("suffocation of the mother"), and hysteria (literally, womb disease), were believed to stem from the uterus becoming engorged with unexpended seed, and so wandering the body, in search of release. Orgasm was one of the chosen methods of effecting the release, although the prescription for how orgasm was brought about varied. Over the centuries, the methods physicians prescribed to induce orgasm in so-called hysterical women included advocating being "strongly encountered by their husbands" if they had one. Alternatively, if a woman was single, widowed or confined to a nunnery, the recommendation could be horseriding, pelvic rocking in swings, chairs or hammocks, or vaginal massage— the latter to be provided by the patient's physician or midwife.

Over the centuries it was practised, vaginal or vulval massage to orgasm became just another skill that male physicians and midwives must perfect for the benefit of their patients. Galen advised how to rub a woman's genitalia until she felt the "pain and at the same time the pleasure" associated with intercourse—and had emitted a quantity of thick seed. Not surprisingly, different approaches to providing the orgasmic conclusion were suggested. The method Giovanni Matteo Ferrari da Gradi (d. 1472) prescribed was to rub the woman's chest and cover it with large cupping glasses, after which "the midwife would be instructed to use sweet-smelling oil on her finger and move it well in a circle inside the vulva." A successful treatment, according to da Gradi, was when the woman experienced *"simul…delectatio & dolor,"* that is, pleasure and pain at the same time, another description of orgasm that contains echoes of St. Teresa's ecstasy.

Many male medics felt it necessary to ask women to help them in their exertions. In his influential early-seventeenth-century medical compendium, Dutch physician Pieter van Foreest recommends to medics confronted with a case of *suffocatio ex semine retento* (suffocation because of retained seed): "we think it necessary to ask a midwife to assist, so that she can massage the genitalia with one finger inside, using oil of lilies, musk root, crocus, or [something] similar. And in this way the afflicted woman can be aroused to the paroxysm."

As well as providing descriptions of orgasm, the many discussions of medical vaginal massage provide a rare, intimate and surprising insight into how the vagina was viewed and treated in the last two millennia. Using pleasant or aphrodisiacal aromas seems to have been common, as was applying a particular type of stimulation. In the following case, the recommendation appears to be to stimulate the cervix: "Let the mydwife anoint her fingers with…spike mixed with musk, ambergreese, civet and other sweet powders, and with these let her rub or tickle the top of the neck of the wombe which toucheth the inner orifice."

Significantly, some accounts touch on what physical effect their actions had on female genitalia, as well as the technique they applied. Äetius of Amida (502–75) describes the moment of orgasmic release as characterised by uterine contractions, muscular spasms throughout the entire body, and the secretion of vaginal fluids. Rhazes, the tenth-century Arabic author of a practical textbook of medicine, details how, when the mouth of the womb is rubbed

with a well-oiled finger, there is the sensation "as if something is pulled up."

It's important to note, though, that not all doctors were comfortable with providing vulval massage to orgasm for health—from both a moral and practical perspective. The word orgasm is noticeably absent from the majority of descriptions of genital massage, with most orgasm-providing medics preferring to talk about relieving the "hysterical paroxysms" of women. In 1883, the French physician Auguste Tripier would only admit that what was known as the convulsive crisis of hysteria *"est de même quelquefois que la crise vénérienne"*—"is sometimes the same as the orgasm."

One of the few physicians to refer, in print, to the type of relief his profession was routinely providing was Nathaniel Highmore. In his 1660 manuscript *De Passione Hysterica et Affectione Hypochondriaca* he uses the word *orgasmum,* which can only mean one thing in Latin. Highmore also detailed how blood rushed to a woman's genitals during arousal and how the contractions of orgasm seemed to return that blood to the rest of the body. This seventeenth-century doctor was also more direct (and humorous) than most in describing the skill required to effect orgasm via vaginal massage, commenting: "it is not unlike that game of boys in which they try to rub their stomachs with one hand and pat their heads with the other." Nearly two and a half centuries later, in 1906, fellow physician Samuel Spencer Wallian was bemoaning not just the expertise called for, but the time taken up too. Manual massage, he complains, "consumes a painstaking hour to accomplish much less profound results than are easily effected by the *other* in a short five or ten minutes."

"AIDS THAT EVERY WOMAN APPRECIATES"

The *other* in question was the latest tool of the medical profession—the vibrator. Vibration therapy, as detailed beautifully in Rachel Maines' book *The Technology of Orgasm: "Hysteria," the Vibrator and Women's Sexual Satisfaction,* was the answer to all tired medics' prayers. Whether steam-powered, water-propelled, foot-operated or, from 1883 onwards, thanks to English doctor and inventor Joseph Mortimer Granville, electromechanical, vibrators provided much-needed relief for physicians and their patients. Female orgasms could now be provided at the flick of a switch. Business, it seemed, boomed. In 1873, it was estimated that in the U.S. "more than three-fourths of all the practice of the [medical] profession are devoted to the treatment of diseases peculiar to women," with the annual estimated aggregate income which "physicians must thank frail women for" totalling around $150 million. This is not surprising, considering vulval massage to orgasm was by the end of the nineteenth century a staple medical practice, with some doctors recommending women come in for "treatments" on a weekly basis. A lucrative outcome indeed.

The difference that the electromechanical vibrator made to the medical profession's treatment of "hysterical" women was summed up in 1903 in a book by Dr. Samuel Howard Monell discussing medical uses of vibration. "Pelvic massage (in gynaecology)," he wrote, "has its brilliant advocates and they report wonderful results, but when practitioners must supply the skilled technic with their own fingers the method has no value to the majority." However, he adds, "Special applicators (motor driven) give practical value and office convenience to what otherwise is impractical."

Vibrators took off at home, as well as in the doctor's surgery. In the U.S. in the 1890s, women could purchase a $5 portable vibrator—"perfect for weekend trips," ran the advertisement—rather than paying at least $2 a pop for a visit to the physician. Delightfully, the vibrator was the fifth household appliance to be electrified, after the sewing machine, fan, kettle and toaster. And as vibrators became available for home use, the ancient art of physician-prescribed vaginal massage to orgasm slowly became defunct. Male medical hands were increasingly freed to perform other healing tasks. Unfortunately, it's not known precisely how many late-nineteenth-century and early-twentieth-century home vibration kits were sold; however, they were certainly popular enough to feature in many mail-order magazines in the U.S., the U.K., and Canada up until the 1920s.

The pages of the magazine *Modern Priscilla,* in April 1913, sold vibrators with the promise of "a machine that gives 30,000 thrilling, invigorating, penetrating, revitalizing vibrations per minute." Not surprisingly, perhaps, vibrator advertisements (whether directed at doctors or women), did not mention orgasms or sexual pleasure, just the "health benefits" of vibration. An 1883 text entitled *Health for Women* recommends vibrators as they can treat "pelvic hyperemia"—congestion of the genitalia. Quite why vibrators fell from medical and public grace and use during the first half of the twentieth century is also unclear, although it has been suggested that their exposure in the early erotic films of the 1920s may have changed medical and public opinion as to their "health" role and highlighted their sexual one. And sadly, the morals of the day were not in favour of females sexually pleasuring themselves

Ironically, the orgasm industry in the west was thriving in a time when many medics and men felt confident enough to put forward, and publish, the notion that women were passionless creatures, not much troubled by sexual feelings. While some male doctors were charging women for orgasm provided by them on health grounds, others were promulgating the view that women that did have sexual feelings were mad, bad, dangerous and abnormal. In 1896, Richard von Krafft-Ebing, in *Psychopathia Sexualis,* famously said, "Woman, however, when physically and mentally normal and properly educated, has but little sensual desire." He adds that "if it were otherwise marriage and family life would be empty words," a sentiment that seems to express a fear of what would happen to society if women gave free rein to their sexuality.

The following are just a few comments from other male doctors in this particularly hypocritical period in medicine's history.

Women have less sexual feeling than men...as a rule women have nothing of what is understood as sexual passion. (Charles Taylor, 1882)

The appearance of the sexual side in the love of a young girl is pathological . . . half of all women are not sexually excitable. (Hermann Fehling, 1893)

Only in very rare circumstances do women experience one tithe the sexual feeling which is familiar to most men. Many of them are entirely frigid. (Nineteenth-century American physician George Napheys)

Meanwhile, writing in 1871, British doctor William Acton did not deny that some women were capable of being aroused; however, he suggested that they were "sad exceptions," and on a fast track to a "form of insanity that those who visit lunatic asylums must be fully conversant with."

MEDICAL MASSAGE GOOD, WOMEN MASTURBATING BAD

Equally astonishingly and outrageously, while male doctors were manipulating women to orgasm in their surgeries and charging them for it, other male physicians were publishing papers on the problems of female doing it for themselves—manually or mechanically. "The Neuropsychical Element in Conjugal Aversion," that is, why women say no to sex with their husbands, is the title of an article published in 1892 in the *Journal of Nervous and Mental Disease.* This paper suggested that a common "source of marital aversion seems to lie in the fact that substitution of mechanical and iniquitous excitations [vibrators and masturbation] affords more satisfaction that the mutual legitimate ones do."

Other medical journals published articles detailing ways in which male doctors could spot if their female patients were suffering from the "masturbatory disease." "Signs of Masturbation in the Female," by E. H. Smith in *The Pacific Medical Journal* of 1903, is essentially a guide for doctors on how to detect if women have been masturbating. One sign, according to E. H. Smith, was one labium being longer than the other. Other signs of masturbation were that women were more sexually sensitive than they should be. Horrifically, to figure out whether a woman was more sexually sensitive than she should

be, the medical journal advocated sending a "mild faradic current," i.e. an electric shock, through the urethra.

It seems that western women couldn't win—they were either inferior to men because they were lacking in sexual feeling, or abnormal because they enjoyed and displayed their feelings of sexual pleasure. Many doctors appear to have been very confused. The late-nineteenth-century gynaecologist Otto Adler wrote that up to 40 percent of women suffered from sexual anaesthesia. However, the women who made up this "sexually anaesthetic" category included women who said they did masturbate to orgasm; women who said they had strong sexual desires (although they were unable to satisfy them); and a woman who was reported to have had an orgasm as she was being examined by the doctor. Adler's categorisation of what constituted sexual anaesthesia in women seems peculiar indeed, and not particularly robust. Meanwhile the 1899 edition of the reference guide for physicians, the *Merck Manual,* on one page recommended massage as a treatment for hysteria, while on another it suggested sulphuric acid as a remedy for nymphomania. This brings to mind the barbaric idea of pouring carbolic acid on the clitoris as a "cure" for female masturbation.

This state of confusion in the medical world as to how to understand female orgasm and sexual pleasure is, in part, perhaps explained by the differing messages being received from the authorities of the day. On the one hand, science said female orgasm had no role to play in sexual reproduction, therefore in the eyes of moral and church-going men, sexual pleasure could not be sanctioned in women, as it did not lead directly to procreation. However, on the other hand, science was still teaching (at least up to the end of the nineteenth century) that female orgasm was necessary for health—surely medical ethics demanded doctors do their job? Ultimately, though, just as with the clitoris, the loss of an obvious and immediate role in ensuring successful sexual reproduction meant that it was possible for the medical and scientific community to ignore the troublesome concept of the female orgasm. And in the main, they did, despite having recently routinely provided female orgasms on health grounds....

THE ELIXIR OF LIFE

Before looking at what science today has to say about female orgasm and its connection with female genitalia, what about outside the Christian western world? How is orgasm understood elsewhere? Moreover, do views of female orgasm differ in cultures where sex is viewed as sacred? Fascinating, eastern belief systems, such as Taoism, which developed in China, and Tantra, from northern India, also viewed female orgasm as essential for health. First Tantrism. Orgasm in Tantric terms is understood as a resolution of two forces—call them expansion and contraction, or female and male—which results in cosmic harmony. Tantra, which teaches that Buddhahood, some say nirvana, resides in the vagina, places great emphasis on *maithuna*—a Tantric sex rite. During *maithuna,* which is often called *yoni-puja* (worship of the vagina), a man's goal is to feed or fuel himself off the woman's sexual/spiritual energy. In this way, it is said he can revitalise himself and achieve longevity. There's one sticking point though. Having sex is not enough. Successful sexual vampirism is only accomplished by ensuring the woman has an orgasm (and that the man does not ejaculate his semen).

There is also another reason why Tantrism perceives female orgasm to be essential. This stems from the idea that it is orgasm that releases a woman's *rajas*—her vivifying vaginal secretions. Indeed, in some Tantric schools, the main aim of *maithuna* is the production and collection of the woman's *rajas,* which the man will then ingest. Somewhat peculiarly, this can be done by collecting the vaginal juices on a leaf, mixing them with a little water and then drinking the genital cocktail. Or, if a man has truly mastered his Tantric sexual techniques, he can enhance his hormonal system by absorbing the *rajas* directly through his penis—a practice known as *vajroli-mudra.*

Female orgasm is also considered to have benefits for health and a long life within Taoism, which

was founded by the sixth-century bce prophet Lao Tzu. In fact, Taoism teaches that sex is seen as one of the prime ways to come closer to the Tao, that is, ultimate reality, energy, movement and constant change, where the polar opposites of yin (female) and yang (male) are balanced and harmonious, continually uniting and metamorphosing into each other. Indeed, the basic principle of traditional Chinese philosophy says that "the interaction of the female essence [yin] with the male essence [yang] is the Way of Life [Tao]." Moreover, as Taoist sexual lore teaches that death is caused by the imbalance of yin and yang, sex is seen as a major force for rebalancing the body and thus cheating death.

For men, the way to garner longevity sexually is by the process of gathering and absorbing essential yin essence (*cai Yin pu Yang*), while withholding their own ejaculation. And just as in Tantric thought, this female elixir (known as *khuai*) is only produced when a woman has an orgasm. However, there is a slight twist. According to the Taoist sex manual *A Popular Exposition of the Methods of Regenerating the Primary Vitalities,* this life-giving essence can be supped from three places: a woman's mouth, her breasts and her vagina—hence it's called The Great Medicine of the Three Peaks. Regarding the vaginal juices, the manual states that it "is called the Peak of the Purple Agaric, also the Grotto of the White Tiger, or the Mysterious Gateway. Its medicine is called Black Lead, or Moon Flower. It is in the vagina. Usually it does not flow out....Only the man who can control his passion and sexual excitement in coitus can obtain this medicine and achieve longevity."

But what about women? Their orgasms may benefit men, but are orgasms good for female health as well? Well, in Taoist thought, the answer is a resounding and emphatic yes. In fact, in Taoism women seem to have a remarkable win–win situation. Not only are they understood to gain in energy and longevity from their own orgasms, but they can also nourish themselves by gathering a man's essence too (*cai Yang pu Yin*). In contrast, men can only gain from women's orgasms, not their own. Women, it is said, gain longevity via orgasm by allowing their sexual or creative energy (symbolised as the Kundalini serpent) to rise from the vagina, up the spine and to the brain. This type of nourishing whole body orgasm (where altered levels of consciousness are reached) is understood as a moment of union with the supreme Tao, or universe, and is called an "orgasm of the valley." Women are taught that they can help themselves to experience these profound and consciousness-altering orgasms by developing an awareness of and connection with their genital musculature (both vaginal and uterine).

WHO HAS THE BEST ORGASM?

Curiously, eastern and western theories of female orgasm have something else in common—other than considering it a health boon. This sharing of ideas surrounds a question that we've all asked ourselves at one time or another—namely, who has the best orgasm, or greatest pleasure during sex? The answer it seems is unanimous—women do. Tellingly, it is a general belief in Greek mythology, Hinduism, Islam, Taoism, Christianity and western medicine that women enjoy greater pleasure during sexual activity. Within Taoist thought, this belief is expressed in the idea of a woman's yin energy being like water, or k'an, vast and inexhaustible, and very slow to cool, whereas a man's yang energy is like fire, or li, volatile and flaring up quickly, but easily spent and extinguished. Taoism also explains that it is easier for women to draw sexual orgasmic energy up from their genitals as their energy is on balance more yin. That is, as they are more focused inwards, they have a greater ability to be in touch with their internal sensations, hence their greater orgasmic capacity.

The idea that women have greater sexual pleasure is recorded in Greek mythology in the story of Teiresias, a man who was famous for having spent seven years of his life as a woman, during which time he became a celebrated courtesan. Because of his sexual experiences as both a woman and a man, Teiresias was one day called by the Greek god Zeus to settle a dispute between Zeus and his wife, Hera.

The married couple were arguing over who enjoyed the greatest pleasure, or the better orgasm (*major voluptas*) during sex. Teiresias' answer was simple:

> If the parts of love-pleasure be counted as ten,
> Thrice three go to women, one only to men.

The tale of Teiresias and his championing of women's greater enjoyment of the pleasures of the flesh is echoed, almost uncannily, in many cultures. Very similar words and numbers are attributed to Ali ibn Abu Taleb, who was the husband of the Muslim prophet Muhammad's daughter, Fatima, and also the founder of the Shiite sect of Islam. According to him: "Almighty God created sexual desire in ten parts; Then he gave nine parts to women and one to men."

The legend of Bhangasvana, recorded in the Hindu saga the *Mahabharata,* contains many elements of Teiresias' myth too. Bhangasvana is a powerful king, a tiger among men, but he angers the god Indra, who punishes him by turning him into a woman. As a woman, Bhangasvana cannot rule his kingdom and is forced to live as a hermit. Years later, when Indra forgives the ex-king, the god grants Bhangasvana the choice of becoming a man once more, or remaining as a woman. Bhangasvana's reply? "The woman has in union with man always the greater joy, that is why...I choose to be a woman. I feel greater pleasure in love as a woman, that is the truth, best among the gods. I am content with existence as a woman."

Other Indian stories, including the companion epic the *Ramayana,* convey similar messages—women are capable of enjoying sex more than men, they are more sexual, and are insatiable sexually. Entertainingly, one Indian proverb tells how woman's power in eating is twice as great as a man's, her cunning or bashfulness four times as great, her decisions or boldness six times as great, and her impetuosity or delight in love eight times as great. Going back to the third century bce, the text of the Old Testament both recognises the voluptuousness of the vagina and warns against it with the following lines: "There are three things that are never sated...Hell, the mouth of the vulva, and the earth."

DOUBLE PLEASURE EQUALS DOUBLE TROUBLE?

Why did all these different civilisations consider women's sexual pleasure or orgasmic capacity to be so much greater than men's? Well, western medicine, with its emphasis on analysis, made a brave attempt to explain why this should be. In fact, the question appears to have aroused the minds of many men of science, causing great consternation and, perhaps, a little envy and fear. *On Coitus,* a medical treatise written by Constantine the African, an eleventh-century doctor (and possibly the west's first sexologist), suggests that "Pleasure in intercourse is greater in women than in males, since males derive pleasure only from the expulsion of a superfluity. Women experience twofold pleasure: both by expelling their own sperm and by receiving the male's sperm, from the desire of their fervent vulva." In other words—women experience double the pleasure as a result of the thrill of both receiving warming male seed and emitting their own.

This idea of women's double pleasure is a frequent theme in western medicine, in particular from advocates of the two-seed theory of orgasm and conception (both women and men ejaculate semen). However, even those medical minds that insisted only men emitted seed during sex stated that women's sexual joy was the greater. According to medieval medic Albertus Magnus, a proponent of the one-seed theory, this greater delight came from "the touch either of the man's sperm in the womb or of the penis against her sexual part." Avicenna, on the other hand, upped the stakes and suggested that woman's sexual pleasure was threefold. Women, Avicenna claimed, have "three delights in intercourse: one from the motion of her own sperm, a second from the motion of the male sperm, and a third from the motion or rubbing that takes place in coitus."

SEXUAL VAMPIRISM

Sadly for women, the hints of sexual vampirism that are found in the east's beliefs about female orgasm are also present in western ones—with a twist. It was not unusual for male medics to write of how women, via their vaginas, could feed sexually off men. For example, sixteenth-century physician Lemnius, writing of woman's greater sexual excitement, describes not only how "she draws forth the man's seed and casts her own with it," but also how she "takes more delight and is more recreated by it." But in this sex-negative society, where sex was sanctioned only for procreative purposes, men got indignant about being used in this way. It appears that the idea that women have a greater capacity for sexual pleasure seems to have been more threatening than welcoming.

Not surprisingly, perhaps, vampiric associations were made clear. Women, it was said, could use sex to "suck the vigour of their menfolk, like the vampire." Today, of course, it is always women that are vamps, never men. And, indeed, the definition of a vamp is a woman who exploits a man. The idea of women as sexually insatiable and vampiric is also very much to the fore in the earlier medieval medical compendium *De Secretis Mulierum* (*Women's Secrets*), which was still popular in the eighteenth century. Written to instruct celibate monks on the facts of life, *Women's Secrets* warns that:

> The more women have sexual intercourse, the stronger they become, because they are made hot by the motion that the man makes during coitus. Further, male sperm is hot because it is of the same nature as air and when it is received by the woman it warms her entire body, so women are strengthened by this heat. On the other hand, men who have sex frequently are weakened by this act because they become exceedingly dried out.

However, *Women's Secrets* is a deeply misogynistic text, with a very strong subtext extolling the evil nature of women. Significantly, it added a very negative flavour to the western medical world's notions of women's greater, boundless sexual pleasure. Woman, the treatise warns, has "a greater desire for coitus than a man, for something foul is drawn to the good." Furthermore, it states, "one should beware of every woman as one would avoid a venomous serpent and a horned devil, for if it were right to say what I know about women, the whole world would be astounded."

Indeed, it is argued that this text on women and the workings of their genitalia directly influenced the *Malleus Maleficarum,* the fifteenth-century inquisitorial treatise on witches, which includes the memorable maligning line: "All witchcraft comes from carnal lust, which is in women insatiable."

THE PLEASURE PRINCIPLE

I would like to finish this book with a comment on a person's capacity for genital pleasure and orgasm. Everyone begins their life with an infinite capacity to experience and enjoy pleasure. This is as true of genitally focused pleasure as it is of any other source. Foetuses orgasming in the womb underline this. Significantly, though, it is increasingly recognised that how an individual responds to sexual pleasure (or any kind of pleasure) during their life is a mixture of both the physical processes the body is undergoing, and a completely subjective perception of what those processes represent. That is, a person's perception of sexual pleasure can be as contingent on their past experiences of genital pleasure (or lack of pleasure), and the rules and values their society promotes, as it is on the sea of chemicals that arousal and orgasm send coursing through their bloodstream.

First of all, how experience influences the enjoyment of genital pleasure. A lifetime, or merely a childhood, of being told to ignore genital sensations, or, on the other hand, never having anyone in "authority" explain that genital pleasure is to be valued, can and does have a blunting effect on how an individual responds to the build-up and release of genital/sexual sensations in their body. For some lucky individuals, these sensations are taught as ones to be valued and are therefore rated as pleasurable; for others, their previous experiences teach them to ignore or suppress these stimuli or label them negatively. How subjective the perception of pleasure can be is illustrated by people's responses to orgasm. Some descriptions of orgasm talk of the sensation as being frightening; others speak of it being the most exciting, fulfilling and enjoyable sensation imaginable. The flood of chemicals may be the same, but

the emotional response to that rush differs depending on a person's history.

The brain is, in fact, an amazingly powerful sexual organ, perhaps the most powerful, and is supremely capable of overriding sexual signals, if a person's past has taught them that it may be "safer" or "better" to do so. Indeed, studies have shown that the physical effects of female arousal and orgasm can be "overlooked" or ignored. And ignoring or suppressing feelings of genital arousal is, it's suggested, easier for women to do, as they do not have an obvious visual sign of arousal to underline or emphasise how their body is actually feeling. Men, on the other hand, have in their erect penises a very handy feedback device, reminding them of how they feel, and making it a lot harder to "ignore" genital sensations.

Secondly, society's role in valuing genital pleasure and orgasm. In the western world and the majority of societies, knowledge about genitalia and sexual pleasure has, until very recently, been shrouded under layers of religious and scientific ideology, much of it misleading or damaging. This is particularly true when it comes to discussions about female genitalia and female sexual pleasure. For these reasons, I don't find it particularly surprising that not all women enjoy their vaginas as much as they could. Anthropological evidence contrasting different cultures' attitudes towards information about sex and genital pleasure have revealed over and over again striking variations in orgasmic response. In societies where little or no sex education is given, and sex is decreed to be for procreation not pleasure, female orgasm and sexual pleasure can be relatively unknown. Yet, in those societies where women and men are taught from an early age to appreciate their own, and each other's, genitalia, as well as the pleasure genitals give, orgasm is achieved virtually universally and without difficulty for both sexes.

In 1948, the anthropologist Margaret Mead, after observing several Pacific Island societies, made some remarkably astute observations on the cultural factors that affect a woman's capacity to experience sexual pleasure and orgasms (they also apply to men). Mead wrote that in order for a female to find sexual fulfilment:

1. She must live in a culture that recognises female desire as being of value.
2. Her culture must allow her to understand the mechanics of her sexual anatomy.
3. Her culture must teach the various sexual skills that can make women experience orgasm.

Fortunately for women (and men) the three tenets of this vital sex education message are starting to come across in the west, albeit slowly. Unbiased information about female genitalia and their role in sexual pleasure and reproduction is increasingly available, and the vagina is beginning to be viewed as valuable, from both a scientific and a cultural perspective—just as mythology tells us it should be. Unlike the sixteenth-century St. Teresa, women can, and do, rejoice in their genitals and the pleasure they bring, as the following twentieth-century description of female orgasm shows: "Without any effort or trying on my part, my body was moved from within, so to speak, and everything was right. There was rhythmic movement and a feeling of ecstasy at being part of something much greater than myself and finally of reward, of real satisfaction and peace." Pride, pleasure and the miracle of creation—this view of the vagina is the real story of V.

---

25 • *Shelly A. McGrath and Ruth A. Chananie-Hill*

"BIG FREAKY-LOOKING WOMEN"
Normalizing Gender Transgression through Bodybuilding

DISCUSSION QUESTIONS

1. What is the central "contradiction" faced by women bodybuilders?
2. How do the women in this study attempt to resolve this contradiction? How do their experiences differ based on race and class?
3. Do you think women active in other sports face similar contradictions?
4. What other factors do you think might impact the pressures women athletes face to maintain their femininity?

> I think femininity exists on a continuum and I think that society can accept women I would say like one or two standard deviations from the normal curve, but those who are the outliers, when you get closer to the plus three and you are kind of skewing stuff—I think that is when it becomes a problem. (Carla)

Shelly A. McGrath and Ruth A. Chananie-Hill, "'Big Freaky-Looking Women': Normalizing Gender Transgression through Bodybuilding." *Sociology of Sport Journal* 26:235–254. © 2009 *Human Kinetics Journals*. Reprinted with permission of the publisher.

Do hypermuscular women transgress normative gender boundaries, or do they merely reinforce the current gender order? The answer depends upon who you ask, although the most recent scholarly works on women's bodybuilding and other sports involving visible female muscle tend to agree that they do both (Boyle, 2005; Brace-Govan, 2004; George, 2005; Grogan, Evans, Wright, & Hunter, 2004; Krane, Choi, Baird, Aimar, & Kauer, 2004; Schippert, 2007). Both question and answer are slippery and resist definitive analysis, as do other social issues requiring "both/and" discourses rather than "either/or" binaries (Hill Collins, 2000). Contemporary feminist and postmodern theorists continue to examine the gendered, sexed, and raced complexities, confusions, and contradictions of the lived experience of female athletes often labeled as "muscular" in popular discourse.

In this paper, we investigate the extent to which female bodybuilders intend to subvert cultural gender norms, and the effects such transgressions have on their everyday worlds. Through participant observation and interviews with ten amateur female bodybuilders attending a university in the Midwestern U.S., we explore this question and the intersection of transgression and complicity with cultural conceptions of sex, gender, race, and sexual preference. As authors, our view is one of pragmatic optimism—we acknowledge limits on female bodybuilding's subversive potential, but we also seek greater insights into the mechanisms of its transformative power.

TRANSGRESSING GENDER NORMS

…Despite increased empowerment, the prominent theme of female bodybuilders' experience is one of contradiction, often leading to attempts to "balance" popular notions of femininity and muscularity. Critical feminists, postmodernists, and sport sociologists describe how female bodybuilders balance contradictory demands of muscular development versus expectations of normative femininity. These include regulating muscular size to avoid being labeled as "too big," "mannish," or lesbian (Bolin, 1992; Boyle, 2005; Grogan et al., 2004; Lowe, 1998; Monaghan et al., 1998; Wesely, 2001); using body technologies such as breast enlargements, plastic surgeries, and feminizing hairstyles, outfits, and accessories to counteract "masculinizing" effects of steroid use or loss of breast tissue (Bolin, 1992; Lowe, 1998; Shea, 2001; Schippert, 2007; Wesely, 2001; Williams, 2000); and emphasizing heterosexual desirability by posing for erotic photo spreads or performing choreographed heterosexy routines during competition (Boyle, 2005; Choi, 2000; Heywood, 1998; Ryan, 2001).

Many laypeople perceive hypermuscular women as possessing more "masculine" personality characteristics (Ryckman, Dill, Dyer, Sanborn, & Gold, 1992), and as more likely to have an "ambiguous sexual orientation" than other women (Forbes, Adams-Curtis, Holmgren, & White, 2004, p. 499). As Halberstam (1998) asserts, female masculinity (such as large musculature) clearly equates with lesbianism, while female femininity assumes heterosexuality. Although critical feminist theorists argue persuasively that sex, gender, and sexuality should not be conflated (Lorber, 1996; West & Zimmerman, 1987), other scholars point out that this is still the case in the context of female bodybuilding (Boyle, 2005; Fisher, 1997; Schippert, 2007; Schulze, 1997; Wesely, 2001; Williams, 2000). However, as Cahn (1994b) maintains, this is a fairly recent development. Early in U.S. women's sporting history, "mannish" female athletes were not viewed as particularly threatening and/or were believed to be "over-eager" heterosexuals. The increased sexual freedom for men and women and the rise of a sexualized economy in the 1930s influenced the conflation of gender and sexual preference.

In addition to gendered expectations, class and race affect social constructions of female bodybuilders. Boyle (2005) explains that white, heterosexual middle-class expectations of feminine sexual morality shape stage routines, such that competitors who pose in sexually overt positions are considered too "low class" for what is defined as a "family affair" (p. 145). However, middle-class respectability on stage is often undercut by oversexualized media images (Boyle, 2005). Although "tan"—not white—is the ideal skin color for most competitors, darker skin tones and other "ethnic" features remain a liability in bodybuilding (Williams, 2000). As Cahn (1994a) writes, "African American women's work history as slaves, tenant farmers, domestics, and wageworkers constructed them as more 'animalistic' and disqualified them from white middle class standards of femininity" (p. 127). Contemporary social perceptions of black bodybuilders as more "masculine" reflect historical constructions of race (Boyle, 2005; Williams, 2000) as do media portrayals of black, Asian, Native American, and Latina bodybuilders as sexually "exotic" (Heywood, 1998).

Perceived sexual preference intersects with race and ethnicity. Visibly muscular female athletes of color are more likely to be labeled "mannish" or lesbian and less likely to gain positive media attention (Boyle, 2005; Cahn, 1994a; Holmlund, 1994; Patton, 2001; Williams, 2000) unless they follow the "heterosexual imperative" (Griffin, 1998). As Williams (2000) discusses, black female sexuality is often conflated with lesbianism because of the so-called sexual excesses assigned to both lesbians and black women by the early scientific community. The success of black women in bodybuilding offers a positive model of strong, black femininity. Yet these women also work extra hard to obtain the "hyperfeminine" look of "done hair" and use feminizing accessories to subvert the "gender and sexuality confusion among the general public" (Williams, 2000, p. 109). Williams argues, "If the questioning begins with gender, it inevitably segues to sexuality" (p. 109)....

The line may not be as clear as many may assume. First, there is a common misconception that women cannot "naturally" develop large muscles without the use of drugs. This belief is often accompanied by a paradoxical fear that lifting heavy weights will make women "huge." These contradictory notions are reflected in fitness magazines (Aoki, 1996; Schulze, 1997), general gym settings (Dworkin, 2001; Markula, 1995), bodybuilding and weightlifting subcultures (Brace-Govan, 2004; Heywood,

1998; Lowe, 1998), and other female sport participation (George, 2005; Krane et al., 2004). Wesely (2001) argues that steroid use and other body technologies should be viewed as a continuum between "natural" and "unnatural." She points out that the gender line between men and women is negotiable and changes over time and within contexts. In sum, "[female] muscles clearly have meaning, but exactly what they mean and how they are valued is not agreed upon even among feminists" (St. Martin & Gavey, 1996, p. 47).

There is very little agreement in extant literature on the cultural meaning of stereotypical gender attributions or in what ways their usage is connected to meanings given to homosexuality. There are numerous anecdotes in the studies about how hypermuscular women are "trying to look like men" (Wesely, 2001, p. 173), or cross the line into "irretrievably male" (Schulze, 1997, p. 26) or look "identical" to a man (Choi, 2000, p. 60), which prompt reactions from (mostly) men such as "I wouldn't mess with you" (Grogan et al., 2004, p. 54). Despite these generalizations, few scholars explore the curious fact that most female bodybuilders are not actually believed to be men. Audience members generally do not perceive female bodybuilders as (literally) male-to-female transsexuals, although they have occasionally been compared with "transvestites" or "drag queens." Perhaps this is an attempt to point out some "failed" attempt at "passing" as a natural woman (Aoki, 1996; Roussel & Griffet, 2000; Schulze, 1997). Like drag queens, female bodybuilders are sometimes perceived as engaging in somatic practices that "mimic and almost exaggerate the traditional requirements of femininity" (St. Martin & Gavey, 1996, p. 55). However, as Aoki (1996) asserts, it is more accurate to say she looks "*something like* a man," which also means she looks something like a woman: "Then the female bodybuilder looks like a woman who fails to look like a man who fails to look like a woman; she is performing a failed impersonation of a failed impersonation" (p. 61–64, emphasis his). But she does not look exactly like a man in drag, either, since she is often read as a "woman wearing a man's body," which Aoki (1996) argues is "much more disturbing" to mainstream audiences (p. 70).

Thus, while Ian (2001) argues that the most muscular women do not "win" bodybuilding contests, Aoki (1996) counters that those who do win are often perceived as somatically disturbing as (failed) attempts to "completely codify the un-mainstream body" (p. 65), and are therefore transgressive—because to some, they look more like men than many men do. This conclusion reaffirms Kane's (1995) conception of sport performance as a continuum, where "many women routinely outperform many men" (p. 193), and supports Schippert's (2007) interpretation of female muscle as having queer "slippage" potential (p. 167). In our data analysis, we explore these themes and draw upon participants' voices to connect notions of gender transgression through purposeful rebellion with patterns of gender attribution in female bodybuilding....

FINDINGS

...In this analysis, we explore a synthesis of previously discussed patterns in the data and an elaboration of insufficiently explored ideas, which we refer to as: gender rebellion, somatic normalization, racialized bodies, and gender attribution. These "categories" provide ease of analysis, and should not be interpreted as discrete experiences in female bodybuilders' lives. In short, we recognize that bodybuilders' lived experience tends to be "ideologically messy" (Schulze, 1997, p. 28). Therefore, we attempt to find a balance between honoring the women's voices and interpreting them in theoretical context.

GENDER REBELS

Gender rebellion explores *intentional* transgression of cultural expectations of femininity as discussed by participants. Nine women we interviewed expressed distaste with or distance from normative femininity requirements. These include embracing muscular women as "beautiful" (Michelle), breaking up with a boyfriend because of his disapproval of her bodybuilding activities (Rachel), disparaging the "boob femininity connection" (Carla), and telling her friends she did not care what they thought of her as a bodybuilder (Kendra).

Participation in female bodybuilding is a gender transgression in itself (Wesely, 2001), so we argue that the participants are all rebels, even as they are all conformists. For example, most interviewees assert their right to be women and bodybuilders, to take up space in the gym, to be muscular, and to be nonnormative in various other ways, although they occasionally contradict themselves, thus returning to the realm of normative femininity. In general, our findings debunk the idea that female bodybuilders *either* rebel *or* conform to demands of traditional femininity, and reinforce Hill Collins' (2000) concept of *both/and* along a continuum of individual variation.

Bev is our most outspoken "gender rebel," and she is the most experienced and the most muscularly developed bodybuilder of the group. Bev is short, muscular, lean, striated, and has dark olive skin and long dark hair. She has won several contests and has set amateur world powerlifting records. Judging from comments several of our interviewees made about Bev, others perceive her as "mannish," arrogant, and sometimes intimidating. However, each of the participants has a working relationship with Bev, because she is a recruiter and one of the judges for the university competition. Thus, she spends time with each participant, advising and guiding them in training and contest preparation. We believe that Bev, a former gymnast from Kuwait, is accustomed to negative comments from others, including her Palestinian family:

> The people who go to the gym are mostly scared of me....They just don't like me cause they can't get themselves to my level cause it takes a little time to get to an advanced level. The people who go to the Nautilus room are idiots and don't like muscular women....Yeah, sometimes my brothers don't like it but I tell them I don't care....They think I am doing too much and they think I am getting too strong because I am stronger than them....I honestly don't see myself as being too big. (Bev)

In this passage, Bev says she doesn't "care" what her brothers think of her. In addition, she interprets others' reactions to her appearance and physical strength as based on fear, ignorance, or jealousy. These are primarily individual or psychological explanations.

Brittney, in contrast, takes a critical feminist view and blames media images for influencing what "society thinks" of muscular women:

> I am going to keep lifting weights and if I get bigger than I am then I won't quit lifting just because others think I am getting too big and because society thinks it is gross or because magazines put Photoshop women on their covers for the ideal body type. The media is what makes people have certain views. (Brittney)

Brittney is relatively inexperienced, although she is already outspoken regarding anyone else's idea of how she should look and what she should do with her body. She told us that her boyfriend "had a problem" with her losing her breast tissue during training, but that she "just didn't care" because she has "no respect" for women who get breast implants. Likewise, several women express a certain enjoyment from participating in an activity that is considered less "socially acceptable" (Rachel) for women than men:

> I like the look so I keep working towards looking better, or what I think is better. I also participate because people think it's kind of strange. It's not something people necessarily want to do because it's not an easy thing to do. (Jeanie)

Clearly, Jeanie takes pleasure from others thinking that what she does is "kind of strange," and she exudes pride in her muscular body and the work it takes to get it in condition. For Jeanie, who has very pale skin and long blond hair, developing muscles is a definite improvement over her earlier body type, which she describes as "weak and skinny, like skin and bones." She detests her "genetics" and has worked hard to build muscle on her tall but slender frame.

SOMATIC NORMALIZATION

In some instances gender rebellion stems from or results in what we call somatic normalization, or

the emergence of new social norms related to the athletic and muscular female body (Grogan et al., 2004; Monaghan et al., 1998). Our use of the word "new" reflects Dworkin's (2001) observation that women continue to "push gently" on the glass ceiling of acceptable female muscle—and that socially constructed ideals of femininity and attractiveness related to the female body continue to change over time. In other words, others begin to perceive a wider range of female muscle and female body types as normal and even attractive, rather than deviant or pathological. Our interviewees' accounts affirm our conceptualization across several contexts, such as changing attitudes of family and friends, changes in self-perceptions, and childhood socialization:

> Yeah they [my parents] don't care I have done stuff like this before. They were more crazy about me doing a pageant than they were about me doing a power lifting competition. I have been an athlete for so long that it is pretty much like you know whatever....I saw them [bodybuilders] so early in life I can't remember. My dad was a workout buff guy and he did that stuff....So when I see it on television it was normal, well I guess it became normal. (Kendra)

Several interviewees have been athletes all their lives. For their families, female sport participation is normative. Bodybuilding is just another healthy activity in a long line of sports in which their daughters have been involved. Kendra is medium height, has medium brown skin and shoulder length, usually braided black hair with a stocky, compact athletic build and a body that responds quickly to weight training. She told us that she is a "tomboy" and that her father "wanted a son" as a way of explaining to us that her muscular physique is "normal" in her family. In Kendra's case, being in a beauty pageant was the rebellion that made her parents "crazy."

Similarly, Carla's parents, who are Catholic, are more concerned with the morality of her extracurricular activities than with her muscular appearance:

> My parents think it is cool um because my parents are very—they like the idea that I am doing something that I am passionate about. As long as I am not

stripping or doing pornography or something that is morally questionable then yeah they are happy that I am doing something I like. (Carla)

Carla, who was raised partially in Ghana (where she was born) and partially in Canada before coming to the U.S. for college, is a lifelong athlete and has a well-developed musculature. Carla is tall and lean, has very dark skin, wears long, braided hair extensions, and considers herself very feminine. Like Kendra, she has participated in beauty pageants, but seems unsure as to the moral and personal value of this activity. She prefers to compete in fitness or figure competitions, which to her are worthier pursuits. Although these two women hail from very different cultural backgrounds, it is interesting to note that they share a similar range of experiences from pageants to bodybuilding competitions, and that both sets of parents frown on the pageants but view their daughters' bodybuilding involvement as just another "healthy" athletic activity.

Kendra and Carla's accounts support Cahn's (1994a) argument that community expectations of black women's femininity encompass a wider gender spectrum than their white counterparts. Indeed, several of our white interviewees articulate their family members' initial negative reactions before their "resocialization" and increased acceptance of their loved one's activities. For instance:

> She [grandmother] was worried in the beginning because she didn't know what I looked like and when she heard the word bodybuilding she looked it up and I am sure that whatever she saw when she looked was not good... after she saw pictures from my last show.... She is now better about it. She shows every one at church pictures.... I didn't look any weirder I just looked athletic. (Kelly)

Kelly's anecdote illustrates a general pattern in the data among Caucasian American women: initial resistance from family and friends followed by their realization that the woman in question does not look big and "freaky" (Rachel) like the media images they have seen. One participant mentions that her strength training "opened up [her friends']

eyes that muscular women look nice as opposed to stick women" (Cathy). In addition, several women note that not only do they feel better about their bodies since being involved in competition and training, but their general perceptions of the ideal feminine body have shifted to encompass a more muscular frame. As Dworkin (2001) might say, they are "tapping on the glass ceiling" of female muscle, and by so doing often alter the opinions of those around them.

RACIALIZED BODIES

Interpretations of the ideal feminine body remain subject to stereotypes and cultural beliefs based on race and ethnicity, which alter perceptions and expectations of the female bodybuilder (Balsamo, 1994; Boyle, 2005; Heywood, 1998; Williams, 2000). Although lived experiences of race and culture are constantly shifting and blending, there remain discernable differences in gendered expectations as reflected in our data. For example, Carla's traditional Ghanaian family has responded positively to the change in her appearance and behavior and even joined her in exercise for health's sake:

> I went back [to Ghana] three years ago and... it was interesting because... I ran with my nephew and every time we would run by they [villagers] looked a little curious [as to] why would you get up and run just for the heck of running, are you going to the store to buy bread and we would come back with empty hands.... The village is a little behind and they have not developed as quickly.... I ended up running fitness classes for the women because I would come back and do push ups and squats and my grandmother decided one day she was going to join me and then my mom joined in and we had a little class going on. Usually when people run in Ghana, they do it for a purpose. It is so different there. (Carla)

In marked contrast to most Western cultures, Ghanaians consider strenuous physical activity a necessary part of everyday labor, rather than as a way to lose weight, get in shape, or stay healthy. Carla tells us that because of increased access to "Western [media] programming," Ghanaian women are "learning that there are more options available to them than traditional soft roles." Therefore, although many Ghanaian women's bodies are hardened from working, they do/did not view this form of strength and muscularity as freedom from traditional female gender roles. Thus, Carla's cross-cultural experience as a black female bodybuilder is part of the current shift in Ghanaian beliefs about femininity. Now, Carla's brother shows pictures of her to his friends and "brags how his sister can beat them up," which pleases her.

In contrast to Carla's family, Bev's Palestinian family gives her a hard time about her increasing muscularity and her "intense" dedication to the sport:

> Some of my family they think I am overworking. I am doing it too intense or too much. But I told them that it is my life and my body and when I listen basically to my body and when it is too much on my body I will back off. (Bev)

Although Bev doesn't discuss her cultural experiences in detail, she repeatedly mentions how her brothers criticize and make fun of her body. This is consistent with traditional Palestinian views regarding female gender roles in a culture where women are not expected to perform hard labor as part of their everyday lives, especially in the middle and upper classes. Thus, Bev is forced to rebel against an even stricter code of acceptable female appearance and behavior than Carla and our American born interviewees.

Another indicator of difference in racialized gender expectations emerges from interaction with friends and significant others. Kendra relates an interaction she had with an African American male friend, who "was doing the head shaking thing" when she told him about her involvement in bodybuilding and makes fun of her because she told him she "didn't care" what he thought about the possibility that she might "lose her ass." This mutual friend expressed the identical concern to Michelle, who is white, because he admired her (ample) backside and did not want her to work it off. His

preference for the large female posterior reflects a racialized concept of what is constructed as sexually attractive to heterosexual black men (hooks, 1992). Carla's interaction with her boyfriend corroborates this as she discusses the point at which she feels she has "gone too far" with her training:

> Well too big is when I have no shape in my butt when my boobs are reduced to nothing and when my friends start making little remarks about me and my boyfriend starts making remarks about he has nothing to hold on to. And when the girls are like, oh my god look at her butt; there is nothing there but muscle. It makes me feel like a freak generally and that is when I feel like I have gone too far. (Carla)

Carla's significant others reinforce ideals of black femininity by remarking on her "reduced" breast size and her "butt," which has "nothing there but muscle." Unlike Bev, however, Carla responds to the criticism by "holding back" on her workouts (Dworkin, 2001) and utilizing feminizing body technologies and accessories (Williams, 2000):

> I have some issues with [labeling]. . . . That is one reason why I wore braids in my hair because I used to wear my hair short and you know—still lifting and with my musculature—I think sometimes people doubted my [sexual] orientation and that bothered me cause they—you know, potential come-ons, and I figured that if I just avoid the confusion at all then I don't have to deal with it one way or another. When I got the braids, it conforms to some ideal of black femininity—long hair—that seems to be pretty much universal, so I got the braids and then I um at one point I had considered getting breast implants. (Carla)

In short, Carla reacts to American culture by conforming to "some ideal of black femininity," whereas in Ghana, which is "a little behind" the times, she is more rebellious. Perhaps this is because she has more investment in what her current cultural contemporaries think of her. Although "in Ghanaian culture women are supposed to be full figured and have huge butts," so standards of black femininity are similar.

In addition, Carla's reference to people doubting her sexual preference and her reaction to that supports Williams' (2000) argument that black women bodybuilders are especially prone to being read as lesbians. The fact that Carla responds by lengthening her hair and considering breast implants suggests that gender attribution (in this case, butch) is conflated with sexual preference (in this case, lesbian). In other words, she believes if she looks sufficiently feminine, people will assume she is heterosexual.

GENDER ATTRIBUTION

As we define and expand it here, gender attribution (Kessler and McKenna, 1978) is based on how people interpret themselves and each other not only in terms of their sex (male ↔ female), but of their gender presentation (feminine ↔ masculine) as compared with generally dominant Western norms. In other words, we use the concept as a heuristic device to represent the sometimes complex process of attributing sex and gender characteristics to an "other" to render them understandably human (and therefore sexed and gendered) in terms of existing social norms. We explore and analyze the curious but widespread practice surrounding female bodybuilding of correct sex attribution (female) mixed with ambiguous gender attribution (female masculinity). Our results are similar to those of Boyle (2005), Fisher (1997) and Wesely (2001), who found that gender expression is linked with sexual preference. In other words, females attributed as displaying "feminine" characteristics are typically assumed to be "normal" heterosexuals, whereas those perceived as more "masculine" are generally assumed to be lesbian and/or pathological (see Halberstam, 1998). In our study, participants typically criticize those they perceive as "mannish" females:

> I think people like the big freaky looking men but they don't like the big freaky looking women. I mean I just hear more and more people making comments about, um, the women that don't look feminine anymore; no one wants to see that really. I have respect for them and for what they do, but I think people are

turned off to what they have done to themselves. I think people want to see dedicated muscular people but without that going over the edge. (Rachel)

Rachel, who is tall, thin, and has light olive skin and long brown hair that she wears in a ponytail, is a lifelong athlete with a well-developed upper body, slender legs, and squarish facial features. She initially became involved in bodybuilding to "lose weight" but stayed because she enjoys the training and being on stage during competitions. Like many of the women we interviewed, she is vocal about the existence of a gender "edge" that when crossed results in something "freaky" that "no one wants to see." Brittney echoes the sentiment: "I think...the [Ms.] Olympia women you know that do bodybuilding...I actually think that they are crossing gender lines." This comment contradicts her earlier statement criticizing media-driven norms of femininity, providing a clear instance of both subversive and normative gendered attitudes (Hill Collins, 2000). Elaine, also in bodybuilding to lose weight and tone up, says, "I don't want to do bodybuilding I want to do overall fitness. I don't want to dewomanize myself." Her description of her mother's reaction to learning what she was doing is striking and may help explain her intense fear of looking like a "man":

> My mom...thought I would be a man at the end of it. She was like "I don't want her to look like that" but I can't get any bigger than I am now unless I take drugs. When she saw Ms. Olympia, she almost threw up. I want to keep losing fat and getting leaner, but I don't want to look like that. She [Ms. Olympia] looks like that from years of steroid use. (Elaine)

As others have stressed, steroid use is linked to perceptions of female bodybuilders as masculine (Grogan et al., 2004; Patton, 2001) or unnatural (Wesely, 2001), although steroid use in itself is not sufficient for such attribution. As Cathy (correctly) observes, "some girls can take stuff and not even look like they are taking stuff." Nevertheless, when others interpret a woman's musculature as "huge" and "bulging" (Michelle), they tend to assume she is using steroids and therefore "screwing with nature" (Jeanie). Whether she is using or not is often unknown. However, if she looks like she is using, they label her "mannish" or call her a man:

> I would say Bev is basically a man; she does as much steroids as the guys.... There is not a doubt in my mind that she is on steroids...and her jaw line. Her muscularity is unbelievable for her. I mean look at her family her sister is tiny. Genetically no way girls will get that big. There is no way a girl can increase her bench press by fifty pounds in one summer. (Cathy)

Cathy, who is also a rugby player and is characterized by others as "uppity," is nevertheless one of several in our sample who are outspokenly critical of Bev's size and other physical attributes. Here, Cathy is not literally making a mistaken sex attribution. She knows that Bev is a "she," which we interpret to mean that to Cathy, Bev is like a man but is not synonymous with one. Rather, she is making a gender attribution that Bev is a masculine female, and therefore deviant. Jeanie echoes the sentiment:

> I know for sure one woman [Bev] who does them and she looks scary. You can tell that she is a woman but her acne is so bad on her back and...the steroids actually make you lose hair and give you a receding hairline, which makes your forehead look like it has gotten bigger. I don't respect people who do steroids it is like cheating, but of course people cannot look like that naturally they need something to help them out. Since steroids that bodybuilders use is a male hormone then I would consider it unnatural for a woman to take them. (Jeanie)

...Although our interviewees rebel against traditional feminine gender norms in various ways, they all draw the line somewhere between "beautiful," muscular, "natural" women (Michelle) and women who are "disgusting," "all veiny and steroidy," (Michelle), "unnatural," "hulking" (Jeanie), and "freaky" (Rachel). Thus, hypermuscular women are often targets of accusations of steroid use and masculine gender attributions, which are typically based on interpretations of appearance.

The problem with finding a balance between femininity and muscular development is not only social but structural—built into a sport which rewards women for developing large, striated, lean muscles and punishes them for looking too big, too bulky, losing their breast tissue, or other somatic consequences of training. If the female bodybuilder wishes to be successful, she must constantly negotiate between gender extremes, especially at elite levels (Heywood, 1998). As Bev comments, "people pay that money for a ticket to see good and muscular people not to see skinny people." In the world of bodybuilding, it is insufficient for a woman to be *only* muscular or *only* feminine—she must be *both/and*.

REFERENCES

Aoki, D. (1996). Sex and muscle: The female bodybuilder meets Lacan. *Body & Society, 2*(4), 59–74.

Balsamo, A. (1994). Feminist bodybuilding. In S. Birrell & C.L. Cole (Eds.), *Women, sport, and culture* (pp. 341–352). Champaign, IL: Human Kinetics.

Bolin, A. (1992). Vandalized vanity: Feminine physiques betrayed and portrayed. In F.E. Mascia-Lees & P. Sharpe (Eds.). *Tattoo, torture, mutilation, and adornment: The denaturalization of the body in culture and text* (pp. 79–99). Albany, NY: State University of New York Press.

Boyle, L. (2005). Flexing the tensions of female muscularity: How female bodybuilders negotia te normative femininity in competitive bodybuilding. *Women's Studies Quarterly, 33*(1/2), 134–149.

Brace-Govan, J. (2004). Weighty matters: Control of women's access to physical strength. *The Sociological Review, 52*(4), 503–531.

Cahn, S.K. (1994a). *Coming on strong: Gender and sexuality in twentieth-century women's sport.* New York: The Free Press.

Cahn, S.K. (1994b). Crushes, competition, and closets: The emergence of homophobia in women's physical education. In S. Birrell & C.L. Cole (Eds.). *Women, sport, and culture* (pp. 327–339). Champaign. IL: Human Kinetics.

Choi, P.Y.L. (2000). *Femininity and the physically active woman.* London, UK: Routledge.

Dworkin, S.L. (2001). 'Holding back': Negotiating a glass ceiling on women's muscular strength. *Sociological Perspectives, 44*(3), 333–350.

Fisher, L.A. (1997). "Building one's self up": Bodybuilding and the construction of identity among professional female bodybuilders. In P.L. Moore (Ed.), *Building bodies* (pp. 135–161). New Brunswick, NJ: Rutgers University Press.

Forbes, G.B., Adams-Curtis, L.E., Holmgren, K.M., & White, K.B. (2004). Perceptions of the social and personal characteristics of hypermuscular women and the men who love them. *The Journal of Social Psychology, 144*(5), 487–506.

George, M. (2005). Making sense of muscle: The body experiences of collegiate women athletes. *Sociological Inquiry, 75*(3), 317–345.

Griffin, P. (1998). *Strong women, deep closets: Lesbians and homophobia in sport.* Champaign, IL: Human Kinetics.

Grogan, S., Evans, R., Wright, S., & Hunter, G. (2004). Femininity and muscularity: Accounts of seven women body builders. *Journal of Gender Studies, 13*(1), 49–61.

Halberstam, J. (1998). *Female masculinity.* Durham, NC: Duke University Press.

Heywood, L. (1998). *Bodymakers: A cultural anatomy of women's body building.* New Brunswick, NJ: Rutgers University Press.

Hill Collins, P. (2000). *Black feminist thought: Knowledge, consciousness, and the politics of empowerment* (2nd ed.). New York, NY: Routledge.

Holmlund, C.A. (1994). Visible difference and flex appeal: The body, sex, sexuality, and race in the *Pumping Iron* films. In S. Birrell & C.L. Cole (Eds.), *Women, sport, and culture* (pp. 299–313). Champaign, IL: Human Kinetics.

hooks, b. (1992). *Black looks: Race and representation.* Boston, MA: South End Press.

Ian, M. (2001). The primitive subject of female bodybuilding: Transgression and other postmodern myths. *Differences: A Journal of Feminist Cultural Studies, 12*(3), 69–100.

Kane, M.J. (1995). Resistance/transformation of the oppositional binary: Exposing sport as a continuum. *Journal of Sport and Social Issues, 19*(2), 191–218.

Kessler, S.J., & McKenna, W. (1978). *Gender: An ethnomethodological approach.* Chicago, IL: The University of Chicago Press.

Klein, A.M. (1993). *Little big men: bodybuilding subculture and gender construction.* Albany, NY: State University of New York Press.

Krane, V., Choi, P.Y.L., Baird, S.M., Aimar, C.M., & Kauer, K.J. (2004). Living the paradox: Female athletes negotiate femininity and muscularity. *Sex Roles, 50*(5/6), 315–329.

Lorber, J. (1996). Beyond the binaries: Depolarizing the categories of sex, sexuality, and gender. *Sociological Inquiry, 66*, 143–159.

Lowe, M.R. (1998). *Women of steel: Female bodybuilders and the struggle for self-definition.* New York, NY: New York University Press.

Markula, P. (1995). Firm but shapely, fit but sexy, strong but thin: The postmodern aerobicizing female bodies. *Sociology of Sport Journal, 12*, 424–453.

Monaghan, L., Bloor, M., Dobash, R.P., & Dobash, R.E. (1998). Bodybuilding and sexual attractiveness. In J. Richardson & A. Shaw (Eds.), *The body in qualitative research* (pp. 39–55). Aldershot, UK: Ashgate.

Patton, C. (2001). Rock hard: Judging the female physique. *Journal of Sport and Social Issues, 25*(2), 118–140.

Roussel, P., & Griffet, J. (2000). The path chosen by female bodybuilders: A tentative interpretation. *Sociology of Sport Journal, 17*, 130–150.

Ryan, J. (2001). Muscling in: Gender and physicality in weight-training culture. In N. Watson & S. Cunningham-Burley (Eds.), *Reframing the body* (pp. 166–186). Hampshire, UK: Palgrave.

Ryckman, R.M., Dill, D.A., Dyer, N.L., Sanborn, J.W., & Gold, J.A. (1992). Social perceptions of male and female extreme mesomorphs. *The Journal of Social Psychology, 132*(5), 615–627.

Schippert, C. (2007). Can muscles be queer? Reconsidering the transgressive hyper-built body. *Journal of Gender Studies, 16*(2), 155–171.

Schulze, L. (1997). On the muscle. In P. L. Moore (Ed.), *Building bodies* (pp. 9–30). New Brunswick, NJ: Rutgers University Press.

St. Martin, L., & Gavey, N. (1996). Women's bodybuilding: Feminist resistance and/or femininity's recuperation? *Body & Society, 2*(4), 45–57.

Wesely, J.K. (2001). Negotiating gender: Bodybuilding and the natural/unnatural continuum. *Sociology of Sport Journal, 18*, 162–180.

West, C., & Zimmerman, D.H. (1987). Doing gender. *Gender & Society, 1*, 125–151.

Williams, C. (2000). Hardcore: The radical self-portraiture of black female bodybuilders. In J. Frueh, L. Fierstein, & J. Stein (Eds.), *Picturing the modern Amazon* (pp. 104–116). New York, NY: Rizzoli.

LOOSE LIPS SINK SHIPS

DISCUSSION QUESTIONS

1. Do you think women and men face the same expectations to possess aesthetically "appealing" genitalia? Why or why not?
2. Could this type of plastic surgery for women be compared to male circumcision? Why or why not?
3. Do you find similarities between the cosmetics and/or diet industries and this type of plastic surgery for women? What underlying ideas about women's bodies do they seem to share and promote?

[They are] two excrescences of muscular flesh which hang, and in some women, fall outside the neck of the womb; lengthen and shorten as does the comb of a turkey, principally when they desire coitus....

–Ambroise Paré (1579), quoted in Lisa Jean Moore and Adele E. Clarke,
"Clitoral Conventions and Transgressions: Graphic Representations in
Anatomy Texts, c1900–1991,"
Feminist Studies 21 (summer 1995)

DESIGNER VAGINAS

Perhaps you noticed some of the articles in women's magazines that came out in 1998; *Cosmopolitan, Marie Claire,* and *Harper's Bazaar* each carried one, as did *Salon* on-line, articles with titles like "Labia Envy," "Designer Vaginas," and "The New Sex Surgeries." More recently, *Jane* magazine covered the topic, and Dan Savage's nationally syndicated advice column, "Savage Love," stumbled explosively upon it as well. These pieces all discussed labiaplasty, a relatively recent plastic surgery procedure that involves trimming away labial tissue and sometimes injecting fat from another part of the body into labia that have been deemed excessively droopy. In contrast to the tightening operation known as "vaginal rejuvenation," labiaplasty is sheerly cosmetic in purpose and purports to have no impact on sensation (unless something were to go terribly awry).[1] Throughout coverage here and in Canada, the aptly named Doctors Alter, Stubbs, and Matlock shared much of the glory and the public relations. In the name of consumer choice, these articles provoke consumer anxiety. The *Los Angeles Times* quotes Dr. Matlock:

"The woman is the designer...the doctor is just the instrument....Honestly, if you look at *Playboy*, those women, on the outer vagina area, the vulva is very aesthetically appealing, the vulva is rounded. It's full, not flat....Women are coming in saying, I want something different, I want to change things. They look at *Playboy*, the ideal woman per se, for the body and the shape and so on. You don't see women in there with excessively long labia minora."[2]

All the popular articles about the "new sex surgeries" that I've reviewed also include remarks from skeptical colleagues and from polled readers who feel okay about their labia. (In an unfortunate turn of phrase, one plastic surgeon describes Dr. Matlock as a bit too "cutting edge.") Despite this apparently balanced coverage, a brand-new worry is being planted, with the declaration in *Salon* that "many women had been troubled for years about the appearance of their labia minora," and with the use of words like "normal" and "abnormal" to describe non-pathological variations among genitalia. The November 1998 article in *Cosmopolitan* has an eye-catching blurb: "My labia were so long, they'd show through my clothes!" Having taken *that* in, the reader suddenly looks up at the accompanying photo with new eyes: the photograph is of a slim woman in fairly modest underwear; because of the picture's cropping, she is headless, but the posture is distinctive, awkward. She's somewhat hunched forward, her hands are both crotch-bound, and one finger slips beneath the edge of her panties. Having read the caption, you think, "My God, she's tucking in her labia!"[3]

Ellen Frankfort's 1972 book, the women's liberationist *Vaginal Politics*, begins with the following scene.[4] Carol from the Los Angeles Self-Help Clinic "slips out of her dungarees and underpants," hops onto a long table in an old church basement and inserts a speculum into her vagina. The 50 other women present file up and look with a flashlight, and learn, too, how to self-examine with a speculum and a dimestore mirror. This self-exploration of what has often been referred to as "the dark continent" or just "down there" seemed the perfect symbol for the early claim of women's liberation

that "the personal is political." How could a woman call for sexual autonomy without self-awareness? To reverse the phrasing of one of Second Wave feminism's most famous byproducts, how could we know "our selves" without knowing "our bodies" first?[5] This image of women using a well-placed mirror to demystify and reclaim their own bodies is rooted dimly in my teen-years memory. I found it eerily resurrected when the *Salon* piece by Louisa Kamps came up on my computer screen. Kamps starts off like this: " 'Ladies, get out your hand mirrors,' begins a curious press release I find at my desk one Monday morning. 'Yes, it is true...the newest trend in surgically enhanced body beautification: Female Genital Cosmetic Surgery.' " The hand mirror this time is used to alert the would-be vagina shopper to any deficiencies "down below" that she may have been blithely ignoring. From 1970s' consciousness-raising groups and Judy Chicago's dinner plates, through Annie Sprinkle's speculum parties of the 1980s, and on to Eve Ensler's collaborative *Vagina Monologues*,[6] we came at the end of the 1990s to Dr. Alter and Dr. Stubbs. What's the trajectory from Second Wave feminist "self-discovery and celebration" to the current almost-craze for labiaplasty? And does the fact of this trajectory provide us with a warning?

THE CLEAN SLIT

The vagina. According to Freud, its first sighting is the first scandal. It is *the* secret, invariably broken, that, once seen, changes you forever, especially if "you" are a little boy in turn-of-the-century Vienna, stumbling in upon your mother *en déshabillé*. You discover, all at once, in a rude shock, that she lacks a penis. You tremble at the threat that her missing phallus implies to *your* little member: if it happened to her, it could happen to you (especially because you've got the gall to compete with your father for your mother's affections). For Freud, his followers, and even many of his feminist revisionists, the "scandal" of a woman's genitals is supposed to be due to what *isn't* there, not what is. This article is not about lack, however. It is about excess. And it is not (exactly) about what Jacques Lacan and Hélène Cixous celebrated as *jouissance.* It's about labia.

So the vagina betokens the horror of castration, we're told. Many have remarked that perhaps this scandal is more accurately defined as one of interiority. In a society that revolves around the visual, an orgasm that doesn't include ejaculation can seem maddeningly uncontrollable: you can't prove it (outside of a laboratory), and thus it can be faked.[7] Discussing hard-core cinematic pornography, Linda Williams claims that "[t]he woman's ability to fake the orgasm that the man can never fake…seems to be at the root of all the genre's attempts to solicit what it can never be sure of: the out-of-control confession of pleasure, a hard-core 'frenzy of the visible.'"[8]

In the Amero-European world of the late-eighteenth and the early-nineteenth centuries, an earlier notion of women's natural lustiness was transformed into the myth of feminine modesty.[9] This purported lady-like decorum has always been depicted as simultaneously innate for the female *and* a massively big job. For the same social world that generated the mythos of the delicate, proper lady has also continually spawned and recycled dirty jokes about "vagina dentata," fatal odors, and other horror-story imagery about female genitalia.[10] The off-color disgust has always been tied in a complex way to a vast, off-color desire, and these both have been concomitant with the prescription to stay dainty—no matter what–for at least three hundred years. The paradoxical welding of abhorrence and adoration is often "resolved" socially through a stereotyped decoupling of the two, although mythologies of the lurid and the pure female are in fact too interdependent ever to be truly unbraided. Women have been branded good or bad, refined or fallen, on the basis of their race, their profession, their station in life, and so forth, with the judgments conveniently supporting the political, economic, and racial status quo (about which, more later). That being said, the paradox is also one that women negotiate individually, and this has been so for a remarkably long time. To see this conundrum's longevity, take a look at Jonathan Swift's eighteenth-century "dressing-room poems," animated by

voyeuristic disgust for the female body, and compare them with "What Your Gynecologist Didn't Tell You about the Smell," a now-defunct joke web site that made fun of Dr. Matlock but did so via misogynist aversion—an aversion familiar to all women who feel compelled to contain this supposed foulness and to approximate the required delicacy.[11]

Although "feminine modesty" used to be the answer to this subtextual concern about vaginas, now the shameful zone needs to be brought into line for display, rather than hidden. The vulva is becoming a pioneer territory for cosmetic enhancement—surgical practitioners need above all to capitalize both on that preexisting shame and on the ever-greater need to provide a cyborgian spectacle of porno-gloss. The relative mainstreaming of the sex industry (think of Demi Moore in *Striptease,* for example) and the blurring of the lines between hard-core and advertising imagery (think Calvin Klein) have led to a perpetually increasing sense of pressure among many women, the pressure to develop and present a seamlessly sexualized, "airbrushed" body.[12] Drs. Alter, Stubbs, and Matlock want that sought-after body to include a specific labial look, one desirable enough to be worth "buying."

Before people will spend money on something as expensive and uncomfortable as cosmetic surgery, they need to be motivated not only by desire but by concern or self-doubt. Bringing the authoritative language of medical science to the aestheticization of the vagina is one key way to trigger such anxiety. Advertisers have frequently invoked and generated medicalized norms to sell products. Roland Marchand describes perhaps the classic example of this phenomenon: after the liquid known as Listerine proved a lackluster general antiseptic, it was decided to dramatize its function as a mouthwash. Foul tasting as it was, consumer incentive would be needed. The term "halitosis" was "exhumed from an old medical dictionary" by an advertising firm and became the driving force behind a subsequent, energetic scare campaign about the medical, social, and romantic risks of bad breath.[13] Advertisers have always been both matter-of-fact and explicit about delineating and then steadily working to create a sense of deficiency where once there was indifference or even, God forbid, enjoyment, working to incite new arenas of insecurity, new personal anxieties, so that more things can be marketed and sold.

Cosmetic surgery has worked with the same principles throughout its more than 100-year history, as detailed in histories of the profession by Kathy Davis, Elizabeth Haiken, and Sander Gilman.[14] For instance, in a particularly unnerving chapter on "micromastia" (the "disease" of flat-chestedness) and the surgeries developed to "correct" it, Haiken quotes a 1958 article by plastic surgeon Milton T. Edgerton and psychiatrist A.R. McClary, on "the psychiatry of breast augmentation": "Literally thousands of women in this country alone, are seriously disturbed by feelings of inadequacy in regard to concepts of the body image. Partly as a result of exposure to advertising propaganda and questionable publicity, many physically normal women develop an almost paralyzing self-consciousness focused on the feeling that they do not have the correct size bosom."[15] The rationale laid out here, which explains *but also helps create* "inferiority complexes," can be applied across the full topography of the human form, as borne out by the increasing prevalence of liposuction, face-lifts, buttock and tummy tucks. The latest realm to be scoured for "abnormalities" is the vagina, formerly spared from the scrutiny of the market because it was considered both too reviled and too quakingly desired to be addressed commercially.

These days, in part because of the video dissemination and the mainstreaming of pornography, women, regardless of gender preference, can see the vaginas of a lot of different other women. They may desire those vaginas, they may simultaneously identify with them, but if they are rich enough or have great credit, they can definitely have them built.[16] A 1997 article in the Canadian magazine *See* interviews a patient of Dr. Stubbs in Toronto. Deborah "has had her eyes done and had breast implants and some liposuction. She says that she started thinking about her labia when her first husband brought home porn magazines and she started comparing herself. 'I saw some other ones that were cuter

than mine' and I thought, 'Hey, I want that one,' she laughs."[17] Of course, the images we relish or bemoan in pornography are almost always tweaked technically. As Deborah did her "catalog shopping," the women she was admiring were perhaps themselves surgically "enhanced," but additionally, they were posed, muted with makeup and lighting, and the resultant photographic images were then edited with an airbrush or the digital modifications of Photoshop.

This is especially true of pornography that presents itself as "upscale," whether soft or hard core. As Laura Kipnis helps us realize, there's a crucial link between *Hustler's* targeting of a working-class market and its being the first of the big three glossy "wank mags" to show what it called "the pink."[18] *Hustler's* aggressive celebration of vulgarity informed its initial rejection of soft-core decorum about genitals; thus, its representations of vaginas were matter-of-fact, and often enough contextualized with very explicit, poorly lit Polaroid shots sent in by readers. When the vagina finally came to the pages of *Penthouse,* by contrast, it was as flaw-free and glossy as the rest of the models' figures. In "The Pussy Shot: An Interview with Andrew Blake," sex writer Susie Bright discusses the classed aesthetics of this pornographer, whose trademarks are his lavish sets (straight out of *Architectural Digest,* Bright remarks) and high-end production values: in this posh setting, it comes as no surprise that the star's labia are small and her "pussy is perfectly composed, with every hair in place."[19]

The evolution of a new strict standard of "beauty," rigid enough to induce surgery, does not occur in a vacuum. Among other factors, economics are in play—not just in the eagerness of a few cosmetic surgeons to up their patient load but in a far more intricate web of drives and desires intersecting with technological shifts and cultural and financial power plays. I will only nod here to the complexity of this phenomenon. A first example: in *Venus Envy: A History of Cosmetic Surgery,* Haiken points out that research catalyzed by World War I and II led to technological innovations that furthered the cosmetic surgery industry. Wars, which maim and disfigure people, increase the demand for and respectability of plastic surgery, allowing surgeons the grim opportunity to improve their skills and their public relations. Additionally, war means the invention and/or increased availability of new materials, like silicone and polyurethane, both of which were used for breast augmentation in the wake of World War II.[20] Could this new material on hand have *led* (in part) to the 1950s' notorious obsession with large breasts?

Here is a more recent example of the subtle interplay of cultural and economic forces that can help shape changes in beauty standards: Perhaps Rudolph Giuliani's New York City should be thought of as undergoing an urban labiaplasty. In this zoned, regulated era, newly comfortable for tourists if not for New Yorkers, the sex industry has been radically curtailed. This change has meant, tellingly enough, that almost all the sex clubs "connected" enough to remain open after 1998 favor "clone" women—Caucasian bodies, tidy tan lines, big blonde hair, collagen lips, surgically removed ribs, liposucked bottoms, and implanted breasts. With time, their labia may also be ubiquitously trimmed. Many women with bodies that diverge from the approved stereotype—biker chicks, Latina and Black dancers, plump or small-breasted women, the pierced girl with the monster tattoo—women who used to be able to dance erotically for an income, have been "sheered away," forced into unemployment, prostitution, or departure. These days in New York, only the clones can dance, and it is clone bodies alone that New York City strip club patrons now ogle.[21] The ripple effects such a change works, no doubt, multiply, and the Bloomberg era will see them continue.

In part because of the prevalence of just such a mainstreamed *Penthouse* and *Playboy* aesthetic, labias in pornography are often literally tucked away (in the most low-tech variant of body modification).[22] If you review enough porn, however, especially lesbian porn or that which is unsqueamishly "déclassé" as in *Hustler,* you will see a wide variety in the female genitalia on display—wide enough to evoke the "snowflake uniqueness" analogy that is bandied around in popular coverage of the new

cosmetic enhancement surgeries. And indeed the before-and-after shots available at some of the surgeons' web sites that I've found so far do reveal, unsurprisingly, that the single favored look for these "designer vaginas" is...the clean slit. Louisa Kamps of *Salon* magazine agrees: "What strikes me in the 'after' shots is the eerie similarity between the women...their genitalia are carbon copies of each other."

In a subtle but nontrivial way, this particular aesthetic and the surgery that manifests it cut back on women's experience of self-on-self contact, of tactility: Luce Irigaray celebrates the nonvisual, sensory experience women perpetually enjoy as their vaginal lips press and move against one another. She suggests that this physiological status makes women psychologically less invested in the myth of the monadic, self-reliant individual than are men. Irigaray's "two lips which are not one" would not touch each other much in a world of women "Altered."[23] What do the aesthetics of a streamlined vulva signify? The smooth groin of our favorite plastic android prototype, Barbie? A desire to approximate prepubescence? A fastidious minimization of marginal zones?[24]

Mary Russo writes of "the female grotesque" in terms that are relevant here: "The images of the grotesque body are precisely those which are abjected from the bodily canons of classical aesthetics. The classical body is transcendent and monumental, closed, static, self-contained, symmetrical, and sleek....The grotesque body is open, protruding, secreting, multiple and changing...."[25] Russo's contrasting of the grotesque with the classical is particularly resonant in this context, as plastic surgeons often invoke classical aesthetics and the metaphor of surgeon-as-sculptor; Stubbs even illustrates his site with photographs of classical statuary and presents his "before-and-after" shots in a "Surgical Art Gallery" captioned by Hippocrates: "'*Ars longa, vita brevis*'—Art is long and life is short."[26] Elizabeth Haiken discusses "the classical context in which [early plastic surgeons] wished to place themselves; the term *plastic surgery* derives from the Greek *plastikos,* to shape or mold."[27] The asymmetries, protrusions, and changeability of Russo's grotesque are what the labiaplasty is meant to "shape or mold" and *cut* away.

Bodies do change with the passage of time, of course. If the living body is to approximate sculpture, change itself must be managed, *fixed*. Reading the following quote from Dr. Alter's web site, one is reminded of the Renaissance theory of the wandering womb, whereby female hysteria and misbehavior were deemed the results of a uterus that had dislodged and begun to storm about internally, wreaking havoc. A woman's "womb was like a hungry animal; when not amply fed by sexual intercourse or reproduction, it was likely to wander about her body, over-powering her speech and senses." [28] In Dr. Alter's prose, the older woman, "in dialogue with gravity," [29] may find her previously pleasing vagina dangerously "on the move": "The aging female may dislike the descent of her pubic hair and labia and desire re-elevation to its previous location," Dr. Alter warns. So, it is woman's work to make sure her genitalia are snug, not wayward.

We are talking about vaginal aesthetics, and aesthetic judgments almost always evidence socially relevant metaphors at work on the material and visual planes. Ideas about feminine beauty are ever-changing: the classic example is a comparison of Rubens's fleshy beauties and the wraithlike supermodel Kate Moss (who succeeded Twiggy). But, in a world where many women have never thought about judging the looks of their genitals, even if they care about their appearance more generally, we should ask what criteria make for a good-looking vagina, and who is assigned as arbiter. These (mutating) criteria should tell us something about the value system that generates them. To tease out some answers to these questions, this article goes on to put the labiaplasty phenomenon in a contextual frame with other vaginal modifications.

MODIFYING/CLASSIFYING

What representations of vulvas circulate in our society? And who, beyond Dr. Tight, is modifying the female genitalia, how and why? For one, among alternative youth (and the not-so-alternative, not-so-youthful, too) piercings are being sought to modify and decorate the labia, sometimes to extend them, and, ideally, to add to clitoral stimulation. What sensibilities mark these changes? Among body modifiers on the Web, conversation about body image, self-mutilation, and, contrarily, healing, is common, with an accepted understanding that many turn to piercing as a means of overcoming perceived past abuse. " 'Most folks use Bod-Mod to get back in touch with the parts of themselves that were hurt or misused by others.' 'BodMod has helped me undemonize pain.... I was able to handle [childbirth] better, knowing that I'd survived...two ten-gauge labial piercings....' " Changing one's relationship to one's genitalia by becoming their "modifier" leads here to an aesthetic reassessment: " 'You know, I never liked to look at my puss until I got my rings. I have well-developed inner labia that always show, and I was always envious of those women who seemed to have nice neat little pussies with everything tucked inside. My puss looked like an old whore's cunt to me! So one reason I *know* I wasn't mutilating myself when I got my privates pierced was how much I liked to look at myself after the work was done. You might actually say I'm *glad* my labia are the way they are now.' " [30]

"Glad" is what the cosmetic surgeons do *not* want you to be about prominent labia minora. If you look at the opening paragraph of Ensler's *Vagina Monologues,* you begin to wonder if the unruliness now coming under the governance of the cosmetic surgeon isn't at least as symbolic as it is aesthetic. This is Ensler, introducing her project (interviews with real women, transcribed, performed onstage, and then collected in a book):

> I was worried about vaginas. I was worried about what we think about vaginas, and even more worried that we don't think about them....So I decided to talk to women about their vaginas, to do vagina interviews, which became vagina monologues. I talked with over two hundred women. I talked to old women, young women, married women, single women, lesbians,

college professors, actors, corporate professionals, sex workers, African American women, Hispanic women, Asian American women, Native American women, Caucasian women, Jewish women. At first women were reluctant to talk. They were a little shy. But once they got going, you couldn't stop them.[31]

Just as Ensler's own catalog of interviewees seems to burgeon and proliferate, so too the women with whom she spoke were "unstoppable." With a similar metaphoric expansion, in the cosmetic surgeons' promotional material, not only are women's *labia* depicted as in danger of distention, but one woman customer also described her *"hang-up"* about her preoperative labia as "just growing and growing," until the doctor cut it short, that is. Loose lips sink ships.

I received a "free consultation" from one doctor who performs labiaplasties, and this doctor explained to me that the ideal look for labia minora was not only minimal and unextended but also symmetrical, "homogeneously pink," and "not wavy."[32] To the dangers and allures of what's hidden about the vagina, now is added the "too muchness" of labial tissue. In their heterogeneous dappling and their moist curves, labia mark the lack of tidy differentiation between inside and outside and that's just *too much.* One effect of this procedure is to reduce this sense of a "marginal" site between exterior and interior corporeality. Labia can be seen as "gateway" tissue, in other words, tissue that is somewhat indeterminate in texture and hue, yielding slowly from outer to inner and blurring the boundary between the fetishized gloss of the outer dermis and the wet, mushy darkness of the inside. This indeterminacy, actually a function of the labia's protective role, may be part of their association with excess.[33] In *Public Privates: Performing Gynecology from Both Ends of the Speculum,* Terry Kapsalis "reads" the images in a widely used medical text, *Danforth's Obstetrics and Gynecology.* She is struck by the lack of representations of healthy vaginas in *Danforth's* and argues that ultimately the work's visual logic pathologizes female genitalia per se. Using language parallel to that which I have used here, she writes: "Perhaps

it is not a lack that is threatening, but an excess. The fact is that even if no pathology exists, there *is* something there—namely, a vulva with labia, a clitoris, and so on, a marginal site occupying both the inside and the outside, an abject space (according to Julia Kristeva) that threatens to devour the penis (vagina dentata)."[34]

In the medical realm, much effort is expended to overcome the mysterious liminality of the vagina. Since the eras of the ancient anatomists Galen and Hippocrates and especially since the rise of gynecology in the nineteenth century, vaginas have been diagrammed and cataloged in medical textbooks. Running parallel, a variant of pornography has always picked up and parodied the objectifying eroticism of scientific conquest.[35] In this realm, large labia have often been associated with deviance—at least since the sixteenth century they have indicated to doctors the alleged presence of hypersexuality, onanism, and possible "tribadism" or lesbian tendencies. Jennifer Terry discusses a 1930s' study conducted in New York City, "under the auspices of the Committee for the Study of Sex Variants," in order "to identify, treat, and prevent homosexuality." A moderate-sized group of self-proclaimed lesbians were examined by a battery of experts, so that their "traits" could be characterized and profiled. These experts included gynecologists. The overseer of the project, one Dr. Dickinson, ultimately "identified ten characteristics which he argued set the sex variant [lesbian] apart from 'normal' women: (1) larger than average vulvas; (2) longer labia minora; (3) 'labia minora protrude between the labia majora and are wrinkled, thickened, or *brawny';* (4) 'the prepuce is large or wrinkled or in folds'; (5) the clitoris is 'notably erectile'...; (6) 'eroticism is clearly in evidence on examination, as shown by dusky flush of the parts, with free flow of clear, glairy mucus, and with definite clitoris erection....'" The study concludes that all "these findings can be the result of strong sex urge [presumably an innate or congenital condition], plus: (a) Vulvar and vulvovaginal self-friction; or (b) Homosexual digital or oral play; or (c) Heterosexual manual or coital techniques, singly or in any combination."[36] Terry rightly emphasizes the researchers' apparent fascination with the concept that homo/hypersexual desire (often conflated) could be strong enough that it could make the vulva a site of transformation. The prurience behind this possibility that perverted sex play could "rebuild" a vagina, seems great enough that it is allowed to overshadow the theory of a congenital distinction between heterosexual and homosexual anatomy.

Many American and British clitoridectomies and female castrations (the removal of healthy ovaries) were performed in the nineteenth century and as recently as the 1970s, as a response to just such indicators.[37] Isaac Baker Brown began to perform clitoridectomies in Britain in 1858, in order to reduce "hysteria" and other nervous ailments, but particularly to combat "excessive" masturbation. He was, by the 1860s, soundly critiqued in his own country and indeed expelled from Britain's Obstetrical Society in 1867; but his procedure (and its milder variant, circumcision of the clitoral hood) became popular in the United States by the late 1860s and was performed in this country for decades. Although experimentation in the development phases of sexual surgeries generally was exacted on the bodies of poor and disenfranchised women (mostly African American), the lady of leisure became the expressed target for these operations. Upper-middle-class and upper-class women had disposable incomes and time on their hands (to masturbate . . . or to recover from genital surgery). Robert Battey developed the practice of removing healthy ovaries to address a whole slew of complaints, from kleptomania to epilepsy, and this procedure was surprisingly widespread, particularly between 1880 and 1910. One 1893 proponent of female castration claimed that "the moral sense of the patient is elevated. . . . She becomes tractable, orderly, industrious and cleanly." Although depleted misrule seems an unsurprising "benefit" of such operations, one would not expect *aesthetics* to spring up as a concern in this context, but Ben Barker-Benfield cites some clitoridectomy and castration patients who thought of the trend as a "fashionable fad" and found their scars "as pretty as the dimple on the cheek of sweet sixteen."[38]

In the 1970s and 1980s, James Burt, an Ohio gynecologist, gained notoriety—and eventually lost his license—performing what he called "the surgery of love" on more than 4,500 patients, apparently often without even garnering the pretense of informed consent, while they were anesthetized and "on the table" for another procedure. This procedure included a clitoral circumcision and a vaginal reconstruction that changed the angle of the vagina; he insisted before and after the malpractice suits that he had enhanced the sexual pleasure of 99 percent of the women upon whom he'd operated and that he was "correcting" the female anatomy, which he saw as God's mistake, by repositioning the genitalia. Women were left with loss of erotic sensation, enormous pain during intercourse, chronic bowel and urination problems requiring regular catheter use, and ongoing serious infections; the same set of medical sequelae have been reported among infibulated women.[39] In 1997, the Ohio Supreme Court ultimately awarded forty women compensation amounting to a total of $20 million. This award came after spectacular struggles in the courts over an eleven-year-period. The organization Patients-in-Arms, led by Carla Miller (who describes herself as "a victim of FGM" [female genital mutilation]), is devoted to helping women speak out about abuse and disfigurement at the hands of gynecologists. A review of the cases toward which Ms. Miller can direct one makes it excruciatingly clear both that this phenomenon is quite widespread and that it is made possible by the common and interlinked phenomenon of the "white wall of silence" that reduces the doctors' risk of being brought to task.[40]

In a related phenomenon that persists to this day, the erotic tissue of "intersexed" or ambiguously gendered babies and children is routinely, in fact just about ubiquitously, modified through surgery without the minor's consent, in what the medical profession calls a "psychosocial emergency." These modifications have been shown to leave behind serious psychological scarring; often enough, the surgeries profoundly compromise the sexual sensation of the people forced to undergo them. In a piece called "The Tyranny of the Aesthetic: Surgery's Most

Intimate Violation," Martha Coventry explains that "girlhood is [almost always] the gender approximated through surgery in such circumstances." "It's easier to poke a hole than build a pole," as one surgeon remarks. Coventry quotes Suzanne Kessler, whose work represents an important contribution to the study of intersexed experience: "Genital ambiguity is corrected not because it is threatening to the infant's life, but because it is threatening to the infant's culture." [41]

The genitalia are cultural terrain that must conform to identificatory norms; this has been driven home by the historians of gynecological science. When mid-nineteenth-century physician Marion Sims developed the duck-billed speculum and an examination protocol that gave him a good view, he used the language of an imperial conquistador, beholding still uncharted territory: "I saw everything, as no man had seen before." [42] Much has been written, particularly by Irigaray, about the mythologization of female genitalia as "the dark continent," the "nothing to see," an Unknown supposedly waiting to be penetrated by pioneering masculine experts; Mary Ann Doane and Anne McClintock are among those who have etched out the linkage that such a metaphor immediately suggests between gender politics and racial imperialism. [43]

What if the "nothing," the furor about female absence, is in part a stand-in scandal for the *something* that is the vaginal bloom—just as the "vast wildernesses" of the Americas and Africa were an invader's myth that suppressed the inconvenient fact of inhabitation? It is exactly in the realms where gender and race intersect that we can see this being played out. Sander Gilman and Michele Wallace are among those who have discussed Saartjie (or Sara) Baartman, dubbed the Hottentot Venus. She and other African women were taken from their homes and put on show in the early nineteenth century; in this display, their labial "aprons" were rumored about and peeked at with as much eroticized condemnation as were their "steoptygic" buttocks, although the latter were more plainly in view. [44] When George Cuvier, Geoffrey St. Hilaire,

and Henri de Blainville, eminent naturalists all, attempted to force a scientific examination of Baartman, de Blainville reported that "she hid her apron carefully between her thighs—her movements were brusque and capricious like those of apes.... It was only with great sorrow that she let drop her handkerchief for a moment." [45] The outrage of invasion so evident here is aggravated by the dehumanization of Baartman that drove the tragic endeavor. In the same commentary, Cuvier describes elements of her appearance as being "like an orangutan," "like an animal," and "like a dog." [46] Eager to inspect her labia, particularly as they were seeking a classificatory wedge that would distinguish the Hottentot from the European on the level of species, the scientists spent three days trying to convince Baartman to submit to the physical, even offering her money, which she refused. Alas, her early death afforded them ready access to her private parts, however, and Cuvier made a plaster cast of her body and had her brain and genitals preserved in jars. Although the skeleton remains at Paris's Musée de l'Homme, her body is due to be returned to South Africa for burial ... and her brain and genitals have disappeared. [47]

It is no coincidence that the aforementioned Marion Sims, early American gynecologist, developed his surgery techniques only by repeated, public operations on the bodies of African American slaves and poor, white "washerwomen." [48] Doing symbolic work, nonwhite women in the Euro-American context have endured the exposure of their bodies only to have them decried and desired, first as heathenish, then as "abnormal." Meanwhile, the nonprostitute white woman's vagina was hidden, protected—shamed, too, but out of the limelight.

OUR VULVAS, OUR SELVES

Perhaps this context needs to be kept in mind when we consider another role played contemporarily by images of female genitals: among activists opposed to the circumcision of African females, even among those who are extremely sensitive to the liabilities of cultural bias, the documenting photo has a special, and somewhat problematic, status. In "Desiring the 'Mutilated' African Woman," Wacuka Mungai points out that there is a heated and eerily prurient interest expressed over the Web in accessing documentary photos of girls and women who have undergone clitero-dectomies, excisions, and infibulation.[49] Although photographs of excised and infibulated vaginas are available at "kinky" web sites alongside other images deemed freakish or gory, I agree with Mungai that, even beyond the overtly pornographic, their status as emblems of an "Othered" barbarity is also tinged with unacknowledged eroticism. As Mungai explains, these photos are typically taken with something like consent, but under circumstances when a girl would be hard pressed to withhold permission—in exchange for treatment, a foreign, light-skinned doctor who doesn't speak your language asks that you let her photograph you. You are not likely to refuse her, even though there may be trauma in the taking, and even though the photos then circulate the globe, representing only the wounded status of the African female. Like the gynecological diagram, like Baartman's genitals so long on formaldehyde display in Paris, like the "monster shot" in porn flicks, these images are partial, headless...vaginas emphatically disseevered from whole people, made creatures of their own—treated, perhaps, as the essence of the woman, the cut vagina the truest thing about her, a dangerous metonymy. Mungai points out that, by the same token, in media coverage of the debates over female circumcision among immigrants, the portraits of "cut" women's faces that accompany articles decrying the practice often serve to bring about the same delimiting reduction.

One North American woman with whom I spoke who had elected to have a labiaplasty laughed uproariously with me at the nerve of a European television news program that had approached her to ask if she'd like to do a segment on their show about her operation. The very *thought* of her face being linked to her imagined, modified vagina was preposterous to her, and she would certainly never have consented to being part of the show. Our

laughter should continue to ring until it has turned livid, as we think about the many African girls and women who experience just this representational conflation.

[In keeping with the concerns voiced here about circulating images of "cut" female genitalia, I have decided not to present illustrations like those at the plastic surgeons' web sites mentioned here or those found in some anti-FGO (female genital operations) materials....]

CONFOUNDING THE BOUNDARIES

The U.S. Congress passed a measure criminalizing the circumcision of a minor female in 1996, and nine or ten states have passed anti-FGO acts since 1996 as well. In Illinois, Minnesota, Rhode Island, and Tennessee, this legislation felonizes operations performed on adults as well as on minors. But *which* operations? Anti-FGO laws that now exist in a number of U.S. states describe procedures that would definitely include those practiced by Drs. Alter and Matlock, but they use only language that addresses the "ritual" or custom and belief-based cutting of African immigrant bodies. Meanwhile, this legal language either elides or okays both the "corrective" cutting of the intersexed child and the surgery sought by the unsettled consumer who has been told by plastic surgeons that her labia are unappealing and aberrant. Thus American law marks out relations between the state and its citizen bodies that differ depending on birthplace, cultural context, and skin color.

In fact, however, it is a (prevalent) mistake to imagine a quantum distinction between Euro-American and African reshapings of women's bodies: far too often, they are measured with entirely different yardsticks, rather than on a continuum. Nahid Toubia, executive director of the advocacy group Rainbo, remarks that "[t]he thinking of an African woman who believes that 'FGM is the fashionable thing to do to become a real woman' is not so different from that of an American woman who has breast implants to appear more feminine."[50] In keeping with Toubia's remark, I propose here that a subtler and less culturally binaristic analysis of such phenomena will lead, not to political paralysis in the name of cultural relativism, but to deeper understanding of core issues like the nature of consent, of bodily aesthetics and social control, and of cross-cultural activist collaboration.[51]

Soraya Miré, Somali maker of the film *Fire Eyes*, remarks in Inga Muscio's (wo)manifesto, *Cunt: A Declaration of Independence:* "[Western women] come into conversations waving the American flag, forever projecting the idea that they are more intelligent than I am. I've learned that American women look at women like me to hide from their own pain.... In America, women pay *the money that is theirs and no one else's* to go to a doctor who cuts them up so they can create or sustain an image men want. Men are the mirror. Western women cut themselves up voluntarily."[52] Significantly, in Miré's construction, consent to genital surgery does *not* okay it so much as it marks the degrading depths of women's oppression. Although consent is at the heart of the issue of genital operations on children, a topic both urgent and not to be downplayed, we must also look at the social and cultural means whereby consent is manufactured, regardless of age, in the West as well as in African and other countries engaging in FGOs. In the North American popular imagination, the public address of advertising is not understood as infringing upon our power of consent. Indeed, the freedom to "pay the money that is [one's] own" is too often inscribed as the quintessential exemplar of life in a democracy. Perhaps due to that presumption, beauty rituals hatched on Madison Avenue or in Beverly Hills do not bear the onus of "barbarism" here, despite the social compulsions, psychological drives, and magical thinking that impel them.

By the same token, American oversimplifications suppress the fact that African women's relations to female genital operations are complex and variable, as are the operations themselves, of course. The operations can be roughly grouped into four sorts: circumcision, the removal of the clitoral hood or "female prepuce"; clitoridectomy, "the partial or total removal of the clitoris"; excision, "the removal of the clitoris and all or part of the labia minora"; and infibulation, "the removal of all external genitalia followed by the stitching together of most of the vaginal opening."[53] As will be discussed, motivations for any of these practices are highly variable across time and between individuals as well as between cultures. Vicki Kirby points out the distortions that come with Western monolithizing: "What is 'other' for the West must thereby forfeit its own internal contradictions and diversities in this singular and homogenizing determination of alterity."[54]

Additionally, African vaginal aesthetics are not limited to such sheerings away of vulvular tissue. Although now it is predominantly the members of the royal family who still practice this technique (which is thus a sign of status), the Buganda people in Uganda have a tradition of stretching and massaging the labia and clitoris from childhood to extend them (for feminine beautification). As Londa Schiebinger describes, some say that the "Hottentot aprons," so fetishized by Europeans, were also the result of cosmetic manipulations, on the part of African women seeking beauty.[55]

If one considers all female circumcision practices in Africa to be analogous, as is too commonly the case in popular American analysis of the phenomenon, not only does one miss the dramatic differences between the different forms of FGO, but one also fails to understand the relevant differences between people who practice it as a part of their cultural life and those who experience it as a part of their religious life. Crucial issues of consent are blurred with such elisions. Western critics of African genital surgeries can also miss completely the role that it often plays in the symbolism of resistance and political struggle, both colonial and tribal.[56] In *Facing Mt. Kenya: The Tribal Life of the Kikuyu* (1953), Jomo Kenyatta remarks that "the overwhelming majority of [the local people] believe that it is the secret aim of those who attack this country's old customs to disintegrate their social order and thereby hasten their Europeanization."[57] An additional point: although female circumcision is not explicitly directed by any religious text, it is practiced as an expression of Muslim, Christian, and Jewish religious observance among various African populations. Overall, it should not be imagined as concomitant with Islam (which it regularly is, often in an anti-Arab conflation), or even as a primarily religious practice.

In most regions, female circumcision practices are determined more by cultural factors, and by ethnic, national, tribal, and postcolonial politics, than by religion. They are by no means solely or exotically "ritualistic" in a way that entirely distinguishes them from nonimmigrant American operations on vaginas. Female genital operations are understood, variously, as hygiene, as beautification, as a curb to female sexuality, as a clarification of the difference between the sexes, as an enhancement of male sexual pleasure, as conducive to fertility and/or monogamy, as disease prevention, and as a means of conforming with social norms and ensuring that one's daughter will be marriageable, that she will be able to take her place among her age set, and that the solidarity and social strength of older women's organizations will be able to flourish.[58]

SURGERY, SISTERLINESS, AND THE "RIGHT TO CHOOSE"

Among the key motivating factors raised by African women who favor female genital surgeries are beautification, transcendence of shame, and the desire to conform; these clearly matter to American women seeking cosmetic surgery on their labia, as well. Thus, the motivations that impel African-rooted FGOs and American labiaplasties should not be envisioned as radically distinct. Not only does such oversimplification lead to a dangerous reanimation of the un/civilized binary, but it also leaves the feminist with dull tools for analysis of either phenomenon. There are aesthetic parallels between the Western and the African procedures. The enthusiasm for the clean slit voiced so vigorously by the American plastic surgeon I consulted is echoed among a group of Egyptian mothers discussing female genital operations for their daughters in the 1990 documentary, *Hidden Faces*. Although several

of the women laughingly nudge each other and say they wouldn't want the excisers to interfere much with "the front" (showing a clear zest for clitoral pleasure), one woman voices an aesthetic principle about which she feels strongly. Energetically, she decries the ugliness of dangling labia, and explains to the filmmaker, with appropriate hand gestures, "Do you want her to be like a boy, with this floppy thing hanging down? Now, it should be straight Shhh. Smooth as silk." This aesthetic judgment is in keeping not only with the views of labiaplasters in the United States but also with the vocabulary of Mauritanian midwives: one such woman, who has argued to her colleagues for a milder version of circumcision in place of vigorous excision, "use[s] two words to refer to female circumcision, 'tizian,' which means to make more beautiful, and 'gaaad,' which means to cut off and make even."[59]

The group of women chatting on a rooftop in *Hidden Faces* invokes another continuum between African and American women's approaches to feminine beauty rituals and vaginal modifications. Simplistic depictions of a global patriarchy, wherein men curb, cow, cut, and dominate "their" women, may drive home the ubiquity of female subjugation, but they leave out an important factor at the same time: although both labiaplasties and African female circumcision should be (and are here) investigated through a feminist lens, that feminism should be informed by an awareness of women's agency. A knee-jerk celebration of that agency misleads, but its disavowal in the name of victimhood leads to dangerous blind spots. Across many different cultural contexts, female genital operations are contemplated and undergone by girls and women in a social and psychological framework shaped *in part* by other women.

The plastic surgeon whose office I visited provided me with two referrals, patients who had had the procedure done by him. As part of what seemed a well-worn sales pitch, he referred often to "self-help groups," a network of supportive, independent women helping each other find the professional care they wanted and deserved, in the face of an unfeeling, disbelieving medical profession. I was interested by what seemed an invocation of rather feminist sensibilities and wondered about this swelling, grassroots support group he seemed to be conjuring up for me. And, indeed, the image of the surgery consumer as a liberated woman and an independent self-fashioner did provide a crucial spin for the doctor, throughout his consultation. The consumer-feminist in support of other women he condoned; by contrast, he expressed an avowed disapproval of the women who came to him solely to please a domineering partner. He brought up this posited bad, weak, man-centric woman three times as we spoke, and each time his face clouded, he frowned, and his brow furrowed: he said that it was only this type of woman who complained of pain after the procedure, for instance, just to get the attention of her partner, whereas for most women, he insisted, the pain was minimal. He seemed to use these diverging models of female behavior to answer in advance any reservations the prospective client might have about a cosmetic operation on the genitalia (such as, "Should I really do something so drastic to my body just to please men?"). By insisting on his antipathy toward women who kowtowed to the male perspective, and celebrating the fearless vision of the pioneer consumer of "cutting edge" surgery, the doctor tried, I suspect, to ward off potential surges of feminist resistance to the procedure.

In the same spirit, one web site advertising the surgery fuels itself on a long-standing feminist call for a more responsive medical establishment by contrasting the surgeon being advertised with other doctors less sensitive to the needs of women. "Very few physicians are concerned with the appearance of the female external genitalia. A relative complacency exists that frustrates many women."[60] Rachel Bowlby has addressed the theoretical conflations between feminist freedom and the "freedom" to choose as a consumer.[61] The surgeon to whose sales pitch I listened and the creators of the web site noted here certainly understood that the feminist discourse of choice can be appropriated, funneled toward the managed choosing-under-duress of the consumer, becoming saturated along the way with commodity culture's directives.

One goal of this article is to raise the question of this ready appropriation. In *States of Injury: Power and Freedom in Late Modernity,* Wendy Brown examines some of the liabilities of the Left's reliance on the rhetoric of identity, injury, and redress, suggesting that it can result in a politics of state domination.[62] From Bakke on, we have certainly seen the language of affirmative action hauled into the arena of "reverse racism." Perhaps by the same token, the language of choice, as central to the feminist project in this country as we could imagine, sprang up in a culture where the glories of consumer "choice" had already been mythologized. Revisiting and perhaps refiguring the conceptual framework behind "choice" in the face of manufactured consent, then, is to enable, not critique feminism. The hand mirror that allowed feminists of the 1960s and 1970s to get familiar with "our bodies, our selves" is positioned again so that we can see our vaginas. Only, it comes now with the injunction to look critically at what we see and to exert our selfhood through expenditure and remodeling of a body that is not "ourself" any longer but which is "ours," commodified and estranged, to rebuild.

Although the approach of the doctor I visited seemed agenda-driven and rather theatricalized, when I talked with the women to whom he referred me, I was struck by how very friendly and supportive they *did* seem. I had found the doctor likable but showy, like a much rehearsed salesman, but these women were engaged, candid, and genuinely warm. They were generous with their time (and with their permission to be cited anonymously in the present article), and they made it clear that they really did want to help other women with their "experience, strength, and hope." Perhaps these women were "incentivized" to speak well of the doctor (about whose care they raved): maybe they received discounted work in exchange for talking with prospective clients. Even with this possibility in mind they seemed sincerely ready to assume a common perspective, in fact an intimacy, between women discussing their bodies and body image. To overlook their candor, generosity, and *sisterliness* in order to critique the misogynist judgments that may have driven them to surgery would be to mis-characterize the phenomenon of gender display. We typically learn about and develop a gendered bod-ily performance, not in isolation, but as members of both real and imagined female "communities."[63] And in 2002, one senses the cultural shading that twentieth-century feminism has, ironically, brought to this community building: the rhetoric of choice making and of solidarity developed during the Second Wave ghosts through our conversations. It's a stereotypical joke that women *really* dress for each other—a deeper look at how this female-to-female hodgepodge of peer pressure and peer support really manifests itself is useful. And again, a look at the web of relations among women is helpful in under-standing African female genital operations as well.

One on-line World Health Organization report discusses the impact of female circumcisions on girls' psychological health. Importantly, it men-tions not only "experiences of suffering, devalua-tion and impotence" but also the "desirability of the ceremony for the child, with its social advantage of peer acceptance, personal pride and material gifts." Claire Robertson points out that among the func-tions of the circumcision ceremony in Central Kenya is the role female initiation plays in maintaining the social strength of organizations of older women.[64] The flip side of approving support, of course, is peer pressure. "When girls of my age were looking after the lambs, they would talk among themselves about their circumcision experiences and look at each oth-er's genitals to see who had the smallest opening. If there was a girl in the group who was still uninfibu-lated, she would always feel ashamed since she had nothing to show the others."[65]

A reminiscent bodily shame lurks behind the support for labial modifications that my American patient contacts expressed. One (heterosexual) woman explained to me that although none of her boyfriends had ever remarked on her labia, "ever since I was fourteen, I felt like I had this abnormalcy; I felt uncomfortable changing in front of girlfriends." She went on to say that she felt she had to hide her vagina around other women and could never enjoy skinny-dipping because of her concerns about other women judging her appearance. Another labiaplasty patient reported a "120% shift" in her "mental atti-tude," and a "night-and-day" improvement in the looks of her genitalia, thanks to the surgery. "As sad as it is, it makes you feel inferior," she commented.[66] Her use of the second person (or the ethical dative, as it's known), so intimate in its extension of sub-jectivity, meant that her language included me. . . . I too felt sad, I too felt inferior. And for a fee, the kind doctor was there to correct me.

NEW RITES

It is probably obvious from this piece that, even in the age where both informational and medical tech-nology have led to bodies being reshaped, extended, reconfigured, and reconceptualized like never before, I believe that erotic tissue is far better enjoyed than removed.[67] In approaching the politics of female genital operations, however, I would argue that it is imperative that both consent issues and vaginal modifications themselves be considered *on a con-tinuum* that is not determined along hemispheric, national, or racial lines. Instead, we peer at female genital operations with a prurient, bifurcating tunnel vision and pretend a clean break between the "primi-tive barbarism" of "ritual" cutting of African women, who are far too often represented as undifferentiated victims, and the aesthetic or medical "fixings" of those Amero-European women who are presented as either mildly deformed people in the wise hands of experts or consumer-designers of a cyborgian gender display.

In "Arrogant Perception, World-Traveling, and Multicultural Feminism: The Case of Female Genital Surgeries," Isabelle R. Gunning attempts to define and model a responsible approach to thinking about genital operations across cultures. She urges activists "to look at one's own culture anew and identify [. . .] practices that might prove 'culturally challenging' or negative to some other," and "to look in careful detail at the organic social environment of the 'other' which has produced the culturally challenging prac-tice being explored."[68] I have tried, in this article, to meet her first criterion, and I hope that rendering

American cosmetic surgery strange through a heedful look at this latest, not-yet-naturalized procedure can aid us in contextualizing and understanding genital surgeries born in other contexts as well.

Gunning examines some of the ramifications of legal "remedies" for African genital operations and concludes that criminalization of FGOs, whether on the grounds of violating human rights, women's rights, or children's rights, can seem to characterize African women and men as morally blighted, criminally bad parents, and blinded by a cultural tradition that would best be replaced with Western values. Stan Meuwese and Annemieke Wolthuis of Defense for Children International remark that a "legal approach to the phenomenon ... especially the use of criminal law, shows very clearly the limitations of the juridical system to combat historically and socially deeply-rooted behavior." One Somali woman points out that "if Somali women change, it will be a change done by us, among us. When they order us to stop, tell us what we must do, it is offensive to the black person or Muslim person who believes in circumcision. To advise is good, but not to order." [69]

Gunning, Robertson, and writers at Rainbo's web site are among those who advise that the socioeconomic dependency of women upon men is perhaps the key context for understanding and ultimately abandoning female genital surgeries. [70] They call for a two-pronged strategy: (1) work to improve women's socioeconomic autonomy, both globally and locally and (2) facilitate autonomous, community-generated cultural evolution rather than imposing punitive restrictions. These do seem fruitful emphases, as applicable in the American as in the African context. That they are realizable can be seen with the following story.

In 1997, Malik Stan Reaves reported in the *African News Service* about an alternative ritual that was replacing female circumcision in some rural sections of Kenya. I quote from his article:

A growing number of rural Kenyan families are turning to an alternative to the rite of female circumcision for their daughters. "Circumcision Through Words" grows out of collaborations between rural families and the Kenyan national women's group, Maendeleo ya Wanawake Organization (MYWO), which is committed to ending FGM in Kenya, ... with the close cooperation of the Program for Appropriate Technology in Health (PATH), a nonprofit, nongovernmental, international organization which seeks to improve the health of women and children. ...

"People think of the traditions as themselves," said Leah Muuya of MYWO. [71] "They see themselves in their traditions. They see they are being themselves because they have been able to fulfill some of the initiations." ... Circumcision Through Words brings the young candidates together for a week of seclusion during which they learn traditional teachings about their coming roles as women, parents, and adults in the community, as well as more modern messages about personal health, reproductive issues, hygiene, communications skills, self-esteem, and dealing with peer pressure. The week is capped by a community celebration of song, dancing, and feasting which affirms the girls and their new place in the community. [72]

Willow Gerber, of PATH, confirms that as of December 2001, the Circumcision Through Words program is still ongoing and has been, over the last several years, expanded to other districts by a consortium of donors. [73] Considering this impressive endeavor, which has seen more than 1,900 girls grow to womanhood uncut, one is reminded of the words of Claire Robertson: "Central Kenyan women have been making increasingly successful efforts to stop FGM ... [they show] strengths that U.S. women might well emulate in seeking to better their own status." [74]

How *might* we emulate "Circumcision Through Words"? Newly formed rituals in this country, at least those formally recognized as such, usually emerge in either New Age or evangelical settings and can grate the sensibilities of people beyond those spheres. Initiation of our girls into womanhood is often enough left to the devices of Madison Avenue and magazines like *YM, Teen People,* and *CosmoGirl.* And yet, for all the unconsciousness with which so many of us muddle through our life transitions in this country, nonetheless we too "feel that we have been ourselves" when we fulfill what we see as society's expectations for people at our stage of life. This is not an emotion to be belittled. (One Arabic term for the genital scar is *nafsi,* "my own self.")[75] Without the "years of research and discussion" that helped MYWO develop Circumcision Through Words, we would be hard pressed to generate new ways of bringing "our bodies, ourselves" into a symbolic relation with the social world that would prove both intelligible and affirmative. Just as analogies between genital cuttings are both important and exceedingly difficult to draw, so too is the conscious development of new, performative practices both worth emulating and only circuitously "applicable." Even in rural Kenya, the approach to "circumcision through words" varies dramatically from district to district.[76]

So I will not conclude this article with a glib, faux ritual for American women trained to hate the specificities of their bodies in the interest of capital accumulation. I will see, however, if I can leave you in a performative mode, offering a coda that I hope can "act" upon and through the reader as a textual "rite of antidote," speaking back to the cited language of abnormality, pathology, and sexual distrust with which this article began.

CODA

Dan Savage, syndicated sex advice columnist, responded to one reader concerned about the aesthetic effect of her long labia minora, by suggesting the work of Dr. Stubbs. He received many letters of protest, providing paeans to the appeal of prominent labia and/or suggesting that he advise self-admiration, not surgery. The enthusiastic adjectives these letter writers employed ("lavish," "luscious," "extravagant"), coupled with their emphasis on erotic pleasure, can remind us that perhaps "beauty" results from a harmony between form and function, and one key genital function is *pleasure.* I offer excerpts from some of these letters here.[77]

- ...You might have told Jagger Lips to toss her unappreciative lovers out of bed and find a boyfriend who sees the beauty of her as she exists....

- ...I have long inner labia and most of the women I've seen naked have inner labia that extend past the outer labia....If someone wants to see what vulvas really look like, they should put down *Penthouse* and start sleeping with lots of women.

- ...many men, myself included, don't find a thing wrong with longer labia minora. My girlfriend has one [*sic*] and I find it quite the enjoyable thing to suck on....

- Does female sexual pleasure mean anything to you? Not only do the labia minora engorge during sexual stimulation and have lots of nerve endings, they also increase friction....

- I am writing to Jagger Lips to discourage her from chopping off her labia minora. I prefer long labia. I find that they lend themselves more readily to being tugged, stretched, nibbled, etc....

- ...I remember a gorgeous actor, Savannah, who sadly committed suicide in the mid-1990s, who had a beautiful snatch with extravagant labia spilling (an inch and a half, easy) from her soft and salty cornucopia of love. She was rad, I hope she's resting in peace, and I'd recommend your reader try and rustle up a video....

- Our society tends not to be so pussy-positive, and most commercial pussy pictures are airbrushed on Planet Barbie, and shouldn't be considered reality. Labia (inner and outer) have lots of nerves and feel really good when they get stroked.

- ...Please tell the woman with the lavish labia not to have them removed....You were much too hasty to recommend clipping her butterfly wings!...

NOTES

1. Things certainly can happen. See Louisa Kamps, "Labia Envy," 16 Mar. 1998, <http://www. salon.com/ mwt/feature/1998/03/16feature.html> (9 Dec. 2001).

2. *Los Angeles Times,* 5 Mar. 1998. See, too, the following Internet resources on labiaplasty: Dr. Alter: "Female Cosmetic and Reconstructive Genital Surgery,"

<http://www. altermd.com/female/index.html>
(9 Dec. 2001); Julia Scheeres, "Vaginal Cosmetic
Surgery," 16 Apr. 2001, <http://thriveonline.oxygen.
com/sex/sexpressions/vaginal-cosmetic-surgery.html>
(9 Dec. 2001); Dr. Stubbs, <http://psurg.com>; Laser
Rejuvenation Center of LA, <http://www.drmatlock.
com>; Dan Savage, "Long in the Labia," 16 Dec.
1999, <http://www.the stranger.com/
1999-12-16/savage.html> (13 Dec. 2001); iVillage.
com Archive Message Board, "Cosmetic Surgery," 7
Jan. 2000, <http://boards.allhealth.com/messages/
get/bhcosmeticsx2.html> (13 Dec. 2001); Patients'
chatboard, <http://boards.allhealth.com/messages/get/
bhcosmeticsx2.html>.

3. See Kamps. Also, see Carrie Havranek, "The New Sex
   Surgeries," *Cosmopolitan,* November 1998, 146.

4. Ellen Frankfort, *Vaginal Politics* (New York:
   Quadrangle, 1972). See, too, Julia Scheeres, "Vulva
   Goldmine: How Cosmetic Surgeons Snatch Your
   Money," *Bitch* 11 (January 2000): 70–84.

5. Boston Women's Health Collective, *Our Bodies,
   Ourselves* (New York: Simon & Schuster, 1973).
   Updated editions have continued to be released.
   See Boston Women's Health Collective, *Our Bodies,
   Ourselves for the New Century: A Book by and for Women*
   (New York: Simon & Schuster, 1998).

6. See Amelia Jones, ed., *Sexual Politics: Judy Chicago's
   Dinner Party in Feminist Art History* (Berkeley:
   University of California Press, 1996); Shannon Bell,
   "Prostitute Performances: Sacred Carnival Theorists
   of the Female Body," from her *Reading, Writing, and
   Rewriting the Prostitute Body* (Bloomington: Indiana
   University Press, 1994), 137–84; and Eve Ensler, *The
   Vagina Monologues* (New York: Villard Press, 1998).

7. Although some women enjoy orgasmic ejaculation, it
   remains an exception to the rule.

8. Linda Williams's book is about pornographic films,
   especially those of the 1970s: *Hard Core: Power,
   Pleasure, and the "Frenzy of the Visible"* (Berkeley:
   University of California Press, 1989), 50.

9. See Michel Foucault, *The History of Sexuality,* vol. 1, *An
   Introduction* (New York: Random House, 1978).

10. See Gershon Legman, *Rationale of the Dirty Joke: An
    Analysis of Sexual Humor* (New York: Breaking Point
    Press, 1975), 547.

11. Jonathan Swift's "dressing room poems" include "To
    Betty the Grisette," "The Lady's Dressing Room,"
    "A Beautiful Young Nymph Going to Bed," and
    "Strephon and Chloe." See Jonathan Swift, *The Complete
    Poems,* ed. Pat Rogers (New Haven: Yale University
    Press, 1983), 447–62. Also, see William Ian

Miller, *The Anatomy of Disgust* (Cambridge: Harvard
University Press, 1997).

12. In a mode that both ridicules and familiarizes the
    body modifications of plastic surgery, tabloids
    regularly feature articles about the "work" being done
    on celebrities, with a special emphasis on implant
    disasters. See, for instance, "Hollywood's Plastic
    Surgery Nightmares: When Breast Implants Go Bad,"
    National Enquirer, 4 May 1999, 28–33. Kathy Davis
    discusses popular coverage of celebrity surgeries in
    *Reshaping the Female Body: The Dilemma of Cosmetic
    Surgery* (New York: Routledge, 1995), 18.

13. See the work of the late historian Roland Marchand,
    *Advertising the American Dream: Making Way for
    Modernity, 1920–1940* (Berkeley: University of
    California Press, 1985), 18–20.

14. Davis; Elizabeth Haiken, *Venus Envy: A History of Cosmetic
    Surgery* (Baltimore: Johns Hopkins University Press,
    1997); Sander Gilman, *Making the Body Beautiful: A
    Cultural History of Aesthetic Surgery* (Princeton: Princeton
    University Press, 1999). Also, see Claudia Springer,
    Electronic Eros: Bodies and Desire in the Postindustrial Age
    (Austin: University of Texas Press, 1996).

15. Milton T. Edgerton and H. R. McClary, quoted in
    Haiken, 244.

16. On the thin line between identification and
    desire, between wanting to be like someone and
    wanting to bed down with them (so exploited in
    consumer culture), see Diana Fuss, "Fashion and the
    Homospectatorial Look," in *On Fashion,* ed. Shari
    Benstock and Suzanne Ferriss (New Brunswick, N.J.:
    Rutgers University Press, 1994), 211–32; and Judith
    Butler, *Gender Trouble: Feminism and the Subversion of
    Identity* (New York: Routledge, 1990), esp. 57–72.

17. Josey Vogels, "My Messy Bedroom," *See,* 10 July 1997,
    <http://www.greatwest.ca/ SEE/ Issues/1997/970710/
    josey.html> (13 Dec. 2001).

18. Laura Kipnis, *Bound and Gagged: Pornography and the
    Politics of Fantasy in America* (New York: Grove, 1996).

19. Susie Bright, "The Pussy Shot: An Interview with
    Andrew Blake," *Sexwise* (New York: Cleis Press,
    1995), 82.

20. Haiken, 29–34, 136–45, 237, 246.

21. See Richard Goldstein, "Porn Free," *Village Voice,* 1
    Sept. 1998, 28–34. My own research for a work-in-
    progress, "Choosing the Moves: Choreography in the
    Strip Club," also bears this out.

22. See Nedahl Stelio, "Do You Know What a Vagina
    Looks Like?" *Cosmopolitan,* August 2001, 126–28, on
    sex magazines' doctoring of vaginas and the increased
    prevalence of labiaplasty.

23. Luce Irigaray, *This Sex Which Is Not One,* trans. Catherine Porter (Ithaca: Cornell University Press, 1985), 209. Also see her *Speculum of the Other Woman* (Ithaca: Cornell University Press, 1986).

24. See Mary Douglas on a cross-cultural tendency to approach marginal zones, marginal people, and marginal periods with great apprehension, in *Purity and Danger: An Analysis of the Concepts of Pollution and Taboo* (1966; reprint, New York: Routledge, 1992).

25. Mary Russo, *The Female Grotesque: Risk, Excess, and Modernity* (New York: Routledge, 1994), 8.

26. See <http://www.psurg.com/gallery.html> (13 Dec. 2001).

27. Haiken, 5.

28. Natalie Zemon Davis, "Women on Top," in her *Society and Culture in Early Modern France* (Stanford: Stanford University Press, 1975), 124. See 124–31.

29. Denise Stoklos, remark made in Solo Performance Composition, her course offered by the Performance Studies Department, New York University, Spring 2000. "Our primary dialogue is with gravity," Stoklos says.

30. See Ambient, Inc., "Body Modification: Is It Self-Mutilation—Even if Someone Else Does It for You?" 2 Feb. 1998, <http://www.ambient.on.ca/bodmod/mutilate.html> (13 Dec. 2001). Another web site dealing with body modification is <www.perforations.com> (13 Dec. 2001).

31. Ensler, 3–5.

32. This and all subsequent quotations from this plastic surgeon are from an office visit in a major American city—location to remain unspecified to ensure anonymity—in April 1999.

33. Elizabeth Grosz: "[W]omen's corporeality is inscribed as a mode of seepage." See her *Volatile Bodies: Toward a Corporeal Feminism* (Bloomington: Indiana University Press, 1994), 203.

34. Terri Kapsalis, *Public Privates: Performing Gynecology from Both Ends of the Speculum* (Durham: Duke University Press, 1997), 89. She references Julia Kristeva, *Powers of Horror: An Essay on Abjection* (New York: Columbia University Press, 1982). On the cultural and political implications of representations of genitalia in anatomical textbooks, see Lisa Jean Moore and Adele E. Clarke, "Clitoral Conventions and Transgressions: Graphic Representations in Anatomy Texts, c1900–1991," *Feminist Studies* 21 (summer 1995): 255–301; and Susan C. Lawrence and Kae Bendixen, "His and Hers: Male and Female Anatomy in Anatomical Texts for U.S. Medical Students, 1890–1989," *Social Science and Medicine* 35 (October 1992): 925–36. Also, see Katharine Young, "Perceptual Modalities: Gynecology," in her *Presence in the Flesh* (Cambridge: Harvard University Press, 1997), 46–79.

35. Thomas Laqueur, *Making Sex: Body and Gender from the Greeks to Freud* (Cambridge: Harvard University Press, 1990). And see Lynn Hunt, *The Invention of Pornography* (New York: Zone, 1993).

36. Jennifer Terry, "Lesbians under the Medical Gaze: Scientists Search for Remarkable Differences," *Journal of Sex Research* 27 (August 1990): 317–39, 332 (emphasis added), 333.

37. See Ben Barker-Benfield, "Sexual Surgery in Late-Nineteenth-Century America," *International Journal of Health Services* 5, no. 2 (1975): 279–98; Andrew Scull and Diane Favreau, "The Clitoridectomy Craze," *Social Research* 53 (summer 1986): 243; Barbara Ehrenreich and Deirdre English, *Complaints and Disorders: The Sexual Politics of Sickness* (New York: City University of New York Press, 1973); and Rachel P. Maines, *The Technology of Orgasm: "Hysteria," the Vibrator, and Women's Sexual Satisfaction* (Baltimore: Johns Hopkins University Press, 1999).

38. Barker-Benfield, 287, 298.

39. See Daniel Gordon, "Female Circumcision and Genital Operations in Egypt and the Sudan: A Dilemma for Medical Anthropology," *Medical Anthropology Quarterly* 5 (March 1991): 7.

40. For more on this and similar cases, see Carla Miller's statement at <www.InMemoryoftheSufferingChild.com>. For coverage of the Burt case, see, for instance, Sandy Theis, "His Peers Waved Red Flags: Monitors' Concern Went beyond Love Surgery," *Dayton Daily News,* 4 Aug. 1991, 1A; Rob Modic, "Painful Testimony: Woman Testifies of Trust for Gynecologist Burt," *Dayton Daily News,* 1 June 1991, 1A; Judith Adler Hennessee, "The Love Surgeon," *Mademoiselle,* August 1989, 206; Gerry Harness and Judy Kelman, "A Mother's True Story: 'My Gynecologist Butchered Me!'" *Redbook,* July 1989, 22. Also see <http://www.nocirc.org> (13 Dec. 2001); <http://www.SexuallyMutilatedChild.org/index.html> (13 Dec. 2001).

41. See Suzanne Kessler, *Gender: An Ethnomethodological Approach* (1978; reprint, Chicago: University of Chicago Press, 1985), quoted by Martha Coventry in "The Tyranny of the Aesthetic: Surgery's Most Intimate Violation," <http://www.fgm.org/coventryarticle.html> (20 Dec. 2001).

42. Deborah Kuhn McGregor, *From Midwives to Medicine: The Birth of American Gynecology* (New Brunswick, N.J.: Rutgers University Press, 1998), 149. She is quoting Sims's autobiography. See also Kapsalis, chap. 2.

43. Mary Ann Doane, "Dark Continents: Epistemologies of Racial and Sexual Difference in Psychoanalysis and the Cinema," in her *Femmes Fatales: Feminism, Film Theory, Psychoanalysis* (New York: Routledge, 1991), 209–48; and Anne McClintock, *Imperial Leather: Race, Gender, and Sexuality in the Colonial Context* (New York: Routledge, 1995), esp. 1–4, and 21–31.

44. See Zola Maseko, director, *The Life and Times of Sara Baartman, "The Hottentot Venus,"* videorecording, London: Dominant 7, Mail and Guardian Television, France 3, and SABC 2, 1998.

45. Henri de Blainville, quoted in Maseko.

46. See Londa Schiebinger, *Nature's Body: Gender in the Making of Modern Science* (Boston: Beacon, 1995), chap. 5.

47. Maseko.

48. McGregor, 46–51.

49. Wacuka Mungai, "Desiring the 'Mutilated' African Woman," paper, 1999. Mungai is a doctoral student at New York University and assistant program director at Rainbo, an organization devoted in large part to advocating for African women around the issue of female circumcision.

50. Nahid Toubia, *Female Genital Mutilation: A Call for Global Action,* 3d ed. (New York: Women, Ink, 1995), 35.

51. See Janice Boddy, "Body Politics: Continuing the Anticircumcision Crusade"; and Faye Ginsburg, "What Do Women Want? Feminist Anthropology Confronts Clitoridectomy," both in *Medical Anthropology Quarterly* 5 (March 1991): 15–19.

52. Inga Muscio, *Cunt: A Declaration of Independence* (Toronto: Seal Press, 1998), 134–35.

53. "Female Genital Mutilation: A Human Rights Information Pack" (London: Amnesty International, 1997).

54. Vicki Kirby, "On the Cutting Edge: Feminism and Clitoridectomy," *Australian Feminist Studies* 5 (summer 1987): 35–56.

55. In New York City, March 1999, Wacuka Mungai shared one anecdote with me about a Buganda woman who took one trip to a gynecologist in North America: the doctor was flabbergasted and wanted to rush in a crowd of residents to stare at her. Of course, this reaction was not welcomed by the patient and she shied away from the entire profession afterward, rather than risk a reoccurrence of the circus atmosphere the doctor had created. See also, Lauran Neergard, "Doctors See More Female Circumcision," 17 Sept. 1999, posted at <http://www.worldafricannet.com/news/news7861. html>. And see this web site, that catalogs body modifications across cultures: <http://www.cadewalk. com/mods/modify.htm>. Also, see Schiebinger.

56. See Claire Robertson, "Grassroots in Kenya: Women, Genital Mutilation, and Collective Action, 1920–1990," *Signs* 21 (spring 1996):615–42, on some of the history of circumcision's changing meaning in Kenya over the course of the twentieth century. Mungai suggested that the *tribal* politics, in addition to the politics of colonial resistance, were perhaps more complex than Robertson's article describes. See also, Isabelle R. Gunning, "Arrogant Perception, World Traveling, and Multicultural Feminism: The Case of Female Genital Surgeries," *Columbia Human Rights Law Review* 23 (Summer 1992): 189–248.

57. Jomo Kenyatta, quoted in Gunning, 228.

58. See, for instance, Nadia Kamal Khalifa, "Reasons Behind Practicing Re-Circumcision among Educated Sudanese Women," *Ahfad Journal* 11, no. 2 (1994): 16–32; Anke van der Kwaake, "Female Circumcision and Gender Identity: A Questionable Alliance?" *Social Science and Medicine* 35, no. 6 (1992): 777–87.

59. Claire Hunt and Kim Longinotto, with Safaa Fathay, *Hidden Faces,* videorecording (New York: Twentieth Century Vixen Production/Women Make Movies, 1990). And see Elizabeth Oram, introduction to Zainaba's "Lecture on Clitoridectomy to the Midwives of Touil, Mauritania" (1987), in *Opening the Gates: A Century of Arab Feminist Writing,* ed. Margot Badran and Miriam Cooke (Bloomington: Indiana University Press, 1990), 63–71.

60. See <http://www.altermd.com/female/index.html> (13 Dec. 2001).

61. See Rachel Bowlby, in *Shopping with Freud: Items on Consumerism, Feminism, and Psychoanalysis* (New York: Routledge, 1993), on theoretical conflations between feminist freedom and the "freedom" to choose as a consumer.

62. Wendy Brown, *States of Injury: Power and Freedom in Late Modernity* (Princeton: Princeton University Press, 1995).

63. Anonymous telephone interviews with two West Coast labiaplasty patients, August 1999. For an on-line example of this, see the fascinating archived chat between women about cosmetic surgery at iVillage, "Cosmetic Surgery Archive Board," 7 Jan. 2001, <http://boards.allhealth.com/messages/get/ bhcosmeticsx2.html> (13 Dec. 2001).

64. See Robertson.

65. Anab's story, from "Social and Cultural Implications of Infibulation in Somalia," by Amina Wasame, in *Female Circumcision: Strategies to Bring about Change* (Somali

Women's Democratic Organization), quoted in Toubia, 41.

66. Anonymous telephone interview with author, August 1999.

67. An important caveat: As the transgendered community has made clear, for some individuals, erotic enjoyment is enhanced via the genital modification that comes along with reassigning gender, even if that surgery has resulted in a reduction in nerve endings or sensation.

68. Gunning, 213.

69. See Frances A. Althaus, "Female Circumcision: Rite of Passage or Violation of Rites?" *International Family Planning Perspectives* 23 (September 1997), <http://www.agi-usa.org/pubs/journals/2313097.html#21> (20 Dec. 2001).

70. Alan Worsley, "Infibulation and Female Circumcision," *Journal of Obstetrics and Gynecology of the British Empire* 45, no. 4 (1938): 687.

71. For more information, see the web site for the Gender Learning Network, a partnership between twenty-three women-run NGOs, including MYWO, "working to promote women's rights and status in Kenya," <http://arcc.or.ke/gln/glnl3sec.html> (13 Dec. 2001). And here are two relevant links to PATH's web site: (1) Anonymous, "Alternative rituals raise hope for eradication of Female Genital Mutilation," 20 Oct. 1997, <http://www.path.org/resources/press/19971020-FGM.html> (13 Dec. 2001), and (2) Anonymous, "Modern Rites of Passage," <http://www.path.org/resources/closerlooks/ f_modern_rites_of_passage.htm> (13 Dec. 2001).

72. PATH's Michelle Folsom heads a ten-year office in Kenya, and oversees the organization's collaboration on this and other projects with MYWO, and their work receives the support of the Kenyan government. See "Program for Appropriate Technology in Health," *Promoting a Healthy Alternative to FGM: A Tool for Program Implementers* (Washington, D.C.: PATH, 2001). See also, Davan Maharaj, "Kenya to Ban Female Genital Excision," *Los Angeles Times,* 15 Dec. 2001.

73. Robertson, 615. See also, Carolyn Sargent, "Confronting Patriarchy: The Potential for Advocacy in Medical Anthropology," *Medical Anthropology Quarterly* 5 (March 1991): 24–25.

74. Alan Worsley, 687.

75. See "Modern Rites of Passage,"<http://www.path.org/closerlooks/f_modern_rites_of_passage.html> (13 Dec. 2001).

76. All letters quoted in Dan Savage, "Savage Love," *Village Voice,* 18 Jan. 2000, 126.

27 • *Eithne Luibhéid*

A BLUEPRINT FOR EXCLUSION

The Page Law, Prostitution, and Discrimination against Chinese Women

DISCUSSION QUESTIONS

1. How does our regulation of immigration reinforce systems of race, gender/sexuality, and class oppression?
2. How are gender, sexual, and race inequities reinforced in the construction of the U.S. nation and its citizens?

Eithne Luibhéid, "A Blueprint for Exclusion: The Page Law, Prostitution, and Discrimination against Chinese Women" from *Entry Denied: Controlling Sexuality at the Border.* Minneapolis: University of Minnesota Press, pp. 31–54. Reprinted with permission by the publisher.

3. Why were Chinese prostitutes seen as a threat to white supremacy?
4. Why does Luibhéid argue that the categorization of prostitutes is a socially constructed designation?

The Page Law of 1875 established "the policy of direct federal regulation of immigration by prohibiting for the first time the entry of undesirable immigrants."[1] Immigrants designated as undesirable were those who could be classified as convicts, contract laborers, and Asian women coming to work in prostitution. The provisions regarding convicts and contract laborers had little effect at the time.[2] But the vigorously enforced bar on Asian women coming to work in prostitution had a noticeable effect on the ability of Chinese women to immigrate and served as a harbinger of multiple forms of sexuality based immigration exclusions.[3] The fact that the Page Law targeted Asian women, even when women of other nationalities were significantly involved in prostitution work too, highlights how the sexual monitoring of immigrants intersects with other systems of social hierarchy. . . .

To explain the origins of the Page Law and its profound effects on U.S. immigration control, this chapter first describes how fears about the future of white lives, cultural forms, and nation became channeled into concerns about prostitution among Chinese immigrants. It then maps out how such concerns became concretely incorporated into the immigration control process through the strategies that officials devised to try to identify and exclude Chinese prostitutes. Although these strategies remained incapable of generating reliable information about which Chinese women were prostitutes, they had important effects. The strategies transformed the immigration control apparatus into a system that constructed and regulated sexuality and, moreover, constituted Chinese women, individually and collectively, as subjectified in gender, racial, sexual, and class terms. These effects suggest that immigration control reproduces inequalities not only through individual officials' prejudices but

also through the routine monitoring strategies on which immigration control depends. These strategies, which were pioneered on Chinese women because of fears about their sexuality, gradually became extended to every immigrant who sought to enter America.

"COOLIE LABOR, IMMORAL AND DISEASED HEATHENS, AND UNASSIMILABLE ALIENS"

In order to understand the restrictions that were imposed on Chinese women by the Page Law, the law needs to be situated in relation to the larger, conflicted history of Chinese immigration to the United States. The first Chinese immigrants were overwhelmingly male, and San Francisco was the main port of entry. A majority came from the province of Guangdong and began arriving as part of the California gold rush of 1848. Like many other immigrants, they initially intended to make money and return to China. Thus, "although more than half of them were married, most did not bring their wives and families."[4] . . .

Among this predominantly male Chinese immigrant community, a prostitution industry developed. Chinese prostitution quickly emerged as a contentious issue in San Francisco. Yet prostitution was fairly common in the American West at that time:

For the first few years of the 1850s, the arrival of Chinese female prostitutes accompanied that of European and Anglo-American *filles de joie*. The latter, and a few of the former, were primarily entrepreneurs or aspiring entrepreneurs who flocked to San Francisco to take advantage of the dramatic demand for their services. The temporary and migratory nature of the population, a critical shortage of women for companionship, and the lack of conjugal life stood out as the main features of this male-dominated society....As a consequence, opportunities existed for prostitutes to move both upward in the profession and outward in the wider society.[5]

Despite the widespread existence of prostitution by many nationalities, Chinese prostitution attracted particular public attention, giving rise to negative images and discriminatory institutional structures. According to Judy Yung, "discrimination against Chinese prostitutes, as well as prostitutes from Latin American countries, was most apparent at the institutional level. Both groups of women were ghettoized and, in accordance with the racial prejudice of the day, consistently singled out for moral condemnation and legal suppression, even though white prostitution was more prevalent."[6] Laws explicitly directed at Chinese, rather than all, prostitutes began to develop. For instance, in 1854 municipal authorities in San Francisco passed an ordinance "To Suppress Houses of Ill-Fame Within City Limits" and enforced it mainly against Chinese and Mexican brothels. In 1865 municipal authorities passed an "Order to Remove Chinese Women of Ill Fame from Certain Limits in the City." A year later the state legislature passed "An Act for the Suppression of Chinese Houses of Ill-Fame," which resulted in the geographical confinement of Chinese prostitution, but not its elimination.[7] In 1867 "fourteen owners of houses of ill-fame were arrested—all of them Chinese. In 1869, there were twenty-nine arrests for importing prostitutes—all of them Chinese."[8] In March 1870 the state passed "An Act to Prevent the Kidnapping and Importation of Mongolian, Chinese, and Japanese Females for Criminal or Demoralizing Purposes." The Act stipulated that no Asian woman could land without proof that she had migrated voluntarily and was of good character. However, in 1874 the U.S. Circuit Court ruled that this Act was unconstitutional. The ruling judge added that while he was aware of anti-Chinese sentiment in California, "if their future immigration is to

be stopped, recourse must be had to the federal government, where the sole power over this subject lies."[9]

Advocates for Chinese exclusion had already started looking to their representatives in Washington for assistance. They looked particularly to Horace Page, a Republican who "maintained his seat in the House for ten years, largely at the expense of the Chinese."[10] Although Page was initially unable to convince legislators of the need for full Chinese exclusion, he successfully argued for the passage of a bill that excluded Chinese women who were entering the United States for prostitution. This was the Page Law of 1875.

"AN INJURY AND A CURSE TO US"

Why target Chinese prostitution, in particular? Exclusionists' concerns centered not on the experiences and needs of poor Chinese girls and women who had been sold or tricked into prostitution, but on the fate of white men, white families, and a nation constructed as white. Transcripts of public hearings in San Francisco on Chinese immigration make this clear.[11] Mr. Pixley testified for the city that their concern was for white male laborers. "The true American hero is the man who takes his dinner out in his tin plate, works all day, six days in the week, and brings his wages home for his wife to expend in the maintenance and education of the family, in their clothing and their protection."[12] These American heroes were defined as coterminous with civilization and the U.S. nation in part because of their adherence to particular gender and sexual arrangements:

> Our white laborers are, as a rule, married, and fathers and heads of families, and according to our mode of civilization the poorest laborer with the poorest wife must occupy a room by himself for his bed and must have at least another room to cook and eat in. If he has a boy and a girl, growing to the ages of puberty, the boy must have a room for himself and the girl must have a room for herself, and both must be separate from the parents'

bed. It is the ingrained decency of our civilization. It is as impossible to change it as to change us from the worship of the Christian God to the heathen tablet.[13]

Chinese immigrants were characterized not only as lacking these gender and sexual arrangements but also as threatening white families' ability to maintain them. For instance, Pixley related that Chinese men undercut white men's ability to earn, while Chinese women caused disease and immorality among white men. Testimony also attributed nine tenths of venereal disease in the city to Chinese prostitutes and accused prostitutes of spreading leprosy and incurable forms of syphilis. According to Dr. Charles C. O'Donnell, "the virus of the cooly {sic}, in my opinion, is almost sure death to the white man. That is my opinion because I have seen it. There are cases of syphilis among the whites that originated from these Chinese prostitutes that are incurable."[14] Chinese women were also blamed for encouraging immorality, even among young boys:

I am satisfied, from my experience, that nearly all the boys who have venereal disease contracted it in Chinatown. They have no difficulty there for the prices are so low that they can go whenever they please. The women do not care how old the boys are, whether five years old or more, so long as they have money.[15]

Even those who testified in support of Chinese prostitution were not concerned about the women involved but about how to ensure that Chinese men remained useful laborers who did not threaten white men, white families, and the white nation. Thus, Senator Sargent suggested that since many domestic servants were Chinese men, the fact they could have sex with Chinese prostitutes helped to "protect our own families."[16] On those grounds, "it would be better for the Chinamen if they had more of them."[17] Dr. Stout also believed that Chinese men should have access to more, not fewer, Chinese prostitutes:

That physiological necessity of man must be satisfied or crime must ensue. It is amazing, it is astonishing that such a population of Chinese being in our country, and there being so few women to satisfy that necessity of nature, that so little crime results from it.... That number [of Chinese prostitutes in San Francisco] is too little. There should be more.... It is irrepressible; it is a necessity. If there is a certain supply of women of that character, the family is much more sacred and much more pure.[18]

Such views remained the minority, however. The majority consensus was that Chinese prostitutes represented a distinct threat to the lives of white families.

The association of Chinese prostitutes with danger to the life of white families had been constructed through multiple social and material processes. According to Stuart Creighton Miller, the writings and testimonies of missionaries, traders, and diplomats greatly shaped popular U.S. images of the Chinese. The growth of the popular press and the negative coverage of China during the Opium War "populariz[ed] the anti-Chinese themes developed and polished by diplomats, traders, and missionaries over several decades."[19] Domestic experiences with the Chinese further shaped perceptions. Chinese arrival coincided with debate among race theorists about the monogenetic versus polygenetic origin of humans and the increasing demarcation of racial hierarchies that stamped the Chinese as inferior. Some racial theorists also articulated the belief that biological racial differences could not be changed through exposure to the supposedly ameliorative effects of American institutions and ways of life; instead, racial differences corresponded to an inability to understand the very notion of democracy. Thus, the presence of the "racially distinct" Chinese presented a threat to democratic institutions.[20]...

The common perception that all Chinese women were likely to be enslaved prostitutes had direct connections to scientific racism, because some scientific racists held that the status of women within various groups mirrored larger racial hierarchies. Thus, H. Hotz, whose "copious historical notes" are included in Count A. de Gobineau's tract on *The Moral and Intellectual Diversity of the Races*,[21] argued that the varied treatment of women proves that different races exist and are unequal:

It is said that all barbarians treat their women as slaves; but, as they progress in civilization, woman gradually rises to her legitimate rank....

But I totally disagree that all races, in their first state of development, treated women equally. There is not only no historical testimony to prove that *any* of the white races were ever in such a state of barbarity and moral debasement as most of the dark races are to this day, and have always been, but there is positive evidence to show that our barbarous ancestors assigned to woman the same position that we assign to her now: she was the companion, and not the slave of man.... it is possible to demonstrate not only that all races did not treat their women equally in their first stage of development, but also, that no race which assigned to woman in the beginning an inferior position ever raised her from it in any subsequent stage of development. *I select the Chinese for illustration.*[22]

Clearly, women in China were perceived to be treated particularly poorly, but rather than inspiring efforts on their behalf, the perception served mainly to support racist condemnation of all Chinese people. As Chandra Talpade Mohanty indicates, this perception served to erase any consideration of how racism and imperialism contributed to Chinese women's status, and to racially differentiate and elevate white women.[23]

Chinese arrival also coincided with the development of germ theory, which made North Americans conscious of the connection between germs and disease. Filtered through the lens of racism, germ theory suggested that different racial groups carried distinct germs to which they were immune but others were not. Commentators from the penny press to the American Medical Association (AMA) took seriously the notion that Chinese immigrants carried distinct germs to which they were immune, but from which whites would die if exposed. "The germ theory of disease provided an explanation of the manner in which an obviously inferior group might best a superior one, contrary to the natural law of the social Darwinists."[24] Many of the fears became concentrated in a particularly dense form around the bodies of Chinese women who worked in prostitution. The sexual labor of Chinese prostitutes was believed to be the nexus through which germs and disease could most easily be transmitted to white men (prompting the AMA to study whether Chinese prostitutes were poisoning the nation's bloodstream).[25] Sex with Chinese prostitutes seemed to be the vector through which white supremacy and the perpetuity of "the white race" was directly threatened. Havelock Ellis, one of the most prominent sexologists of the nineteenth century, captured the ways that sexual concerns were inevitably also racial, when he wrote that "the question of sex—with the racial questions that rest on it—stands before the coming generations as the chief problem for solution."[26]

Thus, the Page Law, which mandated the exclusion of Asian women coming to the United States to work as prostitutes, responded to a constellation of what were believed to be serious threats to "white" values, lives, and futures.

DIFFERENTIATING "REAL" WIVES FROM PROSTITUTES

By examining how the Page Law was implemented, we discover the microphysics of power through which sexuality entered U.S. immigration control. The task, as it was presented to officials, was to differentiate "real" wives from women posing as wives but bound for sex work. According to historians, officials found such a differentiation difficult to make and, driven by racism, they implemented the law so harshly that almost all Chinese women ended up being barred from the United States. Such analyses suggest that the problem with the Page Law was officials' racist manner of implementation—but not the law's demand to differentiate among women on the basis of sexuality.

I want to suggest an alternative formulation, which is that officials had difficulty differentiating "real" wives from women bound for sex work because there is no absolute differentiation that can be made....

...Scholarship suggests that distinctions between women who get labeled as prostitutes and other women derive not from any inherent characteristics within the women themselves but from social relations of power. In an article about the history of prostitution in the United States, Miller, Romenesko, and Wondolkowski suggest that there are a myriad of difficulties in trying to define who is a prostitute and "whether or not [women] are so labeled depends more on the political stance of the potential moral entrepreneur who would seek to label them than on the degree to which their actual behavior deviates from some norm of correct conduct."[27] Illustrating their argument, Judith Walkowitz has documented that in Victorian England prostitutes emerged as a distinct social group, separate from regular working-class communities, not because of anything inherent in the women or distinctive about their behavior but because of strategies that officials used to enforce the Contagious Diseases Act, which aimed to control the spread of venereal disease.[28] Gayle Rubin described a similar process that occurred in the nineteenth-century United States. She explains, "prostitution began to change from a temporary job to a more permanent occupation [and distinct social group] as a result of 19th century agitation, legal reform, and police persecution. Prostitutes, who had been part of the general working class population, became increasingly isolated as members of an outcast group."[29]

Yet even as a class of marginalized women who were stigmatized as prostitutes took shape, not all women who sold or bartered sex were labeled as prostitutes. Deborah Rhode highlights the unevenness of the process whereby certain women get labeled and penalized as prostitutes:

> streetwalkers, who tend to come from the lowest socioeconomic group, account for 10 to 15 percent of all prostitutes, and 80 to 90 percent of all arrests. Women of color account for 40 percent of streetwalkers, 55 percent of those arrested, and 85 percent of those receiving jail sentences.[30]

Rhode's analysis makes clear how the label "prostitute" becomes attached to particular groups of women (but not others) through social relations that are racist, classist, and gendered rather than because

of any distinguishing behavioral or moral traits of the women involved.

. . . The sex industry is multitiered and continually changing, but public crackdowns focus disproportionately on streetwalkers rather than on women in other tiers.[31] Thus, streetwalkers remain the paradigmatic image of "the prostitute," while other women are much less likely to be arrested, labeled, or stigmatized, even when they sell sex too.

Streetwalkers are particularly likely to become stigmatized and subjected to efforts at control in times of social transformation. . . . According to Ruth Rosen, discourses about prostitution in the United States have provided a means for people to express concerns about "unrestricted immigration, the rate of venereal disease, the anonymity of the city, the evils of liquor, the growth of working class urban culture, and, most important of all, the changing role of women in society."[32] . . .

. . . But which women become labeled and treated as "prostitutes" as a result depends greatly on what tier of the sex industry they work in, prevailing anxieties of the time, and how these anxieties become directed at some class and racial or ethnic groups but not others. The labels also reflect culture-specific beliefs about how sex and gender systems should operate. For instance, during hard times in China, women and girls were commonly sold into domestic service, concubinage, or prostitution, and one form of sale could lead to another.[33] Yet not all domestic servants, called *mui tsai*, were resold; some continued providing domestic service until freed through marriage. But the practice of selling women, and the difficulties of differentiating between various kinds of sales, led immigration officials to assume that all girls traveling in groups were surely prostitutes, rather than, for example, *mui tsai*.[34] A further source of confusion to officials was the fact that some Chinese men had concubines, in addition to first wives. Concubines, who were usually of lower social status and acquired through purchase, were legal members of the family, and their children were their fathers' legal heirs. But concubinage, which reflected a sex and gender system that was different from the dominant U.S. culture, contributed to officials' beliefs that virtually all immigrant Chinese women were enslaved prostitutes.[35]

The variety of sex/gender arrangements evident among Chinese immigrants actually underscores a more general point, which is that there is no necessary opposition between women who sell or trade sex while occupying various social statuses, and wives.[36] William Sanger's pioneering study of prostitution in New York City in the 1850s showed that among the 2,000 women he identified as prostitutes, 490 (or 25 percent) were also married, and 71 lived with their husbands while working in prostitution.[37] Historians of Chinese women in America have also documented that marriage was one of the routes through which sex workers left the industry. Based on census figures, Benson Tong estimates that "during the 1870s, a large number of Chinese prostitutes left the trade and very likely entered into matrimony."[38] Peggy Pascoe affirms that "the highly skewed sex ratio in immigrant Chinatowns...and the absence of established in-laws, created unusual opportunities for immigrant prostitutes to marry and leave prostitution behind."[39] Indeed, Pascoe further suggests that many Chinese immigrant women "regarded prostitution as a means of finding a husband or making a financial start in the United States, an opportunity that would enable them to lead a better life or support a poverty-stricken family at home."[40] While marriage provided a way out of sex work for some early immigrant Chinese women, a small number of women were both married and engaged in sex work. Sucheng Chan notes that "the 1900 census manuscript showed that some brothels in San Francisco were run by couples, among whom a few wives were apparently continuing their profession [as prostitutes]."[41] Women in other racial and ethnic groups also combined marriage and sex work, too.

IMPLEMENTING THE PAGE LAW

...Racism and sexism ensured that "real" wives became labeled and treated administratively as prostitutes—because that category designates women who occupy positions of social vulnerability, rather than a distinct "type" of woman.

...During the first years after passage of the Page Law, the American Consul in Hong Kong played a pivotal role in its enforcement. Prior to emigration, each Chinese woman had to submit "an official declaration of purpose in emigration and personal morality" statement, accompanied by an application for clearance and a fee, to the American Consul.[42] The declaration was sent to an association of the most prominent businessmen in Hong Kong, the Tung Wah Hospital Committee, for investigation. A list of intending emigrants was also sent to the British colonial government in Hong Kong for investigation. The day before the ship sailed, each woman had to answer questions before the consul. These included such inquiries as:

> Have you entered into contract or agreement with any person or persons whomsoever, for a term of service within the United States for lewd and immoral purposes? Do you wish of your own free and voluntary will to go to the United States? Do you go to the United States for the purposes of prostitution? Are you married or single? What are you going to the United States for? What is to be your occupation there? Have you lived in a house of prostitution in Hong Kong, Macao, or China? Have you engaged in prostitution in either {sic} of the above places? Are you a virtuous woman? Do you intend to live a virtuous life in the United States? Do you know that you are at liberty now to go to the United States, or remain in your own country, and that you cannot be forced to go away from your home?[43]

On the day of sailing, each woman had to answer similar questions about morality and reasons for emigration, this time put by the Harbor Master. Once on board the ship, she was questioned again. Women who passed this rigorous series of interrogations were given a certificate of good moral character, which they had to present on arrival in San Francisco if they wanted to land. While the ship sailed, the Consul sent a photograph of each woman who had been approved, along with a letter testifying to her character, to the ship's destination.

Sometimes he also sent a letter urging further investigation of a particular woman.[44]

Information about how women were processed on arrival in San Francisco after passage of the Page Law is somewhat sketchy. But transcripts of a habeas corpus hearing involving several Chinese women, held in San Francisco just prior to the passage of the Chinese Exclusion Act in 1882, provide some indication. According to testimony by Colonel Bee, the American Consul for the Chinese, he met all arriving ships from Hong Kong. Accompanied by his Vice Consul and interpreter and by the Deputy Surveyor of the Port of San Francisco, he boarded the ship, and "[got] access to the women before anyone else."[45] He gathered copies of their paperwork with the photographs attached and, using the interpreter, he asked each woman the same questions that she had been asked in Hong Kong. The replies given in Hong Kong were included in each woman's paperwork, and these replies were cross-checked against what she said on arrival in San Francisco.[46] According to Bee's testimony, the questions asked of the women had changed somewhat since Consul Bailey's tenure. For the court, Bee listed the questions that women were asked:

> Native residence in Hong Kong; number of the storeys to the house; name of the people in the house; when and from what place I came to Hong Kong; person or persons with whom I came; name, country, and occupation of my father; name, country, and occupation of my husband; names and addresses of sureties; relatives or friends from whom inquiries can be made; the person or persons with whom I am going; the object of my going; the place to which I am going; the street and number of the house where I can be seen.[47]

If the women answered the questions with the same information that was included in their paperwork, and if they matched the photographs, "we have no authority whatever to detain them."[48] But if women did not answer the questions the same way, or did not match the photographs, or carried paperwork that was incompletely filled out, they were liable to be detained. George Peffer estimates that between 1875 and 1882 at least one hundred and perhaps

several hundred women were sent back as a result of these procedures.

...In the case of Chinese women seeking to immigrate to the United States, biographical details were elicited only after they had been corralled into carefully controlled spaces. The first two interrogations were carried out in the Consul's and Harbor Master's offices, and on their terms. The third interrogation took place immediately before the ship sailed, in a manner designed to ensure that the woman who answered the officials' questions "correctly" was also the one who sailed for San Francisco (rather than a substitute being sent in her place). On arrival in San Francisco, the women were confined on the ship to ensure that Colonel Bee "[got] access to them before anyone else." Only after answering questions to Bee's satisfaction were the women permitted to join relatives and friends waiting on the dock. The strategic control of space that Chinese women endured was intended by officials to generate the "truth" of their sexual pasts and likely sexual futures. Spatial control was designed to minimize opportunities for the women to be "coached" about what to say to officials, to avoid substitutions, and most likely to provide women who had been kidnapped with an opportunity to speak openly outside the hearing of their procurers. Yet, as Benson Tong suggests, the likelihood of kidnapped women speaking openly to an unknown official was small (though it did sometimes happen).[49] Furthermore, the whole process was shaped by the larger, explicitly racist assumption that "a Chinaman prefers a lie to the truth" and that Chinese women were equally dishonest.[50] As Stuart Creighton Miller describes, a founding image among Western traders, diplomats, and missionaries was that the Chinese were dishonest, tricky, and sneaky, and this image led to the development of exhaustive regimes of questioning, conducted through strictly controlling space and minimizing contact with other Chinese people, which were believed to be the best way to elicit "truth" from Chinese immigrants.[51] Judy Yung underscores that this process was "different not only in degree but in kind" from that endured by other immigrants.[52] The process was not just racist but also racializing, in the sense of helping to literally construct the Chinese as a distinct and racialized group. After passage of the Page Law, Chinese women became subjected to an early form of this racializing process.[53]

The questioning to which Chinese women were subjected involved gender and class dimensions, too. For instance, although the women's individual histories mattered, their fathers' and husbands' mattered more. Officials assumed that women's likelihood of becoming sex workers in the United States depended on their family background and husbands' occupations. Therefore, they wanted to be sure that women came from "respectable" families and were joining husbands who were demonstrably able to support them. To some extent, the officials' approach was cognizant of the realities of limited economic possibilities for immigrant women of color in the U.S. economy at that time. It also took into account the fact that Chinese women did often enter the United States believing that they were joining husbands, only to find that they had been tricked and sold into prostitution. But rather than challenging these conditions, officials simply accepted that male intentions and actions were more likely to determine a woman's sexual future than her own actions and intentions, and processed her case accordingly. Thus, ironically, officials further institutionalized the structures of patriarchy for which they condemned Chinese men. Their processes also institutionalized a distinct class bias regarding Chinese women's possibilities for immigration.[54]

...Individual Chinese women's testimonies never enabled a reliable differentiation between "real" wives and prostitutes. But the testimonies' circulation structurally changed the organization of immigration control.

Biographical data, however, was made fully subjectifying only when it was attached to a photograph. Photographs provided one of the earliest methods for officially recording the body's distinctiveness and using the record to control an individual's mobility. This system was used on Chinese women before any other group of immigrants, because of the "threat" of their sexuality to the United States. A photograph was attached to each woman's consular clearance, and another photograph was sent in advance of the ship, so that when the ship arrived, officials already had in their possession photographs of the women who had been approved for migration. Women who arrived without photographs, or who did not match the photographs that had been sent in advance, were detained and returned to Hong Kong. Through these very simple techniques, officials tried to ensure that if a particular woman was cleared for immigration on the basis of biographical data provided, another woman was not sent in her place.[55]

By contrast, officials did not attempt to link together specific biographies and bodies in the case of Chinese men or anyone else who immigrated at the same time. In testimony before Congress in 1877, the collector of the port related that if one thousand Chinese men were authorized to land and twelve hundred arrived, officials let any thousand land, without trying to determine exactly which thousand were cleared.[56] Some five years later, Colonel Bee testified in court that immigrating Chinese men were still treated less rigorously than women. "We go through the steerage and ask them if they are free laborers, if they come under contract to anybody or under bond to any one and if any one says he is not free we send him back."[57] Mr. Quint, the attorney representing several Chinese women who had been denied landing because they were suspected of coming to the United States for prostitution, asked, "are not each one of these [men] required to have papers the same as females?" But Bee affirmed, "No, I believe not, sir."[58] Men were also not required to carry photographs, nor to match photographs that had been sent in advance to San Francisco port authorities.

Thus, Chinese women were the first group of immigrants whose mobility was regulated by the exchange of photographs between officials. Photographs tied a specific body to biographical data that had been approved by officials for migration. Only as of the second decade of the twentieth century, according to John Torpey, would such a system become broadly implemented in the United States through passport controls.[59] Until then, racialized, gendered, and sexualized Others disproportionately bore the burden of such techniques, as the experience of Chinese women shows.

Other techniques also supplemented (and in some cases supplanted) the use of photography as a means to anchor a body to a specific biography in ways that ensured official control. For instance, Bertillionage, a system of taking nine measurements of different parts of the body and recording these measurements in file cards, was certainly used on Chinese immigrants by the turn of the century.[60] Immigrants who left and wanted to reenter had to submit to being remeasured; if their measurements matched those recorded in the file cards, they were let in. Fingerprinting also came to provide an unchangeable physical mark that officials used to tie individuals to specific biographies in ways that controlled them.[61] More recently, the INS has pioneered a biometric data system called INPASS. As Daniel Sutherland describes:

> An INPASS is available to U.S. citizens and resident aliens who fly internationally on a regular basis. The [person] provided the INS with biographical data—home address, date of birth, office address, position in his company, and number of international trips he anticipates making—so the agency could verify that he is authorized by the government to travel. The INS then took an image of his hand geometry (a type of "biometric" data—physical characteristics that are unique to each person, such as a person's voice or retina pattern) and electronically recorded it on a plastic card. The agency also stored the biographical and biometric data in a central computer. Although INPASS is currently a voluntary program, it is designed to demonstrate the feasibility of including machinereadable biographical and biometric data on U.S. passports.[62]

The *New York Times* also reports that the INS has begun to rely on dental and bone X rays when trying to determine how to process people who arrive at airports without documents, or with questionable documents.[63] The X rays are intended to determine whether the person is under eighteen, because adults and minors are processed differently. At some large U.S. airports, arrivals with problematic or missing documents are brought directly to the airport dentist, where the dental drill and row of medicine bottles is their first glimpse of America, and where they are X-rayed. The use of X rays as a means to definitively determine age has been disputed, but nonetheless continues. Through these and other techniques, which were initially used against Chinese women after passage of the Page Law, official techniques for recording the body's distinctiveness and anchoring it to specific biographical data became the locus for new forms of subjection....

I noted above that scientific racism and popular prejudice facilitated the assumption that bodies that "looked" Chinese were likely to be involved in prostitution. Of course, the idea that Chinese bodies "look" a particular way had to be constructed by scientific racism and then disseminated into popular wisdom.[64] At the risk of stating the obvious, these bodies also had to "look" female, in order to be presumed to be prostitutes. Little has been written about the significance of seeming to have a female, rather than a male, body when being processed for immigration, but there can be no doubt that gender appearance mattered.[65] The salience of gender is suggested by Lucie Cheng's description of how some Chinese tongs smuggled women into the United States for work in prostitution by dressing them as boys.[66] The strategy would be effective only if females and males were subjected to different regimes of processing, regardless of their common "Chineseness." Therefore, "looking" both Chinese and female was what triggered official suspicions that the immigrant was likely a prostitute.

Yet the conflation of Chinese women's bodies with prostitute bodies was never absolute, or officials would not have needed to try to differentiate prostitutes from "real" wives. Accordingly, other signs were also sought. A series of "scientific" discourses, which predated the Page Law, suggested that prostitute bodies carried distinct marks, in addition to features that we are accustomed to thinking of as racial or gendered, which set them apart. For instance, Dr. Alexandre Parent-Duchatelet published an 1836 book about Parisian prostitutes, describing his efforts to delineate a distinct prostitute physiognomy.[67] Subsequent work by the

St. Petersburg physician Pauline Tarnowsky claimed that over the course of their lives, the faces of prostitutes looked more degenerate and more mannish, and their genitalia became visibly altered.[68] In 1893 Cesare Lombroso published a study that suggested that prostitutes had distinct genitalia and prehensile feet.[69] By the early twentieth century, eugenicists argued that prostitutes suffered from feeblemindedness and that this condition might be discerned from looking at the face, but could also be objectively diagnosed through use of the Binet intelligence test.[70] In these and other ways, prostitute bodies were believed to be visibly distinct, though no one could agree on what was a reliable differentiating mark.

But testimonies before Congress and reports in immigrant case files show that one of the physical marks that officials often seized upon when inspecting Chinese women was bound feet. At an 1877 hearing before the Joint Special Committee to Investigate Chinese Immigration, dissenting opinions were expressed about the extent to which bound feet were a reliable indicator of "respectability." But Judy Yung suggests that at least some inspectors relied heavily on bound feet when determining whether a Chinese woman was likely to be a prostitute:

> Only women such as my great grandmother who had bound feet and a modest demeanor were considered upper class women with "moral integrity." As one immigration officer wrote in his report, "There has never come to this port, I believe, a bound footed woman who was found to be of immoral character, this condition of affairs being due, it is stated, to the fact that such women, and especially those in the interior, are necessarily confined to their home and seldom frequent the city districts."[71]

This interpretation of the significance of bound feet was not necessarily accurate.[72] But for some officials, bound feet came to serve as a physical mark on which to rely when trying to differentiate prostitutes from "real" wives, as is evident from the extent to which immigration records regularly contain questions and notes about Chinese women's feet.

No doubt, questions of "prettiness," youth, demeanor, and how she walked, were among other bodily "clues" that shaped officials' responses to a Chinese woman seeking to immigrate. As Yung relates, the inspector who processed her great grandmother also wrote, "the present applicant No. 14418 is a very modest appearing woman whose evident sincerity, frankness of expression, and generally favorable demeanor is very convincing."[73]

Officials looked not only at the body but also at the woman's clothes when making judgments about her. Prostitutes have a history of dressing distinctively,[74] sometimes because they were required to, or as a means to advertise their services, display subcultural solidarity, or express class aspirations.[75] It is not entirely surprising, then, that immigration officials carefully examined the clothing of women seeking entry to the United States. At a hearing on Chinese immigration, one official asked, "I have heard there is a difference in the coloring of the lining of the sleeves of the gown [of prostitutes], and that they are distinguished by different costumes?"[76] Though differences in dress were not substantiated, dress remained another aspect of appearance that inspectors carefully examined.

In sum, the appearance of the body and clothing supposedly offered a range of possible clues about "inner character," on which some officials drew when trying to differentiate prostitutes from "real" wives. Though this approach, too, failed to yield any reliable differentiations, it ensured that the dominant philosophical paradigm of the time and the "scientific" studies it generated were centrally though informally incorporated into immigration control. The photographs that were employed to constrain Chinese women's mobility serve as traces of the incorporation of these other processes into immigration control....

The Page Law, which particularly targeted working-class Chinese immigrant women, required officials to differentiate "real" wives from women bound for sex work and to deny entry to the latter. It was an impossible task. The idea that such a differentiation could be made was, as Foucault puts it, a "ruse" that both marked and facilitated particular arrangements of power. But these arrangements were sanctioned because Chinese prostitutes had become popularly identified with multiple dangers to white lives, institutions, and nation. As a result, officials developed techniques for trying to differentiate "real" wives from prostitutes through the elicitation of biographical details, photography, and the creation of case files. Although these techniques never enabled officials to reliably differentiate among women, they had several important effects. For one, the techniques concretely introduced concerns about sexuality into U.S. immigration control processes. They compelled the production of discourses about sexuality and gave rise to varied circuits for exchanging and evaluating these discourses. The circuits linked together bureaucrats, experts, politicians, and the public in new ways, around preoccupations with sexuality, immigration, and nation. The techniques also enabled officials to constitute Chinese women as subjectified and disciplined in racial, gendered, class, and sexual terms. Over time, the policing of immigrants around sexuality, which the Page Law inaugurated, became extended to all newcomers. It remains a central feature of immigration control today.

A focus on the problematic effects of techniques for trying to differentiate prostitutes from other women suggests the need to revise traditional analyses about how immigration control reproduces social inequalities. Certainly, discriminatory laws and officials' prejudices have substantially ensured that U.S. immigration control functioned to sustain racial, gender, sexual, and class hierarchies. But even if the laws were overturned and prejudiced officials let go, immigration control would still reproduce social hierarchies. This is because the techniques and systems of knowledge on which its daily operations depend are deeply rooted in histories of racism, sexism, imperialism, and exploitation, as the history of restrictions on Chinese immigrant women shows. To create real transformation, these techniques and systems of knowledge must also be analyzed and changed.

NOTES

1. U.S. Immigration and Naturalization Service, *Statistical Yearbook of the Immigration and Naturalization Service, 1991*, A1–2.

2. Three of the five provisions of the Page Law dealt with prostitution. E. P. Hutchinson summarizes, "The first section made it a duty of consular officials at any port from which subjects of China, Japan, or other Oriental nations were to depart for the United States to determine whether such travel was 'free and voluntary,' and to ascertain whether any such travelers were under contract or agreement to serve for 'lewd and immoral purposes' in the United States, and in the latter case, to refuse to grant the required permit for travel. The third section of the act forbade the importation of women for prostitution, outlawed all contracts and agreements for such importation, and made illegal importation a felony subject to imprisonment of up to five years and a fine of up to $5,000. The fifth section included 'women imported for the purposes of prostitution' as one of the excluded classes." See E. P. Hutchinson, *Legislative History*, 419–20. About the provisions for convicts and contract laborers, see Salyer, *Laws Harsh as Tigers*, 260 n. 76, and Peffer, *If They Don't Bring Their Women Here*, 8.

3. As chapter 1 shows, laws subsequently mandated the exclusion of prostitutes of every nationality, "immoral" women, single women who "arrived in a state of pregnancy," lesbians and gay men, polygamists, and other people considered undesirable as immigrants on sexual grounds.

4. Judy Yung, *Unbound Feet: A Social History of Chinese Women in San Francisco* (Berkeley: University of California Press, 1995), 18.

5. Benson Tong, *Unsubmissive Women: Chinese Prostitutes in Nineteenth-Century San Francisco* (Norman: University of Oklahoma Press, 1994), 4–5. Similarly, Judy Yung writes: "The scarcity of women in the American West, the suspension of social and moral restraints, and the easy access to wealth during the early years of the gold rush attracted women from different parts of the world. The first prostitutes to arrive were women from Mexico, Peru, and Chile; these were followed by women from France and other European countries, as well as women from American cities such as New York and New Orleans" (*Unbound Feet*, 26).

6. Yung, *Unbound Feet*, 31. Sucheng Chan corroborates this analysis, writing that "during the gold rush and for several decades thereafter, prostitutes of many nationalities lived and worked in San Francisco. Municipal authorities tried sporadically to suppress prostitution and they singled out Chinese women for special attention from the beginning" ("The Exclusion of Chinese Women," 97). See also Tomás Almaguer, *Racial Fault Lines* (Berkeley: University of California Press, 1994), 177–78.

7. Benson Tong notes that the city of San Francisco passed another anti-prostitution ordinance in 1869, this time directing that the doors of brothels should be kept shut (presumably so that passers-by could not see what was going on inside, and perhaps to also prevent women from advertising).

8. Jacqueline Barker Barnhardt, *The Fair but Frail: Prostitution in San Francisco 1849–1900* (Reno: University of Nevada Press, 1980), 49.

9. Quoted in Sucheng Chan, "Exclusion and Chinese Women," 103.

10. George Peffer, *If They Don't Bring Their Women Here*, 33.

11. *Chinese Immigration; Its Social, Moral and Political Effects*, Report to the California State Senate of its Special Committee on Chinese Immigration (Sacramento: State Printing Office, 1878), 272.

12. *Report of the Joint Special Commission to Investigate Chinese Immigration*, Rpt. 689, 44th Cong., 2d Sess., Senate (Washington, D.C.: USGPO, 1877), 19. (Hereafter *Report*.)

13. *Report*, 19.

14. *Report*, 1097.

15. *Report*, 14.

16. *Report*, 143.

17. *Report*, 143.

18. *Report*, 652.

19. Stuart Creighton Miller, *The Unwelcome Immigrant: The American Image of the Chinese* (Berkeley: University of California Press, 1966), 112.

20. Audrey Smedley, *Race in North America* (Boulder: Westview Press, 1993), 269.

21. De Gobineau was one of the preeminent scientific racists of the nineteenth century.

22. *The Moral and Intellectual Diversity of the Races*, from the French by Count A. De Gobineau, with an analytic introduction and copious historical notes by H. Hotz (Philadelphia: J.B. Lippincott and Co., 1865), 385, 386, 287. My emphasis.

23. Chandra Talpade Mohanty, "Under Western Eyes: Feminist Scholarship and Colonial Discourses" in Chandra Talpade Mohanty, Ann Russo, and Lourdes Torres, eds., *Third World Women and the Politics of Feminism* (Bloomington: Indiana University Press, 1991), 51–80.

24. Miller, *The Unwelcome Immigrant*, 166.

25. Ibid., 163.

26. Quoted in Siobhan Somerville, "Scientific Racism and the Emergence of the Homosexual Body," in *Journal of the History of Sexuality* 5, no. 2 (1994), 246.

27. Eleanor Miller, Kim Romenesko, and Lisa Wondolkowski, "The United States," in *Prostitution: An International Handbook of Trends, Problems, and Policies*, ed. Nanette J. Davis (Westport, Conn.: Greenwood Press, 1993), 309.

28. Judith Walkowitz, *Prostitution and Victorian Society: Women, Class, and the State* (Cambridge: Cambridge University Press, 1980).

29. Gayle S. Rubin, "Thinking Sex: Notes for a Radical Theory of the Politics of Sexuality," in *The Lesbian and Gay Studies Reader*, ed. Henry Abelove, Michele Aina Barale, and David M. Halperin (New York: Routledge, 1993), 17–18.

30. Deborah Rhode, *Justice and Gender: Sex Discrimination and the Law* (Cambridge: Harvard University Press, 1989), 261.

31. According to Priscilla Alexander, tiers in the sex industry include streetwalking, massage parlors, bar and café prostitution, brothels, and "call girl" or escort services. Priscilla Alexander, "Prostitution: A Difficult Issue for Feminists," in Frederique Delacoste and Priscilla Alexander, eds., *Sex Work: Writings by Women in the Sex Industry* (Pittsburgh, PA: Cleis Press, 1987), 189–90. These tiers may have been modified since Alexander described them, with new tiers emerging.

32. Ruth Rosen, *The Lost Sisterhood: Prostitution in America, 1900–1918* (Baltimore: The Johns Hopkins University Press, 1982), xiii.

33. Alternatively, poor families might put their daughters up for adoption rather than sell them. Adoption took two forms: as a future daughter-in-law, which was considered a betrothal, or as a real daughter, in which case the girl became part of the family. See Sue Gronewold, *Beautiful Merchandise: Prostitution in China 1860–1936* (New York: Haworth Press, 1982), 39.

34. See Peffer, *If They Don't Bring Their Women Here*, 71.

35. For more information on the sex/gender system in nineteenth-century China, see Gronewold, *Beautiful Merchandise*; Kay Ann Johnson, *Women, the Family, and Peasant Revolution in China* (Chicago: University of Chicago Press, 1983); Olga Lang, *Chinese Family and Society* (New Haven: Yale University Press, 1946); Rubie S. Watson and Patricia Buckley Ebrey, eds., *Marriage and Inequality in Chinese Society* (Berkeley: University of California Press, 1991). On marriage resistance among women in Guangdong, which was the home of most early Chinese immigrants to California, see Janice Stockard, *Daughters of the Canton Delta* (Stanford: Stanford University Press, 1989). According to Gronewold (and contrary to dominant U.S. ideologies of the time), "the rite of marriage

was almost universally regarded as a sad occasion" for Chinese women (p. 41).

36. Gail Hershatter puts the point more forcefully, arguing that both prostitution and marriage have to be situated on a shared continuum of claims to women's sexual services. See Gail Hershatter, "Prostitution and the Market in Women in Early 20th Century Shanghai," in Watson and Ebrey, eds., *Marriage and Inequality in Chinese Society*, 258. Hershatter's essay examines "similarities between marriage and prostitution in Shanghai, as well as the movement of individuals from one to the other" (259).

37. Sanger characterizes the existence of these 71 as "an announcement so disgraceful to humanity that . . . it would scarcely be credited." He also offers an analysis of why, in his view, married women might work as prostitutes: "Sufficient {sic} has been proved to show that in many cases, prostitution among married women is the result of circumstances which must have exercised a very powerful influence over them. The refusal of a husband to support his wife, his desertion of her, or an act of adultery with another woman, are each occurrences which must operate injuriously upon the mind of any female, and, by the keen torture that such outrages inflict on the sensitiveness of her nature, must drive her into a course of dissipation. Many women thus circumstanced have actually confessed that they made the first false step while smarting from injuries inflicted by their natural protectors, with the idea of being revenged upon their brutal or faithless companions for their unkindness. Morality will argue, and very truly, that this is no excuse for crime; but much allowance must be made for the extreme nature of the provocation, and the fact that most of these women are uneducated, and have not sufficient mental or moral illumination to reason correctly upon the nature and consequences of their voluntary debauchery, or even to curb the violence of their passions." See William W. Sanger, *The History of Prostitution: Its Extent, Causes, and Effects Throughout the World* (New York: Eugenics Publishing Company Edition, 1937), 475–76.

38. Tong, *Unsubmissive Women*, 159.

39. Peggy Pascoe, *Relations of Rescue* (New York: Oxford University Press, 1990), 95.

40. Pascoe, *Relations of Rescue*, 96. Pascoe adds, "their employment as sexual 'slaves'—the fact that so troubled mission women—did not in itself lead them to request help; for the most part, they contacted missionaries only when they felt that their owners had treated them particularly badly."

41. Sucheng Chan, *This Bittersweet Soil: The Chinese in California Agriculture, 1860–1910* (Berkeley: University of California Press, 1986), 390. Chan also includes statistics on the small numbers of married Chinese women who worked as prostitutes, according to census data for the Sacramento Delta in 1880 and 1900. See 392–393.

42. George Peffer, "Forbidden Families: Emigration Experiences of Chinese Women under the Page Law, 1875–1882," *Journal of American Ethnic History* 6, no. 1 (fall 1986), 33.

43. Peffer, "Forbidden Families," 32. David Bailey, the American consul in Hong Kong between 1875 and 1877, asked these questions of women applicants who appeared at the consulate on the day that he got word of the Page Law's passage. Over time, he likely altered the questions somewhat, but this is one sample of what the questions covered.

44. Peffer, "Forbidden Families," 31–35; Tong, *Unsubmissive Women*, 34–77. According to Peffer, these procedures were developed by David Bailey. Peffer relates that Bailey's successor, Sheldon Loring, who served until 1879, was also reasonably diligent in following these procedures, as was his successor, John Mosby, until 1881. After 1881 Mosby decided that he would no longer examine Chinese women departing on non-U.S. vessels, even if they were bound for the United States, and in June 1882 he declared that he had abolished the entire procedure established by his predecessors. However, Mosby's abolition of procedure "occurred too near the implementation of the [1882 Chinese] Exclusion Act to exert an impact on Chinese female immigration" (54). See Peffer, *If They Don't Bring Their Women Here*, 43–56.

45. Testimony of Col. F. A. Bee, in U.S. District Court, Northern California District, *In The Matter of Wah Ah Chin and Others for Their Discharge on Writ of Habeas Corpus*, No. 2495, March 1882, 19.

46. According to the ship's captain, Colonel Bee also had duplicates of the women's paperwork and photographs in his possession when he boarded the ship, which had presumably been sent to him from Hong Kong.

47. Testimony of Col. F. A. Bee, *In The Matter of Wah Ah Chin and Others*, 19–20.

48. Ibid., 20.

49. Tong suggests that most of the women "belonged to a different cultural and legal environment and had been brought up to believe that all 'foreign devils' were 'barbarians'—a belief reinforced by their agents during the voyage to America." This would have discouraged

many of them from seeking assistance from U.S. officials. (*Unsubmissive Women*, 64.)

50. *Report*, 987.

51. Miller, *The Unwelcome Immigrant*, 14. Miller writes that "the allegedly universal dishonesty in China [was] mentioned by 37 [of 50] of the sample" of traders' accounts and echoed in books published by diplomats. See *The Unwelcome Immigrant*, 29–30.

52. Yung, *Unbound Feet*, 66.

53. In the years following the Page Law, control of space and detailed questioning were combined in acute forms to try to produce the "truth" of all Chinese immigrants' testimonies. For instance, "during his term as collector [of the port of San Francisco] between 1889 and 1893, Timothy Phelps devised a system of investigation which attempted to expose fraudulent testimony. The inspectors questioned the applicant and his [or her] witness separately and in great detail about their family and village in China. Inspectors would ask questions such as, How many steps were there out of the family's back door? How many houses were there in the village? Did the mother have bound feet? If discrepancies existed in the testimony, the inspectors assumed that the parties did not know each other and that the applicant's claim was false. Chinese immigrants dreaded the inspector's investigations. Over the years, the inspector's drilling became longer and more refined" (Salyer, *Laws Harsh as Tigers*, 59). These interrogations easily lasted weeks and even months, and while they were going on, immigrants were kept carefully separated from family and friends. They were detained either in the Pacific Mail steamship shed, or, after 1910, on Angel Island. In these locations, their movements were carefully circumscribed. For instance, exercise was barely permitted and sharply supervised so that immigrants could not talk to anyone else. Parcels and visitors were denied. Even food parcels were denied, because officials feared that information that coached immigrants in what to say to officials might be included in the food. Stories of ingenious Chinese methods for smuggling coaching information are legion; one story, related in an immigration report, sheds light on the reasons for the restrictions against outside food. According to the report, "the device adopted to deliver the coaching letter was this: the letter was written in small characters on a slip of tissue paper, which was rolled tightly and placed inside of a large peanut shell, the two halves of which were carefully glued together, and then placed in a bag and sent to the Chinaman." (See *Facts Concerning the Enforcement of Chinese Exclusion Laws*,

House Document 847, U.S. House of Representatives, 59th Congress, 1st Sess., 25 May 1906 [Washington, D.C.: U.S. Government Printing Office], 10.) Contact with Chinese staff was also restricted to the greatest degree possible, for fear that staff had been paid to pass on coaching information. The authors of *Island* also relate that "a different interpreter was used for each session" of a case, to forestall collusion. See Him Mark Lai, Genny Lim, and Judy Yung, *Island: Poetry and History of Chinese Immigrants on Angel Island, 1910–1940* (San Francisco: HOCDOI, 1982), 22.

54. Under the Chinese Exclusion Act of 1882, this class bias would be extended to men.

55. As John Torpey expressed it, the principle involved is that "the person's body is used *against* him or her." *The Invention of the Passport*, 17.

56. See *Report*, 392–93.

57. Testimony of Col. F. A. Bee, *In The Matter of Wah Ah Chin and Others*, 24.

58. Ibid. Bee further told the court that "I have never sent any males back. We have sent females" (24).

59. Torpey, *The Invention of the Passport*, 117–118.

60. On the use of Bertillionage in the United States, see Donald C. Dilworth, ed., *Identification Wanted: Development of the American Criminal Identification System, 1893–1943* (Gaithersburg, Md.: International Association of Chiefs of Police, 1977); Alan Sekula, "The Body and the Archive," in Richard Bolton, ed., *The Contest of Meaning: Critical Histories of Photography* (Cambridge: MIT Press, 1989), 343–89; Shawn Michelle Smith, *American Archives* (Princeton: Princeton University Press, 1999), 68–93. I have found little information about the use of Bertillionage as a technique for immigration control. The one reference I found concerned using Bertillionage to control Chinese immigrants' entry, specifically between 1903 and 1906. See *Facts Concerning the Enforcement of Chinese Exclusion Laws*, 31.

61. According to Paul Rabinow, "the first practical use of fingerprints took place in Bengal. As Major Ferris of the India Staff Corps put it, 'the uniformity in the colour of the hair, eyes, and complexion of the Indian races renders identification far from easy.' The proverbial 'prevalence of unveracity' of the Oriental races provided another motivation for these gentlemen to perfect a reliable identification system, one whose basis lay in a marker beyond or below the cunning will of the native or criminal." (See Paul Rabinow, "Galton's Regret," in Rabinow, *Essays on the Anthropology of Reason* [Princeton: Princeton University Press, 1996], 113.) Although fingerprints are a

mark of the body that cannot be altered and result in precise identitications, Rabinow relates that Galton's regret was precisely that fingerprints could not reveal anything about the "race" or "inner character" of the person.

62. Daniel W. Sutherland, "The High-Tech ID Menace," *The American Spectator* 32, no. 2 (February 1999), 60. Teeth X rays have been recently used as a means to determine the age of people seeking asylum who claim to be minors but are suspected of lying. See Chris Hedges, "Crucial INS Gatekeeper: The Airport Dentist," *New York Times*, 22 July 2000, A1.

63. See Chris Hedges, "Crucial I.N.S. Gatekeeper: The Airport Dentist," *New York Times*, 22 July 2000, A1, A14.

64. Robyn Wiegman refers to "the cultural training that quite literally teaches the eye not only how but what to see" (22), and she analyzes the role of visual regimes in "making race real" (21) in *American Anatomies: Theorizing Race and Gender* (Durham: Duke University Press, 1995). See especially "Economies of Visibility," 21–78.

65. Readers should keep in mind that beliefs that bodies can be divided unambiguously into male and female are culturally constructed, and, furthermore, there are differences between seeming to have a body that is culturally coded as male or female versus an individual's own bodily identifications.

66. Lucie Cheng Hirata, "Free, Indentured, Enslaved: Chinese Prostitutes in Nineteenth-Century America," in Lucie Cheng Hirata and Edna Bonacich, eds., *Labor Immigration under Capitalism: Asian Workers in the U.S. Before World War II* (Berkeley: University of California Press, 1984), 410.

67. Sander Gilman, *Difference and Pathology: Stereotypes of Sexuality, Race, and Madness* (Ithaca: Cornell University Press, 1985), 94.

68. Ibid., 95–96.

69. Gilman, *Difference and Pathology*, 98; Steven Jay Gould, *The Mismeasure of Man* (New York: Norton, 1981), 129.

70. According to Mark Haller, "The Massachusetts Commission for the Investigation of White Slave Traffic, in one of the most significant investigations of Vice, gave Binet tests to one hundred young prostitutes and two hundred experienced prostitutes. Not only did more than half test feebleminded, but the behavior of the prostitutes confirmed what the tests indicated: 'The general lack of moral insensibility, the boldness, egotism, and vanity, the love of notoriety, the lack of shame or remorse, the absence of even a pretense of affection for their own children or their parents, the desire for immediate pleasure without regard for consequences, the lack of forethought or anxiety about the future—all cardinal symptoms of feeblemindedness—were strikingly evident in every one of the 154 women.'" (See Mark H. Haller, *Eugenics: Hereditarian Attitudes in American Thought*, 103.) Eugenicists became directly involved in immigration administration. For instance, in 1912 Henry Goddard, a leading eugenicist, was invited to assist at Ellis Island in selecting immigrants who might be feeble-minded or mentally deficient and should be denied entry. See Alan M. Kraut, *Silent Travelers*, 74.

71. Yung, *Unbound Feet*, 24.

72. Gail Hershatter, for instance, has documented that courtesans in Shanghai sometimes had bound feet. See *Dangerous Pleasures*, 84. See also Wang Ping, *Aching for Beauty: Footbinding in China* (Minneapolis: University of Minnesota Press, 2000).

73. Yung, *Unbound Feet*, 24.

74. See Fernando Henriques, *Prostitution and Society*, 3 vols. (London: McGibbon and Kee, 1962, 1963, 1968), for a history of how prostitutes have used (or been required by authorities to use) clothing and other visual signs as a means to differentiate themselves.

75. See Walkowitz, *Prostitution and Victorian Society*, 26. See also Christine Stansell, *City of Women: Sex and Class in New York, 1789–1860* (New York: Knopf, 1986), 187, where she writes, "fancy dress signified a rejection of proper feminine behaviors and duties. For [working class] girls who donned fine clothes, dress was en emblem of an estimable erotic maturity, a way to carry about the full identity of an adult, and a sign of admission into heterosexual courting."

76. *Report*, 1146.

28 • *Melanie Heath*

STATE OF OUR UNIONS
Marriage Promotion and the Contested Power of Heterosexuality

DISCUSSION QUESTIONS

1. Why is there a "state interest" in heterosexual marriage? How has that interest manifested itself?
2. How has the state's interest reinforced race, class, gender, and sexual orientation inequality?
3. Heath examines the Oklahoma Marriage Initiative; can you identify other examples of state-sponsored marriage promotion?

STATE INTEREST IN HETEROSEXUAL MARRIAGE

Nation-building strategies tied to the white, nuclear family have a long history in the United States. Federal and state law has shaped marriage as a form of inclusion and exclusion by determining who can marry, the rights and obligations involved in marriage, and the conditions under which a marriage can end. Historian Nancy Cott (2000: 3) identifies how in the United States the government has promoted a particular model of marriage: "life-long, faithful monogamy, formed by the mutual consent of a man and a woman, bearing the impress of the Christian religion and the English common law in its expectations for the husband to be the family head and economic provider." The ideal of the nuclear family in the United States evolved by separating "productive labor" from the home, creating a new social category: the "housewife" (Pascale 2001). Domesticity attributed to wealthy white women became the standard for all women, and the "Cult of True Womanhood" elevated the submissive housewife as morally superior (Brown 1990; Pascale 2001). In contrast, racial ethnic women have systematically been relegated to do the "dirty work" in domestic service and industry (Duffy 2007). Protecting the family and nation has meant maintaining boundaries of racial and sexual purity. In building the nation, the federal and state government sought to "civilize" American Indians by instituting monogamous households, instilling a work ethic among men and domesticity among women (Cott 2000). Slaves were denied the right to marry, signifying their lack of civil rights that would entail the freedom to consent to marriage's obligations. Before and after slaves' emancipation, many states passed laws to ban marriage across the color line, as the specter of sexual relations between white women and African American men created moral panic. Concerns about race and morality also motivated the evolution of immigration law, which largely restricted the entry of Chinese and Japanese women.

Governmental intervention has changed over time in how it envisions protecting "the family," but the thread in this history can be traced to the need to safeguard the boundaries of the nation along the lines of race, class, gender, and sexuality (McClintock 1997). In recent years, federal and state concern has focused on "family breakdown." Sharp rises in female labor force participation, divorce, cohabitation, and single parenting have triggered a "deinstitutionalization" of marriage (Cherlin 2004). These changes, together with the growing movement to legalize same-sex marriage, call into question what constitutes "normal" family life in the United States (Stacey 1996). In the 1960s, President Lyndon Johnson drew on a report from a little-known senator, Daniel Patrick Moynihan, to address the problem of the "breakdown of the Negro family structure" (quoted in Blankenhorn 2007: 5). Controversy about the report ultimately led to a new consensus between conservative and liberal policy makers about what they viewed as the bad behavior of impoverished single mothers inherent in "welfare dependency" (Reese 2005). More recently, marriage advocate David Blankenhorn (2007: 5) has identified a united policy stance to address "the breakdown of *white* family structure" that he believes has followed the trends purportedly undermining Black families. These concerns now motivate federal and state policy to promote marriage. While race and class are visible in these policies, below the surface are anxieties about changing gender relations and the challenge to heterosexuality presented by the increased visibility of lesbian and gay families....

STUDYING MARRIAGE PROMOTION

To study marriage promotion, I conducted ethnographic research for 10 months in 2004 in Oklahoma. Oklahoma is home to the most extensive statewide marriage initiative in the nation, and consequently its policy "extends out" and is influenced by national marriage promotion politics (Burawoy 1998). In 1999, the governor employed the marriage promotion provisions of the Personal Responsibility and Work Opportunity Reconciliation Act to pioneer the Oklahoma Marriage Initiative at a time when few states opted to exercise this option. The Oklahoma Department of Human Services (OKDHS) committed $10 million from its federal TANF block grant and contracted with Public Strategies, Inc. (a private, for-profit firm) to develop and manage the initiative. The Oklahoma Marriage Initiative trains state employees, community leaders, and other volunteers to offer marriage education workshops throughout the state. The workshops use the Prevention and Relationship Enhancement Program (PREP), a research-based curriculum created by Howard Markman and Scott Stanley that teaches communication skills, conflict management, and problem solving. The initiative also trains volunteers to offer a Christian version of the PREP curriculum in settings that are not state funded. In exchange for receiving free workshop training, volunteers pledge to provide at least four free workshops in their communities.

In addition to its groundbreaking marriage initiative, Oklahoma is also well known for being a Bible Belt state. Nearly 60 percent of registered voters say they attend church regularly, compared to the national average of 40 percent (Campbell 2002). Oklahoma's high religiosity would appear to render it exceptional with respect to wide-ranging marriage promotion activities across the nation. Indeed, Oklahoma's social and cultural environment is likely one reason that the marriage initiative was able to take root in the early years of welfare reform, as a Republican governor initiated it with little political resistance. While there are many unique aspects to the formation of the marriage initiative, Oklahoma has nevertheless served as a model for state and community marriage promotion programs across the nation. In recent years, Alabama, Georgia, North Carolina, New Mexico, New York, Ohio, Texas, and Utah have also designated portions of their TANF block grants for marriage promotion. Texas legislated $7.5 million a year.[1]

The Oklahoma Marriage Initiative blends two models of marriage promotion. On the one hand, it seeks to blanket the state with messages about marriage by providing free marriage workshops to as many Oklahomans as possible. On the other, it targets specific populations, including welfare recipients, low-income parents, high school students, the prison population, the military, and Native Americans....

Fears about the declining significance of the nuclear family have spurred the Oklahoma Marriage Initiative to offer marriage education to the public as a mechanism to reinstitutionalize marriage. As one report puts it, the strategy of the marriage initiative is to provide marriage education services to all Oklahomans to effect "specific behavior change at the individual level" and to "restore support for the institution of marriage as a valued social good" (Dion 2006). When I interviewed the OKDHS director, he described being enlightened by reading Barbara Dafoe Whitehead's (1993: 84) *Atlantic Monthly* article "Dan Quayle Was Right," which explains "family breakup" as breeding behaviors that "damage the social ecology, threaten the public order, and impose new burdens on core institutions." Whitehead goes on to express concern that the once isolated breakup of Black families is now spreading to white ones. This implicit (and sometimes explicit) racial comparison is a common theme in the discourse of the marriage movement. Kay Hymowitz (2006: 78), the author of *Marriage and Caste in America*, argues that educating the young to be "self-reliant" members of a democratic society is "The Mission" of white, middle-class families and that poor Black parents are not "simply middle-class parents *manqué;* they have their own culture of child-rearing, and—not to mince words—that culture is a recipe for more poverty." This philosophy harks back to nation-building principles that analogize marriage and the state as a necessary form of governance to produce worthy (white, middle-class) citizens (Cott 2000).

In the national discussion, the poor Black family remains an invisible standard of deviancy. As the focus of policy has turned to family breakdown, the mostly unspoken concern of marriage promotion leaders is the norm of the white, middle-class family and the harm caused to this norm. During our interview, the OKDHS director outlined the cost of "fractured families":

> Another piece of this, when you sit back and think about it, we spend $40 million in this state to run our child support enforcement division. Every one of those faces is a fractured relationship. So, we are spending $40 million in the state to do nothing but administer the transfer of cash from noncustodial parents to custodial parents who have experienced fractured relationships. You can see the high cost of having fractured relationships. It's worth the investment.

The director's words suggest that the "deviancy" of fractured families hurts middle-class families that consist of good citizens who pay taxes and embrace Hymowitz's (2006) "Mission."

The focus on fractured families reinforces a boundary around the normalcy of the white, middle-class, nuclear family. One of the top managers of the marriage initiative, a social worker who maintains a more critical stance, offered this evaluation:

> The way Governor Keating attached lowering the divorce rate through a poverty-funded program, who are we blaming for the divorce rate? I mean that kind of message is real strong in my mind. I've got an education so I was concerned about people living in poverty being blamed for the divorce rate and the state of families and that kind of thing.

Attaching marriage promotion to TANF shifts attention away from transformations taking place among white, middle-class families and places it on poor ones. Moreover, the welfare-to-work provisions in TANF, which enforce stringent work requirements and set time limits for receiving aid, help to ensure that poor "dependent" women (most often U.S.-born and immigrant women of color) are bound to low-wage jobs in service industry.

Marriage promotion follows a long history in the United States of defending the ideal gendered family to preserve a bounded space of normalcy against "deviant" others, with attendant social consequences of race and class inequalities. While positioning fractured families as a social problem, the marriage initiative's practices on the ground predominantly focus on white, middle-class couples to promote a bounded heterosexual space to define the ideal family. In the marriage workshops, issues of race and class disappear, and the focus turns on the problematic of gender relations for heterosexual couples. Heterosexuality is the unexamined backdrop to teach about the "opposite sexes" within the ideal family.

TEACHING THE IMPORTANCE OF GENDER (AND HETEROSEXUALITY)

A dominant ideology of marriage promotion, and its historical presumption in the gendered behavior of the opposite sexes, view it as form[ing] the foundation of a cohesive and stable society. Crisis tendencies, in the form of growing marriage activism by gays and lesbians, are beneath the surface of this ideology, informing the need to strengthen heterosexual relationships. When I asked the OKDHS director, for example, about the goal of the marriage initiative, he confirmed the ideal of marital heterosexuality: "In terms of the marriage initiative, it's relationships between men and women which are committed preferably for life." His use of the words "relationships between men and women" announces the kind of relationships applicable—a declaration that would have been unnecessary 20 years ago—and suggests the prohibition of nonheterosexual love.

With heterosexuality as the unquestioned footing, the marriage workshops for the general population represent a forum to teach the mostly white, middle-class couples who attend about gender as *the* visible problem. The instruction encourages self-discipline and motivation to do gender in the manner compelled by the ideology of the "natural" family (Hay 2003). PREP, the secular version of the curriculum, engages communication and problem-solving skills. One of its main features is the speaker/listener technique, which instructs the speaker, who holds the "floor"—a tile that lists the rules of communication—to make brief "I" statements and the listener to paraphrase what he or she has heard. Despite the mostly gender-neutral curriculum, the 30 workshops I attended stressed gender relations in marriage.

The three-day, state-sponsored workshop leader training of PREP and its Christian version, taught by its creators—Howard Markman and Scott Stanley—and Vice President Natalie Jenkins, established the importance of gender to an implicit heterosexuality. Volunteers attending the training were predominantly white, many of them counselors and educators receiving continuing education units. Throughout, the three presenters focused on what men versus women do in relationships. Scott Stanley told the audience that he wanted to talk about gender differences and explained how researchers have found a pattern that involves women's pursuing an issue and men's withdrawing. He attributed this to men's tendency to be more physiologically reactive and women to be more emotionally aroused. Stanley acknowledged that these patterns of behavior are complex and that researchers have difficulty deciding what is physiological and what is not. Yet he suggested that the pattern seems to reflect a greater need for men not to argue with their mates. He conveyed that a central goal for teaching PREP is helping couples manage gender differences.

Stanley explained the impact of the decline of marriage on men and women. He argued that today, young people think that cohabiting is a good first step to test marriage but that in reality, practicing serial nonmonogamy hurts women because marriage is the only means to ensure a man's commitment. Citing research, Stanley told us that a young man who lives with his girlfriend tends to think she is not the "one," while a young woman thinks just the opposite. He explained, "We have talked young people out of thinking that marriage matters, particularly young women. Women get the worse deal if men don't marry them." Although it is not clear what he meant by the "worse deal," Stanley implied that women are naturally more committed to men, whereas men need the institution of marriage to become self-disciplined practitioners of lifelong monogamy. A dominant script of marital heterosexuality is that men know to settle down—that is, no longer act on their sexual urges—after they marry.

The curriculum includes a number of videos of real couples fighting. One shows a young African American couple who argue over the amount of time the man spends watching sports. During the young man's explanation for why his sport watching is not excessive, Howard Markman stopped the video to point out the way he lifts his hands up and "gazes towards heaven." Markman called this the "beam me up Scotty response." He explained, "This really is an appeal to God. We have a special message to the women in the room. If your partner, husband, son has this response, you might mistakenly think that he is withdrawing, but he is having a spiritual moment." I laughed along with the audience, but what makes this statement funny is the cultural assumption of an embattled masculinity. Markman implied that women cannot really understand the nature of men, which leads to the kind of exasperation shown in the video. Later, Scott Stanley told us that the young man is asking for his wife to accept this important part of him—the part that lives on sports. Statements like this place the onus on the wife to understand the "nature" of men.

Throughout the training, the presenters performed gender and made jokes that drew on the innate differences between men and women, providing a message about handling gender within heterosexual relationships (Butler [1990] 1999; West and Zimmerman 1987). These performances and dialogue subtly suggest a gender hierarchy compelling women to put up with men's idiosyncrasies since ultimately men are the stronger sex. At one point, Howard Markman told a joke about how many men it takes to change the toilet paper. The punch line: There is no scientific answer because it has not happened. Underneath the humor is the suggestion that men have more important things to do than change toilet paper. Several moments later, he flipped the remote as if he were surfing television channels, distracting from Natalie Jenkins' presentation. She told him to "sit" and informed us that she forgot to take the batteries out of the men's toy. She quickly qualified that she "needed" these guys because she is not the most technologically advanced. As we watched a video of a couple fighting over the way the husband put the laundry soap in the washer, Jenkins asserted that the wife is "missing the miracle. He's doing the laundry!" Later, Jenkins discussed expectations and how, when she was first married, she wanted flowers because all her friends were getting them. She and her husband were having financial difficulties, so she found a 99-cent coupon for a dozen carnations. She put four quarters and the coupon on the fridge with a note saying, "Honey, if this coupon expires so will you."

All of this gender work solidifies the importance of the differences between men and women. Men play with toys (and are technologically advanced); women want flowers (and do laundry). The state's promotion of marriage makes visible the importance of these gendered practices, teaching men and women to monitor and accept the differences between men and women. At heart is a lesson about gender difference as the glue that keeps two people of the opposite sex together. The ideal for white, middle-class families is a configuration of gender hierarchy premised on institutionalized heterosexuality. Tying gender difference to understandings of bodies solidifies marital heterosexuality.

The union of gender differences and bodies together with institutionalized heterosexuality was even more pronounced in the breakout training session of the Christian version of PREP. Scott Stanley discussed how gender differences originate in the Genesis passage of the Bible. He explained,

> I think it is interesting that it says man [will leave his mother and father] and not man and woman. I have come to believe from science—and this is going to sound sexist—why males are called to a higher level of commitment and sacrifice, biologically and scripturally. Women are inherently made more vulnerable than men because they have babies. Males need to protect. Unfortunately, in our culture, we have gutted that, and women bear the most burden by the lack of a sacrificial ethic.

His statement makes explicit the often implicit instruction on gender difference throughout the training—men are naturally less emotional and better equipped for certain responsibilities in marriage, namely, the need to protect their families. The interaction of gender and heterosexuality is important to position men and women hierarchically as part of a social order that rewards married, heterosexual (and mostly white, middle-class) men as husbands and often as the primary breadwinner.

Linking ideas of gender and heterosexuality directly to bodies, the instructor presented the definition of marriage as a union of male and female. According to Stanley,

> God meant something when he specified that there should be male and female and what to do with bodies. I don't just mean sex and physical union, but I mean oneness. They covered up where they are most obviously different. We don't cover up where we are similar. We fear rejection in relationships because of the possibility of difference. Difference symbolizes physical union, which is now apparent to them.

The heterosexual footing implied by the idea of the opposite sexes is also the ground for the performance of gender hierarchy. Through the state-sponsored instruction, potential instructors of PREP and the Christian version of PREP are taught to present ideas about gender and sexuality to encourage self-monitoring in relation to the ideal of the "natural," married family.

REHEARSING THE POWER OF HETEROSEXUALITY

...In the 30 marriage promotion workshops I attended, most included heterosexual married or engaged couples and sometimes a single woman or man. In two of the six-week workshops, however, there was one lesbian couple.[2] The first of these included 14 white heterosexual couples, one interracial heterosexual couple, and three female coaches, two white and one Black. Tammy and Chris, white lesbians in their fifties, had introduced themselves as "life partners" on the first day. They had a number of issues with communication. After hearing about the workshop on the radio, Tammy enrolled herself and "a friend." They told me they were relieved they were not asked to leave. The next workshop included Amanda and Jennifer, a white lesbian couple in their late twenties, among the 18 white couples, two white single men, and two female coaches, one white and one Black. Amanda and Jennifer were less talkative, but with their severe communication problems, by their own admission, they monopolized much of the coaches' energy during the practice exercises....

The focus on gender within the confines of marital heterosexuality ensured that the same-sex couples' presence remained invisible. This was true even in the case of Tammy and Chris, who were very vocal. The last class of the first six-week session on sensuality/sexuality offered one of the more poignant examples. David asked people to share how their families of origin had discussed sexuality with them when they were young. I was sitting at an end table with Tammy and Chris. David began at the table opposite us and stopped at the table next to ours to talk about his own upbringing, skipping Tammy, Chris, and myself. This omission did not deter the two from participating. When David asked about sensuality and touch, Tammy spoke up: "We assume that what we like, the other person likes." Her words drew attention to the fact that her partner is a woman and not a man. While it is probably true that heterosexuals and nonheterosexuals make this kind of assumption, her statement stood in bold relief to the dominant message of managing difference in heterosexual relationships. Comments such as this one challenge taken-for-granted assumptions of gender and sexuality.

All the participants I interviewed acknowledged awareness of the lesbian couples without my asking, and most admitted feeling a little uncomfortable due to either their disapproval of or their inexperience dealing with same-sex relationships. Tom, a white man in his mid-twenties who attended with Suzanne, said he was caught off guard by "the two girls who were there together. They were like lesbians. I was surprised, I guess." Becky, a white woman in her thirties who was married and had four children with Martin, an African American man in his early forties, answered my question about whether anything in the workshop made her uncomfortable:

> Mmm. I did feel uncomfortable with the fact that there were couples in there of the same sex, just because I feel strongly about family values and what the traditional family is. But I know it is something that is happening in the United States, and there is really nothing I can do about it. And, I mean, they are human. They have needs too. It doesn't mean that I agree with them.

Norm, a white man in his sixties who attended with his third wife, moved from talking about men's responsiveness to his disapproval of homosexuality. He said,

> At first, the unknown [was uncomfortable]. When you go around and there is more and more interaction, I felt like there was a quality of responses and information given by the men in that class that usually doesn't happen. [Pause] I do consider homosexuality a sin, but I'm not here to judge that. I have a lot of patients that are gay, and they have a lifestyle I do not approve of. But I thought even the gay couple had a lot of good information to toss out.

Some of the other participants expressed a subtle resentment about dealing with same-sex couples in the marriage workshop but admitted that these couples "have needs too."...

CONCLUSION

This research contributes to feminist theories of the state by problematizing the assumption of a male state with unidimensional control of its citizens or subjects. Instead, it reveals polycentric state practices that are structured as gendered and sexualized, and that uphold the dominance of the white, middle-class family and its importance to a cohesive national identity. In the case of marriage promotion, diverse state practices focus policy concerns on "deviant" (coded Black) single-mother families

while resources are allocated to teach about gender hierarchy to predominantly white, middle-class couples. Putting feminist state theory and critical heterosexuality studies in dialogue demonstrates the importance of an unspoken heterosexuality to state control. State actors who seek to promote marriage rely on a particular, and conservative, interpretation of social scientific research on families as a noncontroversial way to focus policy concerns on the need to promote "healthy" (heterosexual) families. These policies demonstrate a perceived need on the part of the state to safeguard the health of the nation by strengthening the "mission" of white, middle-class (heterosexual) marriage. The race and class assumptions of this reasoning are largely made invisible as marriage promotion leaders use the rhetoric of health and social capital.

On the ground, marriage education becomes a tool to teach self-monitoring gendered practices within the confines of heterosexual marriage. In the workshops I attended, instruction on the "opposite" sexes signaled heterosexuality to reaffirm the sexual outsider status of same-sex couples as well as that of single-mother families. The on-the-ground practices of promoting heterosexual marriage mirror antigay countermovements, such as the ex-gay movement, which encourages individuals to police their behavior according to scripted gender and heterosexual norms (Robinson and Spivey 2007). This strategy provides states and social movements the ability to govern the behavior of citizens and members from a distance.

Marriage workshops rehearse dominant scripts on gender polarity to reinforce expectations of men's and women's "nature" to make marital heterosexuality appear instinctive and effortless. The decline of marriage and women's increased workforce participation during the past 40 years has challenged traditional norms that created social cohesion through gender hierarchy and implicit heterosexuality. Marriage workshops offer a forum to revisit ideas on hierarchical relationships between men and women. State training for workshop leaders teaches that managing gender differences is essential to a harmonious marriage. The trainers provide examples and offer gendered performances to focus on indisputable differences between men and women that cater to cultural ideas of men as rational (strong) and women as emotional (weak). These performances provide simple answers to complex negotiations that many families face as they juggle tight work schedules along with raising children and try to manage households that often bring children from previous marriages or relationships. The gendered performances teach that wives need to allow "men to be men" and that husbands need to cater to their wives' emotional needs.

NOTES

1. Many of these states, including Texas, have incorporated the "one percent solution," putting 1 percent of their Temporary Assistance to Needy Families money toward marriage promotion. From my calculations, Oklahoma designates roughly 5 percent of its Temporary Assistance to Needy Families block grant per year.

2. One of the initiative leaders told me that she knew of other same-sex couples attending marriage workshops. There was no way to find out how many actually did attend since the "All about You" forms that participants fill out at the beginning of the workshops do not ask about sexual orientation or same-sex relationships.

REFERENCES

Blankenhorn, David. 2007. *The future of marriage*. New York: Encounter Books.

Brown, Gillian. 1990. *Domestic individualism: Imagining self in nineteenth-century America*. Berkeley: University of California Press.

Burawoy, Michael. 1998. The extended case method. *Sociological Theory* 16:4–33.

Butler, Judith. [1990] 1999. *Gender trouble*. New York: Routledge.

Campbell, Kim. 2002. Can marriage be taught? *Christian Science Monitor*, July 18.

Cherlin, Andrew J. 2004. The deinstitutionalization of American marriage. *Journal of Marriage and Family* 66:848–61.

Cott, Nancy. 2000. *Public vows: A history of marriage and the nation*. Cambridge, MA: Harvard University Press.

Dion, Robin. 2006. *The Oklahoma Marriage Initiative: An overview of the longest-running statewide marriage initiative in the U.S.* ASPE research brief. Washington, DC: Office of the Assistant Secretary for Planning and Evaluation, U.S. Department of Health and Human Services.

Duffy, Mignon. 2007. Doing the dirty work: Gender, race, and reproductive labor in historical perspective. *Gender & Society* 21:313–36.

Hay, James. 2003. Unaided virtues: The (neo) liberalization of the domestic sphere and the new architecture of community. In *Foucault, cultural studies, and governmentality*, edited by Jack Z. Bratich, Jeremy Packer, and Cameron McCarthy. Albany: State University of New York Press.

Hymowitz, Kay S. 2006. *Marriage and caste in America: Separate and unequal families in a post-marital age*. Chicago: Ivan R. Dee.

McClintock, Ann. 1997. "No longer in a future heaven": Gender, race, and nationalism. In *Dangerous liaisons: Gender, nation, and postcolonial perspectives*, edited by Anne McClintock, Aamir Mufti, and Ella Shohat. Minneapolis: University of Minnesota Press.

Pascale, Celine-Marie. 2001. All in a day's work: A feminist analysis of class formation and social identity. *Race, Gender & Class* 8:34–59.

Reese, Ellen. 2005. *Backlash against welfare mothers*. Berkeley: University of California Press.

Robinson, Christine M., and Sue E. Spivey. 2007. The politics of masculinity and the ex-gay movement. *Gender & Society* 21:650–75.

Stacey, Judith. 1996. *In the name of the family: Rethinking family values in the postmodern age*. Boston: Beacon.

West, Candace, and Don Zimmerman. 1987. Doing gender. *Gender & Society* 1:125–51.

Whitehead, Barbara Dafoe. 1993. Dan Quayle was right. *Atlantic Monthly*, April, 47–84.

29 • *Lionel Cantú, Jr.*

DE AMBIENTE
Queer Tourism and Shifting Sexualities

DISCUSSION QUESTIONS

1. Why does Cantú argue that gay and lesbian tourism facilitates both sexual colonization *and* liberation?
2. Why does Cantú situate sexual tourism within an analysis of the political economy of the border? How does he link gay Mexican identity itself to transnational dynamics?
3. How do the dynamics of class and race delimit the experiences of gay Mexicans seeking the utopic "fantasy of gay life in the United States"?

> The coastal regions all around the country are noted for their sensual ambience. Perhaps it's the heat; but just about anywhere there's a beach and a city, there's action. Acapulco, Cancun, Vallarta, Mazatlan, and Veracruz are all hot, and so are the men.
>
> —Eduardo David, *Gay Mexico: The Men of Mexico*

"Do you know Mexico?" coyly poses the opening page of Mexico's official tourist web site.[1] Do you? Perhaps not. This is not a Mexico of social inequality, economic turmoil, indigenous uprisings, and mass emigration. No; this is a different Mexico—a sexy Mexico. Additional headers entice the reader to "Come Feel the Warmth of Mexico" where "...beaches are such as moods: bays that with happy smiles, beaches that spread in straight line, as to remind its steadiness, female beaches, smooth and with cadence, frisky beaches, that open and close, decline and go up [sic]." The sexual imagery of the web site leaves the reader (presumably heterosexual) with a sort of coquettish frustration and a desire for more than a "virtual tour" can provide. While it may seem otherwise, Mexico's flirtation with tourists is not limited to straight travelers.... The nation has become a major destination of gay and lesbian tourists, particularly Americans, in a growing global tourism industry. In turn, Mexico's *ambiente* (homosexual subculture...) is undergoing its own transformation, intimately linked to queer tourism.

The purpose of this chapter is to examine two sides of queer tourism "south of the border": (1) the development of gay and lesbian tourism in Mexico and (2) the effects of this industry on Mexican sexualities. As a point of clarification, I should also state up front that I refer to gay and lesbian tourism as an identity-based industry, and queer tourism as a larger market that encompasses a multitude of identities, including both native and foreign heterosexuals, bisexuals, and transgendered people. I argue that the relationship between gay and lesbian tourism and Mexican sexualities is a complex one in which dimensions of both sexual colonization and sexual liberation are at work. Furthermore, I assert that in order to understand Mexican sexualities we must move away from one-dimensional cultural models and instead examine them from a more complex and materialist perspective that recognizes that culture, social relations, and identities are embedded in global processes.

...I soon realized that tourism was not only an important factor in the lives of the men I interviewed but also a form of migration itself (in a broader sense of the word). While my ancestry is Mexican and I am fluent in Spanish, I am a Chicano—I am not Mexican. Thus, although my purpose in Mexico was entirely academic, I was a tourist. Despite the voyeuristic tendencies of both, there is a difference between my roles as ethnographer and as tourist that I think is relevant to this chapter and my analysis. My gaze as an ethnographer was armed at understanding the political economy of sexuality in Mexico as it differentially shapes the lives of men. I was not in Mexico on vacation; nonetheless, Mexicans often read me in the public spaces of the plazas, the bars, and the streets, not as a researcher but as a tourist. Thus, it is the intersection of my ethnographic and tourist roles that informs my analysis of queer tourism in Mexico....

...I address the following questions in this chapter: First, to what extent are Mexican sexualities and the dimensions that shape them "Mexican," and to what extent are they global? Furthermore, if tourism is to be understood as a modernist project built upon mediated representation and space, as Dean MacCannell (1999 [1976]) asserts, then how might these dimensions shape "native" identities and experiences? This chapter attempts to examine the complexities of Mexican sexualities from a political economic perspective, with a particular focus on queer tourism, in order to understand, in turn, how these dimensions are shaping the sexual identities of Mexican men.

ENCLACES/RUPTURAS FRONTERIZAS *(BORDER LINKAGES/RUPTURES)*

The border that delineates the nations of Mexico and the United States has been since its creation with the Treaty of Guadalupe in 1848 "an open wound." But as Anzaldua (1987) makes clear, *la frontera* is both real and imagined. It is a geopolitical boundary that links even as it separates the two nations, but it is also a metaphor for the spaces in which hybridity is created (in an often violent manner). In this section, my purpose is to highlight the political–economic linkages between the United States and Mexico that have given rise to the development of gay and lesbian tourism in Mexico. In addition, I highlight the border ruptures that are created through "tolerance zones"—a sexual "borderlands" in which Mexican male sexualities are fixed even as they are transformed.

Tourism has become an increasingly important sector of the Mexican economy. Beginning in the late 1960s Mexico created its own Ministry of Tourism (SECTUR), which is responsible for tourism as a whole, and FONATUR (in the early 1970s), which is responsible for infrastructure development projects in particular and has sponsored annual tourism trade fairs since 1996. In 1999, the World Trade Organization ranked Mexico seventh among the top ten destinations and tenth in foreign currency generated from tourism, and a majority of Mexican tourists continue to be from the United States (Guenette 2000). More precisely, more than 90 percent of Mexican tourists are from the United States (Arellano 1996). While it is impossible to know in any definitive way what proportions of Mexican tourists are gay, lesbian, or bisexual, there are factors that point to the development of queer tourism in the country.[2] These include the development and commodification of Mexican "gay" culture and space, and the rise of a Mexican gay and lesbian movement.

Gay bars in Mexico are a relatively new phenomenon, although they seem to be historically linked to urbanization and the development of *zonas de tolerancia* in the early part of the century.... *Zonas de tolerancia* (tolerance zones, or red light districts) developed after the revolution to control what were defined as forms of social deviance that included prostitution and homosexuality. The *zonas* were thus both gendered and sexualized spaces for those who transgressed gender norms and where men could satisfy their "licentious" desires. The spaces included areas where both male homosexual and transvestite bars were located and provided an escape from moral restraint for men who otherwise led more public heterosexual lives. Once established, the *zonas* became a legitimized space for "immoral activity" that attracted sexual tourism from north of the border where morality was more closely policed. For example, "Boys Town" brothels on the Mexican side of the border remain to this day rites of passage for young American men who cross the border looking for mostly heterosexual adventure. Thus, by the mid-twentieth century, the Mexican border towns were already firmly established as sites of sexual tourism for men on both sides of the border.[3]

Various scholars have mentioned the growing popularity of the term "gay" as an identity label in Mexico by both men and women (who also use the term "lesbian") (see Lumsden 1991; Murray 1995; Prieur 1998). While the label is sometimes written as "gai," it is clear that it refers to a sexual identity, culture, and movement and is thus similar in many ways to the term "gay" as used in the United States. Lumsden (1991) explains this shift in identity constructions as a consequence of several political factors. The combination of urbanization/industrialization, along with the creation of *zonas de tolerancia*, in all probability provided the social spaces whereby sexual minorities could establish social networks and, at least to some degree, create "community."

This spatial segregation resulted in queer zones or ghettoes in some cities like Guadalajara and Puerto Vallarta.[4] In Puerto Vallarta, the south side of the city has become the de facto "gay side" with bars, hotels, and other establishments that cater to a gay male—especially tourist—clientele. It should also be stated, however, that as is the case in the United States, an entire city has also become identified as a "gay space."... The city of Guadalajara itself has over time become known as the San Francisco of Mexico due to its gay and lesbian population. As one middle-aged gay man told me, "in Guadalajara all the men are either *mdriachis* or *maricones* [fags]." However, the development of a gay and lesbian community in Guadalajara, along with the movement for gay rights, has been hotly contested by conservative forces in the community.

Guadalajara and Acapulco were common vacation destinations for gay men from Mexico City in the 1980s and early 1990s (Sanchez-Crispin and Lopez-Lopez 1997).[5] However, since that time, Puerto Vallarta has developed into Mexico's premier gay resort town as a sort of satellite gay space for its big sister (Guadalajara), much as Fire Island is to New York and Palm Springs is to Los Angeles.[6]

Another factor that has contributed to the development of queer tourism in Mexico is the slow but steady rise of a Mexican gay and lesbian rights movement. Lumsden (1991) argues that the student movement in 1968 and the firing of a Sears department store employee can be understood as catalysts for challenging social oppression on the basis of sexual orientation in Mexico. Whether incidents like these were indeed the cause of the Mexican gay rights movement or not, what is clear is that the movement is not "new" to the Mexican political arena. Since the 1970s various gay and lesbian organizations have been created (and disbanded) throughout Mexico. Gay pride festivities are held in various Mexican cities and have become a tourist attraction in themselves. In fact, Cancun hosted the International Gay Pride Festival in 2001. These examples illustrate that a gay (and lesbian) identity exists in Mexico; and although it is not a clone of American constructions, there are many similarities.[7]

The rise of a gay identity is linked to the transnational ties of globalization between Mexico to the United States, in particular the gay United States. My interviews with Mexican men in Guadalajara and migrants in the Los Angeles area were particularly useful in shedding light on this matter. These transnational links gave rise to a sexual identity label in the 1980s (still used to a certain degree)—*internacional*. Carrier reported use of the *internacional* (international) label by the then "hipper" and younger homosexual men during his field research.[8] The label, which referred to men who were versatile in their sexual repertoire, obviously has transborder connotations. Clearly, then, Mexican sexualities are being transformed through transnational processes and linkages, including that of tourism.

QUEER TOURISM IN MEXICO

> The reason why a million or more American visitors have traveled to Mexico in the course of recent years is that the average practical-minded person regards recreation travel from the angle of maximum returns at a minimum outlay of money and time. It is upon this purely practical consideration that Mexico makes its bid to the recreation-bent traveler.
>
> —Anonymous, "The Lure of Mexico"

While a growing body of literature has examined the impact of tourism and globalization on sexuality in the Pacific Rim (Truong 1990; Hall 1994a, 1994b), the way these phenomena are influencing Latin American countries has been largely ignored.[9] However, the fact that gay and lesbian tourism is a rapidly growing market in every part of the world—estimated at $17 billion (U.S.) dollars by the International Gay and Lesbian Travel Association (IGLTA)—demands greater attention.[10] With its proximity to the United States and the relatively low cost compared to other international sites, Mexico has become a desired destination for many gay and lesbian tourists. The recently created

Tourist Promotion Board of Mexico plans to market "a number of product clubs featuring destinations and services *for certain types of people* like honeymooners, fishing buffs or nature lovers" (Guenette 2000, 42). Although the gay and lesbian market niche is not mentioned specifically by the government organization, there are signs of strategic growth, including a growing number of gay and lesbian travel companies with travel programs in Mexico and publications that cater to the gay and lesbian tourist in Mexico.

Although Mexico has long been a favored site for vacationing among Americans, the growing popularity of Mexico as a *gay and lesbian* tourist destination is due in large measure to the marketing efforts of the gay and lesbian tourist industry. Founded in 1983, the IGTLA is an international organization with member organizations throughout the world and growing representation in Latin America,[11] including Mexico. The development of gay and lesbian cruise companies, such as Atlantis, RSVP, and Olivia, have also contributed to making Mexico a popular destination.[12] In addition, there are a number of travel magazines and web sites that cater to gay and lesbian patrons, as do a growing number of gay and lesbian travel agencies that offer packages throughout Mexico. *The Ferrari Guides Gay Mexico* (Black 1997) lists more than forty businesses that offer travel arrangements throughout Mexico aimed at gay and lesbian clientele; not surprisingly, nearly all of these are based in the United States (mostly, but not exclusively, in major urban centers) (Cordova 1999). Among the numerous international travel guides for gay and lesbian tourists—including comprehensive guides by Spartacus, Ferrari, Odysseus, and Damron—are several that focus on travel information for the queer tourist in Mexico. There are three queer tourist guide books that focus exclusively on Mexico and for the most part target a male audience: *Gay Mexico: The Men of Mexico* (David 1998), *The Ferrari Guides Gay Mexico: The Definitive Guide to Gay and Lesbian Mexico* (Black 1997),[13] and *A Man's Guide to Mexico and Central America* (Cordova 1999). Each of the guides gives both general information useful to any tourist (i.e., money exchange information and maps) and information specific to the queer tourist (e.g., bath house locations and helpful Spanish phrases for meeting men).

All three guides provide city-by-city information. Senor Cordova's *Man's Guide* lists fourteen cities, Eduardo David's *Gay Mexico* has listings for twenty-five, and Richard Black's *Ferrari Guide* lists forty-three. While Mexico's urban centers (e.g., Mexico City, Guadalajara, and Monterey) and mainstream tourist destinations (i.e., Cancun, Acapulco, Los Cabos) are among the cities listed, the guides also list towns and cities that are more "off the beaten path," especially for the queer tourist. These include cities such as Leon in the state of Guanajuato (known as the shoe capital of the world) and the city of Oaxaca with its neighboring villages. The distinction between these sites and gay tourist sites is supposedly one of "authenticity." But while the travel guides forewarn gay tourists of the potential dangers of crossing into these native grounds, they are in reality tourist sites, too. Thus, "off the beaten path" does not necessarily mean that the sites are nontourist spaces but rather that they are more "mainstream," catering to a more "straight" clientele.

An examination of these guides and tourist services suggests that two "sides" of Mexico are most commonly represented: the "just like home" and the exotic. As Black (1997) explains in *The Ferrari Guides*, "For Americans, Mexico is close, yet foreign. For any traveler, it's different yet has many of the comforts of home. It offers something for everyone! You're in for a great time!" (14). While both the "just like home" and the exotic representations emphasize the homoerotic aspects of different sites in Mexico, one targets American tourists who want to vacation with all the gay comforts of home while the other seeks to attract those who seek an erotic adventure not to be found in any suburban American home life. Both speak to MacCannell's (1999 [1976]) insight that

> [t]he frontiers of world tourism are the same as the expansion of the modern consciousness with terminal destinations for each found throughout the colonial,

ex-colonial, and future colonial world where raw materials for industry and exotic flora, fauna, and peoples are found in conglomeration. The tourist world has also been established *beyond* the frontiers of existing society, or at least beyond the edges of the Third World. A *paradise* is a traditional type of tourist community, a kind of last resort, which has as its defining characteristic its location not merely outside the physical borders of urban industrial society, but just beyond the border of the peasant and plantation society as well. (183)

Yet for queer tourism there also exists a "border" tension between the lure of an exotic "paradise" and the dangers of homophobia in foreign lands. Here, Mexico seems to represent a homosexual paradise free of the pressures of a modern "gay lifestyle"; where sexuality exists in its "raw" form yet where the dangers of an uncivilized heterosexual authority also threaten.

Gay and lesbian cruises seem to target those more inclined to a mediated adventure where one can enjoy prefabricated representations of the exotic and always return to one's "home away from home" either aboard ship or in a hotel. The cruise destinations tend to be located either in the "Mexican Caribbean" on the east coast or in the Baja area on the west. Take, for instance, Atlantis's description of its services:

> Atlantis vacations are designed for the way we enjoy ourselves today. We created the concept of an all-gay resort vacation and are the leaders in all-gay charters of first class resorts and cruise ships. All at exotic locations, exclusively ours for these special weeks, with an emphasis on friendship and camaraderie. Places where you can always be yourself and always have fun. That's the way we play.

The "home-away-from-home" approach to gay travel thus allows for the "best of both worlds" where one can "play" on exotic beaches but under controlled conditions. A new *zona de tolerancia* is born—a queer space that protects inhabitants from the threat of cultural mismatch, including homophobia. Thus, in this queer borderland, the tourist can enjoy

Mexico's pleasures under a controlled environment free from the less "civilized" world *del otro lado* (on the other side) of tourist boundaries.

In comparison to the vacation cruise advertisements, gay guide books are more apt to give stereotypical representations of Mexican men. Consider David's (1998) description:

> Many Mexican men are often breathtaking in their beauty. They are sensual and often unabashedly sexual. Proud to be male, aware of their physical nature, they are often ready to give of themselves and sometimes receive in return....
>
> The adventurous visitor may want to go farther afield in search of the men for whom Mexico is particularly famed: the butch *hombres* who would never walk into a place known to be gay, but who are ready to spring to attention when they catch a man's eye. These are men who must be pursued. (27–28)

This excerpt exemplifies a *colonial desire* that Robert Young (1995) defines as the dialectic of attraction and repulsion, to conquer (and be conquered by) the hypermasculine and sexually charged racial Other. The colonial message is reinforced in the guide books by advice on "rewarding" Mexican men for their services with gifts or money, suggesting that financial compensation for homosexual sex is a cultural norm.

Such representations are reminiscent of what is commonly referred to as "Spanish fantasy heritage" (see McWilliams 1948). At the end of the nineteenth century and in the first half of the twentieth century, the prevailing image of Mexicans (both in the United States and Mexico) was of "gay *caballeros*" and "dark and lovely *senoritas*" lazily dancing the night away under Spanish tile roofs. These representations were utilized to sell a romantic and exotic image of California and Mexico to tourists in the early decades of the twentieth century. Contemporary gay tourist images seem to either play up the "Latin lover" image or place greater emphasis on a bit rougher and more "savage" version of the gay *caballero*, both of which abound in gay travel guides. Compare, for instance, the cover images of the three travel guides.

The images on the covers of both Black's guide (Figure 29.1) and Cordova's (Figure 29.2) represent the "Latin lover" look, a light-complected (though tanned) young man in romantic settings, at least partially clothed and waiting to give the queer male tourist a *bienvenida* (a welcoming). The image on the cover of David's guide (Figure 29.3) is a darker *mestizo* with facial hair in an ambiguous setting and framed suggestively (the reader is not sure of the model's state of dress). Not surprisingly, it is David's book that contains more information for the traveler looking for experiences "off the beaten path." Beyond the stereotypes of Latino masculinity, these images represent contradictions of internalized homophobia and the quest for the elusive "real" man among gay tourist themselves.

Figure 29.1

Figure 29.2

Figure 29.3

One of the ironies of this search is that as more gay male tourists look for these exotic places—virgin territory, off the beaten path of mainstream gay tourist sites—the sites become, in effect, conquered territory—gay tourist spots. This type of "invasion" is complicated, of course, by the tensions between a certain level of sexual liberation versus sexual conquest. That is, as gay and lesbian tourists become more common to an area, there is a certain level of normalization that occurs through visibility. However, it is not clear to what extent the opening of more legitimized queer space is a positive effect for Mexico's queer population and to what extent this space is framed as "American."

The expansion of the gay and lesbian tourism industry in Mexico is but one of the more visible manifestations of this queer manifest destiny.... Other signs of this development are the gay bars that now operate throughout Mexico, some with American-sounding names like Relax (Acapulco), Blue City (Cancun), MN'MS (Ciudad Juarez), and The Door (Mexico City). In each case, these Mexican gay bars are located in sites commonly visited by foreign gay tourists. While they are not technically or legally off-limits to queer Mexican nationals, only those of at least a middle-class background and with more sophisticated tastes who might mix better with tourists are commonly found in such bars/discos. *Zonas de tolerancia*, yes, but within limits.

The question of how this tourism is influencing the lives and sexual identities of Mexican men and women remains to be researched, but Murray (1995; see also Black 1997) reports that the hospitality industry is a common employer of Mexican gays and lesbians.[14] In addition, male prostitution (as either an occupation or "part-time" activity) is obviously linked to gay male tourism (Carrier 1995). And more recently, epidemiologists have become more concerned with tourism and the spread of HIV in the country. In the following section I explore these questions more directly through the voices of Mexican men themselves.

GAY CABALLEROS AND PHALLIC DREAMS: LIFE IN THE SEXUAL BORDERLANDS

> In...coordination of and responsibility for the diverse efforts of the nation, tourism has its place, a place that is characterized by its diversification, for it is indifferent to nothing and affects all, the local as much as the foreign.... And that does not refer only to foreign tourism, those visitors from afar who discover new realities, even as they offer them.
>
> —Hector Manuel Romero, "Nada es indiferente al turismo"

Mexico's Gay *ambiente* has changed dramatically over the last decade. What was once an underground world of private parties in the homes of homosexual men has become a more public and therefore more visible phenomenon, as Santiago's observation (as noted in the previous chapter) that "anybody can be gay now" illustrates. The commodification of Mexican gay spaces presents a complex set of factors in the lives of queer Mexican men. The spaces created allowed for the development of an identity and community that served as the foundation of the gay and lesbian movement in Mexico. Queer tourists shape this space both through their contact with Mexicans and through the creation of new space to serve their needs. Contact provides an exchange of cultural and political information around issues of

queerness that has an impact on men's lives.

Some men use this information as a rationale for migrating to the United States, which they construct as a more tolerant space/place. Armando is a 32-year-old man from Jalisco who lives in the Los Angeles area, where he works in HIV services. He is the oldest of eight children and moved to the United States in 1990. In 1995, he was living in Santa Ana after having moved from Los Angeles, where he had been living with his brother. At the time of the interview he was an undocumented immigrant. Armando learned about the United States through tourism, indirectly at first and later through his own experiences. In Mexico, Armando was a seminarian studying to be a priest. In the seminary he heard stories of gay life in the United States from friends (including other seminarians) who had visited the "north," and later he himself visited the United States for missionary exchange programs. It was after he was advised by a priest to move to the north, where he could live more openly as a gay man, that Armando migrated.

Lalo, a 33-year-old gay-identified man from Guadalajara, is a similar case. The fifth of nine children, Lalo comes from what he describes as a "very poor" class background. Lalo explained that after being rejected by his family for being gay, he moved to Puerto Vallarta for a time, where he worked in hotels. He explained that many of his coworkers were also gay and that they helped him get by to the extent of giving him an apartment in which to live. He migrated to Southern California on the advice of his friends in 1983. He is now a legal resident and lives in Fountain Valley. He explained,

> The people in the hotel would tell me "Go to the United States, it's beautiful, you make good money and there are a lot of homosexuals. You can hold [your lover's] hand and kiss in public and nothing happens."
> I thought it was an ideal world where homosexuals could be happy. [But I] learned that it wasn't true that homosexuals were free, that they can hold hands or that Americans liked Mexicans.

The reality that awaited Lalo was not a utopia but rather more of a nightmare. Soon after moving to the United States with the assistance of gay friends, he discovered not only that homophobia does exist in the United States but also that racism was a fact of life he would have to deal with, which is just one of the many tribulations and hardships that queer immigrants must face (see Luibheid 1998). The fantasy of gay life in the United States reported to Lalo is a common one. As mentioned, in my interview with Santiago he referred to it as the *sueizo falico*, or "phallic dream," in which queer men in Mexico envision the United States as a sexual utopia, an erotic land of milk and honey. The irony, of course, is that many American gay tourists have a similar dream when they visit Mexico's gay resorts.

For those Mexican men who have the resources, travel to "gay-friendly" places is also an option, as in the case of Marcos discussed in the previous chapter. Another such case is that of Franco, who travels about once a year to the Los Angeles area to visit family. He and Angel, a gay cousin, always go to gay bars together and Franco admits to having a good time, but his real love is Cuba. With a grin he related, "The men in Cuba are fantastic. I always take some extra things like cologne and clothes. Cuban men will fuck you for a Nike baseball cap." Thus, like his American counterparts in Mexico who are tourists with expendable income, Franco seeks sexual conquest in exotic lands, in this case Cuba. The excerpt helps to highlight not only the diversity of Mexican male sexual experiences with tourism but also the importance of class in shaping the power relations of these experiences. Apparently, the phallic dream knows no borders.

But the road to the phallic dream that some Mexican men pursue is a two-way street, and the reality of racism in the United States is the slap that wakes them. Juan and Miguel, both in their midtwenties, are two Mexican men I met during my research in the Los Angeles area. They actually returned to Mexico in part because of the difficulty of living in the United States but also because of social and economic opportunities they felt existed in Mexico. Although Juan was a naturalized citizen of the United States, Miguel was an undocumented immigrant. On a return visit to the United States Juan explained,

> The situation for us here in the United States was just too difficult. The type of work that Miguel could find here, without papers, was very hard and did not pay well, and everything is so expensive too. We decided that it was better to go to Cancun and work with gay tourists there. I know English and I've learned a little French too. We have a very small apartment and it isn't always easy, but we are happy there.

Juan and Miguel chose to return to Mexico to pursue their dreams and a more comfortable life as gay men. That is, with some of the social and economic capital (although it was limited) they acquired in the United States, Juan and Miguel were able to move to Cancun and begin anew in a better class position.

Some of the Mexican men whom I interviewed in the United States felt the same discomfort that Juan and Miguel expressed, but rather than return to Mexico to live, they vacation there. Julio, a Guadalajara native in his early forties, lives in Orange County, California. He migrated to the United States through a network of gay friends and soon after married a lesbian friend who is a U.S. citizen. Now a legal resident, he works as an accountant for most of the year and saves money so that he can return to Mexico for months at a time. Like his Mexican contemporaries, Julio also uses vacations and tourism as a strategy of escape, but from his American context.

> The men here are superficial and I haven't been able to meet someone that I can have a long-term relationship with. When I go to Mexico I visit my family and friends and I feel their warmth and love. I still have a lot of gay friends in Guadalajara and I always spend time in [Puerto] Vallarta too. I feel like I can be myself there and that people appreciate me for who I am.

The frustrations that Julio expressed to me were in reference to his experiences with American gay scenes in general, but he was also critical of gay Latino culture and norms in the United States. Julio feels that the affective connections and sense of community that he knows in Guadalajara are largely missing in the United States—even among gay Latinos. In addition, he feels that American gay culture, and American men in particular, are too superficial.

Mexican men's relationships with American men are not always contentious. Roberto is in his early forties and has resided in the United States since moving from Mexico City in 1996. The fourth of five children, he comes from a prestigious and well-to-do family in Nayarit, Mexico. Although never married, Roberto has a teenaged son who lives in Mexico with the son's mother. Roberto lives in Long Beach and works as an AIDS educator for a Latino community organization. Roberto explained to me that he was quite happy with his life in Mexico as a civil servant but that people had begun to gossip about his sexual orientation and he feared for his job security. Roberto had met a man from the United States who was vacationing in Mexico and had maintained a friendly relationship with the man. When the American suggested to Roberto that he move to the United States to live with him in the Los Angeles area, Roberto took advantage of the opportunity and moved to L.A. Although he is no longer in a relationship with the American, they continue to be friends.

My own experience researching issues of sexuality and migration has taught me that Roberto's experience is a common one. Many men become involved in "binational relationships" (i.e., relationships where partners are of different nationalities). Such relationships are not recognized by U.S. immigration policy, which therefore does not allow for the legal migration of same-sex spouses. Despite the "illegitimacy" of these relationships for immigration purposes, gays and lesbians do migrate from foreign countries any way they can to be with their partners.

Although he is not sure when and how he got infected, Roberto's story also speaks to the issue of HIV/AIDS and its connection to queer tourism (see Haour-Knipe and Rector 1996; Clift and Carter 2000). It is impossible to determine to what extent queer tourism is responsible for the spread of HIV in Mexico, but it would be foolish to suggest that there is no connection. However, queer tourism does play another important role related to HIV/AIDS. Condoms, lubricants, medications, and literature on safer sex that foreign tourists bring to Mexico are also shared with Mexican men. It should also be noted that the gay Mexico travel guides mentioned here even suggest that their readers assist Mexican men in such a manner (David 1998, 70). That is, travel guides recommend that gay American men take "plenty" of "lube and condoms" with them and leave any extras to Mexican "friends" they've met along the way.

As discussed previously, the image of the "gay *caballero*" marketed by gay travel guides is a fantasy that has very real implications for Mexican masculinities and sexualities. The frustration that many Mexican men feel over the racist macho stereotype that Americans have of them is a complaint that I heard time and again during my research. For instance, Javier is a bisexual man in his late twenties whom I met in Guadalajara. Javier is married and has two children but enjoys having sex with men. Javier bemoaned,

> I don't like to have sex with Americans. They always seem to want a sex machine. They want a big penis that screws them all night long. I don't have a big penis and I want someone who will hold me and kiss me. I don't want to be the *activo*. I just want a man to make love to me.

Throughout my interview with him, I was struck by the way in which Javier expressed his sexuality in a manner that was compatible with his masculine identity. Despite the fact that he admittedly enjoyed being *pasivo*, and contrary to much of the literature on the topic, he securely expressed a masculine nonhomosexual identity. As a married bisexual man, Javier has social privileges that many other men who have sex with men do not. His sense of sexual repression is based not in Mexican norms but in American ones. In Javier's experience, American tourists come to Mexico seeking a stereotype of Mexican masculinity that Javier cannot meet and yet it is a gendered performance that is demanded time and again by gay American tourists' search for the macho.

CONCLUSION

…Mexico seems to represent a place fixed in time, where "real" men can be found. The stereotype of the Mexican macho is alive and well in the imagination of American tourists. However, far from being culturally stagnant, Mexico has undergone profound changes in the last several decades. These changes shape the everyday experiences of Mexican men and the meanings and identities of gender and sexuality. While anthropologists working in Mexico in the 1970s and 1980s asserted that "gay" identities did not exist as we understand them in an American context this is no longer the case in the twenty-first century. The boundaries of Mexican sexual identities are changing even as the spaces that produce them are remapped. The development of gay and lesbian tourism in the country is a key factor linked to these changes. The relationship between queer tourism and Mexican male sexualities is complex and multiply constituted, but in this chapter I have highlighted some of these dimensions, particularly as they are linked to a sexual political economy.

…My purpose in this chapter has been to point to some of the diversity of Mexican male sexualities that is shaped by a number of factors, including culture. By using a political–economic framework for understanding Mexican male sexualities, I assert that we might be able to better understand how Mexican men who have sex with men are differentially positioned in Mexico's *ambiente*. I have also argued that Mexico's *ambiente* is embedded not only in a nationalist development project but also in a global political economy. Although I have privileged the public sphere in my discussion, public and private spheres are neither clearly delineated nor mutually exclusive, especially in the realm of sexuality.

The geopolitical border that the United States and Mexico share is an often overlooked dimension in studies of Mexican and U.S. sexualities (epidemiological studies of HIV/AIDS being an exception). Historically, the Mexican border towns and "tolerance zones" have served as "safe spaces" wherein Americans could escape strict sexual mores and prying eyes in the United States. This early version of sexual tourism included space for homosexual activity that would gradually expand to other areas such as urban centers. These border zones and their linkages to a national development project are crucial to understanding the shifting boundaries of Mexican sexualities.

Mexico's modernization projects, including its industrialization and urbanization, have in part created the conditions for the development of commodified and more legitimized same-sex sexuality in urban centers. While space for same-sex sexuality is not necessarily "new," the greater visibility, legitimacy, and even identity basis of these spaces are. Queer communities such as those in Mexico City have been instrumental in the creation of a Mexican gay and lesbian movement. Such changes helped to establish the conditions that would allow the establishment of a formal queer tourist industry. In addition, as part of its strategy for national development, the Mexican government prioritized tourism with aspirations for economic growth and controlled urbanization, and one of the "side effects" of this strategy is that it also contributed to the development of queer tourism.

As I discussed, gay and lesbian tourism in Mexico has resulted in an expansion of commodified space, which has had the dual effect of creating sites in the country that are both sexually liberating and exploitative. In some instances, segregated spaces are actually created for gay and lesbian tourists through specialized cruises and/or resorts. In other instances, gay and lesbian tourists are encouraged to "mix with the natives" and in so doing transform queer Mexican space. These spaces both reproduce and rupture the racialized politics of the U.S./Mexican border. While creating spaces by which identities and community may form, commodification also brings with it exclusionary norms and practices. "Gay Mexico" is marketed to mostly foreign tourists through organizations such as the IGLTA and venues such as travel guides and web sites. Part of the "sell" to this market relies upon stereotypes of Mexican men with racist undertones and images and the idea that Mexican men are "for the taking," particularly in those areas deemed to be more authentic than the controlled spaces of queer resorts.

The commodification of Mexican gay space presents a complex set of factors in the lives of Mexican men. While gay and lesbian tourist markets do not exclude Mexican nationals, socioeconomic constraints often do. Thus for many Mexican men, contact with gay tourists may occur more regularly not through leisure activities but through their labor as service workers. Such spaces, however, have their own boundaries or borders, whereby someone such as Lalo who worked in the industry had no "real" contact with Americans until he migrated to the United States. However, sometimes native/tourist contact brings with it information that serves as incentive for some Mexican men to emigrate to other countries and for some men to form binational relationships through tourist contacts, too.[15] Roberto is a case in point. However, the experiences that Lalo and Roberto had with American gay tourists should not be read as simply different. Class differences between the two men no doubt shaped these trajectories.

Gays and lesbians in Mexico have responded to social regulation and oppression in a number of ways depending upon their social locations. These responses range from the creation of a subculture and communities to social protest. While Mexico's gay and lesbian movement does have a long history (although this is not often acknowledged in the literature), gay and lesbian tourism is also a factor in the shifting boundaries of space and place for queer Mexicans. The growing visibility of the gay and lesbian tourist market (including events such as the IGLTA conference in Cancun) and the dependence of both local and national economies on tourism are important factors in the political environment for gays and lesbians in Mexico.

Tourism can also be a response to one's marginality. By traveling to other cities and countries some Mexican homosexual men are able to "escape" temporarily the constraints of their marginalized status. Again, social class is a key factor in determining the avenues by which the constraints of marginality might be maneuvered. Thus, while this chapter has focused on dimensions of American tourism to Mexico, the dynamics of Mexican queer tourism are not restricted to foreign tourists. Thus the tensions of sexual liberation/colonialism that arise with gay and lesbian tourism in Mexico are reproduced by Mexican upper-class men in other parts of the world as well.

Although the rise of gay and lesbian tourism in Mexico was not a planned outcome of the nation's tourist development project, it is an end result with important social and political reverberations. It is significant that those on the margins of Mexican society (*los otros*) and those on the margins of other nations, especially the United States (i.e., gays and lesbians) should come together under a nationalist project. However, as the border reminds us, and as I have argued here, life in these queer sexual borderlands has elements that are both liberating and oppressive. However, a central question remains: To what extent is the Mexican nationalist project willing to consciously embrace not only its gay and lesbian tourists but also, more importantly, its gay and lesbian citizens? The answer may ultimately lie not in the demands of Mexican gays and lesbians but rather in the demands of a queer market and the political economy of space.

NOTES

1. The web site has text in both English and Spanish. Interestingly, however, the messages are completely different. The text in English is extremely erotic; in Spanish, however, the discourse focuses on national treasures and seems to target tourism within Mexico (http://www.mexico-travel.com).
2. Although, to my knowledge, there are no statistics on the countries of origin of gay and lesbian Mexican tourists, one may assume (given the marketing tactics of the industry and Mexican tourism statistics) that their demographics reflect those of tourists in general, i.e., a majority are from the United States.
3. This phenomenon seems consistent with Chauncey's discussion of homosexuality in pre–World War II New York, where marginal (racially segregated) areas became havens for different types of "deviance," including homosexuality, and a sort of playground for the more well-to-do. However, it is not clear how prevalent the *zonas* were in areas other than border towns and the urban center of Mexico City.
4. To my knowledge, there does not exist any literature on the demographics of this community. However, traditional Mexican culture makes it easier for unmarried men (as opposed to women) to live apart from their families, and both economic conditions and the growing popularity of the area are also factors that affect the demographics of its residents.

5. Sanchez-Crispin and Lopez-Lopez (1997) also argue that the liberalization of Acapulco for gays and lesbians was due to its popularity among international gay and lesbian tourists.

6. The satellite space status of Puerto Vallarta is supported by the fact that many (if not all) bars in Guadalajara carry the Puerto Vallarta gay paper/flyer with all its ads and a map.

7. Even in the United States, the "gay" label fails to capture the numerous experiences and identities that are commonly grouped under it.

8. This terminology is reportedly also used by lesbians.

9. The Caribbean, particularly Cuba, is one area that is beginning to be studied. See, for instance, Davidson (1996) and Lumsden (1996).

10. International Gay and Lesbian Travel Association, 2000, http://www.iglta.com. Tourism Industry Intelligence estimated the global market at $10 billion (U.S.) dollars in 1994 (as reported in Holcomb and Luongo 1996), and an industry survey by Community Marketing (2008) estimates the American gay and lesbian market alone to be worth more than $64.5 billion.

11. The IGLTA is represented in Argentina, Brazil, Chile, Bolivia, Venezuela, Colombia, Ecuador, Panama, and Costa Rica as well.

12. While Atlantis and RSVP advertise as open to both men and women, their main market seems to be men, while Olivia targets a lesbian clientele.

13. While the *Ferrari Guide* does have some information for women, the guide is aimed mostly at men. This is due in part, no doubt, to the greater visibility of gay men as opposed to lesbians in Mexico.

14. Madsen Camacho (2000), who has conducted research on the Mexican tourist industry in Huatulco, Mexico, reports that businesses in the hospitality industry, particularly hotels, often desire gay men as workers due to their perceptions that gay men have a "higher" cultural aesthetic and more cultural capital, which serves the hospitality industry's needs (personal communication).

15. These dynamics are also transforming queer space in Los Angeles; thus my argument is not unilateral.

REFERENCES

Anzaldua, Gloria. 1987. *Borderlands/LaFrontera: The New Mestiza.* San Francisco: Aunt Lute.

Black, Richard. 1997. *The Ferrari Guides Gay Mexico: The Definitive Guide to Gay and Lesbian Mexico.* Phoenix, AZ: Ferrari Guides.

Clift, Stephen, and Simon Carter, eds. 2000. *Tourism and Sex: Culture, Commerce, and Coercion.* London: Pinter Press.

Cordova, Señor. 1999. *A Man's Guide to Mexico and Central America.* Beverly Hills, CA: Centurion Press.

David, Eduardo. 1998. *Gay Mexico: The Men of Mexico.* Oakland, CA: Floating Lotus Press.

Davidson, Julia. 1996. "Sex Tourism in Cuba." *Race and Class* 8(1): 39–49.

Guenette, Louise. 2000. "Touting Tourism." *Business Mexico* 10(3):42–47.

Hall, C. Michael. 1994a. "Gender and Economic Interests in Tourism Prostitution: The Nature, Development, and Implications of Sex Tourism in South-East Asia." Pp. 142–63 in *Tourism: A Gender Analysis*, edited by Vivian Kinnaird and Derek Hall. New York: Wiley.

Hall, C. Michael. 1994b. *Tourism in the Pacific Rim: Development, Impacts, and Markets.* New York: Halsted Press.

Haour-Knipe, Mary, and Richard Rector, eds. 1996. *Crossing Borders: Migration, Ethnicity, and AIDS.* London: Taylor & Francis.

Luibheid, Eithne. 1998. " 'Looking Like a Lesbian': The Organization of Sexual Monitoring at the United States-Mexican Border." *Journal of the History of Sexuality* 8(3):477–506.

Lumsden, Ian G. 1991. *Homosexuality, Society, and the State in Mexico.* Mexico: Solediciones, Colectivo Sol.

Lumsden, Ian. 1996. *Machos, Maricones, and Gays: Cuba and Homosexuality.* Philadelphia: Temple University Press.

MacCannell, Dean. 1999 [1976]. *The Tourist: A New Theory of the Leisure Class.* Berkeley: University of California Press.

Madsen Camacho, Michelle E. 2000. "The Politics of Progress: Constructing Paradise in Huatulco, Oaxaca." Ph.D. dissertation, University of California, Irvine.

McWilliams, Carey. 1948. *North from Mexico: The Spanish-Speaking People of the United States.* New York: Praeger.

Murray, Steven O. 1995. *Latin American Male Homosexualities.* Albuquerque: University of New Mexico Press.

Prieur, Annick. 1998. *Mema's House, Mexico City: On Transvestites, Queens, and Machos.* Chicago: University of Chicago Press.

Sanchez-Crispin, Alvaro, and Alvaro Lopez-Lopez. 1997. "Gay Male Places of Mexico City." Pp. 197–212 in *Queers in Space: Communities, Public Places, Sites of Resistance*, edited by Gordon Brent Ingram, Anne-Marie Bouthillette, and Yolanda Retter. Seattle: Bay Press.

Truong, Thanh-Dam. 1990. *Sex, Money, and Morality: Prostitution and Tourism in Southeast Asia.* Atlantic Highlands, NJ: Zed.

Young, Robert J.C. 1995. *Colonial Desire: Hybridity in Theory, Culture and Race.* New York: Routledge.

30 • *Kamala Kempadoo*

WOMEN OF COLOR AND THE GLOBAL SEX TRADE
Transnational Feminist Perspectives

DISCUSSION QUESTIONS

1. How does the global sex trade support "development" in "underdeveloped" nations?
2. How have feminist approaches to prostitution changed over time?
3. What unique insights does Kempadoo's intersectional, transnational, post-colonial feminist approach offer that are distinct from the other analyses she reviews?
4. Why does Kempadoo argue that concepts and theories of prostitution and the sex trade need to be more fluid and local?

The global sex trade has received increasing attention since the mid-1990s from a variety of researchers, activists, organizations, law and policy makers, and international agencies, particularly under the rubrics of "trafficking" and "sexual slavery." The assumption commonly underpinning the widespread interest it has aroused is that the sex trade is premised upon a universal principle of male violence to women. Indeed, even though several feminists and scholars, including this author, have argued for more complex and nuanced approaches, we are often asked to participate in discussions on the subject in the context of conferences and public events that concentrate on violence to women. Similarly, among non-governmental organizations and increasingly in the mainstream media, the global sex trade is more often than not portrayed through this one dimension, with the women involved represented as "victims" of male sexual violence.

In this article, I expand the argument that the global sex trade cannot be simply reduced to one monolithic explanation of violence to women. Research and theorizing require a framework that embraces the realities, contradictions, and intersections of various global relations of power. To illustrate this point, I draw on recent feminist studies showing that colonialisms, recolonizations, and cultural imperialisms, as well as specific local cultural histories and traditions that shape the sexual agency of women are important for any account of global manifestations of sex work. The goal is to articulate a framework that will allow us to explore and theorize differences and commonalities in meanings and experiences in the sex trade. Here, I focus particularly on experiences of, and definitions by, women of color,[1] tracing the contours of what may be named a "transnational feminist" framework for studies of prostitution and sex work. While this article

Kamala Kempadoo, "Women of Color and the Global Sex Trade: Transnational Feminist Perspectives." *Meridians: Feminism, Race, Transnationalism* 1(2):28–51. Copyright © Spring 2011 by Smith College. Reprinted with permission by the author.

may offer to some readers new insights and arguments, it does not represent a new study. Rather it aims to bring together and further circulate ideas and knowledge produced by and about women of color in the global sex trade and to make explicit the framework that underpins this current trend of feminist theorizing.[2]

REPRESENTATIONS OF WOMEN OF COLOR IN THE GLOBAL SEX TRADE

In the late 1980s, when I first started investigating the global sex trade, I was struck by the apparent over-representation of women of color in sex industries in western Europe. Living in Amsterdam—in the midst of the red-light district—I could not help but notice the preponderance of Thai, Dominican, Colombian, and Ghanaian women in sex work in clubs, behind windows, or in massage parlors. This concentration of non-Dutch and non-European women in the district was simultaneously a focus of attention for a Dutch prostitution research organization (Brussa 1989). The research indicated that around 60 percent of the population working in red-light districts in Amsterdam and other large Dutch cities were foreign/migrant/Third World women. My initial work built upon some of the insights from this research as well as from my own observations in the red-light district, exploring the mechanisms that drew women from Latin America and the Caribbean into the Dutch sex industry and forcing an engagement with the interplay of global relations of power around gender, race, nationality, and the economy (Kempadoo 1994, 1996, 1998).

While the situation in the Netherlands has drastically changed "color" since the late 1980s due to a movement of Eastern European and Russian women into Western European sex industries after the collapse of the Soviet Union, it appears that the concentration of women of Asian, African, Caribbean, and Latin American descent in the global sex trade is a continuing, if not escalating, trend as we enter a new century. This claim is difficult to substantiate

with figures, given that sex work occurs for the most part underground and in informal sectors, and is invisible in most accounts of women's work, commercial activities, and economic and labor force reports. It is also complicated by the fact that sex work is commonly a highly stigmatized activity; the women who provide the sexual services and labor are the subjects of discriminatory, often criminalizing, policies, laws, and ideologies. Nevertheless, three features of the global sex trade combine to illuminate the overrepresentation of women of color.

In the first place, prostitution around military bases has been well documented in "Other" (that is, non-Western/non-European) countries, most notably in Asia and the Pacific. In India, Hawaii, Vietnam, the Philippines, Japan, and Korea, the operation of foreign—colonial, imperial, or Allied—troops at various times in history has produced particular forms of prostitution where the military, often in collusion with the local state or government, tolerated, regulated, or encouraged the provision of sexual services by local women to the troops (Pivar 1981; Enloe 1989; Sturdevant and Stoltzfus 1992; Bailey and Farber 1992; Moon 1997; Lim 1998). In the Caribbean militarized prostitution has also been noted in various social studies as well as in calypsos and other cultural productions in places such as Trinidad, Curacao, Belize, Puerto Rico, and Cuba (Del Omo 1979; Kane 1993; Kempadoo 1996; Martis 1999; Findlay 1999; T. Hall 1994). Here too, Brown and Black women provided sexual labor and services, whether they were "native" to the specific countries or worked as migrants. Militarized prostitution in the Caribbean, while scantily researched, continues through U.S. military activities in the region in the late twentieth century, Martis notes:

> In 1996 St. Maarten became the homeport for an U.S. Navy ship that docks at the port every three months and stays for about a week. The crew of this ship consists of between 4,000 and 5,000 men (and some women). It is accepted and expected that the sailors need entertainment and release of their physical needs, and the brothels and bars overflow with

customers. The demand for sex workers is so great that more women are flown in during the week the ship stays in port. The Commissioner of Tourism calculates that the navy personnel spend around U.S. $1,000,000 on each visit. (1999, 209)

The stationing of UN peacekeeping troops in Haiti during the 1990s also raised questions about a renewed arena for prostitution activities, and HIV/AIDS specialists and health agencies have flagged militarized prostitution as an increasing area for concern.[3] Furthermore, while only a few studies have addressed militarized prostitution in African countries in the past, the recent deployment of UN peacekeeping troops in Congo and Sierra Leone has led to a concern in UN circles about the transmission of HIV/AIDS via visits to brothels and other prostitution activities.[4] Irrespective of the tasks assigned overseas military troops, sexual access to local women (of color) remains important.

Sex with local women has a longstanding history for armed forces. Not only has access to women's sexuality and regular sexual intercourse been considered within dominant discourse integral to the making of men under heteropatriarchy, but the specific construction of militarized masculinity demands heterosexual sex on a regular basis. That a large number of women upon whose bodies and labor such constructions of masculinity depend are of nations, "races," and ethnicities other than those of the men is a contemporary reality that cannot be neglected or ignored.

Second, in the context of discussions of "trafficking" of women for sex work, domestic service, marriage, sweatshop labor, farming, and other un- or semi-skilled work, Third World women appear as the most frequent "victims." While estimates of the number of trafficked persons vary from anywhere between one to four million per year, the predominant focus has been on the trade of young women that takes place from Nepal to India, from Sri Lanka and Bangladesh to Saudi Arabia, from the Philippines to Italy, Thailand to the Netherlands, or from the Dominican Republic to Spain for work in sex industries and domestic service. The UN estimated in 1999 that of the approximately 700,000 women and girls trafficked into Western Europe, the Middle East, Japan, Australia, and North America, 75 percent were drawn from countries in Latin America, Africa, South Asia, and Southeast Asia (*Gender Matters* 1999).

A 1999 CIA report indicated that around 50,000 women per year were brought into the U.S. for work in sex industries, domestic labor, and sweatshops. At least twenty-six American cities have been reported to employ trafficked female labor, with the primary "sending" countries identified as Thailand, Vietnam, China, Mexico, Russia, and the Czech Republic, followed by the Philippines, Korea, Malaysia, Nigeria, Latvia, Hungary, Poland, Brazil, and Honduras (O'Neill 1999). Reports on trafficking to Canada also signal that the concern revolves around women from Asia and Latin America, as well as Eastern Europe (*National Post* 17 May 2000). In England, where the trafficking of Filipinas and Thai women is not unknown, the case of the fifty-eight Chinese men and women who were found dead in a container on arrival at Dover in June 2000 spurred further probes into both the trafficking and smuggling of Asians into Britain. In other Western European countries, Eastern Europeans and Russians are thought to be cornering the sex work market, but Italy's pronounced concern is about migrant women trafficked from Africa, while the Spanish government similarly has called for a crack down on the traffic of persons from sub-Saharan Africa (*Guardian Weekly* 31 August 2000).

The representation of women from Third World or postcolonial countries as "trafficked victims" combines with descriptions of conditions of excessive force and violence. Debt-bondage, where sums of up to $20,000 are loaned to families and paid back by women and girls through work in underground or informal sectors; indentureship, where women are forced into prostitution, domestic work, or sweatshops and are required to pay the trafficker for travel and documents[5]; and slavery-like conditions, where women are locked into rooms or a building, chained up, or otherwise held against their will, forced to have sex both with clients and their "protectors" and traffickers, are raped and abused by their "managers," and are starved or are not allowed freedom of movement, are most commonly linked with Third World and non-western women's experiences in the global sex trade. The dominant image in the West of the trafficked, victimized sex worker is of a young Brown, Asian, or Black woman, an image refracted through mainstream television programs and newspaper reports, as well as in some feminist writings and in international debates on trafficking.[6]

Third, "sex tourism" takes place for the most part in "exotic" (i.e., "Third World") countries, where Western European, Japanese, and North American men (primarily) buy sex in various ways from women, men, boys, and girls who, in turn, are "encouraged" by local governments to bring in foreign exchange and to sustain the image of their country as an appealing vacation destination. In the 1960s tourism was promoted by the United Nations as a way for the "developing world" to participate in the global capitalist economy and since then has been heavily promoted and adopted as a development strategy for and by national governments of "poor countries" around the world. Studies of tourism in various parts of Asia, for example, have documented how governments have not simply embraced tourism but have deliberately relied upon longstanding racist stereotypes of Asian women as exotic and erotic to attract tourists. It is through the reliance on the sexuality and sexual labor of Asian women that sex tourism has become vital to the national economies (Truong 1990; Lim 1998).

With the economic restructuring that many former Third World countries have been forced to accept under International Monetary Fund (IMF) and World Bank dictates—so-called structural adjustment programs that rest upon neoliberal free-market policies—tourism has received an even greater boost, as these countries can no longer depend upon their participation in the global markets on the basis of agricultural production or the exploitation of other resources. Sex tourism, a service that caters to the new leisure demands by citizens of the wealthy, as well as to more traditional types of travelers, such as businessmen, has for some countries become an integral part of the tourism industry that sustains the nation (see also Bishop and Robinson 1998, and Kempadoo 1999).[7]

The global sex trade leans heavily on the bodies of women of color. Sex work of Brown and Black women is drawn upon as a way to "develop" "underdeveloped" regions of the world, either by attracting foreign exchange or as an export commodity servicing industries abroad. Remittances from migrant women to their families and home communities also are fast becoming a staple of small national economies. Bodies of women of color are employed to sustain underground sex industries such as massage parlors and exotic dance clubs in "over-developed" countries, to boost militarized masculinity, to secure profits for multinational elites and corporations that govern tourism industries, as well as to keep local economies and underdeveloped nations afloat.

The flip side of this development is that sex work has become so embedded in social relations that it is often seen as one of the few options for women of postcolonial societies to keep their heads above water in a world where the highly unequal distribution of wealth and power on an international scale, as well as the agencies and classes that defend this inequality, induce poor people and nations to seek alternative, sometimes underground, strategies for survival. For many Black and Brown women, and increasingly for more young men of color, sex work is more lucrative than Free Trade Zone work, domestic service, export processing, farm work, or other hard manual labor (Cabezas 1999; Mayorga and Velasquez 1999). Sex with an "exotic" is desired and valued among many tourists, and exoticized subjects devise strategies to benefit from this situation to the best of their ability. Their sexual labor is often a supplement to meager wages or incomes from other sources of work, or can provide the sole financial contribution to the household. . . .

FEMINIST THEORIZING

If we take into account the apparent importance of women of color's sexual labor in the maintenance of the contemporary global sex trade as well as to the survival of whole communities and families in developing countries, where does this place feminist theories of prostitution? Can we ignore the evidence, and continue to adhere to twentieth-century ideas about the universality of prostitution as violence to women, or can we begin to entertain the idea that, in the twenty-first century, in a world steeped in global restructuring, postmodern and postcolonial conditions "social relations, subjects, and subjectivities are undergoing profound changes" and that "concepts and categories of prostitution and prostitute are not static" but also are subject to change? (Marchand et al. 1998, 959, 963)....

Feminist accounts of prostitution have barely scratched the surface here. Too often we still rely heavily on older feminist formulations. In the 1970s, prostitution, along with marriage and the family, was defined by Western feminism as an expression of patriarchy and violence to women, illustrating the way in which female sexuality and the female body were controlled, subordinated, and exploited by male and masculine interests. Kathleen Barry made popular the term "sexual slavery" to refer to some of the conditions that women faced under patriarchy, asserting that sex constituted the primary basis for power and authority in society (1984, 194). The concepts of sex and gender were given primacy in this analysis of prostitution, and the cause for prostitution defined as universal in nature....

Since the 1980s sex work has been made synonymous with sexual slavery by various women's organizations in various parts of the world. The notion of sexual slavery has been widely used in relation to "comfort women" who were "drafted" from Korea, China, Taiwan, Indonesia, Thailand, the Philippines and Japan to sexually service Japan's Imperial Army during the 1930s and 1940s, and to agitate for compensation for these abused and exploited women (Hicks 1994; Howard 1995; Bang-Soon Yoon 1997; Henson 1999). The international circulation of ideas about prostitution and other forms of sex work exclusively in terms of "violence to women" or "sexual slavery" has also more generally informed the contemporary discourse of international human rights agencies....

While these definitions of the sex trade have been contested by other African and Asian women and sex workers in these locations,[8] they are nevertheless often assumed to represent the condition for all women in the sex trade....

It is critical to keep in mind that the reduction of prostitution to masculine violence and sexual slavery also has been viewed by other feminists as inadequate to capture the various histories, oppressions, and experiences of women of color. In Japan, against the dominant feminist trend, Sisterhood—a group of feminist intellectuals and lawyers—has argued the necessity of defining prostitution as labor. Masumi Yoneda states:

> It is all the more necessary to recognize prostitution as work and improve working conditions for these women. Isn't it our job to secure a liveable environment where they won't be exploited illegally, to create a situation where they can network among themselves, and where they can voice their demands, and to help them build up the power to get out of prostitution when they want to? They are not going to accept us as long as we work on the premise that they are victims who are forced into prostitution, something that humans shouldn't practice, that our mission is to protect and rehabilitate them, that we should abolish prostitution from the face of the earth! That's simply a nuisance to them. If I were a prostitute I would say to hell with the do-gooders. The situation won't go away by telling them that they were forced into it and that they are victims. (Group Sisterhood 1998, 94)

Others have pointed out that legacies of racism, colonialism, and imperialism have produced conditions and situations for women that are experienced, and can be read, in quite different ways. This needs to be taken into consideration when theorizing prostitution. Ofreneo and Ofreneo, for example, insist that "Imperialism, militarism and racism provided the 'geopolitical-economic' context of military prostitution and sex tourism" in the Philippines (1998, 104)....In this framework sexual labor/sex work is viewed as having been, and continuing to be, performed and organized in a variety of ways, with no universal expression or meaning.

... In other words it would seem erroneous, if not socially irresponsible, to ignore these national and geo-political contexts, as well as specific histories and experiences, when talking about women in the global sex trade. Reducing sex work to a violence inflicted upon women due to notions of a universality of patriarchy and masculinist ideologies and structures, or through the privileging of gender as the primary factor in shaping social relations, dismisses the great variety of historical and socio-economic conditions, as well as cultural histories, that produce sexual relations and desire.

Challenges to the prevalent reductionistic discourse on prostitution parallel those that took place over feminist conceptualizations of "the family" and "the household" during the 1980s. At that time the dominant Euro-American definition of the family, domestic work and the household as exclusive sites of oppression for women were opposed by Black and anti-imperialist feminists and redefined to encompass different women's histories and legacies of and resistance to slavery, colonialism, and racism. As Hazel Carby so poignantly stated in her article "White Women Listen!" in 1982:

> We would not want to deny that the family can be a source of oppression for us but we also wish to examine how the black family has functioned as a prime source of resistance to oppression. We need to recognize that during slavery, periods of colonialism and under the present authoritarian state [Britain in the 1980s], the black family has been a site of political and cultural resistance to racism.

The meaning of the family to Black women in light of a history of racialized and colonial oppression needed special attention and could not simply be covered by a blanket definition that had emerged from a white, Euro-American middle class experience.

Similarly, Angela Davis addressed the relationship between domestic work and Black struggles against racism. She argued that it was

> precisely though performing the drudgery which has long been a central expression of the socially conditioned inferiority of women [domestic labor] the Black woman in chains could help to lay the foundations for some degree of autonomy both for herself and her men. Even as she was suffering under her unique oppression as female, she was thrust into the center of the slave community. She was, therefore, essential to the survival of the community. (1982, 17)

Examinations of particular colonial, imperial, and neocolonial histories in the construction of prostitution and of the "erotic–exotic" woman of color are needed for feminist frameworks that purport to study, analyze, and produce knowledge about sex work and the global sex trade, for without taking these relations of power and dominance into account, commonalities and differences in social histories, lives, and experiences of women around the world are erased, and various complicities and contestations ignored. . . .

The notion of Black women as "breeders" on plantations during slavery throughout the Americas has not gone unnoticed in feminist historiography. Abraham-van der Mark notes about the Jewish male elite in nineteenth-century Curaçao in the Dutch Caribbean, that "concubinage gave them the benefits of a category of children which, if necessary, provided labor but could not make any legal demands and were excluded from inheritance" (1973, 46). In other instances in the Caribbean, Black slave women were put to work as prostitutes by the owner or plantation manager during slumps in the plantation economy and when extra cash was needed for the plantation household (Beckles 1989). In these and other studies a continuous theme is the unconditional sexual access that white men had to Black and Brown women's bodies and the force and coercion that was involved. . . .

The positioning of Asian, African, Caribbean, and Latin American women as sexual objects, and the obfuscations of their agency, in particular relations of power and domination, have not ground to a halt but rather can be seen to extend into the twenty-first century in both theory and practice. Women of color remain in various ways racialized as highly sexual by nature, and positioned as "ideal" for sex work. They continue to be overrepresented globally in "body-work"—as sexual, domestic, and un- or semi-skilled manual workers—and are underrepresented in intellectual activities in which social theory is produced. The agency of Brown and Black women in prostitution has been avoided or overlooked and the perspectives arising from these experiences marginalized in dominant theoretical discourse on the global sex trade and prostitution. Our insights, knowledges, and understandings of sex work have been largely obscured or dominated by white radical feminist, neo-Marxist, or Western socialist feminist inspired analyses that have been either incapable or unwilling to address the complexities of the lives of women of color. Third World, transnational, or postcolonial feminisms have offered possibilities for theorizing prostitution within the matrix of gendered, racialized, sexualized, and international relations of power, as well as from the experiences and perspectives of women of color in prostitution (Mohanty 1991; Grewal and Kaplan 1994; Alexander 1997), yet it is remarkable that to date, very little has been explicitly advanced as a transnational or postcolonial feminist approach to the subject of prostitution....

Various inroads are being made on this front, such as in the analyses of Amalia Cabezas, Rama Kapur, Siobhan Brooks, Joan Phillips, Jacqueline Sanchez Taylor, and Jenn Guitart, who extend the tentative steps made earlier in this direction by Truong (1990), Moon (1997), Lim (1998), and this author.[9]...

A transnational feminist theory and politics on prostitution and other forms of sex work also includes a rethinking of practical strategies and programs to address the specific situations for women of color in the global sex trade. The radical feminist strategy to seek the abolition of prostitution can seem to many to be worthwhile, yet has its limitations. Based on a universalistic construction of prostitution, it does not allow space for addressing the multiple ways the sex trade is constituted and the myriad arrangements for the involvement of women's sexual agency. Paralleling the call for the abolition of marriage as an institution of male

power and violence to women, it tends to ignore the strategies that women have undertaken to reform or transform social institutions and relations of power, instead demanding a single, monolithic strategy for change. Those who start from a "victim approach" to prostitution often advocate prosecuting men who participate in the sex trade as pimps, clients, traffickers, or brothel owners, proposing laws that criminalize working women in the belief that they can rehabilitate men who use prostitutes and can "rescue" or "save" women in a missionary fashion.

Little is advanced from this perspective that allows for the empowerment of women who strategically use their sexual labor to secure a place in the modern world, or for the recognition of sex workers' rights. Therefore, while we cannot lose sight of the vicious realities that many women of color face in the global sex trade, it is imperative that we build strategies that start from a recognition that sex work is an integral part of the global economy and is deeply embedded in, and cannot easily be disassembled from, many women's everyday lives, strategies, and identities. By embracing an abolitionist position on the subject, we will certainly ignore the different meanings and daily realities, constraints, and possibilities that sex work affords women in the global economy.

Moreover, in building an appropriate strategy, we need to recognize that oppression in the sex trade is not always experienced and defined as the sex act itself, but rather that it is the conditions that sex workers must endure that often are defined as the problem. Recent research in the Caribbean, for example, found that the problems identified by women in the sex trade emanated from the criminal status of sex work in many of the Caribbean countries that encouraged police harassment and abuse, and from lack of legal access to workers' rights, health care, social security benefits, pensions, appropriate childcare, and so forth (see Mellon 1999). Criminalization and stigmatization of sex workers ensured poor working conditions and sustained notions of prostitutes as disposable people....

These experiences of women of color in the sex trade—their perspectives, visions and dreams—need to be listened to carefully by feminists of color. Rather than simply remaining silent and thus complicit with rendering them as victims or as oversexualized racialized subjects, we could, from our academic and other non-sex work locations, collaborate with sex workers to struggle for everyday changes and transformations in the sex trade and for policies and practices that would strengthen them as autonomous, knowing subjects. We could also acknowledge their efforts as part of the contemporary transnational women's movement. Legacies of Black radical feminism and Third World feminism position us well to listen to our "subaltern" or marginalized sisters and to avoid reproducing the hierarchies, privileges and priorities that characterize much of postmodern academic feminism. It is certainly possible, then, for us to reflect on sex worker demands as part of our feminist theorizing, and to collaboratively build strategies for change.

Feminists of color around the world need also to be more vigilant and attentive to the ways the global economy is pushing increasingly larger numbers of people into marginality and informal sector work, recognizing that to thwart the growth of the sex trade requires a much larger reorganization of the global economy. Without real economic alternatives for women and young men today, attempts to halt or change exploitative situations for women will remain a futile exercise. The 1999/2000 proposals and bills brought before the U.S. Senate and House regarding trafficking richly illustrate this problem. While the 1999 CIA research indicates that the current "epidemic" of trafficking is directly related to the diminishing resources for poor people in developing countries and to the greed of large transnational corporations, the proposals focus on punishing individual traffickers and the local governments of sending countries. They do not address structural global inequalities of wealth and power, the demand being made by industries and corporations in the North for cheap labor, or the fact that unless something else is made available, families will continue to rely on prostitution as an income generator....

Finally, this transnational feminist politics of articulation on sex work examines and contests the ways in which the transnational middle classes and elites—both men and women—construct racialized sexualized ideologies and practices that lock women and men of color into the positions and roles of sexual servants. It examines how some notions of obtaining gender equity among women and feminists in postindustrial world centers also can be highly oppressive to poor women of color, and it interrogates more fully the implications of the emergence onto the global scene of such phenomena as the Western European or North American female sex tourist. It follows a strategy that allows women to probe histories of racialization in the formation of identities, desire, and knowledge and to take responsibility for our varying contemporary positions in international relations of power and privilege. Most important, it asks how feminists can relate to and communicate with sex workers of color to build a sustainable future. A transnational feminism that relinquishes colonizing narratives about prostitution and the global sex trade, draws from women of color's experiences and perspectives in sex work, and builds global alliances, could be a useful theory and practice for many women around the world.

NOTES

1. The term "women of color" is used in this article interchangeably with "Brown and Black," "Third World," "African, Asian, Latin American, and Caribbean," or "Thai, Dominican, Nepalese, Ghanaian, Colombian" women, and could easily be replaced by the notion of "postcolonial women." I am acutely aware, however, that these categories, while speaking to the historical and shared experiences of, and struggles against, colonialism, neocolonialism, Western imperialism, masculine domination, and racialized/ethnicized oppression, may collapse differences between women, may not relate to the self-identification or political identity in particular societies, or could make some nationalities invisible. However, I use them to highlight the significance of the racialization of the global sex trade.

2. I would like to thank an anonymous reviewer for helpful feedback and comments on earlier drafts of this article and for bringing to my attention that

the emphasis on "women of color" may lead to an undertheorizing and strategizing around the roles of white Eastern European and Russian women and "non-U.S., non-European and/or nonwhite men's roles as customers" in the sex trade. This is certainly not my intention, although I am aware that any emphasis on the subjectivity and agency of any single category of people (sex workers, white women, Black men, pink-collar workers, poor women, etc.) can implicitly lead to the invisibility of larger relations of power and to the elision of other subjectivities and actors. However, it would take another article to do full justice to these other dimensions of the sex trade.

I have also chosen to retain my focus on "sex workers of color" in this article in light of a new trend in the media and international discussions, where concern with white Eastern and Russian women in prostitution has begun to eclipse the centrality of "Third World women" in the global sex trade. Furthermore, I can only hope that readers will grasp that while sex tourism, militarized prostitution, and trafficking are premised for a large part on international, racialized, gendered relations between postindustrial and postcolonial societies, the involvement of Sri Lankan women in the contemporary Middle East, Nepali women in India, Brazilian women in Suriname, or Korean and Chinese women serving men in the Imperial Japanese army in the 1940s also poses questions about the significance of cultural/racial/ethnic difference between client and sex worker in constructions of prostitution.

3. According to Dr. Julio Javier Espinola, former PanAmerican Health Organization (PAHO) consultant to Haiti, during a meeting in April 2000.

4. UN press release reported in the *Washington Post* 17 March 2000.

5. Transportation and trafficking fees vary but prices of around $10,000 are common. A Reuters report on 3 July 2000 on trafficking notes "the price for Chinese passage to the United States has risen to about $50,000 a person from $30,000 a few years ago"—one of the highest fees in the world.

6. See Kempadoo and Doezema (1998), and Doezema 1998 and forthcoming for various critiques of this neo-colonial image of Third World women.

7. While the majority of sex tourists appear to be men, women sex tourists are also becoming more common and have been the subject of recent investigations in Asia and the Caribbean. See, for example, O'Connell Davidson and Sanchez Taylor (1999), Dahles (1998),

and Albuquerque (1998).

8. See Kempadoo and Doezema (1998), where sex work is defined as "work" or labor by various individuals and by women's and sex workers' organizations in India, Malaysia, Japan, Thailand, South Africa, Ghana, Senegal, Brazil, the Dominican Republic, Mexico, Ecuador, Suriname, and so forth. These definitions and understandings of sex work are perhaps as widely spread as the "prostitution-as-violence to women" approach in these parts of the world.

9. Some of this work is yet to be published, but I refer here to the Ph.D. dissertation by Amalia Cabezas (1999) on sex work in the Dominican Republic; the presentation by Ratna Kapur at the Fifth LatCrit conference, Breckenridge 5–7 May, 2000 about sex work, the law, and desire in the Indian context; an interview with Angela Davis by Siobhan Brooks (1999) about Black American women's sexuality and prostitution; Joan Phillip's doctoral study on Black male sex workers in Barbados that builds upon her earlier research on this subject; studies by Jacqueline Sanchez Taylor on female sex tourism in the Caribbean; and Jean Guitart's research on sex work in Cuba.

REFERENCES

Abraham-van de Mark, E. E. 1973. *Yu'i Mama: Enkele Facetten van Gexinsstructuur op Curacao.* Assen: Van Gorcum.

Albuquerque, Klaas de. 1998. "Sex, Beach Boys, and Female Tourists in the Caribbean." *Sexuality and Culture* 2: 87–112.

Alexander, M. Jacqui. 1997. Erotic Autonomy as a Politics of Decolonization: An Anatomy of Feminist and State Practice. In *Feminist Genealogies, Colonial Legacies, Democratic Futures*, edited by M. Jacqul Alexander and Chandra Talpade Mohanty. New York: Routledge: 63–100.

Bailey, Beth and David Farber. 1992. "Hotel Street: Prostitution and the Politics of War." *Radical History Review*: 54–77.

Bang-Soon Yoon. 1997. "Sexism, Racism and Militarism: Imperial Japan's Sexual Slavery Case." Paper presented at the First North Texas UN Conference on Women, University of Texas-Dallas, 25 October.

Barry, Kathleen. 1984. *Female Sexual Slavery*. New York: New York University Press.

Beckles, Hilary. 1989. *Natural Rebels: A Social History of*

Enslaved Black Woman in Barbados. London: Zed.

Bishop, Ryan and Lillian S. Robinson. 1998. *Night Market: Sexual Cultures and the Thai Economic Miracle*. New York: Routledge.

Brooks, Siobhan. 1999. "Sex Work and Feminism: Building Alliances through a Dialogue between Siobhan Brooks and Professor Angela Davis." *Hastings Women's Law Journal* 10 (Winter): 181–87.

Cabezas, Amalia Lucía. 1999. *Pleasure and Its Pain: Sex Tourism in Sosúa, the Dominican Republic*. Ph.D. diss. University of California.

Carby, Hazel. 1982. White Women Listen! Black Feminism and the Boundaries of Sisterhood. In *The Empire Strikes Back: Race and Racism in '70s Britain*, edited by the Centre for Contemporary Cultural Studies, London: Hutchinson.

Dahles, Heidi. 1998. Of Birds and Fish: Street Guides, Tourists, and Sexual Encounters in Yogyakarta, Indonesia. In *Sex Tourism and Prostitution: Aspects of Leisure, Recreation, and Work*, edited by Martin Oppermann. New York: Cognizant Communication Corporation: 60–70.

Davis, Angela. 1982. *Women, Race and Class*. New York: Vintage.

Del Omo, Rosa.1979. "The Cuban Revolution and the Struggle Against Prostitution." *Crime and Social Justice* 12: 34–40.

Doezema, Jo. 1998. "Loose Women or Lost Women? The Re-emergence of the Myth of 'White Slavery' in Contemporary Discourses of 'Trafficking' in Women." MA Thesis, University of Sussex.

Enloe, Cynthia. 1989. *Bananas, Beaches and Bases: Making Feminist Sense of International Politics*. Berkeley: University of California Press.

Findlay, Eileen J. Suárez. 1999. *Imposing Decency: The Politics of Sexuality and Race in Puerto Rico, 1870–1920*. Durham: Duke University Press.

Gender Matters. 1999. USAID Office of Women in Development, GenderReach Project, Issue. 1, February.

Group Sisterhood. 1998. "Prostitution, Stigma, and the Law in Japan: A Feminist Roundtable Discussion." In Kempadoo and Doezema 1998:87–98.

Hall, Tony. 1994. "Jean and Dinah . . . Who Have Been Locked Away in the World Famous Calypso Since 1956 Speak Their Minds Publicly." Lord Street Theatre Company, Trinidad and Tobago.

Henson, Maria, Rosa. 1999. *Comfort Woman: A Filipina's Story of Prostitution and Slavery Under the Japanese Military*. Boulder: Rowman and Littlefield.

Hicks, George. 1994. *The Comfort Women*. New York: W.W. Norton.

Howard, Keith. 1995. *True Stories of the Korean Comfort Women*. Testimonies Compiled by the Korean Council for Women Drafted for Military Sexual Slavery by Japan and the Research Association on the Women Drafted for Military Sexual Slavery in Japan. London: Cassell.

Kane, Stephanie C. 1993. "Prostitution and the Military: Planning AIDS Intervention in Belize." *Social Science and Medicine* 36: 965–79.

Kempadoo, Kamala. 1994. *Exotic Colonies: Caribbean Women in the Dutch Sex Trade*. Ph.D. Diss. University of Colorado.

———. 1996. "Prostitution, Marginality, and Empowerment: Caribbean Women in the Sex Trade." *Beyond Law* 5.14: 69–84.

———. 1998. "Globalizing Sex Workers' Rights." In Kempadoo and Doezema 1998: 2–28.

——— ed. 1999. *Sun, Sex and Gold: Tourism and Sex Work in the Caribbean*. Lanham, MD: Rowman and Littlefield.

Kempadoo, Kamala and Jo Doezema, eds. 1998. *Global Sex Workers: Rights, Resistance, and Redefinition*. New York: Routledge.

Lim, Lin Lean, ed. 1998. *The Sex Sector: The Economic and Social Bases of Prostitution in Southeast Asia*. Geneva: International Labour Office.

Marchand, Marianne H., Julian Reid and Boukje Berents. 1998. "Migration, (Im)mobility and Modernity: Toward a Feminist Understanding of the 'Global' Prostitution Scene in Amsterdam." *Millennium* 27.4: 955–83.

Martis, Jacqueline. 1999. "Tourism and the Sex Trade in St. Marten and Curacao." In Kempadoo 1999: 201–15.

Mayorga, Laura and Pilar Velasquez. 1999. "Bleak Pasts, Bleak Futures: Life Paths of Thirteen Young Prostitutes in Cartagena, Colombia." In Kempadoo 1999: 157–82.

Mellon, Cynthia. 1999. "A Human Rights Perspective on the Sex Trade in the Caribbean and Beyond." In Kempadoo 1999: 309–22.

Mohanty, Chandra Talpade. 1991. Cartographies of Struggle: Third World Women and the Politics of Feminism. In *Third World Women and the Politics of Feminism*, edited by Chandra T. Mohanty, Ann Russo, and Lourdes Torres. Indiana University Press: 1–50.

Moon, Katharine. 1997. *Sex Among Allies: Military Prostitution in U.S.-Korea Relations*. New York: Columbia University Press.

O'Connell Davidson, Julia and Jacqueline Sanchez Taylor. 1999. "Fantasy Islands: Exploring the Demand for Sex Tourism." In Kempadoo 1999: 37–54.

O'Neill, Amy. 1999. *International Trafficking in Women to the United States: A Contemporary Manifestation of Slavery and Organized Crime.* U.S. Center for the Study of Intelligence.

Ofreneo, Rene E. and Rosalinda Pineda Ofreneo. 1998. Prostitution in the Philipines. In *The Sex Sector: The Economic and Social Bases of Prostitution in Southeast Asia*, edited by Lin Lean Lim. Geneva: International Labour Office: 100–30.

Pivar, David J. 1981. "The Military, Prostitution and Colonial Peoples: India and the Phillipines, 1885–1917." *Journal of Sex Research* 17.3: 256–67.

Sturdevant, Saundra Pollock and Brenda Stoltzfus. 1992. *Let the Good Times Roll: Prostitution and the U.S. Military in Asia.* New York: New Press.

Truong, Than-Dam. 1990. *Sex, Money and Morality: The Political Economy of Prostitution and Tourism in South East Asia.* London: Zed.

31 • *Andrea Smith*

RAPE AND THE WAR AGAINST NATIVE WOMEN

DISCUSSION QUESTIONS

1. How much of the history Smith provides was new to you? Why do you think issues such as forced sterilization and medical experimentation are often not included in history classes or other courses? Should all students learn this history?

2. Does the Ivory soap advertisement surprise you? Do you think our culture continues to equate cleanliness with whiteness? Consider phrases like "forces of darkness" and "she was shown the light." Do you think these phrases reinforce notions of white cleanliness, purity, and superiority? Can you think of other similar phrases?

3. What does the author mean when she says Indian people "learn to internalize self-hatred"? Do you think this is a common occurrence among oppressed groups?

4. The author asserts that white feminists have failed to call attention to the rapes and murders of indigenous people in Guatemala, despite being outraged at similar events in Bosnia. Why do you think this elision has occurred?

In Indian Country, there is a growing "wellness" movement, largely spearheaded by women, that stresses healing from personal and historic abuse, both on the individual and the community level. This wellness movement is based on the fact that Native peoples' history of colonization has been marked on our bodies. In order to heal from personal abuse, such as sexual abuse, we must also heal from the historic abuse of every massacre, every broken treaty, that our people have suffered. As Cecelia Fire Thunder states:

> We also have to recognize and understand that we carry the pain of our grandmothers, mothers, and the generation that came before us. We carry in our heart the pain of all our ancestors and we carry in our hearts the unresolved grief [and] the loss of our way of life.... There is no way we can move forward and be stronger nations without recognizing the trauma and pain that took place within our nations, our families, and within ourselves.[1]

One of the barriers, however, to healing from violence in Native communities is the reluctance to openly address violence against Native women. Native women who are survivors of violence often find themselves caught between the tendency within Native communities to remain silent about sexual and domestic violence in order to maintain a united front against racism and colonialism and the insistence on the part of the white-dominated antiviolence movement that survivors cannot heal from violence unless they leave their communities. The reason Native women are constantly marginalized in male-dominated discourses about racism and colonialism and in white-dominated discourses about sexism is the inability of both discourses to address the inextricable relationship between gender violence and colonialism. That is, the issue is not simply that violence against women happens during colonization but that the colonial process is itself structured by sexual violence. It is not possible for Native nations to decolonize themselves until they address gender violence because it is through this kind of violence that colonization has been successful. It is partly because the history of colonization of Native people is interrelated with colonizers' assaults upon Indian bodies. It is through the constant assaults upon our bodily integrity that colonizers have attempted to eradicate our sense of Indian identity.

As a multitude of scholars such as Robert Allen Warrior, Albert Cave, H. C. Porter, and others have demonstrated, Christian colonizers[2] often envisioned Native peoples as Canaanites, worthy of mass destruction as they went about the task of creating a "New Israel."[3] What makes Canaanites supposedly worthy of destruction in the biblical narrative and Indian peoples supposedly worthy of destruction in the eyes of their colonizers is that they both personify sexual sin. In the Bible, Canaanites commit acts of sexual perversion in Sodom (Gen. 19:1–29), are the descendants of the unsavory relations between Lot and his daughters (Gen. 19:30–38), are the descendants of the sexually perverse Ham (Gen. 9:22–27), and prostitute themselves in service of their gods (Gen. 28:21–22; Deut. 28:18; 1 Kings 14:24; 2 Kings 23:7; Hos. 4:13; Amos 2:7).

Similarly, Native peoples, in the eyes of the colonizers, are marked by their sexual perversity.[4] Alexander Whitaker, a minister in Virginia, wrote in 1613, "They live naked in bodie, as if their shame of their sinne deserved no covering: Their names are as naked as their bodie: They esteem it a virtue to lie, deceive and steale as their master the divell teacheth them."[5] Furthermore, according to Bernardino de Minaya, "Their [the Indians'] marriages are not a sacrament but a sacrilege. They are idolatrous, libidinous, and commit sodomy. Their chief desire is to eat, drink, worship heathen idols, and commit bestial obscenities."[6]

Because they personify sexual sin, Indian bodies are inherently "dirty." As white Californians described in the 1860s, Native people were "the dirtiest lot of human beings on earth."[7] They wore "filthy rags, with their persons unwashed, hair uncombed and swarming with vermin."[8] The following 1885 Procter & Gamble ad for Ivory Soap also illustrates this equation between Indian bodies and dirt.

We were once factious, fierce and wild,
 In peaceful arts unreconciled,

Our blankets smeared with grease and stains
From buffalo meat and settlers' veins.
Through summer's dust and heat content,
From moon to moon unwashed we went,
But IVORY SOAP came like a ray
Of light across our darkened way
And now we're civil, kind and good
And keep the laws as people should,
We wear our linen, lawn and lace
As well as folks with paler face
And now I take, where'er we go,
This cake of IVORY SOAP to show
What civilized my squaw and me
And made us clean and fair to see[9]

Because Indian bodies are "dirty," they are considered sexually violable and "rapable." That is, in patriarchal thinking, only a body that is "pure" can be violated. The rape of bodies that are considered inherently impure or dirty simply does not count. For instance, prostitutes have almost an impossible time being believed if they are raped because the dominant society considers the prostitute's body undeserving of integrity and violable at all times. Similarly, the history of mutilation of Indian bodies, both living and dead, makes it clear to Indian people that they are not entitled to bodily integrity. Andrew Jackson, for instance, ordered the mutilation of approximately 800 Muscogee Indian corpses, cutting off their noses and slicing long strips of flesh from their bodies to make bridle reins.[10] Tecumseh's skin was flayed and made into razor straps.[11] A soldier cut off the testicles of White Antelope to make a tobacco pouch.[12] Colonel John Chivington led an attack against the Cheyenne and Arapahoe in which nearly all the victims were scalped; their fingers, arms, and ears were amputated to obtain jewelry; and their private parts were cut out to be exhibited before the public in Denver.[13]

In the history of massacres against Indian people, colonizers attempted not only to defeat Indian people but also to eradicate their very identity and humanity. They attempted to transform Indian people from human beings into tobacco pouches, bridle reins, or souvenirs—an object for the consumption of white

people. This history reflects a disrespect not only for Native people's bodies but also for the integrity of all creation, the two being integrally related. That is, Native people were viewed as rapable because they resemble animals rather than humans. Unlike Native people, who do not view the bodies of animals as rapable either, colonizers often senselessly annihilated both animals and Indian people in order to establish their common identity as expendable. During the Washita massacre, for example, Captain Frederick W. Benteen reported that Colonel Custer "exhibits his close sharpshooting and terrifies the crowd of frightened, captured squaws and papooses by dropping the straggling ponies in death near them. . . . Not even do the poor dogs of the Indians escape his eye and aim, as they drop dead or limp howling away."[14] Whereas Native people view animals as created beings deserving of bodily integrity, Bernard Sheehan notes that Europeans at that time often viewed animals as guises for Satan.[15] As one Humboldt County newspaper stated in 1853, "We can never rest in security until the redskins are treated like the other wild beasts of the forest."[16] Of course, if whites had treated Native people with the same respect that Native people have traditionally treated animals, Native people would not have suffered genocide. Thus, ironically, while Native people often view their identities as inseparable from the rest of creation, and hence the rest of creation deserves their respect, colonizers also viewed Indian identity as inseparably linked to that of animal and plant life, and hence deserving of destruction and mutilation.

Today, this mentality continues in new forms. One example is the controversial 1992 hepatitis B trial vaccine program conducted among Alaska Native children. In this experiment, almost all Alaska Native children were given experimental vaccines without their consent. Dr. William Jordan of the U.S. Department of Health has noted that virtually all field trials for new vaccines in the United States are first tested on indigenous people in Alaska, and most of the vaccines do absolutely nothing to prevent disease.[17] As Mary Ann Mills and Bernadine Atcheson (Traditional Dena'ina) point out, this constant influx of vaccines into Native communities is a constant assault on their immune systems. They are particularly concerned about this hepatitis B vaccine because they contend it might have been tainted with HIV. They note that even Merck Sharp & Dohme seems to acknowledge that the vaccine contained the virus when it states in the *Physicians' Desk Reference* (PDR) that "clinical trials of HEPTAVAX-B provide no evidence to suggest transmission of...AIDS by this vaccine, even when the vaccine has been used routinely in infants in Alaska."[18] According to Mills and Atcheson, alarming cases of AIDS soon broke out after these experiments, mostly among women and children, and now some villages are going to lose one-third of their population to AIDS.[19]

The equation between indigenous people and laboratory animals is evident in the minds of medical colonizers. The PDR manual notes that Merck Sharp & Dohme experimented both on "chimpanzees and...Alaska Native children."[20] Mills and Atcheson question why these drugs are being tested on Native people *or* chimpanzees when Alaska Native people did not have a high rate of hepatitis B to begin with.[21] Furthermore, they question the precepts of Western medicine, which senselessly dissects, vivisects, and experiments on both animals and human beings when, as they argue, much healthier preventative and holistic indigenous forms of medicine are available. This Western medical model has not raised the life expectancy of indigenous people past the age of forty-seven. States Mills, "Today we rely on our elders and our traditional healers. We have asked them if they were ever as sick as their grandchildren or great-grandchildren are today. Their reply was no; they are much healthier than their children are today."[22]

Through this colonization and abuse of their bodies, Indian people learn to internalize self-hatred. Body image is integrally related to self-esteem.[23] When one's body is not respected, one begins to hate oneself. Thus, it is not a surprise that Indian people who have survived sexual abuse say they do not want to be Indian. Anne, a Native boarding school student, reflects on this process:

You better not touch yourself....If I looked at somebody...lust, sex, and I got scared of those sexual feelings. And I did not know how to handle them....What really confused me was if intercourse was sin, why are people born?...It took me a really long time to get over the fact that...I've sinned: I had a child.[24]

As her words indicate, when the bodies of Indian people are inherently sinful and dirty, it becomes a sin just to be Indian. Each instance of abuse we suffer is just another reminder that, as Chrystos articulates, "If you don't make something pretty / they can hang on their walls or wear around their necks / you might as well be dead."[25]

While the bodies of both Indian men and women have been marked by abuse, Inés Hernández-Avila (Nez Perce) notes that the bodies of Native women have been particularly targeted for abuse because of their capacity to give birth. "It is because of a Native American woman's sex that she is hunted down and slaughtered, in fact, singled out, because she has the potential through childbirth to assure the continuance of the people."[26] David Stannard points out that control over women's reproductive abilities and destruction of women and children are essential in destroying a people. If the women of a nation are not disproportionately killed, then that nation's population will not be severely affected. He says that Native women and children were targeted for wholesale killing in order to destroy the Indian nations. This is why colonizers such as Andrew Jackson recommended that troops systematically kill Indian women and children after massacres in order to complete extermination.[27] Similarly, Methodist minister Colonel John Chivington's policy was to "kill and scalp all little and big" because "nits make lice."[28]

Because Native women had the power to maintain Indian nations in the face of genocide, they were dangerous to the colonial world order. Also, because Indian nations were for the most part not patriarchal and afforded women great esteem, Indian women represented a threat to colonial patriarchy as they belied the notion that patriarchy is somehow inevitable. Consequently, colonizers expressed constant outrage that Native women were not tied to monogamous marriages and held "the marriage ceremony in utter disregard,"[29] were free to express their sexuality, had "no respect for...virginity,"[30] and loved themselves. They did not see themselves as "fallen" women as they should have. Their sexual power was threatening to white men; consequently, they sought to control it.

> When I was in the boat I captured a beautiful Carib woman....I conceived desire to take pleasure....I took a rope and thrashed her well, for which she raised such unheard screams that you would not have believed your ears. Finally we came to an agreement in such a manner that I can tell you that she seemed to have been brought up in a school of harlots.[31]

> Two of the best looking of the squaws were lying in such a position, and from the appearance of the genital organs and of their wounds, there can be no doubt that they were first ravished and then shot dead. Nearly all of the dead were mutilated.[32]

> One woman, big with child, rushed into the church, clasping the altar and crying for mercy for herself and unborn babe. She was followed, and fell pierced with a dozen lances....the child was torn alive from the yet palpitating body of its mother, first plunged into the holy water to be baptized, and immediately its brains were dashed out against a wall.[33]

> The Christians attacked them with buffets and beatings....Then they behaved with such temerity and shamelessness that the most powerful ruler of the island had to see his own wife raped by a Christian officer.[34]

> I heard one man say that he had cut a woman's private parts out, and had them for exhibition on a stick. I heard another man say that he had cut the fingers off of an Indian, to get the rings off his hand. I also heard of numerous instances in which men had cut out the private parts of females, and stretched them over their saddle-bows and some of them over their hats.[35]

American Horse said of the massacre at Wounded Knee:

> The fact of the killing of the women, and more especially the killing of the young boys and girls who are to make up the future strength of the Indian people, is the saddest part of the whole affair and we feel it very sorely.[36]

Ironically, while enslaving women's bodies, colonizers argued that they were actually somehow freeing Native women from the "oppression" they supposedly faced in Native nations. Thomas Jefferson argued that Native women "are submitted to unjust drudgery. This I believe is the case with every barbarous people....It is civilization alone which replaces women in the enjoyment of their equality."[37] The *Mariposa Gazette* similarly noted that when Indian women were safely under the control of white men, they "are neat, and tidy, and industrious, and soon learn to discharge domestic duties properly and creditably."[38] In 1862, a Native man in Conrow Valley was killed and scalped, his head twisted off, with his killers saying, "You will not kill any more women and children."[39] Apparently, Native women can only be free while under the dominion of white men, and both Native and white women need to be protected from Indian men rather than from white men.

While the era of Indian massacres in their more explicit form is over in North America, in Latin America, the wholesale rape and mutilation of indigenous women's bodies continues. During the 1982 massacre of Mayan people in Rio Negro (Guatemala), 177 women and children were killed; the young women were raped in front of their mothers, and the mothers were killed in front of their children. The younger children were then tied at the ankles and dashed against the rocks until their skulls were broken. This massacre was funded by the U.S. government.[40] While many white feminists are correctly outraged by the rapes in Bosnia, organizing to hold a war crimes tribunal against the Serbs, one wonders why the mass rapes in Guatemala or elsewhere against indigenous people in Latin America has not sparked the same outrage. In fact, feminist legal scholar Catherine MacKinnon argues that in Bosnia "the world has *never* seen sex used this consciously, this cynically, this elaborately, this openly, this systematically...as a means of destroying a whole people."[41] She seems to forget that she lives on this land only because millions of Native people were raped, sexually mutilated, and murdered. Is perhaps mass rape against European women genocide while mass rape against indigenous women is business as usual? In even the white feminist imagination, are Native women's bodies more rapable than white women's bodies?

In North America, while there does not seem to be the same wholesale massacres of Indian people as in Latin America, colonizers will revert back to old habits in times of aggravated conflict. In 1976, Anna Mae Aquash (Micmac), who had been fighting U.S. policies against Native people as a member of the American Indian Movement (AIM), was found dead—apparently raped. Her killer was never brought to justice, but it is believed that she was killed either by the FBI or as a result of being badjacketed by the FBI as an informant. After her death, the FBI cut off her hands. Later, when the FBI pressured Myrtle Poor Bear into testifying against political prisoner Leonard Peltier, they threatened that she would end up just like Anna Mae if she did not comply.[42] In the 1980s when I served as a nonviolent witness for the Chippewa spearfishers, who were being harassed by white racist mobs, one white harasser carried a sign saying "Save a fish; spear a pregnant squaw."[43] Even after 500 years, in the eyes of the colonizers, Native women's bodies are still rapable. During the 1990 Mohawk crisis in Oka, a white mob surrounded the ambulance of a Native woman who was attempting to leave the Mohawk reservation because she was hemorrhaging after having given birth. She was forced to "spread her legs" to prove she had given birth. The police at the scene refused to intervene. An Indian man was arrested for "wearing a disguise" (he was wearing jeans), and he was brutally beaten, his testicles crushed. Two women from Chicago WARN (Women of All Red Nations, the organization I belong to) went to Oka to videotape the crisis. They were arrested and held in custody for eleven hours without being charged and were told they could not go to the bathroom unless the male police officers could watch. The place they were held was covered with pornographic magazines.[44]

This colonial desire to subjugate Indian women's bodies was quite apparent when, in 1982, Stuart Kasten marketed a new video game, "Custer's Revenge," in which players get points each time they, in the form of Custer, rape an Indian woman. The slogan of the game is "When you score, you score." He describes the game as "a fun sequence where the woman is enjoying a sexual act willingly." According to the promotional material,

> You are General Custer. Your dander's up, your pistol's wavin'. You've hog-tied a ravishing Indian maiden and have a chance to rewrite history and even up an old score. Now, the Indian maiden's hands may be tied, but she's not about to take it lying down, by George! Help is on the way. If you're to get revenge you'll have to rise to the challenge, dodge a tribe of flying arrows and protect your flanks against some downright mean and prickly cactus. But if you can stand pat and last past the strings and arrows—You can stand last. Remember? Revenge is sweet.[45]

Just as historically white colonizers who raped Indian women claimed that the real rapist was the Indian man, today white men who rape and murder Indian women often make this same claim. In Minneapolis, a white man, Jesse Coulter, raped, murdered, and mutilated several Indian women. He claimed to be Indian, adopting the name Jesse Sittingcrow and emblazoning an AIM tattoo on his arm.[46] This is not to suggest that Indian men do not rape now. After years of colonialism and boarding school experience, violence has also been internalized within Indian communities. However, this view of the Indian man as the "true" rapist obscures who has the real power in this racist and patriarchal society.

Also, just as colonizers in the past targeted Native women for destruction because of their ability to give birth, colonizers today continue their attacks on the reproductive capabilities of Native women. Dr. Connie Uri, a Cherokee/Choctaw doctor, first uncovered sterilization abuses of Native women when a Native woman requested from her a "womb transplant." Dr. Uri discovered that this woman had undergone a hysterectomy for sterilization purposes but was told the procedure was reversible. The doctor began investigating sterilization abuses, which led Senator James Abourezk to request a study on IHS (Indian Health Services) sterilization policies. The General Accounting Office released a study in November 1976 indicating that Native women were being sterilized without informed consent. Dr. Uri conducted further investigations, leading her to estimate that 25 percent of all Native women of childbearing age had been sterilized without their informed consent, with sterilization rates as high as 80 percent on some reservations.[47]

While sterilization abuse has been curbed somewhat with the institution of informed consent policies, it has reappeared in the form of dangerous contraceptives such as Norplant and Depo-Provera.[48] These are both extremely risky forms of long-acting hormonal contraceptives that have been pushed on Indian women. Depo-Provera, a known carcinogen that has been condemned as an inappropriate form of birth control by several national women's health organizations,[49] was routinely administered to Indian women through IHS before it was approved by the FDA in 1992.[50] There are no studies on the long-term effects of Norplant, and the side effects (constant bleeding—sometimes for over ninety days—tumors, kidney problems, strokes, heart attacks, sterility) are so extreme that approximately 30 percent of women on Norplant want the device taken out in the first year, with the majority requesting it be removed within two years, even though it is supposed to remain implanted in a woman's arm for five years.[51] To date, more than 2,300 women suffering from 125 side effects related to Norplant have joined a class action suit against Wyeth Pharmaceuticals, the manufacturer of the product.[52] The Native American Women's Health Education Resource Center conducted a survey of IHS policies regarding Norplant and Depo-Provera and found that Native women were not given adequate counseling about the side effects and contraindications.[53]

Native women (as well as other women of color) are seen by colonizers as wombs gone amok who threaten the racist world order. In 1979, it was discovered that seven in ten U.S. hospitals that performed voluntary sterilizations for Medicaid recipients violated the 1974 DHEW guidelines by disregarding sterilization consent procedures and by sterilizing women through "elective" hysterectomies.[54] One recently declassified federal document, National Security Study Memorandum 200, revealed that even in 1976 the U.S. government regarded the growth of the nonwhite population as a threat to national security.[55] As one doctor stated in *Contemporary Ob/Gyn:*

> People pollute, and too many people crowded too close together cause many of our social and economic problems. These in turn are aggravated by involuntary and irresponsible parenthood....We also have obligations to the society of which we are part. The welfare mess, as it has been called, cries out for solutions, one of which is fertility control.[56]

Consequently, Native women and women of color, because of their ability to reproduce, are "overpopulating the world" and pose "the single greatest threat to the health of the planet."[57] Consequently, Native women and women of color deserve no bodily integrity—any form of dangerous contraception is appropriate for them so long as it stops them from reproducing.[58]

Finally, completing the destruction of a people involves destroying the integrity of their culture and spirituality, which forms the matrix of Native women's resistance to sexual colonization. Native counselors generally agree that a strong cultural and spiritual identity is essential if Native people are to heal from abuse. This is because a Native woman's return to wellness entails healing from not only any personal abuse she has suffered but also from the patterned history of abuse against her family, her nation, and the environment in which she lives.[59] Because Indian spiritual traditions are holistic, they are able to restore survivors of abuse to the community, to restore their bodies to wholeness. That is why the most effective programs for healing revolve around reviving indigenous spiritual traditions.

In the colonial discourse, however, Native spiritual traditions become yet another site for the commodification of Indian women's bodies. As part of the genocidal process, Indian cultures no longer offer the means of restoring wholeness but become objects of consumerism for the dominant culture. Haunani-Kay Trask, Native Hawaiian activist, describes this process as "cultural prostitution."

> "Prostitution" in this context refers to the entire institution which defines a woman (and by extension the "female") as an object of degraded and victimized sexual value for use and exchange through the medium of money....My purpose is not to exact detail or fashion a model but to convey the utter degradation of our culture and our people under corporate tourism by employing "prostitution" as an analytical category....
>
> The point, of course, is that everything in Hawai'i can be yours, that is, you the tourist, the non-native, the visitor. The place, the people, the culture, even our identity as a "Native" people is for sale. Thus, Hawai'i, like a lovely woman, is there for the taking.[60]

Thus, this "New Age" appropriation of Indian spirituality represents yet another form of sexual abuse for Indian women, hindering its ability to help women heal from abuse. Columnist Andy Rooney exemplifies this dominant ideology when he argues that Native spiritual traditions involve "ritualistic dances with strong sexual overtones [that are] demeaning to Indian women and degrading to Indian children."[61] Along similar lines, Mark and Dan Jury produced a film called *Dances Sacred and Profane,* which advertised that it "climaxes with the first-ever filming of the Indian Sundance ceremony."[62] This so-called ceremony consisted of a white man, hanging from meat hooks from a tree, praying to the "Great White Spirit" and was then followed by C. C. Sadist, a group that performs sadomasochistic acts for entertainment. Similarly, "plastic medicine men" are often notorious for sexually abusing their clients in fake Indian ceremonies. Jeffrey Wall was recently sentenced for sexually abusing three girls while claiming this abuse was part of American Indian spiritual rituals that he was conducting as a supposed Indian medicine man.[63] David "Two Wolves" Smith and

Alan "Spotted Wolfe" Champney were also charged for sexually abusing girls during supposed "cleansing" ceremonies.[64] That so many people do not question that sexual fondling would be part of Indian ceremonies, to the point where legitimate spiritual leaders are forced to issue statements such as "No ceremony requires anyone to be naked or fondled during the ceremony,"[65] signifies the extent to which the colonial discourse attempts to shift the meaning of Indian spirituality from something healing to something abusive.

Nevertheless, as mentioned earlier, Native women resist these attacks upon their bodies and souls and the sexually abusive representations of their cultures through the promotion of wellness. The University of Oklahoma sponsors two national wellness and women conferences each year, which more than 2,000 Indian women attend (it also sponsors smaller gatherings for Native men). These conferences help women begin their healing journeys from various forms of abuse and teach them to become enablers for community healing. The Indigenous Women's Network also sponsors gatherings that tie together the healing of individuals and communities from the trauma of this nation's history. At the 1994 conference, each of the four days had a different focus: individual healing, family healing, community healing, and political struggles in North America and the world.

I belonged to a wellness and women circle where Native women share their stories and learn from each other as they travel on the road toward wellness. At one circle, where we discussed the effect of hormonal contraceptives on our bodies, women talked about the devastating effects these hormones were having on their bodies, but the response of their medical providers was simply to give them more hormones. We began to see that we do not need to rely on the "experts" who have their own agendas; we need to trust our bodies, which colonizers have attempted to alienate from us. Our colonizers have attempted to destroy our sense of identity by teaching us self-hatred and self-alienation. But through such wellness movements, we learn to reconnect, to heal from historical and personal abuse, and to reclaim our power to resist colonization.

NOTES

1. Cecelia Fire Thunder, "We Are Breaking a Cycle," *Indigenous Woman* II (1995): 3.
2. I shall not discuss how Jewish traditions have interpreted the Canaanite narratives, nor whether there even was a wholesale conquest of the Canaanites, which many scholars doubt. I am describing how the Christian appropriation of Canaanite narratives has impacted Native people; I make no claims either for or against Jewish colonialism.
3. Albert Cave, "Canaanites in a Promised Land," *American Indian Quarterly* (Fall 1988): 277–297; H. C. Porter, *The Inconstant Savage* (London: Gerald Duckworth, 1979), pp. 91–115; Ronald Sanders, *Lost Tribes and Promised Lands* (Boston: Little, Brown, 1978), pp. 46, 181, 292; Djelal Kadir, *Columbus and the Ends of the Earth* (Berkeley: University of California Press, 1992), p. 129.
4. Richard Hill, "Savage Splendor: Sex, Lies and Stereotypes," *Turtle Quarterly* (Spring/Summer 1991):19.
5. Robert Berkoher, *The White Man's Indian* (New York: Vintage, 1978), p. 19.
6. David Stannard, *American Holocaust* (Oxford: Oxford University Press, 1992), p. 211.
7. Charles Loring Brace (1869), quoted in James Rawls, *Indians of California: The Changing Image* (Norman: University of Oklahoma, 1984), p. 195.
8. Hinton Rowan Helper (1855), quoted in Rawls, *Indians of California*, p. 195.
9. Andre Lopez, *Pagans in Our Midst* (Mohawk Nation: Akwesasne Notes), p. 119. It should be noted, as Paula Gunn Allen points out, that Native people in fact bathed much more frequently than did Europeans; see Paula Gunn Allen, *The Sacred Hoop* (Boston: Beacon, 1986), p. 217.
10. Stannard, *American Holocaust*, p. 121.
11. William James, *A Full and Correct Account of the Military Occurrences of the Late War between Great Britain and the United States of America* (London: printed by the author, 1818), Vol. 1, pp. 293–96, in *Who's the Savage?* ed. David Wrone and Russet Nelson (Malabar: Robert Krieger, 1982), p. 82.
12. U.S. Congress. Senate, Special Committee Appointed under Joint Resolution of March 3, 1865. *Condition of the Indian Tribes,* 39th Congress, Second Session, Senate Report 156, Washington, DC, 1867, pp. 95–96, quoted in *Who's the Savage?* p. 113.
13. John Terrell, *Land Grab* (New York: Dial Press, 1972), p. 13.
14. Terrell, *Land Crab,* p. 12.
15. Bernard Sheehan, *Savagism and Civility* (Cambridge: Cambridge University Press, 1980).
16. Rawls, *Indians of California*, p. 200.
17. Traditional Dena'ina, *Summary Packet on Hepatitis B Vaccinations* (Sterling, AK, November 9, 1992).
18. *Physicians' Desk Reference* (PDR) (Oradell, NJ: Medical Economics, 1991), pp. 1292–93.
19. Traditional Dena'ina, *Hepatitis B.*
20. PDR, pp. 1292–93.
21. Traditional Dena'ina, *Hepatitis B.*
22. Mary Ann Mills (speech delivered at a WARN Forum, Chicago, IL, September 1993).
23. For further discussion on the relationship between bodily abuse and self-esteem, see Ellen Bass and Laura Davis, *The Courage to Heal* (New York: Harper and Row, 1988), pp. 207–222, and Bonnie Burstow, *Radical Feminist Therapy* (London: Sage, 1992), pp. 187–234.
24. Celia Haig-Brown, *Resistance and Renewal* (Vancouver: Tilacum, 1988), p. 108.
25. Chrystos, "The Old Indian Granny," in *Fugitive Colors* (Cleveland: Cleveland State University Press, 1995), p. 41.
26. Inés Hernández-Avila, "In Praise of Insubordination, or What Makes a Good Woman Go Bad?" in *Transforming a Rape Culture,* ed. Emilie Buchwald, Pamela R. Fletcher, and Martha Roth (Minneapolis: Milkweed, 1993), p. 386.
27. Stannard, *American Holocaust,* p. 121.
28. Stannard, *American Holocaust,* p. 131.
29. *Cattaraugus Republican,* II February 1897, in Lopez, *Pagans in Our Midst,* p. 9.
30. Dominican monk Thomas Ortiz, quoted in Kirkpatrick Sale, *The Conquest of Paradise* (New York: Penguin, 1990), p. 201.
31. From Cuneo, an Italian nobleman, quoted in Sale, *Conquest of Paradise,* p. 140.
32. U.S. Commissioner of Indian Affairs, *Annual Report for 1871* (Washington, DC: Government Printing Office, 1871), pp. 487–88, cited in *Who's the Savage?* p. 123.
33. Le Roy R. Hafen, ed. *Ruxton of the Rockies* (Norman: University of Oklahoma Press, 1950), pp. 46–149, cited in *Who's the Savage,* p. 97.
34. Bartolome de Las Casas, *The Devastation of the Indies,* trans. Herma Briffault (Baltimore: Johns Hopkins University Press, 1992), p. 33.
35. Lieutenant James D. Cannon, quoted in "Report of the Secretary of War," 39th Congress, Second Session, Senate Executive Document 26, Washington, DC, 1867, printed in *The Sand Creek Massacre: A Documentary History* (New York: Sol Lewis, 1973), pp. 129–30.
36. James Mooney, "The Ghost Dance Religion and the Sioux Outbreak of 1890." In *Fourteenth Annual Report*

of the United States Bureau of Ethnology (Washington, DC: U.S. Government Printing Office, 1896). p. 885, quoted in Stannard, *American Holocaust,* p. 127.

37. Roy Harvey Pearce, *Savagism and Civilization* (Baltimore: Johns Hopkins University Press, 1965), p. 93.

38. Robert Heizer, ed., *The Destruction of California Indians* (Lincoln: University of Nebraska Press, 1993), p. 284.

39. Rawls, *Indians in California,* p. 182.

40. Information gathered by the Guatemalan Forensic Anthropology team and posted by Stefan Schmitt, online at garnet.aces.fsu.edu/~sss4407/RioNeg.htm.

41. Catherine MacKinnon, "Turning Rape into Pornography: Postmodern Genocide," *Ms. Magazine* 4, no. 1: 27 (emphasis mine).

42. Johanna Brand, *The Life and Death of Anna Mae Aquash* (Toronto: Lorimer), pp. 28, 140.

43. "Up Front," *Perspectives: The Civil Rights Quarterly* 14, no. 3 (Fall 1982).

44. Personal conversations with author (Summer 1990).

45. Promotional material from Public Relations: Mahoney/ Wasserman & Associates, Los Angeles, CA, n.d.

46. Mark Brunswick and Paul Klauda, "Possible Suspect in Serial Killings Jailed in N. Mexico," *Minneapolis Star and Tribune,* 28 May 1987, IA.

47. See "The Threat of Life," *WARN Report,* pp. 13–16 (available through WARN, 4511 N. Hermitage, Chicago, IL 60640); Brint Dillingham, "Indian Women and IHS Sterilization Practices," *American Indian Journal* (January 1977): 27–28; Brint Dillingham, "Sterilization of Native Americans," *American Indian Journal* (July 1977): 16–19; Pat Bellanger, "Native American Women, Forced Sterilization, and the Family," in *Every Woman Has a Story,* ed. Gaya Wadnizak Ellis (Minneapolis: Midwest Villages & Voices, 1982), pp. 30–35; "Oklahoma: Sterilization of Native Women Charged to I.H.S." *Akwesasne Notes* (Mid Winter, 1989): 30.

48. For a description of the hazards of Depo-Provera, see Stephen Minkin, "Depo-Provera: A Critical Analysis," Institute for Food and Development Policy, San Francisco. He concludes that "the continued use of Depo-Provera for birth control is unjustified and unethical." For more information on the effects of Norplant, see *Womanist Health Newsletter,* Issue on Norplant, available through Women's Health Education Project, 3435 N. Sheffield, #205, Chicago, IL 60660.

49. For a statement on Depo-Provera from the National Black Women's Health Project, National Latina Health Organization, Native American Women's Health Education Resource Center, National Women's Health Network, and Women's Economic Agenda Project, contact NAWHERC, PO Box 572, Lake Andes, SD 57356–0572.

50. "Taking the Shot," series of articles from *Arizona Republic* (November 1986).

51. Debra Hanania-Freeman, "Norplant: Freedom of Choice or a Plan for Genocide?" *EIR* 14 (May 1993): 20.

52. Kathleen Plant, "Mandatory Norplant Is Not the Answer," *Chicago Sun-Times,* 2 November 1994, p. 46.

53. "A Study of the Use of Depo-Provera and Norplant by the Indian Health Services" from Native American Women's Health Education Resource Center, South Dakota, 1993.

54. "Survey Finds Seven in 10 Hospitals Violate DHEW Guidelines on Informed Consent for Sterilization," *Family Planning Perspectives* II, no. 6 (Nov/Dec 1979): 366; Claudia Dreifus, "Sterilizing the Poor," *Seizing Our Bodies,* ed. and intro. by Claudia Dreifus (New York: Vintage Books, 1977), pp. 105–20.

55. Debra Hanania-Freeman, "Norplant," p. 20.

56. *Akwesasne Notes,* p. II.

57. Population Institute, *Annual Report,* 1991. See also Zero Population Growth, fundraising appeal, undated; "Population Stabilization: The Real Solution," pamphlet from the Los Angeles chapter of the Sierra Club—Population Committee; and Population Institute fund-raising appeal, which states that the population growth is the root cause of poverty, hunger, and environmental destruction.

58. For a more detailed discussion of the population control movement and its impact on communities of color, see Andy Smith, "Women of Color and Reproductive Choice: Combating the Population Paradigm," *Journal of Feminist Studies in Religion* (Spring 1996).

59. Justine Smith (Cherokee), personal conversation, 17 February 1994.

60. Haunani-Kay Trask, *From a Native Daughter: Colonialism & Sovereignty in Hawai'i* (Maine: Common Courage Press, 1993), pp. 185–94.

61. Andy Rooney, "Indians Have Worse Problems," *Chicago Tribune,* 4 March 1992.

62. Jim Lockhart, "AIM Protests Film's Spiritual Misrepresentation," *News from Indian Country* (Late September 1994): 10.

63. "Shaman Sentenced for Sex Abuse," *News from Indian Country* (Mid June 1996): 2A.

64. David Melmer, "Sexual Assault," *Indian Country Today* 15 (30 April–7 May 1996): 1.

65. Michael Pace, in David Melmer, "Sexual Assault," *Indian Country Today* 15 (30 April–7 May 1996): 1.

DOING GENDER AND DOING GENDER INAPPROPRIATELY

Violence against Women, Gay Men, and Lesbians

DISCUSSION QUESTIONS

1. How does violence against women serve as a form of social control over all women? Why does Perry argue that sexual violence is also gendered violence? Do you think violence against women should be considered a "hate crime"?
2. How is violence against women shaped by race and class dynamics?
3. How is men's violence against both women and other men tied to the construction of gender? Why do you think violence against gay men is more common than violence against lesbians?

GENDER-MOTIVATED VIOLENCE: KEEPING WOMEN IN "THEIR PLACE"

Gender-motivated violence is predicated upon widespread assumptions regarding gender and gender-appropriate deportment. In particular, these assumptions revolve around constructions of gender that represent polar extremes inhabited by masculine and dominant men, and feminine and subordinate women. Violence is but one means by which men as a class enforce conformity of women as a class. Moreover, it is not necessary for all men to engage in violence against women, since the very threat of violent censure is constantly with women. Violence against women, then, is indeed a "classic" form of

hate crime, since it too terrorizes the collective by victimizing the individual. In so doing, hate crime against women reaffirms the privilege and superiority of the male perpetrator with respect to the female victim.

Feminist scholars acknowledge the parallel between violence against women—especially sexual violence—and the lynching of black males as means to exert control and create identity (Brownmiller, 1974; Rothschild, 1993; Pendo, 1994). There is little difference in the motives. Both groups are victimized because of their identity, often for very similar illusionary "violations": "for being uppity, for getting out of line, for failing to recognize 'one's place,' for assuming sexual freedoms, or for behaving no more provocative than walking down the wrong road at night in the wrong part of town and presenting a convenient isolated target for group hatred and rage" (Brownmiller, 1974: 281). Just as racially motivated violence seeks to reestablish "proper" alignment between racial groups, so too is gender-motivated violence intended to restore men and women to "their place." Victims are chosen because of their gender and because of the assumptions about how they should enact their gender. The gender polarization that permeates U.S. culture is taken as a "natural," "given" fact, wherein women are expected to enact deference, men dominance. This dichotomy presupposes mutually exclusive scripts for males and females—scripts that constrain everything from modes of dress and social roles to ways of expressing emotion and experiencing sexual desire. It also defines any person or behavior that deviates from these scripts as problematic: unnatural, immoral, biologically anomalous, or psychologically pathological. Gender-motivated violence is a key means by which men and women rehearse their scripts, ensuring that women act "like women" in the bedroom, in the kitchen, in the workplace, and on the street.

GENDER, POWER, AND VIOLENCE

In each of these domains, gendered relations of power are enacted, albeit in slightly disparate forms. What unites the home, the workplace, and the street is that each historically has been a crucial site in efforts to establish an "appropriate" hierarchy in which men are dominant, women subordinate. Each has been the locus of struggles that have contributed to the empowerment of men and the relative disempowerment of women.

The United States is a male supremacist society wherein gender difference is constructed as gender inferiority and, ultimately, gender disadvantage. Consequently, women garner less power, prestige, and economic reward than men, who have consistently retained leadership and control in government, commerce, and family matters (Lorber, 1994). This is readily apparent in the legal history

that has helped shape gendered relations of power. Male privilege has long been guaranteed by legal proscriptions and silences that have simultaneously excluded women from involvement in the public sphere, while failing to protect them in the context of their private lives (Taub and Schneider, 1990). On the one hand, legal exclusions on women's enfranchisement, ownership of property, and employment (in law and medicine, for example) have meant that until well into the twentieth century, women were unable to participate fully in politics or the economy. Even today, restrictions on access to abortion or to social security provisions, for example, limit the participatory power of women.

On the other hand, law has also enabled the subordination of women within the home. The same nineteenth- and twentieth-century provisions that limited (married) women's ownership of property meant that married women, in particular, ceded autonomy to their husbands upon marriage. The historical tendency to exclude from criminal proceedings husband's rapes or assaults on wives similarly ensured the dominance of men who were merely exercising their "marital rights." The continued failure to recognize the value of women's domestic labor through some form of income support likewise helps to maintain women's economic dependence on men, both during and subsequent to marriage. This is exacerbated by inequitable divorce settlements and the intractable wage disparities between men and women.

At least with respect to family and domestic violence, men's perceived sense of "ownership" continues to provide a context for the victimization of girls and women. The structured inequality of women leaves them vulnerable to the presumption of male control by whatever means necessary. It establishes an environment in which men freely manipulate the terms of a relationship. Violence becomes one such means for him to prove that he is "the man" and therefore in control. This even extends to relationships with daughters, as in the case of incestuous assaults. Research consistently suggests that child sexual abuse within families is disturbingly common (Baskin and Sommers, 1998; Belknap, 1996).

It is not unlike woman battering in the home, to the extent that it too is a display of men's control over women, and especially women's sexuality. As Elizabeth Stanko (1985) contends, incestuous assaults are an assertion of male "rights" of access to and control of the powerless female. Young girls especially are vulnerable to such victimization due to their place in the family, their lack of experience, and their femaleness, which Stanko equates with powerlessness.

The extensive research of R. Emerson Dobash and Russell Dobash has led them to identify four interrelated "sources of conflict" that, they argue, are most predictive of woman battering: "men's possessiveness and jealousy; men's expectations concerning women's domestic work; men's sense of the right to punish 'their' women for perceived wrongdoing; and the importance, to men, of maintaining or exercising their position of authority" (1998: 268). Uniting these four triggers is the sense that the man has the right, perhaps the duty, to express his masculine power through violent repression. The female partner in such a relationship is seen to have challenged the masculine authority of her partner. She is seen to have transcended the boundaries of appropriate behavior and deference—perhaps she spoke too long with another man, or sought employment outside the home, contrary to the "demands" of her partner. Such behaviors throw into question the masculinity of the perpetrator. If he cannot control "his woman," perhaps he is not really a manly man after all. By striking out in violence, he reasserts his dominant and aggressive masculinity.

This male concern with taking charge and taking control of the heterosexual relationship emerges repeatedly in research on domestic violence (Websdale and Chesney-Lind, 1998; Weisburd and Levin, 1994; Wolfe and Copeland, 1994; Dobash and Dobash, 1998). This is especially true for patriarchal and usually lower-class families. In such situations, the "essential" nature of the patriarch is interpreted as the responsibility to "dominate and control their wives, and wife beating serves both to ensure continued compliance with their commands and as a resource for constructing a 'damaged'

patriarchal masculinity. Thus, wife beating increases (or is intended to do so) their control over women" (Messerschmidt, 1993: 147).

That a great deal of domestic violence is in fact motivated by a presumed loss of control and ownership is apparent in the increased likelihood of victimization as women attempt to exit a relationship. When women seek to empower themselves, when they seek to achieve some personal autonomy by escaping an abusive relationship, they often become dangerously vulnerable to stalking, assault, even murder (Browne, 1995; Chaiken, 1998; Tjaden and Thoennes, 1998). In many relationships, separation is the moment when the quest for control becomes lethal. Browne's interviews with battered women who killed their partners revealed the extent to which men's attempts to retain control outlast the relationship. One participant maintained that "we were separating but I don't think that would have solved anything. Don always said that he would come back around—that I belonged to him" (Browne, 1995: 232). The spouse of another of Browne's subjects once wrote in his journal, "Every time, Karen would have ugly bruises on her face and neck. She would cry and beg me for a divorce, and I would tell her, 'I am sorry. I won't do it again. But as for the divorce, absolutely not. If I can't have you for my wife, you will die. No one else will have you if you ever try to leave me'" (Browne, 1995: 232). Men who batter attempt to assert their proprietary masculinity through violence. It is as if they fear that all appearance of masculinity, of dominance, of control is lost in the face of women's challenges to their authority. Their violence simultaneously reestablishes the appropriate place of the male and female partners; it is both male prerogative and female punishment.

Moreover, not all men need to engage in battering for it to have a debilitating effect on women. Indeed, the power of domestic violence is that—like other forms of bias-motivated violence—it is embedded in a systemic pattern of real and potential violence against women. The violence against a particular woman in the home is a reminder that any woman in society is subject to violent control by men. In other words, "Men's power is not an individual, but a collective one. Women's lives are bounded by it. The threat of male violence outside the home . . . is an acutely intimidating reality to women who endure violence within their own homes" (Stanko, 1985: 57). Men correspondingly enact their "will to power" outside the home. Assaults, rapes, or homicides that are outside the bounds of an intimate relationship tend to be directed at individual women as proxies for the combined threats to masculine domination represented by women as a class. In their daily lives, all women, at any time, may be vulnerable to gender-motivated harassment, intimidation, and violence because they are women and because they represent the devalued, often threatening Other. Wherever a particular act lies on the continuum of violence, it is a "ritual enactment of domination, a form of terror that functions to maintain the status quo" (Caputi, 1993: 7).

As with racially motivated violence, gender-motivated violence often emerges in the context of what is perceived by men as a loss of relative position. Challenges to the collective hegemony of men often are met with aggressive attempts to reassert the "natural" dominance of men. It is, in these terms, a reactive expression of insecurity in the face of reconstituted femininities. It is no coincidence that violent crime perpetrated against women has risen so steadily in the three decades corresponding to the rise of the women's movement. Marilyn French (1992) and Susan Faludi (1991) carefully document what they refer to as the "War Against Women" and the antifeminist backlash, respectively. Both authors point to the increasing harassment and intimidation of women through violence and the threat of violence. As women have collectively striven to redefine themselves as autonomous actors, some men have been compelled to meet the challenge by resorting to the readily available resource of violence.

Marc Lepine is a case in point. On December 6, 1989, Lepine entered a classroom at Montreal's Ecole Polytechnique, systematically separated the male and female engineering students, and opened fire on the women. Before he killed himself, Lepine had murdered fourteen women and seriously injured nine others. In his verbal harangue during the shooting and in his suicide note, Lepine made it clear that his assault was intended to punish the feminists he held responsible for his personal failures—in particular, his inability to get into engineering school. Lepine's response was extreme, but nonetheless illustrative of the male response to the "erosion of white male exclusivity and privilege" (Caputi and Russell, 1992: 13). . . .

Neil Websdale and Meda Chesney-Lind's (1998) review of recent domestic violence literature reveals the consistency with which researchers are able to identify a relationship between patriarchal ideals and wife battering. For example, studies by Dobash and Dobash have revealed that battering is most likely to occur where women challenge their partners about household (economic) decisions, and where women are perceived as having failed in their "wifely duties"—refusing sex, serving cold meals, or neglecting the vacuuming. In other words, violence is a reactive performance of masculinity in the face of oppositional performances of femininity.

Interviews with batterers and their victims are illuminating in this regard. Often, both are very much aware of the existence of shared patriarchal beliefs, and the role of violence in enforcing them. A Kentucky woman interviewed by Websdale makes astute observations on the consequences of her "inappropriate" performance of an oppositional form of femininity:

TAMARA: The man is the head of the household. The woman has no say. It doesn't matter about her morals and her feelings. Nothing.

WEBSDALE: Was your husband like that?

TAMARA: He tried to be. That was our biggest problem. I talked back. I had an opinion and I wasn't allowed to have an opinion. And I'd say, "I don't care if you agree or not, honey, that's how I feel." That's one reason I was hit.

Male batterers express the same ideological position, as is the case with this abusive male interviewed by Peter Adams, Alisa Towns, and Nicole Garvey:

> Well, you got the male and you got the [laughing] female. And the male earns the bread and the woman brings up the family and that.... And it's a fact of life that only women can be a mother. There's no, there's no other way around it. And the man's still gotta go and earn the bread and the woman's still gotta have the children. (1995: 390)

Interviews with both battered women and their partners conducted by Dobash and Dobash (1998) reflect the paramount importance men place on their needs and their partners' ability to fulfill them. Often the only provocation to violence was the woman's failure to anticipate or fulfil her partner's expectations of her domestic femininity. One woman reported that

> He was late and I'd started cooking his meal but I put it aside, you know, when he didn't come in. Then when he came in I started heating it. I was standing at the sink and he just came up and gave me a punch in the stomach....It was only because his dinner wasn't ready on the table for him. (1998: 147)

This theme appears again in Diana Russell's interviews with victims of marital rape. One participant revealed that

> Oftentimes, he'd ask "where's my supper?" If it wasn't there, he'd hit me, even though I never knew when he'd be home because he was out with other women. (1990: 129)

A final illustration of the relationship between patriarchal beliefs and gendered violence is cited by Jane Caputi and Diana Russell:

> In 1989, Curtis Adams was sentenced to 32 years in prison for torturing his wife in a ten-hour attack. After she refused anal sex, Adams handcuffed his wife, repeatedly forced a bottle and then a broomstick into her anus and hung her naked out the window— *taking breaks to make her read biblical passages adjuring women to obey their husbands.* (1992: 18, emphasis added)

In such patriarchal relationships, male batterers use violence to simultaneously prove their manliness and remonstrate "their women" for failing to prove their corresponding womanliness. An essential nature and set of roles is assumed for each, and when they are not forthcoming—when his ability to be a real man is thwarted by her refusal to be a real woman—violence often ensues. The enactment of violence is an enactment of masculine power and control, where it might otherwise be eroding.

Intuitively, this analysis implies that domestic violence perpetrated against women of color may be especially problematic. Christine Rasche (1995) maintains that many of the ethnic communities that have shaped the United States—Latinos, African Americans, Asians, and Native Americans in particular—are structured by rigid patriarchal norms that tend to render familial violence tolerable, if not invisible. However, Kimberlé Williams Crenshaw (1994) highlights the problematic nature of this assumption in light of the academic neglect of the "intersection of racism and patriarchy." What Crenshaw does make clear is that women of color are uniquely vulnerable to gendered violence because of their multiply determined structural disempowerment. They are often simultaneously oppressed by their class, gender, and racial position. That this is the case is also suggested by recent trends toward increasing domestic violence among the Navajo of the Southwest, for example (Zion and Zion, 1996). The traditionally egalitarian nature of these people has been distorted by their more recent history of racial discrimination and disempowerment. Racial and economic disadvantage, coupled with the incursion of Anglo gender ideals, has dramatically altered the place of Navajo women. Increasingly, like their white counterparts, Navajo women are expected to perform the rituals of domestic femininity as a complement to the male performance of patriarch.

Contrary to popular mythology, African-American gender politics are characterized by neither the extreme matriarch nor the extreme patriarch. Rather, the performance of gender historically has been fluid. According to Beverly Greene (1997), rigid expectations of femininity and masculinity have been "impractical" against the backdrop of economic marginalization of black men. While the importance of the family has been a constant, idealized notions of masculinity and femininity nonetheless have varied by class, region, and ethnicity.

This is not to say that domestic violence has not also been a constant. hooks' volumes consistently draw attention to the sexism that seems to permeate African-American culture, even where patriarchal performances of masculinity are not in question. hooks agrees that male-as-breadwinner has not always been a viable option as a resource for most young black males. Proof of masculinity instead is embedded in their aggression, their sexuality, or in their ability to discipline the family. Combine these options with the tendency to share with white males a devalued and disdainful perception of women, and the climate is ripe for domestic violence against "uppity black women" (hooks, 1981; 1992). Contemporary African Americans also can find legitimation for their violent subjugation of women in the Muslim glorification of the "feminine ideal." Women are expected to defer to men's natural superiority. Violence in this context allows men to exercise at once their aggressiveness, dominance, and holiness (hooks, 1981).

Espiritu's (1997) examination of the gender politics of Asian Americans also highlights the intersection of race, gender, and class. In contrast to what is often a very traditional division of labor and power in their homeland, Asian immigrants to the United States find that their abilities to maintain such boundaries are compromised. As Espiritu contends, Asian-American women are more likely to be employed, albeit in low-wage occupations, than either their counterparts at home or their male partners in the United States. Consequently, they assume an elevated position in the family as breadwinner and decision maker—a clear threat to the masculinity authority and place of their husbands. As in the parallel white patriarchal family, violence can come to represent a leveling influence....

SEXUALITY AND VIOLENCE

Paralleling the presumption of a normative division of labor, there exists the presumption of normative sexualities. The latter is especially crucial in helping us to understand sexual violence as gendered violence. Sexual assault serves a particularly dramatic role in the policing of gender boundaries and the control of women's sexuality, for it is the place wherein women become objectified as predominantly sexual beings in the service of men.

To the extent that women are sexualized—in the workplace, on the street, in the home—they are held accountable to a femininity that requires sexual responsivity to men's advances. Just as the relative performance of masculinity and femininity assumes male proprietary rights, so too does it assume that sex with the woman of his choice is a man's right. Herein lies the context for gender-motivated sexual violence. As one rapist put it,

> Rape is a man's right. If a woman doesn't want to give it, the man should take it. Women have no right to say no—women are made to have sex. That's all they're good for. (Curran and Renzetti, 1994: 207)

Just as a sense of entitlement underlies domestic violence, so too does it underlie sexual violence within and outside intimate relationships. As the above quote suggests, sexual access to women as a class is perceived as the inalienable right of men as a class. Sexual assault, then, is an institutionalized, rather than aberrant, means by which men can perform their masculinity while "symbolizing and actualizing women's subordinate position" (MacKinnon, 1991: 1302). Women's sexuality is a ready commodity, available to all. In other words, "all women are whores and, therefore, fair game; sexual violence is normal and acceptable" (Caputi and Russell, 1992: 18).

Entitlement takes on a special meaning in the context of sexual assault by intimates—both rape in marriage and acquaintance rape. In these situations, sexual assault takes on an additional validity, reinforcing the gendered power of men to control even the most intimate dimensions of women's lives. Earlier, I discussed the family as a preeminent site for the regulation of the sexual division of labor, through violence if necessary. The marital relationship is no less important for the regulation of sexuality, and women's sexuality in particular. It is the site at which men most readily and forcefully exercise their (hetero) sexual rights to a woman's body. Women are expected to "exchange" their sexual favors for a share of their husbands' paychecks, or for the dinner and a movie provided by their dates. This, according to tradition, is the appropriate way for a woman to express her gratitude, and of course, her femininity. Should she adopt an oppositional femininity—by saying "no"—she becomes vulnerable to violent reprobation. Such is the normativity of sexual entitlement, that rapists—and their victims—often don't acknowledge intimate rape as rape. Robin Warsaw (1994) reports that 84 percent of men who had committed date rape asserted that their actions definitely did not constitute rape. A victim of rape clearly articulates her victimizer's failure to recognize the severity of his assault:

> He left me a note with one of those smile faces drawn on it. The note read "Denise, I woke up and you were gone. Catch ya later! Have a nice day. Bob." Minutes later, the phone rang. The voice belonged to a cheerful Bob. I think I called him a bastard or a fucker and I told him not to ever call me again, and then hung up. He called back, sounding surprised, asking, "Hey, what's the matter?" (Warsaw, 1994: 91).

Similar assumptions of the unobstructed right of men to women's bodies is evident in sexual assault within cohabiting and marital relationships. Even more so than dates or boyfriends, husbands hold their wives to the presumption of unrestricted sex-on-demand. That is part of her "role" as prescribed by narrow and rigid constructions of femininity. She is the sexual companion, often sexual property, of her mate. When women rebel against such prescriptions, they become vulnerable to the violent reassertion of their partners' aggressive sexuality and manhood, in a way that also is intended to remind them how they are expected to perform. This was the interpretation of rape offered by many of Russell's (1990) subjects:

> I consented to sex with him when I didn't want to....It was out of duty, I guess you'd say. He somehow conveyed to me that he expected it of me because I was his wife. (52)

> With a husband, you feel forced. I have an obligation to my husband which is very bad. It's always been a man's world. (81)

> He used to call me at work to come to him at once because he wanted sex. I used to work on Saturday and he didn't so he wanted me home. (92)

> It was a very brutal marriage. He was so patriarchal. He felt he owned me and the children—that I was his property. In the first three weeks of our marriage, he told me to regard him as God and his word as gospel. If I didn't want sex and he did, my wishes didn't matter. (123)

Women and men learn very young that male sexual access to women is "naturally" unrestricted. In some cases, this lesson is learned in the home, when young girls become the victim of child sexual abuse. This practice normalizes sexual assaults against women. It also sexualizes them very early on, so that they become defined by their "sexual capital"; girls learn that their most valuable and manipulable asset is their sexuality. As Stanko puts it, "One basic part in some children's lives, however, can be a source of confusion: as part of the pink world, incestually assaulted children learn that their female role also entails sexual availability to men" (1985: 20). Perhaps, then, it is no accident that those victimized as children are vulnerable to revictimization as adults (Belknap, 1996).

These lessons are reinforced as girls and boys enter adolescence. Barrie Thorne's (1994) work on gender socialization in school settings suggests that adolescent girls are encouraged to cultivate a "culture of compliance and conformity" with respect to boys that may very well leave them vulnerable to sexual victimization. Conversely, boys begin to develop a sense of self that is predicated on mastery of their environment, including girls.

If women have not learned during earlier courtships that "their sexuality is not their own," the lesson often is driven home after marriage (Stanko, 1985: 73). In fact, sexual assault is the ultimate abrogation of women's choice, autonomy, and self-determination. Forced sex reproduces masculine dominance and control like few other activities. It victimizes women in ways to which they are "uniquely vulnerable" (Rothschild, 1993: 270). Men's ability to overpower women sexually—by right—establishes them as master.

O'Sullivan's comparison of gang rapists and batterers suggests that in some respects, there are remarkable similarities in the dynamics of marital rape and gang rapes. Both appear to turn on "general beliefs in male supremacy, hostility toward women, and different standards for sexual behavior in men and women" (O'Sullivan, 1998: 89). However, there is also a crucial difference: "Gang rape is 'about' the relationship among men doing it rather than their relationship to they woman they are abusing.... [Marital rape] is more instrumental than expressive, with the goal of regulating the relationship between the man and his wife" (O'Sullivan, 1998: 105). In other words, gang rape has a different audience in mind, with a slightly different purpose. It is a display of sexual prowess for the group. It is a communal exercise whereby men degrade women while simultaneously proving their solidarity, their sexuality, and their manhood. They share in one another's sexuality through their sharing of the victim (O'Sullivan, 1998; Martin and Hummer, 1995; Sanday, 1998). Moreover, that gang rapes are especially likely in college fraternities should not come as a surprise, since these groups tend to be consumed with constructing and displaying masculinity. Few contexts are so meticulously orchestrated around a conception of hegemonic masculinity that "stresses competition, athleticism, dominance, winning, conflict, wealth, material possessions, willingness to drink alcohol, and sexual prowess vis à vis women" (Martin and Hummer, 1995: 473). In brief, few contexts provide such a ready recipe for gang rape as a display of heterosexuality, misogyny, and loyalty.

Just as in other situations involving coerced sex, gang rapists perceive their victims as sexual commodities. Patricia Yancey Martin and Robert Hummer's (1995) investigation of fraternities suggests that sexual violence against women is seen by members as a sport or game in which women collectively are pawns, and in which the goal is to score sexually. Non-fraternity rapists share this notion of using a woman—any woman—as a vessel for a group adventure. The challenge is to perform for the group, regardless of the wishes of the interchangeable victim. As expressed by one such rapist,

> We felt powerful, we were in control. I wanted sex and there was peer pressure. She wasn't like a person, no personality, just domination on my part. Just to show I could do it—you know, macho. (Scully and Marolla, 1993: 39)

Male sexual prowess is performed at the expense of the victim's autonomy. The victims are natural and ready outlets for the satisfaction of males' "explosive" or "insatiable" sexual appetites (Sanday, 1998; Messerschmidt, 1993). While men voluntarily and enthusiastically enact what is for them normal masculinity, their female victims are involuntarily and unwillingly forced to play the feminine role into which the culture has cast them: sexual conduits whose own pleasure is unimportant.

Women who are victims of gang rape are not in a position to exercise their autonomy. The sheer fact of being outnumbered by two, three, or seven men is itself an obstacle to resistance. Peggy Sanday cites one such case, where the victim was virtually paralyzed with fear:

> The 17–year-old freshman woman went to the fraternity "little sister" rush party with two of her roommates. The roommates left early without her. She was trying to get a ride home when a fraternity brother told her he would take her home after the party ended. While she waited, two other fraternity members took her into a bedroom to "discuss little sister matters." The door was closed and one of the brothers stood blocking the exit. They told her that in order to become a little sister she would have to have sex with a fraternity member. She was frightened, fearing they

would physically harm her if she refused. She could see no escape. Each of the brothers had sex with her, as did a third who had been hiding in the room. During the next two hours, a succession of men went into the room. There were never less than three men with her, sometimes more. (1998: 498)

Alternatively, the victim's ability to consent may be compromised by her state of intoxication, a factor that is unfortunately often used to "blame the victim." If she had been a "good girl," if she had acted "like a lady," she would not have put herself in the position to be so dramatically violated. Chris O'Sullivan traces this to the cultural perception that women who do not adhere to their roles as gatekeepers of sexuality are "fair game for exploitation" (1998: 85). Such popular interpretations, however, deny the complicity of the offenders in providing the liquor and in exploiting the victim when she is vulnerable.

The literature on campus gang rape, in particular, reveals the normativity of alcohol use as a precedent to gang rape (O'Sullivan, 1998; Sanday, 1998). Offenders often plan and coordinate their victims' excessive consumption of alcohol. One fraternity member boasted that

> We provide them with "hunch punch" and things get wild. We get drunk and most of the guys end up with one.... Hunch punch is a girl's drink made up of overproof alcohol and powdered Kool-Aid, no water or anything else, just ice. It's very strong. Two cups will do a number on a female. (Martin and Hummer, 1995: 477–478)

The "number" that such drinks do on women is to render them incapable of resistance, either because of a loss of coordination or a loss of consciousness. That women are but the vessel of men's sexuality is especially evident here, where women could not possibly be expected to attain any pleasure from the act. This bothers the participants not at all; it is in fact seen as an extension of women's normative sexual passivity. A couple of examples will suffice to illustrate the dynamics whereby fraternity men take advantage of their intoxicated victims.

In the Florida State case, the ringleader met the victim at an off-campus drinking club and invited her back to his fraternity for a "party."... At the fraternity house, her host gave her a bottle of wine, which she finished. He carried her unconscious to the communal shower room and summoned three other men. His best friend left his own date waiting downstairs in the hall to join in the assault. After sexually assaulting her, the four classy men wrote fraternity slogans and "hatchet gash" on her thighs, dumped her in the entry hall of another fraternity and called 911. At the hospital, her blood alcohol level was found to be potentially lethal and semen from several different men was found in her vagina. (O'Sullivan, 1998: 101)

It was her first fraternity party. The beer flowed freely and she had much more to drink than she had planned. It was hot and crowded and the party spread out all over the house, so that when three men asked her to go upstairs, she went with them. They took her into a bedroom, locked the door and began to undress her. Groggy with alcohol, her feeble protests were ignored as the three men raped her. When they finished, they put her in the hallway, naked, locking her clothes in the bedroom. (Sanday, 1998: 498)

Whether drunk or sober, the victim's sexuality often is invoked to justify the perpetrator's behavior. As noted previously, victims often are portrayed as "whores" or "sluts" who have violated the standards of femininity, and so deserve to be themselves violated for their impropriety. In such contexts, women are presumed to enjoy gang rape. This allows the construction of the perpetrators as men involved in the legitimate performance of heterosexuality with willing participants. Their behavior is a natural reaction to the seductress in their midst. It is not they who have schemed to assault the victim, but the victim who has somehow schemed to "fire them up." The following example illustrates the presumption of consent:

> A 19-year-old woman student was out on a date with her boyfriend and another couple. They were all drinking beer and after going back to the boyfriend's dorm room, they smoked two marijuana cigarettes. The

other couple left and the woman and her boyfriend had sex. The woman fell asleep and the next thing she knew she awoke with a man she didn't know on top of her trying to force her into having sex. A witness said the man was in the hall with two other men when the woman's boyfriend came out of his room and invited them to have sex with his unconscious girlfriend. (Sanday, 1998: 498)

That victimized women are presumed to be always willing, available, and receptive to male "advances" also is apparent in the rationales of gang rapists interviewed by Diana Scully and Joseph Marolla (1993). Rapes of women hitchhikers were justified under the pretext that they must have been prostitutes and therefore "enjoyed it." Gang date rape involved the planned communal assault of one group member's date. This, too, was rendered acceptable by impugning the sexual promiscuity—read inappropriateness—of the victims: "Usually the girl had a bad reputation, or we know it was what she liked" (Scully and Marolla, 1993: 40). One participant admitted to committing twenty or thirty such assaults on "girls who were known to do this kind of thing." He also believed that "it might start out as rape, but then they [the women] would quiet down and none ever reported it to the police" (Scully and Marolla, 1993: 40). Obviously, the women "enjoyed" or even "invited" their victimization. Consequently, men imagined themselves to have established their sexual prowess by their demonstrated ability to satisfy even a protesting woman.

Such demonstrations are at the core of gang rapes. To themselves and their peers, such behavior is not deemed aberrant or deviant. Quite the contrary, it is a show of manliness and comaraderie among friends. Again, it is apparent that the intended audience is not the woman involved. She is a secondary player, interchangeable with any other available woman. What is important is that the men involved solidify their individual and collective identities as heterosexual performers. The show is for the coparticipants. The communal activity permits the concurrent display of sexuality, fearlessness, and comaraderie. O'Sullivan expresses the value of gang rape to its participants as "a performance put on for other men, proving one's masculinity through heterosexual dominance and exploitation of women. It is a way of co-operating and competing with male friends through a shared risky and risqué, socially sanctioned (in the sense that it's something to brag about among men, although not something to write home to mother about) behavior" (1998: 105). Gang rape signifies the commitment of the participants to the group and to masculine norms of behavior. It is a very public enactment of loyalty to the brotherhood of Man over Woman. And it is a confirmation of the aggressive sexuality of each of the group members. That it is seen as a crucial test of one's heterosexual mastery is evident in the finding that those who refuse to participate are branded "unmanly," possibly homosexual (Sanday, 1998; Martin and Hummer, 1995).

CULTURAL PERMISSION TO HATE

An implicit thread has run throughout this discussion of gender-motivated violence: cultural permission to hate and to victimize women is typically bestowed upon men. Abundant myths, stereotypes, images, and ideologies simultaneously support gendered and unequal relations of power, labor, and sexuality as well as the resultant gender-motivated violence. Cultural assumptions about men, women, and the relationships among and between them condone and often encourage victimization of women as women, because they commonly objectify and minimize the value of women. In other words, "men physically and emotionally abuse women because they *can,* because they live in a world that gives them permission" (Pharr, 1988: 14). For example, actual and potential victims of sexual violence are all too often portrayed as fantasizing about and therefore enjoying their victimization. Movie images, pornographic magazines, even commercial advertising often paint a portrait in which women may initially resist, but ultimately willingly and enthusiastically participate in their own violation. Hence, "No Means Yes" and other such rape myths abound to distance the offender from culpability. "Boys will be boys," after all!

This discussion of gender-motivated violence began with the acknowledgment that our culture assumes a masculine and feminine essence—traits, characteristics, capacities that clearly distinguish Man from Woman. Part of that binary is the construction of women as either "good" or "bad," depending upon their adherence to their prescribed role (Sheffield, 1987). If femininity is enacted through nurturing, submissive, passive behavior, then the woman is good; if it is enacted through selfishness, aggression, promiscuity, or resistance, the woman is bad and so deserves whatever she gets by way of violent retribution. The Bad Woman is herself to blame for male violence directed at her: "women who are beaten by their intimate partners, raped by strangers or acquaintances, or even killed somehow deserve their victimization because of their own fallibility, misjudgement or provocation" (Miller, 1995: 232–233).

Cultural constructs surrounding women's experiences of violence overwhelmingly lay blame on the victim. If only she had not been out alone; if only she had prepared a hot, appetizing meal; if only she had not dressed so provocatively, she would not have been assaulted, battered, or raped. In other words, if she had "done femininity" appropriately rather than oppositionally, she would not have suffered. Violence is a predictable response to women who violate the gender order. In contrast, the male offender is exonerated, often rewarded. He is "doing masculinity" normally; he is performing masculinity in a socially sanctioned, legitimate manner, in accordance with his right and duty to chasten non-conforming women.

Sheffield (1989) identifies what she refers to as "gender violence myths" that perform this function of releasing males from culpability. Rape myths include:

- all women want to be raped
- no woman can be raped if she doesn't want it
- she asked for it
- she changed her mind *afterward*
- she said no but meant yes
- if she's going to be raped, she may as well lie back and enjoy it

Among the wife-battering myths:

- some women need to be beaten
- a good smack will straighten her out/shut her up
- she needs a beating to keep her in line
- she must have provoked it

Sexual harassment is often justified because:

- she was seductive/flirting
- she was in a workplace where she didn't belong
- she misunderstood "friendliness"

In the context of a culture that holds so tenaciously to these sorts of excuses, women who are assaulted become suspect. She must have done something "inappropriate" to incite the violence. Moreover, it is not just the perpetrators who cling to the popular mythologies. Friends and family of the victim are likely to question her role in the process; police officers carry the assumptions into their investigation of reports of gender-motivated violence; and judges and attorneys are infamous for their tendency to try the victim rather than the offender in cases of sexual assault and domestic violence.

Sheffield (1987) argues elsewhere that the good/bad woman dichotomy is especially problematic for women of color, who, according to strictures of the racial hierarchy, can never achieve "goodness." It is the presumption of the inherent inferiority of black women that long left them vulnerable to unpunished and unpunishable rape at the hands of white men. That black women are uniquely vulnerable to gendered violence is implicit in Opal Palmer Adisa's observation that "African American women are more likely to be raped than any other woman, are least likely to be believed, and most often watch their rapists treated with impunity or mild punishment" (1997: 196). Women of color typically are not viewed as "real" victims. More so even than white women, women of color are characterized as inviting violent assault. The latitude allowed them for enacting femininity is even more circumscribed than that allowed white women. African-American women, for example, are "safe" only when enacting the roles of "mule" or "Mammy." So narrow are these notions of black womanhood that few women could possibly live up to them. Consequently, black women are assigned the label—often by black and white cultures alike—Jezebels, matriarchs, or uppity black women. It is this intersection of race, gender, and sexuality that shapes the victimization of black women and other women of color (Crenshaw, 1994; Collins, 1993). As noted earlier, it is the Jezebel image of the black prostitute that is perhaps most damning. It constructs black women as sexually promiscuous and therefore enticing, seductive. It is "impossible" to rape a prostitute since she is always on the job.

Aída Hurtado confirms the contrasting imagery of white and black femininity. While the former share in the privilege of white men through their enactment of emphasized femininity, the latter are denied such access and are instead the objects of white masculine power and aggression:

> In many ways the dual conception of women based on race—"white goddess/black she-devil, chaste virgin/nigger whore, the blond blue-eyed doll/the exotic 'mulatto' object of sexual craving"—has freed women of color from the distraction of the rewards of seduction. Women of color "do not receive the respect and treatment—mollycoddling and condescending as it sometimes is—afforded to white women." (Hurtado, 1989: 846; quoting Joseph, 1981)

In other words, race conditions the gender imagery to which women are held accountable, especially in terms of their sexuality. While both white women and women of color are vulnerable to gendered violence, the cultural permission for such victimization varies dramatically. As argued above, white women are often victimized because they are perceived to have crossed some boundary of appropriate feminine behavior; women of color because they are perceived to be, "by nature," sexually available and provocative. In short, white men's subordination of white women and women of color "involves holding them accountable to normative conceptions of essential womanly nature in different ways" (West and Fenstermaker, 1993: 168).

ANTI-GAY VIOLENCE AND THE CONSTRUCTION OF GENDER

As the foregoing discussion suggests, the contemporary practices of gender politics result in a situation where *men in general* benefit from the subordination of women. Clearly, a dominant masculinist project is the subordination of women by men. However, no less important is the "denial of authority to some groups of men" (Connell, 1987: 109). Significantly, the intersection of the division of labor, power, sexuality, and culture, as outlined above, means that there also exists a hierarchy of masculinities in which some are subordinated to others. Relations of power operate between masculinities and femininities, but also between an array of masculinities. Not all men share in the ability to exercise control at either the macro- or microsocial level. Below a hegemonic masculinity are arrayed a series of subordinated masculinities. Working-class men are subordinate to capitalists; black men to white; homosexuals to heterosexuals. Goffman may have overstated the case only slightly when he identified ideal—or "hegemonic"—masculinity as "a young, married, white, urban, northern, heterosexual Protestant father, of college education, fully employed, of good complexion, weight and height, and a recent record in sports.... Any male who fails to qualify in any of these ways is likely to view himself—during moments at least—as unworthy, incomplete and inferior" (1963: 128). The crucial point here is that the nonqualifiers not only "feel" inferior, but are so judged. This is the standard according to which the hierarchy of masculinities is created, resulting in stigmatized and marginalized "out-groups." It is among these subordinated masculinities that we find homosexuals.

Herek explicitly places homophobic violence in its sociocultural context: "Anti-gay violence is a logical, albeit extreme extension of the heterosexism that pervades American society. *Heterosexism* is defined here as an ideological system that denies, denigrates and stigmatizes any nonheterosexual form of behavior, identity, relationship or community" (1992: 89). From this point of reference,

Herek goes on to trace the ideological and institutional practices that serve to denigrate and marginalize gay men and lesbians. From the exclusion of gays from civil rights and hate crime protections, to biblical condemnations of homosexuality as "unnatural," to curricular constraints on positive presentations of homosexuality, heterosexism is transmitted through cultural institutions (Herek, 1992: 90). The implication of this is that gays are subsequently rendered invisible at best, worthy of persecution at worst.

As one potential resource in the accomplishment of gender, gay-bashing plays the dual role of reaffirming the perpetrator's ability to "do gender," while simultaneously punishing the victim's propensity to "do gender inappropriately." At one and the same time, this practice serves to define, regulate, and express sexuality. It is a forceful resource by which young men, in particular, can regulate challenges to the binaries of gender and sexuality. In short, both hegemonic and subordinate forms of masculinity are shaped and maintained through active homophobia. In particular, hegemonic masculinity is accomplished through the simultaneous valuation of aggressive heterosexuality and the denunciation of homosexuality.

GAY-BASHING AS A RESOURCE FOR CONSTRUCTING MASCULINITIES

Violence against homosexuals is not a new problem (Bensinger, 1992). Historically, it has been a legally sanctioned policy, as in medieval Europe or the colonial United States where sodomy was punishable by various forms of mutilation, or even death. Homosexuals were imprisoned and exterminated alongside German Jews in Nazi death camps (Herek and Berrill, 1992: 1). Some American "liberators," noting the pink triangles worn by gay men in the camps, returned the "deviants" to their prisons in sympathy with the Nazis' intentions (Gran, 1995; Heger, 1980; Plant, 1986). The McCarthy era in the United States was a period of extensive legal and extralegal persecution of gay men and lesbians (Duberman, 1993; Adam, 1995).

While most (but not all) American states have eliminated legislation that would criminalize the sexual practices of gays and lesbians, the gay community continues to suffer as victims of hatred, harassment, and violence. Moreover, attacks against homosexuals tend to be among the most brutal acts of hatred. They often involve severe beatings, torture, mutilation, castration, and sexual assault. They are also very likely to result in death (Comstock, 1991; Levin and McDevitt, 1993). NGLTF annual audits consistently report disproportionate evidence of "overkill" in gay-related homicides (1996; 1997; 1998). In fact, more than 60 percent of such homicides show evidence of "rage/hate-fueled extraordinary violence...(such as dismemberment, bodily and genital mutilation, use of multiple weapons, repeated blows from a blunt object, or numerous stab wounds)" (NGLTF, 1995: 18). Frequently, the mutilation or dismemberment follows death, as if to wipe out the victim's identity.

What accounts for the persistence of violence against gays? Perhaps a consideration of the common traits shared by its perpetrators provides some insight. Consistently, the data show that they are "predominantly ordinary young men" (Comstock, 1991: 2; Hamm, 1994). In particular, they are young white men or adolescents, often from working-class or middle-class backgrounds (Berk, Boyd, and Hamner, 1991; Berrill, 1992; Hamm, 1994). With this in mind, Comstock is quite right to insist that sociological and sociocultural, rather than psychodynamic, processes are at work. It is vital to recognize anti-gay violence as an active exercise in the construction of gender. Such an understanding allows us to examine hate crime in its immediate subjective context by drawing attention to the interactions and implied meanings of actors and their audiences. Yet it also demands that we consider the historical and cultural contexts that inform those meanings, so that we might understand the ways in which identities are shaped both by our engagement with others and by our structural background.

Gay-bashing provides young men in particular with a very useful resource for doing gender, especially for accomplishing hegemonic masculinity.

It is an interesting paradox that while masculinity is assumed to be "natural," it also appears to be so fragile "that one must always guard against losing it" (Hopkins, 1992: 123; Kaufman, 1992). Gay-bashing thus allows perpetrators to reaffirm their own masculinity, their own aggressive heterosexuality, in opposition to this nonconformist threat. As an activity, it is tailor-made for this construction of masculinity, since it allows the visible demonstration of the most salient features of manliness: aggression, domination, and heterosexuality.

Recall West and Zimmerman's (1987) contention that gender is situationally managed. Doing gender is to be understood in the context in which it occurs. The task of gender is reaccomplished in a diversity of social settings, each of which may demand different accountable activities. Thus, "even though one is recognized as a man (or boy) prior to evidenced masculinity, evidence must also be forthcoming in order to merit that continued 'unproblematic' status" (Hopkins, 1992: 124). In this context, the practice of violence against gays provides one such situational resource for men to establish their masculinity. And it does so in both negative and positive terms: by establishing what a man *is not* and what he *is*.

Gay-bashing provides proof of manhood, which is especially important for young males who are constantly challenged to prove their virility. The perpetrator proves, by his actions, that he is unafraid to fight, as any real man must be. And, he is unafraid of engaging in illegal attacks on his victims—again a sign of his manhood.

Like all social actors, gay-bashers act with an eye to their audience (Herek, 1992; 1992b). How will they be evaluated? What is the message their actions carry? In part, violence against gays provides visible, documented proof of offenders' unquestionably straight sexuality. As Messerschmidt contends, physical violence against gay men in front of other young, white, working-class men reaffirms what they define as natural and masculine sex—heterosexuality (1993: 100). Karen Franklin takes a similar position, arguing that "in group assaults the homosexual victim can be seen as fundamentally

a dramatic prop, a vehicle for a ritualized conquest through which assailants demonstrate their commitment to heterosexual masculinity and male gender norms" (1998: 12). Gay-bashing provides a resource through which young men can confirm not only what is natural, but what is culturally *demanded* of them in performance of their particular style of masculinity.

Thus, while violence against gays serves as a verification of the perpetrator's bravery and machismo, it also serves as a disclaimer of his homosexuality. The taunts the young adolescent males often favor—such as, "What are you, a fag?"—are frequent reminders of the inviolability of the artificial boundaries between the sexes. Hostility against homosexuals can be accounted for as an assertion of its opposite, that is, heterosexuality. The gay-basher could not possibly be mistaken for a homosexual, since he willingly assaults homosexuals. The active substantiation of his homophobia simultaneously removes any doubt about the offender's sexuality. Similarly, the epithets cast by the perpetrator distance him from the dreaded Other, once again offering obvious proof that he is of the "in-group" rather than the "out-group" constituted by homosexuals. The Blue Boys, an avowed homophobic group of young men interviewed by Michael Collins, offer an extreme illustration of this point:

> We chose the blue baseball bat because it's the color of the boy. The man is one gender. He is not female. There is no confusion. Blue is the color of men, and that's the color that men use to defeat the anti-male, which is the queer. (1992: 193)

As this statement implies, gay-bashing also provides the ideal context in which young men can conclusively establish what they *are,* in other words, manly, virile men. Recall the importance of accountability here: one must be seen (and interpreted) to be masculine in the prevailing sense of the term. And violence is a tried and true means to this end....

As outlined previously, "doing gender" explicitly is concerned with structuring differences between males and females, with creating "essential" natures specific to each gender. Consequently, contemporary sexuality (and marriage) is predicated upon the normalcy of opposite-sex relationships. Homosexuals apparently refuse to play this game. They do not sufficiently accomplish either maleness or femaleness; they have not even attempted to become one of the "natural" sexes. Homosexuals refuse to be forced into these binary categories of masculine or feminine. Thus, by definition, homosexuality transcends the boundaries our culture has so conscientiously erected between the genders, lapsing into the category of deviance. Additionally, gays violate the sanctity, the "naturalness" of established gender identities. That is, they are sanctioned for *presumably* failing to practice either absolute femininity or masculinity. Such violations ultimately make them vulnerable to stigmatization and finally to violent repression. William Hassel's two teenage assailants clearly were hostile to his refusal to "be a man." Throughout the attack—at knifepoint—the pair challenged his masculinity, beating him for crossing the gender line, for being a failed man. They threatened to complete his emasculation physically. According to Hassel's account,

> They made me address them as "Sir." They made me beg them to be made into a real woman. They threatened to castrate me. They threatened to emasculate me. They called me "Queer," "Faggot." One of them urinated on me. They threatened me with sodomy. (1992: 144–145)

. . . Because homosexuality challenges the fundamental assumptions of what it is to "be a man," it inevitably is assigned an inferior status in this gender hierarchy. The institutional norm of heterosexual masculinity is affirmed in the media, legislation and social policy, and police practices, to name but a few (Kaufman, 1987; Carrigan et al., 1987). The 1978 Briggs Initiative was an early attempt to expel homosexuals from the education system. Restrictions on "domestic partner" benefits disadvantage gay couples. And tax status is based on the traditional heterosexual marriage—doubly problematic since most states outlaw gay marriages.

At the level of the informal social order, gay-bashing serves a no less effective, but certainly more violent, disciplinary mechanism. Violence is used as a tool of subordination intended to maintain the powerlessness of homosexuals. Tim Carrigan et al. are worthy of a lengthy quotation on this point:

> The history of homosexuality obliges us to think of masculinity not as a single object with its own history but as being constantly constructed within the history of an evolving social structure, a structure of sexual power relations. It obliges us to see this construction as a social struggle going on in a complex ideological and political field in which there is a continuing process of mobilization, marginalization, contestation, resistance, and subordination. It forces us to recognize the importance of violence, not as an expression of subjective values or of a type of masculinity, but as constitutive practice that helps to make all kinds of masculinity. (1987: 89)

Violence simultaneously conditions both hegemonic and subordinate masculinities. As such, it is an integral weapon within the structure of power relations. This is especially obvious when gays collectively challenge their subordination. The last decade has seen a dramatic increase in the activity and visibility of a vibrant gay and lesbian movment. This visibility has been a two-edged sword. On the one hand, it has resulted in valuable gains in gay rights. On the other hand, it has engendered great hostility and backlash. Just as Native Americans and women, for example, are at increased risk of victimization during periods of activism, so too are gays more vulnerable when they find their voice. This is evident in the increased violence leading up to gay rights referenda in Maine, Colorado, and Oregon. Kathleen Sarris's experiences in Indiana are not atypical. She had played a leadership role in Justice, Inc.'s efforts to promote pro-gay activities. Following a widely publicized press conference, Sarris suffered weeks of telephone harassment and hate mail. The harassment culminated in a brutal beating and sexual assault by a man claiming to be acting for God; that what he was doing was God's revenge on me because I was a "queer," and getting rid of me would save children and put an end to the movement in Indiana. (Sarris, 1992:202)

...Ultimately, then, gay-bashing is a practice motivated by the discomfort, even hostility toward those Others who cross the gender boundaries of sexuality, power and labor, who refuse to "do gender appropriately." In almost Durkheimian fashion, violence against gays reasserts the normative order around gender by rewarding the perpetrators (explicitly or implicitly) for accomplishing masculinity in a "manly manner" while punishing the victims for refusing to do so.

REFERENCES

Adam, Barry. 1995. *The Rise of a Gay and Lesbian Movement.* New York: Twayne Publishers.

Adams, Peter, Alisa Towns, and Nicole Garvey. 1995. "Dominance and Entitlement: The Rhetoric Men Use to Discuss Their Violence Towards Women." *Discourse and Society.* 6(13): 387–406.

Adisa, Opal Palmer. 1997. "Undeclared War: African American Women Writers Explicating Rape," in *Gender Violence: Interdisciplinary Perspectives,* ed. Laura O'Toole and Jessica Schiffman. New York: New York University Press, 194–208.

Belknap, Joanne. 1996. *The Invisible Woman: Gender, Crime and Justice,* Belmont, CA: Wadsworth.

Bensinger, Gad. 1992. "Hate Crime: A New/Old Problem." International Journal of Comparative and Applied Criminal Justice 16: 115–123.

Berk, Richard, Elizabeth Boyd, and Karl Hamner. 1992. "Thinking More Clearly about Hate-Motivated Crimes," in *Hate Crimes: Confronting Violence against Lesbians and Gay Men,* ed. Gregory Herek and Kevin Berrill. Newbury Park, CA: Sage, 123–143.

Berrill, Kevin. 1993. "Anti-Gay Violence: Causes, Consequences and Responses," in *Bias Crime: American Law Enforcement and Legal Responses,* ed. Robert Kelly. Chicago: Office of International Criminal Justice, 151–164.

————. 1992. "Anti-Gay Violence and Victimization in the United States: An Overview," in *Hate Crimes: Confronting Violence against Lesbians and Gay Men,* ed.

Gregory Herek and Kevin Berrill. Newbury Park, CA: Sage, 19–45.

Browne, Angela. 1995. "Fear and the Perception of Alternatives: Asking 'Why Battered Women Don't Leave' Is the Wrong Question," in *The Criminal Justice System and Women,* ed. Barbara Price and Natalie Sokoloff. New York: McGraw-Hill, 228–245.

Brownmiller, Susan. 1974. *Against Our Will.* New York: Simon and Schuster.

Brownworth, Victoria, 1991. "An Unreported Crisis," *The Advocate,* November 5: 50, 52.

Caputi, Jane. 1993. "The Sexual Politics of Murder," in *Violence against Women,* ed. Pauline Bart and Eileen Moran. Newbury Park, CA: Sage, 5–25.

————, and Diana Russell. 1992. "Femicide: Sexist Terrorism against Women," in *Femicide: The Politics of Woman Killing,* ed. Jill Radford and Diana Russell. New York: Twayne Publishers, 13–21.

Carrigan, Tim, Bob Connell, and John Lee. 1987. "Toward a New Sociology of Masculinity," in *The Making of Masculinities: The New Men's Studies,* ed. Harry Brod. Winchester, MA: Allen and Unwin, 63–100.

Chaiken, Jan. 1998. *Violence by Intimates: Analysis of Data on Crimes by Current or Former Spouses, Boyfriends and Girlfriends.* Washington, DC: Bureau of Justice Statistics, NCJ 167237.

Collins, Michael, 1992. "The Gay-Bashers," in *Hate Crimes: Confronting Violence against Lesbians and Gay Men,* ed. Gregory Herek and Kevin Berrill. Newbury Park, CA: Sage, 191–200.

Collins, Patricia Hill. 1993. "The Sexual Politics of Black Womanhood," in *Violence against Women,* ed. Pauline Bart and Eileen Moran. Newbury Park CA: Sage, 85–104.

————. 1990. *Black Feminist Thought: Knowledge, Consciousness and the Politics of Empowerment.* New York: Routledge.

Comstock, Gary. 1991. *Violence against Lesbians and Gay Men.* New York: Columbia University Press.

Connell, Robert. 1987. *Gender and Power.* Stanford, CA: Stanford University Press.

Crenshaw, Kimberlé Williams. 1994. "Mapping the Margins: Intersectionality, Identity and Violence Against Women of Color," in *The Public Nature of Private Violence,* ed. Martha Albertson Fineman and Roxanne Mykitiuk. New York: Routledge, 93–118.

Curran, Dan, and Claire Renzetti. 1994. "Introduction: Gender Inequality and Discrimination on the Basis of Sexual Orientation," in *Contemporary Societies: Problems and Prospects,* ed. Dan Curran and Claire Renzetti. Englewood Cliffs, NJ: Prentice Hall, 204–209.

Dobash, R. Emerson, and Russell Dobash. 1998. "Cross-Border Encounters: Challenges and Opportunities," in *Rethinking Violence against Women,* ed. Rebecca Dobash and Russell Dobash. Thousand Oaks, CA: Sage, 1–22.

Duberman, Martin. 1993. *Stonewall.* New York: Penguin Books.

Editors of the *Harvard Law Review.* 1990. *Sexual Orientation and the Law.* Cambridge: Harvard University Press.

Espiritu, Yen. 1997. *Asian American Women and Men.* Thousand Oaks, CA: Sage.

Faludi, Susan. 1991. *Backlash.* New York: Anchor Books.

Fenstermaker, Sarah, Candace West, and Don Zimmerman. 1991. "Gender Inequality: New Conceptual Terrain," in *Gender, Family and Economy: The Triple Overlap.* ed. Rae Lesser Blumberg. Newbury Park, CA: Sage, 289–307.

Franklin, Karen, 1998. "Unassuming Motivations: Contextualizing the Narratives of Anti-Gay Assailants," in *Stigma and Sexual Orientation,* ed. Gregory Herek. Thousand Oaks, CA: Sage.

French, Marilyn. 1992. *The War against Women.* New York: Summit Books.

Goffman, Erving. 1963. *Stigma: Notes on the Management of Spoiled Identity.* New York: Touchstone Books.

Grau, Günter, 1993. *Hidden Holocaust?* London: Cassell.

Greene, Beverly. 1997. "Ethnic Minority Lesbians and Gay Men: Mental Health and Treatment Issues," in *Ethnic and Cultural Diversity among Lesbians and Gay Men,* ed. Beverly Greene. Thousand Oaks, CA: Sage, 216–239.

Hamm, Mark, 1994. *American Skinheads: The Criminology and Control of Hate Crime.* Westport, CT: Praeger.

Heger, Heinz. 1980, *The Men with the Pink Triangles.* Boston: Alyson Publications Inc.

Herek, Gregory. 1992. "The Social Context of Hate Crimes: Notes on Cultural Heterosexism," in *Hate Crimes: Confronting Violence against Lesbians and Gay Men,* ed. Gregory Herek and Kevin Berrill. Newbury Park, CA: Sage, 89–104.

———, and Kevin Berrill, 1992. "Introduction," in *Hate Crimes: Confronting Violence against Lesbians and Gay Men,* ed. Gregory Herek and Kevin Berrill. Newbury Park, CA: Sage, 1–10.

hooks, bell. 1992. Black Looks. Boston: South End Press.

———. 1981. *Ain't I A Woman: Black Women and Feminism.* Boston: South End Press.

Hopkins, Patrick, 1992. "Gender Treachery: Homophobia, Masculinity and Threatened Identities," in *Rethinking Masculinity: Philosophical Explorations in Light of Feminism,* ed. Larry May and Robert Strikwerda. Lanham, MD: Rowman and Littlefield, 111–131.

Hurtado, Aída. 1989. "Relating to Privilege: Seduction and Rejection in the Subordination of White Women and Women of Color." *Signs* 14: 833–855.

Kaufman, Michael. 1992. "The Construction of Masculinity and the Triad of Men's Violence," in *Men's Lives,* ed. Michael Kimmel and Michael Messner. New York: Macmillan, 28–49.

Kinsman, Gary. 1992. "Men Loving Men: The Challenge of Gay Liberation," in *Men's Lives,* ed. Michael Kimmel and Michael Messner. New York: Macmillan, 483–496.

Levin, Jack, and McDevitt, 1993. *Hate Crimes: The Rising Tide of Bigotry and Bloodshed.* New York: Plenum.

Lorber, Judith, 1994. *Paradoxes of Gender.* New Haven, CT: Yale University Press.

MacKinnon, Catharine. 1991. "Reflections on Sex Equality under Law." *Yale Law Journal* 100: 1281–1319.

Martin, Patricia Yancey, and Robert Hummer. 1995. "Fraternities and Rape on Campus," in *Race, Class and Gender: An Anthology,* ed. Margaret Anderson and Patricia Hill Collins. Belmont, CA: Wadsworth, 470–487.

Messerschmidt, James. 1997. *Crime as Structured Action.* Thousand Oaks, CA: Sage.

———. 1993. *Masculinities and Crime.* Lanham, MD: Rowman and Littlefield.

Miller, Jean Baker. 1995. "Domination and Subordination," in *Race, Class and Gender in the United States* (3rd ed.), ed. Paula Rothenberg. New York: St. Martin's Press, 57–63.

National Gay and Lesbian Alliance. 1995. *Anti-Gay/Lesbian Violence, Victimization and Defamation in 1994.* Washington, DC: NGLTF Policy Institute.

National Gay and Lesbian Task Force. 1999. *Anti-Gay/Lesbian Violence, Victimization and Defamation in 1998.* Washington, DC: NGLTF Policy Institute.

———. 1998. *Anti-Gay/Lesbian Violence, Victimization and Defamation in 1997.* Washington, DC: NGLTF Policy Institute.

———. 1997. *Anti-Gay/Lesbian Violence, Victimization and Defamation in 1996.* Washington, DC: NGLTF Policy Institute.

———. 1996. *Anti-Gay/Lesbian Violence, Victimization and*

Defamation in 1995. Washington, DC: NGLTF Policy Institute.

———. 1995. *Anti-Gay/Lesbian Violence, Victimization and Defamation in 1994.* Washington, DC: NGLTF Policy Institute.

———. 1994. *Anti-Gay/Lesbian Violence, Victimization and Defamation in 1993.* Washington, DC: NGLTF Policy Institute.

———. 1993. *Anti-Gay/Lesbian Violence, Victimization and Defamation in 1992.* Washington, DC: NGLTF Policy Institute.

O'Sullivan, Chris. 1998. "Ladykillers: Similarities and Divergences of Masculinities in Gang Rape and Wife Battery," in *Masculinities and Violence,* ed. Lee Bowker. Thousand Oaks, CA: Sage, 82–110.

Pendo, Elizabeth. 1994. "Recognizing Violence against Women: Gender and the Hate Crimes Statistics Act." *Harvard Women's Law Journal* 17: 157–183.

Pharr, Suzanne. 1995. "Homophobia as a Weapon of Sexism," in *Race, Class and Gender in the United States* (3rd ed.), ed. Paula Rothenberg. New York: St. Martin's Press, 481–490.

———. 1988. *Homophobia: A Weapon of Sexism.* Inverness, CA: Chardon Press.

Plant, Richard. 1986. *The Pink Triangle: The Nazi War against Homosexuals.* New York: Henry Holt and Company.

Rasche, Christine. 1995. "Minority Women and Domestic Violence: The Unique Dilemmas of Battered Women of Color," in *The Criminal Justice System and Women,* ed. Barbara Price and Natalie Sokoloff. New York: McGraw-Hill, 246–261.

Rothschild, Eric. 1993. "Recognizing Another Face of Hate Crimes: Rape as a Gender-Bias Crime." *Maryland Journal of Contemporary Legal Issues* 4(2): 231–285.

Russell, Diana. 1990. *Rape in Marriage.* Bloomington: Indiana University Press.

Sanday, Peggy. 1998. "Pulling Train," in *Race, Class and Gender in the United States* (4th ed.), ed. Paula Rothenberg. New York: St. Martin's Press, 497–503.

Scully, Diana, and Joseph Marolla. 1993. "Riding the Bull at Gilley's: Convicted Rapists Describe the Rewards of Rape," in *Violence against Women,* ed. Pauline Bart and Eileen Moran. Newbury Park, CA: Sage, 26–46.

Sheffield, Carde. 1989. "Sexual Terrorism," in *Women: A Feminist Perspective,* ed. Jo Freeman. Mountain View, CA: Mayfield, 3–19.

———. 1987. "Sexual Terrorism: The Social Control of Women," in *Analyzing Gender,* ed. Beth Hess and Myra Marx Ferree. Newbury Park, CA: Sage, 171–189.

Stanko, Elizabeth. 1985. *Intimate Intrusions.* London, England: Routledge and Kegan Paul.

Taub, Nadine, and Elizabeth Schneider. 1990. "Women's Subordination and the Role of Law," in *The Politics of Law,* ed. David Kairys. New York: Pantheon, 151–176.

Thorne, Barrie. 1994. *Gender Play: Boys and Girls in School.* New Brunswick, NJ: Rutgers University Press.

Tjaden, Particia and Nancy Thoennes. 1998. *Stalking in America: Findings from the National Violence against Women Survey.* Washington, DC: Centers for Disease Control and Prevention.

von Schulthess, Beatrice. 1992. "Violence in the Streets: Anti-Lesbian Assault and Harassment in San Francisco," in *Hate Crimes: Confronting Violence against Lesbians and Gay Men,* ed. Gregory Herek and Kevin Berrill. Newbury Park, CA: Sage, 65–75.

Warsaw, Robin. 1994. *I Never Called It Rape.* New York: HarperPerennial.

Websdale, Neil, and Meda Chesney-Lind. 1998. "Doing Violence to Women: Research Synthesis on the Victimization of Women," in *Masculinities and Violence,* ed. Lee Bowker. Thousand Oaks, CA: Sage, 55–81.

Weisburd, Steven Bennett, and Brian Levin. 1994. "On the Basis of Sex: Recognizing Gender-Biased Bias Crimes." *Stanford Law and Policy Review,* spring: 21–47.

West, Candace, and Sarah Fenstermaker. 1995. "Doing Difference." *Gender and Society* 9(1): 8–37.

———. 1993. "Power, Inequality and the Accomplishment of Gender: An Ethnomethodological View," in *Theory on Gender/Feminism on Theory,* ed. Paula England. Hawthorne, NY: Aldine de Gruyter, 151–174.

West, Candace, and Don Zimmerman. 1987. "Doing Gender." *Gender and Society* 1(2): 125–151.

Wolfe, Leslie, and Lois Copeland. 1994. "Violence against Women as Bias-Motivated Hate Crime: Defining the Issues in the USA," in *Women and Violence,* ed. Miranda Davies. London: Zed Books, 200–213.

Zion, James, and Elsie Zion. 1996. "Hazko's Sokee'—Stay Together Nicely: Domestic Violence under Navajo Common Law," in *Native Americans, Crime and Justice,* ed. Marianne Nielsen and Robert Silverman. Boulder, CO: Westview, 96–112.

NTOZAKE SHANGE, WITH NO IMMEDIATE CAUSE

every 3 minutes a woman is beaten
every five minutes a
woman is raped/every ten minutes
a lil girl is molested
yet i rode the subway today
i sat next to an old man who
may have beaten his old wife
3 minutes ago or 3 days/30 years ago
he might have sodomized his
daughter but i sat there
cuz the young men on the train
might beat some young women
later in the day or tomorrow
i might not shut my door fast
enuf/push hard enuf
every 3 minutes it happens
some woman's innocence
rushes to her cheeks/pours from her mouth
like the betsy wetsy dolls have been torn
mensis red & split/every
three minutes a shoulder
is jammed through plaster & the oven door/
chairs push thru the rib cage/hot water or boiling sperm decorate her body
i rode the subway today
& bought a paper from a
man who might
have held his old lady onto
a hot pressing iron/i dont know
maybe he catches lil girls in the
park & rips open their behinds
with steel rods/i cdnt decide
what he might have done i only know every 3 minutes
every 5 minutes every 10 minutes/so
i bought the paper
looking for the announcement
there has to be an announcement
of the women's bodies found yesterday/the missing little girl
i sat in a restaurant with my
paper looking for the announcement
a yng man served me coffee
i wondered did he pour the boiling
coffee/on the woman cuz she waz stupid/
did he put the infant girl/in

---

the coffee pot/with the boiling coffee/cuz she cried too much
what exactly did he do with hot coffee
i looked for the announcement
the discovery/of the dismembered
woman's body/the
victims have not all been
identified/today they are
naked & dead/refuse to
testify/one girl out of 10's not
coherent/i took the coffee
& spit it up/i found an
announcement/not the woman's
bloated body in the river/floating
not the child bleeding in the
59th street corridor/not the baby
broken on the floor/

  "there is some concern
  that alleged battered women
  might start to murder their
  husbands & lovers with no
  immediate cause"

i spit up i vomit i am screaming
we all have immediate cause
every 3 minutes
every 5 minutes
every 10 minutes
every day
women's bodies are found
in alleys & bedrooms/at the top of the stairs
before i ride the subway/buy a paper/drink
coffee/i must know/
have you hurt a woman today
did you beat a woman today
throw a child cross a room
  are the lil girl's panties
  in yr pocket
did you hurt a woman today

i have to ask these obscene questions
the authorities require me to
establish
immediate cause

every three minutes
every five minutes
every ten minutes
every day

PART FOUR

(Re)Envisioning Community and Social Change

INTRODUCTION

In the preceding sections of this book, we have examined a variety of theoretical perspectives on sex, gender, and sexuality and presented narrative pieces that challenge many of these constructions; discuss the importance of context and location with regard to behavior, identity, and performance; and delve into the politics of power vis-à-vis the discourses surrounding sex, gender, and sexuality. We know that these classifications and their hierarchies are not concrete, absolute, and unchanging; rather, they are created differently in distinctive historical periods and maintained by various social institutions for the benefit of some and to the detriment of others. At this point, you may be asking, What can we do? Now that we have this knowledge, how can we create change? If so, you are in good company with many of our students, and this section will hopefully address those questions for you.

Our constructions of sex, gender, and sexuality have had and continue to have real-life consequences, and they remain a continuing feature of public and legal discourse. One of the most salient examples today is the dialogue around gay marriage. As of November 2011, Massachusetts, Connecticut, Iowa, Vermont, New York, New Hampshire, and the District of Columbia legally allow same-sex marriages; however, ten states have constitutional amendments banning same-sex marriage, 17 states have constitutional amendments banning both same-sex marriage and civil unions, and both Michigan and Virginia have constitutional amendments banning same-sex marriage, civil unions and *any* contract that approximates marriage in any way. These constitutional amendments are only reversible by the United States Supreme Court. The consequences for gay people who are unable to marry are manifold; marriage comes with a package of more than a thousand federal rights and benefits, ranging from issues of hospital visitation to inheritance to adoption of children. Moreover, LGBTQI people still face a number of basic inequalities along economic, social, medical, and legal lines, which grind exceedingly small.

However, there is reason to be hopeful about social progress in matters of sex, gender, and sexuality. During his three-year tenure, President Obama has repealed the military's "Don't Ask, Don't Tell" policy regarding the right of gays to serve openly in the armed forces. He has also urged Congress to repeal the Defense of Marriage Act, which currently prohibits states from offering "full faith and credit" for same-sex marriages performed in states where gay marriage has been legalized. The decision is likely to be made in early 2012, and it will be interesting to see what, if any, effect it will have on increasing civil rights for LGBTQI individuals.

The increased visibility of queer folks in the political sphere has also given the general populace an unprecedented look into our lives, augmenting our humanity and the reality of our experiences; however, there is evidence to suggest that legal progress and media exposure vis-à-vis LGBTQI folks may be simultaneously affirmative and dangerous. The social stigma surrounding gay, lesbian, bisexual, and trangender-sexual persons still carries myriad and severe consequences for their personal safety. According to the National Coalition of Anti-Violence Programs (NCAVP), there were 27 anti-LGBTQI murders in 2010, a 23 percent increase from 2009 and the second highest number ever recorded, with the majority of victims being HIV-affected and/or LGBTQ people of color. The NCAVP also reported a 13 percent overall increase in LGBTQI-directed hate violence in 2010 (http://www.avp.org/ncavp).

Rape and sexual assault also occur at alarming rates in the United States—more so than in any other developed nation in the world. One in eight women in this country will be raped in her lifetime, and more than a quarter will be assaulted in some way. More alarming, these statistics underestimate the reality, since the vast majority of rapes and sexual assaults go unreported, thus making accurate statistical data impossible to gather. Even without accurate data, it is clear that rape and sexual assault have reached epidemic proportions, and something must be done to reverse this trend.

The bottom line is that while we may have much to celebrate in the way of progress in 2012, we still have a long road ahead of us to reach equality. Many readers may be thinking, "What can I do? The problems seem so vast, and I am only one person." These sentiments have been echoed by our students countless times. Whereas many of the pieces from other parts either theorize or problematize our current constructions of sex, gender, and sexuality, the authors in Part Four provide some theoretical and practical tools for creating positive social change. Some of the following chapters, like the contribution by

Navalta, are personal narratives that share stories of people who have engaged in resistance and social change. Others are more academic, offering suggestions and guidance. They provide a snapshot of contemporary sexual politics and are both informative and inspirational.

Gutierrez discusses an alternative school created for LGBT youths, many of whom had experienced violence in their own schools. Despite issues endemic to segregation, the youths in this context were able to discuss their experiences and to learn in an environment that was free of the violence and harassment they often faced in a public school setting. This case emphasizes the significance of institutional change. By contrast, Woolfe takes a more individual approach, discussing appearance and positive body image among lesbian, gay, bisexual, and transgender persons. In a similar vein, Solomon discusses her positive experiences as a self-identified androgynous lesbian Christian, despite the prevailing social belief that Christianity and gay identification are both mutually exclusive and "wrong." Each of these chapters makes clear the complex linkages among sex, gender, and sexuality, as well as other aspects of identity, in contemporary political and social movements.

Many of the articles in this part also discuss the contributions to social change by groups who have been ignored or elided from the historical record. For instance, Cohen discusses the exclusion of black gays and lesbians from the civil rights movement and the crucial importance of forming coalitions even among people who are facing multiple marginalizations. Chauncey, on the other hand, shows how he and other academics utilized the history of discrimination based on sexuality and sexual practices counter-discursively to overturn anti-sodomy laws that targeted gay men in *Lawrence v. Texas*. Similarly, both Rochlin and Skolnik offer simple rhetorical questionnaires designed to counter-discursively shed light on the privileges held by heterosexual and cis-gendered people, respectively.

Still other authors in Part Four offer concrete solutions and an alternative vision of a society that values social justice and freedom For instance, Lorber argues that we must "degender" society and offers instructions for people to resist strict gender prescriptions in the workplace, family and home, and everyday social interactions. These, she argues, are practical steps that individuals can implement in their daily lives, which can produce profound change over time, bringing men and women closer to full equality and broader human experience. Feinberg also offers a vision of a socially just world in which classifications of sex, gender, and sexuality do not limit and constrain us, but free us for better and more positive possibilities of human experience.

As you read the chapters in this final part, think about the ways that you and the people you know can begin to effect social change in your communities, on your campuses, in your homes, and elsewhere. What kinds of changes need to be made? Think about change at both the theoretical level of knowledge and the level of practice and the ways that these levels are intertwined. Thinking back to the chapters in Part One, how should we conceptualize these identities and practices? Do our current theories and definitions help us to understand, or actually obscure, the realities of sex, gender, and sexuality? Which theoretical perspectives do you now find most useful? How can we embrace social activism from an intersectional perspective? Are you a member of any of the movements discussed in these chapters? If so, what have you contributed, and in what ways can you continue to do so? What does it mean to be an ally? Are there movements or causes that appeal to you? If you are involved, in what ways is your activist community exclusive? How can the community reach out to those who are not represented in the movement? How do your political actions further marginalize those who are already in precarious situations? Whatever your involvement, remember the words of Margaret Mead: "Never underestimate the power of a small group of committed people to change the world. In fact, it is the only thing that ever has."

ONE IN FRONT OF THE OTHER

DISCUSSION QUESTIONS

1. How does the author reconcile her religion and her sexual identity?
2. How do religion, race/ethnicity, and sexuality intersect in Navalta's life? Can we understand her experience as a lesbian without also examining these other aspects of her identity?
3. Which facets of your identity and background do you think have the greatest impact on your sexuality? Why?

We march.

Our hearts provide the beat to which

my feet your feet our feet

march.

Boom-boom-boom-boom.

"Dyke!"

Yeah, so what.

"But you're Catholic. You're Filipino. You're YOU."

And?!

I march on, annoyed, perturbed.

I hold my sign high; Sappho would be pleased.

"Sinners!"

God, where do these people come from?

Boom-boom-boom-boom.

What color do you bleed?

Red. Yellow. Rainbow.

Choose one—call me what you like.

I am queer. I am Asian.

I am, I am, I am.

I "came out" in the spring of my junior year of high school. Perhaps I should set the scene: large Texan city with sprinklings of Filipinos, richly Roman Catholic, and, consequently, ridiculously conservative. So where's a queer gal like *me* gonna fit in?

Church.

Of all places, church had to accept me. Unfortunately, this only lasted until the winter of my high school senior year but three extremely good things came out of it. I learned to listen to God, to fight what I believe is wrong in the Church, and to love; I found someone to love. The separatist in me drives me to see the difference between homosexual and heterosexual relationships but the truth is if love is there, it doesn't matter who's radiating that fire. After all, love has no gender.

We all have different reasons for falling in love. I fell in love with her heart. Together, we formed such a formidable team that no one dared to question our morals. It's always amazing to see the link love forms between two people because this link never breaks, even if the couple breaks. You should admire one sometime. It's a sight to see.

My queerness is a gift from God. But being born a queer Catholic Asian is a curse, for me, at least. Restrictions bombard me every minute of my life.

There is no respite in my life as a gay Asian, especially a Catholic gay Asian. When I was a child, I used to wish I were a different race because it seemed like my friends had fewer restrictions on their lives. Nowadays, I know that some rules were for my own good but restrictions on my heart and on my body were not.

I love being Asian. The smells from the kitchen before potlucks, the traditions during holidays, the clothes, the people, the music, and the languages always intoxicate me. Imagine how incredibly boring it would be if everyone were white or black. Yellow or red. Gay or straight. Although most Asians' smiles quickly turn to disapproving frowns when confronted with homosexuality, I still cannot help being drawn into my culture. These colors, smells, and sounds—this is me.

I have been told I am going straight to hell for who I am. *Putang ina mo*, how can people do this to their fellow human? And this, also, from the woman who sponsored me during my Confirmation (a Catholic sacrament in which we are "confirmed" in our Catholic faith). Yet, I feel the fire of the Holy Spirit in me every day. Is this the fire that awaits me at the end? If so, then I welcome it with open arms.

To you homophobic people, what drives you to condemn us? Is it born within you to single us out, to point your grubby little fingers at our pride parades, our public displays of affection, and our work? I am driven to dismantle your stereotypes because I am everything but the things you consider to represent a typical lesbian. I don't bash men. I don't dress like a man. I'm not even angry! (Frustrated, yes, but angry? Far from it.)

At times I feel like a walking abortion clinic. This isn't because of the abortion part, but because of the protests that occur at those clinics. (And while I'm staunchly pro-life, I do not in any way condone violent protests.) Thankfully, no one has become violent with me, but I am aware of the dangers as the daily news is filled to the brim with hate crimes directed at gays.

And so I enjoy women. Is that a crime? Is it a mortal sin? We all have crosses to bear, but this isn't mine. My queerness is a gift. It is branded on my Asian identity. I'm in love and she happens to be a woman. Try to blow me up. Just try it. I'm already on fire, baby—and in the meantime, I'll continue marching, one in front of the other. *Boom. Boom. Boom-boom.*

34 • *Nova Gutierrez*

VISIONS OF COMMUNITY FOR GLBT YOUTH

Resisting Fragmentation, Living Whole: Four Female
Transgender Students of Color Speak about School

DISCUSSION QUESTIONS

1. The alternative school identifies the students as transgender, but the students themselves resist the transgender label. Why?
2. What factors enabled these students to speak about their racial, class, sexual, and gender identities so effortlessly?
3. The students in this article experienced harassment and violence in their schools. What suggestions do you have to create a more inclusive educational environment for all students? Looking back on your own experience in high school, would these suggested changes have made a difference for you?

Although race, class, and gender each are recognized and serve as the basis for curriculum and other services (clubs, counseling, mentoring) in many urban schools, particularly progressive, alternative, or charter schools, sexuality is not. However, GLBT schools, like any of the other *segregated* schools, are not by virtue of their existence progressive, radical, or challenging to systemic norms. Although GLBT schools address sexuality, they often fail to effectively address issues of race, class, and gender. For students whose survival, in life and in school, depends on how they navigate their complex and completely integrated identities, a better school is one that provides a space for community-building, role models, historical grounding, and opportunity for active and involved project-based learning; challenges their critical thinking; and raises consciousness and self-awareness.

This paper presents interviews with four male-to-female transgender students of color under the age of 21 at an alternative school for lesbian, gay, bisexual, and transgender youth in the Northeast. The student population of the school is predominantly gay male, with a small number of lesbians. Most of the students are transgender in dress or behavior, but only a small number of them *live as the other gender* or are on hormone therapy. Racially, nearly all of the students are black and Latino, most with backgrounds in the Caribbean. At least one student is an English as a Second Language student;

a few are classified as learning disabled. Many of the students are living on their own, and work in addition to attending school. A few have been homeless at some point in their lives.

The interviews expose the need to advocate for education that acknowledges and addresses the ways that race, sexuality, class, ethnicity, and gender together inform life experience and identity, especially within the context of educational institutions. These interviews point to an additional need to include an activist-oriented curriculum in schools and to include diverse faculty and staff representative of the student population.

I taped interviews in the fall of 2000 with four students who are identified by their alternative school as transgender, but who identify themselves in a variety of terms. I chose to interview transgender students specifically because, according to some of the teachers, the transgender students appeared to be the ones struggling the most to be successful in this school. Some were hustling, and many had begun getting illegal silicone injections to look more like *real* females. Some were angry and volatile; others chronically absent or late. Some were drug users while some were living and working completely on their own in addition to attending school. At least three were doing well in their classes in terms of grades.

At the time of these interviews, there were no transgender employees at the school, so there were no adult mentors who intimately understood what these students were going through on a daily basis. I chose to interview these students so they could speak about their particular experiences in their former schools as well as their experiences at this alternative school. It is crucial to honestly examine alternative schools for GLBT students that are labeled progressive in order to assess whether the education happening in these schools is truly liberatory for all student populations. Within the gay and lesbian community, the subjective voices of transgender people are often marginalized or ignored (Currah & Minter, 2000). Although they have been the objects of study, their life experiences and ideas as subjects are conspicuously absent (Beemyn

& Eliason, 1996). Therefore, the assessment and interpretation of their own school and social experiences as transgender students of color should reveal much about how power operates in their lives and how they resist in a variety of settings, both progressive and traditional.

I interviewed each of the four students—Shari, Cassandra, Debbie, and Marisol—for about an hour and a half in cafes near the school. They were interviewed individually and as a group, in order to have the opportunity to also be in conversation with each other. They seemed very eager to share. Cassandra had recently been expelled from the alternative school, but continued to visit the after-school program. Shari was enrolled in the GED program, while Debbie and Marisol were students in the school. All were students of color and identified as black, Latino, or both. Although the school identified them as transgender (male-to-female), all four of the students criticized the use of the word. Shari commented,

> I never used it [the word] because I never liked it. It sounded like a science project....Oh, you're *transgender,* Shari. Not transgender, Shari. But, like, oh you, we have this transgender [this or that]....They [the school] always refer to you as being transgender...I understand the word and why people use it. That...a lot of times people need labels to better understand things....

Cassandra described her feelings about the label more in depth:

> Honestly I've never heard of the word transgender until I went to [the alternative school]. I've heard of a transsexual and a drag queen. But I never heard of a transgender or a femme queen....Before I went there I always considered myself a woman. To this day I still consider myself a woman. I don't consider myself transgendered, you know. I feel like me. We're women. We're not transgendered. We're who we are. That word transgender. It really does irk me. But I can't say anything about it.
>
> Like after school, the [program] they have there, I'm gonna use the word they use, the transgender

people, when they come in, when you stand there and they take your name and your age and sex, they'll put female, but when you walk away, they slash it and they'll put transgender. TG, and a lot of females and males that are transgender, they get very offended by it. I got offended by it too. But they explained why they do it, like, so I kind of paid it.

The reason why they do that is so that they could get funding for the building, so they could know how many transgender people are coming. How many gay people. But for that I mean they could just put something else. Transgender makes it sound like I'm a transformer, or something, or a toy that could change into something to another, okay, like Cassandra, change. Transform. Like a cartoon or something. It's a label that shouldn't be used. I think if someone's gonna portray themselves as a woman they should be considered as a woman.

Each one of the girls felt a strong desire to operate outside of the label *transgender*, though in their interviews, they recognized the ways that they had been treated differently in the gay, lesbian, and straight communities because they are transgender. Debbie, in particular, spoke about how other people perceive transgenders as wanting to be "legitimate" in the eyes of society. Debbie's analysis of her own identity in relationship to her girlfriend, who identifies as a woman and is lesbian, illustrates a nuanced understanding of the relational nature of identity:

I don't like the fact that you have to be labeled as a transgender, I feel that transgender shouldn't even be a word at all.... Another thing I don't like about that, that if you're transgender, the reason you're transgender is to get with the opposite sex, with the same sex, it's to be approved by the society, whatever. I don't think that's true.... People feel comfortable dressing and being the person they want to be.

You know, because I date a girl, people think that's not right, because, you're a male trying to be a female, because that's one of the reasons you're trying to be a female. You know I don't think of it that way. I think of myself as a female that likes females. A female that likes males and females, just a female at

the moment. I don't think of myself as a female with transgender experience.

If she [my girlfriend] considered herself a male, then I would consider myself to be straight at the moment, [if] I consider myself a female, and she considers herself a male. But, since she considers herself as a female, I consider myself as a lesbian.

When asked about their experiences in the traditional schools they attended before this alternative school, each of the girls spoke about how race and class in addition to their sexuality affected them. Cassandra recalled:

Elementary school was ok. I was trying to figure out my sexuality then. But nobody really bothered me then. My trouble getting spooked, as Marisol puts it, was during junior high, but guys still wanted me anyway. That was in [another state]. Also, it was very nice. I graduated with honors, um, the students were a****; the teachers, forget it, they were jerks. I had really rough teachers that really, really didn't understand children....

In junior high school, when I decided I wanted to be a girl, my teachers gave me a hard time because I was growing nubs for some reason. I don't know why. They were like, oh, we can't call you a different name. And we have to call you *he* and this, that, and the third. And it really hurt me, because, you know, I'm trying to be something else and they're bringing reality into my face and it really bothered me a lot.

Marisol, more explicitly, speaks about her family's economic situation and how it affected which schools she attended. When these students spoke about the different aspects of their racial, class, sexual, and gender identities, they did so effortlessly. Just as they expressed their aversion to the label transgender because it does not capture how they perceive themselves, they spoke of their identities in holistic, completely integrated terms. The identities they speak of depend rather on the contexts of their experiences.

Marisol: [At my elementary school] I made good friends.... I hung out with the boys, I hung out with the girls. I didn't know I was gay. Then one day I just told my mother I wanted to move with my father. And...[when] I went to...[a new] school,...all these people was thinking I was a girl. Like, what's your name, what's your name? So I fell into the role, "My name is Cindy." So I fooled the whole damn school into thinking my name was Cindy.

I was dating my classmates. The teachers were nice to me, I don't know what the hell they said behind my back....So, I went to junior high school. Child, that was the worst experience of my life....I got my a** beat from the time I got there to the time I left, child....It was really severe. Girls used to follow me home and throw rocks to me, like I'm some witch. Like I'm gonna cast some spell on their a**. But anyways, I just felt bad. Nobody cared about me.

Like by eighth grade, I just got more bold. Whatever happens happens. So I was just like, whatever. I just started fighting them and then they started to respect me. That's how I saw it. If I had to defend myself by any means necessary, then that's what I had to do to protect myself....And then I got a nasty...attitude. Cuz I just picked it up off the streets....

When Marisol talks about moving back with her mother, she recalls not fitting into her new high school, in particular because of the racial composition of the school:

Three years ago, I was in a high school [in the northside of the city] and it was cute. At first it was rocky, cuz of the straight boys calling me names or whatever, but then I started to meet gay people there and I started to build friendships....Everybody was hanging out with me and they got used to it, and they paid it no more. I was hanging out with the [girls], I was hanging out with the boys. It felt nice there.

But then I kept messing up on my grades, so they moved me back upstate with my mother so I could live with her. So I was up there like a couple of months, and I was going to this school, and I knew right when I walked in, I did not fit in. Because the students were just so white, it was a white school, and it was like so damn preppy. White students would give you dirty looks. And I got harassed I would say like an average of twenty times, in like four months.

The students were like, it's not that they didn't understand what I was, it was just that they wanted to be mean for no reason. So they was like calling me names. So I felt real bad and I would tell the teachers, and they played it like it was nothing. And I was like, if I fight, do I get suspended and kicked out? I mean what?

So one day me and my mother had a fight, whatever, and I just ran away. I couldn't take it no more. I ran back to the city....I was going from house to house, with my aunts and my mother's friends...it was hurtful....I hadn't been in school to close to like a year and a half. One day I was just talking to Sarah [a counselor] and I told her I wanted to join [the alternative school]. And she was like, okay, I'll see what I can do. Since you are like a member here, since you been here for a long time, you'll be highly recommended by all of the staff here.

This is my first year. It's been decent.

Again, all of the students I interviewed had learned to fight to defend themselves. Cassandra had a black belt in karate. The traditional schools they had all attended before the alternative school had forced them to perfect tough attitudes and sassy mouths as well as fighting skills. Shari had attended a traditional high school in the northside of the city and ran around with a clique of girls who would get into fights along with her, often defending her against harassers. She eventually got expelled for fighting a girl in her school. They all seemed to want a place where they "wouldn't have to use their skills," as Cassandra phrased it.

In so many of the schools, it wasn't only harassment from students that was a hindrance. Teachers, principals, and even security guards posed threats. Debbie recalled the incident that got her expelled from her high school. One of the security guards had called her a "faggot" and pushed her, so Debbie grabbed the guard's stick and slapped her with it. Debbie was suspended, but the guard was not.

When Cassandra began to really explore her sexuality in high school, she was living with her cousin's family, who eventually kicked her out. She moved in with her grandmother and continued to experiment with wearing women's clothing and her coming-out process, for which she was attacked by her uncle, who also went to jail for "busting her eye open." The incident that resulted in her expulsion from her former high school involved Cassandra breaking another student's nose on the lunchroom table after he had harassed and hit her. But she says she didn't really want to come to the alternative school. In fact, Cassandra was expelled from the school a month before our interview.

> I really never wanted to come [here]. How can I say this? It wasn't by choice that I got selected to that school. I was placed there because of my sexuality. And I feel that was very disrespectful on the Board of Education's behalf. Because I really didn't want to go to that school. I was accepted in 1997 and I didn't want to go. I explained that to them and they just put me there anyway....
>
> I had already joined the after-school program and I saw how kids were, how shady [aggressive] they were, and I wasn't shady then, and I didn't know how to throw shade, I was very quiet. I just didn't like that area....Being in my other school for so long, it made me more aggressive and it made me more fighting because I had skills that I never really wanted to use, you know, and I had to use them. After I used them so many times, I felt like I was big and bad because nobody beat me...so that's how my attitude, that's how my stronger attitude came along, and to this day my attitude is still, *No one can beat me.*

Most of the students simply seemed to be demanding respect for their identities—their *whole* identities, not just fragments. They wanted to be acknowledged, listened to, and accepted as whatever gender or persona they chose to put forward. Debbie recalled:

> And then I applied to [the alternative school] and I really didn't get chosen, but the Board of Ed sent me there. And I was like, well, I'm gonna go there any way, because I wanted to start my transformation from a boy to a girl. So when I'm done with my transformation I want to go back to a straight school, to a regular school, where they treat you more fairly than how they do in [the alternative school].

> Well, if they know that I'm a boy they wouldn't treat me fairly, but if they think I am what I appear to be, then they will treat me fairly, but everything else, like...I came [to the alternative school] as a boy, but then I started dressing like a girl. They'll give me all "he's" and push my birth name. And all the other transgenders that came in as transgender, they'll respect them and call them the name they want to be called and they won't do that for me, and I feel that that isn't right.

Given their experiences, the students had very clear ideas about the kind of schools they envisioned as ideal. Their experiences in a place like the alternative school described here show that creating a school around a particular, singular identity might not be the solution. Progressive schools serving these populations must come up with other strategies for education and not rely on traditional systems in nontraditional settings. In a physical sense, adequate facilities and resources are needed to be able to meet the needs of large populations, but also, a diverse faculty and staff, representative of the student population, is needed to provide mentors and role models.

Curriculum must be engaging and activity-centered, with explicit links made between content and real, lived experience. Students who have been disenfranchised and who are on the outside of the political structure of society must receive an education that will help them learn how to organize and build communities that will be able to struggle for justice. Students need safe spaces where they can build trust, talk with each other, talk with caring and empathetic adults, process and theorize about their daily experiences, and use those discussions in classroom activities that are structured to help them actively build new social and academic spaces.

Many of these issues came up when I asked students to describe the schools they envisioned as well as their future aspirations:

SHARI: There's not really much I want to do that I don't think I can. Maybe there's something I haven't thought of that might be hard for me to do, but everything's hard. Nothing is impossible.

DEBBIE: I want a school where everyone is equal, is accepted. It wouldn't be another [school like this]. It would just be equal . . . [everybody] all in one school. I don't think any of that should be segregated at all. And one class I would really want to be in there is gender studies, because a lot of people don't really know much about gender. They just know what's on the television, you know, the media. . . . I read that it's not just what's between your legs, it's what's inside your mind. So, it's like, that's one thing I would have. So that everyone will have an understanding of the gay life. The transgender life. So there will be more of an understanding and there will be more of an acceptance in the community, in the world.

Cassandra spoke about the difficulty of living as a "transgender" and remarked on how society is not accepting of her, either legally or socially. The students recognized the injustice of society, that the rights of citizenship, like marriage, are denied them:

> It's really hard for transgenders more than regular gay men who walk off as men. It's harder for transgenders to be accepted by society because of the way they dress and present themselves to be. . . . For us to walk out of our house it takes a lot of guts, to walk out of our houses like this, cuz I mean, we're trying to be women, and some guys could tell that we're not, and they be like, oh you . . . fag, that's a man or whatever, it's really hard sometimes. Sometimes guys want to bash you. . . .
>
> There's a lot of things in this society that just aren't right. You can't even get married in this society. Gay people can't even get married. And I think that's wrong. Like you can get married, but not legally. . . . I congratulate a lot of transgenders, even females who look like guys, we give them a very big applause because it takes a lot of guts to walk out of your house like that knowing that society will not accept them more than regular gay people.

Marisol spoke at great length about her vision, which was one that summed up the spirit of an inclusive education quite well:

> If I was to make a school, child, you know I would have a school for every sexual orientation, whether gay, straight, lesbian, bisexual, questioning, and transgender youth. I would have a class like Debbie said, gender studies. The reason I would have that class is cuz I feel even though people will know about gay and lesbian and transgender youth and adults, I think they know about it, but they don't fully understand it.
>
> There's some of us out there who actually want to make a difference. I feel that people just don't understand that. They just have a one-track mind. They really don't even really care to understand. Like my grandparents. So I wish there was a school back then that actually taught them about that stuff. It wouldn't be so narrow minded when I speak to them now about it cuz they don't understand what I'm saying. They try to interpret what I'm saying. But I don't think they fully understand. . . .
>
> I would have a school like that. I want everybody to feel comfortable with one another. The straight people could just walk by the gay people and be like, "hey wassup" . . . give them five . . . not be like, that's a fag, watch out for your a** . . . all that other stuff, that's stupid, that's ignorant. . . . I've dealt with that s*** for a long time and I really think it's stupid.
>
> I actually really wanted to become a singer and an actor. A female singer or actor. I see that as, I don't think I would be accepted like that. So really, I want to work more in gay activism and stuff like that. Cuz I want to pave the way for people who have the dreams that I have to like, become a singer or an actor, to don't get judged by it. I want to pave the way to make a difference. . . . it's like people who are actually making a difference, I don't feel like they're reaching out to people like they should, they don't try as hard as they should. . . . I mean it's cute that we have a couple of laws about sexual orientation and things like that and you can't be judged about how you dress or how you act on a job. But there's so much more stuff that people seem to forget.
>
> I just really want to make a difference I just feel that before I die I just want to touch a lot of people and let them know that gay people are not what people interpret us to be . . . we really have minds. We're really strong people. We have ideas. We don't think about all the things that people think we do. I really

want to prove to people that we can also make a difference....

FINAL THOUGHTS

More research is needed: more oral histories, personal narratives, focus groups, ethnographies. The voices of gay, lesbian, and transgender students of color must be part of academic theorizing, especially where education is concerned. Race, class, gender, sexuality, ethnicity, and nation must all be simultaneously addressed in any research about the culture of any school. There need to be spaces within educational institutions and academic literature where students can communicate freely. Ideally, those spaces should be in every classroom. Curriculum ought to be relevant to their lives. Young people need to see adults taking stands, posing critical questions, encouraging dialogue, self-critiquing. That is the first step in building a community of activists within schools. Young people need adults on their side who are willing to model activism and encourage it.

REFERENCES

Beemyn, B., & Eliason, M. (Eds.). (1996). *Queer studies: A lesbian, gay, bisexual, and transgender anthology.* New York: New York University Press.

Currah, P., & Minter, S. (2000). *Transgender equality: A handbook for activists and policymakers.* New York: The Policy Institute of the National Gay and Lesbian Task Force.

35 • *Kate Woolfe*

IT'S NOT WHAT YOU WEAR
Fashioning a Queer Identity

DISCUSSION QUESTIONS

1. How did gendered norms and expectations of lesbians contribute to the author's acceptance within the lesbian community?
2. Why do you think some of the author's friends objected to the heterosexual privilege she "could claim with him" when she fell in love with a man?
3. Explain what the author means when she asserts that the "Lesbian Look" is less about sexual preference than it is about redefining traditional notions of female beauty.
4. How did the bisexual movement make it possible for the author to claim a new identity more easily?

Oddly enough, it was my boyfriend Travis who spotted the first signs of lesbianism in me. "Men's jeans," he would say gloomily, "You know what *that* means." I didn't. I grew up in a white-bread, suburban town where lesbians were invisible. No one ever talked about lesbians, and as far as I knew, I had never seen a lesbian in person or in the media. I don't even remember hearing lesbian jokes growing up, although the hatred toward gay men expressed around my house through fag jokes seemed generally directed at women as well as men.

Somehow I had an idea that lesbians, as women-loving women, were hyperfeminine, with long, wavy hair and flowing, gauzy skirts, à la Stevie Nicks. It wasn't until my first Two Nice Girls concert that I glimpsed The Lesbian Look—short hair, funky glasses, maybe a little leather. Lesbians seemed a homogeneous group at that time, and I wanted nothing more than to be a part of them. Recognizing that I loved women was like finally giving reign to something long buried inside of me.

A series of transformations over the next year brought me closer to the Look, each one punctuated by a defeated sigh from Travis. I had stopped wearing makeup and shaving my legs a few years earlier when I discovered feminism, and the haircut and clothes followed quickly. I found the Look surprisingly liberating, discovering to my amazement that mascara, high heels, long hair, and fingernails were cumbersome in their own way and that without them I was free to be myself: to be intellectual, athletic, messy, hysterical, anything, without worrying about smudged makeup or torn stockings. I loved the serious, capable side of myself that emerged when I was free of those restraints. It was around that time that I stopped measuring my waist size, trying to get a tan, or worrying about the size of my breasts. I had always liked my body as it was, and if anything, I feared and disliked the unwelcome attention from men that came from having a body that more or less fit their expectations. Men now left me alone, which suited me just fine.

Travis and I parted amicably, and I immersed myself fully in lesbian culture. kd lang and Phranc were my new idols, and striding through campus in my Doc Martens and spiky haircut made me feel as if I could conquer the world. I saw myself reflected, validated, and loved through the queer images all around me, from Dykes To Watch Out For to my own girlfriends. I both loved and hated being mistaken for a man, and I pitied straight women, teetering on their high heels and fussing with their makeup. My greatest joy was that glance of recognition while passing another lesbian on the street that said, "I'm one, too." I was in the club, and the secret password was my image. Nothing thrilled me more.

Still, the Look had a certain tyranny of its own. Because it brought recognition and status as a lesbian, those women who deviated from it were often ignored or considered less worthy. Just as women are punished by society at large for stepping out of the traditionally feminine image created for them, I often saw that dykes who didn't look like dykes were considered unenlightened at best and traitors at worst.

My own dyke appearance, while crucial to my sense of self-worth at the time, seemed a little silly even to me at times. I wrote a country song for a high-profile lesbian in town called "Too PC For Me," about my unrequited love for her. Some of the lyrics went, "So I'm wearing turtlenecks and Birkenstocks/ And I'm reading Rita Mae Brown/ The hair is growing in under my arms/ But you're still not around / I even quit eating meat for you/ And I threw away my eye shadow..." and on it goes. My desire to be accepted was so powerful that I probably would have done anything to my appearance. Thankfully, I loved the way my dyke friends and I looked, and playing around with my image led to some truly exhilarating experiences.

One night I went in a rented tuxedo to a fundraiser for the rape crisis center where I volunteered. My date, who bore a striking resemblance to me in the right light, wore a femme, formal dress. Periodically throughout the evening, we would rush to the bathroom to change clothes. We would reemerge in each other's outfits and watch the heads spin. One rape crisis center staffer who was also a photographer adored us and photographed us all night. We played with our roles as well, alternating between butch and femme and feeling free to be anyone and everyone that we could be. I love those photos and the memory of our role-plays— the cavalier, Southern gentleman, the nagging wife, the nervous date. We were beautiful and brave and perfect that night. Being a dyke was a rare and wonderful thing to me, and my sexual identity was inextricably tied up in how I looked.

Much to my surprise, I fell in love with a man around that time. I tried at first to ignore it, and when that proved unsuccessful, I resolutely determined that I would identify as a "lesbian in love with a man," whatever that means. I feared losing my community's approval as well as my own identity. I had dreams that my hair had grown long again, and no matter how often I cut it, it kept coming back. Scott, the object of my affections, told me later that every woman he had ever dated initially thought he was gay, I suppose because of his sensitive, soft-spoken nature. This time, I was too caught up in misgivings about my own sexuality to worry about his.

We began a relationship, and I struggled with my identity constantly. He could never belong in my beloved lesbian community, and I shuddered at the thought of being mistaken for heterosexual. It was that fear that led me to be more out than I had ever been as a lesbian, and I found myself strolling through the supermarket, holding hands with Scott, and wearing a Queer Nation T-shirt.

I knew that my separatist friends objected to the heterosexual privilege I could claim with him, but that privilege seemed more like a curse to me. I hated the way I was treated with him. People could make all kinds of assumptions about our relationship—assumptions about power, sex, who did the dishes. I found it repulsive, and so did Scott, but it haunted me all the same. Perhaps that's why I clung so tightly to my dyke look. While I managed to look like a lesbian to straight people, I was still heterosexual to the queers who saw me with Scott, and I hated that.

As much as I feared assimilating into the heterosexual, mainstream world and losing my hard-won identity, our relationship was so untraditional that

I didn't really have anything to worry about. Scott and I once stayed in a motel outside Houston, where we had gone to see a Paul Simon concert. We walked out of our room that evening, hand in hand, past a bunch of beer-swilling rednecks. As we passed, I heard them whisper, "Those are *fags!*" I had been mistaken for a man many times before, and people always thought my lover was gay, but together we faced a new and unusual form of gay-bashing.

Rednecks weren't the only ones who thought I was a boy. One night Scott and I went to eat in an Italian restaurant that was covered in mirrors on one wall. I hadn't bothered to look around the room very carefully, and I assumed that the reflection next to me was actually another dining room. Out of the corner of my eye, I glimpsed a fellow diner and said to Scott, "You know, that little red-haired boy looks a lot like me!" When I turned for a closer look, I realized I had seen my own reflection and mistaken it for a boy. I never again got mad at anyone for calling me "sir."

After a year or so, Scott and I moved to California, and I finally managed to claim the label "bisexual," thanks largely to the queer politics happening in San Francisco. "Coming out" to me now meant telling my gay and lesbian friends about Scott. I still feared rejection from lesbians and did encounter hesitation from some queer women, but my gay male friends loved our relationship, flirting with Scott and puzzling over how he could really be straight. The bisexual movement had made it acceptable for queers to talk about their sexual encounters with those of the opposite sex, so I began to know lesbians and gay men who slept with men or women without feeling that it diminished their identity or politics. With their support, I've begun to get my queer identity from within, and not necessarily from my clothes or haircut, or from the approval of my peers. I've even toyed with the idea of growing my hair out, taking on a more femme image, just because I love the look and feel of long hair.

I still feel a little distanced from the lesbian community, tending to idolize lesbians and pine away for those dyke days. I was amazed one day when my lesbian housemate, who looks quite femme but is always the consummate lesbian in my mind, said to me, "I love being out in public with you because then I get recognition as a lesbian." Sure enough, other dykes gave us that *look* that she didn't get when out on her own. I had begun to take that thrilling second of eye contact for granted and was amazed to consider that she didn't experience that in public. It seemed crazy to me that she got that recognition when she was out with me, who has been in a relationship with a man for four years now, but not on her own.

On the night I started writing this chapter, I was browsing in a bookstore in Berkeley and ran across *Out in America,* a collection of photographs of queers. I opened the book to a photo of Greg Louganis, looking for all the world like kd lang, with an impish grin and boyish hair. I couldn't believe it was a man and not a dyke I was so attracted to. I rushed to show Scott this beautiful person and remarked, "You know, the more bisexual I become, the less I even bother to figure out the gender of people I'm attracted to." (Don't worry, kd, Greg's got nothing on you, it was probably just a momentary lapse on my part.)

Over the years, I've come to find my own essential truth about the Lesbian Look: it has less to do with one's sexual preference and more to do with a rejection of our culture's values about women. The Look frees us up to be more than decorative, while pointing to new beauty standards for ourselves and other women. As we continue to expand the word "queer" to include gay, lesbian, bisexual, transgendered, etc., I am thrilled to see women of all sexual orientations looking queer as a way of reclaiming their own beauty and value. Still, we can hurt each other by trying to judge each other's politics and sexuality on those terms. A woman as dykey as myself can sleep with men, and someone as femme as my housemate can be the most radical, lesbian feminist.

As for me, it's been years since I even pretended to fuss over my looks, and I love the sight of large, strong, unadorned women. My haircut, clothes, tattoo, and glasses all represent my freedom to define beauty on my own terms and to respect other women's ability to do the same. I know now, however, that if I ever do let go of my look, my politics and identity will stay with me and could never be carted off to Goodwill with my dyke outfits.

36 • *Cindy Solomon*

ANDROGYNY AND FAITH

DISCUSSION QUESTIONS

1. Solomon explains that the Bible depicts various forms of love and marriage. What are some of the examples she gives, and how do these problematize contemporary discourse surrounding "traditional" marriage?
2. In addition to being a lesbian and a Christian, the author also claims an androgynous identity. What does this mean to her?

Cindy Solomon, "Androgyny and Faith." Written for this volume.

3. How does the author reconcile her faith and sexual and gender identities amidst popular discourses that often claim Christianity and homosexuality/gender variance are mutually exclusive?

My favorite picture of myself is me at three years old standing in the hallway at my grandparents' home wearing my grandfather's bathrobe and glasses, holding his well-worn Bible upside down and preaching. Whether that was some sort of omen or prophecy, I don't know. But I did turn out to be a preacher and a person who identifies primarily as androgynous. Being queer and Christian has always placed me squarely in the middle of two warring camps: many Christians say I can't be one of them as I am a lesbian (they can't even wrap their heads around the androgynous thing), and many in the LBGTQ community are so at odds with Christianity that they can't understand how I can maintain my faith.

I can certainly understand my queer sisters' and brothers' sentiments. So many in our community have been not only shunned, but actively damaged by the "church" that it is little wonder that they desire to be as far as possible from anything "Christian." I have seen great changes in this over the years as more and more churches take up the struggle with centuries of homophobia and reconcile their doctrines around sexuality and faithful witness. There is still so far to go, but I have hope when I see ever more denominations grappling with their witness in authentic ways. I believe they will one day look back on their own biases much as the Baptists, Presbyterians, and Methodists have tried to distance themselves from their pro-slavery past. Schisms in those denominations led to North–South divisions. Today, denominations have occasionally split along ideological lines regarding sexuality and gender expression, though modern upheavals have tended to be less dramatic as smaller contingents within denominations opt out of the larger bodies.

While I disagree over standards of scriptural interpretation, I can also understand my Christian sisters and brothers who follow doctrines they have been raised to believe have "always" existed. For many of them the arguments relating to sexual orientation and gender expression are simply nonexistent when their own, personal lives are untouched by such struggles. It is easy for them to swallow the party line that what the religious right calls "traditional marriage" is a Biblical norm. Of course, the Bible presents all kinds of models for families and relationships, including sexual variations. Jonathan loved David more than he ever loved any woman (his words); Ruth declared her love for Naomi with words that heterosexuals have co-opted into their own weddings (whither thou goest, I will go, whither thou stayest, I will stay; thy people shall be my people and thy God my God...till death do us part—paraphrased from the King James for clarity). Thanks to my surname (Solomon) I have always contemplated with wonder my namesake's more than 800 wives and concubines (talk about scheduling issues!). Paul liked the idea of celibacy because he was just too busy evangelizing to have time for a family and Jesus said that family consisted of those who loved him and did God's will. Don't even get me started on Jacob, Leah, and Rachel and the idea of having to marry within the same family line! Turns out traditional models of family are actually pretty rare in the Bible.

As a historian, I recognize that arguments for models of almost anything that date back more than two thousand years must include recognition of how societies, groups, families, and even faiths have changed. To pretend that everything we hold as "normal" or even common today existed in a similar form during Biblical times (which itself encompasses more than fifteen hundred years of writing time) is nonsensical. In fact, I believe that denying the truth of scriptural descriptions of family—in all its variety—in order to try to make scripture support modern arguments for a narrow definition of marriage or family is an affront to God. The third commandment tells us we shouldn't use God's name to reinforce our own biases (using God's name in vain). Those who argue that marriage is between one man and one woman (already ignoring Biblical models of marriage discussed earlier) have to do theological contortions to escape what is plain in the Biblical text: families come in all kinds of combinations!

As if being a lesbian and a minister weren't complicated enough, I also understand myself to be primarily androgynous. For me that means that even though I have a body that functions as female (though I certainly do not fit the stereotype of "feminine"—just ask any of the numerous people who have done double-takes as I enter/leave the women's restroom), I do not identify as female. I do not feel like a man or a woman, but a bit of both. I consider my breasts an annoyance at best, but have no desire to trade my clitoris for a penis. I believe that there are differences in how men and women think at times, but that just as our sexuality flows along a continuum, so does gender for some of us.

As a Christian, I believe Jesus took on bodily form to be one of us and was a gender rebel in the process. Jesus certainly did not fit the model of a typical Jewish man of his century. He did not marry and confounded those who sought to follow a rigid set of rules around issues of sexuality and gender. For those in the queer community (and certainly for those of us who fall under the umbrella of transgender), Jesus' words in Matthew 19:12 (King James Version) give a great deal of confidence that we are exactly who God made us

to be. Jesus said, "For there are some eunuchs, which were so born from their mother's womb: and there are some eunuchs, which were made eunuchs of men: and there be eunuchs, which have made themselves eunuchs for the kingdom of heaven's sake. He that is able to receive it, let him receive it." If one believes that Jesus was God incarnate and omniscient, then one must acknowledge that Jesus would certainly have been aware that the word eunuch often referred to gay men and/or those whose genitalia reflected something other than the male/female view of gender. In this passage I believe Jesus is saying something more, though. He describes eunuchs of different kinds (some are born that way, some become eunuchs at the hand of others, and still others make themselves eunuchs to further the realm of God). Jesus seems to be saying that there are people who are different for different reasons, yet all fall into the same category and all are acceptable. Whether he is referring specifically to gays, castrati, the intersexed, or some other form of gender-identified people, he understands that not everyone will be able to "receive" this word. Some people will "get it," while others needn't worry about it.

Standing between worlds—gay/straight, male/female, Christian/non-Christian—can be uncomfortable. It is certainly never boring. It presents challenges and opportunities. There are so many things about myself that I have yet to learn, but I believe my faith gives me room to explore without fear. If God didn't limit me, why should others think they can limit me? And why should I limit myself? When I get the funny looks as I enter a public restroom, I think, "And isn't it great that God made us all so different?!"

CONTESTED MEMBERSHIP
Black Gay Identities and the Politics of AIDS

DISCUSSION QUESTIONS

1. What does the author mean by "indigenous" membership among African Americans? How does indigenous racial identity influence the distribution of resources, services, access, and legitimacy within communities, according to the author?

2. How did the system of racism render black gays and lesbians silent during the civil rights era? How did this silence become life threatening in the late 1980s?

3. Why does the author suggest that the black community has not mobilized in response to the AIDS epidemic? Why is sexuality policed and guarded so strictly within the black community? How does this reflect the specific contours of black history?

4. How do marginal groups build a unified sense of political identity in the face of increasing stratification and cross-cutting identities? Do you think constructing a unified identity is important to building a movement for social change?

Only fairly recently have scholars in the social sciences begun to recognize that the concept of group identity in its essentialist core is in crisis. Influenced by postmodern and deconstructive discourse, historical analyses focusing on marginal groups, and a new emphasis on identity in social movement theories, researchers are beginning to understand that the idea of group identity that many of us now employ is markedly different from the conception of a stable, static, and homogenous group previously assumed in the social sciences. Just as most scholars have finally become accustomed to including in their analyses simple conceptions of identity coded in binary form (e.g., white/black; man/woman), we now face the realization that identities of difference (race, class, gender, sexuality) are themselves fragmented, contested, and of course, socially constructed.

Social constructionist theory provides the framework and the intellectual incentive to identify and examine those social, political, and economic processes that lead to the promotion of certain conceptualizations of group membership and group meaning at particular historical moments. Social constructionist models can also be used to analyze internal debates over membership within marginal communities. Using this approach, constructionist frameworks help us recognize and understand indigenous definitions of group membership and group meaning encapsulated under the rubric of group identity.

While previously, most of the work on the social construction of group identity came from scholars in the humanities, researchers in the social sciences, especially those of us interested in the topics of race, gender, class, and sexuality, must find ways to incorporate such insight into our analyses. Moreover, we are being challenged by a rapidly expanding understanding of group identity not only to recognize and examine the socially constructed character of group identity, but also to investigate the stratification found in groups and the implications of such fragmentation on attempts at group mobilization and political action. Thus, beyond examining the ways in which dominant groups and institutions change or alter their imposed definitions of marginal groups within different historical contexts, we must also understand how marginal group members define and redefine themselves, setting their own standards for "full group membership."

This article takes up the topic of indigenous constructions of group membership and its impact on the political attitudes and mobilization of marginal group members. In particular, I am interested in how the concept of "blackness," as it is defined and refined within black communities, is used to demarcate the boundaries of group membership. As a second point of examination, I want to know how these indigenous definitions of blackness influence, shape, and lend legitimation to the political attitudes and behavior of community leaders and members.

Indigenous definitions of blackness, while of course building on dominant ideas or definitions of who *is* black, employ a more expansive, but at the same time often less inclusive, understanding of black group identity. They center not merely on easily identifiable biologically rooted characteristics, but also use moralistic and character evaluations to appraise membership. Individuals employ a "calculus" of indigenous membership that can include an assessment of personal or moral worth, such as an individual's contribution to the community, adherence to community norms and values, or faithfulness to perceived, rewritten, or in some cases newly created African traditions. Thus, indigenously constructed definitions of black group identity seek to redefine and empower blackness to the outside world by policing the boundaries of what can be represented to the dominant public as "true blackness." And it is through *public policing,* where the judgments, evaluations, and condemnations of recognized leaders and institutions of black communities are communicated to their constituencies, that the full membership of certain segments of black communities are contested and challenged.

Let me be clear that examples of the indigenous construction of blackness and contests over such definitions abound in our everyday interactions. Whether it be the challenge to the authenticity of those black students who choose not to sit at "the black table" in the cafeteria or the looks of contempt or concern encountered by black group members seen walking with their white mates, informal or "hidden transcripts" of blackness guide interactions in black communities, as they undoubtedly do in all communities. However, in most cases full-scale contestation is not the norm in black communities. Instead, those whose position in the community is challenged exist silenced and regulated for years. Only when the subgroup experiencing ostracization or *secondary marginalization* has alternative means for securing resources, such as an external network of support, will the full battle over inclusion be fought. Thus, in most cases those individuals deemed to be on the outside of "acceptable blackness"—either because of their addiction, their sexual relationships, their gender, their financial status, their relationship with or dependency on the state, etc.—are left with two choices: either find ways to conform to "community standards" or be left on the margins where individual families and friends are expected to take care of their needs.

Again, my concern here is not that these group members will be rejected by dominant groups as not being part of the black community. Most marginal group members know that racism in the dominant society functions with essentialist principles in its assessment of black people. Thus, men and women who meet basic dominant ideas of what black people look like and "act" like rarely have their "blackness" evaluated, except to have it negated as a reward for assimilation into dominant white society (e.g., Michael Jackson, Clarence Thomas, and formerly O. J. Simpson). Instead, my concern is with the process employed by other marginal group members to evaluate someone's blackness. Will certain group members be rejected by other marginal group members because of their inability to meet indigenous standards of blackness? Are there processes through which the full "rights" or empowerment of group members becomes negated or severely limited *within* black communities because of a stigmatized black identity?

As stated earlier, the objective of this analysis is not only to understand the processes through which indigenous constructions of group membership come about, but also to explore how these definitions impact on the behavior, in particular the political behavior, of marginal group members. To this end, I have chosen to center this analysis on the black community's response to the AIDS epidemic. Specifically, I will explore how indigenous contests over black gay male identity have framed and influenced black communities' conception of and response to AIDS.

Throughout this article I use examples and quotes from community leaders in black churches, electoral politics, activist organizations, and the academic communities. Has the emergence of a public, empowered black gay identity, perceived and defined by many community leaders, activists, and members, as standing outside the bounds of generally recognized standards of blackness been used by these leaders to justify their lack of an aggressive response to this disease? Do community leaders interpret a public black gay identity as a direct threat to the acceptability or "cultural capital" gained by

some in black communities, in particular by the black middle class? In the minds of indigenous leaders and activists, does embracing or owning AIDS as a disease significantly impacting on members of black communities also mean owning or finally acknowledging that sexual contact and intimate relationships between men are something found in, and inherently a part of, black communities?

My central claim is that contestation over identity, in this case indigenous racial identity, has tangible effects, influencing the distribution of resources, services, access, and legitimacy within communities. In the case of AIDS, without the support of established leaders and organizations in black communities, underfunded community-based education programs encounter limited success, facilitating the continued infection and death of black men, women, and children. Further, in the absence of political pressure from leaders, organizations, activists, and mobilized members of the black community, the federal government is allowed to continue its shameful dealings, neglecting to provide the full resources needed to effectively fight this disease in black communities. Thus, those failing to meet indigenous standards of blackness find their life chances threatened not only by dominant institutions or groups, but also by their lack of access to indigenous resources and support. Therefore, scholars who profess to be concerned with the conditions of marginal group members face the monumental challenge of recognizing and examining indigenous group definition without reifying the group as an essentialist and exclusionary category.

Furthermore, the importance of disputes over community membership and the importance of groups should not be understood only at an abstract, theoretical level where discussions of identity, authenticity, and essentialism are often held. This examination of the intersection of AIDS, black gay identity, and indigenous constructions of "blackness" provides us with an empirical example of the importance of group membership and group resources for marginal group members, as well as the dangers of identity politics. In this case we must be concerned with politics that only recognize and respond to the needs of those segments of black communities judged by our leaders to meet indigenous standards of group membership. This issue is of critical importance because it represents what I believe to be one of the more pressing political challenges currently facing marginal communities in the twenty-first century, namely, how to maintain and rebuild a principled and politically effective group community. How do marginal communities, still struggling for access and power from dominant institutions and groups, maintain some pseudo-unified political base in the face of increasing demands to recognize and incorporate the needs and issues of members who were previously silenced and made invisible in structuring the politics of the community? How do marginal communities make central those who are the most vulnerable, and often the most stigmatized, members of the community, when many of the previous gains of marginal group members have been made through a strategy of minimizing the public appearance of difference between the values, behavior, and attitudes of marginal and dominant group members? How do we build a truly radical, liberating politics that does not re-create hierarchies, norms, and standards of acceptability rooted in dominant systems of power? These are the questions that frame this analysis.

DECONSTRUCTION AND THE CRISIS OF ESSENTIALISM

Before proceeding, I want to take up what I consider an important criticism of group analysis. For some scholars, attention to the construction of identity, instead of the deconstruction of such bounded categories, seems misplaced. These researchers call for the deconstruction of both dominant and indigenous categories that are viewed as excluding certain marginal group members and reinforcing hierarchies of power. Thus, activists and academics adhering to a deconstructionist framework embrace a more fluid and transgressive understanding of identity. In the case of black Americans, these scholars argue that the variation found in definitions of who qualifies as black and what that is to mean, as well as the

variation in the actual life chances and lived experience of those identified through history as black, demands that we abandon the use of race as a category of analysis. Barbara Jeanne Fields, who I doubt would label herself a deconstructionist, writes at the end of her essay "Slavery, Race and Ideology in the United States of America":

> Those who create and re-create race today are not just the mob that killed a young Afro-American man on the street in Brooklyn or the people who joined the Klan and the White Order. They are also those academic writers whose invocation of self-propelling "attitudes" and tragic flaws assigns Africans and their descendants to a special category, placing them in a world exclusively theirs and outside history—a form of intellectual apartheid no less ugly or oppressive, despite its righteous (not to say self-righteous) trappings, than that practiced by the bio- and theo-racists; and for which the victims like slaves of old are expected to be grateful.

In contrast to Fields, I argue that calls for the deconstruction of categories and groups ignore not only the reality of groups in structuring the distribution of resources and the general life chances of those in society, but also ignore the importance of group membership in promoting the survival and progress of marginal group members. If one exists, as many of us do, without the privilege and the resources to transgress socially erected boundaries or categories, then we learn at an early age to rely on, and contribute to, the collective material resources/power/status of other group members who share our subject position. Thus, to argue that race or blackness is not "real" in some genetic or biological form (which I do) is not to believe that race or blackness, in particular as an ideological construct of grouping and separation, has not massively structured the lives of those designated black as well as the rest of American society. Omi and Winant in their book *Racial Formation in the United States* write, "The attempt to banish the concept [of race] as an archaism is at best counterintuitive....A more effective starting point is the recognition that despite its uncertainties and contradictions, the concept of race continues to play a fundamental role in structuring and representing the social world."

Nonetheless I share some of Fields's concerns about the re-creation and legitimization of categories used primarily to exploit and oppress. Many within black communities, whether they be cultural nationalists, religious leaders, politicians, or the average person trying to make it day to day, adhere to some form of a less stigmatized notion of group essentialism. Scholars ranging from Molefi Kete Asante to Patricia Hill Collins to those of us who use statistical analyses to examine the condition and progress of black people invoke some nonbiologically based definitions of "*the* black experience." Undoubtedly, much of our focus on a unified black community reflects that, compared to white communities, black people do in fact exhibit a significant political cohesiveness. Clearly, this observed homogeneity of black political attitudes, for instance, is forced in part by the survey questions that researchers ask, and more forcefully by the shared history of oppression that has framed our worldviews. However, we have reached a time when the issues faced by black communities demand that we look below the unified surface so often referenced by social scientists. Issues that currently frame the political agenda of black communities are often rooted in those points of social cleavage—class, gender, sexuality, language, country of origin—that problematize, at the very least, any conception of a unified, essential core of blackness as well as any assumption of shared lived experience.

Thus, it seems that this examination and others like it must be understood as an attempt to walk the thin line between two important constraints. First is a recognition that essentialist theories of the black community have at best limited relevance to understanding the structure and condition of black communities. Second, we must also understand that strict adherence to deconstructive approaches, which call for the complete negation of groups as a unit of analysis, risks ignoring the importance of indigenous group structure to the living conditions of marginal groups.

EMERGENCE OF A VISIBLE BLACK GAY IDENTITY

The perceived existence of a unifying group identity cannot be overstated when trying to explain the structured politics of black communities. Systems of oppression from slavery to redemption, to legal and informal Jim Crow segregation, and other more recent forms of segregation and deprivation have dictated that most African-Americans share a history and current existence framed by oppression and marginalization. However, even as a unifier, blackness, or what qualifies as indigenously constructed blackness, has always been mediated or contested by other identities that group members hold. And at no time did both the primacy and the fragility of a unified group identity become more evident than in the liberation politics and social movements of the late 1960s and early 1970s. Whether it be civil rights institutions, black liberation organizations, or even the electoral campaigns of black candidates, one primary identity—"blackness"—was understood to be the underlying factor joining all these struggles. Each organization espoused in its own way a commitment to the liberation of black people, and anything thought to detract from this goal was dismissed and in some cases denounced. However, the uniformity during this period of such a political worldview can also be challenged.

During the 1960s and 1970s the black community experienced increasing stratification. Whether that stratification was based in the deindustrialization experienced in urban centers or the politicized nature of the times, which helped to promote consciousness of members' multiple identities, a segregated and seemingly unified black community had to deal openly with fragmentation. All across the country we witnessed the beginning of extreme bifurcation in black communities, with an expanding middle class and an expanding segment of poor black people. However, beyond economic segmentation, other identities or social locations became visible in defining the lived experience of black people. In black communities, as well as in the political groups of the time, individuals increasingly began to recognize and acknowledge the multiplicity of identities upon which their oppression was based. Unfortunately, it was the inability of many of the race-based organizations to recognize and act on perceived tears in "unity" that led in part to the dismantling of many of these organizations. However, it was also in this changing environment that the visibility of lesbian and gay people, including black lesbian and gay people, began to take shape in the community.

It is important to recognize that black gay men and lesbians have always existed and worked in black communities, but these individuals had largely been made invisible, silent contributors to the black community. When faced with the devastation of racism, the cost of silence and invisibility seemed a willing payment from lesbian and gay community members for the support, caring, and protection of members of the black community and, more importantly, the support and acceptance of immediate family members. In her book *Talking Back,* bell hooks discusses the dilemma that many black lesbians and gay men confronted:

> The gay people we knew did not live in separate subcultures, not in the small, segregated black community where work was difficult to find, where many of us were poor. Poverty was important; it created a social context in which structures of dependence were important for everyday survival. Sheer economic necessity and fierce white racism, as well as the joy of being there with the black folks known and loved, compelled many gay blacks to live close to home and family. That meant however that gay people created a way to live out sexual preferences within the boundaries of circumstances that were rarely ideal no matter how affirming.

Thus, if one was willing not to "flaunt" one's sexual orientation in front of family members and neighbors (although many would secretly suspect that you were "that way"), the primarily verbal abuse—like taunts of "faggot" and "bull dyke"—was generally kept to a minimum. Again, I do not want to minimize the importance of even such conditional support on the part of family, friends, and

community. The prospect of facing continuous residential, occupational, and social exclusion as a manifestation of widespread racism, even in primarily white lesbian and gay communities, underscores the importance of some feelings of safety and familiarity. These were the feelings of support bought by our silence.

However, the willingness and ability of black lesbians and gay men to remain quiet and invisible has radically changed. These changes have resulted in part from many of the factors that have spurred new identities as well as politicized identities of old. One major factor has been the proliferation of liberation and social movements demanding access and control for groups long pushed out of dominant society. Cornel West speaks of this situation when he argues, "During the late fifties, sixties, and early seventies in the USA, these decolonized sensibilities fanned and fueled the Civil Rights and Black Power movements, as well as the student antiwar, feminist, gray, brown, gay, and lesbian movements. In this period we witnessed the shattering of male WASP cultural homogeneity and the collapse of the short-lived liberal consensus."

Closely connected to involvement and association with organized social movements was the more formal establishment of an institutionalized, socially connected, and in many cases monetarily secure gay community in many of the nation's urban centers. These "ghettos" provided a space in which ideas of rights and political strategies of empowerment could be generated and discussed. These enclaves, as well as other dominant institutions such as universities, were integral in creating space for the exploration of independence away from local communities and families.

In conjunction with the continued development of gay enclaves was the emergence of an outspoken and brave black lesbian and gay leadership who openly claimed and wrote about their sexuality (Audre Lorde, Cheryl Clarke, Barbara Smith, Pat Parker, Joseph Beam, Essex Hemphill ...). These individuals were intent on creating new cultural voices. When they were denied the right to speak openly through traditional avenues in black communities, these cultural leaders found and created new avenues to affirm their presence and connection to black communities. Books such as *This Bridge Called My Back, Home Girls, Brother to Brother, In the Life,* and more recently videos such as *Tongues Untied* all sought to detail from various perspectives the struggle to consistently mesh one's black and gay identities. All of these factors helped create an environment in which the silence that had structured the lives of many black lesbian and gay men seemed unacceptable.

The conditions listed above, however, did not lead to a massive coming out in black communities. In fact, the level of silence among black lesbian and gay men is still an immediate and pressing concern for those organizing in the community today. However, the environment that developed through the sixties and seventies created a situation in which some black women and men choose to identify publicly as black *and* gay. The choice, or in many cases the perceived need, to embrace publicly a black gay male or black lesbian identity undoubtedly escalated with the emergence of AIDS, an issue that demands either recognition and empowerment or death. Thus, after spending years affirming themselves, building consciousness, and contributing to black communities that had too often refused to embrace their particular needs, gay brothers and lesbian sisters faced an issue, AIDS, that threatened to kill black gays and lesbians as well as generally wreak havoc throughout black communities if we did not speak out and demand recognition.

It would be this political, social, and economic environment that would heighten the contestation over an open black gay male identity. This social context, where black gay men in particular were experiencing the destruction of AIDS, produced many of the early pioneers who saw it as their responsibility to provide the first level of response to AIDS in the black community. Ernest Quimby and Samuel Friedman, in their article "Dynamics of Black Mobilization against AIDS in New York City," document much of the early organized activity around AIDS in people-of-color communities. The authors note, "In the epidemic's early days, media reports that AIDS was a disease of white gay men reduced the attention blacks paid to it.... By 1985, however, some leaders of the minority gay and lesbian community began to challenge this denial and helped set up some of the first minority-focused AIDS events."

Two of the earliest national conferences on AIDS in people-of-color communities were organized by lesbians and gay men of color. The Third World Advisory Task Force, a primarily gay group out of San Francisco, organized a Western regional conference in the early part of 1986. The National Coalition of Black Lesbians and Gays, a progressive national membership organization structured around local chapters, organized the National Conference on AIDS in the Black Community, in Washington, D.C., in 1986. This conference, which was cosponsored by the National Minority AIDS Council and the National Conference of Black Mayors, was funded in part from a grant from the U.S. Public Health Service. Further, black gay men across the country, from Washington, D.C., to New York to Oakland to San Francisco to Los Angeles, were instrumental in establishing some of the first AIDS service organizations explicitly identifying minority communities as their target population. Additionally, black gay organizations such as Gay Men of African Descent (GMAD) of New York City have been and continue to be essential in educational efforts seeking to reach large numbers of black men.

A number of factors were helpful in laying the groundwork for the response from black gay men and lesbians. The information this group received from white gay activists was extremely helpful. The realization that some black gay men and lesbians also possessed limited access and economic privilege was useful in developing contacts and pooling resources. Further, the personal experiences of loss that brought together and raised the awareness of black lesbians and gay men were undoubtedly instrumental in motivating some response. Finally, "out" black gays and lesbians were less vulnerable to the moral judgments of traditional institutions in the black community. Because of their public identity as black lesbians or gay men, these individuals stood ready to challenge the marginalizing ideology associated with AIDS. Thus, as they attempted to speak to the entire black community about the dangers of this growing epidemic, the silence and invisibility that had once been a part of the survival contract of black lesbians and gay men could no longer exist if lives were to be saved.

AIDS AND POLICING BLACK SEXUALITY

In spite of the activities initiated by black lesbian and gay men in response to AIDS, it has devastated black communities, which is clearly represented in the numbers. In New York City, as in other major metropolitan areas AIDS is now the number one killer of black men ages 25–44 and women ages 18–44. Nationally, over one hundred thousand (114,868) black Americans have been diagnosed with AIDS, accounting for 32 percent of all AIDS cases, nearly three times our 12 percent representation in the general population. Black women comprise 54 percent of all women with AIDS nationally, with black children constituting 55 percent of all children with AIDS, and black men accounting for 28 percent of men with AIDS. If these numbers were not sobering enough, the trend of increasing representation of those with AIDS from people-of-color communities suggests that these numbers will only continue to increase.

Thus, in the face of such substantial and increasing devastation being visited upon the black community by AIDS, one might expect members or at least leaders of black communities to mobilize community support for more resources, attention, and action in response. However, the evidence suggests that the response from black community leaders and activists has been much less public, confrontational, collective, and consistent than the statistics might dictate. Further, any cursory comparative examination of the political response emanating from predominately white lesbian and gay activists to this disease suggests that black organizations and institutions have been less active. Over the years, members of gay and lesbian communities have found old and new ways to make officials, institutions, and at times the general public answer some of their demands. Gay activists have developed sophisticated political tactics to respond to the indifference and hostility that the government and other institutions display toward people with AIDS. Rallies, sit-ins, lobbying, private meetings, civil disobedience, "phone zaps"—few things seem too far out-of-bounds to make people listen and respond.

And while the gay community has mounted a coordinated effort of traditional politics and public collective action to the AIDS epidemic, the response in the black community has been much less pervasive, public, and effective. Again, through the work of primarily black gay activists, important conferences and forums have been sponsored to educate members of black communities on the dangers of AIDS. Organizations such as the Minority Task Force on AIDS and the Black Leadership Commission on AIDS have been established to provide services and develop educational programs for members of black communities. National leaders have even on occasion made mention of AIDS in their speeches to black constituents. However, generally there has been no substantial and sustained mobilization around this crisis in African-American communities. There have been few, if any, rallies, sit-ins, or petitions in black communities to bring attention to the devastation created by AIDS. There has been no sustained lobbying effort by national black organizations such as the NAACP or the Urban League. Instead, many in the black community continue to see AIDS as a horrible disease, believing that we should extend sympathy and compassion to its "victims," but claim no ownership as a community. AIDS is generally not understood as an internal political crisis that necessitates the mobilization of black communities. Even when AIDS is seen as a conspiracy against black communities, by the government or some other entity, no mobilization accompanies such suspicion. For most in black communities, AIDS is still a disease of individuals, usually "irresponsible, immoral, and deviant" individuals, some of whom happen to be black.

Quite often, when trying to explain the response to AIDS in black communities, authors retreat to the familiar and substantively important list of barriers preventing a more active response from community leaders and organizations. Regularly topping this list is the claim that because black communities have fewer resources than most other groups, they cannot be expected to respond to AIDS in a manner similar to "privileged" lesbians and gay men. And while there is truth to the claim that most black people operate with limited access to resources, this explanation is based on a narrow conception of resources and a limited understanding of the history of the black community. Most of the cities hardest hit by this disease (New York, Los Angeles, Washington, D.C., Detroit, Chicago, Atlanta) have been or are currently headed by black mayors. Thus, while black individuals suffer from limited resources, black elected officials control, or at least have significant input into, decisions about how resources will be allocated in their cities. Further, while individuals in the black community still suffer from marginalization and oppression, organizations such as the NAACP, the SCLC, and the Urban League have been able to gain access to national agencies and policy debates. Thus the claim that black people have fewer resources than other groups, while accurate at the individual level, does not appropriately account for the institutional resources controlled or accessed by black elected officials and traditional organizations.

A second explanation that is sometimes offered focuses on the numerous crises plaguing black communities. Proponents of this view argue that members of the black community suffer from so many ailments and structural difficulties, such as sickle-cell anemia, high blood pressure, diabetes, homelessness, persistent poverty, drugs, crime, discrimination...that no one should expect community leaders to turn over their political agenda to the issue of AIDS. Again, this position has merit, for we know that black communities do suffer disproportionately from most social, medical, economic, and political ills. It is, however, specifically because of the inordinate amount of suffering found in black communities that we might expect more attention to this disease. Because AIDS touches on, or is related to, so many other issues facing, in particular, poor black communities—health care, poverty, drug use, homelessness—we might reasonably expect black leaders to "use" the devastation of this disease to develop and reinforce an understanding of the enormity of the crisis facing black communities. Rarely does an issue so readily embody the life-and-death choices facing a community and rarely is an issue so neglected by the leadership of that community.

Another explanation suggested is that the dominant media sources as well as many community papers portray AIDS as a disease of white gay men, which thus does not threaten and need not interest the majority of black people. Further, when coverage around AIDS and black communities is provided, it often continues the historical practice of associating black people/Africa with disease (e.g., discussion of the origin of AIDS in Africa) and helps reinforce a look-the-other-way attitude by indigenous leaders and organizations. Again while both of these factors clearly play a part in understanding the community's response, I contend they still leave vacant a central component in this puzzle over black communities' lack of mobilization around AIDS.

Recently, scholars who study AIDS and black communities have begun to point to homophobia in the black community as the missing piece in our puzzle. Their concern is not just with homophobia among individuals, but more importantly with the homophobia rooted in indigenous institutions such as the black church, fraternal and social organizations, as well as some national political organizations. Different variants of this argument suggest that the black community's homophobia significantly structures its response, or lack thereof, to AIDS.

While homophobia in the black community is something we must pay attention to, I do not believe that the concept or explanation of homophobia adequately captures the complexity of sexuality, in particular lesbian and gay sexuality, in black communities. This is not to say that homophobia, which we all endure in socialization, is not a part of black communities. However, homophobia as the fear or even hatred of gay and lesbian people does not represent the intricate role that sexuality has played in defining blackness throughout the years. Sexuality, or what has been defined by the dominant society as the abnormal sexuality of both black men and women—with men being oversexed and in search of white women while black women were and are represented as promiscuous baby producers when they are not the direct and indirect property of white men—has been used historically and currently in this country to support and justify the marginal and exploited position of black people.

Scholars such as Takaki, Steinberg, Davis, Lewis, and Omi and Winant have all attempted, through various approaches, to detail the ways in which dominant groups, often with state sanctioning, have defined and redefined racial classification for their benefit and profit. Whether it be the one-drop rule, one's maternal racial lineage, simplistic evaluations of skin color, or some other combination of biological, cultural, or behavioral attributes, ideas of who is to be classified as black have had a long and varied history in this country. However, beyond the mere designation of who belongs in a particular group, dominant groups have also defined racial-group meaning. Those characteristics or stereotypes propagated as representing the "essence" of black people have been constructed by particular historical needs. Ideas about the laziness, inferiority, and in particular the sexual or abnormal sexual activity of black people have been advanced to justify any number of economic, political, and social arrangements.

This systematic degradation, stereotyping, and stigmatization of black Americans has all but dictated that attempts at incorporation, integration, and assimilation on the part of black people generally include some degree of proving ourselves to be "just as nice as those white folks." Thus, leaders, organizations, and institutions have consistently attempted to redefine and indigenously construct a new public image or understanding of what blackness would mean. This reconstruction or (im)provement of blackness relies not only on the self-regulation of individual black people, but also includes significant "indigenous policing" of black people. In the writings of black academics we consistently hear reference to the role of the black middle class as examples and regulators of appropriate behavior for the black masses. Drake and Cayton, in their 1945 classic, *Black Metropolis,* discuss the attitude of the black upper class toward the behavior of black lower classes:

> The attitude of the upper class toward the lower is ambivalent. As people whose standards of behavior approximate those of the white middle class, the members of Bronzeville's upper class resent the tendency of outsiders to "judge us all by what ignorant Negroes do." They emphasize their *differentness.* . . . The whole orientation of the Negro upper class thus becomes one of trying to speed up the process by which the lower class can be transformed from a poverty-stricken group, isolated from the general stream of American life, into a counterpart of middle-class America. [Emphasis in original.]

Regulation of the black masses was often pursued not only by individuals, but also by an extensive network of community groups and organizations. James R. Grossman details how the Urban League in conjunction with black and white institutions worked to help black migrants "adjust" to urban standards of behavior:

> The Urban League and the *Defender,* assisted by the YMCA, the larger churches, and a corps of volunteers, fashioned a variety of initiatives designed to help—and pressure—the newcomers to adjust not only to industrial work, but to urban life, northern racial patterns, and behavior that would enhance the reputation of blacks in the larger (white) community. . . . The Urban League, through such activities as "Stranger Meetings," leafleting, and door-to-door visits, advised newcomers on their duties as citizens: cleanliness, sobriety, thrift, efficiency, and respectable, restrained behavior in public places. . . . Under the tutelage of the respectable citizens of black Chicago, migrants were to become urbanized, northernized,

and indistinguishable from others of their race. At the very least, they would learn to be as inconspicuous as possible.

It is important to remember that a substantial amount of indigenous policing focused on what would be represented publicly as the sexual behavior of black people. Community leaders and organizations, fighting for equal rights, equal access, and full recognition as citizens, struggled to "clean up" the image of sexuality in black communities. Cornel West in *Race Matters* discusses the unwillingness of most black institutions to engage in open discussions of sexuality in black communities.

> But these grand yet flawed black institutions refused to engage one fundamental issue: *black sexuality....*
>
> Why was this so? Primarily because these black institutions put a premium on black survival in America. And black survival required accommodation with and acceptance from white America. Accommodation avoids any sustained association with the subversive and transgressive—be it communisms or miscegenation.... And acceptance meant that only "good" negroes would thrive—especially those who left black sexuality at the door when they "entered" and "arrived." In short, struggling black institutions made a Faustian pact with white America: avoid any substantive engagement with black sexuality and your survival on the margins of American society is, at least, possible.

Thus, individuals who were thought to fulfill stereotypes of black sexuality as something deviant or other often had their morality questioned by leading institutions in black communities. For instance, sexuality thought to stand outside the Christian mores as set down by the black church was interpreted as an indication of the moral character of that individual and his or her family as well as an embarrassment to the collective consciousness and cultural capital of the black community. Hazel Carby discusses the moral panic and threat to the collective respectability of black communities attributed to uncontrolled migrating black women in her article "Policing the Black Woman's Body":

The need to police and discipline the behavior of black women in cities, however, was not only a premise of white agencies and institutions but also a perception of black institutions and organizations, and the black middle class. The moral panic about the urban presence of apparently uncontrolled black women was symptomatic of and referenced aspects of the more general crises of social displacement and dislocation that were caused by migration. White and black intellectuals used and elaborated this discourse so that when they referred to the association between black women and vice, or immoral behavior, their references carried connotations of other crises of the black urban environment. Thus the migrating black woman could be variously situated as a threat to the progress of the race; and as a threat to the establishment of a respectable urban black middle class; as a threat to congenial black and white middle-class relations; and as a threat to the formation of black masculinity in an urban environment.

While these examples may seem dated, we need only look around today to see the great efforts many black leaders and academics engage in to distance themselves from those perceived to participate in "inappropriate immoral sexual behavior." Examples of such distancing efforts are evident not only in the absence of any sustained writing on black lesbians and gay men by black authors and academics, but is also found in the counterexperience of unending writing and policy attacks on the "inappropriate" and "carefree" sexuality of those labeled the "underclass" and more generally black women on welfare.

I want to be clear that contests or opposition to the public representation of black gay male sexuality in particular and nonnormative sexuality in general is significantly motivated by a genuine threat to the cultural capital acquired by some in black communities, where cultural capital symbolizes the acceptance, access, and privilege of primarily black middle- and upper-class people. Thus, for many black leaders and activists, visible/public black homosexuality is understood to threaten that "cultural capital" acquired by both assimilation and protest. The policing or regulation of black gay and lesbian behavior/visibility is seen as the responsibility not only of dominant institutions, but also of leaders of indigenous institutions, who can claim that they are protecting the image and progress of "the race/community." Through the fulfillment of these communal duties, internal ideas and definitions of blackness, thought to help with the task of regulation, emerge. These definitions set the rules that to be a "good" or "true" black person you must adhere to some religious standards of appropriate sexual behavior. To be a true black man is antithetical to being gay, for part of your duty as a black man is to produce "little black warriors in the interest of the black nation." The rules suggest that to be gay is to be a pawn of a white genocidal plot, intent on destroying the black community. To be gay is to want to be white anyway, since we all know that there is no tradition of homosexuality in our African history. Thus, to be gay is to stand outside the norms, values, and practices of the community, putting your "true" blackness into question.

In his article "Some Thoughts on the Challenges Facing Black Gay Intellectuals," Ron Simmons details just some of the arguments made by national (and nationalist) black leaders such as Nathan Hare, Jawanza Kunjufu, Molefi Asante, Haki Madhubuti, Amiri Baraka, and Yosuf Ben-Jochannan that seek to undermine claims of an empowered, fully recognized black gay identity. Specifically, Simmons outlines what he considers the four major reasons provided by these scholars for the development of homosexuality in the black community:

> In reviewing African-American literature, one finds that black homophobic and heterosexist scholars believe homosexuality in the African-American community is the result of (1) the emasculation of black men by white oppression (e.g., Staples, Madhubuti, Asante, Farrakhan, and Baraka); (2) the breakdown of the family structure and the loss of male role models (e.g., Kunjufu, Madhubuti, Farrakhan, and Hare); (3) a sinister plot perpetuated by diabolical racists who want to destroy the black race (e.g., Hare); and (4) immorality as defined in biblical scriptures, Koranic suras, or Egyptian "Books of the Dead" (e.g., Farrakhan and Ben-Jochannan).

It is important to recognize that while these authors all see homosexuality as something devised and infiltrated from outside the black community, none or few are advocating directly that black gay men and women be fully rejected and excluded from the community. And that is not the claim I seek to make with regards to the contested nature of black gay identities. Instead, many of the scholars in Simmons's analysis argue that homosexuality must be understood as a threat to the survival of the black community. Thus, they ask that black lesbians and gay men suppress their sexuality, keep quiet, remain undemanding, and make their needs subservient to the "collective" needs of the community. Simmons cites Molefi Asante as directly promoting such a subservient position in his book *Afrocentricity:*

> Afrocentric relationships are based upon...what is best for the collective imperative of the people....All brothers who are homosexuals should know that they too can become committed to the collective will. It means the submergence of their own wills into the collective will of our people.

Simmons identifies similar ideas of inclusion without empowerment for black gay men and lesbians in Nathan and Julia Hare's book *The Endangered Black Family:*

> On the other hand—and this is crucial—we will refuse to embark on one more tangent of displaced contempt and misdirected scorn for the homosexualized [*sic*] black brothers or sisters and drive them over to the camp of white liberal–radical–moderate-establishment coalition. What we must do is offer the homosexual brother or sister a proper compassion and acceptance *without advocacy....* Some of them may yet be saved. And yet, we must declare open warfare upon the sources of [their] confusion. [Emphasis added.]

Again, the proscription these authors offer is not the complete rejection of black lesbian and gay men. Instead, they suggest a quiet acceptance "without advocacy." It is within this analysis that we again see the conflictual nature of black gay identity as it has been repeatedly defined in the black community. It is an identity that allows inclusion, but only under certain restrictions—denying any attempt at the empowerment of this segment of the black community. For these leaders, homophobia or the hatred of black gays and lesbians does not fully explain their position of silent inclusion. Thus, the "sin" that black lesbians and gay men commit is not just rooted in the inherent wrongness of their sexual behavior, but instead or just as importantly in their perceived weakness and cost to black communities.

We can now understand why homophobia, as a simple makeshift explanation to represent the complexity of sexuality in black communities, is inadequate. Instead, to analyze black communities' response to AIDS we must address a whole set of issues, including dominant representations of black sexuality, how these ideas/stereotypes have been used against black communities, and the perceived need to regulate black sexuality through indigenous definitions of blackness. From this starting point we may be better able to understand, although never accept, the range of opposition black gay men encounter as stemming not only from people's repudiation of the idea of sex between men, but also from the use of sexuality by dominant groups to stigmatize and marginalize further a community already under siege.

Again, it is important to note that what is at stake here is the question of membership, full empowered membership in black communities. Thus, visibility, access to indigenous resources, participation and acknowledgment in the structuring of black political agendas—all are put into question when one's blackness is contested. Undoubtedly, many factors contribute to the black community's response to AIDS, including a real deficiency in community resources as well as a real mistrust of government-sponsored information on health care and disease in black communities. However, I believe that a significant part of the explanation for the lack of forceful action around AIDS is directly tied to ideas and definitions of "black identity" put forth by indigenous leaders, institutions, and organizations. These definitions of blackness stand in direct contrast to the images and ideas associated with those living with AIDS or HIV in black communities. In particular, these indigenous constructions of blackness

define behavior linked to the transmission of HIV as immoral and an embarrassment, threatening to the status and survival of community members.

Having laid out this argument concerning the contestation of black gay identity and its impact on political responses to AIDS in black communities, it is important to provide, even briefly, a concrete example of the way an indigenous institution such as the black church defines and responds to the needs of black gay men in the era of AIDS. I will also try to highlight a few of the ways black gay men have responded to the secondary marginalization they have experienced through black churches. Again, I use the church merely as an illustration of the marginalization and identity contestation in which numerous indigenous institutions engage.

THE BLACK CHURCH

Activists and scholars have often focused on the activity of the black church to understand and explain the political behavior of members of the black community, since traditionally the church has been perceived as the glue and motor of the community. If any activity was to touch every segment of the community, it was believed that such efforts had to be based in the black church. The work of Aldon Morris linking the black church to the civil rights movement is a classic example of the role the black church is thought to play in struggles for liberation and rights. However, even prior to the civil rights movement the black church was used to build movements of freedom. The black church acted as meeting space, school, health care facility, and distributor of food from slavery to Reconstruction, through the years of Northern migration and the decades of Jim Crow segregation. In her article on the new social role of black churches, Hollie I. West comments, "African-American churches have traditionally served as a refuge from a hostile white world, beehives of both social and political activity."

However, with the advent of AIDS, drug epidemics, and the increasing poverty and stratification of black communities, some organizers and activists are beginning to question the central authority given to the church. West suggests in her article that AIDS is a problem that pulls the church in two directions: "Some clergymen privately acknowledge the dilemma. They recognize the need to confront AIDS and drugs, but conservative factions in their congregations discourage involvement." A conservative ideology, based on strict norms of "moral" behavior, has often framed the church's response to many of the controversial social issues facing black communities. Gail Walker briefly delineates the contradictory nature of the black church: "The dual—and contradictory—legacy of the African-American church is that it has been among the most important instruments of African-American liberation and at the same time one of the most conservative institutions in the African-American community."

While the position of the black church on homosexuality has seemed fairly straightforward, it has both public and private dimensions. Holding with the teaching of most organized religions, members of black churches assert that homosexual behavior is immoral and in direct contrast to the word of God. Black ministers have consistently spoken out and preached against the immorality and threat posed to the community by gays and lesbians. Recently, black ministers from numerous denominations in Cleveland, Ohio, organized in opposition to federal legislation to include gay men and lesbians under the protection of the 1964 Civil Rights Bill. These ministers, representing themselves as "true leaders" of the black church, wrote in the local black newspaper, the *Call and Post*:

> We as members and representatives of African American protestant congregations reaffirm our identity as THE BLACK CHURCH....
>
> We view HOMOSEXUALITY (including bisexual, as well as gay or lesbian sexual activity) as a lifestyle that is contrary to the teaching of the Bible. Such sexual activity and involvement is contrary to the pattern established during creation. Homosexual behavior in the Bible is forbidden and described as unnatural and perverted....

> Our attitude toward any individuals that are involved in/with a HOMOSEXUAL LIFESTYLE is expressed through tolerance and compassion. The church's mission is to bring about RESTORATION....

However, at the same time that condemnation of gay and lesbian sexual behavior is a staple of the black church, it is also well-known that black gay men, in particular, can be found in prominent positions throughout the church. Thus, black gay men in black churches can be quietly accepted as they sing in the church choir, teach Sunday school, and in some cases even preach from the pulpit, or they can be expelled for participating in blasphemous behavior. Nowhere does the idea of inclusion as fully recognized and empowered members exist. Thus, according to religious doctrine, black lesbian and gay members of the community are to be embraced and taken care of in a time of need. However, their gay identity places them outside the indigenously constructed boundaries of both Christian and black identification as recognized by the church.

Nowhere recently has this principle of silent acceptance and care at the expense of a public denunciation of homosexuality been more evident than in struggles around the church's response to AIDS in black communities. The contradictory nature of church actions and rhetoric continues to frustrate many AIDS activists, who looked to the church initially for a swift, compassionate, and empowering response. Activists and those providing services claim that the church did little to nothing early in response to the epidemic. Further, when members of the church elite finally did mobilize, it was with negative judgments and pity.

Dr. Marjorie Hill, former director of New York City's Office of Lesbian and Gay Concerns under Mayor David Dinkins, explains that the church's history of activism is muted with regards to AIDS because of its insistence on denying public recognition of lesbian and gay community members: "Historically, activism in the black community has come from the church. However, the reluctance of the church to respond to AIDS means they are not following the mission of Christ.... The church has not dealt with the issue of homosexuality. Many have gays who sing in the choir and play the organ and that is fine until they need the church's help and recognition....Denial only works for so long; the reality of gay men and women will eventually have to be dealt with."

Others argue that the church is making progress. Church members point to the numerous AIDS ministries that have been established to deal with AIDS in black communities. They highlight what seem like revolutionary strides in the ability of black ministers to even mention AIDS from the pulpit. And while black lesbian and gay leaders commend those attempting to identify comfortable ways for black ministers and congregations to deal with the devastation of AIDS in their communities, they still contend there's no full recognition of the rights and lives of those infected with this disease. The saying "love the sinner, hate the sin" is paramount in understanding the limited response of black clergy. Gay men are to be loved and taken care of when they are sick, but their loving relationships are not to be recognized nor respected. Most individuals affected by this disease can tell at least one story of going to a funeral of a gay man and never having his being gay recognized as well as never hearing the word AIDS mentioned. Family members and ministers are all too willing to grieve the loss of a son or church member, without ever acknowledging the total identity of that son. Lost to AIDS is not only the son loved so dearly, but the totality of his life, which included lovers and gay friends who also grieve for that loss.

The fundamental obstacle to the church's wholehearted response to AIDS is its adherence to a strict middle-class Christian code that holds behavior that transmits the virus is immoral, sinful, and just as importantly for the argument presented here, costly to the community's status. Until church leaders are ready to discuss issues of sexuality, drug use, and homosexuality in an inclusive discourse, their ability to serve the entire community as well as confront, instead of replicate, dominant ideologies will be severely inhibited. The Reverend James Forbes of

Riverside Church in New York City has been one of the few black clergy who has openly called on the church to open up its dialogue concerning AIDS. In a keynote address at the 1991 Harlem Week of Prayer, he declared that until the black church deals with fundamental issues such as sexuality in an inclusive and accepting manner, it will never be able to deal adequately with the AIDS epidemic in the black community.

While ministers like the Reverend Mr. Forbes preach the need for the church to reevaluate its stance on fundamental judgments of human sexuality, others believe that we may have seen the church move about as far as it's going to go. Except for those exceptional congregations committed to a liberation theology, the provision of services for those with AIDS may be the extent of the church's response, because for many clergy there is no way to reconcile behavior that can lead to the transmission of the virus to the doctrine of the Christian church. The Reverend Calvin Butts of Abyssinian Baptist Church in Harlem explains:

> The response of the church is getting better. At one time the church didn't respond, and when the church did respond, it was negative. Ministers thought that a negative response was in keeping with the thinking that AIDS was transmitted by homosexual transmission, drugs, you know. But as more thoughtful clergy became involved, issues of compassion entered the discussion and we used Jesus' refuge in the house of lepers as an example. People became more sympathetic when people close to the church were affected. Also the work of BLCA [Black Leadership Commission on AIDS] brought clergy together to work on our response. Unfortunately, there are still quite a few who see it as God's retribution.

However, in an environment where their identity is contested and their full rights and connection with black communities is negated, many black lesbian and gay leaders are actively developing ways to ignore the dictates and challenge the power of the church, especially as it affects AIDS organizing. One such strategy has focused on how black gay and lesbian leaders as well as

AIDS activists can do effective work in the community without the help of the church. Some suggest that it does not matter whether the church responds because the church no longer touches those parts of the community most at risk for this disease. Colin Robinson, former staff member at Gay Men's Health Crisis and currently executive director of Gay Men of African Descent, explains, "The church is still hooked on sin, but compromised by sin. They will take care of you when you get sick, but they won't talk about it, and that is no way to provide effective education." George Bellinger Jr., a member of GMAD and former education director of the Minority Task Force on AIDS in New York, suggests, "We put too much status in the church. They aren't connected to the affected populations, and they bring with them all kinds of middle-class values."

Others in the community have gone beyond developing AIDS education strategies to focus directly on challenging the teaching of the church about homosexuality, especially as black gay identities are offered as a contrast to the indigenous constructed image of "good black Christian folk." These individuals seek out leaders inside the community, such as the Reverend James Forbes, who have publicly challenged the representations of more conservative clergy. These activists seek a leadership that will embrace an empowered black lesbian and gay community. In the absence of these individuals, black gay activists have begun building their own religious institutions, in such cities as New York, San Francisco, and Los Angeles, to put forth a different interpretation of the Bible.

All of these oppositional strategies contest the stigma of a black gay identity as constructed by the black church. Black gay activists understand that to engage the black community on AIDS as well as lesbian and gay rights they must contest and challenge the church's labeling of gay and lesbian lifestyles as immoral. Further, black lesbian and gay activists must redefine themselves as integral, connected, and contributing members of the community, so as to access the community support we most desperately need.

CONCLUSION: A FEW LAST COMMENTS

The goal of this paper was to explore, in some concrete fashion, the contested nature of identity within marginal communities. For far too long we have let assumptions of a stable, homogeneous group direct our attention to a framework of analysis that focuses on struggles between dominant and marginal groups. Left largely unexplored by social scientists are the internal struggles within marginal communities threatening to severely change the basis and direction of group politics. Throughout this paper I have attempted to explore how identities are constructed and contested, and how in this case such disputes influenced the politics of AIDS in black communities. Central to this entire discussion has been the idea that group identity, or at least the way many of us conceptualize it, has changed over the years. We can no longer work from an essentialist position, in which all marginal people, in particular all black people, are assumed to have the same standing within their communities. Instead, we must pay attention to the battles for full inclusion waged within these communities, because these battles provide important signals to the future political direction of the community. In the case of AIDS, the vulnerable status and contested identities of those most often associated with this disease in the black community, IV-drug users and gay men, severely impacts the community's response to the epidemic. And while indigenous institutions and leaders have increasingly demonstrated a willingness to fight political battles over AIDS funding and discrimination, these same leaders have made few attempts to redefine the community's battle against AIDS as a political fight for the empowerment of the most marginal sectors of the community.

However, the battle around AIDS and who has full access to the resources and consciousness of the community does not stand alone. Similar battles are being waged around other issues, such as the "underclass." Those on the outside, those designated "less than, secondary, bad or culturally deviant," are developing new ways to politically challenge a cohesive group unity that rejects their claims at representation and in many cases ignores their needs. These individuals, like the black gay men discussed in this paper, can no longer afford to support a leadership that is content to have them seen, in some cases blamed, but not heard.

Thus, if there is one larger implication of this work that needs further investigation, it is how marginal groups facing increasing stratification and multiple social identities will adjust to build a somewhat unified identity for the pursuit of political struggles. The importance of groups in our political system cannot be denied. In a pluralistic political system access is usually based on the grouping of individuals with some shared interest, with these individuals pooling resources and influence to impact policy. Collective mobilization becomes especially important for marginal groups with a history of being denied access to dominant political structures. These marginal groups often find themselves excluded and defined out of the political process. Thus, African-Americans grouped together by the socially constructed category of race have found their political access restricted. Only through coming together to redefine their marginal identity into a new identity that both unified and empowered the multiple segments of the community could any political battles be won.

In black communities the presence of increasing stratification and heterogeneity, as is evident in the community's mixed response to AIDS, raises the question of the utility of race as a basis upon which to build political movements. Some scholars suggest that race is of dwindling importance in understanding the life choices and conditions of most black people and instead argue that class as it interacts with urban (inner-city) residency should be regarded as the defining explanation of the "black experience" in the contemporary United States. While I do not subscribe to the school that race is unimportant, I do believe that African-Americans face a crisis in identity. Other social identities, such as gender, class, sexual orientation, and geographic location, are taking on greater significance in determining the experiences of group members. Without

some increased recognition of the broadening of identities through which people exist in and understand the world, black leaders, scholars, and activists may end up so out of touch with the experiences of most people that they fill no real function in the community and thus are left to talk to themselves.

Thus, as social scientists we must proceed with our study of groups and group identity in new and innovative ways. First and foremost, we must again see the group as a unit of analysis with special attention paid to the internal structure of marginal groups. Second, we must pay attention to and recognize new or newly acknowledged identities. Where once we struggled to include gender, race, and class into our multivariate regressions as well as our classroom discussions, we now have the opportunity to explore group identities, such as lesbian and gay identities, that were once thought to be outside the realm of importance to "real" political scientists. And finally, as we focus on the group and include more groups in the picture, we must accept that ideas of essentialist, stable identities in which homogenous groups act as one in calculating risk and determining strategy must be dismissed or revised. Gone are the biological and essentialist conceptions of group formation. They have been replaced with an emphasis on social construction and contextual meaning.

Overall, I believe that we must develop a new approach to understanding identity and its role in structuring politics and political behavior. This new approach assumes that identities are not only constructed, they are also challenged and contested. As reluctant as we political scientists often are to incorporate change into our understandings of politics, this new approach to understanding and studying group identity both promises and threatens to reconstruct our social science playing fields. There are new players to identify, there are old groups to redefine, and there are new actions that should be interpreted as political. Undoubtedly, our old favorites of race, class, and gender will remain, but the internal restructuring of those identities may change as common agendas and assumed "unity" are challenged. In the end what all of this may mean is that those of us interested in the group as a unit of analysis, those of us interested in the developing agenda of marginal groups as they struggle for inclusion and/ or equality, even those interested primarily in the individual, assessing the role of group identity through dummy variables representing race, class, and gender in multivariate equations, may have to look a bit closer at what is really happening in these communities and groups. Who is being counted? Who is shaping the political agenda? How are stratification and contests over identity impacting on the internal unity needed to address a dominant system? And finally, how will this affect the politics of these groups as well as the larger society in the twenty-first century?

38 • *George Chauncey*

"WHAT GAY STUDIES TAUGHT THE COURT"
The Historians' Amicus Brief in *Lawrence v. Texas*

DISCUSSION QUESTIONS

1. How did the authors/contributors to the amicus brief use legal history to demonstrate how the word "sodomy" was usurped to specifically criminalize gay male sex?
2. How is the amicus brief an example of social justice via academic work? How might academics use their research to further social progress in other arenas?
3. In what other ways might we look to history to better understand our current constructions of sex, gender, and sexuality, as well as other identities?

INTRODUCTION

The historians' amicus brief reprinted here was submitted by a group of ten professors of history to the U.S. Supreme Court as it considered the constitutionality of Texas's "homosexual conduct law" in the case of *Lawrence v. Texas*. The Court cited the brief in the decision it issued on June 26, 2003, which overturned that law and the rest of the nation's sodomy laws. Although legal observers immediately began to debate the implications of the decision and the merits of its legal reasoning, there is no doubt that it constituted a major victory for the gay movement. Although the two plaintiffs in Texas were not the only ones to face such charges, few consenting adults had been prosecuted for sodomy even before the decision. But by criminalizing homosexual activity, the sodomy laws had effectively criminalized all lesbians and gay men, and opponents of gay rights had regularly used this imputation of criminality in public debates and court decisions to justify everything from the exclusion of gays from the military to the removal of children from the homes of their lesbian mothers. Sodomy laws were an ideological cornerstone in the legal edifice of antigay discrimination.

In declaring those laws unconstitutional, the Court repudiated its decision in *Bowers v. Hardwick*, then only seventeen years old, which had upheld Georgia's sodomy statute. The Court is generally reluctant to reverse itself so quickly and therefore needed to offer an extensive explanation of why it had done so. To the surprise of the brief's authors, many commentators credited it and two other historically oriented amicus briefs (filed by the American Civil Liberties Union and the Cato Institute) with giving the *Lawrence* majority the scholarly grounds it needed. The press took notice. "What Gay Studies Taught the Court," ran the headline over the *Washington Post* article that provided the best analysis of how the historical briefs had influenced the Court's decision. "When Six Justices Changed the Law of the Land, They Turned to Its History," declared the *New York Times* when it published excerpts from our brief under the subheading "Educating the Court."[1] ...

Ahistorical assumptions about the unchanging character both of homosexuality and of hostility to homosexuality had undergirded the *Bowers* decision. As many observers noted at the time, the majority in *Bowers* treated Georgia's sodomy law as if it applied only to homosexual conduct, when in fact it also prohibited oral or anal sex between men and women and between married as well as unmarried couples. This astonishing misreading of the statute under review was linked to the majority's misreading of the entire history of sodomy laws as distinctly antihomosexual measures, which Chief Justice Warren Burger, in a famous concurring opinion, claimed had the sanction of "millennia of moral teaching" against homosexual conduct.

His error was not unusual. In the common parlance of the 1980s (and of today), most people, not just the chief justice, assumed that sodomy laws referred only to homosexual conduct, even though most of them did not—and in fact could have been used to imprison millions of happily married heterosexuals.

Our brief sought to correct the historical errors used to bolster the majority's reasoning in *Bowers* by demonstrating the historical variability of sexual regulation and the historical specificity of the antigay hostility animating the Texas law (and, by extension, the *Bowers* decision itself). Part I of the brief shows that the medieval and colonial sodomy regulations alluded to by the Court did not provide evidence of a consistent preoccupation with the prohibition of homosexual conduct; they were concerned instead with a wide, inconsistent, and historically variable range of nonprocreative sexual practices, which typically included sexual acts between men and women or men and animals as well as between men and men, and which typically did not include sexual acts between women. Although such laws often involved some of the behavior that would today be classified as "homosexual," sodomy as these statutes usually defined it was not the equivalent of homosexual conduct. Part II then argues that while sodomy laws had regulated various forms of sexual conduct, in which anyone (or at least any male person) could engage, it was only in the twentieth century that the state began to classify and discriminate against certain of its citizens on the basis of their status as homosexuals.

This argument laid the basis for our contention that the decision of Texas and several other states in the 1970s to enact new laws singling out "homosexual sodomy" for penalty at the very moment that they decriminalized "heterosexual sodomy" recast the historical purpose of sodomy laws by adding them to the distinctly twentieth-century array of discriminatory measures directed specifically at homosexuals....

The Court accepted this argument. As Associate Justice Anthony M. Kennedy wrote in his majority opinion, in a rebuke to the reasoning in *Bowers*, "[F]ar from possessing 'ancient roots,' American laws targeting same-sex couples did not develop until the last third of the twentieth century." He elaborated this premise in a historical survey that closely followed the outline of our brief, but he drew as well on supplemental research conducted by his own law clerks. He even cited John D'Emilio and Estelle B. Freedman's book *Intimate Matters* and Jonathan Ned Katz's *Invention of Heterosexuality* to acknowledge the claim that the category of the homosexual dated only from the nineteenth century....

...I found writing the brief a useful exercise, because it required the crafting of a single analytic narrative linking the regulation of sodomy to the rise and fall of antigay discrimination in the twentieth century. Doing so highlighted two historical phenomena with special force. First, it emphasized the degree to which the state's policy of systematically classifying and discriminating against certain people on the basis of their homosexual status was an invention of the twentieth century. We continue to live with the legacy of this discrimination, in the laws still on the books and in the hostility that such laws have expressed, legitimized, and perpetuated. But although we generally perceive such discrimination as both timeless and inevitable, in fact it is of remarkably recent origin and remarkably short duration. Most of the discriminatory laws and regulations that were put in place between the 1920s and the 1950s were dismantled between the 1960s and the 1990s....

We reprint the brief here because it provides a short synthesis of historians' present understanding of the history of the regulation of sexual practices and identities. I hope that it will prove useful as such in courses and that it will encourage additional research and critical reflection on these questions. We print it also as a reminder that our scholarship matters and that it is both possible and incumbent on us to engage, as scholars, with the world beyond the academy....

NOTE TO INTRODUCTION

1. "What Gay Studies Taught the Court," *Washington Post*, July 13, 2003; "When Six Justices Changed the Law of the Land, They Turned to Its History," *New York Times*, July 20, 2003.

THE HISTORIANS' AMICUS BRIEF IN *LAWRENCE V. TEXAS*

. . .

INTRODUCTION AND SUMMARY OF ARGUMENT

Amici, as historians, do not propose to offer the Court legal doctrine to justify a holding that the Texas Homosexual Conduct Law violates the U.S. Constitution. Rather, *amici* believe they can best serve the Court by elaborating on two *historical* propositions important to the legal analysis: (1) no consistent historical practice singles out same-sex behavior as "sodomy" subject to proscription, and (2) the governmental policy of classifying and discriminating against certain citizens on the basis of their homosexual status is an unprecedented project of the twentieth century, which is already being dismantled. The Texas law at issue is an example of such irrational discrimination.

In colonial America, regulation of nonprocreative sexual practices—regulation that carried harsh penalties but was rarely enforced—stemmed from Christian religious teachings and reflected the need for procreative sex to increase the population. Colonial sexual regulation included such nonprocreative acts as masturbation, and sodomy laws applied equally to male–male, male–female, and human–animal sexual activity. "Sodomy" was not the equivalent of "homosexual conduct." It was understood as a particular, discrete, act, not as an indication of a person's sexuality or sexual orientation.

Not until the end of the nineteenth century did lawmakers and medical writing recognize sexual "inversion" or what we would today call homosexuality. The phrase "homosexual sodomy" would have been literally incomprehensible to the Framers of the Constitution, for the very concept of homosexuality as a discrete psychological condition and source of personal identity was not available until the late 1800s. The Court in *Bowers v. Hardwick* misapprehended this history.

Proscriptive laws designed to suppress all forms of nonprocreative and nonmarital sexual conduct existed through much of the last millennium. Widespread discrimination against a class of people on the basis of their homosexual status developed only in the twentieth century, however, and peaked from the 1930s to the 1960s. Gay men and women were labeled "deviants," "degenerates," and "sex criminals" by the medical profession, government officials, and the mass media. The federal government banned the employment of homosexuals and insisted that its private contractors ferret out and dismiss their gay employees, many state governments prohibited gay people from being served in bars and restaurants, Hollywood prohibited the discussion of gay issues or the appearance of gay or lesbian characters in its films, and many municipalities launched police campaigns to suppress gay life. The authorities worked together to create or reinforce the belief that gay people were an inferior class to be shunned by other Americans. Sodomy laws that exclusively targeted same-sex couples, such as the statute enacted in 1973 in Texas, were a development of the last third of the twentieth century and reflect this historically unprecedented concern to classify and penalize homosexuals as a subordinate class of citizens.[1]

Since the 1960s, however, and especially since the *Bowers* decision in 1986, official and popular attitudes toward homosexuals have changed, though vestiges of old attitudes—such as the law at issue here—remain. Among other changes, the medical profession no longer stigmatizes homosexuality as a disease, prohibitions on employment of homosexuals have given way to antidiscrimination protections, gay characters have become common in movies and on television, 86 percent of Americans support gay rights legislation, and family law has come to recognize gays and lesbians as part of nontraditional families worthy of recognition. These changes have not gone uncontested, but a large majority of Americans have come to oppose discrimination against lesbians and gay men.

In this case, the Court should construe the Equal Protection Clause and the Due Process Clause with a thorough and nuanced history of the subject in mind.

ARGUMENT

I. Bowers v. Hardwick *Rests on a Fundamental Misapprehension of the History of Sodomy Laws*

In *Bowers v. Hardwick*, this Court concluded, by a 5–4 vote, that the Constitution does not confer a fundamental right to engage in "homosexual sodomy." The majority's conclusion was based, in large measure, on the "ancient roots" of laws prohibiting homosexuals from engaging in acts of consensual sodomy.[2] The Court stated that in 1791 "sodomy" "was forbidden by the laws of the original thirteen States," that in 1868 "all but 5 of the 37 States in the Union had criminal sodomy laws," and that, "until 1961, all 50 States outlawed sodomy."[3] Accordingly, the Court reasoned, the right of homosexuals to engage consensually in the acts that have been labeled "sodomy" is not "deeply rooted in this Nation's history and tradition."[4] . . .

Recent historical scholarship demonstrates the flaws in the historical accounts endorsed by the Court and Chief Justice Burger. We concur with the accounts given of the history of sodomy laws and of their enforcement in colonial America and the United States by the American Civil Liberties Union and the Cato Institute in their amicus briefs. We will not endeavor to replicate their historical accounts here, but we do wish to stress two points about this history.

First, contrary to the Court's assumption in *Bowers*, sodomy prohibitions have varied enormously in the last millennium (and even since our own colonial era) in their definition of the offense and in their rationalization of its prohibition. The specification of "homosexual sodomy" as a criminal offense does not carry the pedigree of the ages but is almost exclusively an invention of the recent past.

Prohibitions against sodomy are rooted in the teachings of Western Christianity, but those teachings have always been strikingly inconsistent in their definition of the acts encompassed by the term. When the term "sodomy" was first emphasized by medieval Christian theologians in the eleventh century, they applied it inconsistently to a diverse group of nonprocreative sexual practices. In subsequent Latin theology, canon law, and confessional practice, the term was notoriously confused with "unnatural acts," which had a very different origin and ranged even more widely (to include, for example, procreative sexual acts in the wrong position or with contraceptive intent). "Unnatural acts" is the older category, because it comes directly from Paul in Romans 1, but Paul does not associate such acts with (or even mention) the story of Sodom (Genesis 19) and appears not to have considered that story to be concerned with same-sex activity.[5]

Later Christian authors did combine Romans 1 with Genesis 19, but they could not agree on what sexual practices were meant by either "unnatural acts" or "sodomy." For example, in Peter Damian, who around 1050 championed the term "sodomy" as an analogy to "blasphemy," the "sins of the Sodomites" include solitary masturbation. In Thomas Aquinas, about two centuries later, "unnatural acts" cover every genital contact intended to produce orgasm except penile–vaginal intercourse in an approved position.[6] Many later Christian writers denied that women could commit sodomy at all; others believed that the defining characteristic of unnatural or sodomitical sex was that it could not result in procreation, regardless of the genders involved.[7] In none of these authors does the term "sodomy" refer systematically and exclusively to same-sex conduct. Certainly it was

not used consistently through the centuries to condemn that conduct. The restrictive use of the term in the Texas law at issue must itself be regarded as a historically recent innovation.

The English Reformation Parliament of 1533 turned the religious injunction against sodomy into the secular crime of buggery when it made "the detestable and abominable vice of buggery committed with mankind or beast" punishable by death. The English courts interpreted this to apply to sexual intercourse between a human and animal and anal intercourse between a man and woman as well as anal intercourse between two men.[8]

Colonial American statutes variously drew on the religious and secular traditions and shared their imprecision in the definition of the offense. Variously defining the crime as (the religious) sodomy or (the secular) buggery, they generally proscribed anal sex between men and men, men and women, and humans and animals, but their details and their rationale varied, and the New England colonies penalized a wider range of "carnall knowledge," including (but by no means limited to) "men lying with men." Puritan leaders in the New England colonies were especially vigorous in their denunciation of sodomitical sins as contrary to God's will, but their condemnation was also motivated by the pressing need to increase the population and to secure the stability of the family. Thus John Winthrop mused that the main offense of one man hanged in New Haven in 1646 for having engaged in masturbation with numerous youths—not, in other words, for "sodomy" as it is usually understood today—was his "frustratinge of the Ordinance of marriage & the hindringe the generation of mankinde."[9]

Another indication that the sodomy statutes were not the equivalent of a statute against "homosexual conduct" is that with one brief exception they applied exclusively to acts performed by men, whether with women, girls, men, boys, or animals, and not to acts committed by two women. Only the New Haven colony penalized "women lying with women," and this for only ten years. For the entire colonial period we have reports of only two cases involving two women engaged in acts with one another. As one historian notes, both cases "were treated as lewd and lascivious behavior, not as potential crimes against nature."[10]...

It was only beginning in the 1970s that a handful of states, including Texas, passed legislation specifying homosexual sodomy while decriminalizing heterosexual sodomy. This legislation had no historical precedent, but resulted from a uniquely twentieth-century form of animus directed at homosexuals, which will be detailed in the next section of this brief.

Second, throughout American history, the authorities have rarely enforced statutes prohibiting sodomy, however defined. Even in periods when enforcement increased, it was rare for people to be prosecuted for consensual sexual relations conducted in private, even when the parties were of the same sex. Indeed, records of only about twenty prosecutions and four or five executions have surfaced for the entire colonial period. Even in the New England colonies, whose leaders denounced "sodomy" with far greater regularity and severity than did other colonial leaders and where the offense carried severe sanctions, it was rarely prosecuted....

The relative indifference of the public and the authorities to the crime of sodomy continued in the first century of independence. For instance, only twenty-two men were indicted for sodomy in New York City in the nearly eight decades from 1796 to 1873.[11] The number of sodomy prosecutions increased sharply in the last two decades of the nineteenth century and in the twentieth century. This was made possible by the decision of many states to criminalize oral intercourse for the first time. But it resulted in large measure from the pressure applied on district attorneys by privately organized and usually religiously inspired anti-vice societies, whose leaders feared that the growing size and complexity of cities had loosened the constraints on sexual conduct and increased the vulnerability of youth and the disadvantaged....

Thus, the majority in *Bowers* misinterpreted the historical record. Laws singling out sexual (or "sodomitical") conduct between partners of the same sex for proscription are an invention of our time, not the legacy of "millennia of moral teaching." And in practice, regulating sodomy has never been a major concern of the state or the public....

Furthermore, in its analysis of the Equal Protection Clause issue in this case, the Court should recognize what the foregoing history shows: sodomy laws have not only varied in content over time, but have also depended on the kinds of status-based distinctions and shifting justifications that are typical of irrational discrimination. Neither millennia of moral teaching nor the American experience teach *any* consistent message about which sexual practices between consenting adults should be condemned and why....

II. Discrimination on the Basis of Homosexual Status Was an Unprecedented Development of the Twentieth Century

Over the generations, sodomy legislation proscribed a diverse and inconsistent set of sexual acts engaged in by various combinations of partners. Above all, it regulated *conduct* in which *anyone* (or, at certain times and in certain places, any male person) could engage. Only in the late nineteenth century did the idea of the homosexual as a distinct category of person emerge, and only in the twentieth century did the state begin to classify and penalize citizens on the basis of their identity or *status* as homosexuals....

The unprecedented decision of Texas and several other states, primarily in the 1970s, to enact sodomy laws singling out "homosexual sodomy" for penalty, is best understood historically in the context of these discriminatory measures. The new sodomy laws essentially recast the historic purpose of such laws, which had been to regulate conduct generally, by adding them to the array of discriminatory measures directed specifically against homosexuals. Such discriminatory measures against homosexuals, although popularly imagined to be longstanding, are in fact not ancient but a unique and relatively short-lived product of the twentieth century.

It was only in the late nineteenth century that the very concept of the homosexual as a distinct category of person developed. The word "homosexual" appeared for the first time in a German pamphlet in 1868, and was introduced to the American lexicon only in 1892.[12] As Michel Foucault has famously described this evolution, "the sodomite had been a temporary aberration; the homosexual was now a species."[13]

The discriminatory measures we will describe responded to the growing visibility of gay and lesbian subcultures in American cities in the late nineteenth and early twentieth centuries. It should be noted, though, that many Americans responded to gay life with fascination and sympathy. Many people regarded the increasing visibility of gay life as simply one more sign of the growing complexity and freedom from tradition of a burgeoning metropolitan culture. Thousands of New Yorkers attended the drag balls organized by gay men in Harlem in the 1920s and 30s, for instance, and two of the most successful nightclubs in Times Square in 1931 featured openly gay entertainers.[14]

Others regarded the growing visibility of lesbian and gay life with dread. Hostility to homosexuals was sometimes motivated by an underlying uneasiness about the dramatic changes under way in gender roles at the turn of the last century. Conservative physicians initially argued that the homosexual (or "sexual invert") was characterized as much by his or her violation of conventional gender roles as by specifically sexual interests....

Anti-vice societies organized in the late nineteenth century also opposed the growing visibility of homosexuality, which they regarded as an egregious sign of the loosening of social controls on sexual expression in the cities. They encouraged the police to step up harassment of gay life as simply one more part of their campaigns to shut down dance halls and movie theaters, prohibit the consumption of alcohol and the use of contraceptives, dissuade restaurants from serving an interracial mix of customers, and otherwise impose their vision of the proper social order and sexual morality. As a result of this pressure, the police began using misdemeanor charges, such as disorderly conduct, vagrancy, lewdness, loitering, and so forth to harass homosexuals....

In some cases, state officials tailored these laws to strengthen the legal regulation of homosexuals. For example, in 1923 the New York State legislature specified for the first time one man's "frequent[ing] or loiter[ing] about any public place soliciting men for the purpose of committing a crime against nature or other lewdness" as a form of disorderly conduct.[15] Many more men were arrested and prosecuted under this misdemeanor charge than for sodomy. Between 1923 and 1967, when Mayor John Lindsay ordered the police to stop using entrapment to secure arrests of gay men, more than 50,000 men had been arrested on this charge in New York City alone.[16]...

The persecution of gay men and lesbians dramatically increased at every level of government after the Second World War. In 1950, following Senator Joseph McCarthy's denunciation of the employment of gay persons in the State Department, the Senate conducted a special investigation into "the employment of homosexuals and other sex perverts in government."[17] The Senate Committee recommended excluding gay men and lesbians from all government service because homosexual acts violated the law.[18] The Committee also cited the general belief that "those who engage in overt acts of perversion lack the emotional stability of normal persons,"[19] and that homosexuals "constitute security risks."[20]...

...In 1953, President Eisenhower issued an executive order requiring the discharge of homosexual employees from federal employment, civilian or military.[21] Thousands of men and women were discharged or forced to resign from civilian and military positions because they were suspected of being gay or lesbian.[22]

In addition, President Eisenhower's executive order required defense contractors and other private corporations with federal contracts to ferret out and discharge their homosexual employees.[23] "Other private industries adopted the policies of the federal government...even though they had no direct federal contracts."[24] Furthermore, the FBI initiated a widespread system of surveillance to enforce the executive order. As one historian has noted, "The FBI sought out friendly vice squad officers who supplied arrest records on morals charges, regardless of whether convictions had ensued. Regional FBI officers gathered data on gay bars, compiled lists of other places frequented by homosexuals, and clipped press articles that provided information about the gay world.... Federal investigators engaged in more than fact-finding; they also exhibited considerable zeal in using information they collected."[25]...

Lesbians, gay men, and their supporters challenged police harassment and state discrimination throughout this period, but with little success before the 1960s and 1970s. Through much of the twentieth century, gay men and lesbians suffered under the weight of medical theories that treated their desires as a disorder, penal laws that condemned their sexual behavior as a crime, and federal policies and state regulations that discriminated against them on the basis of their homosexual status. These state practices and ideological messages worked together to create or reinforce the belief that gay persons were an inferior class to be shunned by other Americans. Such forms of discrimination, harassment, and stigmatization were so pervasive and well established by the 1960s that it was widely imagined that they were the inevitable "residue of an age-old, unchanging social antipathy toward homosexuality."[26] But recent historical scholarship tells a different story. Discrimination on the basis of homosexual status was a powerful but unprecedented development of the twentieth century. Public conceptions and attitudes had changed, and they would change again.

III. Tolerance toward Homosexuals Has Increased, Resulting in Acceptance by Many, but Not All, Mainstream Institutions

Since the 1960s, official and popular attitudes toward homosexuals have changed significantly, with a dramatic attitudinal shift since *Bowers* was decided in 1986. Homosexuality remains a contentious moral and political issue and we still live with the legacy of the many discriminatory measures put in place between the 1930s and 1960s, but a significant number of those measures have been repealed in recent years as large segments of the American public have become more understanding and accepting of lesbians and gay men.

The widespread consensus in the first half of the twentieth century that homosexuality was pathological and dangerous has given way, with growing numbers of expert and ordinary Americans regarding it as a normal and benign variation of human sexuality. Major institutions that once helped legitimize antigay hysteria have changed their positions. Medical writers and mental health professionals whose stigmatization of homosexuality as a disease or disorder had been used to justify discrimination for decades—as discussed in Part II above—were among the first to change their views. In 1973, the American Psychiatric Association voted to remove homosexuality from its list of mental disorders.[27] The American Psychological Association and the American Medical Association soon followed suit.[28]

Religious attitudes toward homosexuals and homosexuality also began to change. The place of lesbians and gay men in religious life is still vigorously debated, but since the 1970s many mainline Protestant denominations have issued official statements condemning legal discrimination against homosexuals and affirming that homosexuals ought to enjoy equal protection under criminal and civil law. Several of these groups descended from the historically influential denominations whose religious authority had been invoked to justify colonial statutes against sodomy.[29]...

The federal government, which once prohibited the employment of homosexuals, now prohibits its agencies from discriminating against them in employment. The U.S. Civil Service Commission lifted its ban on the employment of gay men and lesbians in 1975.[30] President Clinton signed executive orders banning discrimination in the federal workplace on the basis of sexual orientation... and barring the use of sexual orientation as a criterion for determining security clearance.... Hundreds of companies have adopted similar measures. A survey of 319 of America's largest companies found that approximately "92 percent of the firms surveyed prohibit workplace discrimination against gays and lesbians."[31] ...

Even those who are hostile to or made uneasy by homosexuality are against discrimination and intolerance. A 2002 Gallup Poll found that, while 44 percent of the people said homosexuality was unacceptable, 86 percent of those surveyed said homosexuals should have equal rights in terms of job opportunities.[32] Only 56 percent of Americans supported gay rights legislation in 1977. The figure jumped to 83 percent in 1989, and increased to 86 percent in 2002.[33] ...

Gay men and lesbians who parent together or as individuals have also become more numerous and visible. This has led to greater familiarity with and acceptance of gay parents. The experience of family courts that consider the best interests of individual children is revealing. Over the several decades in which courts have considered the rights of gay, lesbian, and bisexual parents, experience has led the vast majority of states to adopt custody standards that are neutral as to sexual orientation.[34] Acceptance has increased in part because research studies have led numerous influential medical and mental health groups, including the American Academy of Pediatrics, to endorse nondiscriminatory standards.[35] ...

Additionally, laws permitting overt intolerance and discrimination against homosexuals, including same-sex sodomy laws in a handful of states, remain in force, with severe consequences for people's lives and livelihoods. For example, a review of twenty surveys conducted across America between 1980 and 1991 showed that between 16 and 44 percent of gay men and lesbians had experienced discrimination in employment.[36] Cheryl Summerville's separation notice from Cracker Barrel read: "This employee is being terminated due to violation of company policy. This employee is gay."[37] Labeling gay people criminals—as same-sex sodomy laws do—also leads to the imposition of many legal disabilities "because the law permits differential treatment of criminals."[38] Some—but by no means all—of the most important disabilities arise in parents' efforts to maintain relationships with their children.[39]

We ask the Court to consider the findings of recent historical scholarship on the history of sexual regulation, sodomy prohibitions, and antigay discrimination as it considers this case. In our judgment as historians, the lessons of this history are clear. The history of antigay discrimination is short, not millennial. In early American history, "sodomy" was indeed condemned, but the concept of "the homosexual" and the notion of singling out "homosexual sodomy" for condemnation were foreign. Through most of our Nation's history, sodomy laws prohibited some forms of same-sex conduct only as one aspect of a more general (and historically variable) prohibition.

It was only in the twentieth century that the government began to classify and discriminate against certain of its citizens on the basis of their homosexual status. An array of discriminatory laws and regulations targeting lesbians and gay men were put in place in a relatively short period of time. In recent years, a decisive majority of Americans have recognized such measures for what they are—discrimination that offends the principles of our Nation—yet a number of them remain in place. The 1973 Texas Homosexual Conduct Law at issue is an example of such discriminatory laws. They hold no legitimate place in our Nation's traditions.

CONCLUSION

The judgment of the court of appeals should be reversed.

Respectfully submitted,
ROY T. ENGLERT, JR.
Counsel of Record
ALAN UNTEREINER
SHERRI LYNN WOLSON
Robbins, Russell, Englert,
Orseck & Untereiner LLP
1801 K Street, N.W.
Suite 411

Washington, D.C. 20006
(202) 775–4500
Counsel for Amici Curiae
JANUARY 2003

NOTES

1. Texas, *General Laws* (1973), c. 399, see. 1, 3.
2. Bowers v. Hardwick, 478 U.S. 186, 192 (1986).
3. Ibid., 192–93.
4. Ibid., 192–94.
5. Cf. *Ezekiel* 16:49–50, where the sin of Sodom is the arrogant and inhospitable refusal to share wealth and leisure.
6. Mark D. Jordan, *The Invention of Sodomy in Christian Theology* (Chicago: University of Chicago Press, 1997), 46, 144–45.
7. Mark D. Jordan, *The Silence of Sodom* (Chicago: University of Chicago Press, 2000), 62–71.
8. William Eskridge, Jr., "Law and the Construction of the Closet: American Regulation of Same Sex Intimacy, 1880–1946," *Iowa Law Review* 82 (1997): 1007, 1012; Ed Cohen, "Legislating the Norm: From Sodomy to Gross Indecency," *South Atlantic Quarterly* 88 (1989): 181, 185.
9. John Murrin, " 'Things Fearful to Name': Bestiality in Early America," in *American Sexual Histories*, ed. Elizabeth Reis (Malden, MA: Blackwell, 2001), 17; see also Robert F. Oaks, " 'Things Fearful to Name': Sodomy and Buggery in Seventeenth-Century New England," *Journal of Social History* 12 (1978): 268; Jonathan Ned Katz, "The Age of Sodomitical Sin, 1607–1740," in *Gay/Lesbian Almanac* (New York: Harper and Row, 1983), 23.
10. Murrin, 15; Katz, 29–30.
11. D'Emilio and Freedman, *Intimate Matters*, 123.
12. Jonathan Ned Katz, *The Invention of Heterosexuality*, with a foreword by Gore Vidal (New York: Dutton, 1995), 10. For a detailed philological explication, see David M. Halperin, *One Hundred Years of Homosexuality, and Other Essays on Greek Love* (New York: Routledge, 1990), 15 and n. 155.
13. Michel Foucault, *The History of Sexuality*, trans. Robert Hurley (New York: Pantheon Books, 1978), 43.
14. Chauncey, *Gay New York*, 258, 320.
15. Chauncey, *Gay New York*, 172.
16. George Chauncey, "A Gay World, Vibrant and Forgotten," *New York Times*, 26 June 1994, E17.
17. Congress, Senate, *Senate Report* 241, 81st Cong., 2d sess., 1950.
18. Ibid., 3.
19. Ibid., 4.
20. Ibid., 5. As historian David Johnson noted, however, the Senate Committee "could only uncover one example of a homosexual who was blackmailed into betraying his country, and for that, investigators had to reach back to World War I and beyond America's shores, to a Captain Raedl, chief of the Australian Counterintelligence Service in 1912." David Johnson, "Homosexual Citizens: Washington's Gay Community Confronts the Civil Service," *Washington History* (Fall 1994/Winter 1995): 45, 48.
21. D'Emilio, *Sexual Politics, Sexual Communities: The Making of a Homosexual Minority in the United States, 1940–70* (Chicago: University of Chicago Press, 1983), 44.
22. Ibid.; Robert D. Dean, *Imperial Brotherhood: Gender and the Making of Cold War Foreign Policy* (Amherst: University of Massachusetts Press, 2001).
23. Johnson, 45, 53.
24. Ibid.
25. D'Emilio, *Sexual Politics*, 46–47.
26. Chauncey, *Gay New York*, 355.
27. Gary B. Melton, "Public Policy and Private Prejudice," *American Psychologist* 44 (1989): 933. See "Resolution of the American Psychiatric Association, Dec. 15, 1973," in Ibid., appendix A, 936.
28. "Resolution of the Council of Representatives of the American Psychological Association," *American Psychologist* 30 (1975): 633.
29. Statements in support of equal legal protection for homosexual persons were also adopted by the Central Conference of American Rabbis and the Union of American Hebrew Congregations as early as 1977. See Lutheran Church in America, "Social Statement: Sex, Marriage, and Family" (5th Biennial Convention, 1970); United Methodist Church, "Revision of 'Social Principles' " (General Conference, 1972), codified in Book of Discipline of the United Methodist Church, 162H (2000); United Church of Christ, "Pronouncement on Civil Liberties without Discrimination Related to Affectional or Sexual Preference" (10th General Synod, 1975); Protestant Episcopal Church (now Episcopal Church), "Resolution A-71: Support Right of Homosexual to Equal Protection of the Law" (65th General Convention, 1976), in *Journal of the General Convention of the Episcopal Church* (Minneapolis, 1976): C-109; Christian Church (Disciples of Christ), "Resolution 7747" (General Assembly, 1977); United Presbyterian Church in the U.S.A. (now Presbyterian Church

[U.S.A.]), *Minutes of the 190th General Assembly* (1978), 265–66; American Lutheran Church, "Human Sexuality and Sexual Behavior" (10th General Convention, 1980), G(5); Central Conference of American Rabbis, "Resolution on Rights of Homosexuals" (88th Annual Conference, 1977); Union of American Hebrew Congregations, "Resolution on Human Rights of Homosexuals" (54th General Assembly, 1977).

30. D'Emilio and Freedman, *Intimate Matters*, 324.
31. Kirstin Downey Grimsley, "Rights Group Rates Gay-Friendly Firms," *Washington Post*, 14 August 2002.
32. Newport, "Homosexuality."
33. Ibid.
34. Stephanie R. Reiss, Meghan Wharton, and Joanne Romero, "Child Custody and Visitation," *Georgetown Journal of Gender and the Law* 1 (2000): 383, 392–97; see Jacoby v. Jacoby, 763 So. 2d 410 (Fla. Dist. Ct. App. 2000).

35. American Academy of Pediatrics, "Technical Report: Coparent or Second-Parent Adoption by Same-Sex Parents," *Pediatrics* 109 (2002): 341.
36. Statement of Anthony P. Carnevale, Chair, National Commission for Employment Policy, quoted in Congress, Senate, Committee on Labor and Human Resources, *Employment Discrimination on the Basis of Sexual Orientation: Hearings on S. 2238 before the Senate Committee on Labor and Human Resources*, 103d Cong. 2d sess. 1994, 70.
37. Ibid., 6.
38. Christopher R. Leslie, "Creating Criminals: The Injuries Inflicted by 'Unenforced' Sodomy Laws," *Harvard Civil Rights–Civil Liberties Law Review* 35 (2000): 103, 115.
39. See Bottoms v. Bottoms, 457 S.E. 2d (Va. 1995), 102, 108 (although "a lesbian mother is not *per se* an unfit parent [,]...[c]onduct inherent in lesbianism is punishable as a Class 6 felony in the Commonwealth...; thus, that conduct is another important consideration in determining custody").

39 • *Martin Rochlin*

HETEROSEXISM IN RESEARCH
The Heterosexual Questionnaire

DISCUSSION QUESTION

1. What are your first reactions upon reading this questionnaire?

Purpose: The purpose of this exercise is to examine the manner in which the use of heterosexual norms may bias the study of gay men's and lesbians' lives.

Instructions: Heterosexism is a form of bias in which heterosexual norms are used in studies of homosexual relationships. Gay men and lesbians are seen as deviating from a heterosexual norm, and this often leads to marginalization and pathologizing of their behavior.

Read the questionnaire below with this definition in mind. Then respond to the questions that follow.

* * *

1. What do you think caused your heterosexuality?
2. When and how did you first decide you were a heterosexual?
3. Is it possible that your heterosexuality is just a phase you may grow out of?
4. Is it possible that your heterosexuality stems from a neurotic fear of others of the same sex?
5. If you have never slept with a person of the same sex, is it possible that all you need is a good gay lover?
6. Do your parents know that you are straight? Do your friends and/or roommate(s) know? How did they react?
7. Why do you insist on flaunting your heterosexuality? Can't you just be who you are and keep it quiet?
8. Why do heterosexuals place so much emphasis on sex?
9. Why do heterosexuals feel compelled to seduce others into their lifestyle?
10. A disproportionate majority of child molesters are heterosexual. Do you consider it safe to expose children to heterosexual teachers?
11. Just what do men and women *do* in bed together? How can they truly know how to please each other, being so anatomically different?
12. With all the societal support marriage receives, the divorce rate is spiraling. Why are there so few stable relationships among heterosexuals?
13. Statistics show that lesbians have the lowest incidence of sexually transmitted diseases. Is it really safe for a woman to maintain a heterosexual lifestyle and run the risk of disease and pregnancy?
14. How can you become a whole person if you limit yourself to compulsive, exclusive heterosexuality?
15. Considering the menace of overpopulation, how could the human race survive if everyone were heterosexual?
16. Could you trust a heterosexual therapist to be objective? Don't you feel s/he might be inclined to influence you in the direction of her/his own leanings?
17. There seems to be very few happy heterosexuals. Techniques have been developed that might enable you to change if you really want to. Have you considered trying aversion therapy?
18. Would you want your child to be heterosexual, knowing the problems that s/he would face?

40 • *Avy Skolnik with the Colorado Anti-Violence Program (CAVP)*

PRIVILEGES HELD BY NON-TRANS PEOPLE

DISCUSSION QUESTION

1. What are your reactions to these statements?
2. What do these statements assume as they exemplify cisgender privileges?
3. In an exercise to consider how other types of privileges manifest in your everyday life experience, write your own list of privileges based on gender.

1. Strangers don't assume they can ask me what my genitals look like and how I have sex.
2. My validity as a man/woman/human is not based upon how much surgery I've had or how well I "pass" as a non-transperson.
3. When initiating sex with someone, I do not have to worry that they won't be able to deal with my parts or that having sex with me will cause my partner to question his or her own sexual orientation.
4. I am not excluded from events which are either explicitly or de facto* men-born-men or women-born-women only. (*basically anything involving nudity)
5. My politics are not questioned based on the choices I make with regard to my body.
6. I don't have to hear "so have you had THE surgery?" or "oh, so you're REALLY a [incorrect sex or gender]?" each time I come out to someone.
7. I am not expected to constantly defend my medical decisions.
8. Strangers do not ask me what my "real name" [birth name] is and then assume that they have

a right to call me by that name.
9. People do not disrespect me by using incorrect pronouns even after they've been corrected.
10. I do not have to worry that someone wants to be my friend or have sex with me in order to prove his or her "hipness" or good politics.
11. I do not have to worry about whether I will be able to find a bathroom to use or whether I will be safe changing in a locker room.
12. When engaging in political action, I do not have to worry about the *gendered* repercussions of being arrested. (i.e., what will happen to me if the cops find out that my genitals do not match my gendered appearance? Will I end up in a cell with people of my own gender?)
13. I do not have to defend my right to be a part of "Queer," and gays and lesbians will not try to exclude me from OUR movement in order to gain political legitimacy for themselves.
14. My experience of gender (or gendered spaces) is not viewed as "baggage" by others of the gender in which I live.

Avy Skolnik with the Colorado Anti-Violence Program "Privileges Held by Non-Trans People."
Reprinted with permission by the authors.

15. I do not have to choose between either invisibility ("passing") or being consistently "othered" and/or tokenized based on my gender.

16. If I get pulled over or have to present my driver's license, I don't have to worry about the consequences if the officer notices the "F" or "M" on the ID. If I'm travelling abroad, I don't have to worry about being detained because my appearance doesn't "match" the gender on my passport.

17. I am not told that my sexual orientation and gender identity are mutually exclusive.

18. When I go to the gym or a public pool, I can use the showers.

19. If I end up in the emergency room, I do not have to worry that my gender will keep me from receiving appropriate treatment nor will all of my medical issues be seen as a product of my gender.

20. My health insurance provider (or public health system) does not specifically exclude me from receiving benefits or treatments available to others because of my gender.

21. When I express my internal identities in my daily life, I am not considered "mentally ill" by the medical establishment.

22. I am not required to undergo extensive psychological evaluation in order to receive basic medical care.

23. The medical establishment does not serve as a "gatekeeper" which disallows self-determination of what happens to my body.

24. I don't have to worry about losing my house, my job, or my children if someone checks my credit history.

25. People do not use me as a scapegoat for their own unresolved gender issues.

41 • *Judith Lorber*

A WORLD WITHOUT GENDER
Making the Revolution

DISCUSSION QUESTIONS

1. Why does Lorber argue that there is "ambivalence" about contemporary gender divisions?
2. Do you agree with Lorber that we need to work toward a "gender-free" society? What do you find most appealing about this idea? What do you find most uncomfortable? What can you do in your own life to begin working toward abolishing gender?
3. Would a "degendering" of society lead to the erasure of differences among men and women?

4. How would degendering society change our conceptions of sexual identity?

But what is it that is impossible to think, and what kind of impossibility are we faced with here?

—Michel Foucault

With all the diversity and divisions of gender identities and gender practices, the ultimate paradox is that gender systems are still binary. Societies in developed and developing countries with vastly different cultures, complex economies, and a variety of family groupings organize their members into categories of people who have different statuses, roles, access to economic resources and skills training, and opportunities for leadership and political power. Gender is only one of those sorting mechanisms, but it is virtually universal. The ubiquity of gender as an organizing principle of social life leads to the belief that the man–woman division is a male-female division. It is not. Societies are not divided into "penises" and "vaginas" or "wombs" and "nonwombs" or "ovaries" and "testes." Nor are most modern societies divided into child bearers and non-child bearers. When gender as a social institution organizes a society, the divisions are "women" and "men"— social identities whose breaches are possible but often punishable. The comparative social categories for "woman" and "man" are not body types but social divisions like "slave" and "free man," "peasant" and "aristocrat," "Black" and "White." In societies that do not have third genders, you pass at great peril as a person of the gender category opposite the one you are legally assigned, but it is done easily, especially when all it takes is a clothing change.

The insidiousness of such deeply embedded social categories is that they control our lives. They create differences between one group and its supposed opposite and designate the first group as primary, the norm, and the second as subordinate, the other. The differences are established through the contrast of socially created opposites. As Joan Wallach Scott notes, "Any unitary concept in fact contains repressed or negated material; it is established in explicit opposition to another term." Because the categorical opposites contain elements of the other, similarities must be suppressed; if the similarities were allowed to emerge, they would blur the boundaries between the two groups and undermine the distinction of one as dominant.

The distinctions between women and men and the dominance of men are hard to justify in modern Western societies, but they persist. Tracing the rise in women's status in the United States in the last 150 years, Robert Max Jackson argues that thanks to increasing bureaucratization and rationalization of many areas of modern life, women have substantial equality with men in jobs, legal rights, education, and voting power. Despite these marks of formal equality, what he calls residual inequalities are still to be tackled—the rarity of women in high political office and at the top levels of prestigious and lucrative professions, the widespread imbalance in domestic labor, greater costs to women in divorce and staying unpartnered, sexual harassment, rape, physical violence, and the persistent belief that women and men are inherently different.

Modern Western societies are comparatively less gender-divided and more gender-egalitarian than feudal, aristocratic, or eighteenth- and nineteenth-century bourgeois societies were. But the areas of inequality are stubbornly resistant to change. Most men living in households with adult women do not share equally in domestic work and child care, so most women have a double work shift, or they hire to do "their" work another woman from the supply of those disadvantaged by poor education or immigrant status. This unequal domestic division of labor diminishes women's worth in the paid work-place and cuts into opportunities to wield political power. Yet with modern technology, women and men can do much of the same work in home maintenance, child care, and the paid marketplace, and the presence of women at the top echelons of governments is becoming routine.

Nonetheless, the gender schema of male-female differences and men's dominance bubbles away beneath the public rhetoric of respect for individual differences and legal equality. The continued social endorsement of men's dominance over women spills out in sexual entitlement—harassment of subordinates for sexual favors, sly and overt groping, date rape, gang rape, rape as an instrument of war, prostitution. It is also manifest in population and abortion policies that give women little choice in when and whether to procreate. The continued belief in the biological origin of differences between women and men continues to justify the gender divisions of family and paid work and the resulting inequality of economic resources and political power.

The ambivalence over gender divisions and allocation of responsibilities for child care, household maintenance, and paid work characterizes a social order in transition. In many respects, women and men are so equal that the gender divisions seem unnecessary, and then, when they are ignored, major aspects of inequality thwart women's ambitions. The infamous glass ceiling that allows women to see the road to the top and then bump their heads on invisible barriers is a case of perennial gender inequality. Gender segregation in the workplace is another. Women and men more and more do similar work, but dominant men continue to monopolize the better jobs, and the work world continues to replicate occupational gender segregation even as women move into jobs formerly considered men's work. During the 1970s and 1980s, women who went into occupations where the employees were predominantly men soon found that their co-workers became predominantly women because the men left. The entry of women did not drive the men out; it was because the men were

leaving increasingly unattractive work sectors that positions for women opened. Similarly, women's and men's wages have become more equal because men's wages have declined, not because women's wages have increased; men still get the highest-paying jobs.

At the other end of the spectrum from the increase in formal equality in the Western world is the deepening of the gendered divisions of work in the global economy. Financed by capital from developed countries, work organizations around the world exploit the labor of poor, young, unmarried women under sweatshop-like conditions while reserving better-paid jobs and support for entrepreneurship for middle-class men. The policies of the International Monetary Fund and other financial restructuring agencies do not include gender desegregation or encouraging women's education and access to health resources, which would allow women to break into men's occupations. In many of these countries, violence and sexual exploitation, as well as the spread of AIDS heterosexually, seriously undermine efforts to upgrade the lives of women and girls. Population policies are embedded in gendered stratification systems. Feminist work here has all it can do to prevent women's lives from worsening and to influence the programs of development agencies to be attentive to the needs of women and girls.

The persistence of gender inequality makes it necessary to have a gendered perspective on how work and family are organized, how resources are awarded, and how power is distributed. However, I think that we also have to include in this perspective the other major social statuses intertwined with gender—at a minimum, social class, racial ethnic group, and sexual orientation. For many purposes, age, parental and relational status, physical ability, education, and religion have to be included as well. This multiple perspective fragments gender and breaks the hold of binary categorization. I think that for feminists in modern Western civilizations, going beyond gender is a needed step toward gender equality, with the immediate target for change the legal rigidity of gender statuses, their constant use in the allocation of family work and paid jobs, and the embedded notion of men's entitlement to women's services and sexuality.

FEMINISM AND SOCIAL CHANGE

Feminists have described the history and changing content of gender categories—the fluidity of "masculinity" and "femininity," the switches of tasks and jobs, the turnabouts of beliefs about what is "natural." Many feminists have intensively documented the practices that sustain the gendered social order in an effort to change the processes, expectations, and value systems that blight women's lives. But few feminists are now challenging the binary divisions themselves, perhaps because they, too, believe in their ultimate biological underpinnings. As Christine Delphy says, "Feminists seem to want to abolish hierarchy and even sex roles, but not difference itself." That is, while feminists want women and men to be equal, few talk now about doing away with gender divisions altogether. One who does is Sandra Lipsitz Bem, who advocates "a vision of utopia in which gender polarization...has been so completely dismantled that—except in narrowly biological contexts like reproduction—the distinction between male and female no longer organizes the culture and the psyche."

Eradicating the social division of women and men is hardly a new idea for feminists. In 1971, Shulamith Firestone said that "the end goal of feminist revolution must be . . . not just the elimination of male *privilege* but of the sex *distinction* itself: genital differences between human beings would no longer matter culturally." In 1972, Lois Gould's classic tale of childhood degendering, "X: A Fabulous Child's Story," was published in *Ms.* magazine. In 1980, Monique Wittig challenged lesbians and gay men to deny the divisive power of heterosexuality by refusing to think of themselves as women and men. In 1986, I said we needed to dismantle "Noah's ark"—lockstep binary thinking. Since 1990, postmodernists and queer theorists, following Judith Butler's lead in *Gender Trouble,* have questioned the twofold divisions of gender, sexuality, and even sex, undermining the solidity of a world built on men/women, heterosexuals/homosexuals, and male/female. Currently, in *Undoing Gender,* Butler argues that gender is a fluid, psychological, and sexual category but that collective social norms sustain gender divisions and the power intrinsic in gender hierarchies.

Yet feminism as a movement, in the fight for equal treatment within the present gender structure, has lost sight of the revolutionary goal of dismantling gender divisions. The present drive toward gender balance or mainstreaming gender continues the attempts to undo the effects of gender divisions, but it is these divisions that perpetuate gender inequality. The distinctions between women and men may be deceptive, as Cynthia Fuchs Epstein argues, but they are unlikely to wither away by themselves.

Part of the reason the dismantling of gender divisions was abandoned was that some feminists began to focus on women's bodily, sexual, and emotional differences from men and to valorize those differences, taking joy and pride in being a woman. Moving away from the goal of liberal feminists—to gain equality in the public world of work and politics—difference feminists insisted that what women gave men and children, and each other, in nurturance and emotional sustenance should not be relegated to secondary labor but should be rewarded as a primary contribution to society. In the debate over gender theory and politics, difference feminists and gender feminists became opposing factions.

GENDER, WOMEN, AND DIFFERENCE

Gender feminists argue for the value of the generality of the concept, contending that gender encompasses the social construction of masculinities as well as femininities, the interrelations of women and men, the division of labor in the economy and in the family, and the structural power imbalances of modern Western societies. Difference feminists argue that the concept of gender minimizes the body and sexuality, the significance of women's procreative and nurturing capacities, and the violent potentialities of men's control of women's bodies, sexuality, and emotions. Difference feminists, using psychoanalytic and linguistic analyses of bodies, sexualities, psyches, and cultural representations, have eschewed a concept of gender for a deconstruction of the symbolic social order as deeply divided between the dominant possessors of the phallus and oppressed others.

Standpoint feminism, a theoretical perspective that links the gendered division of labor in the work world and in the home to gendered consciousness, incorporates marxist and psychoanalytic theories of difference. Standpoint feminism locates the source of differences between women and men in the gendered structure of family work and paid work, as well as in bodies and sexualities. As physical and social reproducers of children, women use their bodies, emotions, thoughts, and physical labor, and so they are grounded in material reality in ways that men are not. Women are responsible for most of the everyday work, even if they are highly educated, while highly educated men concentrate on the abstract and the intellectual. Because women's lives connect them to their bodies and emotions, their unconscious, as well as their conscious, the view of the world is unitary and concrete. If women produced knowledge, what we know would be much more in touch with the everyday material world, with bodies, procreative rhythms, and the connectedness among people, because that is what women experience in the gendered social world.

Standpoint feminism privileges women's viewpoint; multicultural feminism asks, Which women? Multicultural and postcolonial feminists, addressing the national and international sources of women's oppression, claim that they are enmeshed in complex systems of class and racial ethnic dominance and subordination, in which some men are subordinate to other men and to some women as well. Feminist studies of men show that all men may have a "patriarchal dividend" of privilege and entitlement to women's labor, sexuality, and emotions, but some men additionally have the privileges of whiteness, education, prosperity, and prestige. These analyses see gender hierarchies as inextricable from the hierarchies of class and racial ethnic statuses.

In this sense, *difference* is expanded from men versus women to the multiplicities of sameness and difference among women and among men and within individuals as well. All these differences arise from different social locations or standpoints, and it is hard to justify privileging one over others. Joan Wallach Scott points out that within-gender differences are especially compatible with "an equality that rests on differences—differences that confound, disrupt, and render ambiguous the meaning of any fixed binary opposition." Working with these differences, feminist philosophers and political scientists have developed gendered theories of justice and have located gender in the matrix of complex inequality.

Feminist theories of justice contend that gender is a different form of inequality from social class or racial ethnic disadvantage because of women's responsibility for family work. Gendering family work produces inequality in the home because of the imbalance of the division of domestic labor. It also produces inequality in the workforce because women workers carry the extra baggage of care for husband, home, and children. Where they don't, there are other forms of inequality similar to those for men—in social class, racial ethnic categorization, sexual orientation, education, occupation, immigration. Thus, women as a group suffer from both public and private forms of injustice. As Leslie McCall says, "The discussion of inequality must therefore be expanded from one revolving around a unitary term—the new inequality—to one involving an open question about the overlapping and conflicting manifestations of gender, race, and class inequality."

DEGENDERING AND FEMINIST THEORIES

Many feminists have implicitly called for a gender-free society by urging the minimization of the effects of gender, to the point of gender's practical disappearance. I am arguing here for a gender-free society to be an *explicit and primary goal*. This goal is not incompatible with feminist theories of difference, standpoint feminism, psychoanalytic theories, or feminist theories of justice. In fact, in many ways it is the logical outcome of these theories.

Difference feminists argue that gender feminists neglect the valued qualities of women's lives that come from their bodies, sexualities, and intimate parenting—nurturance, interrelatedness, emotionality. The basis of standpoint feminism is that women live in a world in touch with bodies, children, and hands-on physical labor. Difference and standpoint feminists may argue that degendering will create a masculine world—objective, instrumental, and bureaucratic. However, men also do physical labor, for pay or as volunteers and do-it-yourselfers, so they are not all detached from the material world.

Men also do far more caring for others, including elderly parents and infants, than is recognized by gendered norms for masculine behavior. These norms expect men to look out for their buddies in times of war and danger, but men also care for elderly parents and sick spouses and partners. Degendering policies would encourage men to routinely care for children, the elderly, and each other and not leave emotional sustenance for family and friends to women. Thus, men as well as women would develop the valued qualities of nurturance, relatedness, and emotional expression.

Work relations in the modern world are both formal in organization and informal in practice, rule-based and relational, rational and emotional at the same time, and so are women and men workers. Organizational bureaucracies necessitate objectivity, rationality, and adherence to rules. The parallel informal organization of work creates circles of colleagues built on trust and loyalty and networks of sponsors, mentors, and novices, the "families" that make work life so attractive to men and women. Diminution of gender divisions as an organizing principle of workplaces would not turn warmhearted women into coldhearted men any more than it would turn warmhearted men into coldhearted women. It would, rather, degender the best—and the worst—qualities of people so that good and bad characteristics are no longer seen as "the way women are" or "the way men are."

Gender feminism has been accused of superficiality in that it does not attend to unconscious desires and deeply embedded personality patterns. In psychoanalytic theories of parenting, those are the outcome of women's primary parenting. These theories argue that women's openness to others and child-care capabilities are produced by continued identification of daughters with their mothers to the point of blurred ego boundaries. Men's repression of emotionality emerges from their need to separate from their mothers and from their hostility toward women, which in turn emerges from their fears that they, too, will lose their penises, just as their mothers must have. Sons develop the ego boundaries encouraged by identification with an emotionally distant father and demanded by the competitiveness of the world of men they enter as his heir. Castration fears are sublimated into control of emotions and dominating relationships with women.

Degendering parenting is a way of cutting into this loop of the reproduction of gendered children by gendered parents. Boys close to fathers who "mother" would not have to repress emotions to be masculine, and girls could identify with fathers and mothers. Misogynist views of women as castrated inferiors and potential castrators would also be diminished by boys' not having to reject everything womanly to be masculine. Degendering parenting would undercut distinct personality structures—objective and rational men, relational and emotional women—allowing boys and girls to develop the characteristics to compete and be authoritative, as well as to cooperate and befriend.

Feminist multicultural, social-class, and racial ethnic studies, as well as feminist studies of men, have long called for a perspective that locates gender in stratification systems of multiple domination or intersectionality. Degendering places gender within the matrix of complex inequality and calls for erasure of all invidious divisions and open access to economic resources, educational opportunities, and political power. These multiviewed perspectives have to be translated into praxis by seeking solutions to problems in ways that do not rely on conventional categories and conventional assumptions. As Carol Lee Bacchi warns, when we ask, what is the problem? we need to challenge "deeply held cultural assumptions, given specific historical, economic and cultural locations."

Gender balance—putting women's as well as men's needs and perspectives into public policies—perpetuates gender divisions and women's subordinate position, since women as a group are matched against dominant men. Since separate is never equal, we need gender "mainstreaming" policies built on the assumption that all groups are equally entitled to public resources but not in exactly the same way. The groups that are compensated in the fight for equality need to be carefully constructed to reflect multiple sources of disadvantage. Advantages only to women, just like a single-minded focus on the needs of disadvantaged racial ethnic or social-class groups, can too easily be undercut by protesters who invoke the needs of the other groups.

Iris Marion Young says that a just heterogeneous society would attend to the needs of different groups, not erase differences: "Justice in a group-differentiated society demands social equality of groups, and mutual recognition and affirmation of group differences." A policy of degendering would recognize people of different social classes, racial ethnic categories, ages, sexual orientations, parental and relational statuses, and so on, as shifting groups, cooperating and conflicting, depending on the situation and the policy question.

There is a testable equation in degendering. I am arguing that it is only by undercutting the gender system of legal statuses, bureaucratic categories, and official and private allocation of tasks and roles that gender equality can be permanently achieved. In the countries that are the most degendered in the sense of treating women and men the same, legally and bureaucratically, women and men have more equal statuses. They are more likely to be comparably educated, work in comparable occupations and professions, have comparable political power and economic resources, and have shared responsibility for the care of children.

Degendering is already common in many gender-equal societies, such as Sweden and Norway. The extent of degendering in those countries is in sharp contrast to the forcefulness of gendering in such countries as Saudi Arabia, where every aspect of women's and men's lives is controlled by gender, to women's marked disadvantage. The feminist task of gaining citizenship rights and economic equality for most of the world's women is undeniably of first priority, but a second task can be done where women are not so terribly unequal—challenging the binary structures just a little bit more by asking why they are necessary at all.

Degendering will not do away with wars and hunger and economic disparities. But I do think that degendering will undercut the patriarchal and oppressive structure of Western societies and social institutions and give all of us the space to use our energies to demilitarize, work for peaceable solutions to conflicts, grow and distribute food, and level the gaps between social classes.

A WORLD WITHOUT GENDER

In an essay about why war is futile, Jonathan Schell, recalling Marx's "all that was solid melted into air," begins:

> There are moments in history when a crack in time seems to open and swallow the known world: solid-seeming institutions, rotted from within, collapse or are discarded, settled beliefs are unsettled; old truths are discovered to be provisional; acts that were forbidden are permitted or even required; boundaries thought impassable are passed without comment; and outrageous and unreal events…flood in profusion from some portal of future that no one was guarding or even watching.

I think that in the not-too-far future, we will see this crumbling of gender divisions and statuses.

Throughout this book, I have suggested ways to think about families, work, political regimes, and political action from the perspective of multiple gendering. I have said that these multiplicities challenge the solidity of the binary gender order and provide examples of degendering practices. Now I would like to think beyond gender to the possibilities of a totally nongendered social order.

In *Paradoxes of Gender,* I described two thought experiments that render gender irrelevant. In the first, an imaginary society divided into two genders treats them strictly equally, with half of all jobs held by men and half by women, family work done half by women and half by men, men and women serving alternately as heads of governments, equal numbers of women and men in the officer corps and ranks of armed forces, on sports teams, in cultural productions, and so on throughout society. In the second imaginary society, all work is equally valued and recompensed, regardless of who does it, and families and work groups are structured for equality of control of resources and decisions. Either path would render gender irrelevant—strict parity by the interchangeability of women and men and strict equality by making no category of people more valuable than any other. Strict parity would make it pointless to construct and maintain gender differences; strict equality would contradict the purpose of gender divisions by undercutting the subordination of women by men. As Christine Delphy says:

> If we define men within a gender framework, they are first and foremost dominants with characteristics which enable them to remain dominants. To be like them would be also to be dominants, but this is a contradiction in terms.... To be dominant one must have someone to dominate.

At the end of *Paradoxes of Gender,* I asked the reader to envisage a scrupulously gender-equal world. Here I am going further and trying to imagine a world without genders at all. Can we think the impossible and envisage societies where people come in all colors, shapes, and sizes and where body characteristics are not markers for status identification or for predetermined allocation to any kind of activity? Here is my vision of such a world:

Love and sexuality, friendships and intimacies revolve around people with a mutual attraction to each other's bodies, intellects, interests, and personalities. Males inseminate willing females through copulation or provide sperm for insemination. Females who want to, give birth to infants. These infants become part of families of different kinds of kinship groups and households composed of a variety of responsible adults. They are breast-fed by lactating females and cared for by competent child minders. They receive love and affection from the older children and adults in their circles of relationships. Their favorites and role models vary over time, but there is at least one legally responsible adult for every child.

Children are not sexed at birth—their genitalia are irrelevant in the choice of names, blankets, and clothing. "A child is born to...," the announcements read. In play groups and schools, children are organized by age, size, talents, skills, reading ability, math competence—whatever the needs of the group. Children's talents, skills, and interests shape their choices of further education and job training.

If we can assume nonassortment by other invidious categories, such as racial ethnic group, people are hired on the basis of their credentials, experience, interviewing skills, and connections. The salary scales and prestige value of occupations and professions depend on various kinds of social assessments, just as they do now, but the positions that pay best and are valued most are not monopolized by any one type of person. Science is done by scientists, teaching by teachers, cultural productions by writers, artists, musicians, dancers, singers, actors, and media producers. The beliefs and values and technologies of the time and place govern the content.

Positions of public authority in corporations, bureaucracies, and governments are attained by competition, sponsorship and patronage, networking, and other familiar forms of mobility. Charity, honesty, and competence are as evident as corruption, double-dealing, and shoddy work—people are people.

So there are still murders, wars, and other forms of violence although perhaps through an ethical evolution, societies might develop in which people are taught how to handle anger and conflict in positive ways. But rules are made to be broken, so there is still a need for police and soldiers, judges and prison guards.

Games and sports are played for fitness and fun. New games are devised that put less emphasis on body shapes and more on skill. In competitions, people of different levels of body functioning and abilities compete against one another in a variety of "Olympics."

In the major and minor religions, new liturgies and rituals are in use, but old ones are turned to for their historical cultural value, as are the old novels, plays, songs, and operas. Those who have the calling and the talent lead congregations and prayer services and speak for the god(s).

New language forms develop that do not mark or categorize the speaker or the spoken about. The old forms of language and literature are studied for their archaic beauty and what they tell us about the way people used to live and behave and think.

People group and identify themselves on the basis of all sorts of similarities and disdain others on the basis of all sorts of differences. Sometimes those who identify with each other wear similar clothing or hair styles or jewelry or cosmetics. Sometimes these displays become fashions for all who consider themselves chic. Group and individual ways of speaking, dressing, and behaving serve as cues for interaction and distancing.

There are no women or men, boys or girls—just parents and children, siblings and cousins and other newly named kin, and partners and lovers, friends and enemies, managers and workers, rulers and ruled, conformers and rebels. People form social groups and have statuses and positions and rights and responsibilities—and no gender. The world goes on quite familiarly but is radically changed—gender no longer determines an infant's upbringing, a child's education, an adult's occupation, a parent's care, an economy's distribution of wealth, a country's politicians, the world's power brokers.

To go back to the kabbalistic metaphor of broken bowls, a commentator on kabbalah said of Miriam the prophet, who led the women in dance at the shore of the Red Sea after the Israelites' safe passage, "By making a circle dance, she drew down the supernal light [from the source] where the categories of masculine and feminine do not exist." The goal of *tikkun olam*—repair of the world—is to gather the scattered points of light so all the world will be one. If we apply this metaphor of unification to degendering, at least one human division can be erased.

---

42 • *Leslie Feinberg*

WE ARE ALL WORKS IN PROGRESS

DISCUSSION QUESTIONS

1. Do you think that trans liberation should be a goal of the women's movement? Why or why not?
2. Why does the author argue that the struggles facing transgender people should be important to gender-normative people as well?
3. In your own life, how can you be involved in creating positive social change in the struggle against sex, gender, and sexual oppression?

The sight of pink-blue gender-coded infant outfits may grate on your nerves. Or you may be a woman or a man who feels at home in those categories. Trans liberation defends you both.

Each person should have the right to *choose* between pink or blue tinted gender categories, as well as all the other hues of the palette. At this moment in time, that right is denied to us. But together, we could make it a reality....

I am a human being who would rather not be addressed as Ms. or Mr., ma'am or sir. I prefer to use gender-neutral pronouns like *sie* (pronounced like *"see"*) and *hir* (pronounced like *"here"*) to describe myself. I am a person who faces almost insurmountable difficulty when instructed to check off an "F" or an "M" box on identification papers.

I'm not at odds with the fact that I was born female-bodied. Nor do I identify as an intermediate sex. I simply do not fit the prevalent Western concepts of what a woman or man "should" look like. And that reality has dramatically directed the course of my life.

I'll give you a graphic example. From December 1995 to December 1996, I was dying of endocarditis—a bacterial infection that lodges and proliferates in the valves of the heart. A simple blood culture would have immediately exposed the root cause of my raging fevers. Eight weeks of round-the-clock intravenous antibiotic drips would have eradicated every last seedling of bacterium in the canals of my heart. Yet I experienced such hatred from some health practitioners that I very nearly died.

I remember late one night in December my lover and I arrived at a hospital emergency room during a snowstorm. My fever was 104 degrees and rising. My blood pressure was pounding dangerously high. The staff immediately hooked me up to monitors and worked to bring down my fever. The doctor in charge began physically examining me. When he determined that my anatomy was female, he flashed me a mean-spirited smirk. While keeping his eyes fixed on me, he approached one of the nurses, seated at a desk, and began rubbing her neck and shoulders. He talked to her about sex for a few minutes. After his pointed demonstration of "normal sexuality," he told me to get dressed and then he stormed out of the room. Still delirious, I struggled to put on my clothes and make sense of what was happening.

The doctor returned after I was dressed. He ordered me to leave the hospital and never return. I refused. I told him I wouldn't leave until he could tell me why my fever was so high. He said, "You have a fever because you are a very troubled person."

This doctor's prejudices, directed at me during a moment of catastrophic illness, could have killed me. The death certificate would have read: Endocarditis. By all rights it should have read: Bigotry.

As my partner and I sat bundled up in a cold car outside the emergency room, still reverberating from the doctor's hatred, I thought about how many people have been turned away from medical care when they were desperately ill—some because an apartheid "whites only" sign hung over the emergency room entrance, or some because their visible Kaposi's sarcoma lesions kept personnel far from their beds. I remembered how a blemish that wouldn't heal drove my mother to visit her doctor repeatedly during the 1950s. I recalled the doctor finally wrote a prescription for Valium because he decided she was a hysterical woman. When my mother finally got to specialists, they told her the cancer had already reached her brain.

Bigotry exacts its toll in flesh and blood. And left unchecked and unchallenged, prejudices create a poisonous climate for us all. Each of us has a stake in the demand that every human being has a right to a job, to shelter, to health care, to dignity, to respect.

I am very grateful to have this chance to open up a conversation with you about why it is so vital to also defend the right of individuals to express and define their sex and gender, and to control their own bodies. For me, it's a life-and-death question. But I also believe that this discussion will have great meaning for you. All your life you've heard such dogma about what it means to be a "real" woman or a "real" man. And chances are you've choked on some of it. You've balked at the idea that being a woman means having to be thin as a rail, emotionally nurturing, and an airhead when it comes to balancing her checkbook. You know in your guts that being a man has nothing to do with rippling muscles, innate courage, or knowing how to handle a chain saw. These are really caricatures. Yet these images have been drilled into us through popular culture and education over the years. And subtler, equally insidious messages lurk in the interstices of these grosser concepts. These ideas of what a "real" woman or man should be straightjacket the freedom of individual self-expression. These gender messages play on and on in a continuous loop in our brains, like commercials that can't be muted.

But in my lifetime I've also seen social upheavals challenge this sex and gender doctrine. As a child who grew up during the McCarthyite, Father-Knows-Best 1950s, and who came of age during the second wave of women's liberation in the United States, I've seen transformations in the ways people think and talk about what it means to be a woman or a man.

Today the gains of the 1970s women's liberation movement are under siege by right-wing propagandists. But many today who are too young to remember what life was like before the women's movement need to know that this was a tremendously progressive development that won significant economic and social reforms. And this struggle by women and their allies swung human consciousness forward like a pendulum.

The movement replaced the common usage of vulgar and diminutive words to describe females with the word *woman* and infused that word with strength and pride. Women, many of them formerly isolated, were drawn together into consciousness-raising groups. Their discussions—about the root of women's oppression and how to eradicate it — resonated far beyond the rooms in which they took place. The women's liberation movement sparked a mass conversation about the systematic degradation, violence, and discrimination that women faced in this society. And this consciousness raising changed many of the ways women and men thought about themselves and their relation to each other. In retrospect, however, we must not forget that these widespread discussions were not just organized to

talk about oppression. They were a giant dialogue about how to take action to fight institutionalized anti-woman attitudes, rape and battering, the illegality of abortion, employment and education discrimination, and other ways women were socially and economically devalued.

This was a big step forward for humanity. And even the period of political reaction that followed has not been able to overturn all the gains made by that important social movement.

Now another movement is sweeping onto the stage of history: Trans liberation. We are again raising questions about the societal treatment of people based on their sex and gender expression. This discussion will make new contributions to human consciousness. And trans communities, like the women's movement, are carrying out these mass conversations with the goal of creating a movement capable of fighting for justice—of righting the wrongs.

We are a movement of masculine females and feminine males, cross-dressers, transsexual men and women, intersexuals born on the anatomical sweep between female and male, gender-blenders, many other sex and gender-variant people, and our significant others. All told, we expand understanding of how many ways there are to be a human being.

Our lives are proof that sex and gender are much more complex than a delivery room doctor's glance at genitals can determine, more variegated than pink or blue birth caps. We are oppressed for not fitting those narrow social norms. We are fighting back.

Our struggle will also help expose some of the harmful myths about what it means to be a woman or a man that have compartmentalized and distorted your life, as well as mine. Trans liberation has meaning for you—no matter how you define or express your sex or your gender.

If you are a trans person, you face horrendous social punishments—from institutionalization to gang rape, from beatings to denial of child visitation. This oppression is faced, in varying degrees, by all who march under the banner of trans liberation. This brutalization and degradation strips us of what we could achieve with our individual lifetimes.

And if you do not identify as transgender or transsexual or intersexual, your life is diminished by our oppression as well. Your own choices as a man or a woman are sharply curtailed. Your individual journey to express yourself is shunted into one of two deeply carved ruts, and the social baggage you are handed is already packed.

So the defense of each individual's right to control their own body, and to explore the path of self-expression, enhances your own freedom to discover more about yourself and your potentialities. This movement will give you more room to breathe—to be yourself. To discover on a deeper level what it means to be your self.

Together, I believe we can forge a coalition that can fight on behalf of your oppression as well as mine. Together, we can raise each other's grievances and win the kind of significant change we all long for. But the foundation of unity is understanding. So let me begin by telling you a little bit about myself.

I am a human being who unnerves some people. As they look at me, they see a kaleidoscope of characteristics they associate with both males and females. I appear to be a tangled knot of gender contradictions. So they feverishly press the question on me: woman or man? Those are the only two words most people have as tools to shape their question.

"Which sex are you?" I understand their question. It sounds so simple. And I'd like to offer them a simple resolution. But merely answering woman or man will not bring relief to the questioner. As long as people try to bring me into focus using only those two lenses, I will always appear to be an enigma.

The truth is I'm no mystery. I'm a female who is more masculine than those prominently portrayed in mass culture. Millions of females and millions of males in this country do not fit the cramped compartments of gender that we have been taught are "natural" and "normal." For many of us, the words *woman* or *man, ma'am* or *sir, she* or *he*—in and of themselves—do not total up the sum of our identities or of our oppressions. Speaking for myself, my life only comes into focus when the word *transgender* is added to the equation.

Simply answering whether I was born female or male will not solve the conundrum. Before I can even begin to respond to the question of my own birth sex, I feel it's important to challenge the assumptions that the answer is always as simple as either-or. I believe we need to take a critical look at the assumption that is built into the seemingly innocent question: "What a beautiful baby—is it a boy or a girl?"

The human anatomical spectrum can't be understood, let alone appreciated, as long as female or male are considered to be all that exists. "Is it a boy or a girl?" Those are the only two categories allowed on birth certificates.

But this either-or leaves no room for intersexual people, born between the poles of female and male. Human anatomy continues to burst the confines of the contemporary concept that nature delivers all babies on two unrelated conveyor belts. So are the birth certificates changed to reflect human anatomy? No, the U.S. medical establishment hormonally molds and shapes and surgically hacks away at the exquisite complexities of intersexual infants until they neatly fit one category or the other.

A surgeon decides whether a clitoris is "too large" or a penis is "too small." That's a highly subjective decision for anyone to make about another person's body. Especially when the person making the arbitrary decision is scrubbed up for surgery! And what is the criterion for a penis being "too small"? Too small for successful heterosexual intercourse. Intersexual infants are already being tailored for their sexuality, as well as their sex. The infants have no say over what happens to their bodies. Clearly the struggle against genital mutilation must begin here, within the borders of the United States.

But the question asked of all new parents: "Is it a boy or a girl?" is not such a simple question when transsexuality is taken into account, either. Legions of out-and-proud transsexual men and women demonstrate that individuals have a deep, developed, and valid sense of their own sex that does not always correspond to the cursory decision made by a delivery-room obstetrician. Nor is transsexuality a recent phenomenon. People have undergone social sex reassignment and surgical and hormonal sex changes throughout the breadth of oral and recorded human history.

Having offered this view of the complexities and limitations of birth classification, I have no hesitancy in saying I was born female. But that answer doesn't clear up the confusion that drives some people to ask me "Are you a man or a woman?" The problem is that they are trying to understand my gender expression by determining my sex—and therein lies the rub! Just as most of us grew up with only the concepts of *woman* and *man*, the terms *feminine* and *masculine* are the only two tools most people have to talk about the complexities of gender expression.

That pink-blue dogma assumes that biology steers our social destiny. We have been taught that being born female or male will determine how we will dress and walk, whether we will prefer our hair shortly cropped or long and flowing, whether we will be emotionally nurturing or repressed. According to this way of thinking, masculine females are trying to look "like men," and feminine males are trying to act "like women."

But those of us who transgress those gender assumptions also shatter their inflexibility.

So why do I sometimes describe myself as a masculine female? Isn't each of those concepts very limiting? Yes. But placing the two words together is incendiary, exploding the belief that gender expression is linked to birth sex like horse and carriage. It is the social contradiction missing from Dick-and-Jane textbook education.

I actually chafe at describing myself as masculine. For one thing, masculinity is such an expansive territory, encompassing boundaries of nationality, race, and class. Most importantly, individuals blaze their own trails across this landscape.

And it's hard for me to label the intricate matrix of my gender as simply masculine. To me, branding individual self-expression as simply feminine or masculine is like asking poets: Do you write in English or Spanish? The question leaves out the possibilities that the poetry is woven in Cantonese or Ladino, Swahili or Arabic. The question deals only with the system of language that the poet

has been taught. It ignores the words each writer hauls up, hand over hand, from a common well. The music words make when finding themselves next to each other for the first time. The silences echoing in the space between ideas. The powerful winds of passion and belief that move the poet to write.

That is why I do not hold the view that gender is simply a social construct—one of two languages that we learn by rote from early age. To me, gender is the poetry each of us makes out of the language we are taught. When I walk through the anthology of the world, I see individuals express their gender in exquisitely complex and ever-changing ways, despite the laws of pentameter.

So how can gender expression be mandated by edict and enforced by law? Isn't that like trying to handcuff a pool of mercury? It's true that human self-expression is diverse and is often expressed in ambiguous or contradictory ways. And what degree of gender expression is considered "acceptable" can depend on your social situation, your race and nationality, your class, and whether you live in an urban or rural environment.

But no one can deny that rigid gender education begins early on in life—from pink and blue color coding of infant outfits to gender-labeling toys and games. And those who overstep these arbitrary borders are punished. Severely. When the steel handcuffs tighten, it is human bones that crack. No one knows how many trans lives have been lost to police brutality and street-corner bashing. The lives of trans people are so depreciated in this society that many murders go unreported. And those of us who have survived are deeply scarred by daily run-ins with hate, discrimination, and violence.

Trans people are still literally social outlaws. And that's why I am willing at times, publicly, to reduce the totality of my self-expression to descriptions like masculine female, butch, bulldagger, drag king, cross-dresser. These terms describe outlaw status. And I hold my head up proudly in that police lineup. The word *outlaw* is not hyperbolic. I have been locked up in jail by cops because I was wearing a suit and tie. Was my clothing really a crime? Is it a "man's" suit if I am wearing it? At what point—from field to rack—is fiber assigned a sex?

The reality of why I was arrested was as cold as the cell's cement floor: I am considered a masculine female. That's a *gender* violation. My feminine drag queen sisters were in nearby cells, busted for wearing "women's" clothing. The cells that we were thrown into had the same design of bars and concrete. But when we—gay drag kings and drag queens—were thrown into them, the cops referred to the cells as bull's tanks and queen's tanks. The cells were named after our crimes: gender transgression. Actual statutes against cross-dressing and cross-gendered behavior still exist in written laws today. But even where the laws are not written down, police, judges, and prison guards are empowered to carry out merciless punishment for sex and gender "difference."

I believe we need to sharpen our view of how repression by the police, courts, and prisons, as well as all forms of racism and bigotry, operates as gears in the machinery of the economic and social system that governs our lives. As all those who have the least to lose from changing this system get together and examine these social questions, we can separate the wheat of truths from the chaff of old lies. Historic tasks are revealed that beckon us to take a stand and to take action.

That moment is now. And so this conversation with you takes place with the momentum of struggle behind it.

What will it take to put a halt to "legal" and extralegal violence against trans people? How can we strike the unjust and absurd laws mandating dress and behavior for females and males from the books? How can we weed out all the forms of trans-phobic and gender-phobic discrimination?

Where does the struggle for sex and gender liberation fit in relation to other movements for economic and social equality? How can we reach a point where we appreciate each other's differences, not just tolerate them? How can we tear down the electrified barbed wire that has been placed between us to keep us separated, fearful and pitted against each other? How can we forge a movement that can bring about profound and lasting change—a movement capable of transforming society?

These questions can only be answered when we begin to organize together, ready to struggle on each other's behalf. Understanding each other will compel us as honest, caring people to fight each other's oppression as though it was our own.